Strategic Marketing

Todd A. Mooradian
The Mason School of Business
The College of William and Mary

Kurt Matzler
Department of Strategic Management, Marketing and Tourism
University of Innsbruck

Lawrence J. Ring
The Mason School of Business
The College of William and Mary

D1378512

Prentice Hall

Boston   Columbus   Indianapolis   New York   San Francisco   Upper Saddle River   Amsterdam
Cape Town   Dubai   London   Madrid   Milan   Munich   Paris   Montreal   Toronto   Delhi
Mexico City   Sao Paulo   Sydney   Hong Kong   Seoul   Singapore   Taipei   Tokyo

Editorial Director: Sally Yagan	**Cover Designer:** Suzanne Duda
Editor in Chief: Eric Svendsen	**Manager, Visual Research and Permissions:** Karen Sanatar
Executive Editor: Melissa Sabella	**Manager, Rights and Permissions:** Laura Town
Editorial Project Manager: Kierra Bloom	**Cover Art:** Angel_Vasilev 77/shuttertock
Editorial Assistant: Elisabeth Scarpa	**Full-Service Project Management:** Sudip Sinha/Aptara®, Inc.
Director of Marketing: Patrice Lamumba Jones	**Composition:** Aptara®, Inc.
Marketing Manager: Anne Fahlgren	**Printer/Binder:** Edwards Brothers
Marketing Assistant: Melinda Jensen	**Cover Printer:** Lehigh-Phoenix/Hagerstown
Project Manager: Renata Butera	**Text Font:** Minion
Operations Specialist: Renata Butera	
Creative Art Director: Jayne Conte	

Credits and acknowledgments borrowed from other sources and reproduced, with permission, in this textbook appear on appropriate page within the text.

Copyright © 2012 Pearson Education, Inc., publishing as Prentice Hall, One Lake Street, Upper Saddle River, New Jersey 07458. All rights reserved. Manufactured in the United States of America. This publication is protected by Copyright, and permission should be obtained from the publisher prior to any prohibited reproduction, storage in a retrieval system, or transmission in any form or by any means, electronic, mechanical, photocopying, recording, or likewise. To obtain permission(s) to use material from this work, please submit a written request to Pearson Education, Inc., Permissions Department, One Lake Street, Upper Saddle River, New Jersey 07458.

Many of the designations by manufacturers and seller to distinguish their products are claimed as trademarks. Where those designations appear in this book, and the publisher was aware of a trademark claim, the designations have been printed in initial caps or all caps.

Library of Congress Cataloging-in-Publication Data

Mooradian, Todd A.
    Strategic marketing / Todd A. Mooradian, Kurt Matzler, Lawrence J. Ring.
       p. cm.
    ISBN-13: 978-0-13-602804-8
    ISBN-10: 0-13-602804-7
    1. Marketing—Management.   2. Strategic planning.   I. Matzler, Kurt.   II. Ring, Lawrence J.   III. Title.
    HF5415.13.M663 2011
    658.8'02—dc22
                                                                              2010020497

10 9 8 7 6 5 4 3 2 1
Prentice Hall
is an imprint of

www.pearsonhighered.com

ISBN 13: 978-0-13-602804-8
ISBN 10:   0-13-602804-7

To Paula, Addison, and Andie
—Todd Mooradian

To Maximilian and Felix
—Kurt Matzler

To Kathleen
—Larry Ring

BRIEF CONTENTS

CONTENTS

PREFACE

INTRODUCTION AND ORIENTATION

Strategic marketing is the essential marketing activity—it organizes and directs all other marketing activities and aligns the firm with its customers. This book presents an all-purpose approach to strategic marketing management: a comprehensive and effective "way of thinking" suitable for addressing any and all strategic marketing opportunities and challenges. This framework is not revolutionary or complicated; it involves four essential stages: (1) situation assessment; (2) strategy formation; (3) implementation (positioning and the marketing mix); and (4) documentation, assessment, and adjustment (Figure 1-1). Each stage includes several subordinate steps and can necessitate the application of any number of specific tools or analyses, depending on the situation. The essence of strategic marketing, the fundamental objective, is to *meet some specific needs of some specific customers better than the competition within profitable relationships.* This essence is sometimes summarized in two key questions: "*Where's the pain?*" and "*Where's the magic?*" That is, *what customer needs does the firm serve* (the pain) and *how does the firm solve those needs better than the competition* (the magic)?

The Organization of This Book

"Nothing is particularly hard if you divide it into small jobs."

Henry Ford[1]

This book, the Strategic Marketing, presents a general approach to analysis and planning for strategic marketing management. By 'general' we mean this is all-purpose or *universal* approach can and should be applied as a starting point to *every* strategic marketing situation, challenge, or opportunity. This framework organizes the myriad basic tools of strategic

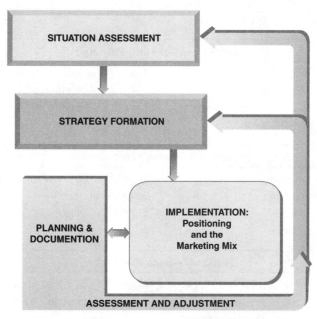

FIGURE 1-1   Summary of the Strategic Marketing Analysis and Planning Process

[1]Quoted in Reader's Digest 24, 143 (March, 1934): 52.

marketing within its basic structure. This framework clarifies the key issues and identifies the tools required to address a given situation. All those specific tools will not be relevant to *every* case or situation, but every situation will require *some* more detailed analyses. This framework clearly points the user to the specific tools and detailed analyses required by a particular situation, opportunity, or threat.

This book is organized logically so that the user will (a) thoroughly understand the general problem solving framework, and then (b) be able to quickly find and understand the specific tools needed to "drill down" into a particular situation, task, or problem. Section I presents the analytic problem solving framework and makes the connections to specific tools clear in the text, in shaded callouts, and in graphic "maps" linking each stage to the relevant tools. The remaining sections, Section II through Section VI, comprise a comprehensive, organized compendium of brief notes, each describing a specific tool of strategic marketing analysis and planning. Table 1-1 lists those tools and frameworks and shows the organization of the book. Together, these materials make up the essential knowledge of strategic marketing.

TABLE 1-1: Organization of Notes on Specific Analytic Tools and Frameworks

Section II—Situation Assessment

Note 1: Market Definition
Note 2: Context—PEST Analysis
Note 3: Customer Assessment—Trends and Insights
Note 4: Customer Assessment—Consumer and Buyer Behavior
Note 5: Competitor Analysis—Competitive Intelligence
Note 6: Company Assessment— Missions and Visions
Note 7: Company Assessment—The Value Chain

Note 8: Industry Analysis
Note 9: The Product Life Cycle
Note 10: Experience Curve Effects
Note 11: Economies and Diseconomies of Scale
Note 12: Economies of Scope/Synergies and Virtuous Circles
Note 13: Market Share Effects
Note 14: Scenario Analysis

Section III—Marketing Strategies

Note 15: The Marketing Concept
Note 16: What is a Marketing Strategy?
Note 17: Generic Strategies—Advantage and Scope
Note 18: Generic Strategies—The Value Map

Note 19: Generic Strategies—Product-Market Growth Strategies
Note 20: Specific Strategies

Section IV—Strategy Formulation

Note 21: Market Segmentation
Note 22: Loyalty-Based Marketing
Note 23: Customer Lifetime Value
Note 24: Competitive Advantages

Note 25: SWOT Analysis
Note 26: Targeting
Note 27: Positioning

Section V—Implementation

Note 28: Customer-Oriented Marketing Research
Note 29: Brands and Branding
Note 30: Products—New Product Development
Note 31: Products—Innovations
Note 32: Products—Product Portfolios

Note 33: Pricing Strategies
Note 34: Promotion and People—Integrated Marketing Communications
Note 35: Place—Distribution

Section VI—Documentation, Assessment and Adjustment	
Note 36: Forecasts, Objectives, and Budgets	Note 37: Assessment and Adjustment

Appendices	
Appendix A: The Basic Financial Math for Marketing Strategy	Appendix B: Strategic Market Plann Exercise
Appendix C: Case Analysis and Action-oriented Decisions	

The high-level analytic approach (presented in Section I) is *essential* to strategic thinking and should become second nature to every marketing executive. The first section, which presents the framework, is not a difficult read—but it is indispensable and should be reviewed often. When you've mastered this material, you understand how to "think strategically" from a marketing perspective. In comparison, it may not be especially important that a manager commit each and every specific tool to memory (Sections II through VI and the Appendices), although familiarity and experience applying those tools will be invaluable. This book explains the most important tools in short, accessible notes. Additionally, more extensive information on these tools is available from a variety of sources. Thus, a good, effective approach to taking the greatest value from this book will be to *study this first section thoroughly* and commit the process to memory, practice applying the paradigm to problems and opportunities, and then make a convenient place on the bookshelf for frequent reference to this *Strategic Marketing*.

INSTRUCTOR SUPPORT

Resources to accompany this text are available for download for instructors only at our Instructor Resource Center at www.pearsonhighered.com/irc. Resources include an Instructor's Manual and a PowerPoint presentation.

ACKNOWLEDGMENTS

We are appreciative of the support, advice and contributions from our colleagues at the College of William and Mary's Mason School of Business, including Scott Gibson, Michael Luchs, James M. Olver, Roy Pearson, Lisa Szykman, and K. Scott Swan. In particular, Michael was instrumental in developing the materials on customer analysis and marketing research, and Scott helped create the note on Scenario Analysis.

This book would not have been possible without the tireless research support from Don Welsh, Mary Molineux, and Martha E. Higgins in Reference Services at the College of William and Mary's Swem Library.

We are indebted to the partners of IMP Consulting, especially Franz Bailom, Markus Anschober and Josef Storf from IMP Austria, Stephan Friedrich von den Eichen from IMP Germany, Dieter Tschemernjak from IMP Switzerland, and Artur Bobovnický from IMP Slovakia. We thank them for supporting us in the development of this book, offering many practical examples and cases, and helping us clarify the managerial usefulness of theories and concepts.

The whole team of the Strategy Group at Innsbruck University School of Management provided valuable support. We thank especially Andrea Mayr, Dagmar Abfalter, Julia Hautz, Melanie Hoppe, Katja Hutter, Julia Müller, Sarah Plank, and Margit Raich.

The following leading business experts and scholars offered invaluable feedback in the development of this book: Harold Babb (University of Richmond); Anne Brumbaugh; College of Charleston); Susan Fournier (Boston University); Bradley T. Gale (Harvard Business School and Customer Value, Inc.); Dominique M. Hanssens (Marketing Science Institute and University of California at Los Angeles); Johny K. Johansson (Georgetown University); Dale F. Kehr (University of Memphis); Jean-Claude Larreche (INSEAD); Hans Mühlbacher (University of Innsbruck); Michael E. Porter (Harvard Business School and the Institute for Strategy and Competitiveness); Scott M. Smith (Brigham Young University); Hennie Visser (University of South Africa [UNISA]);

We are indebted to several successful executives who supported the development of this book with their feedback and their keen insights into marketing strategy and its implementation in the "real world": Chad Baker and Eric Esch (Smithfield Foods); Johann Füller (Hyve AG); J. Barry Golliday (Polaris Group); Catesby Jones (PeaceFrogs Inc.); Shane Kent (Unilever); David Lennarz (FDA Registrar Corporation), Michael Mirow (Siemens [Retired]); D. J. (Don) Moloney (General Motors of Canada); Michael J. Morecroft (Hamilton Beach); Ken Rogers (Mars Incorporated [Retired]); Franz Rotter (Böhler Uddeholm); Richard Spatz (Publicis [Retired]); Tiffany Stone (The Coca-Cola Company); and James E. Ukrop (First Market Bank).

Reviewers

Ron Borreici
Embry-Riddle Aeronautical University (Visiting Asst. Professor)

David Bourff
Boise State University

E. Vincent Carter
California State University, Bakersfield

Linda Crosby
Davenport University

Dale F. Kehr
University of Memphis

Ashok Lalwani
UNIV OF TEXAS – SAN ANTONIO

Marilyn Leibrenz-Hines
George Washington University

Robert Loeffler
NOTRE DAME COLLEGE OF OHIO

Abe Qastin
Lakeland College

Tim Reisenwitz
Valdosta State University

Victoria Szerko
Dominican College of Blauvelt

Mario Zaino
Claflin University

ABOUT THE AUTHORS

Todd A. Mooradian Todd A. Mooradian is an associate professor of marketing at the College of William and Mary's Mason School of Business and a partner in Innovative Management Partners (IMP) Consulting. He holds a Bachelor of Science in Business Administration from the University of New Hampshire, a Masters of Business Administration from Wake Forest University, and a Doctorate in marketing from the University of Massachusetts. He has been a Visiting Professor at the University of St. Andrews (Scotland), at the University of Innsbruck (Austria), at the University of Klagenfurt (Austria), at Management Center Innsbruck (MCI; Austria), at Aoyama Gakuin University (Japan), at Wirtschaftsuniversität Wein (Austria), and at the Instituto Centroamericano de Administracion de Empresas (INCAE; Costa Rica). He was a Fulbright Scholar at the University of Innsbruck in Austria in 2005.

Doctor Mooradian teaches Marketing Management, Marketing Strategy, and Branding. Professor Mooradian has been recognized for teaching excellence, including being honored with the Mason School of Business Faculty Excellence Award (1993, 1997, 2003, 2006, and 2009), the Dungan Fellowship for Teaching Innovation at William and Mary, the College of William and Mary Alumni Teaching Fellowship (1998), and the Faculty Advisor of the Year Award (2002). Professor Mooradian has published numerous articles on marketing strategy, consumer behavior, customer satisfaction, and innovation, in a wide range of academic journals.

Professor Mooradian consults with an assortment of clients on issues of marketing strategy across industries and in both Europe and the United States.

Kurt Matzler Kurt Matzler is Professor of Strategic Management at the Innsbruck University School of Management and is a partner in Innovative Management Partners (IMP) Consulting. He holds a Doctorate and a Magister degree in Business Administration from the University of Innsbruck. He has also been a professor of International Management at Johannes Kepler University Linz and professor of Marketing at Klagenfurt University in Austria. He is academic director of the Executive MBA Program at the Management Center Innsbruck (MCI) and teaches at several MBA programs in Austria, Germany, and Switzerland. He was Visiting Scholar at the Wharton School, University of Pennsylvania in 1996. Dr. Kurt Matzler was Visiting Professor for International Business at the School of Business of Fairfield University, Connecticut, USA (1998), at Southeast Missouri State University (2000), and was visiting scholar at Bocconi University, Milan. In 2010 Kurt Matzler received the Emerald Citation of Excellence Award for his Article "Avatar-based Innovation" in Technovation.

Doctor Matzler's primary research and teaching interests are in the area of customer satisfaction, marketing strategy, strategic leadership, and innovation. Professor Matzler is author of four books and editor of ten books in his research areas; he has published numerous articles in scholarly journals. Kurt Matzler has received the research award of the "Stiftung der Südtiroler Sparkasse" (1996), the Erwin Schrödinger Research fellowship (2000), and the award of the "Stiftung für junge Südtiroler im Ausland" (2008).

Professor Kurt Matzler has consulting experience in a wide variety of industries, in small- and medium-sized firms as well as in international companies in Europe and in the United States.

Lawrence J. Ring
Lawrence J. Ring is Chancellor Professor of Business and the Executive MBA Alumni Professor of Executive Education, Mason School of Business, The College of William and Mary, Williamsburg, Virginia. Professor Ring received the Bachelor of Science in Industrial Management degree, the Master of Science in Management degree, and the Ph.D. in Industrial Administration degree from the Krannert School of Management at Purdue University. He was the founder and first director of William and Mary's Executive MBA Program and also served the business school as Associate Dean for Academic Affairs. He has previously held academic appointments at the University of Toronto, the University of Virginia, and Purdue University, as well as seminar appointments at Nijenrode University (Netherlands), the International Management Institute (Switzerland), Mt. Eliza/Melbourne Business School (Australia), Monash University (Australia), Trinity College (Dublin), IAE (Argentina), and the Singapore Retail Institute.

Professor Ring's teaching and research interests center on the areas of marketing management and marketing and retailing strategy. He has received various MBA Program Outstanding Teaching Awards seven times at William and Mary and once at the University of Toronto. He is co-author of the books *Decisions in Marketing* (1984, 1989) and *Retail Management* (2004), and has published a variety of scholarly articles, technical notes, and cases.

Professor Ring is co-founder of the executive program *Strategic Planning and Management in Retailing*. This program has been conducted over 300 times on both an open-enrollment basis and a customized/corporate basis to numerous world-class retailing organizations. In addition to an active consulting practice that serves a variety of US and international clients, Professor Ring is a member of the Boards of Directors of Mr. Price Group Ltd., Durban, South Africa; and Retail Ventures Incorporated, Columbus, Ohio. He previously served as a board member at Acme Markets of Virginia, Bon Ton Stores Inc., C. Lloyd Johnson Company Inc., Sportmart Inc., and the Williamsburg Landing Corporation. He was also a member of the International Advisory Board of Angus and Coote Limited, Sydney, Australia.

Overview of Marketing Strategy and the Strategic Marketing Process

Before examining the strategic marketing problem-solving framework that is the core of this book, it is useful to understand the role of marketing strategy in the firm and to specify exactly what a marketing strategy is. In this note we specify what a strategy should include—that is, what elements make up a complete and effective marketing strategy—and we define the range or universe of all possible marketing strategies. It is also important to understand why a customer-orientation is beneficial and why aligning the strategic activities of the firm around the customers' needs is both efficient and effective—that is, it is important to understand the "marketing concept"—so this chapter will begin by clarifying the marketing concept and its value.

Marketing strategy is about the "big picture"—"the view from 30,000 feet." It is about whether the firm (or product or business unit) is:

- Moving in the right direction;
- Setting appropriate objectives;
- Competing for the right customers (and *avoiding* those it should avoid); and
- Developing the right skills, resources, and capabilities for success.

If specific marketing tactics are the "trees," so to speak, then marketing strategy is the "forest." It is easy for busy managers to "lose sight of the forest for the trees," to get caught up in the details, and to forget that those details are worthwhile only if they are part of a coherent, overarching strategy.

WHAT IS A MARKETING STRATEGY?

"Marketing strategy" may refer to a *process* or to its *outcome*. This book addresses *both*. The majority of the first section of the book deals with the *process* of formulating, implementing, and maintaining a marketing strategy. Before digging into that process, however, we should know where it leads. What should the outcome of the process be? *What is a "marketing strategy"?*

A comprehensive marketing strategy specifies the *who, what, when, where, why,* and *how* of the business:

1. *Who* the firm will serve—the customers and segments the business will serve;
2. *When* the firm will serve those customers and those needs—that is, what "occasion(s)" the firm will target;
3. *Where* the firm will do business—the geographic markets the firm will serve;
4. *What* needs the firm will meet;
5. *How* the firm will serve those customers and needs—the means (resources and distinctive competencies) the firm will bring to bear to serve those customers and their needs better than the competition; and
6. *Why* the firm will do these things—the compelling business model that specifies how long-term revenues will exceed costs by a reasonable rate of return on the capital employed.

A complete marketing strategy will stipulate each of these essential aspects of the way the company goes to market. A sound strategy must, eventually, reduce to *meeting some specific needs of some specific customers better than the competition within profitable relationships.* That is, the six questions above define a customer-driven strategy and can be summarized as three high-level decisions:

- *Target Segments.* Questions about *who* the firm serves, *when* the firm meets those needs (i.e., on what occasions), *where* it does these things (i.e., geographic markets) and, especially, *what* needs the firm meets are all essentially about what segments the business serves. *Where's the pain?*
- *Competitive Advantages.* Questions about *how* the firm serves those target segments and

their needs better than the competition, and *why* the firm does that (the business model or profit logic), are all really about what competitive advantages (resources or capabilities) the firm has or will build. *Where's the magic?*

- *Singularity.* The idea that a strategy must specify how the firm meets some set of customer needs better than the competition doesn't mean that the firm has to be better than the competition on *all* elements of the offering. Rather, the firm's offering must, in the end, be *different from the competition's in some way that some segment of customers will value.* The strategy must be *unique* or *singular* and not in an inconsequential way. It does no good to be "just like" the competition—copycats may or may not survive, but they won't triumph. It also does no good to be better than the competition on attributes customers don't value. Michael Porter, the renowned strategy expert, summarized this requirement: "Competitive strategy is about being different. It means deliberately choosing a different set of activities to deliver a unique mix of value."[1]

THE MARKETING CONCEPT AND A CUSTOMER FOCUS

At its core, strategic marketing involves crucial decisions about *which customers* and *what needs* the firm will serve and *what means* the firm will employ to serve those needs. In other words, strategic marketing is the creation and maintenance of a *market-oriented strategy,* focusing the organization on the customers it serves and the needs it meets. This is the essence of the "marketing concept." Peter Drucker famously summarized this idea: "There is only one valid definition of business purpose: *to create a customer* [emphasis added]. . . . It is the customer who determines what a business is. . . . He alone gives employment."[2] This simple statement is sometimes misunderstood; it does *not* mean that a company should try to meet the needs of *all customers* or try to meet *all of the needs* of any customer. It doesn't mean that "the customer is always right," or that serving a customer is disconnected from generating *profits.* Drucker"s advice and "the marketing concept" it summarizes are best understood as focusing the business on *meeting some specific needs of some specific customers better than the competition within profitable relationships.* The crux of this message is incontrovertible: the customer and the customer's needs should be primary in defining the purpose and strategy of the business. *Customer needs come first.*

That is not some abstract theory or altruistic philosophy—companies should be driven by the customers they serve and the needs they meet because *that is the most effective approach.* The marketing concept suggests that if we take good care of our customer, everything else, such as sales and profits, will follow. Extensive research has linked a market orientation to higher long-term profits but, while this is certainly true, it is true in the *long term.* Unfortunately, most firms and most managers are measured in the *short term,* and therein lies a conflict. Balancing the short term with the long term is one of the tough parts of being a strategic marketing manager.

"GENERIC" FRAMEWORKS OF MARKETING STRATEGIES

Answers to the these basic questions that drive a marketing strategy—what customers and customer needs to serve, and how to profitably serve those needs better and differently than the competition—can result in countless, almost literally infinite specific strategies across products, companies, and industries. There are, however, a few universal characteristics and distinctions that serve to describe *all* possible strategies, creating general taxonomies. These taxonomies organize the infinite specific strategies that could possibly come out of the basic strategic questions into a summary set of "strategy types."

One fundamental way to distinguish and organize generic marketing strategies is by *competitive advantage* and *competitive scope.*[3] Competitive advantages or "bases of competition" can be broadly categorized as *either* some form of differentiation *or* as cost leadership. Differentiation means that the product or brand offers some characteristic, quality, or attribute that alternatives cannot or do not offer, the characteristics which some segment of customers

value—things like performance (which can mean many different things across product categories and even within a product category), conformance (invariability across units), image, service, reliability, convenience, or unique combinations of these differentiating attributes. Because differentiating characteristics almost always cost money to deliver, it is generally true that a firm can't pursue both differentiation and cost leadership simultaneously. Cost leadership—which is "price leadership" from the customers' perspectives—means developing the lowest cost structure in order to offer the lowest price or garner higher margins (or both).

Competitive scope includes segment scope (the breadth of customers and customer needs served) and the extent to which value-creating activities are performed by the firm itself versus being outsourced (that is, the degree of forward and backward integration). In general, competitive scope can range from mass marketing (targeting very large markets or market segments or even treating the whole world as a target market in a "global" strategy) to niche or focused strategies that identify relatively small segments of customers and serve their needs very specifically (a "customer intimacy" strategy). Because scale is so closely associated with cost advantage, a focused or niche cost-leadership strategy may be the most difficult to implement and sustain, but there are instances of firms serving niches that respond to an absolute low cost/low price in markets where the large-scale entrants, the entrants that could pursue a lowest-cost strategy, do not offer a "barebones" lowest-possible-cost alternative.

These two dimensions—competitive advantage and competitive scope—correspond with the two components of a marketing strategy specified above: "target segments" and "competitive advantages" (see Table 1-1, above). By simplifying the two attributes of generic strategies, competitive advantage and competitive scope, to two broad alternatives each (differentiation versus cost and narrow versus broad, respectively), it is easy to organize the resulting possibilities as shown in Figure 1-1. A firm can differentiate its offerings or compete on price (overall cost), and it can do that at a broad or "mass" scope or at a narrow or "niche" scope. It is unusual for a price strategy to succeed at a narrow/niche scope because competing on costs usually necessitates

TABLE 1-1 What Is a "Marketing Strategy"?

Basic Elements	"5Ws and 1H"	Porter, 1985
Target Segments *Where's the pain?*	**Who?** The customers and segments the business will serve	***Strategic Target or Competitive Scope***
	Where? The geographic markets the firm will serve	
	When? The occasions the firm will serve	
	What? The needs that the firm will meet.	
Competitive Advantages *Where's the magic?*	**How?** The *means* (resources and distinctive competencies) the firm will use	***Strategic Advantage or Competitive Advantage***
	Why? The compelling business model that specifies how long-term revenues will exceed costs by a reasonable rate of return on the capital employed	

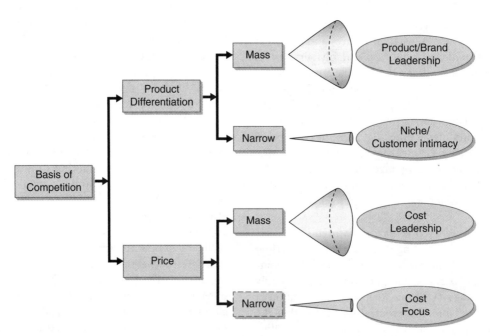

FIGURE 1-1 Generic Strategies—Competitive Advantage and Competitive Scope

achieving high scale in production, but it is feasible in certain circumstances.[4]

Another general framework organizing all possible strategies is the "value map" or "value frontier." "Value" is defined as *what the customer gets* (performance or quality) adjusted for *what the customer gives* (price):

$$\text{Value} = \frac{\text{Relative Performance}}{\text{Relative Price}}$$

The value-map framework plots performance and price as the axes of the two-dimensional space as shown in Figure 1-2. These are customer *perceptions* of performance and price, making this one type of "perceptual map," and these are *relative* dimensions; price and performance are perceived as high or low *relative to other offerings in the marketplace* ("offering" refers to a specific bundle of performance or "give" and price or "get"). Products in a market will tend to form a frontier within this space along which there is equilibrium between changes in performance and

changes in price. People are willing to pay more for higher performance (better quality) but the market will punish firms charging more or offering less for the same price. This two dimensional space highlights three potentially effective strategies—premium (high price/high performance), high-customer-value (lower prices/high performance), and economy (low prices/low performance)—and one unsustainable strategy: inferior customer value (higher prices/lower quality). Within this framework, successful innovations can be viewed as the creation of ways either to offer the same performance for a lower price or to offer more performance for the same price. In fact, innovation, shown as arrows in Figure 1-2, is constantly shifting the value frontier and its underlying equilibrium toward the right.

A third framework organizes "growth strategies"—strategies specifically seen as expanding sales—based on their relationship with existing company offerings and existing markets. At any given time a firm is selling its existing products to its existing

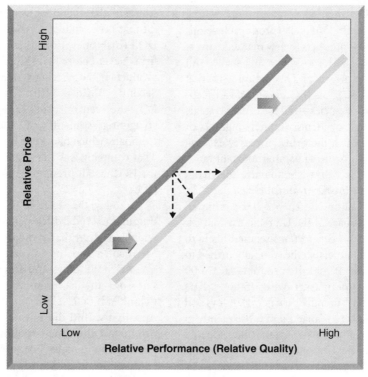

FIGURE 1-2 Value Frontier

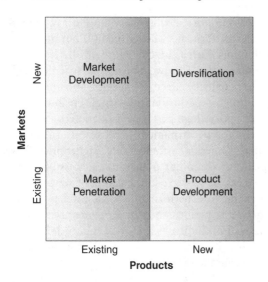

FIGURE 1-3   Product-Market Growth Strategies[6]

markets. Logically, growth can come from selling more of the firm's existing products to its existing markets (market penetration), selling existing products to *new markets* (market development), selling *new products* to existing markets (product development), or selling new products to new markets (diversification; Figure 1-3). This logic was first spelled out by Professor Igor Ansoff.[5] The product-market growth framework suggests the concept of "adjacencies" and core competencies—the idea that strategic growth is best found by identifying new markets or new products for which the firm can parlay existing core strengths into growth. Thus, an important question is how portable or transferable are the firm's strengths, and *where are they transferable to?*

For example, at one time, Toys-Я-Us achieved nearly a 25 percent share of the US retail toy market. Further gains (*market penetration*) seemed likely to cannibalize existing outlets, so the company turned to *market development*. It took its product—a 35,000 square foot toy supermarket with 15,000 SKUs ("stock-keeping units" or individual items) of toys and games to a new market—Canada, and subsequently to Europe and eventually to Asia. Later, it developed a new product, Kids-Я-Us, a category killer retail concept for kids clothing, and it located the Kids-Я-Us stores next to its Toys-Я-Us outlets. This was product

development, offering a new product to existing customers. Still later, they followed with Babies-Я-Us.

RECOGNIZING A STRATEGIC DECISION

As important as it is to know what constitutes a "marketing strategy" and what a strategic "marketing orientation" entails, it is just as important to understand what a "strategic decision" is—and how to recognize a strategic decision when faced with one. A strategic decision is a decision you make today that impacts your ability to compete at some point in the future. It is *not* a future decision. There are two kinds of strategic decisions—those we *know* are strategic when we make them and those which are *ad hoc* and only recognized as strategic *later* in the game. Perhaps the most famous example of the latter was IBM's entry into personal computers. IBM introduced the original IBM PC, legitimizing the PC as a real business tool, in 1982. The company did two things differently with the PC than it had done with any product before it. First, IBM effectively "outsourced" the operating system to a small company (at that time) called Microsoft, ceding ownership of DOS (disk operating system) to Bill Gates' young firm. Never before had IBM done that—all previous products had operating systems proprietary to IBM. Second, IBM also outsourced the "brains" of the PC—the "central processing unit" or CPU—to a struggling spin-off of the Fairchild Camera Company which had some microprocessor expertise. That company was Intel. Once again, this was a first for IBM, as all previous products had proprietary CPUs.

Today, the IBM PC platform has become the dominant standard for personal computers worldwide. However, that standard isn't really IBM's; it's Microsoft's and Intel's—sometimes referred to as "Wintel" (Windows-and-Intel). In the end, IBM itself sold the last remnants of its PC business (ThinkPad) to the Chinese company Lenovo in 2004. Apparently, IBM did not view the PC as a strategic product at the time—looking at it more through "mainframe goggles." Many have wondered what IBM would do differently if it had those decisions back to do over again.

OVERVIEW OF THE STRATEGIC MARKETING PROCESS

Effective marketing strategy is all about the marketer maintaining a high-level strategic perspective while at the same time dealing with the never ending urgencies of day-to-day management. Making that perspective more difficult is the fact that strategic questions don't arrive neatly labeled—"this is a product development opportunity," "this is a distribution problem," or "this is a competitive threat"—marketing managers must first figure out what the question is before they can analyze it, address it, exploit it, or fix it. We have now established a general definition of a marketing strategy, reviewed the marketing concept, and considered some universal frameworks of possible strategies. In the next chapters we introduce a general framework for gaining a high-level perspective, figuring out what the important questions are, and then formulating, implementing, and assessing a marketing strategy.

An assessment of the various strategic planning and management practices at firms that do these tasks well suggests that there are certain things that *all* effective approaches have in common. The framework we present integrates and organizes those shared elements. This model is not revolutionary or complicated. It can be applied easily and often, and *it should become second nature to successful marketers*. There are four essential stages to this process (diagrammed in Figure 1-4):

1. Situation Assessment;
2. Strategy Formation;
3. Implementation (Positioning and the Marketing Mix); and,
4. Documentation, Assessment, and Adjustment.

The remainder of this first section—Section I, Chapters I-3 through I-6—presents that framework and links the process to the more specific tools and frameworks required to drill down into specific marketing situations and opportunities.

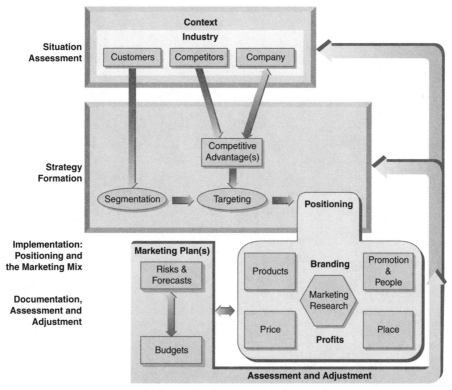

FIGURE 1-4 The Strategic Marketing Analysis and Planning Process

Endnotes

1. Michael E. Porter "What is Strategy," *Harvard Business Review* (November–December, 1996): 61–78: 64.

2. Peter Drucker, *Management* (New York: Harper & Row, 1973), 61. Emphasis original.

3. See Michael E. Porter, *Competitive Strategy: Techniques for Analyzing Industries and Competitors* (New York: Free Press, 1980); and Michael Treacy and Fred Wiersema, *The Discipline of Market Leaders: Choose your customers, narrow your focus, dominate your market* (New York: Perseus Publishing, 1995).

4. Ibid.

5. H. Igor Ansoff, "Strategies for Diversification," *Harvard Business Review* 35, no. 5 (September–October, 1957): 113–124.

6. Figure is from H. Igor Ansoff, "Strategies for Diversification," *Harvard Business Review* 35, no. 5 (September–October, 1957): 113–124; figure is at page 114.

2

Situation Assessment: The External Environment

"A good hockey player plays where the puck is. A great hockey player plays where the puck is going to be."

WAYNE GRETZKY[1]

Situation assessment involves monitoring the environment (external forces) while also scrutinizing the company itself (internal factors), including its core competencies, resources, and strategic directions. Understanding external and internal factors at a given time and, importantly, *anticipating future events, trends, and conditions* is critical to creating and advancing effective strategies. Situation assessment can be divided into these two basic categories, external and internal, and can be further organized into the four Cs (Customers; Competition; Context, and the Company; Figure 2-1). External assessment also includes the analysis of the dynamics of the specific *industry* within which the firm operates and the understanding of some prominent and powerful regularities or "laws of marketing"; by laws of marketing we refer to to fixed patterns that are observed across situations and across time in the marketplace, such as changes in the market as it evolves, the cost benefits of economies of scale, or the profitability advantages of market share.

Before any situation analysis can be done effectively, it is crucial to carefully and strategically define the market the firm competes in or may choose to compete in—that is, to define *what situation should be assessed.* This chapter first explains that crucial step of market definition and then focuses on external situation assessment and those laws of marketing strategy; the next chapter explains internal analysis of the situation within the company itself.

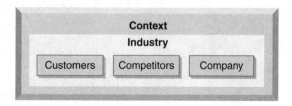

FIGURE 2-1 Situation Assessment

MARKET DEFINITION

Before assessing "the situation" it is necessary to first specify *exactly what situation should be assessed.* In what market does the firm participate? Who are its competitors? Who are its customers? How the market or the submarket as defined is critical to all marketing activities? If we define the market too broadly, our marketing activities lose focus. If we define the market too narrowly, we risk missing opportunities. Market definition is the basis upon which we measure our participation, or market share. Even the labeling of the market tends to define the boundaries of the firm's efforts and its vision. Because all markets are constantly evolving, market definition is also important to understand the dynamics in the market. Is the market growing or declining, and how do these dynamics relate to customer needs, wants, expectations, and requirements?

Managers usually have a routine answer to the question *"In what market does your business compete?"* Unfortunately, the familiar answer is often narrow, reflecting the target of the latest marketing mix rather than a strategic perspective. Often, it is backward looking—describing where the firm has been, not where it is headed. Irrespective of whether that answer is accurate or inaccurate, it is useful to periodically reexamine the boundaries of the firm's markets and to consider the ways those boundaries influence strategy. The market definition becomes the optics with which the firm determines who its customers are, who the competitors are, and a lot about the company itself. Thus, thorough and accurate market definition is a critical precondition to strategic thinking and strategic planning.

Markets can be thought of as having concentric boundaries (Figure 2-2), beginning at the core with

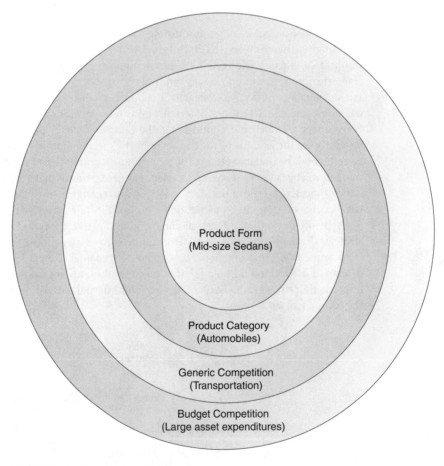

Product Form
(Mid-size Sedans)

Product Category
(Automobiles)

Generic Competition
(Transportation)

Budget Competition
(Large asset expenditures)

FIGURE 2-2   Concentric Markets

product form (small sedans, for example) and moving outward to product category (cars), generic competition (transportation), and finally, at the broadest level, to budget competition (money spent on a car could be spent on a number of other things, from a vacation to home improvements). Traditional approaches to market definition have been "supply side" perspectives, often based on the industry or product (e.g., "railroads," "automobiles", "airlines"). These definitions are limiting; while they may help identify traditional competitors, they may obscure opportunities, potential competitors, and substitutes. A second, complimentary approach is to define markets from the customers' perspectives—that is, the "demand side" perspective: *Which consumers (segments and/or occasions) does the product serve? What needs does the product meet? Who else and what else (competitors; alternative products) could meet those same needs?*

The scope of a market definition should be flexible, adjusting to the purpose at hand. For some purposes, a relatively narrow market definition is appropriate: *Who are our customers and competitors today?* Other tasks require a broader view and may include nearby and potential customers or competitors: *Who is likely to buy our existing offerings but is not currently buying them?* For long-term planning and growth, the broadest outlook is appropriate: *Where can we find long-term growth and profitability? What needs do (or could) our strengths meet? What needs* could *they meet? What technologies might supplant our strengths?*

COMPETITIVE INTELLIGENCE

"Rommel, you magnificent bastard! I read your book!"
George S. Patton[2]

Knowing the plans, intentions, and capabilities of existing and potential competitors is essential to understanding your own organization and to anticipating *the future of the market*. Understanding your competitors is necessarily imperfect. Even the most transparent firm with the most inept security has activities and plans that the competition cannot detect. There are several areas that are important to understand about competitors: corporate level missions and objectives; current marketing strategies;

strengths and weaknesses along the value chain; current tactics; and the directions those missions, strategies, and tactics might take. Finally, one should also try to understand how competitors act and react, for example, will they grimly defend their position, will they aggressively attack, or will they inconspicuously capture market share? Table 2-1 outlines these areas of inquiry, emphasizing the need to anticipate *future* strategies and tactics.

The marketing strategist, in a real sense, "chooses" the competition, deciding where to direct strategic energies and scarce marketing resources. Early in the product lifecycle, you may choose to target alternative products or technologies; in a mature market, competition often comes in direct, same-product forms. For example, satellite television providers such as Sky in Europe and DirecTV in America focus a large share of their strategic efforts against alternative technologies (cable television, and terrestrial services). Later in the lifecycle, as satellite television matures, it is likely that these firms will compete more directly and more intensely against other satellite television services (such as UPC in Europe and Dish Network in the US).

TABLE 2-1 Questions in Competitive Assessment

Strategic Questions

- Who are the competitors?
- What are their corporate missions, goals, and strategies?
- What are their marketing strategies and objectives?
- What are their objectives (at each business level)?
- What are the firm's operational strengths and weaknesses?
- How badly do they want to play this game?

Tactical Questions

- What does their marketing plan look like?
- What are their attribute-level product strengths and weaknesses? What are their product *line* strengths and weaknesses?
- Can they execute? Do they have (or can they acquire) the skills?

TABLE 2-2 Elements of the Context: PEST

Political/Regulatory Context

Marketers operate in powerful, complex regulatory and legal environments that are shaped by political processes. These include tax codes, liability structures, operating rules, product-labeling regulations, purity and conformance requirements as well as government subsidies, and government procurement itself. Some firms also operate under nongovernment regulations and even informal guidelines (equipment rules in golf and informal bans on television advertising in the liquor industry).

Economic Context

Economic variables such as interest rates, unemployment rates, currency exchange rates, and inflation impact marketing strategies in substantial and complex ways.

Social/Cultural Context

Social and cultural values, attitudes, norms, manners, and tastes all affect customer needs and thereby must be considered in developing marketing strategies and tactics. Demographics and lifestyles of the population (for example, age, education, and social class) are important components of the social/cultural context that change across time.

Technological/Physical Context

Technology, innovation, and technological progress impact strategies in many ways. New technologies can replace or become direct or indirect substitutes for a product form or product category. Technological changes can alter the way a product is distributed and/or consumed. The physical environment includes the natural environment, population density, physical infrastructure, and commercial infrastructure.

CONTEXT

The general "context" or environment within which a firm, product, or brand operates has pervasive and complex effects on strategy and results. It is useful to begin with a succinct classification of the environmental factors that influence strategy. This classification imposes discipline on the assessment, stimulates brainstorming, and assures completeness. The mnemonic "PEST," for Political/Regulatory, Economic, Social/Cultural, and Technical/Physical (see Table 2-2) is a good, comprehensive partitioning of the "big picture," macro-level business environment. Changes in the general context are often the fundamental cause of problems and also the root of important opportunities. Failure to relate symptoms such as sales declines to underlying causes can blur strategic decision making. For example, declining sales due to an economic recession can be expected to rebound; declining sales tied to deep-seated changes in social values or fundamental technological changes related to demand may not rebound so quickly or so surely.

CUSTOMER ASSESSMENT

The tasks and considerations associated with *customer assessment* as well as *segmentation* (within strategy formulation), *marketing research* (at the center of positioning with the marketing mix) and, finally, strategic *assessment* (within assessment and adjustment) all emphasize keen attention to and deep understandings of customers and their responses to marketing actions (differentiated in Table 2-3 and highlighted in Figure 2-3). The pervasive role of customer understandings and research in our strategic marketing framework is no accident. As we have argued, effective and efficient strategies begin with and are continuously aligned with a customer focus or "market orientation."

Organizing Customer-Focused Research

Throughout this book we use "customers" to refer to *both* direct customer—that is, business-to-business customers, distributors, or retailers—*and* the ultimate

TABLE 2-3 Organizing Customer-Focused Research

Customer-Oriented Marketing Research			
	Situation Assessment	*Customer Assessment*	The broad, exploratory, and inductive study of customers in general to identify (a) *trends* in needs and demand, and (b) *customer insights*.
	Strategy Formation and Implementation	*Segmentation*	Focused research indentifying meaningful differences across customers/consumers with regard to needs and descriptive characteristics.
		Marketing Mix Development and Testing	Focused research to pretest and hone tactics, including price, promotions, advertising, new products or product modifications, and merchandising programs.
		Customer Relationship Management (CRM)	Ongoing data collections tied to specific accounts, customers, or consumers that serves to tailor offerings (personalize or customize offerings) and direct investments and efforts toward the "right" customers and segments.
	Assessment & Adjustment	*Customer- and Market-Oriented Metrics*	Focused and ongoing research collecting information on customer responses to the marketing mix, including measures of satisfaction, loyalty, profitability, and revenues.

customer or consumer of a product. The term "consumers" is reserved for the ultimate user of a final product. We use customer assessment to refer to broad exploration for macro trends and customer insights. We reserve "marketing research" for issue-focused research that is directly and deliberately linked with specific marketing decisions and problems. The ongoing collection of customer-related data for targeting and for assessment (Customer Relationship Management [CRM] systems) falls under marketing research. Others may use these labels differently—all of these activities do require gathering and processing information about customers—but customer assessment and marketing research have different priorities, each requires different types of information, and each relies on different methods. Customer assessment, which is part of situation assessment, is the *broadest* consideration of the firm's current customers, the competitors' customers, and customers not yet in the market (poten-

tial customers). It draws on both secondary and primary data to: identify emerging trends in the market, understand how products deliver value and how customers consume the products, and, especially, *anticipate future patterns of customer needs and consumption.*

IDENTIFYING CUSTOMER TRENDS. Trends are broad-based changes in the marketplace that occur over time. Trends represent significant marketing opportunities that are grounded on substantive transformations such as changes in values, lifestyles, or technology, and are accessible to the "mainstream" or the majority of the market.[3] Monitoring the environment for trends can be highly quantitative and can include traditional, statistical methods for econometric forecasting as well as emerging methods of "data mining."[4] Data mining involves the analysis of large databases using diverse analytic methods to identify patterns, associations, and emerging trends.

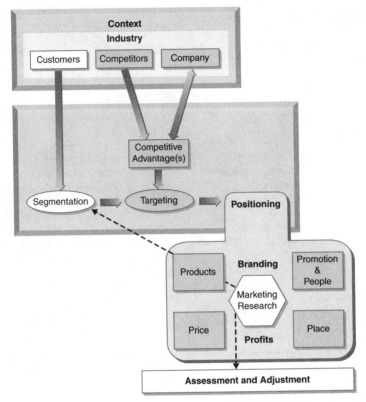

FIGURE 2-3 Customer Knowledge throughout Strategic Marketing Management

Research firms such as ACNeilsen, Information Resources Inc. (IRI), and Catalina Marketing and mega-retailers like Wal-Mart collect multi-terabytes of data across billions of transactions. These data create new opportunities for insights but also ever-increase the possibility that strategic marketers will be swamped by them. Searching for trends also entails scanning across media and across settings. That broad and subjective search for trends is sometimes called "trendspotting" or "coolhunting";[5] it should be wide ranging, inclusive, and unstructured. Uncertain trends and indefinite patterns of future customer needs can be included in the factors that define "possible futures" in scenario planning (discussed in more detail below).

DISCOVERING CUSTOMER INSIGHTS.   Gary Hamel and C. K. Prahalad have argued that "to realize the potential that core competencies create, a company must also have the imagination to envision markets that do not yet exist and the ability to stake them out ahead of the completion." The realization of exceptional returns often means disregarding mature, competitive markets for truly new ones. Finding markets that do "not yet exist" often begins with a "customer insight." A customer insight is a penetrating, discerning understanding of customer needs, the ways that customers derive value from products, and the ways customers *might* derive value from products; it is an insight that unlocks an opportunity.[6] Customer insights should be fresh, relevant, enduring, and inspiring.[7]

"If I had asked people what they wanted, they would have said faster horses," Henry Ford once said.[8]

Identifying customer insights requires more than painstakingly asking customers what they know or think they want—insights often necessitate customer intimacy with an eye toward discovering solutions customers could not have envisioned or articulated. Customer assessment includes "deep dives" required to understand the customers' perspective and to identify unmet and even unrecognized customer needs. Toward that end, customer assessment draws on qualitative methods, including depth interviews, anthropological methods such as ethnographies, and "total immersion sessions."[9] These are *inductive* research methods—they let observations shape conclusions, rather than imposing preconceived structure on the research or the findings. These methods also produce rich but not very generalizable findings—the results are specific to the customers observed.

INDUSTRY ANALYSIS

An analysis of the industry or industries within which the firm operates is a more specific "micro" perspective embedded within the broader, "macro" setting of situation assessment and the four Cs. There are five forces that drive industry analysis (Figure 2-4): the bargaining power of suppliers and the bargaining power of customers, the threat of substitute products, and the threat of new entrants. The fifth force that influences industry competitiveness is the intensity of the rivalry among existing competitors in the industry. The five forces together influence *industry profitability*.

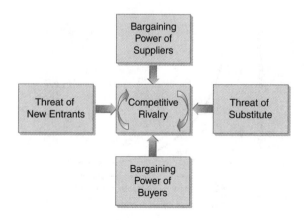

FIGURE 2-4 Five Forces Industry Analysis

LAWS OF STRATEGIC MARKETING

Physicists know that an object will stay at rest or continue at a constant velocity unless acted upon by an external, unbalanced force and that the total energy in a system remains constant over time. These observed regularities are the "*laws of physics*" (Newton's First Law of Motion and the Law of Conservation of Energy, respectively); they're "truths" that describe underlying realities that do not change.[10] In strategic marketing there are similar "truths"—the "laws of marketing strategy," so to speak—that describe essential regularities in the way things work and the way things relate. These generalizations include: the product lifecycle (product-market evolution), scale effects (cost leverage), and market share effects (share leverage). Managers may choose a strategy that builds directly on one of these generalizations, or they may choose a strategy that is less directly tied to a given generalization, but *they can't change the reality*. For example, Toyota builds its strategy on the benefits of scale effects; they produce more cars than anyone else in the world based on a set of common core processes. Although another car company, such as Porsche, may choose to forego scale to compete on high performance using small-scale production, *it can't change the reality of scale effects*.

Product Lifecycle

All products and all markets are in a constant state of evolution. Some evolve in fairly smooth and expected patterns while others evolve less predictably, such as when "disruptive technologies" cause unexpected, sharp declines. Nevertheless, the biological analogy of birth, growth, maturity, and decline is generally reliable. The S-shape of the product lifecycle (see Figure 2-5) describes this market evolution—the vertical axis is the percent of the total market and the horizontal axis is time; but distinct lifecycles exist for industries, products, and product forms.

Markets behave differently at different stages: competitors compete differently, sales are more profitable or less profitable, customers buy differently, and different customers buy. Different strategies and tactics work better than others at various stages in the

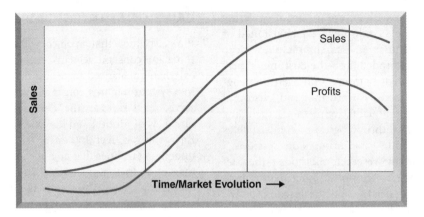

FIGURE 2-5   The Product Lifecycle

product lifecycle. Most major strategic gains and losses occur in the growth phase of a market. Share gains while all competitors are growing can frequently be achieved without significant competitive reaction. Share building in mature markets is tougher and frequently results in rapid competitive reaction, often in the form of price competition. Those who have achieved lower costs have an advantage at this stage. Thus, understanding where a product and an industry are in the lifecycle facilitates better prediction of competitor actions, of customer responses, and of sales trends and will inform considerations about what strategies are typically effective. Recognizing when the market is evolving from one "stage" to another—that is, anticipating "inflection" points—can create a significant advantage; missing such a shift can be a substantial disadvantage.

Scale Effects/Cost Leverage

Cost leverage can be achieved by both scale and experience. Scale is related to volume and time. It is axiomatic that as volume in a given time period increases, fixed expenses as a percentage of sales decline. This effect is referred to as economies of scale. Similarly, the more units a company produces of anything, *the lower per-unit costs* will be. With each doubling of accumulated volume, costs decline by a determinable percentage. That is, experience effects are generally expressed as a percentage (e.g., 10%, 15%, 17%) decline in costs realized with every dou-

bling of units produced (i.e., moving from 1 to 2, 2 to 4, 4 to 8 . . . 1.6 million to 3.2 million, etc.); that relationship between unit costs and volume produced forms the experience effects curve, shown in Figure 2-6. This percentage decline varies from industry to industry, but, regardless of the industry, *significant cost advantage can be achieved by the competitor who moves down the experience curve faster.* We can visualize that advantage as the "distance" between one competitor's position on the experience curve and another's.

Too often, *any* reduction in cost as units-produced increases is mislabeled as an "economy of scale." In fact, at least four distinct sets of forces *with differing implications for strategy* can drive scale ef-

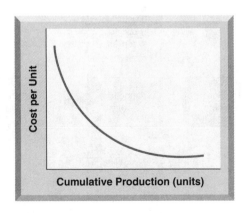

FIGURE 2-6   Experience Curve

TABLE 2-4 Sources of Scale Effects

Learning Curve Effects or Experience Curve Effects	The effects of the organization, its suppliers, and its employees literally *learning*—becoming more knowledgeable and more skilled and thereby doing things more *efficiently*.
Economies	The lowering of per-unit costs as the number of units produced increases via the spreading of fixed costs across units.
Diseconomies of Scale	Diseconomies of scale are the realization of *inefficiencies*, that is, of *increases* in unit costs as production increases.
Economies of Scope	The lowering of unit costs realized when producing *more than one product* lowers the cost of production of all products.
Synergies	Synergies are two (or more) inputs or activities ("factors") coming together or acting together to result in output that is greater than the sum of the two factors taken separately (i.e., $(1+1) > 2$).
Network Effects	When a product provides more value to *each customer* when more *overall customers* own it or use it.
Virtuous Circles	Systems of factors that provide feedback on themselves. For example, the more people buy a product, the more retailers will want to stock the product, leading to higher sales. A "vicious circle" is the opposite—the feedback of negative factors exacerbating problems.

fects: learning- or experience-curve effects, economies and diseconomies of scale, economies of scope and synergies, and network effects and virtuous circles (these distinct sources of benefits from scale are clarified in Table 2-4). These different sources of scale effects are important in that they have different bases. They respond differently to managerial actions, and they are more or less enduring. For example, learning curve effects can contribute to both lower unit costs and higher quality (especially reliability and conformance quality). They endure across time, and can be increased by enhancing institutional learning and knowledge retention. Economies of scale, on the other hand, lower costs but do not relate to quality, are less enduring, and are increased by one thing: higher units of production in a given time period.

Market Share Effects/Share Leverage

One of the best known observations in the strategy literature is that firms with higher market share tend to be more profitable. This share-profitability association is real; it has been replicated empirically many times in well known pooled-business data, such as the "PIMS" data (the Profit Impact of Marketing Strategy database[11]). The share-profitability association is also logical; market share will *correlate with* advantages of scale, discussed above. Scale generally leads to lower unit costs, and lower unit costs should lead to higher profits (firms with lower unit costs can lower price and gain sales volume or maintain price and realize higher per unit margins). Nevertheless, shaping strategy around market share ignores the ambiguity in the share-ROI findings: The causal direction of the relationship is unclear and the relationship is undoubtedly complex. For example, many other factors such as product quality and managerial skill should lead to *both* market share and profitability, rendering market share a dubious starting point for strategy. Still, share building activities in the market growth phase do pay off in superior competitive position during maturity.

Summary

Marketing strategy involves developing an effective marketing mix for a *given marketplace reality* and then adapting that mix to *changes* in those environmental forces. Therefore, marketing strategy demands a thorough analysis of the context, the competition, and the customers. If marketing strategy is marketing mix evolution in response to the environment, really *good* marketing strategy is marketing mix evolution in *anticipation* of changes in those forces—that is, anticipating *future* configurations of the forces in the environment and developing effective marketing mixes in advance of those future realities (which underscores Wayne Gretzky's notion of skating to "where the puck is going to be"). This chapter has organized and explained tools and frameworks for analyzing the environment—the external situation—and anticipating where it may be headed. The next chapter deals with analyzing the *internal situation*—that is, analyzing the company itself, including its missions and visions, strengths and weaknesses, and competitive advantages.

Endnotes

1. Wess Moss, *Make More, Worry Less* (Upper Saddle River, NJ: FT Press 2008), 160.
2. As portrayed by George C. Scott in Franklin J. Schaffner (Producer), Francis Ford Coppola and Edmund H. North (screenplay), *Patton* [Motion Picture], USA, 20th Century Fox, 1970.
3. Irma Zandl, "How to Separate Trends from Fads," *Brandweek* 41, no. 41 (23 October, 2000): 30–35.
4. Jiawei Han and Micheline Kamber have defined data mining as "uncovering interesting data patterns hidden in large data sets" (page 1) and have noted that, in the past several years, available data have grown "from terabytes to petabytes," in *Data Mining: Concepts and Techniques*, 2nd ed. (San Francisco: Morgan Kaufmann Publishers, 2006).
5. Peter A. Gloor and Scott M. Cooper, *Coolhunting: Chasing Down the Next Big Thing* (AMACOM, a division of American Management Association, 2007); Malcolm Gladwell, "The Coolhunt," *The New Yorker* (March 17, 1997): 78–88.
6. David Taylor, "Drilling for Nuggets: How to use insight to inspire innovation," *Brand Strategy* (March 24, 2000),
7. Ibid.
8. Quoted in James G. Barnes, *Build Your Customer Strategy* (New York: John Wiley and Sons, 2006), 106
9. See, for example, Research, "Total Immersion: Researchers can be wary of them, but businesses seem to love them. Essential Research's Stuart Knapman investigates customer immersion sessions and clients tell us how they have made them work," June, 2008, www.research-live.com/features/total-immersion/2002001.article. Last accessed June 19, 2010
10. See, for example, Steven Holzner, *Physics for Dummies* (Hoboken, NJ: Wiley Publishing, 2006).
11. See Paul Farris, Michael J. Moore, and Robert Dow Buzzell, *The Profit Impact of Marketing Strategy Project: Retrospect and Prospects* (New York: Cambridge University Press, 2004).

3

Situation Assessment: The Company

"Knowing others is intelligence;
knowing yourself is true wisdom.
Mastering others is strength;
mastering yourself is true power"

LAO TZU, CIRCA SIXTH CENTURY BCE[1]

In the simplest terms, marketing strategy is about matching external opportunities with internal strengths and competitive advantages. The previous chapter developed ideas about analyzing the external situation, the environment within which the firm and the strategy compete. The obvious complement to that external analysis is the development of a thorough and honest understanding of the firm itself. Strategies and tactics must be developed within an understanding of the overarching organizational context and, eventually, should contribute to the overall mission and goals. Company assessment includes four related considerations:

- *Using Guidance Statements: Missions and Values;*
- *Assessing Past Performance and Current Strategy;*
- *Establishing Preliminary Objectives and Targets; and*
- *Identifying Strategic Gap(s) or Planning Gaps.*

USING GUIDANCE STATEMENTS: MISSIONS AND VISIONS

Corporations have unique values and cultures, as well as distinctive resources and competitive advantages; any marketing strategy is supported by and constrained by those parameters. Most firms and business units begin their strategy formulation process with some sort of guidance statement—sometimes called a mission or a vision statement. Some organizations have *both*. Most corporations have a mission that establishes purpose and values that shape their vision. Vision statements, which are sometimes included within mission statements, are the forward-looking part of the mission—"the desired future state of the organiza-tion."[2] Mission/vision statements clarify the firm's identity and purpose and should include at least four elements:

- The core purpose of the company;
- The core values of the company;
- The visionary goal (as noted, vision is some-times pulled out on its own); and
- A vivid description of the envisioned future (specification of *goals*).[3]

Mission and vision statements, therefore, *should* be important documentation of the higher-level corpo-rate context within which the product and business unit operate and to which they should contribute. Unfortunately, mission statements often fail to clar-ify much at all, as one critic observed:

> "The idea—of boiling down a com-pany's essential purpose and character into a short paragraph which can be in-stantly understood by shareholders, workers and customers—sounds like a useful one. . . . But what emerges on to page one of the annual statement is all too often the worst kind of committee drafting, topped and tailed by syntacti-cally-challenged PR copywriters. . . . The typical British mission statement crams so many power-words into one sentence as to be at best inelegant, at worst virtu-ally unreadable."[4]

Nevertheless, despite common poor execution, mis-sion and vision statements should be the primary stipulations and records of what the organization is, why it exists, what its values are, how it does business, and what it intends to become. It is in the mission and vision that the company clarifies its goals. The words goal and objective are synonyms in the English lan-guage, but in the strategic management literature they are used to distinguish desired results and conditions that are longer-term and general (goals) from desired results or conditions that are short-term and specific (objectives). Goals are specified in mission and vision statements; objectives, discussed below, are related to marketing plans, to specified time periods, and to specific marketing mixes.

USING GUIDANCE STATEMENTS: CORPORATE SOCIAL RESPONSIBILITY

As noted, marketing strategies should be anchored in overarching *corporate strategies* which themselves are tied to and are intended to advance *corporate-level missions and visions*. Corporate missions and visions may or may not embrace purposes and goals beyond shareholder value and means to that end, but it is nevertheless important that marketing strategists at least consider the broader issues of *corporate social responsibility* (CSR). Even if the executive and the firm reject broader obligations, that rejection should be deliberate and explicit, especially, given contem-porary social and regulatory scrutiny of corporate behavior. Corporate social responsibility has been defined broadly as involving a firm taking "actions that appear to further some social good, beyond the interests of the firm and that which is required by law"[5] or as concerns about how businesses should deal with *social* and *public policy* matters.[6] Corporate Social Responsibility subsumes concerns for social and environmental outcomes. The term sustainabil-ity—"meeting the needs of the present without com-promising the ability of future generations to meet their own needs"[7]—also applies to both social and environmental matters but is generally understood to focus on sustainable treatment of the natural envi-ronment (or the "planet").

Attitudes about the appropriate role of busi-ness in pursuing social and environmental goals have changed across time, but some broad frameworks may be valuable across trends in framing how firms, marketing strategies, and marketing strategists inte-grate broader social and public policy concerns into strategy formation and day-to-day decision making. Those include "doing well by doing good," the idea that acting in a socially and environmentally respon-sible way may also enhance profitability, stakeholder theory, the triple bottom line, or the three pillars framework.

CHANGING SENTIMENT TOWARD CORPORATE SOCIAL RESPONSIBILITY.   Henry Ford, the indus-trialist and founder of Ford Motor Company, was once sued by his shareholders for putting expansive employment ahead of dividends to shareholders.

Ford was an advocate of and even created, within the Ford Motor Company, a "Sociology Department." He had justified foregoing a dividend payment in order "to employ still more men; to spread the benefits of this individual system to the greatest number, to help them build up their lives and their homes." The Michigan Supreme Court ruled that "A business organization is organized and carried on primarily for the profit of the shareholders. Directors cannot shape and conduct the affairs of a corporation for the mere incidental benefit of shareholders and for the primary purpose of benefiting others."

Later in the twentieth century, Henry Ford II, the founder's grandson and Ford chairman at the time, in apparent appreciation of the Court's ruling against his grandfather, asserted that "The corporation is not an all purpose mechanism. It is a sophisticated instrument designed to serve the economic needs of society and is not well equipped to serve social needs unrelated to its business operations." More recently, Henry II's own grandson, William Ford Jr. argued "I believe very strongly that corporations can and should be major forces for resolving social and environmental concerns in the twenty-first century. Not only do I think this is the right thing to do, I believe it is the best thing to do to achieve profitable, sustainable growth."[8]

Clearly, attitudes toward corporate social responsibility and the scope of "legitimate" commercial interests have evolved and continue to evolve. The Ford family's changing views parallel broader sentiments, including the notion widely held today that the best approach to corporate social and environmental responsibility may be to recognize that doing good—acting in socially responsible and environmentally sustainable ways—can also lead to doing well (realizing profits and sustainable growth).

DOING WELL BY DOING GOOD. This means searching for opportunities to do business in socially and environmentally responsible ways that *also enhance profitability and shareholder value.* An important point is that shareholder value may not be a short-term outcome, although equity markets may act as if it were. A longer-term perspective on shareholder value is more likely to recognize the merit, in tangible terms of shareholder value and profits or

doing "well," of a broad perspective on corporate responsibility or doing "good." There is evidence that fair treatment of workers, attention to the community and society, and producing "green" products all contribute to increased profitability.[9] Bob Willard and John Elkington have organized the various possible benefits of social and environmental responsibility into seven categories:

1. Easier hiring of the best talent;
2. Higher retention of top talent;
3. Increasing employee productivity;
4. Reduced expenses in manufacturing;
5. Reduced expenses at commercial sites;
6. Increased revenue/market share; and
7. Reduced risk, easier financing.[10]

STAKEHOLDER THEORY. Milton Freedman famously said "there is one and only one social responsibility of business—to use its resources and engage in activities designed to increase its profits so long as it stays within the rules of the game, which is to say, engages in open and free competition without deception or fraud"—he later restated that sentiment in a *New York Times* article titled "The Social Responsibility of Business Is to Increase Its Profits."[11] Freedman's words have become emblematic of the extreme position that businesses need consider no consequences of their actions beyond maximizing shareholder value, although his book and essay are more nuanced, asserting that return maximization is moral because profits and the accompanying jobs and well-suited products are *valuable contributions to society in themselves* and because maximizing returns on assets is itself a moral obligation (to the equity holders).

In contrast to Freedman's narrow "shareholder" centered view of the firm's obligations and legitimate concerns, "stakeholder theory" broadens the understanding of the firm's legitimate audiences and responsibilities. It asks two questions: *What is the firm's purpose?* And *what is the firm's obligations to its stakeholders?*[12] Stakeholders are various groups of people or organizations that have an interest (a "stake") in the actions and the success of the firm. Stakeholders can be internal (employees, managers, debt holders, and shareholders) or external (including the community and society, regulators, customers, vendors and suppliers). Stakeholders vary in their interest in the outcomes of the firm's operations and in its success as well as in their power or influence over the firms actions. The fundamental premise of stakeholder analysis is not a proposal, but, rather, a recognition that firms have always had broader groups of interested parties than just shareholders, and that those stakeholders have varying degrees of legitimate claims on the capabilities and resources of the firm and legitimate power to influence the firm's missions, visions, strategies, and actions. Stakeholder theory also asserts that firms will benefit—*do well*—by taking into account the interests of a broader array of stakeholders.

THE TRIPLE BOTTOM LINE.   Profits, people, and the planet (the "three pillars") or economic, social, and environmental concerns have been integrated into "the triple bottom line" ("3BL" or "TBL;" Figure 3-1). This framework highlights three clusters of legitimate concerns for any business, and it is certainly useful for sorting out and clarifying otherwise disorganized considerations and stakeholders. As originally proposed, the triple bottom line was proposed as literally implying multiple reports: Just as firms generate financial statements, the triple bottom line asserted that they should also produce environmental and social impact "statements." Challenges with this framework include the development of valid metrics for nonfinancial

outcomes—social and environmental impact metrics—as well as the question of how performance against those diverse metrics will be motivated and regulated. That is, how will social and environmental performance be measured, and what will happen if the firm performs well or poorly on those measures?

ASSESSING PAST PERFORMANCE AND CURRENT STRATEGY

The strategy formulation process must be grounded in a thorough analysis of past performance. Which objectives over the most recent period have been met? Which ones have been missed? Why? What are the firm's current strengths and weaknesses? Challenge the present strategy, assessing its current competitiveness, and looking for areas of leverage are essential in developing the *next* strategies. Several factors are integrated into assessment of past performance. One is review of ongoing financial and operating performance; another is the review of data from marketing information systems; a third category of factors involves the understanding of the firm's existing competitive advantages (and disadvantages) vis-à-vis the competition. Financial and operating results include firm, business-unit, product-level and account-level data on prices realized and revenues, margins, and profitability as well as operating results such as units shipped,

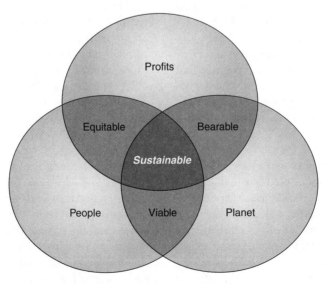

FIGURE 3-1 The Triple Bottom Line[13]

costs, inventory, and defects/reworks. Marketing information systems collect data on an ongoing basis regarding such customer-level measures as customer satisfaction, customer profitability, complaints, and customer loyalty. Satisfaction, profitability, and loyalty are essential markers of quality *from the customers' perspective* and have been shown to mediate the effects of quality—of both goods and services—on corporate outcomes such as profitability and stock price. Marketing information system data address the question "How well are we doing in our customers' eyes?" and are invaluable in troubleshooting malfunctions and failures, gauging the effects of various product attributes and marketing initiatives, and setting cogent, motivating objectives for the organization.

Understanding the company's strengths and weaknesses, or "competitive advantages," is another crucial company-related consideration in creating and maintaining effective strategies. The firm must know *the competition*. That is, strengths and weaknesses are only strengths or weaknesses in comparison to the competition, those assessments require evaluation of competitors' strengths, too. Identifying the company's strengths, weaknesses, and competitive advantages and matching them with opportunities is the essence of strategy formation, the next stage of the planning model described below.

ESTABLISHING PRELIMINARY OBJECTIVES AND TARGETS

A marketing strategy without specific objectives is like a ship without a compass. It can sail, but it cannot be sure whether it sails in the right direction or whether it ever reaches its destination. Having clear marketing objectives enables a company to: (1) focus and organize its efforts; (2) direct day-to-day activities and achieve consistency in decisions; (3) motivate people to strive for excellence; and, most importantly, (4) provide a basis for assessment and control. A simple mnemonic for weighing effective and useful marketing objectives is **"SMART," which denotes that objectives should be:** Specific, Measureable, Achievable, Relevant, and Time-specific. In order to facilitate assessment and adjustment, objectives should have these five qualities (Table 3-1).

Two distinct kinds of objectives are useful and common in developing marketing strategies, *marketing-related* objectives, and *financial* objectives. Some typical marketing objectives, which are often measured both at the market and the segment level, include

- Sales volume and market share (in units and/or dollars);
- Customer readiness variables (for example, awareness, interest);
- Customer behaviors and attitudes (satisfaction, brand attitudes, repeat-purchase intention, recommendations/word-of-mouth, complaints); and
- Accounts and distribution (retailers stocking, SKUs or facings, business-to-business customer accounts opened, approved-vendor lists).

These market-related objectives highlight the need, discussed earlier, to first clearly demarcate what market is being targeted and measured. Metrics like market share and customer satisfaction are meaningless unless the market to be shared and the customers to

TABLE 3-1 SMART Marketing-Plan Objectives

SMART	Description	Example
Specific	What *exactly* is to be achieved?	Dollar sales to new accounts in Italy
Measureable	*What quantitative or quantifiable methods and metrics will define the objective?*	Dollars of shipped merchandise as reported to management by logistics on report XYZ123
Achievable	*Is the objective realistic and demanding/challenging?*	20% increase over last year and the firm has an enhanced product offering
Relevant	*Is the objective under the control of the people or unit for whom it is established?*	This sales team for the new enhanced line calls on new accounts in Italy
Timed or Time-Specific	*When should these objectives be achieved and when will these objectives be assessed?*	Calendar-year 2010

be satisfied have first been spelled out clearly. Typical financial objectives include

- Profits (overall profits, contribution, margins, and contributions by units, products, and lines) and return-on-investment;
- Costs of Marketing (sales costs; costs of goods sold);
- Inventory and logistics (inventory levels and turns, fulfillment time, stock-outs).

In setting objectives there is an important tension between *investing* in long-term strengths—such as in innovation and new product development, building customer loyalty, and the like—and *"harvesting"* short-term profits. Whether or not the strategy is to invest or harvest, that decision must be made deliberately and in the context of a clear understanding of the business model and of consumer responses (for instance, customer stickiness, customer profitability [customer lifetime value], and purchase rates).

IDENTIFYING STRATEGIC GAP(S) OR PLANNING GAPS

One way to think about strategy is to think about the gap that exists between *where we are* and *where we want to be.* Figure 3-2 depicts what has often been referred to as the strategic gap or the planning gap. The horizontal axis represents time, divided into the past and the future. The vertical axis represents performance. As

noted above, there are two types of performance measures and objectives that are important to marketing strategists: market performance and financial performance. Market performance is often measured as sales or market share. Financial performance usually relates to profitability or return on something, such as sales, assets, or capital.

Figure 3-2 is divided into the past and the future, where past performance is past sales or share or past profitability (return). Going into the future we have our marketing and financial objectives (generally heading in an upward direction). Below the objectives we have a momentum forecast of our current strategy; this is where our current course (strategy and programs) will take us if we just keep doing what we have been doing. If there is a difference between the objectives and the momentum of the present strategy, we have a planning or *strategic gap.* The bigger the gap is, the more strategic change is needed in order to reach the objectives.

Closing the Gap

Let us think about the situation in which the organization has a *sales gap*—that is, the planning gap in Figure 3-2 is between the sales objectives and the momentum of the present strategy with respect to sales. *What are the possible ways to close such a sales gap?* One way to think about this would be based on the relationship with existing company offerings and existing markets, as discussed earlier in Chapter 2 as Product/Market

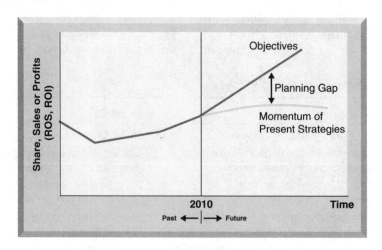

FIGURE 3-2   The Planning or Strategic Gap

Growth Strategies. As discussed above, there are a limited set of possible "growth strategies." At any given time, a firm is selling its existing products to its existing markets. Logically, growth (closing the gap) can come from selling more of the firm's existing products to its existing markets (market penetration); selling existing products to *new markets* (market development); selling *new products* to existing markets (product development); or selling new products to new markets (diversification). One other possible way to increase sales would be to forward integrate—an option open to manufacturers but not to retailers as they are already as forward integrated as possible.

If the gap is a *profitability gap*, that is, if the gap between objectives and momentum in Figure 3-2 is between profitability objectives and the momentum of profits, then another set of generic strategies is suggested. These include the following:

1. *Increasing the yield.* This can be done, perhaps, by improving the sales mix, increasing the price, or reducing distribution margins.
2. *Reducing costs.* This can be achieved through economies of scale, better capacity utilization,

systems and process efficiencies, or out-and-out cost cutting.
3. *Backward Integration.* This implies undertaking value-added activities that had been outsourced to suppliers; that is, making or doing things "in house" that had been purchased. "Backward" refers to integrating toward the source in the channels of distribution.
4. *Reducing Investment Intensity.* This can be achieved perhaps by reducing inventories, factoring accounts receivable, or the sale and lease back of property, plant, and equipment.
5. *Selectivity and Focus.* Abandoning segments we can't win in or rationalizing the product line or the channels of distribution ("rationalizing" generally refers to narrowing the scope by concentrating on the most profitable and effective and cutting inefficient or ineffective products or channels).

Figure 3-3 shows these generic profitability-improvement strategies. There are ten generic strategies. In other words, at a high level there is a finite set of available strategies—some relate to sales or marketing

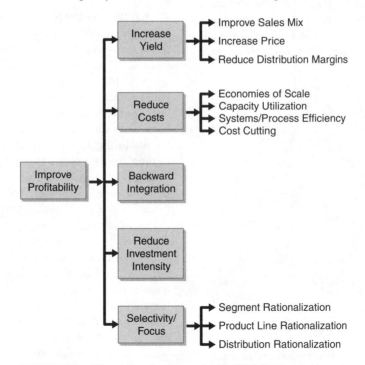

FIGURE 3-3 Alternatives for Improving Profitability

improvement and some relate to profitability improvement. A company might employ several of these strategies simultaneously. For example, we might be pursuing a market penetration and product development strategy along with cost reduction at the same time.

INTEGRATING SITUATION ASSESSMENT

Situation assessments should be wide-ranging and descriptive in the sense that these assessments seek to understand what is going on in the environment and within the firm. But, situation assessments are also *analytical* in the sense that they assess, integrate, and organize vast and potentially overwhelming data into organized information that can be used to drive decision making and action. Figure 3-4 emphasizes the need to sort vast amounts of messy data into organized, useable information which then supports decision making and strategic action. Situation assessment establishes the foundations for planning and strategy formulation. There are at least a couple of straightforward tools for systematically managing and integrating situation assessment and to structure the product of that assessment in ways that facilitate strategic thinking. First, there is

a pervasive "relevance test" that should be applied to all assessments. Second, scenario analysis is an invaluable tool for integrating situation assessment and uncertain possible future trends and events into strategic planning.

RELEVANCE TEST. It is worthwhile to highlight the fact that *not everything in the environment is meaningful,* at least not to every decision or strategy. To avoid "paralysis by analysis," the first job of the strategist is to cull through the tremendous amount of noise to focus on substantive and important information. Because every situation is complex and there are overwhelming amounts of data that *could* be considered, it is important at the outset to emphasize a "relevance test" before assessing the situation. This is the *"so what?"* of strategic marketing analysis. The manager must constantly ask: "*Is this important and relevant to this firm and to this strategy?* In fact, the first job of a manager is to filter the available data down to *useable information.* Time, energy, and attention should be reserved for information that directly affects strategy and ties to decisions.

SCENARIO ANALYSIS. An effective tool for bringing together situation assessment and for planning for future uncertainties is "scenario analysis." When Coca-Cola introduced "New Coke" in the mid-1980s, public response was mixed. Contrary to legend, sales actually went up, but there was also a backlash from consumers who demanded their old Coke back. Coca-Cola responded quickly by reintroducing the old formula as "Coca-Cola Classic" while maintaining New Coke. In the end, Coca-Cola (across both products) had more shelf space in grocers and higher overall sales. Donald Keogh, president of Coca-Cola at the time, said "Some critics will say Coca-Cola made a marketing mistake. Some cynics will say that we planned the whole thing. The truth is we are not that dumb, and we are not that smart."[14] He meant that the company was not smart enough to foresee that introducing New Coke and having customers reject it and then having to reintroduce Old Coke (Classic) was the way to gain market share. He also meant the company was not so dumb as to launch New Coke without a contingency plan to fall back on in the event it wasn't accepted. Coca-Cola

FIGURE 3-4 From Data to Information to Decisions to Action

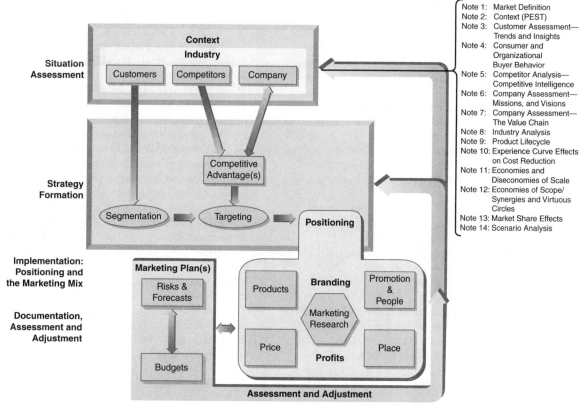

Note 1: Market Definition
Note 2: Context (PEST)
Note 3: Customer Assessment—Trends and Insights
Note 4: Consumer and Organizational Buyer Behavior
Note 5: Competitor Analysis—Competitive Intelligence
Note 6: Company Assessment—Missions, and Visions
Note 7: Company Assessment—The Value Chain
Note 8: Industry Analysis
Note 9: Product Lifecycle
Note 10: Experience Curve Effects on Cost Reduction
Note 11: Economies and Diseconomies of Scale
Note 12: Economies of Scope/Synergies and Virtuous Circles
Note 13: Market Share Effects
Note 14: Scenario Analysis

Linking Situation Assessment to Relevant Tools and Frameworks

had planned for uncertainty by thinking through responses to multiple "possible futures" or "scenarios." Scenario analysis is essentially an elaborate "if . . . then" planning tool—maybe more accurately described as an "if . . . and if . . . and if . . ., then . . ." tool, because it considers multiple factors evolving to shape possible futures or scenarios. It is a powerful method for formalizing situation assessment, for clarifying possible futures, and for preparing the firm's preferred responses to those possibilities.

Endnotes

1. Lao Tzu, (trans. Stephen Mitchell) *Tao Te Ching: An illustrated journey* (London: Frances Lincoln Limited, 1999), 34.
2. Michael E. Raynor, "That vision thing: Do we need it?" *Long Range Planning* 31, no. 3 (June 1998): 368–376 (definition is from page 371).
3. James C. Collins and Jerry I. Porras, "Building your company's vision," *Harvard Business Review* (September–October, 1996): 65–77.
4. Martin Vander Weyer, "Mission Improvable: For Cliched Syntactically-Challenged Copy Mission Statements Are Hard to Beat," *Management Today* (September 1994): 66–68.
5. Abagail McWilliams and, Donald Siegel, "Corporate Social Responsibility: A Theory of the Firm Perspective," *Academy of Management Review* 26, no. 1, (January 2001): 117–127 (definition is from page 117); also see A. McWilliams, D. Siegel, and P. Wright, "Corporate Social Responsibility: Strategic Implications," *Journal of Management Studies* 43, no. 1 (January 2006): 1–18.

6. Duane Windsor, "Corporate Social Responsibility: Three Key Approaches," *Journal of Management Studies* 43, no. 1 (January 2006): 93–114.

7. G. H. Brundtland, *Our Common Future* (Brussels: World Commission on Environment and Development, 1987), 43 (published as annex to General Assembly document A/42/427).

8. These quotes, this reasoning, and the juxtapositioning of the latter two quotes (Henry II's and William Jr.'s), are found in Subhabrata Bobby Banerjee, *Corporate Social Responsibility: The Good, the Bad and the Ugly* (Northampton, MA: Edward Elgar Publishing, 2007), 13, 51. Banerjee cites Henry Ford (1919) for the first quote, *Dodge v. Ford Motor Company*, 204 Mich. 459, 170 N.W. 668 (Mich. 1919), for the second (to the court), Regan, 1998 for the second and Ford 2000 for the third.

9. Oliver Falck and Stephan Heblich, "Corporate Social Responsibility: Doing Well by Doing Good," *Business Horizons* 50, no. 3 (May–June, 2007)), 247–254; A. Hillman and G. Keim, "Shareholder Value, Stakeholder Management and Social Issues: What's the Bottom Line?" *Strategic Management Journal* 22, no. 2 (February 2001): 125–139; and H. Ozcelik, N. Langton, and H. Aldrich, "Doing Well and Doing Good: The Relationship between Leadership Practices that Facilitate a Positive Emotional Climate and Organizational Performance," *Journal of Managerial Psychology* 23, no. 2 (2008): 186–203.

10. Bob Willard and John Elkington, *The Sustainability Advantage: Seven Business Case Benefits of a Triple Bottom Line* (Gabriola Island, BC, Canada: New Society Publishers).

11. Milton Friedman, "The Social Responsibility of Business is to Increase its Profits," *The New York Times Magazine* (September 13, 1970): 32–33, 122–126.

12. Freeman, R. Edward, *Strategic management : A stakeholder approach* (Boston: Pitman 1984); see also T. Donaldson and L. Preston, "The Stakeholder Theory of the Modern Corporation: Concepts, evidence and implications," *Academy of Management Review* 20, no. 1, (January 1995): 65–91; and R. Edward Freeman, Andrew C. Wicks, Bidhan Parmar, "Stakeholder Theory and 'The Corporate Objective Revisited,'" *Organization Science* 15, no. 3 (May–June, 2004): 364–369.

13. Rodrigo Lozano, "Envisioning sustainability three-dimensionally," *Journal of Cleaner Production* 16, no. 17 (November 2008): 1838–1846 (this figure is adapted from Figure 1, page 1839).

14. Mark Pendergrast, *For God, country and Coca-Cola: The definitive history of the great American soft drink and the company that makes it*, 2nd edition (New York: Basic Books, 2000), 358.

4

Strategy Formation

*"And strategy must start with a different value
proposition. A strategy delineates a territory in which
a company seeks to be unique."*

MICHAEL PORTER[1]

Strategy formation is the heart of the strategic marketing process. The overarching objective is to *meet some specific needs of some specific customers better than the competition within enduring, profitable relationships.* There are four substeps within strategy formulation, organized in Figure 4-1:

- *Identifying competitive advantages.* What things *does* the firm do or *could* it do better than the competition and at a profit?
- *Segmenting the Market.* What are the important differences across customers with regard to their *needs* and their *responses to the marketing mix*? How *attractive* are the various segments?
- *Targeting.* Which specific customers and needs (segments) will be served utilizing which specific competitive advantages? How well do segments *fit* or match with the firm's competitive advantages?; and
- *Positioning.* What is the unique position in the marketplace that the firm will claim? How will the firm claim that position? Positioning is the implementation of the strategy (targeting) into specific tactics (the marketing mix—price, product, place or distribution, people/service, and promotion or "integrated marketing communications").

FIGURE 4-1 Strategy Formation

IDENTIFYING COMPETITIVE ADVANTAGES

For long-term viability, every firm must be better than the competition at something. Those things the firm is best at are its "competitive advantages" (sometimes referred to as "core competencies" or "sustainable competitive advantages"). A company has a competitive advantage if it possesses resources or capabilities that are: (1) valuable in the market (who wants to be best at something no one cares about?); (2) rare (competitors don't have the same resources or capabilities); (3) not imitable or substitutable (competitors cannot easily imitate or work-around them); and (4) transferable to other markets or products. In a strengths-and-weaknesses framework, competitive advantages are the strengths.

The "value chain" offers a useful framework for identifying competitive advantages. McKinsey and Company developed a generic value chain consisting of six distinct activities that need to be carried out to bring a product onto the market: technology development, product design, manufacturing, marketing, distribution, and service.[2] Michael Porter offered a somewhat more detailed but similar version of the value chain that distinguishes "primary" value-adding activities the firm performs along the flow of goods from inputs (raw materials) to outputs (products), marketing and sales, and support services as well as the essential "support" activities such as human resource management and research and development that facilitate those primary activities. The essential question is: *How well does the firm perform the various activities of the value chain vis-à-vis the competition?*

Segmenting the Market

> *"The aim of marketing is to know and understand the customer so well the product or service fits him and sells itself."*
>
> Peter Drucker[3]

Because customers within a broadly defined market almost never have the same characteristics or the same needs and requirements, there is, as a rule, an opportunity to subdivide or segment the market. The purpose of market segmentation is to identify subgroups ("segments") of customers that are similar to each other and different from the rest of the market with regard to needs, wants, and responses to the marketing mix. Marketing-mix-response differences are not just responses to *product* differences; customers may respond differently to *price, service levels, advertisements,* and/or *distribution channels.* Differences in responses in regard to *any of these marketing mix elements*—which correspond to differences in underlying needs or wants—are meaningful segmentation differences and an opportunity to gain advantage through targeted marketing mix development.

The primary reason to differentiate customers into segments is to capture the strategic advantage of meeting differing needs with tailored mixes. The objective and the key to successful segmentation is to find differing needs that match the firm's competitive advantages and thus can be served at a profit better than by the competition. If all customers respond to all elements of the marketing mix in the same way, then there is no reason to segment. The objective then would be to develop the single optimal marketing mix for all customers, and there would be only one "winner." Finding substantial differences that others have overlooked can constitute a "customer insight." It can create a significant opportunity for the firm. For example, in the late 1980s Toyota recognized that the automobile industry was treating younger luxury sedan buyers as a homogeneous segment—whether or not they valued performance, reliability, comfort, or service—and BMW was dominating that market. Toyota launched Lexus as a reliable, comfortable luxury sedan with terrific service, and BMW was forced to refocus on the performance luxury sedan buyers.

There are two types of variables to be distinguished in the segmentation process for both consumer (B2C) and business-to-business (B2B) markets: *segmentation bases* and *segment descriptors.* The *bases* of segmentation—the underlying differences that warrant targeting with distinctive marketing programs—should be differing *customer needs,* differences in needs that underlie differences in responses to elements of the product, and marketing program. Table 4-1 clarifies what a "customer need" is as well as what the related ideas "customer wants,"

TABLE 4-1 Needs, Wants, Benefits, and Demand

Definitions	Examples
Needs: The underlying motivation or reason driving consumption. Conceptualized as the difference between customers' perceived current state and their *desired* state. Needs include: basic physiological needs (food, shelter), safety (security, property), social needs (belonging, affection), esteem (self-esteem, respect by others), and self-actualization (intellectual growth, self-expression).[4]	Hunger
Wants: The specific form that customers may desire to address needs, influenced by culture, experiences, situations, and marketing actions; wants are shaped by culture, experience, situations, and individual factors.	Filet Mignon Kung Pau Chicken Risotto al Gargonzola
Benefit or "Benefit Sought": An *outcome* of consuming a product that motivates purchase and consumption. Benefits are the *consequences* of the consumption of the product and of product attributes.	Nourishment/Nutrition Hunger satiation Taste sensations
Demand: A want combined with the ability (including resources such as money and time, and access) to purchase. Demand requires that consumers *want the product* and have *the ability to buy* the product	Hungry customers who want filet mignon, who can afford filet mignon, and who can access filet mignon.

"benefits sought," and "demand" are. All of these can be legitimate segmentation bases. *Descriptors* of segments are observable variables that *correlate with* the differences in needs/wants/benefits-sought and allow the segment to be identified and targeted. Descriptor variables include things like demographics (age, education, income, etc.), geographics (the location of consumers), psychographics (lifestyles), and behaviors (usage rate, stage in buying process or "readiness," loyalty, and profitability or "customer lifetime value"). In business-to-business markets, segments of organizations can be described on "firm demographics" (size, ownership, etc.), behaviors (purchasing histories) and "B2B psychographics," including purchasing processes (buy centers, bidding, etc.), ownership, and strategies.

Although it is important to describe segments in observable and actionable ways—ways that allow the marketer to identify and address the segment—

it is still true that at the root of differences in the way customers respond to the marketing mix are *differing customer needs*. If a segment is, for example, more price conscious than other segments, *that* is the basis of the segmentation (the need for economy). Such a segment may be *described* as older, retired consumers, or busy single-income parents. But age, family status, and employment (retired or full-time homemaker) *don't drive the segment differences*—the need for economy is what differentiates the segment from other customers. Age, family status, and employment are all demographic variables that correlate with the need for economy. They also describe the customers and the segment, and most importantly, allow the segments to be targeted with tailored offerings. The distinction between and intersection of segment descriptors and segmentation bases (underlying customer needs) are illustrated in Figure 4-2.

		Descriptors				
		Age	**Income**	**Location**	**Loyalty**	**Profitability**
Bases (Needs)	Prestige					
	Quality					
	Economy					
	Performance					
	Reliability					
	Conformance					

FIGURE 4-2   Example of Segmentation *Bases* and *Descriptors*

Similarly, product-related behaviors, such as usage rate and loyalty, are important to strategic segmentation but they are, still, only *correlates* of the underlying *needs* that drive the segments' behaviors. For example, it makes strategic sense to develop loyal customers and to target customers who have higher lifetime value. However, loyalty and customer lifetime value are themselves driven by underlying needs, and efforts to build loyalty or target high-value customers will be most successful if they include efforts to thoroughly understand those needs.

SEGMENTATION SCOPE.   Segmentation decisions include not only *which* segments to target but, simultaneously, the *scope* of the targeted segments; that is, decisions about the number and size of the segments and the relationship amongst the segments to be targeted. Some firms target very broad segments with relatively homogeneous offerings; this is based on "global" and "mass" marketing strategies. Other firms target adjacent segments with somewhat differentiated offerings; this is a form of target marketing. Finally, some firms target smaller segments of the market with extremely focused offerings; this is niche marketing. Figure 4-3 graphically presents these alternatives.

DIFFERENTIATED MARKETING.   Differentiated marketing means that a company develops individual marketing programs for different individual target segments (Figure 4-4). As it tailors products and marketing programs to the segments, it can better

meet the segment-specific needs and requirements, and it can, therefore, create superior value and demand price premiums. The downside is a higher complexity of the organization and the product portfolio, lower economies of scale (standardized products and marketing mixes optimize economies of scale, but economies of *scope* can still be achieved across products/programs), and, as a consequence, higher unit costs. Differentiated marketing can consist of:

- *Selected specialization.* The company selects and focuses on one or a few single segments (Case A in Figure 4-4).
- *Segment specialization.* A producer decides to serve several different needs of one segment and develops many products and marketing programs for this segment (Case B in Figure 4-4).
- *Product specialization.* Focus on one product that is tailored to all market segments (Case C in Figure 4-4).
- *Full market coverage.* A company decides to address all market segments and develops all products the segment wants (Case D in Figure 4-4)

SEGMENTATION DYNAMICS.   Segments are dynamic. Segment preferences change—that is, a segment's ideal product can shift over time, sometimes quite rapidly. In addition, segments can split or merge. Groups of consumers that were reasonably treated as homogenous may develop important dif-

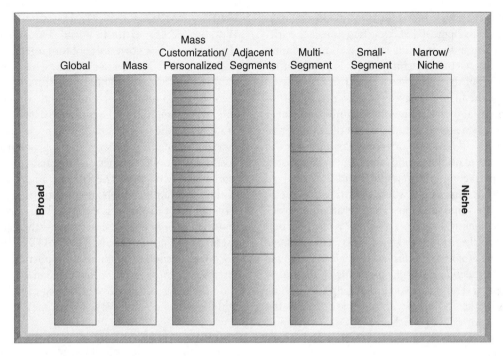

FIGURE 4-3 Segmentation Scope

ferences, and consumers who had differing response profiles may converge around common preferences and behaviors. For example, the luxury sedan market treated affluent professional Americans as relatively homogeneous—and BMW dominated the younger luxury sedan market in the mid-1980s. By the early 1990s, Lexus and other Japanese brands had split the segment by recognizing and serving differing needs:

BMW retained the performance luxury drivers while Lexus carved out a large segment of reliability-comfort luxury drivers.

Targeting

Targeting—matching the firm's competitive advantages with attractive market opportunities—is the

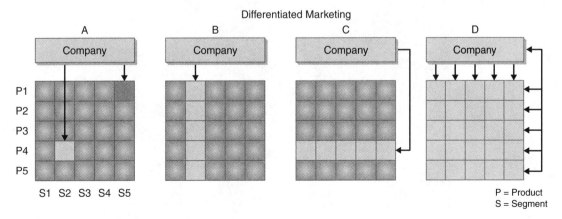

FIGURE 4-4 Differentiated Marketing Approaches[5]

crux of the strategic marketing formulation (shown graphically in Figure 4-1 above). Targeting is the crucial junction in formulating strategy and translating strategy into tactics, matching external opportunities with internal strengths—strengths the firm has or strengths the firm can develop or acquire. Situation assessment and environmental scanning, scenario analysis, segmentation, and analysis of competitive advantages *all feed into targeting.* Positioning, the construction of the brand and deployment of a unique marketing mix, *flows from and is determined by targeting.* Targeting is where the strategy is specified and becomes concrete. The overarching objective is to *identify segments that will value offerings built upon the firm's strengths;* that is, to *meet some specific needs of some specific customers better than the competition within enduring, profitable relationships.* There are several frameworks that help identify attractive markets to target with valuable offerings, the two most powerful of which are: SWOT analysis and the application of strength/ attractiveness matrices to segments.

SWOT ANALYSIS. SWOT analysis—**S**trengths, **W**eaknesses, **O**pportunities, and **T**hreats analysis (Figure 4-5)—is a powerful tool for targeting appropriate markets with effective offerings. It summarizes the juncture of *external* analyses (situation assessment of customers, the context, and competitors) and *internal* analysis (strengths and weaknesses). We can think of the strengths and weaknesses as a summarization of the firm's or offering's competitive position; the opportunities and threats represent the market's attractiveness. The SWOT framework is one of the most familiar tools of strategic planning. An essential point to emphasize about SWOT analyses is that they are *not* merely descriptive—they are most useful as *prescriptive* tools. The SWOT framework organizes strengths, weaknesses, opportunities, and threats *to identify strategic actions to achieve desired ends.* Table 4-5 summarizes the strategic implications of the range of possible SWOT outcomes.

STRENGTH/ATTRACTIVENESS MATRICES. A second powerful tool for identifying exploitable

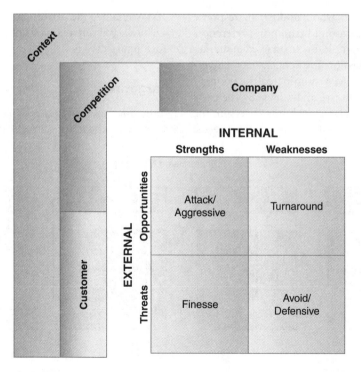

FIGURE 4-5 SWOT Analysis

matches between segments and competitive advantages involves strength/attractiveness matrices, such as the Boston Consulting Group's (BCG) Growth/Share Matrix or the GE/McKinsey Portfolio Planning Grid.[6] These frameworks were originally developed to aid in prioritizing strategic business units (SBUs) and products within a company's "portfolio" (see discussion of product portfolios in Chapter 5 at Product Strategies, below), but the same strength/attractiveness concepts are also effective for *targeting segments with strengths*. Here, in targeting applications, segments are assessed with regard to (a) their general attractiveness (*How good would it be to succeed in this segment if the firm could?*) and (b) the strength of the firm against the segment's particular needs and dynamics (*How likely or well-suited is the firm to succeed in this segment regardless of how attractive it is?*). Some market segments are more attractive than others. Similarly, a firm's distinctive competitive advantages will be

better suited to meet the needs of some segments than others—and some firms' competitive advantages are a poor fit with some segments' needs. A firm may, for example, have access to channels that serve a segment. It may have brands that are well liked by customers in a segment. It may have an installed base in the segment, or production capabilities that make the firm's offering a good fit with the segment's needs. Figure 4-6 illustrates the sorting and prioritizing of segments within a general strengths/attractiveness grid.

TARGETING DISCIPLINE. In many situations it is as important to know who the firm is *not* targeting as it is to know which segments it *is* targeting. No product offering can be right for everybody and a common trap is that, in trying to grow sales toward new customers and new segments, marketers lose their focus and their original advantage in their primary segments. This may be termed "target drift," the loss of

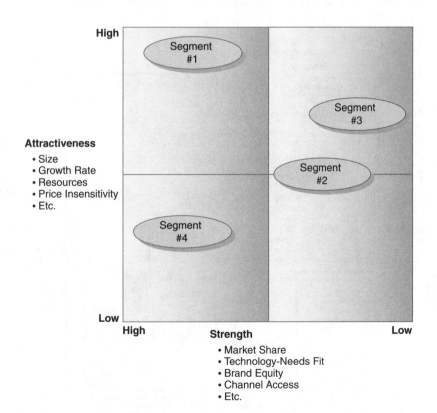

FIGURE 4-6 Strengths/Attractiveness and Segmentation

focus on the target segment in favor of broader or alternative segments.

"If you run after two rabbits, you won't catch either one."
Traditional Armenian Proverb[7]

Closely related to target drift is the temptation to target more than one segment with a single mix; that is, to "straddle" segments or to squat between segments. That strategy may work in the short run, particularly in the early stages of the product lifecycle, but it is unlikely to succeed for long and certain to fail in the long term. The problem with trying to serve two or more segments with a single marketing mix is that the mix isn't *exactly* right for *anyone*—and a competitor will, eventually, offer a mix that *is* exactly right. One solution to straddling may be to revisit the segmentation scheme looking for multiple segments where the original segmentation solution had identified just one. Another alternative to straddling is to offer more than one marketing mix. That is, to focus tailored marketing mixes for each segment. In any case, it usually

turns out that the marketer who targets two segments with a single marketing mix doesn't catch either one.

Positioning

We define positioning as the deployment of the entire marketing mix (products, people, prices, place/distribution, and promotion/integrated marketing communications) to claim a unique, valued, and defensible position in the marketplace. Many experts have highlighted the fact that a product's or brand's position is really something that resides in the consumers' minds. That position is driven by the actions of the marketing firm or brander, and those actions are encapsulated in the "marketing mix." The mix is the totality of tactics and offerings that the firm can use to influence consumers' perceptions of the offering's position and to thereby meet customer needs. The next chapter elaborates on implementing marketing strategy with the marketing mix to claim a position in consumers' perceptions.

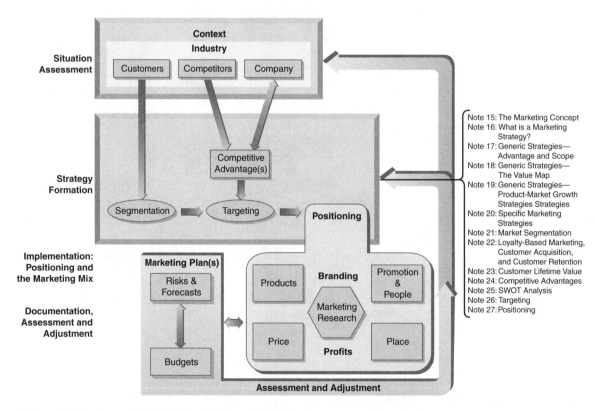

Linking Strategy Formation to Relevant Tools and Frameworks

Endnotes

1. Michael E. Porter, "Toward a Dynamic Theory of Strategy," *Strategic Management Journal* 12, Special Issue: Fundamental Research Issues in Strategy and Economics (Winter 1991): 95–117, 98.
2. See J. B. Barney and W. S. Hesterly, *Strategic Management and Competitive Advantage* (Upper Saddle River, New Jersey: Pearson Education, 2006).
3. Peter Drucker, *Management* (New York: Harper & Row, 1973), 64.
4. See Abraham H. Maslow, "A Theory of Human Motivation," *Psychological Review* 50, no. 4 (1943): 370, 396; and Abraham H. Maslow, *Motivation and Personality* (New York: Harper & Row, 1954).
5. Source: Adapted from Derek F. Abell, *Defining the Business: The Starting Point for Stragic Planning* (Upper Saddle River, New Jersey: Prentice Hall, 1980).
6. See Arnoldo C. Hax and Nicolas S. Majluf, "The Use of the Industry Attractiveness-Business Strength Matrix in Strategic Planning," *Interfaces* 13, no. 2 (1983): 54–71.
7. *Prentice-Hall Encyclopedia of World Proverbs* (Englewood Cliffs, New Jersey: Prentice-Hall, 1986), 399.

5

Implementation

"Some people try to find things in this game that don't exist; but football is only two things—blocking and tackling."

VINCE LOMBARDI, LEGENDARY AMERICAN FOOTBALL COACH[1]

"Many companies want to leapfrog past the basic blocking and tackling of doing the everyday things right. . . . This just won't cut it. If a company can't get the basics down in the delivery of its products and services, other effort will fall on the deaf ears of customers."

JEANNE BLISS, AUTHOR AND FORMER CHIEF CUSTOMER OFFICER AT LANDS' END, MICROSOFT, ALLSTATE, COLDWELL BANKER AND MAZDA.[2]

Blocking and tackling are the basic skills of American football—the "building blocks" so to speak—all other plays and strategies are created by arranging and integrating blocking and tackling. Football coaches and fans too often focus on elaborate strategies and sophisticated techniques, but games are most often won or lost when players execute the basics well—that is, *winning or losing is decided by the unglamorous but crucial fundamentals of blocking and tackling!*

This book is about strategic marketing, and much of it focuses, appropriately, on the high-profile and "exciting" elements of strategy—but this section focuses on the *implementation*. As in football and as emphasized by Jeanne Bliss, the former chief customer officer at five iconic brands, if the tactics and day-to-day details of implementation aren't done well, all the beautiful strategies in the world can't save the effort.

Implementation starts with an understanding of the product or brand's position in the marketplace—that is, the desired "positioning" in customers' perceptions *is the strategy* at the implementation level. Positioning involves developing a tailored marketing mix to target some specific set of customer needs in a *unique* way—a way that no competitor matches—and communicating that position to customers effectively. Positioning is something that, in reality, lives in the customers' *perceptions* of the offering. Customers won't see a brand manager's "positioning statement" or care what the marketing strategist thinks the products position is supposed to be; they'll rely on their own perceptions to decide where it's positioned—and that will be the only product position that matters. Nevertheless, those perceptions are shaped by the marketing mix and its coherence. Thus, the objective of positioning is to "own" a valued place in customers' perceptions. Once the firm has determined *which customers* and *which needs* it is targeting with *which competitive advantages*, it must identify and delineate exactly what "position" those decisions equate to in the marketplace: *In what territory does the product or brand seek to be unique? How does the marketing mix claim that territory?*

Segmentation is the tough job—positioning is the easy job. That is, if you understand the segment's needs well-enough, the positioning challenge should be, if not easy, at least straightforward. If you believe you have a positioning problem, it is probably because you are not sure which segment you are trying to serve or you are serving too many segments.

Positioning aligns the myriad tactical decisions involved in going to market, as shown in Figure 5-1. It is the implementation of strategy into specific brand-building marketing mix elements. These are all of the "details" and specific decisions about the firm's products and services, brands, prices, places (channels and distribution), and promotions (communications with customers). It is important to remember that the fundamental objective of positioning is not the marketing-mix activities themselves, but rather the resulting *customer perceptions.*

Marketing research should lie at the heart of the marketing program and guide all of the tactical elements of the marketing mix (Figure 6-1). Brands are the cumulative sum of all of the marketing tactics and messages across the history of the offering. Brands are the company's and the consumer's shorthand for the overall offering and its position in the market. Therefore, this section on implementation begins with marketing research and then develops the concept of the brand before considering the various elements of the marketing mix and their strategic implications.

MARKETING RESEARCH

Marketing research is a very wide umbrella encompassing an assortment of activities and objectives, including broad, inductive, and exploratory "customer assessment," which is part of situation assessment, as well as *issue- or decision-specific research* that: (1) *describes* markets, segments, and customers; (2) *guides* strategies, programs and tactics; and/or (3) *evaluates* strategies, programs and tactics. This breadth is clarified in Table 5-1. Although all marketing research is focused on understanding the customer and tying the firm's actions to a customer orientation, broad customer assessment and issue-specific market research begin with different objectives, draw on different methods, and result in different sorts of information and guidance. As organized in Table 5-1, market research includes a range of activities from exploring the environment for opportunities and insights to project-based research to hone specific elements of the marketing mix as well as Customer Relationship Management (CRM) systems, which entail the ongoing collection of marketing metrics and customer data for program assessment and customization/targeting.

Too frequently, managers take a "more is better" approach to marketing research and data collection. They collect reams of ill-defined data and *then* sift through those voluminous data hoping to find useable information to support decision making. This is dysfunctional and contributes to "paralysis by analysis," the tendency to over analyze and over research issues and the failure to make decisions and act. To avoid unfocused and ineffective research, the marketing research process stipulates that the decision that will be guided by the research or the problem to be solved by the research *be clearly specified in*

FIGURE 5-1 Positioning Drives Tactics

TABLE 5-1 Organizing Customer-Focused Research

Customer-Oriented Marketing Research	**Situation Assessment**	*Customer Assessment*	The broad, exploratory, and inductive study of customers in general to identify (a) *trends* in needs and demand, and (b) *customer insights*.
	Strategy Formation and Implementation	*Segmentation, Targeting, and Positioning*	Ongoing as well as focused research indentifying differences across customers/consumers with regard to needs and descriptive characteristics and linking those differences to existing or achievable competitive advantages.
		Positioning and the Marketing Mix	Focused research to pretest and refine tactics, including price, promotions, and advertising; new products or product modifications, and merchandising programs; and to gauge the effects of those tactics on achieving the desired positioning.
		Customer Relationship Management (CRM)	Ongoing data collections tied to specific accounts, customers, or consumers that serves to tailor offerings (personalize or customize offerings) and direct investments and efforts toward the "right" customers and segments.
	Assessment & Adjustment	*Customer- and Market-Oriented Metrics*	Focused and ongoing research collecting information on customer responses to the marketing mix, including measures of satisfaction, loyalty, profitability, and revenues.

detail before the research is designed and well before any data are collected. Figure 5-2 shows the basic Marketing Research process,[3] which emphasizes the necessity of early problem and objective specification. Some experts have even recommended actually outlining the "final report" *first*—before designing the study or collecting any data—in order to engage the manager early in the research process and focus efforts on the right questions and on guiding managerially-controllable outcomes.[4]

Questions for Marketing Research

In science there are two well-known types of errors: Type I errors involve finding confirmatory results for hypotheses that are, in fact, not true ("false positives"); Type II errors are rejecting hypotheses that are, in fact, true ("false negatives"). A less well-known sort of error has been labeled "Type III

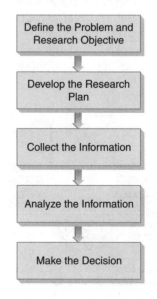

FIGURE 5-2 The Marketing Research Process[5]

error": getting the right answers for the wrong questions.[6] Careful attention to framing the right questions, even going so far as to draft the final report first to emphasize the value of the research, is vital to effective and efficient marketing research. There are three broad categories of questions that marketing research can address:

- Market Questions:
  - Demand forecasting: What is the size of the market?
  - Needs identification and segmentation: What do customers need and care about, and how much do they care? How do customers differ in regards to those needs and "importance weightings"?
- Mix/Program Questions:
  - The effect of various mix elements: What is the best product, message, channel, or price?
- Assessment and Adjustment Questions:
  - Market Share: How are we doing vis-à-vis the competition?
  - Performance: How do our customers feel about us? How loyal are they?

Once the purpose of the research—the question or questions to be addressed—has been carefully defined and delimited, it is useful to reexamine whether or not research is necessary at all. It may be that no research is necessary or justified. There are at least two ways to think about whether investments in marketing research are warranted:

1. *What are the ranges of actions that are possible?* If additional information won't change future decisions in meaningful ways, *don't do the research.* A reality of marketing research is that, too often, managers know what they want to do, what they have to do, what they cannot do, or what they will never do, but they nevertheless conduct research on the decision. That research is a waste of time and resources.
2. *How much will information help?* How much will the research reduce risk and uncertainty or improve accuracy in decision making? One study found, for example, that 92 percent of all new cereals failed despite rigorous marketing research. It turned out to be cheaper to simply

launch new products and "test" them in the actual marketplace. That is, sometimes the best course of action is to "fail fast, fail cheap, and move on."[7] This is, of course, a function of the cost of the research, the cost and potential consequences of failure, and the firm or manager's level of risk aversion.

Marketing Research Designs

Marketing research efforts can have several different types of designs, including *exploratory* (less unstructured research intended to discover deeper understandings and to generate specific issues for future research), *descriptive* (to characterize markets, segments, and even specific customers with regard to size, attitudes and preferences, behaviors, needs, etc.), and *causal* (intended to link variables, such as differences in price or advertising, to outcomes such as sales). We have pulled customer assessment, the prototypical exploratory research, out and dealt with it as a distinct activity with its own objectives, methods, and outcomes. But, exploratory research is also used in more focused marketing research, most often at the front end of projects, to identify issues and generate hypotheses for further study.

Marketing Research Approaches and Data

Many different approaches to marketing research can address certain questions. Marketing research approaches range from reference to existing census data or analysis of in-house archival sales records to highly structured surveys with forced-choice items collected in large, random samples of consumers. Different methods yield different types of data and different sorts of customer understandings. Data can be categorized in many ways, including "secondary" (gathered for some other purpose) and primary (gathered for the specific project at hand), and qualitative versus quantitative. There are also many types of analyses that can be performed on those different data, ranging from the subjective interpretation of open-ended responses to extremely sophisticated statistical analysis of large databases of customer information. Importantly, each sort of marketing research data collection method, data itself, and data analysis yields different types of information which can clarify different sets of strategic issues. Understanding the appropriate research design and method for particular sorts of questions or purposes is a key to managing marketing research and incorporating it into strategic marketing planning.

BRANDS AND BRANDING

Brands are the company's customers' "shorthand" for its product's position and its benefits. A collection of meanings, brands are represented by symbols such as names, logos, spokespeople, and other customers/consumers, packaging and colors, and imagery. Brands can have enormous value to the marketer. Facilitating choice and reducing search and evaluation demands on customers, brands deliver value to customers as well. Brands also deliver assurance, meaning, and self-expressive value to customers and consumers. Drinking a Coca-Cola is very different from merely drinking the carbonated water and (secret) ingredients that make up the tangible core product. Drinking a Coca-Cola is an experience and has meanings that the substance and ingredients do not have on their own. The brand can also have great economic value to the firm. The Coca-Cola brand, for example, was the most valuable brand in the world in 2007, estimated to be worth $ 65.3 billion. From a strategic perspective the importance of branding is that the brand embodies the goodwill or "equity" the firm has earned and can retain with its consumers.

POSITIONING STATEMENTS

Most good brand-building organizations require some summary documentation of what the brand is meant to be, what needs it is meant to serve, and for which specific customers/consumers on what specific occasions. That is, for positioning strategies to be clear, actionable, and enduring they should be documented in "positioning statements." Without working through the process of documenting the intentions of a positioning effort, members of the organization and elements of the marketing mix can drift "off strategy" or "off message." With a positioning statement, it is straightforward to go back to the statement and hold each action up against the original intent. Further, documenting the positioning in a statement facilitates getting people up-to-speed as they join the marketing team and facilitates retention of knowledge when people depart.

Positioning statements are not strategy statements; they're statements about how the strategy should come together *in the perceptions of the customers*. A complete positioning statement usually specifies: the brand/product to be positioned, the market (the "frame of reference"), the target segment(s) and target needs (the "target"), at least one "point of difference" or "brand promise," and the "reason to believe" that support those points of difference.[8] A positioning statement isn't intended for customers to see; it is an internal record of what the brand is meant to be. It serves to keep the various tactics "on strategy" and it fosters institutional memory of what the brand is and, often just as importantly, what it is *not*. Positions can change and migrate to follow customer preferences, but brands that change position too frequently rarely succeed. In any case, a strong, concise, and clear positioning statement reduces ambiguity, ensures "institutional memory" for the positioning decisions, and focuses tactics of the marketing effort discussed in the next sections.

THE MARKETING MIX

Our product, its price, our place (or channels of distribution), our promotion (communications), and our people and sales force are controllable actions that marketing managers direct. The best sales force in the world will have a tough time selling a product that is ill-conceived, ill-designed, or poorly manufactured, or a product with a price that is misaligned with what the customer thinks is good value, or a product that can't be found in the places where the customer shop. These decision variables must be "mixed" correctly. We need the right product at the right price in the right place, and so forth, to serve our target segment in light of all the uncontrollable forces—the situational factors such as the competition, technology, economic conditions, and the political, legal, and regulatory environments. And then, just when we've got the mix right, "[stuff] happens": things change and that mix must evolve and adapt over time. Indeed, marketing strategy may be viewed, from this perspective, as simply *mix evolution.*

As emphasized above, the objective of positioning is to establish the offering's place (position) in customers' perceptions. The marketer does not directly control those customer perceptions, but those perceptions are nevertheless influenced by controllable marketing actions, the "marketing mix." The marketing mix includes *all of the things that marketers can manage and deploy to meet customer needs and to claim a place in customers' minds.* The mix is often summarized as

the product, the price, the distribution of the product (place), the promotions or marketing communications associated with the product and brand, and the people or personal selling effort of the offering (Table 5-2). These are the well-known "five Ps" of marketing, meant to memorably summarize the entire range of actions that a marketing organization can direct at customers to fulfill those customers' needs. The strategic issues related to the mix, including changes in effective tactics across the product lifecycle (Table 5-3), are important to summarize briefly and connect to this strategic planning model.

TABLE 5-2 The Marketing Mix

Mix Element	Definition	Strategic Considerations

Product	*The need satisfying offering of the firm* or "customer solution," includes physical "goods," intangible "services," and myriad combinations of the tangible and intangible.	Product-level considerations:
		  Features and benefits
		  Quality
		  Versions and alternatives
		  Level of technology
		  Packaging
		  Service
		  Warranties
		  Packaging
		Branding and image
		Assortment considerations:
		  Product lines
		  Product portfolios

Price	From the firm's perspective, the money or other value received for the product in an exchange. From the customers' perspective price can include related costs (installation, etc.) and other expenditures such as time, effort, etc.	Objectives and time horizons Business model (Profit and loss considerations) List price(s) Flexibility Discounts and allowances Margins to intermediaries (channels) Terms and financing Bundling

Place	Distribution of the product or service and the location(s) of that distribution. *How does the customer choose and receive the product?*	Length of distribution channel(s)
		Number of distribution channels
		Channel members (types of intermediaries,
		  including ownership and control)
		Channel control and channel conflict
		Functions (logistics, warranties, etc;
		  demands of functions and location in
		  the channel)
		Distribution intensity
		Support and training

(continued)

TABLE 5-2 The Marketing Mix (*continued*)

Mix Element	Definition	Strategic Considerations
Promotion	All communications directed toward customers and customers: 　Advertising 　Media 　Targets 　Content Public relations Electronic/Internet communications 　Web sites 　Viral Point-of-purchase Event marketing Publications, brochures, and materials Buzz Marketing (word-of-mouth encouragement)	Objectives 　Targets 　Reach 　Frequency Promotion emphasis 　Media (television, print, etc.) 　Pull; 　Guerilla, 　Events Messages and meanings (Copy)
People	Personal selling Consultative selling Trade selling Missionary selling Technical selling Entrepreneurial selling Hybrid sales force Retail selling	Objectives 　Targets 　Desired behavior Promotional emphasis 　Push Managerial activities 　Coaching 　Counseling 　Evaluating 　Administrating

TABLE 5-3 The Marketing Mix Across the Product Lifecycle

Mix Element	Introduction	Growth	Maturity	Decline
Product	Initially one; Few	Increased number; Increasing available features and alternatives	Stable number Commoditization	Fewer
Price	Skimming and Penetration	Competitive	Price competition intensifies	Deals and price cutting deepen
Place	Limited distribution; High support required	Building distribution; Moving toward intensive	Intensive	May be reduced
Communication, Including both Promotion and People	Build primary demand; Information needs high	Build selective demand; *Differentiation*	Reminder; Communication budgets reduced	

Products

The first "P" in the marketing mix is products. Products include physical goods, intangible services, and all of the innumerable combinations of tangible and intangible value. Strategically, products can be understood in layers, as shown in Figure 5-3, ranging from:

- The core product (the essential need-fulfilling elements);
- The expected and augmented products (the essential need-fulfilling elements augmented by the peripheral accessories, warranties, service, etc.); and
- The *potential* product, the factors capable of engendering "Wow!" responses from customers—the unexpected factors that, nevertheless, delight customers and lead to satisfaction, loyalty, and positive word-of-mouth—*and that command margins.*

When attributes of the product that once were new and unexpected become expected and even ubiquitous, and all products in a market offer those attributes, it is called "commoditization." Commoditization in a product category often leads to price competition (what else is left to compete on?). Creative marketing strategists succeed in avoiding price competition by finding new "Wow!" attributes—exciting new options or services that augment the core product—thereby differentiating their offerings and avoiding the perils of commoditization.

PRODUCT LINES. A "product line" is an assortment of products offered by the same business unit. Strategies related to product lines include:

- *Price lining*—offering a product for different segments based on preferred price/quality points;
- *Line/brand extensions*—building on the strength of the existing products to add alternatives to the line or brand, including trading-up or trading-down; and
- *"Product platforms"*—common architectures or technologies underlying multiple products in a product line. Such platforms contribute to economies of scope.

PRODUCT PORTFOLIOS. Product strategies include not only decisions about specific products but also decisions about the firm's *overall assortment* or "portfolio" of products, how those multiple products relate to their markets, and how they relate to each other. Many firms manage multiple business units and products lines and must make strategic decisions about which products to invest in, which to harvest, and even whether or not to divest some products or business units.

Product portfolios array discrete business units (strategic business units or SBUs) or products/lines with regard to (a) their strength or competitive position and (b) the attractiveness of the markets they serve. The Growth/Share Matrix (originated by The Boston Consulting Group and often referred to as the BCG Matrix; shown in Figure 5-3) is grounded in the recognition of two fundamental market forces: one is the product life-cycle or product/market evolution, and the other is share leverage (scale effects, including economies of scale and learning curve effects): These are two

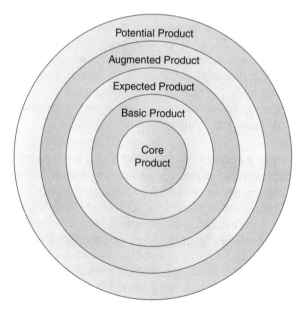

FIGURE 5-3   A Product Hierarchy

of the fundamental regularities or "laws" of strategic marketing discussed above in Chapter I-3. The Growth/Share Matrix identifies four generic strategies for four product/market positions:

- *High share/high growth*—the star, whose share should at least be maintained and which should continue to receive enough investment dollars to maintain or increase its distance from competitors. This quadrant is often to be cash-flow neutral, that is, not generating cash for investment elsewhere, because the company is reinvesting the profits to maintain position and growth.
- *High share/low growth*—the cash cow, which should get just enough investment to maintain share and because of low growth, market maturity, and low cost (further down the cost curve) should throw off significant cash to fund either other stars or problem children.
- *Low share/high growth*—the question mark or problem child, which either needs significant investment to improve position (build share) during market growth, or probably should be divested. Often, this quadrant can be viewed as cash flow negative.

- *Low share/low growth*—the dog, which should eventually die, it's just a question of how fast, because it has neither leverage from cost or share nor the advantages of a growth market.

The Boston Consulting Group Growth/Share Matrix captures attractiveness and firm strength with just two variables (growth rate and relative market share). Most marketing strategists would recognize that many markets are attractive for reasons other than growth rate and that firms may have strengths that go beyond market share. Therefore, various alternatives to the BCG Matrix have been proposed. One of the best known is the GE/McKinsey Portfolio Planning Grid—shown in Figure 5-5—which generalizes the two dimensions to "Business Strength" and "Industry Attractiveness," expanding the single variable chosen by The Boston Consulting Group (growth rate and relative market share) to include many more important drivers of strength and attractiveness (Table 5-4). The GE/McKinsey Portfolio Planning Grid—sometimes called the "Stoplight Grid" due to its adoption of green, yellow, and red to emphasize its strategic implications—breaks the dimensions in finer gradations (three levels each, creating nine "cells") and weights the multiple strength and attractiveness variables to develop scores for each axes. The strategic implications of strengths/attractiveness analysis relate to investment and resource allocation decisions, in particular, and also market-scope decisions. These frameworks guide decisions about what SBUs or products to invest in, and choosing "winnable" races.

NEW PRODUCT DEVELOPMENT.   New product development requires a keen focus on *anticipating* customer needs and even discovering unrecognized (latent) needs. Because it takes time to bring new products to market, there may be no task in the strategic planning process that requires more foresight. The consulting firm Booz, Allen, Hamilton set out a classic new product development model, identifying a flow of seven basic activities required for successful new product development, beginning with idea generation and culminating in commercialization, and involving increasing cumulative investments along the way

FIGURE 5-4   The Boston Consulting Group Growth/Share Portfolio Matrix[9]

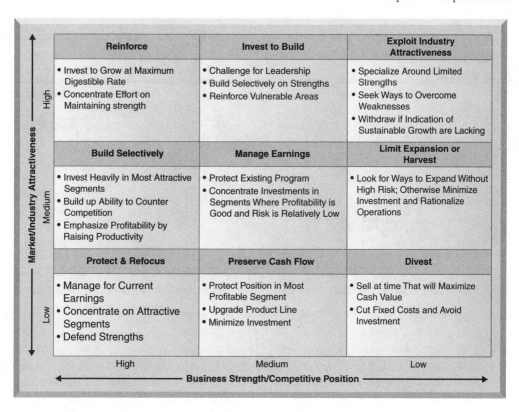

FIGURE 5-5   GE/McKinsey Portfolio Planning Grid[10]

TABLE 5-4 Market Attractiveness and Firm Strength Factors

Market Attractiveness	Strength
• *Real Market Growth*	• Market Share/*Relative Market Share*
• Industry Concentration	• Market Share Rank
• Product Lifecycle Stage	• Relative Price
• Market Differentiation	• Relative Quality
• Percent of Sales Accounted For by New Products	• Relative Direct Costs
• Served Market Concentration	• Relative Percent Sales of New Products
• Capital Intensity	• Patents/Proprietary Products
	• Patents/Proprietary Processes
	• Shared Production Facilities
	• Relative Employee Compensation
	• Labor Productivity

BCG Matrix factors are in **bold italics.**

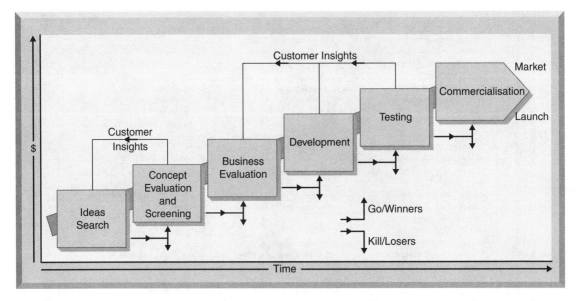

FIGURE 5-6   The Booz, Allen, Hamilton New-Product-Development Process[12]

(Figure 5-6). New product development highlights the need for cross-functional as well as external (customers', vendors', and collaborators') input into the process. Research shows that firms that build "innovation cultures"—cultures in which ideas are valued and failures tolerated—are more successful than their more conservative competitors.[11]

A critical strategic task is planning the "product pipeline;" anticipating needs and preparing to meet *future* needs in the marketplace. In many industries, the lead time required to develop a new product is substantial. Differences across competitors in lead times required to launch new product can constitute a substantial driver of strategic success. It has been estimated, for example, that each single day that a new car launch is delayed can cost the firm a million dollars in lost profits.[13] Therefore, time-to-market and foresight are important considerations in new product development and anticipatory customer assessment, marketing research, and product planning are critical to strategic marketing success.

PRODUCT INNOVATION. Economist Joseph Schumpeter famously equated innovation with "creative destruction"; in effect, innovation and entrepreneurship function to "destroy" existing ways of

doing things in favor of new, *better* ways. Peter Drucker expanded upon that idea: *"Because the purpose of business is to create a customer, the business enterprise has two—and only two—basic functions: marketing and innovation. Marketing and innovation produce results; all the rest are costs."* Innovations can be seen as shifting "the Value Frontier" toward the right—that is, toward greater value for the same price or the same value for a lower price.

Innovations do not always, or even usually, entail "high technology" or technological breakthroughs. Often, innovation involves identifying latent customer needs or seeing customer needs differently than they had been understood before and drawing together existing technologies to meet those needs better than current solutions. Such market-oriented innovation entails identifying customer insights and understanding how innovations spread or "diffuse" through the market. Understanding the diffusion of innovations includes understanding differences across innovations themselves, understanding what aspects of those innovations accelerate or slow their diffusion, and understanding how different consumers respond to innovations:

- Innovations can be distinguished with regard to their degree of newness to the firm and their degree of newness to the customer. Innovations range from "discontinuous" ("radical" or "truly-new;" changing the way customers consume and/or meet the target need) through "dynamically continuous" (noticeable but negligible changes to consumption behaviors) to "continuous" ("incremental;" improving on existing products with no impact or very low impact on consumption patterns and behaviors).

- Various characteristics of those innovations predict the rapidity of their diffusion into the target markets. Things like relative advantage (How much better is the innovation than existing ways to meet the same needs?), "observability" (How easily can others see the innovation in use?), and compatibility with existing lifestyles and consumption patterns all *accelerate* diffusion. On the other hand, characteristics like risk (physical risk or the risk of hurting someone, financial risk, and social risk or the risk of embarrassment) and simple cost will all *slow* the diffusion of an innovation into the market.

- One well-known typology of segments of customers based on their propensity to adopt an innovation: innovators, early adopters, early and late majorities, and laggards.

Promotions/Communications Strategies

Promotions or "integrated marketing communications" include all of the efforts to communicate to the customer. Traditionally, advertising and personal selling were the dominant tools in the communications arsenal. Advertising effectively and efficiently reaches large numbers of consumers and is particularly effective at creating awareness and reminding large audiences about the product or brand. A focus on advertising is a "pull strategy"; it develops demand at the level of the ultimate consumer, and that demand "pulls" sales though the channel.

One reality of advertising in the new millennium is the "death of mass." Media that used to reach truly mass audiences, such as television, radio, and magazines have *fragmented*. There are now literally *hundreds* of television channels and almost infinite alternatives to television, ranging from video games and personal music players to the Internet. This proliferation of media and of technologies that allow consumers to choose what they attend to and what they bypass or ignore has created challenges and opportunities for marketers. On the one hand, it is now nearly impossible to quickly communicate with mass audiences. On the other hand, marketers can now target more defined and refined targets with messages. An advertiser on the World Fishing Network, for example, can connect with many consumers interested in fishing, and will not waste the message on many people who do not.

Changes in paid-for, controlled media and advances in understandings of how markets work has led to an increased emphasis on other communication tools, from electronic to experiential, and to an increasing recognition of the importance of inter-consumer communications, or "word of mouth." Some companies are organizing networks of unpaid "opinion leaders" to stimulate word-of-mouth referral networks. Proctor & Gamble (P&G) has enrolled more than half-a-million woman, mostly mothers and homemakers, into "Vocalpoint," and more than a quarter-million teens into Tremor; these are organized panels of similar consumers who receive samples, news, and coupons from the firm. They are encouraged to offer feedback to the marketer and are expected to act as "brand evangelists," spreading the word about and recommending P&G's products and brands. Such organized word-of-mouth programs raise some ethical issues (one critic called them the "commercialization of human relations"), but they also emphasize the growing emphasis on inter-consumer communications in the new context of fragmented and cluttered media.[14]

People

People is the "fifth P" and refers to personal selling and service provision. Personal paid-for communication is usually the most effective means of communicating large amounts of information and "closing the deal" (moving customers from consideration to purchase). Nevertheless, the cost-per-contact of personal selling is high and its ability to reach mass markets is limited. A communication strategy emphasizing personal selling is a "push" strategy; it develops demand at the immediate next level of the distribution system and, thereby, pushes demand through the channel. In practice, most marketing strategies employ a balance of "push" and "pull."

Managers make a serious mistake when they refer to what salespeople do as merely selling, as though the salesperson's personality alone brings in the sale. Rather, the modern professional salesperson relies on analytic skills as much as on charm and aggressiveness. Getting the order is only the final stage of a complex set of activities involving many people within our own firm as well as within the customer's organization. Modern personal selling is consultative and has become a two-step process: (1) to determine and articulate for the customer the real problem he faces and (2) to present the product or service's benefits as a partial or complete solution to that problem. By helping the customer to define his or her own needs, the salesperson enters the sale at the very beginning and, in this way, can often place his or her products at a considerable advantage. Consultative selling includes four main types of selling tasks: trade, missionary, technical, and entrepreneurial.

Place/Distribution Strategies

Place, or the channel(s) of distribution, involves several categories of decisions, including selecting, motivating, and controlling channel members. These decisions should be based on some basic market-oriented considerations:

- Where, how, and when do customers shop for the product?
- What level of *support* (service, information and training, maintenance, etc.) do customers require for the product?
- What level of *control* does the distribution require to insure quality and to satisfy customer needs?
- How do different means of distribution relate, and how might they *conflict*?

These considerations change across the product lifecycle. Early in the lifecycle, customers require more information and training, especially for technologically-sophisticated products. Later in the product lifecycle, customers may need less hand-holding but may respond more to peripheral services and almost always become more price conscious.

Distribution channels and channel intermediaries can add value for both the consumer and the marketer by performing at least three types of "channel functions:"

- Transactional (buying, selling, holding inventory, and assuming inventory risks such as obsolescence and spoilage),
- Logistical (shipping, breaking bulk, assorting), and
- Facilitating (information gathering and conveyance, including giving information *to customers* and giving information *about customers* to the marketer, financing).

Understanding these functions and how and by whom they are performed in a particular distribution system allows for strategic thinking about how those functions may change. If channel members stop adding value or the functions become unnecessary, they will eventually be bypassed. For example, as technology changes (including Internet-based delivery of product "help" information), it is becoming possible for manufacturers to deliver information directly to customers, bypassing channel partners who specialized in facilitating/information functions. This will reduce the need for intermediaries to educate and provide information and perhaps eventually result in channel reconfiguration.

Pricing Strategies

Viable pricing strategies are linked to the product lifecycle (see Table 5-3, row 2, above). Early in the product lifecycle, as products are being introduced, demand is driven by the value of the innovation—customers are attracted to the new benefits or relative advantage of the product in the new offerings. Pricing can take advantage of that quality-focused demand by "skimming," charging a relatively high price to profit from that newness. A skimming strategy may, however, dampen overall demand. Alternatively, the firm can charge a lower "penetration" price intended to increase volume. Penetration pricing makes the most sense when customers are at least somewhat "sticky" (i.e., can be expected to stay with their initial brand selection due to loyalty or some other source of inertia) and when some benefits of scale can be expected as production increases. Later in the product lifecycle, pricing becomes increasingly competitive.

Profits

Strategy is not successful *unless it is profitable.* This stipulation seems straightforward except for the element of timing. Strategies can be developed with an emphasis on either short-term or long-term profitability. Profitability in the long-term generally requires investment in the short-term; those investments do not preclude short-term profitability but they do rule out *maximizing* short-term returns. Having growth aspirations is important, but it is also wise to remember that "growth for growth's sake is the ideology of the cancer cell."[15] Growth or market share objectives should be set in the context of a specific business model with consideration given to long-term returns. Top-line growth (revenues) can come at the expense of the bottom-line (profits) and can strain the firm's cash flow and other resources. Targeting the "right" customers—customers who are profitable in the long-run, who are relatively likely to

become loyal, and who will appreciate and benefit from the firm's competitive advantages (that is, take value from the firm's unique points of differentiation and competitive advantages) are all at least as important as simple "growth," and require a keen understanding of "cost-volume-profit" logic in the particular context of the firm's business model.

BASIC ECONOMIC LOGIC.   Profits are the outcome of a logical combination of the components of revenues and costs. Disaggregating these components helps thinking about strategy and the sources of profit. For example, distinguishing the components of sales (purchase rate times the number of customers times price per unit) highlights distinct ways to improve profits: raise prices, increase purchase rates, and acquire new customers. Figure 5-7 presents this cost-volume-profit logic and highlights the unit-level contribution margin (the

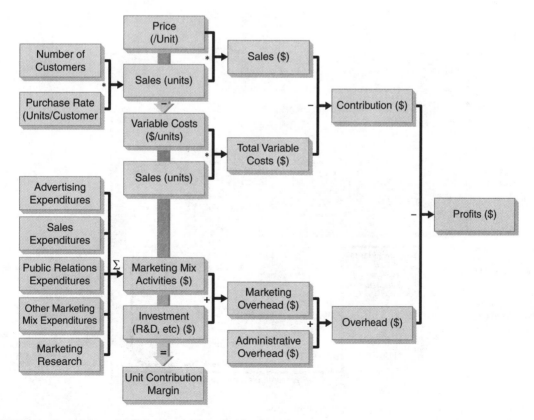

FIGURE 5-7   Cost-Volume-Profit Logic and Contribution Margins

contribution of each individual sale toward covering fixed expenses).

BREAKEVEN ANALYSIS.   The "breakeven point" is the point in sales growth at which revenues equal expenses. That milestone is an important computation in evaluating the feasibility of an endeavor, a marketing plan, or a strategy. Breakeven is defined at the point (in sales) where the sales revenues exactly cover all the expenses. Sales revenues are, of course, the unit price multiplied times the average price. Total costs can be divided into two parts: variable costs (the costs that go up with the sale of each unit) and fixed costs (the overhead and expenses that the firm commits to across a time period and that do not go up with each unit sold). This can be summarized simply in formulas:

$$\text{Revenue} = \text{Price} * \text{Quantity}$$
$$\text{Total Costs} = (\text{Variable Costs} * \text{Quantity})$$
$$+ \text{Fixed Costs}$$

Therefore, if breakeven is where revenues exactly equal expenses, we can set the two equations as equal:

$$\text{Revenue} = \text{Expenses}$$

or

$$(\text{Price} * \text{Quantity}) = (\text{Variable Costs} * \text{Quantity})$$
$$+ \text{Fixed Costs}$$

Solving that equation for breakeven quantity (that is, setting quantity on one side and all other variables on the other) yields the formula for the number of units that must be sold to exactly cover expenses:

$$\text{Quantity}_{\text{Breakeven}} = \frac{\text{Fixed Costs}}{(\text{Price-Variable Costs})}$$

For example, if we are going into business selling something, let's say ice-cream cones, and the variable costs (the cost of the scoop of ice cream, the cone, and the napkin) is $1, the selling price is $2, and we have to pay $150 for our ice-cream-cone-vending

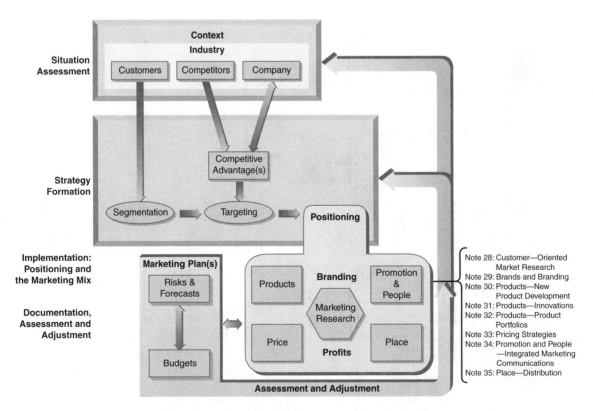

Linking Implementation to Relevant Tools and Frameworks

cart, we would be able to figure out pretty quickly that we need to sell 150 ice-cream cones to "breakeven." That is because we make $1 on each sale (price minus variable costs; $2 − $1—that is called the contribution margin). We need to make $150 just to pay for the vending cart. Once we've paid for the cart (sold 150 cones), we're "in the black" (traditionally, red ink was used to indicate a loss in ledgers and accounting ledgers—so "in the black" means we're profitable). In fact, we're making $1/cone—but what the bank that lent us the money to buy the cart would want to know is: "How many cones do they need to sell to "breakeven" (*and pay us back our money*)?"

Endnotes

1. Vince Lombardi, famous American football coach, describing the role of "blocking and tackling," the two most fundamental "building blocks" of the sport, quoted by Dan J. Sanders and Galen Walters, *Equipped to Lead: Managing People, Partners, Processes, and Performance* (New York: McGraw Hill, 2008), 90.

2. Jeanne Bliss, *Chief Customer Officer: Getting Past Lip Service to Passionate Action* (San Francisco, CA: Jossey Bass, 2006), 80

3. Philip Kotler and Gary Armstong, *Principles of Marketing,* 11th ed. (Upper Saddle River, NJ: Pearson/Prentice Hall, 2009), 106.

4. Johnny K. Johansson and I. Nonaka, "Market Research the Japanese Way," *Harvard Business Review* 65, no. 3 (1987): 16–22.

5. Kotler and Armstrong, *Principles of Marketing,* 106.

6. Allyn W. Kimball, "Errors of the Third Kind in Statistical Consulting," *Journal of the American Statistical Association* 52, no. 278 (June 1957): 133–142.

7. J. Workman Jr., "The State of Multivariate Thinking for Scientists in Industry: 1980–2000," *Chemometrics and Intelligent Laboratory Systems* 60 (Elsevier Science B.V., 2002): 13–23.

8. See Alice M. Tybout and Brian Sternthal, "Brand Positioning," in *Kellogg on Branding,* ed. Alice M. Tybout and Tim Calkins (Hoboken, NJ: John Wiley & Sons, 2005), 11–26.

9. The BCG Portfolio Matrix from the Product Portfolio Matrix, © 1970, The Boston Consulting Group.

10. See Arnoldo C. Hax and Nicolas S. Majluf, "The Use of the Industry Attractiveness-Business Strength Matrix in Strategic Planning," *Interfaces* 13, no. 2 (1983): 54–71; S. Robinson, R. Hitch, and D. Wade, "The Directional Policy Matrix—Tool for Strategic Planning," *Long Range Planning* 11, no. 3 (1978): 8–15; Michael G. Allen, "Diagramming GE's Planning for What's Watt," *Strategy & Planning* 5, no. 5 (1977): 3–9.

11. See, for example, Kurt Matzler, Franz Bailom, and Dieter Tschemernjak, *Enduring Success: What Top companies do differently* (Basingstoke, Hampshire, RG21 6XS, England: Palgrave Macmillan, 2007).

12. Adapted from Simon Knox, "The Boardroom Agenda: Developing the Innovative Organization," *Corporate Governance: International Journal of Business in Society* 2, no. 1 (Emerald Group Publishing Limited, 2002): 27–36.

13. See K. Clark, "Project Scope and Project Performance: The Effect of Parts Strategy and Supplier Involvement on Product Development," *Management Science* 35, no. 5 (1989): 1247–1263.

14. Robert Berner, "I Sold It through the Grapevine: Not Even Small Talk Is Sacred Anymore. P&G Has Enlisted a Stealth Army of 600,000 Moms Who Chat up Its Products," *Business Week* (May 29, 2006), www.businessweek.com/magazine/content/06_22/b3986060.htm. Last accessed June 23, 2010.

15. Edward Abbey, *Voice Crying in the Wilderness (Vox Clamantis in Deserto): Notes from a Secret Journal* (New York: St. Martin's Press, 1990), 98.

6

Planning, Assessment and Adjustment

Strategic and tactical decisions should be documented in a *marketing plan*. A solid marketing plan translates the strategy into specific tactics, catalogues the risks, and establishes forecasts, budgets, and measurable objectives for the marketing effort. Strategic market plans pose and answer three fundamental questions:

1. Where are we now? (situation assessment)
2. Where do we want to go? and
3. How do we get there?

The marketing plan is essential to realizing all of marketing strategy's benefits. These benefits include considering the broad perspective, strengthening a market-orientation, and aligning the many disparate tactics. The marketing plan compels thorough analysis, clarifies and documents assumptions, and records decisions. It helps the marketing manager prioritize issues, goals, and activities.

The marketing plan is also the means by which a marketing manager gains support for her or his brand or product and claims resources. In larger companies, brand or product managers do not usually have authority to demand resources—they must *persuade* the organization to devote resources to their brands and products. In smaller companies the marketing planning process is often the only formal planning mechanism and, therefore, plays a central role in setting expectations, steering resources, and directing activities.

Table 6-1 presents a generic outline for a marketing plan. Much of the marketing plan content derives directly from the strategic marketing process (the focus of this section and the organizing framework of this book). After an executive summary, the marketing plan should proceed through a situation assessment, marketing strategy, and a detailed implementation plan. The marketing plan will present the marketing strategy, including the target segments and target needs (the pain) and competitive advantages to be relied upon (the magic). It will also specify the positioning and spell out the various tactics to be used in time-specific detail. The marketing plan should very clearly establish the size of the target segments and translate the size of the segments, forecasts of market share and sales, and the costs of planned activities into detailed budgets. Finally, the marketing plan should specify the uncertainties and risks inherent to the proposed strategy—and flesh-out contingencies and hedges to those risks.

Much of the content of any marketing plan (outlined in Table 6-1) comes directly out of the strategic marketing process that organizes this book. That is, a good marketing

---

TABLE 6-1 Generic Marketing Plan Outline

Executive Summary
    Target need—*Where's the pain?*
    Solution—*Where's the magic?*
  I. Situation Assessment
    a. Market Definition
    b. Context (PEST)
    c. Customers
    d. Competition
       i. Strengths
       ii. Weaknesses
       iii. Offerings and Target Segments
    e. Industry Analysis
  II. Company
    a. Firm Mission, Vision, and Objectives
    b. Value Chain
    c. Sustainable Competitive Advantages
       (i.e., strengths)
    d. Weaknesses
  III. Strategy
    a. Segmentation
       i. Basis
       ii. Description
       iii. Sizing and Valuation
    b. Basis of Competition (competitive advantages)
    c. Targeting
    d. Positioning(s)
    e. Strategy Summary
  IV. Marketing Mix(s)
    a. Product
    b. Price
    c. Place
    d. Promotions
  V. Projections
    a. Risks
    b. Forecasts
    c. Budgets
    d. Financial and Profit Model (*pro formas*)
    e. Objectives
  VI. Appendices (detailed support for plan)

---

plan includes a thorough situation assessment (including the four Cs of context, customer, company, and competitors), the stipulation of the specific strategy including competitive advantages and target segments, the identification of the desired positioning, and then the details of the marketing mix—all of which are key steps in this strategic planning framework. A good marketing plan will document these decisions and plans and will also:

- Catalog and assess the *risks* and uncertainties inherent to the plan;
- Estimate *forecasts* of sales and market changes;
- Establish *budgets* and *pro forma* financial statements; and
- Specify measurable and motivating *objectives*.

This section reviews these final steps in establishing the marketing plan and accomplishing the marketing strategy.

Risks

The marketing manager should identify risks and develop contingency plans while working on the marketing plan. This application of scenario planning is ongoing and should be a background activity throughout the strategic marketing process. Managers should be cataloging "possible futures," different events and changes that could impact the strategy both in the environment and within the firm. Risk is not to be *avoided* at all cost; risk is to be *managed*.

"Only those who will risk going too far can possibly find out how far one can go."

T.S. Eliot

Managing risk is not simple risk minimization or risk avoidance. Managing risk is evaluating risk and choosing which risks to accept and which to avoid. Risk is an important part of learning what will work. For example, Rowland Macy failed four times in the dry goods business before his Macy's Store in New York City succeeded. Babe Ruth struck out 1,330 times, but he also hit 714 home runs. For the marketing strategist, success will not come from only accepting sure choices, but failure will certainly come from imprudent or ill-considered choices. As the marketing mix is being developed, it is important to assess the risks and potential obstacles to its success.

One important way to examine "possible futures" or contingencies is to assess the *impact* that an event or trend would have on the plan, and the *likelihood* of that event/trend occurring. Figure 6-1 shows an Impact/Likelihood Matrix. The marketing

FIGURE 6-1 Impact/Likelihood Matrix

strategist should spell out all of the assumptions about the way the world will be during a marketing program and the way things might change, and then challenge those assumptions asking: *How likely is X to happen? And what is the impact if X does/does not occur?*

New product development in the cereal industry is a good example of the recognition of "acceptable" risks, and of cost-benefit considerations in regard to reducing uncertainty. The well-known research and consulting firm A.D. Little & Company found that despite the best consumer research efforts, 92 percent of all new cereals introduced failed. In response to that failure rate, many companies reduced their expenditures on consumer research and began to simply launch more new products, letting the market decide what would "stick" and what would not.[1]

Forecasts

Forecasts, objectives, and budgets are interdependent but they must be done *concurrently* and *interactively*. The aim is to optimize the budget and the commitment of resources to maximize expected (forecast) and desired outcomes (objectives). Expectations about outcomes are necessarily based in part on what

actions the firm will take, and those actions are contingent on budgeted resources. At the same time, budgets are based on expectations about their effects. This may seem obvious but it highlights the fact that no forecast, budget, or marketing mix plan stands alone—each impacts the others and so they must be developed concurrently and interactively.

In practice, a number of methods are available for estimating future sales, including assessment of buyer's intentions, sales force estimates, expert opinions, market tests, and time-series analysis. Quantitative methods can be complex but one quantitative tool, regression analysis, and its underlying logic are invaluable to strategic thinking. Regression logic is the idea that some outcome or "dependent" variable can be predicted by multiple inputs or "causes" ("independent" variables). For example, most marketing managers understand that sales are caused by, among other things, sales-force effort and advertising, as well as by the price of competitive products, and interest rates. Sales-force effort and advertising are controlled by the firm; the price of competitive products is an external factor controlled by the competition; interest rates are a macrolevel environmental factor. In this way, the manager can think logically about the relationships and develop sales forecasts based on multiple causal factors in a formula that might look like this:

$$Sales_{t+1} = \beta(\$Selling) + \beta(\$Advertising)$$
$$- \beta(Price_{us} - Price_{Comp}) + \beta(\Delta IntRate) + \cdots$$

In this analysis the firm sets its own selling and advertising budget, estimates the price differential based on competitive intelligence and other inputs, and forecasts changes in interest rates to forecasts sales.

The accuracy of a sales forecast as well as the specificity of objectives can be improved when those forecasts and objectives are decomposed into the components that influence future sales volume. One useful tool is staircase analysis (Figure 6-2). Staircase analysis estimates market potential, actual market, brand awareness, brand image, purchase rate, share of wallet, the repurchase rate, and the cross-buying rate. After having accurate estimates of these factors, a company can more precisely forecast its future sales by predicting the change in market potential, in the actual market, in the brand awareness, purchase rate, repurchase

rate, and so on. These numbers than can also be used to formulate specific marketing objectives.

Budgets

One of the crucial functions of the marketing plan is to convert planned *actions* and *forecasts* into *planned ("budgeted") expenditures*. A budget specifies the money to be spent by area and allocates scarce financial resources across activities. Depending upon the available resources, the strategist can propose a certain marketing mix, make assumptions about competitive and other uncontrollable environmental events, and forecast results. Depending on those forecasts, the objectives and budgets can be reformulated or the mix can be adjusted. Thus, budgeting is interactive with planning and forecasting; like a hydraulic system, raising levels in one (plans, forecasts, or budgets) will change the constraints and outcomes of the others. For this reason, modeling planned actions, forecasts, and budgets interdependently in "sensitivity analyses" is an invaluable exercise.

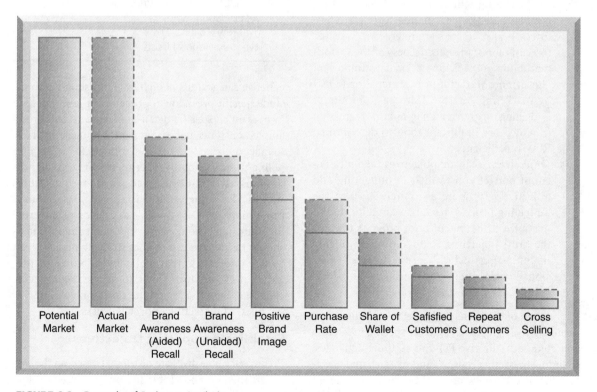

FIGURE 6-2 Example of Staircase Analysis

Budgeting has four defining inputs:

1. *Timeframe.* To be useful, a budget must have a specific timeframe. It would not be enough to determine how much would be spent without knowing when it will be spent. Quarter and annual budgets are common, with assessment happening more often and budget adjustment occurring less frequently.

2. *Allocations.* Firms allocate financial and other resources to marketing organizations. Sometimes that allocation is as a percentage of past sales/profits, other times as a function of objectives and aspirations. This allocation sets a basic limit on budget expenditures. If allocations are based on objectives, it becomes paramount that the marketing organization influences the formation of those objectives with realistic forecasts and well-grounded aspirations.

3. *Forecasts.* Sales forecasts are the expected outcomes of marketing actions and other factors such as market growth, competitor actions, etc. Marketing actions (i.e., the elements of the mix) are based in part on these forecasts. Thus, forecasts and budgets are interactive. Specific forecasts about the effectiveness of the various marketing mix elements (i.e., estimates of "Return on Marketing Investment" or ROMI by marketing mix tool) are basic inputs to budgeting. Regression analysis and "regression thinking" are important tools to determining ROMI coefficients.

4. *Objectives.* Realistic objectives take into account budget constraints, so budgeting and objective-setting are also interactive. In the budgeting process, resources are allocated to maximize achievement of or progress towards the firm's objectives. Factors to be considered in budgeting include corporate-level (missions, goals, etc.) and business-unit-level (profits, sales, growth, etc.) objectives.

Based on forecasts and objectives, budgets are created that assign resources to the specific marketing mix elements (the five Ps) and support activities, including marketing research and research and development (R&D or new product development). To facilitate assessment and adjustment, budgets should be hierarchical; that is, budgets should summarize

TABLE 6-2 Basic Marketing Budget Components
Marketing Communications
Advertising
Electronic Marketing
Direct Marketing
Public Relations
Events
Promotions
Consumer
Trade
Merchandising
Personal Selling
Hiring
Training
Firing
Sales Support and Channel Communications
Marketing Administration
Overhead
Personnel
Marketing Research
Production
Units Produced (units)
Variable Costs (per unit)
Cost of Goods Sold
Inventory Holding Costs
Inventory Disposal Costs

expense categories at a high level but should also include specific breakdowns of each high-level category into as much specific detail as is reasonable. For example, consumer-goods companies' budgets are likely to make a distinction between moneys to be spent on selling/push-side efforts (personal selling, trade promotions, etc.) and consumer-oriented expenditures such as advertising, event marketing, and price-based promotions. It is also possible to categorize "advertising" into television, print, and electronic. Budgets should be constructed so that strategic planners can readily understand that hierarchy from major categories of expenditures down to detailed and specific expenses. Table 6-2 lists some common components or "lines" of marketing budget expenses.

Establishing Specific Objectives

Preliminary objectives are developed based on the corporate mission and vision and on the strategy. More specific objectives tied to detailed metrics and outcomes are developed interactively with forecasts and budgets. *Exactly what does the strategy and the market-ing plan mean to accomplish and how will we know if those objectives have been achieved?* Objectives should be "SMART"—*Specific, Measureable, Achievable, Relevant, and Time-specific*—and should be assessed on an ongoing basis and within timeframes that guide appropriate behaviors and facilitate timely adjustment to performance and changes in the environment.

Three distinct sorts of objectives are useful and common in developing marketing strategies: sales objective, customer objectives, and *financial* or *profit* objectives. Sales and profit objectives are pretty straightforward; sales objectives have to do with units sold, dollar sales, and market share. Customer objectives include things like customer readiness variables (e.g, awareness, and interest), customer sat-isfaction and recommendation behaviors, and cus-tomer loyalty. Financial or profit objectives involve margins, total profits, and returns.

ASSESSMENT AND ADJUSTMENT

> *"However beautiful the strategy, you should occasionally look at the results."*
>
> Winston Churchill

Throughout the strategic marketing process a constant theme has been *specificity* in spelling out tactics, budg-ets, objectives, and forecasts. The specificity, measura-bility/quantification, and time-specific nature of the plan facilitate assessment and adjustment. Recognizing variation from forecasts, objectives, and budgets is a crucial input to assessment. The variables that should be assessed on an ongoing basis include financial, oper-ational, and market- or customer-related outcomes (these are, by design, the same metrics included in ob-jective setting and gap analysis). These various metrics can be considered at the firm, business-unit, product, and account level. Table 6-3 presents some typical fi-nancial and operating metrics. Different industries and different firms use some or all of these along with other idiosyncratic markers of performance.

Market-/Customer-Related Metrics

Customer Relationship Management systems collect, on an ongoing basis, data about customers and their responses to the firm's marketing mix. Those data are used to tailor the firm's offerings and communications

TABLE 6-3 Typical Financial and Operating Metrics

Operating Metrics	• Product quality • Inventory Turns • Fulfillment time • Stock-outs • Process capability • Labor productivity
Financial Metrics	• Overall Profits • Profit Growth • Contribution and Margins • Revenue Growth • Total Operating Cost • Cash-to-Cash cycle • Return on Investment (ROI) • Gross-Margin Return on Investment (GMROI) • Residual Income/EVA [Economic Value Added]

toward profitable customers and to evaluate and ad-just ongoing efforts. In fact, market- and customer-related metrics are essential to assessing and adjusting marketing strategies. Customer-related metrics in-clude things like customer satisfaction, profitability, loyalty, and intention-to-recommend. They also in-clude gauges such as secret-shopper reports—which do not rely on surveying customers.

THE VALUE OF MEASURING RECOMMENDATION INTENTION. Customer satisfaction, repeat-purchase intention, and intention-to-recommend are generally considered to be the three essential markers of how well customers are responding to their experiences with the firm and its offerings. Research efforts have focused on reducing those various customer responses to some more parsimonious measures that can be eas-ily collected and assessed. That is, too many customer-response metrics can be confusing, and it seems evi-dent that all of these things are, at a basic level, tapping into the same underlying customer evaluations. Frederick Reichheld, an authority on strategy and a partner with Bain and Company, conducted research that began with roughly 20 items tapping various post-consumption responses ranging from satisfac-tion, loyalty ("How strongly to you agree that [com-pany X] deserves your loyalty?"), and repeat-purchase intention ("How likely is it that you will continue to purchase products/services from [company X]?") The single item "How likely is it that you would recommend [company X] to a friend or colleague?" on a scale from 1 to 10 (extremely likely) was found to be the most predictive of future behaviors (actual recommendations as well as actual repeat purchase) and, at the firm level, of future growth and profitability.[2] To compute Reichheld's "Net Promoter Index," the firm sums the number of customers who respond with a nine or a ten on the single question (customers are labeled "Promoters") and subtracts the number who responded with anything from a zero to a six (those Reichheld labeled "Detractors"; respondents who gave a seven or an eight are termed "passively satisfied"):

$$Net \; Promoter = \sum(9, 10) - \sum(0, 1, 2, 3, 4, 5, 6)$$

Reichheld has argued that this Net Promoter score is the "ultimate question,"—the "one number you need to grow."[3] Although it is a simplification of the complex array of customer responses that likely begin with some evaluation like "satisfaction," it is certainly a revealing post-consumption marker of customers' appraisals of the marketing programs.

LOYALTY-BASED MARKETING.   Targeting loyal customers—and especially *profitable loyal customers* can lead to dramatic improvements in profitability. Reichheld also conducted numerous studies across industries on the relationship between customer loyalty and firm profits and growth, and found that firms with more loyal customers were more profitable. He attributed that relationship to the related findings that longer-term customers spread acquisition costs across more purchases and continue to provide base profits while increasing their purchases, costing less to serve, referring other customers to the products/brands, and even paying a price premium (see Figure 6-3.[4] Subsequent research has augmented those findings to propose that it is not just loyalty that matters, but, rather, loyalty and profitability. The converse to targeting profitable, loyal customers is also true: although we generally think of firms as ceaselessly seeking to attract more customers, "firing" unprofitable and fickle customers can also improve results.

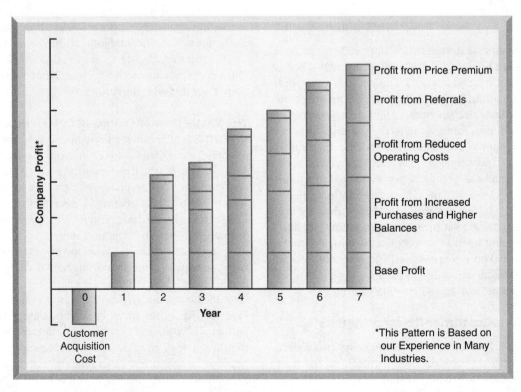

FIGURE 6-3   Why Loyal Customers Are More Profitable[5]

Thus, the core metrics—customer satisfaction, customer loyalty, customer profitability, and "cost to serve"—are all essential in setting objectives and are a key basis of assessment and adjustment for strategic marketing planning. Some of these data come from operational data—sales and shipment records, accounting systems, and the like—and other data come from surveys of current customers. Customer Relationship Management (CRM) systems track and organize those customer data at the segment and the individual customer level for tailoring offerings, targeting communications, and, notably, for assessing and adjusting the strategy and marketing mix.

MONITORING THE ENVIRONMENT.   It is also important to forecast *external* factors related to the strategy and to monitor those factors. Forecasts of economic conditions and market-wide factors used as the bases for planning should be specified during the planning and then assessed continuously. In developing the marketing plan, the strategist should strive to surface assumptions about expected responses by customers, competitors, channel partners, and other constituents. As strategy is established and its implementation begun, those parameters must be monitored, thus beginning anew the situation assessment and strategy formation stages. Assessment and adjustment feeds back into gap analyses of *all* of the earlier steps in strategic marketing analysis and planning—situation assessment, strategy formation, and implementation via positioning and the marketing mix.

Summary

This first section of this book, *Strategic Marketing* has laid out a concise, high-level roadmap for strategic marketing analysis and planning. This is a powerful "way of thinking" that is practical, effective, and complete—shown again graphically in Figure 6-4. *This is how you attack strategic marketing.* This framework identifies and

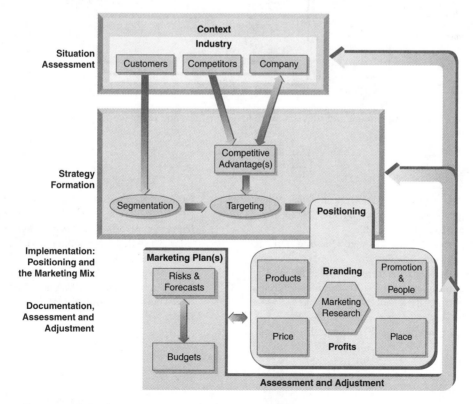

FIGURE 6-4   The Strategic Marketing Process

organizes the tools and frameworks required for drilling down into a particular challenge, and it clearly points the reader to short notes that elaborate on those tools. The

sections that follow will put meat on that skeleton with more detailed notes on how to apply the tools referenced thus far.

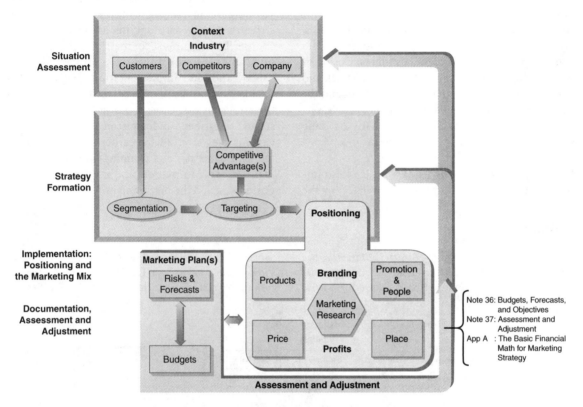

Linking Documentation, Assessment and Adjustment to Relevant Tools and Frameworks

Endnotes

1. Willard I. Zangwill, "Manager's Journal: When Customer Research Is a Lousy Idea," *Wall Street Journal* (March 8, 1993): A12.
2. Fred Reichheld, "The Ultimate Question: Driving Good Profits and True Growth" (Boston, MA: Harvard Business Press, 2006); and Frederick F. Reichheld, "The One Number You Need to Grow," *Harvard Business Review* 81, no. 12 (December 2003): 46–54.
3. Ibid.
4. Frederick F. Reichheld and Thomas Teal, *The Loyalty Effect: The Hidden Force Behind Growth, Profits, and*

Lasting Value (Boston, MA: Harvard Business Press, 1996); Frederick F. Reichheld, "Loyalty-based Management," *Harvard Business Review* 71, no. 2 (March 1993): 64–73; and, Frederick F. Reichheld and W. Earl Sasser Jr., "Zero Defections: Quality Comes to Services," *Harvard Business Review* 68, no. 5 (September–October, 1990): 105–111.
5. Ibid. This figure is found on page 39 of *The Loyalty Effect.*

SITUATION ASSESSMENT

1

Market Definition

Red Bull, the Austrian company that is credited with creating the energy-drinks market in the early 1980s, sells more than four billion units per year and, according to some market analysts, commands a 60 percent market share.[1] However, other sources say that Red Bull's market share is just 12 percent,[2] and others say it is even less. *Which is right?* The answer is: "*all of the above.*" Gauging Red Bull's market share depends, of course, on how you define the market. In the energy drinks market, Red Bull is the clear market leader with approximately 60 percent of the market. In the "functional drinks" market, which also includes sports drinks such as Gatorade, Red Bull has a share of about 12 percent. Ultimately, in the "beverage" market, Red Bull competes with bottled water, colas, and juices, and it has only a tiny market share.

So what is the correct definition of a market? This question is important, and it has a number of implications for marketing. For one, this question defines who the competitors are and what potential substitutes exist for a product. It also defines the competitive position (relative market share) of a product in the product portfolio. If the market is defined too narrowly, a product will have a limited number of competitors and a high market share, and a company might overlook threats or possible substitutes (e.g., sports drinks or functional foods that could serve as a substitute for an energy drink). It might also miss opportunities to meet related customer needs. On the other hand, defining the market too broadly can complicate matters instead of simplifying decision making, by considering too many competitors and substitutes (some of which may be irrelevant).[3]

One way to define a market and identify competition is to examine patterns of substitution.[4] This can be done from a demand-side perspective or from a supply-side perspective. The demand-side perspective analyzes substitutes that are considered by the customer during the buying decision because they offer similar functions. In contrast, the supply-side approach tries to identify all competitors that could serve the needs of a customer group.

CUSTOMER-DEFINED MARKETS

When defining a market, two important premises must be considered.[5] First, it's important to remember that customers seek the benefits that products provide, rather than products per se. Thus, the specific products that customers consider in a buying situation represent the benefits they seek. Second, it's critical to note that customers consider different alternatives in a buying situation, and these alternatives define the market. So, the market also depends on what customers consider as alternatives and substitutions for their specific need.

Based on these two premises, a market can be said to consist of products that both address a customer need and are considered by the customer as alternatives or substitutes. Substitutability, however, is a measure of degree, and there are several levels in a hierarchy of products that represent different substitutions. These substitution levels define five levels of competition (see Table 1-1).

1. The lowest level of competition is the product variant. Variants are items within a product type distinguishable by individual product attributes (e.g., package size, colors, taste) that serve specific needs and pursue the same market segment. One example is the market or segment of customers who seek an energy drink that is low in calories. Hence, the competitive arena for this product would consist of all companies that offer low-calorie energy drinks. To return to an example from earlier in this note, Red Bull's entry in this category is Red Bull Sugar-Free.

2. The second level of competition is the product type. This includes all variants of a product that share the same core features but differ in individual attributes. Here, the market would consist of all drinks that address customers who seek drinks that give them a boost of energy.

3. The next higher level is the product category. This is a group of products with similar features that have certain functional coherence, usually seen as "the industry" by managers. For instance, energy drinks belong to the category of functional beverages, because they all serve similar needs and have a functional coherence. On this level, the market would consist of all beverages that increase physical and mental performance, including colas, juices, and energy drinks.

TABLE NOTE 1-1 Five Levels of Competition

Level of Competition/ Substitution	Description	Market	Example
Product variant	Variants are items within a product type distinguishable by individual product attributes (e.g., size, price, taste) that serve specific needs and pursue the same market segment	Customers who seek an energy drink with low calories	Low-calorie energy drinks
Product type	Product variants within a product category that share the same core features but differ in individual attributes	Customers who seek an energy drink to get a boost of energy	Energy drinks
Product category	A group of products with similar features having certain functional coherence, usually seen as the industry by managers	Customers who seek a functional drink to increase their physical and mental performance	Functional beverages
Generic competition	Product categories that fulfill the same generic need	Customers who want to increase their physical and mental performance via nutrition	Functional nutrition
Budget competition	Products or services that compete for the same customer dollar	Customers who want to improve their health and wellness	Health and wellness

4. The fourth level is generic competition, consisting of product categories that fulfill the same generic need. Here, the generic need is an increase in physical and mental performance, and this need can be achieved by functional beverages, functional food, dietary supplements, and so forth. Therefore, at this generic level, the market would consist of all functional nutrition products, and it would feature energy drinks like Red Bull competing with energy bars and other similar products.

5. Finally, the fifth level is budget competition. Here the market consists of products or services that compete for the same customer dollar. For instance, a customer who has a certain amount of money at his or her disposal might spend it on functional nutrition, sauna and spa, meditation, etc. These products and services that might not compete on the level of generic need (functional nutrition), but they do compete on a higher level—that of health and wellness. Of course, if customers are unconstrained in their spending, many of these products and services might also be complements to one another.

Figures 1-1 and 1-2 illustrate how the market can be defined for Red Bull. Depending on the core benefit sought by customers (e.g., refreshment, increased energy), different arenas of competition are identified. For example, on the product category level (soft drinks), Red Bull competes with colas, juices, and so forth when customers seek a refreshment drink. On the generic competition level, Red Bull also competes with products beyond the category, such as beer, milkshakes, etc. And on the budget competition level, where Red Bull competes for the same customer dollar, people might consider spending their money on a candlelight dinner or a trip to the movies instead of on Red Bull. Hence, at this level, Red Bull's competition consists of food and entertainment in general. In comparison, when the primary benefit sought is a boost of energy (rather than refreshment), Red Bull's competition is different. Here, it competes with sports drinks on the product category level, with functional food (e.g., Powerbar) on the generic competition level, and with meditation, sauna and spa, etc. on the budget competition level.

Which market definition is most appropriate depends on the decisions that have to be made and on their time horizon.[6] For short term, day-to-day tactical decisions such as short-run budgeting or performance evaluation, narrow market definitions

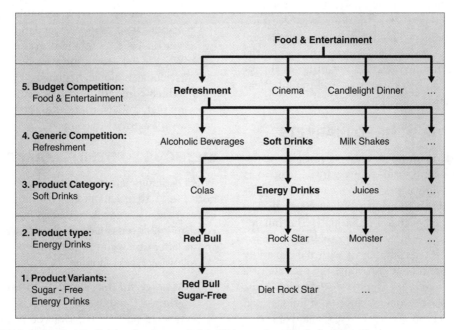

FIGURE NOTE 1-1 Market Definition for Energy Drinks (Primary Benefit: Refreshment)

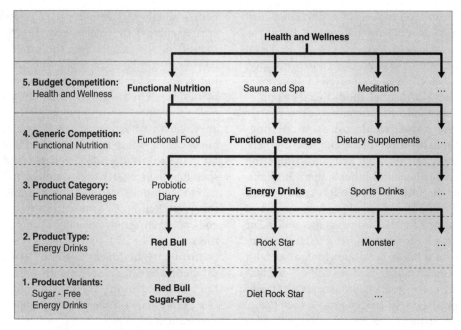

FIGURE NOTE 1-2   Market Definition for Energy Drinks (Primary Benefit: Energy)

based on product variants and product types are most relevant. In such cases, competing products are those that address exactly the same segment, perform the same functions, and are sold through the same channels. In contrast, for strategic, long-term decisions, broader market definitions are necessary. These definitions include market segments that are not currently served and might offer potential growth opportunities, possible substitutions emerging in other product categories, and potential entrants from adjacent markets.

COMPETITOR-DEFINED MARKETS

As previously mentioned, markets can also be defined using a supply-side approach that considers technological similarities between competitors, relative production costs, or distribution coverage. The supply-side perspective of market definition includes all competitors with the capability to serve the customers (i.e., competitors with the capability to design, produce, and distribute the product or a substitute). Therefore, a supply-side definition of the helicopter industry would include both military and commercial helicopters, whereas a demand-side definition would include only one of the two, because customers don't see military and commercial helicopters as interchangeable. In the supply-side approach, the following questions are addressed:[7]

1. Which competitors are serving related product classes with the same technology, the same manufacturing processes, and the same material sources, sales force, and distribution channels?
2. What is the geographical scope of the market (regional, national, or global)?
3. Which competitors are currently serving the market, and who are the potential entrants with a capacity to compete?

METHODS TO DEFINE MARKETS

When defining markets, you can use predefined categories (e.g., SIC [Standard Industrial Classification] codes, categorizations devised by market research companies), or you can develop your own definition[8]. In the latter case, you can base your definition upon the following types of input:[9]

- *Managerial judgment:* With this method, a group of managers judges which product types, product categories, competitors, etc. are or might become direct competitors, or which technologies might become future substitutes for the product in question.

- **Behavioral data:** Among the best known types of behavioral data are cross-elasticities and brand-switching data, and both of these directly measure which products customers consider as substitutes. For example, cross-elasticities based on scanner data from store cash registers can indicate whether two products are substitutes for each other. This is accomplished by measuring the proportional change in the sales of one product due to a specific increase or decrease of sales in the other product (e.g., due to a price reduction). In contrast, brand-switching data indicate the probability of purchasing Brand A, given that Brand B was purchased last time[10]. Here, it is assumed that customers would rather switch between close substitutes than between distant ones, and that these switching probabilities provide a measure for the probability of substitution.

- **Customer judgments:** Customer judgments have also been proven to give usable insights into product-market boundaries. With this method, customers are asked to indicate whether each product on a list is an appropriate substitute and acceptable alternative for satisfying a specific need.

Summary

How a company defines its market is critical to all of its marketing activities. If a company defines the market too broadly, its marketing activities lose focus. If it defines the market too narrowly, it risks missing opportunities. Moreover, market definition is the basis upon which a company measures its market share, and market share is a common metric of success. How the firm labels its market also tends to define the boundaries of its efforts and the horizons of its creative vision. Markets can be defined in customer-oriented (demand-side) terms or in competitor-oriented (supply-side) terms using a variety of methods. No matter which method is used, a company's market definition dictates how it relates to customers' needs, wants, expectations, and requirements.

Additional Resources

Berry, Ben. "Market update: energy drinks in North America." *Agriculture and Agri-Food Canada* (August 2009).

Day, George. "Assessing Competitive Arenas: Who Are Your Competitors?" In *Wharton on Dynamic Competitive Strategy*, George Day and David J. Reibstein and Robert E. Gunther, eds. (Hoboken, NJ: John Wiley & Sons, 1997).

Day, George S., Allan D. Shocker, and Rajendra K. Srivastava. "Customer-oriented approaches to identifying product-markets." *Journal of Marketing* 43 (Fall, 1979): 8–19.

Helm, Burt and Ira Sager. "The sport of extreme marketing." *Business Week* 3924 (March 14, 2005): 14.

Lehmann, Donald R. and Russell S. Winer. *Analysis for Marketing Planning*. New York: McGraw-Hill, 2008. Especially: Chapter 2 Defining the Competitive Set and Chapter 6 Market Potential and Forecasting.

Endnotes

1. Burt Helm and Ira Sager, "The sport of extreme marketing," *Business Week* 3924 (March 14, 2005): 14.

2. Ben Berry, "Market update: energy drinks in North America," *Agriculture and Agri-Food Canada* (August 2009).

3. Donald R. Lehmann and Russell S. Winer, *Analysis for Marketing Planning* (New York: McGraw-Hill, 2008).

4. George Day, "Assessing Competitive Arenas: Who Are Your Competitors?" in *Wharton on Dynamic Competitive Strategy*, George Day, David J. Reibstein and Robert E. Gunther, eds. (Hoboken, NJ: John Wiley & Sons, 1997).

5. George S. Day, Allan D. Shocker, and Rajendra K. Srivastava, "Customer-oriented Approaches to Identifying Product-markets," *Journal of Marketing* 43 (Fall 1979): 8–19.

6. Day, "Assessing Competitive Arenas."

7. Day "Assessing Competitive Arenas."

8. Lehmann and Winer, *Analysis for Marketing Planning.*

9. Day, "Assessing Competitive Arenas."

10. Day, Shocker, and Srivastava, "Customer-oriented Approaches."

2

Context: PEST Analysis

The general context or environment within which a firm, product, or brand operates has pervasive effects on strategy and results. Distinguishing broad categories of environmental factors that affect strategy is helpful but involves simplification of a complex reality. Still, the mnemonic PEST (**P**olitical/regulatory, **E**conomic, **S**ocial/cultural, and **T**echnical/physical) is one helpful, comprehensive tool for partitioning the general business context. The PEST acronym is useful for compartmentalizing and inventorying the environment – but, of course, it is just a tool. The underlying objective is to methodically, thoroughly, and continuously monitor the firm's situation and to probe for connections to opportunities and threats. Although we know that many factors span these four categories (e.g., a recession involves not only economic decline, but also shifts in values and thrift as well as regulatory responses like stimulus spending), beginning with a succinct classification of the environment emphasizes the breadth of issues, imposes discipline on the assessment, stimulates and structures brainstorming, and assures completeness.

UNDERSTANDING THE FOUR PEST CATEGORIES

The four categories of environmental factors influence marketing strategy and tactics, and can pose either opportunities or threats. They also differ between cultures and nations. A marketing strategist, therefore, not only looks at the political/regulatory, economic, social/cultural, and technical/physical aspects of the environment in each country in which the firm operates, but she or he must also try to understand the different factors across nations that shape these forces to predict how they might change in future. Any of these factors can also impact any of the elements of the marketing mix and the overarching marketing strategy as emphasized in Figure 2-1.

Political/Regulatory Context

Marketers operate in powerful, complex regulatory and legal environments that are inseparable from the political systems that shape them. A wide range of political/regulatory factors influence marketing strategy, including tax codes, liability structures, operating rules, product labeling regulations, purity and conformance requirements, government subsidies, and government procurement itself. Some firms also operate under nongovernmental regulations and perhaps even informal guidelines. For example, golf equipment manufacturers must consider the United States Golf Association's rules, and alcohol distillers operated for decades under an informal industry prohibition on television advertising. Thus, political, regulatory, and legal factors encompass a wide

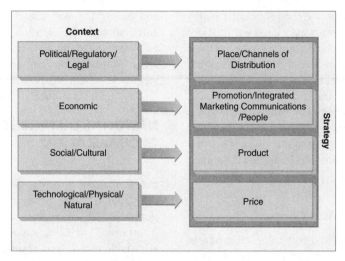

FIGURE NOTE 2-1 The Context and Marketing Strategy/Tactics

range of forces that constrain and direct marketing strategies.

One of the most influential political and regulatory changes of the past half-century has been the liberalization of international trade. Since the end of World War II, trade liberalization treaties and multinational "free trade zones" have substantially lowered barriers to foreign trade, and the volume of world trade has, in turn, increased dramatically. These changes have encouraged organizations to form global marketing strategies that focus on the centralization of decision making and the standardization of marketing programs. Global strategies are important to large firms for which a global strategy is a viable alternative as well as to the smaller firms that must compete against these larger companies. When setting international marketing strategies, adaptation versus standardization is a central tension; in other words, the firm must adapt sufficiently to local contexts, while, at the same time, capturing the benefits of scale (e.g., cost reductions, learning) that may be available from standardization. (International markets and contexts will be revisited later in this note.)

Economic Context

Economic variables, such as interest rates, unemployment rates, currency exchange rates, and inflation, also impact marketing strategies in substantial and complex ways. Some sectors of the economy are affected disproportionally, whereas others are less affected by economic swings. For example, although higher interest rates generally dampen spending and economic activity, some industries, such as housing and automobiles, are more closely tied to interest rates than others. Still other companies, such as pharmaceutical manufacturers, are virtually "recession proof," while yet other businesses, such as do-it-yourself automobile parts suppliers, are countercyclical (i.e., their sales go *up* as the economy falls). Thus, disentangling the relationships between the economy and a particular firm or industry's prospects is important to effective strategy formation.

Social/Cultural Context

Social and cultural values, attitudes, norms, manners, and tastes all affect customer needs and thereby influence marketing strategies and tactics. Cultures vary on values like achievement orientation as well as on attitudes such as those toward wealth and conspicuous consumption. Norms and manners include everything from the formality of business relationships to practices like tipping and gift-giving. The demographics and lifestyles of a population (things like age, education, and social class) are also important components of the social/cultural context.

Culture—or "[t]he set of learned values, norms, and behaviors that are shared by a society and are designed to increase the probability of the society's survival"[1]—is often associated with nations (e.g., Chinese culture, Italian culture) or with ethnic subgroups within nations (i.e., subcultures). Culture can be a powerful moderator of strategic success or failure, because it drives important differences in demand. Cultures are dynamic; in other words, values and aesthetic preferences are constantly changing and are different across generations. Given this situation, it is valuable to understand not only the *state of* but also *trends in* cultural factors.

Technological/Physical Context

Technology, innovation and technological progress, and the available physical and commercial infrastructure additionally impact strategies in many ways. New technologies can replace or become direct or indirect substitutes for an existing product form or product category, and technological changes can alter the way a product is distributed and/or consumed. The physical environment is also part of the strategic context, and it includes climate, population density, physical infrastructure, and commercial infrastructure, all of which interact with social trends such as changing attitudes toward the environment and nature. (Commercial infrastructure includes public infrastructure—such as banking services, e.g., the availability of credit and documentation, roads and water, and mail and shipping services)

Technological changes often have "second-order effects" that are harder to foresee as a technology emerges. For example, cell-phone technology had obvious immediate effects on the world of telecommunications, creating opportunities in wireless service and threatening the business models of traditional telephone companies. Then, wireless converged with GPS technology to threaten stand-alone GPS products such as Garmin and TomTom. Other less obvious effects of cell-phone technology include changes in the way that brick-and-mortar businesses connect with customers. Cell phones created opportunities for real-time "voting," thereby facilitating participative mass media events (such as *American Idol*), and widely available GPS technology changed the manner in which many businesses advertise and reach customers. For instance, Dunkin' Brands, franchisor of Dunkin' Donuts and Baskin Robins Ice Cream shops in the United States

and around the world, reached an arrangement with TomTom, one of the leading producers of stand-alone GPS systems, to put all their shops into the GPS system's "Points of Interest," and many out-of-the-way businesses have similarly begun to take advantage of GPS to "guide" customers to their stores.

NATIONAL DIFFERENCES AND GLOBALIZATION

As previously noted, one major shift in the regulatory environment over the past fifty years has been the liberalization of trade between nations. This liberalization occurred in conjunction with both advances in communication technologies and the proliferation of affordable travel to increase global trade and better connect people across places and cultures. Together, these forces underlie the rise of "globalization" and the associated development of global and multinational marketing strategies. In the words of Theodore Levitt, a professor at Harvard Business School: [2]

> "A powerful force drives the world toward a converging commonality, and that force is technology. . . . The result is a new commercial reality—the emergence of global markets for standardized consumer products on a previously unimagined scale."

In fact, in 1983, these forces of trade, technology, education, and travel led Levitt to predict what he termed the "globalization of markets"—or the emergence of global brands that take advantage of scale to meet broad consumer needs for low-cost, reliable goods, and the related convergence of cultures around common values and understandings. Since then, many of Levitt's predictions have apparently come true. Today, for example, large global producers dominate many industries, and they have afforded consumers the access to a variety of goods unimaginable just a half-century ago. (Note that global marketing strategies— i.e., standardized offerings and centralized processes and decision making—can be contrasted with multinational strategies, in which offerings are adapted to local markets, and processes and decision making is distributed.) Nevertheless, globalization has not been absolute, and it may not be inevitable. Cultures do not seem to be converging to the degree that Levitt and others envisioned,[3] and some industries, such as retailing, appear to resist globalization altogether.[4]

In any case, there is an important connection between thinking about international marketing—whether it be standardized or adapted—and thinking about the context (political, economic, social/cultural, and technological) of marketing strategy. The basic trade-off when making decisions about the adaptation of a marketing program is between accommodating differences in context and exploiting the benefits of standardization. The chief benefits of standardization are cost savings—savings realized by avoiding assembly-line changeovers and via the realization of economies of scale and other efficiencies. However, adaptations to accommodate local tastes and conditions—including local political/regulatory conditions, economic conditions, social/cultural conditions, and technical and infrastructure conditions—have costs and hinder the realization of benefits of scale. Still, marketing mixes are more effective when they are adapted to the distinct needs and demands of local markets. Thus, costs generally go up with marketing mix adaptation, but distinct markets are clearly more responsive to tailored offerings.

As previously mentioned, multinational marketing strategies involve adaption of the marketing mix and offerings and distributed decision making. Therefore, *multinational strategies* can be understood as connecting the 5 Ps of the marketing mix to differences across nations in the PEST framework—that is adjusting to the differences and adapting the marketing mix. In contrast, *global strategies* can, in one sense, be viewed as *disregarding* those same differences in favor of the benefits of standardization and centralization. Interestingly, almost all global strategies make *some* adaptations for different commercial contexts, yet at the same time, almost all multinational strategies seek to standardize and thereby reap the rewards of scale wherever possible.

Summary

Marketing strategy must be built on constant, relentless attention to the firm's industry and sphere of operation, including the *political/regulatory* context, the *economic* context, the *social/cultural* context, and the *technical/physical* context. Certain industries feel the effects of contextual forces especially keenly at specific times. In 2009, for example, the pharmaceutical industry, which has always been closely tied to advances in science and technology, was also attentive to the economy, as the world's industrialized nations struggled through a major recession. Within the United States, pharmaceutical firms were also particularly attentive to the political/regulatory environment, as the federal government undertook efforts toward health care reform. These same environmental factors influence almost all industries, and even if their effects on those industries are less obvious, they are just as real and just as forceful. Therefore, all strategic marketers and brands should continually monitor their general context, probing for connections between events and trends and their own strategy, operations, and tactics. After all, many opportunities and threats alike emerge from these broad spheres.

Additional Resources

Lehmann, Donald R. and Russell S. Winer. *Analysis for Marketing Planning*. New York: McGraw-Hill, 2008. Specifically: Chapter 3 Industry Analysis.

Endnotes

1. American Marketing Association Online Dictionary: www.marketingpower.com/_layouts/Dictionary.aspx?dLetter=C. Last accessed June 18, 2010.
2. Theodore Levitt, "The Globalization of Markets," *Harvard Business Review* 61, no. 3 (May–June, 1983): 92–102, 92.
3. Ibid; *cf.* Marcus Alexander and Harry Korine "When You Shouldn't Go Global," *Harvard Business Review* 86, no. 12 (December, 2008): 70–77 as well as with S. Tamer Cavusgil, Gary Knight, and John R. Reisenberger, *International Business: Strategy, Management, and the New Realities*, Upper Saddle River, NJ: Pearson Prentice Hall, 2008), especially page 147.
4. See, for example, "Global Retailing: Trouble at Till," *The Economist* 381, no. 8502 (November 4, 2006): 18.

3

Customer Assessment— Trends and Insights

This book's pervasive emphasis on the customer and on customers' needs in the strategic marketing framework is deliberate: *effective and efficient marketing strategies begin with and are continuously aligned with customer need.* As synthesized in Table 3-1, the first place at which strategy is informed by and aligned with the customer is customer assessment,

TABLE NOTE 3-1 Customer Consideration in the Strategic Marketing Process

Customer-Oriented Marketing Research	**Situation Assessment**	*Customer Assessment*	The broad, exploratory, and inductive study of customers in general to identify (a) *trends* in needs and demand, and (b) *customer insights*.
	Strategy Formation and Implementation	*Segmentation, Targeting, and Positioning*	Ongoing as well as focused research intended to identify differences across customers/consumers with regard to needs and descriptive characteristics and linking those differences to existing or achievable competitive advantages.
		Positioning and the Marketing Mix	Focused research to pretest and refine tactics, including price, promotions and advertising, new products or product modifications, and merchandising programs; and to gauge the effects of those tactics on achieving the desired positioning.
		Customer Relationship Management (CRM)	Ongoing data collections tied to specific accounts, customers, or consumers that serve to tailor offerings (personalize or customize offerings) and direct investments and efforts toward the 'right' customers and segments.
	Assessment & Adjustment	*Customer- and Market-Oriented Metrics*	Focused and ongoing research collecting information on customer responses to the marketing mix, including measures of satisfaction, loyalty, profitability, and revenues.

defined as the broad, wide-ranging, and exploratory scrutiny of customers and their needs that is a major part of monitoring the situation. Customer assessment can be distinguished from other market research that is focused on specific customers or on particular issues or decisions. Although all of these activities are "market research," customer assessment is different in that it is best done *without* prior hypotheses and should *not* be focused on addressing specific issues. Thus, this note focuses on that exploratory customer assessment, the broadest and most inductive form of market research; this is the "zoom out," wide-angle view of customers and potential customers. Customer assessment has two primary objectives:

1. Identifying trends in the environment that could impact customers and their needs, and "mining" increasingly large internal and external databases for a better understanding of customer behaviors and needs.
2. Discovering customer insights by means of rich, inductive exploratory approaches. (Customer insights are original understandings of the ways customers consume and take value from products connected to innovative ways of meeting those customers' needs.)

These two objectives, identifying trends and discovering customer insights, are distinct but they are also closely related and may overlap.

IDENTIFYING TRENDS: FORECASTING, DATA MINING, AND FUTURING

Identifying marketplace trends and distinguishing trends that have deep, broad, enduring foundations from more ephemeral fads is essential to developing and sustaining effective marketing strategies. Trends are (1) broad-based changes in the marketplace that endure over time; (2) represent significant market opportunities; (3) are grounded on substantive transformations (such as changes in demographics, values, lifestyles, or technology); and (4) are accessible to the mainstream. In contrast, fads are tied to transient shifts in popular culture, in fashion, in the media, or within a subpopulation such as "the trendy crowd."[1] Analyzing the environment for trends can

be highly quantitative, and it frequently includes well-established trend-extrapolation techniques as well as emerging data-mining procedures. Looking for trends sometimes also involves much more subjective "futuring,"[2] or wide–ranging, multidisciplinary exploration of the environment in search of possible future events or trends and consideration of the impact of these possibilities on both customers and markets.

Forecasting

The best known way to look for trends is to perform quantitative analysis of data on past marketplace phenomena and search for patterns and relationships that can be extrapolated to the future. Similar econometric and judgment-based forecasting methods may also be used to explore trends in demographics, attitudes and lifestyles, and cultural and social forces as well as trends in the economy, in competitor actions and strategies, and in the technological and natural environments. Any of these elements can connect with strategy via some related change in customer behaviors or demand patterns. These quantitative forecasting tools are usually focused on projecting one to two years into the future. There are several basic categories of forecasting approaches, which subsume innumerable variations and can get somewhat complex, including trend extrapolation, causal modeling, and judgment-based forecasting:

TREND EXTRAPOLATION   Statisticians often use trend extrapolation or "curve fitting" methods such as moving averages, exponential smoothing, and the like to identify the direction in which customer, economic, and other phenomena are headed. These analyses are relatively straightforward and require few data points, which make them attractive to managers and forecasters. However, they're also dependent on *past* data and *past* market realities, which inextricably ties them to an assumption that the future will be an extension of the past.

Curve fitting frequently involves uncomplicated straight-line extrapolations, but it can also include nonlinear extrapolation, such as geometric and exponential curves, parabolic (polynomial) curves, and even Gompertz or sigmoid (S-shaped) curves.

The latter category consists of S-shaped curves common to natural growth patterns. In marketing, these sorts of curves are often seen in product lifecycles, diffusions of innovations, and other phenomena in which growth is initially slow, gains momentum through some rapid growth phase, and then abates as new growth becomes harder to obtain.

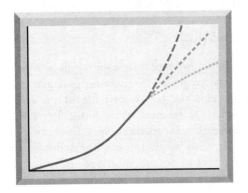

CAUSAL MODELING OR ECONOMETRIC FORECASTING. Regression analysis, the most often used tool of causal modeling and econometric forecasting, identifies the relationships between variables that cause or at least predict some target variable. That is, regressions predict some phenomenon of interest, called the "dependent variable" and usually designated as Y. With this method, the predictors or "independent variables," usually designated with Xs, are the things that cause or at least correlate with Y. A regression relationship is usually expressed as an equation of the form shown here. There may be many independent variables, and the relationship between the independent and dependent variable can be linear, or it can take on nonlinear forms (e.g., exponential curves, Gompertz functions).

$$Y = f(\beta_1 X_1 + \beta_2 X_2 \ldots \beta_n X_n)$$

The difference between causation and prediction is complex. It is usually the topic of an entire course in doctoral programs, but it is not especially important to most marketing managers. Essentially, the question of causation addresses whether two things are related because one leads to the other, or whether the two things simply correlate (move together), perhaps because of some other factor that is causing them both. For example, the value of customers'

houses and the value of customers' cars will correlate; when one is high, the other is likely to be high, and when one is low, the other is likely to be low (with exceptions and variance, of course). In this situation, if one value is known, the other can reasonably be predicted, but *neither one causes the other.* In fact, it's likely that both values are caused by income and wealth. Nevertheless, if we know that two things move together and we also know or can estimate one of the two things, then we can predict the other—and this sort of prediction is usually sufficient for managerial purposes. For example, if a car dealer would like to know what sort of car (e.g., luxury sedans versus economy compacts) to present to a certain customer, knowing the value of that customer's home is good information to have, regardless of the underlying causality or lack of causality.

JUDGMENT-BASED FORECASTING. Although the idea that any single person can foresee future patterns and trends based on "gut feelings" is antithetical to the dominant analytic paradigm of contemporary management, it is nevertheless an alternative—one that is used more often than generally acknowledged, and one that may be underappreciated given emerging evidence that intuition can be a powerful decision-making tool.[3] For instance, a 2002 study found that 45 percent of the executives polled relied "more on instinct than on facts and figures in running their businesses."[4] These and other findings suggest that intuition can be accurate—more accurate than rigorous analysis in some contexts—and they also emphasize the role of unconscious learning and the validity of rapid-processing heuristics.[5]

Nevertheless, rather than relying on a single expert's predictions, formal judgment-based approaches to forecasting typically draw on *panels* of diverse participants. Although individual input to "consensus methods," such as surveys and Delphi panels, may itself be based on intuition or gut feelings, the underlying assumption is that compiling input from multiple and diverse perspectives "cancels out" biases and gleans valid insights from the aggregated perspectives. In fact, there is voluminous evidence that supports the assumption that panels (or "crowds") make better decisions and more accurate forecasts than individuals.[6] One specific sort of judgment-based forecasting is "cool-hunting," or monitoring the environment to identify trends in popular culture, fashion, design, and contemporary lifestyles.[7] Cool-hunting looks for trends *as they emerge*; that is, cool-hunters try to recognize relatively isolated behaviors that will "catch on" and be widely adopted. Cool-hunting is similar to the search for customer insights, discussed in depth later in this note, and it utilizes methods for monitoring culture and fashion similar to those used in ethnography. In particular, ethnography studies consumers in depth in their natural habitat, whereas cool-hunting studies fashion, lifestyles, and contemporary culture on the street, in the office, and in the mall.

One key to identifying trends in popular culture is the recruitment of people well-attuned to emerging tastes. Apparel companies like Nike and North Face as well as branders less obviously entrained to popular culture (such as Wendy's, Coca-Cola, and Nokia), employ "young, bright, culture spies who could roam freely and undetected through the clubs and schoolyards where corporations weren't welcome"[8] in search of "cool." Similarly, research firms look for "observers who "have a taste level that is avant-garde but not so far out that it won't become mainstream."[9] However, the notion of "cool" is fickle and fleeting; once a trend has been spotted and "commercialized" by marketers, it may, unavoidably, be near the point of becoming passé.

Data Mining

Whereas forecasting involves looking at past and current data or behavior to identify trends that can be expected to extend into the future, data mining involves searching through available information to detect relationships among behaviors or to identify original descriptions of consumption phenomena. In particular, data mining is the "extraction of interesting (*nontrivial, implicit, previously unknown* and *potentially useful*) patterns or knowledge from huge amounts of data."[10] Typically, this process involves analysis of large databases using sophisticated computational and statistical methods that consider internal and/or external data to identify interesting relationships. Culling actionable knowl-

edge from such extensive data is a challenge, but today's increasingly large databases can hold valuable information about consumption patterns and preferences.

Harrah's Casinos, for example, collected extensive data on its customers over the years, including information on their spending and gambling patterns, but it took sophisticated data mining to identify actionable understandings in these data. It turned out that Harrah's most valuable customers—the 26 percent of the company's customers who generated a whopping 82 percent of revenues—were *not* the "gold cuff-linked, limousine-riding high rollers" the company might have assumed; instead, they were "former teachers, doctors, bankers, and machinists—middle-aged and senior adults with discretionary time and income who enjoyed playing slot machines."[11] This data-mining "nugget" was readily linked to managerial actions, including the customization of offerings and communications to target these valuable customers.

Futuring

Although forecasting and data mining may *seem* straightforward, the assumption that the future will be an extension of the past or that relationships found in the past will hold into the future is rarely met, at least not directly. The future, it turns out, is usually a function of the past modified by unforeseen factors. In addition, everyone knows about the past—or could and should know about it. Because your competition can see the past as well as you can, forecasts based solely on past data may not yield substantial competitive advantages. Therefore, marketing strategists shouldn't just understand how to extrapolate patterns—they should also consider what things might *disrupt* those patterns and explore the implications of those possible discontinuities. The essential marketing question might therefore be reduced to the following: *If these uncertain but possible things happen at some point in the future, what would we want to have done between now and then to be prepared to take advantage of (or to avoid harm from) such an eventuality?*

Futuring, or "the act, art, or science of identifying and evaluating possible future events,"[12] focuses on the uncertainty of the future and on environmental changes or events that *might* impact customers. Futuring begins with traditional extrapolations from past patterns, but it goes well beyond forecasting by looking further into the future and (especially) by considering what might *disrupt* those patterns. Futuring adopts a broader mindset than traditional forecasting, embracing a multidisciplinary set of more qualitative and judgmental approaches and ways of understanding the world. Despite some common misperceptions, futuring is *not* mystical prophecy, prescience, or clairvoyance. Rather, futuring studies the *possibilities* of the future— what *might* happen—using a wide range of tools and a variety of perspectives. Futuring also studies ways organizations and people can prepare for these possibilities. Thus, futuring is about both anticipation and preparation.

As noted, futuring extends basic forecasting by considering longer time frames, incorporating a broader set of tools (including qualitative and speculative judgment), and looking not only at where trends in past and current data are headed, but also at what might disrupt those trends. For example, a traditional, quantitative forecaster might have forecast that sales of camera film in the early twenty-first century would continue at around $7 million per year, the sales level they'd enjoyed for most of the late twentieth century. Of course, that isn't what happened. Instead, an external disruption—the emergence and rapid adoption of digital photography—changed the existing trend, and sales of film plummeted. Similarly, a forecast of foreign student spending in the United States in 2001 would likely have predicted continued growth in expenditures—at least until the events of September 11, 2001, brought about dramatic changes in federal policies regarding visiting students. Many observers did not foresee digital photography nor did anyone foresee the terrorist attacks of 9/11? Could a futurist have imagined scenarios in which the film industry faced disruptive technology or in which America faced a terrorist attack? *Almost certainly.* Futuring encompasses methods for such imagination or speculation about the future as well as ways to prepare and plan by drawing on that uncertain foresight.

Discovering Customer Insights

"If I had asked people what they wanted, they would have said faster horses."

Henry Ford[13]

Gary Hamel and C. K. Prahalad have argued that "to realize the potential that core competencies create, a company must also have the imagination to envision markets that do not yet exist and the ability to stake them out ahead of the competition."[14] The realization of exceptional returns often means disregarding mature, competitive markets for truly new ones. Finding markets that do not yet exist—that is, identifying and meeting latent needs—begins with the search for customer insights. A customer insight is a penetrating, discerning understanding of customer needs, the ways that customers derive value from products, and the ways customers might derive value from products.[15] Good customer insights are fresh, relevant, enduring, and inspiring.

Identifying customer insights requires more than painstakingly asking customers what they *think* they want; rather, it often necessitate deep customer "intimacy" with an eye toward discovering solutions customers could not have envisioned or articulated themselves. In other words, customer assessment requires "deep dives" to understand customers and to identify unmet and even unrecognized needs. (Needs that have not yet been recognized by the customers themselves are termed latent needs). An important distinction between the search for genuine customer insights and other forms of marketing research is that customer insights come from *inductive* reasoning—exploration that doesn't start with a theory, a hypothesis, or a specific issue to be addressed, but instead attempts to observe in as unbiased and wide-ranging a manner as possible, to "let the data speak," and to identify unexpected insights.

The Customer Value Chain

A useful frame of reference when probing for customer insights is the so-called "customer value chain." The notion of a value chain is well-known in the context of a firm—in particular, it breaks down the series of activities that add value or support the production and delivery of value for the firm. In

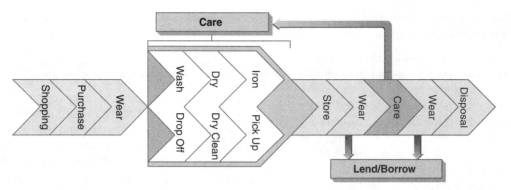

FIGURE NOTE 3-1 A Hypothetical Customer Value Chain for Clothing

comparison, a customer value chain is the series of activities involved in *extracting* value from the good or service; it is how the customer meets a need or needs with the product or by other means. Figure 3-1 is an example of a customer value chain for clothing. As depicted in the figure, the customer may take value from a marketer's offerings anywhere along the chain, from shopping and purchase through wear and care to disposal. Understanding customer value chains and organizing observations and understandings of customers within value chains is useful. Indeed, customer value chains comprise a helpful organizing lens when considering the customer experience and searching for customer insights.

Data Collection Methods for Customer Insights

Marketing researchers who seek to identify customer insights have been encouraged to work like "bricoleurs," a description drawing on the French word *bricoler*,[16] which denotes a tradesman who works with his hands and whatever materials and tools are available. A bricoleur is crafty, resourceful, and able to see known things in new ways; similarly, a marketing researcher who seeks to uncover genuine customer insights must also be creative and resourceful, employing a variety of methods and perspectives to home in on important truths. Searching for customer insights requires a 360-degree view of customers—looking at the way they consume from every possible angle—and a thick description of consumption that includes not only information about

the consumption itself, but also about the consumption's context. For example, if a consumer drinks a glass of wine, the meaning and significance of that consumption, the value derived from the wine, and the needs that are satisfied (and that remain unsatisfied) are dependent on the context, including the social, physical, temporal, and emotional context in which the consumption is situated. Wine consumption would, in most cases, be difficult to understand in a laboratory or simulated setting or via retrospective self-reports.[17] Therefore, customer assessment must draw on a variety of predominantly qualitative methods, such as total immersion, depth interviews, projective techniques, and observation in the consumers' "natural setting" or ethnography.

TOTAL IMMERSION. One method for exploring customers' experiences with a product that, at the same time, ensures that corporate executives get a deep appreciation for those experiences is "total immersion"; this technique involves *executives*, rather than researchers, immersing themselves in the customers' experience and point of view.[18] Sessions, which may not be called "total immersion" sessions—at the BBC, for example, they're called "Meet the Audience"[19]—include deep and rich interactions between the executives and their customers. Some marketing research firms, such as the British firm Essential Research,[20] specialize in facilitating meaningful immersion projects, whereas other marketing researchers criticize these projects as scientifically unsound. Nevertheless, Stuart Knapman, a partner at Essential Research and an expert in total immersion, has observed that total immersion can be invaluable in generating customer insights:

> Immersion helps to bring consumer issues into sharp focus and undoubtedly gets consumer insight into the boardroom. . . . Many researchers and senior execs alike complain that . . . the company is driven by research measures rather than vice versa, and that business metrics have more to do with maintaining the status quo than identifying new and exciting opportunities. . . . Immersion can be the perfect antidote to this insight inertia.[21]

DEPTH INTERVIEWS AND LADDERING. Depth interviewing is a technique in which one or more researchers meets with a single customer and asks that individual about his or her needs, buying behaviors, and experiences with a product category. Depth interviews are resource intensive because they take up researcher time and the qualitative data they generate are difficult to manage and to interpret; also, any

conclusions drawn from these interviews cannot easily be generalized to larger populations. Nevertheless, depth interviews offer deep, rich insight into the customer's motivations, values, and experiences with a product.

Laddering can be an especially effective structure for depth interviews. In laddering interviews, consumers are probed with regard to what makes a product different or attractive and why those qualities are good. In turn, this probing leads to "ladders" or means–end chains (MECCAs) linking product attributes to their consequences and these consequences to the value systems that they support.[22]

For example, Professor Thomas Reynolds of University of Texas at Dallas explored customers' perceptions of and motivations related to express-delivery services and identified the MECCA shown in Figure 3-2. In this example, the customers were secretaries, because they were key decision makers with regard to business express-mail services. Through his interviews, Reynolds learned that the secretaries linked the tangible attribute of drop boxes to the intangible attribute of convenience, which in turn created the consequences of saving time, getting

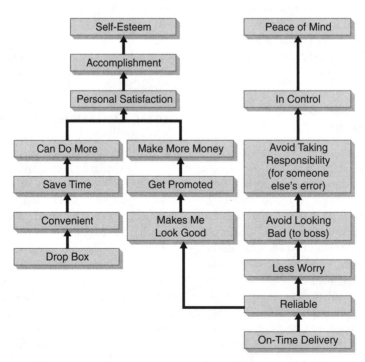

FIGURE NOTE 3-2   Value Map for Express-Mail Services[23]

more done, and achieving a sense of satisfaction. In turn, the consequences of time, productivity, and satisfaction supported the secretaries' values, which included accomplishment and self-esteem. This sort of structured depth interview and the resulting understanding of customers' values can lead to insights via the values that are salient. In addition, this technique reveals the connections between attributes and consequences and consequences and values—connections that motivate purchase behavior and that define consumer–product relationships.

PROJECTIVE TECHNIQUES. Projective techniques, such as word or picture association, sentence completion, and metaphor elicitation, originated in psychology and psychoanalysis and have been applied to understanding consumers since at least the mid-twentieth century. Some of the earliest marketing researchers, including Ernest Dichter in the well-known "motivational research" tradition of the 1940s and 1950s, used projective techniques to dig into consumers' subconscious or covert motives.[24] By asking a decision maker (a buyer or a consumer) to look at a picture, for example, and consider what he or she believes is going on or what he or she thinks someone in that situation would do or want (i.e., by asking the individual to "project" beliefs or motives onto the picture), the researcher avoids defensive reactions and may elicit more honest, deep, and even "subconscious" beliefs and motives.

ETHNOGRAPHY.[25] Ethnographic research methods are drawn from social anthropology—the social science focused on understanding contemporary social interactions and, especially, groups and cultures. Ethnography emphasizes depth and context in observation. Ethnographic observation is done in the context of consumers' "natural habitat"; that is, where the consumers live or consume the product, rather than in a simulated consumption context, in a laboratory, or via self-reports. Ethnography also emphasizes deep, long-term and all-embracing observation, as opposed to other market research methods' narrow, reductionist scopes. Ethnographic studies can recognize realities that customers themselves may be unaware of, cannot articulate, or are unwilling to offer in interviews or surveys.

For example, Moen, a manufacturer of premium plumbing fixtures, hired QualiData, a firm specializing in ethnographic research, to study the way consumers use showers. The resulting study involved watching people take showers—and yes, in order not to bias those observations, these people were naked—and then interviewing them about their shower experiences, the way they felt about the experiences, and ways the experiences might be made better. One outcome of this somewhat voyeuristic study was a unique, easy-to-use dial that allows people—naked people who often cannot see well due to low light, flowing water, and the absence of corrective glasses—to adjust water flow and massaging action.[26]

Interestingly, managers and entrepreneurs have always used this sort of "participant-observer learning," usually without calling it that or even knowing that it has parallels in the study of cultures. In fact, Moen itself is a brand born of customer insight and participant observation. In the 1930s, its founder, Al Moen, was scalded by a rush of hot water from a conventional, two-handled faucet. As the *Washington Post* described it, "Eureka! A flash of genius, a product is born. . . . Al Moen had no research to go on, just his own intuition and life experience."[27] Today, trained ethnographers search for these same types of "eureka" moments using deep, extensive observation of consumers in their natural habitats. When applied to the new product development process, ethnographic research is sometimes called "empathic research," emphasizing the fact that the researchers and the designers try to empathize with customers using the product.[28]

Importantly, all of these methods (total immersion, depth interviews and laddering, projective techniques, and ethnography) intended to identify customer insights are *inductive*. They begin with observations that shape the eventual conclusions, rather than beginning with preconceived structures or setting out to confirm or refute a priori propositions and deductive hypotheses. As a result, one stipulation for the use of these tools is the need to be cautious in extrapolating insights from observations of convenience samples to broader populations. For instance, in the research done by Moen and QualiData on showering, the need to observe consumers showing as they normally shower (i.e., in the nude) required the recruitment of nudists as subjects. Nudists are a unique subpopulation, so generalizing understandings of showering from observations of nudists required an assumption that, although the subjects were from a particular subsegment, their visible consumption (showering) would nevertheless be like that of other consumers in important ways.

Other Sources of Insights

Other sources of customer insights can be customers who are lead users of a product or product category; online collaborators participating in product development via communities of enthusiasts and experts; and even the company's own executives, an often underappreciated source of knowledge and insight into the product and its customers.

LEAD USERS.   In the 1980s, Professor Eric von Hippel of MIT recognized that many innovations come from sophisticated, creative customers. In the manufacture of semiconductors and circuit boards, for instance, the most important innovations did not come from the developers of the relevant process technologies, but from the semiconductor manufacturers themselves. Indeed, almost 80 percent of innovations in scientific instruments came from customers.[29] Of course, there are innovative customers in all product areas, not just in the business-to-business sector. For example, around 20 percent of mountain bikers work on their own mountain bikes and have ideas for solutions that they realize themselves; this figure is almost 40 percent for extreme sports enthusiasts and almost 10 percent for users of outdoor consumer goods.[30] Von Hippel labeled such innovative customers "lead users." Today, lead users are recognized as having the following characteristics:

- Their needs are months or even years ahead of the mass market;
- They are very demanding and have their own ideas for solutions; and
- They are often opinion leaders, using the product they developed themselves with conviction and then making a significant contribution to quickly establishing the innovation on the market.

There are many examples that illustrate how lead users can give insights into customer problems

and needs and become part of the product development process. For instance, in the 1980s, Hilti, a Liechtenstein-based company providing leading-edge technology to the global construction industry, began looking into flexible and easy-to-use fastening systems. Up until that point, there were no functionally efficient systems, but some customers had developed their own solutions. Therefore, Hilti tried to integrate these customers into a development project. Fourteen lead users were selected from a group of 150 users. In a workshop, these lead users then developed an innovative fastening system that formed the basis for a new business unit at Hilti[31]. Another example is Johnson & Johnson Medical, which brought three innovations into the market—innovations that were not developed by the company itself, but by users. In this lead-user project, the company screened the market for lead users, selected them according to well-defined criteria, and brought them together in a workshop. Then, in the two-day lead-user workshop, the users themselves developed a new film for covering robots used in surgery, an all-in-one solution for preventing particulate matter from becoming airborne during operations, and an integrated sterile system for supporting patients' legs during hip operations.[32]

ONLINE COMMUNITIES.   Today, you can find online communities for virtually every product or topic. On the Internet, there are communities for basketball shoes, coffee drinkers, wine connoisseurs, hair loss, outdoor enthusiasts, downhill skiing, and so on and so forth. Consumers gather in these online communities to exchange ideas, discuss their problems, and share enthusiasm for their common interests. For example, in Alt.coffee, a virtual café, coffee connoisseurs discuss how coffee machines and roasters could be improved; in the Outdoorseiten.net online community, hikers and mountain enthusiasts develop their own equipment (e.g., functional jackets and particularly light tents); and at Chefkoch.de, cooking enthusiasts consider how cooking utensils could be improved.[33]

Many companies use these sorts of online communities to get customer insights. Audi, for instance, involved its customers in the conception phase during the development of a new infotainment system. Via several Web sites that are regularly visited by car fans,

Audi reached over 1,600 auto enthusiasts who worked on the virtual development of the infotainment system. This resulted in 219 service ideas, 261 comments on the console, 728 visions of future cars, and the eventual selection of the optimal product configuration.[34] Similarly, during a design competition phase that lasted just four weeks, Swarovski—the Austrian manufacturer of crystal figurines and jewelry—obtained 263 useable motifs for crystal tattoos that were produced by Internet users by means of toolkits.[35]

Sometimes, the company itself may simply observe online discussion without directly participating in it. Consider the example of NikeTalk, a community of more than 50,000 basketball fans that has no official connection with Nike Inc. Thousands of discussions between basketball fans take place in this virtual community every month. Basketball fanatics can be found in the community, as can sports equipment retailers, students of industrial design and Nike fans in general. Some of the subjects these community members discuss include how to customize your basketball shoe, how to distinguish a branded shoe from a fake, what basketball shoes might look like in 2050, and what they think about Nike's latest products.[36] Observing discussions within these communities can provide valuable insights into customers' interests, opinions, problems, acceptance of new products, and so on. In fact, companies such as Munich's Hyve AG specialize in mediating between online innovation seekers and innovation providers in the role of "innomediator." These companies develop tools to harness the innovative power of online communities, using "netnography"—ethnography adapted to the Internet—to identify communities, screen them for innovations, and set up a virtual dialogue with them in order to systematically open up these sources of innovation.

EXECUTIVES AND CHANNEL PARTNERS. Experts, including managers, salespeople, channel partners, and engineers, can also be an invaluable source of customer insights and creative product ideas. Although untested "hunches" can be dangerous, ignoring input from managers and collaborators risks missing important and worthwhile experience-based ideas. In the fast-food industry, for example, the idea for the Egg McMuffin,® one of McDonald's most popular

items, came from a McDonald's franchisee. As McDonald's founder Ray Kroc later wrote, "The advent of the Egg McMuffin opened up a whole new area of potential business for McDonald's, the breakfast trade." Similarly, Subway's "$5 Foot-Long" promotion, in which the sandwich chain sells 12-inch sandwiches for an even five dollars, was a franchisee's idea—and this promotion that is credited with more than $3.8 billion in annual sales.[37]

Integrating Trends and Customer Insights into Strategic Planning

Although following a teenage boy around in his daily life or videotaping people while they shower may seem impractical, significant strategic advantage goes to the firm that first recognizes and capitalizes on a true customer insight. Uncertain trends and indefinite patterns of emerging customer needs can be inputs to scenario analysis. That is, various distinct possible customer outcomes (e.g., changes in attitudes and tastes toward health or thrift) can be included in the factors that define "possible futures" (i.e., scenarios), and contingency plans can be constructed to contend with those possible futures. Cross-impact matrices, for example, are a typical futuring and scenario planning tool. As its name indicates, a cross-impact matrix integrates multiple events to identify their joint impacts; in other words, rather than considering what might happen if one event occurs or a single trend is disrupted, cross-impact matrices consider the interaction of factors and their joint implications (or "impacts"). Cross-impact matrices are similar to scenario analysis; in fact, they are used in scenario analysis. If, for example, the economy improves dramatically, health concerns shift diets toward vegetables and seafood, lifestyles change toward smaller households, and a disruptive technology emerges that dramatically lowers the cost of electricity, then what would the future look like? What are the implications of these events on each other and on other elements of the future? What are the implications of these events on the marketing organization, and how would the organization want to be positioned to respond to this future? These possible futures don't need to be likely (or unlikely); if they are merely *possible* than they are worth thinking about and planning for. However, cross-impact matrices facilitate basic stochastic analysis in which, by estimating the probability of each event and its interactions with the others, the joint probability of any specific future reality can be estimated. Thus, cross-impact matrices are a structured and rigorous examination of *what might happen* tied to consideration of *how the organization should prepare for those possibilities.*

Summary

Trends are important patterns in the past (and up to the present) that indicate or predict changes in the future. Research has shown that the more firms consider and track trends and changes in the environment, the more successful they are.

Customer insights are understandings into customer needs and how customers consume and take value from products tied to ways to meet those needs and deliver that value. Robust evidence has also been found that the more firms focus on their markets and their customers, the more successful they are.

Trend spotting is about looking at past and current phenomena to predict the future; in comparison, searching for customer insights focuses on present (but heretofore unrecognized) customer conditions and needs. Thus, successful marketing strategy is about meeting some specific customer needs better than the competition at a profit. But of course, those customer needs are changing. Thus, adequate marketing strategy can be viewed as marketing mix evolution (changing the "P"s) in response to changes in environmental forces, and *really good* marketing strategy is marketing mix evolution in *anticipation* of changes in those forces.

Additional Resources

Gloor, Peter A., and Scott M. Cooper. *Cool-hunting: Chasing Down the Next Big Thing.* New York: AMACOM, 2007.

Larreche, Jean-Claude. *The Momentum Effect: How to Ignite Exceptional Growth.* Upper Saddle River, NJ: Wharton School Publishing, 2008.

Solomon, Michael R. *Truth About What Customers Want.* Upper Saddle River, NJ: FT Press, 2009.

Vitale, Dona. *Consumer Insights 2.0: How Smart Companies Apply Customer Knowledge to the Bottom Line.* Ithaca, NY, USA: Paramount Market Publishing, 2006.

Endnotes

1. Irma Zandl, "How to Separate Trends from Fads," *Brandweek* 41, no. 41 (23 October, 2000): 30–35

2. Peter A. Gloor and Scott M. Cooper, *Cool-hunting: Chasing Down the Next Big Thing* (New York: AMACOM, 2007); Malcolm Gladwell, "The Cool-hunt," *The New Yorker* (17 March, 1997): 78–88.

3. See, for example, William R. Duggan, *Strategic Intuition: The creative spark in human achievement* (New York: Columbia University Press, 2007).

4. Eric Bonabeau, "Don't Trust Your Gut," *Harvard Business Review* 81, no. 5 (May 2003): 116–123. Quote is from page 116.

5. Gerd Gigerenzer, Peter M. Todd, and ABC Research Group, *Simple Heuristics that Make us Smart* (New York: Oxford University Press 1999).

6. Victor J. Cook, Jr. and David Frigstad, "Take It to the Top: Delphi Sampling is Best for Supply Chain Research" *Marketing Research* 9 (Fall 1997); and James Surowiecki, The Wisdom of Crowds: Why the Many

Are Smarter Than the Few and How Collective Wisdom Shapes Business, Economies, Societies and Nations (New York: Doubleday/Random House, 2004).

7. Gloor and Cooper, "*Cool-hunting*"; and Gladwell, "The Cool-hunt."

8. Douglas Rushkoff, "The Pursuit of Cool," Sportswear International (2001), archived at http://rushkoff.com/articles/articles-and-essays/the-pursuit-of-cool/ Last accessed June 18, 2010.

9. Roy Furchgott, 'For Cool Hunters, Tomorrow's Trend is the Trophy,' *The New York Times* (June 28, 1998).

10. Jiawei Han and Micheline Kamber, *Data Mining: Concepts and Techniques*, 2nd ed. (San Francisco: Morgan Kaufmann Publishers, 2006).

11. Gary Loveman, "Diamonds in the Data Mine," *Harvard Business Review* 81, no. 5 (May 2003): 109–113.

12. Edward Cornish, *Futuring: The Exploration of the Future* (Bethesda, MD: World Future Society, 2004), 294.

13. Quoted in James G. Barnes, *Build Your Customer Strategy* (New York: John Wiley and Sons, 2006), 106.

14. Gary Hamel and C.K. Prahalad, "Corporate Imagination and Expeditionary Marketing," *Harvard Business Review* 69, no. 4 (July–August, 1991): 81–92, page 81.

15. Definition adapted from David Taylor, "Drilling for Nuggets: How to Use Insight to Inspire Innovation," *Brand Strategy* (March 24, 2000); also see Gary Armstrong and Philip Kotler, *Marketing: An Introduction*, 9th ed. (Upper Saddle River, NJ: Pearson/Prentice Hall, 2009), 97.

16. The term "bricoleur" was first used to describe eclectic, make-due qualitative researchers seeking deep insights, by Levi-Straus; see Levi-Strauss, *The Savage Mind* (New York: Free Press, 1966); also see Joe L. Kincheloe, "Describing the Bricolage: Conceptualizing a new rigor in qualitative research," *Qualitative Inquiry* 7, no. 6 (2001), 679–692.

17. Clifford Geertz, "Thick Description: Toward an interpretive theory of culture," in *The Interpretation of Cultures: Selected Essays* (New York: Basic Books, 1973), 3–30.

18. Stuart Knapman, "Customer Immersion: Total Immersion," *Research* (June 2008), 36–37.

19. Ibid.

20. Essential Research's website describes their work, including customer-immersion programs for senior managers (see www.essentialresearch.co.uk/).

21. Knapman, "Customer Immersion"; quote is at page 36.

22. For a thorough review and compilation of research articles, see Thomas J. Reynolds and Jerry C. Olson, eds., *Understanding Consumer Decision Making: The Means-end Approach to Marketing and Advertising Strategy* (Mahwah, NJ: Lawrence Erlbaum Associates, 2008).

23. Figure is from Thomas J. Reynolds and Alyce Byrd Craddock, "The Application of the Meccas Model to the Development and Assessment of Advertising Strategy: A Case Study," *Journal of Advertising Research* 28, no. 2 (April 1988): 43–54, 45.

24. Lynne Ames, "The View From/Peekskill; Tending the Flame of a Motivator," *The New York Times*, August 2, 1998, 14 WC2, New York edition; Linda Obrec, "Marketing, Motives and Dr. Freud," *Detroiter Magazine* (December 1999), available at: www.mktgsensei.com/AMAE/Consumer%20Behavior/Motivational%20Research.doc. Last accessed June 18, 2010. Ernest Dichter, *The Strategy of Desire* (New York: Boardman & Company, 1960); and Ernest Dichter, *The Psychology Of Everyday Living* (New York: Barnes and Noble, 1947). Also see, for example, Martin Zober, "Some Projective Techniques Applied to Marketing Research," *Journal of Marketing* 20, no. 3 (January 1956): 262–268.

25. Richard Durante and Michael Feehan, "Watch and Learn: Leveraging Ethnography to Improve Strategic Decision Making," *Marketing Research* 17, no. 4 (Winter 2005): 10–15.

26. Dana ElBoghdady, "Naked Truth Meets Market Research: Perfecting a New Shower Head? Try Watching People Shower," *The Washington Post*, February 24, 2002, H1, H4, H5.

27. Ibid; quote is from page H1.

28. Dorothy Leonard and Jeffrey F. Rayport, "Spark Innovation through Empathic Design," *Harvard Business Review* 75, no. 6 (November–December 1997): 102–113.

29. Eric von Hippel, *Democratizing Innovation* (Cambridge, London: The MIT Press, 2005).

30. Ibid.

31. Cornelius Herstatt, Christian Lüthje, and Christopfer Lettl, "Wie fortschrittliche Kunden zu Innovationen stimulieren," *Harvard Business Manager* 24, no. 1,(2002): 60–68.

32. Ibid.

33. Johann Füller, Gregor Jawecki, and Michael Bartl, "Produkt- und Serviceentwicklung in Kooperation mit Online Communities," in vol. 5 of *Kundenorientierte Unternehmensführung*, eds. Hans H. Hinterhuber and Kurt Matzler, (Aufl. Wiesbaden: Gabler Verlag, 2006b).

34. Johann Füller and Kurt Matzler, "Virtual Product Experience and Customer Participation—A Chance for Customer-centred, Really New Products," *Technovation* 27 (2007): 378–387.

35. Johann Füller, Michael Bartl, Holger Ernst, and Hans Mühlbacher, "Community Based Innovation: How to Integrate Members of Virtual Communities into New Product Development," *Electronic Commerce Research* 6, (2006a): 57–73.

36. Johann Füller, Gregor Jawecki, and H. Mühlbacher, "Innovation Creation by Online Basketball Communities," *Journal of Business Research* 60, no. 1 (January 2007): 60–71.

37. See Ray Kroc with Robert Anderson, *Grinding It Out: The Making of McDonald's* (Chicago, IL: Contemporary Books, 1977); and Matthew Boyle, "The Accidental Hero: Subway's $5 Footlong, the Brainchild of an Obscure Miami Franchisee, Is the Fast-food Success Story of the Recession," *Business Week* (November 5, 2009).

4

Consumer and Organizational Buyer Behavior

Academic researchers have spent decades studying how consumers and organizations make purchase decisions. Most university-level marketing degrees require a course on "Buyer Behavior" or "Consumer Behavior" that covers that accumulated knowledge. Consumer Behavior usually refers specifically to models of how *the ultimate consumers* make decisions about and consume products. Buyer Behavior is broader; it considers *organizational buyers* (especially businesses, but also not-for-profits and government entities) as well as consumers. Consumer and buyer behavior models and frameworks are theoretical, especially in comparison to market research, which studies the firm's specific customers and specific issues. Consumer and buyer behavior look at *basic processes* that are true for consumers or organizations *in general.*

Despite the theoretical nature of buyer behavior, understanding this body of knowledge is a basic foundation of strategic marketing. Understanding how customers make decisions and the role of customer evaluations and behaviors in determining important market outcomes is essential to segmenting, targeting, positioning, and to developing and assessing an effective marketing mix. This note presents a concise overview of buyer behavior; numerous textbooks[1] and academic research papers are available to drill down into consumer/buyer behavior theory.

CONSUMER BEHAVIOR

Consumers are *the ultimate users of a product.* (We refer to *all* buyers—ultimate consumers and/or organizational buyers and distributors as "customers.") In comparison to organizational buyers, consumers are more numerous (there are many more consumers in most markets than there are buyers in business-to-business markets) and geographically dispersed as well as harder to address or "catalog" (i.e, harder to identify and list with specificity and, therefore, harder to target with personalized communications or offerings), and consumer markets generally involve many more but usually smaller transactions (smaller in quantity and in the dollar value of the transaction). Additionally, consumers use more personal and more emotional purchase criteria in comparison to organizational buyers. In comparison, business-to-business markets generally involve fewer customers (who are often easily listed and readily tied to specific data, such as address, size, and industry) and fewer transactions but transactions of greater size and value. For instance, Coca-Cola is purchased in relatively small quantities by millions and millions of consumers; it would be impossible for Coke to track those customers' purchases with any degree of specificity. In contrast, the maker of aluminum cans can quickly purchase a list, complete with addresses, managers' names, and operating statistics, for all companies producing soft drinks and beer.

Consumer Decision-Making Process

Consumer decision making can be viewed as *a process* moving from the recognition of a need through the search for information about possible ways to satisfy the need and the evaluation of those alternatives on to the purchase and then post-purchase processes (Figure 4-1). Many very similar models have been proposed, some with much more detail, but this basic process or flow is commonly accepted.[2,3] Of course, the degree to which customers engage in effortful thought and search as they move through these steps or stages in the decision-making process varies across consumers, across products and product categories, and across situations.

"Hierarchy of effects" models in communications and advertising management are similar to the consumer-decision-making process framework. However, instead of modeling the flow of a customer *through a purchase decision*—from the recognition of a need through post-purchase processes—"hierarchy of effects" models focus on *the relationship of the consumer with a specific product or brand*, from unaware through degrees of awareness, liking, and bonding toward purchase and adoption or loyalty.[4] One of the earliest hierarchy of effects models is "AIDA"— Awareness, Interest, Desire, Action[5]—although a variety of more detailed models have also been proposed.[6] For example, in the context of the diffusion of innovations, a very similar awareness-interest-evaluation-trial-adoption process is generally accepted.[7] Customer loyalty, the development of long term relationships with valuable customers who may themselves serve as promoters of the brand, was omitted from the brief AIDA summary, but it logically follows after "action" or "trial"; it is important to consider that ultimate loyalty in understanding the flow of relationship intensity.

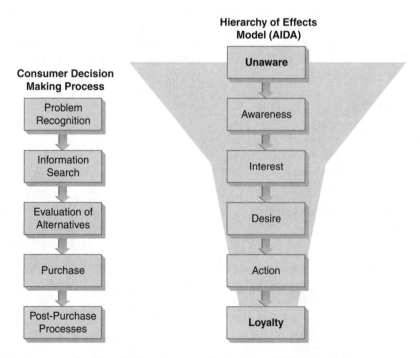

FIGURE NOTE 4-1 Consumer-Decision-Making Process and Hierarchy of Effects Models

Obviously, more customers will become aware of a product than will become interested in it, and more customers will be interested in a product than will ever buy it (take action), and not all customers who buy and try a product will adopt the product or become loyal customers. Therefore, hierarchy of effects models can be viewed as "funnels" into which a large number of customers enter whilst a smaller number, usually quite a bit smaller number, come out the "bottom" as the firm's loyal customer base.

Understanding where different segments of customers are in these decision making or hierarchical flows is invaluable in developing communications and distribution strategies. Different tools and different tactics are more effective at different points in this flow of effects. Advertising is effective, for example, at building awareness but less effective at moving customers to action (to purchase). On the other hand, personal selling is effective at "closing the sale," that is at moving customers to purchase, but personal selling is less effective at generating awareness. Marketing managers are often focused on customers at particular stages in the familiarity/liking ("customer readiness") continuum; they may be concerned with building awareness, inducing trial, or creating loyalty, for example, depending on the strategy and the composition of their markets. Understanding the consumer-decision-making process framework as well as the hierarchy of effects framework is essential in organizing consumer-behavior theory and is also invaluable to marketing strategists as they segment markets and develop effective programs for consumers at different stages in the relationship with the product or brand.

Stages in the Consumer Decision Making Process

As noted, when consumers make decisions, they move through different stages, starting with problem recognition and information search, evaluating alternative, and making the purchase decision. A marketing manager is also concerned with understanding how customers consume and take value from products as well as in post-purchase processes like customer satisfaction, loyalty, or word of mouth.

PROBLEM RECOGNITION. The consumer-decision-making or buying process is initiated by *the recognition of a need or want*. Needs are fundamental human requirements; everybody experiences needs. Abraham Maslow organized human needs in a hierarchical structure (Figure 4-2) in which the most basic and compelling needs are *physiological*—things like food, drink, and shelter.[8] The next level of needs is *safety needs*—the need for physical safety, economic security, and protection from harm. *Social* needs are the needs to be accepted as part of a family or group. The top two categories of needs are ego-driven needs, related to respect and prestige, and self-actualization. Self-actualization needs involve learning, spiritual and personal growth, and self expression. The organization of Maslow's well-known structure indicates prioritization and urgency; lower-level needs are more compelling and meeting those needs takes priority over meeting higher-level needs.

"Needs" can be distinguished from "wants" and other related constructs, including "demands" and "benefits sought." *Needs* are basic human requirements and are *universal*—all people have needs. *Wants* are needs that have been *shaped by the environment*, including the customer's culture, personality, and situation as well as by the actions of marketers. For example, everybody gets hungry—it is a prototypical *physiological* need in Maslow's framework— but everybody doesn't want to meet that need with

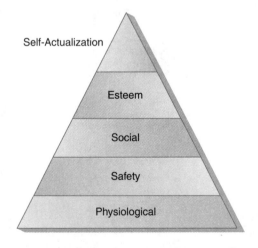

FIGURE NOTE 4-2 Maslow's Hierarchy of Needs[9]

Kung Pau Chicken. Consumers *need* food, they *want* Kung Pau Chicken because of their experiences, their culture, their individual tastes, and the actions of marketers (such as advertisements, price promotions, service personnel recommendations, menu presentation, or even restaurant signage). *Demand* results from the combination of wants and the *ability* of consumers with those wants to buy the product. Ability is a function of both resources and availability/access; that is, consumer demand isn't just having the money to buy the product, it also requires having the opportunity and access.

Benefits or "benefits sought" are closely related to needs and wants. Benefits sought are what the consumer desires to get out of or gain from a purchase or consumption experience. These are *not product attributes*; they're *outcomes* of buying and consuming the product.[10] A customer may buy an electric drill with an 18-volt battery and rubber-cushioned grips, but the benefit he or she seeks is *a hole* or the ability to drill a hole with ease, convenience, and/or comfort. Different customers seek different benefits from a product category, and "benefits-sought segmentation" is a powerful way to distinguish groups of customers based on differing desires and differing responses to the marketing mix.

Problem recognition is generally understood as a form of "gap analysis" related to needs, wants, and the benefits of the product. Customers recognize a need when they recognize, consciously or subconsciously, that there is a gap between their *current* state (the way things are) and their *desired* state (the way they'd like to be). That gap can be between needs, wants, or benefits in their current state versus desired state.

INFORMATION SEARCH. The idea that consumers search for information when making a purchase seems reasonable; in fact, we know it occurs some of the time. The idea that consumers actively search and process information is appealing to marketing managers because of the amount of time that the managers themselves spend thinking about the various attributes and trade-offs that make up their product. But the "information search" stage begins to highlight an important aspect of consumer behavior and of the overall "decision-making process": *consumers don't spend much effort on most purchases, and they spend very little effort on many purchases.*

The amount of time a consumer will spend on a purchase decision, including information search and alternative evaluation, is a function of involvement or *motivation* and *ability*. The term "customer involvement" captures the degree of importance and relevance that a consumer places on a product or a purchase; that is, involvement is the consumer's *motivation* to pay attention to a product and a purchase decision. Involvement or motivation is itself a function of *inherent interest* (some people are just more interested in some products/purchases), *risk* (financial, social, and physical), and *practical importance* (importance to personal well-being or to a job). For example, a consumer's involvement with cars might be due to inherent interest in cars, that is, being a "car enthusiast," or from an event such as the birth of a new child and a resulting heightened attention to safety, or from holding a job that requires reliable transportation; any of these motivations would lead to greater involvement with cars. A second factor, the *ability* to research and evaluate a purchase, also influences the time and energy spent on it. Some consumers, no matter how much they'd like to shop and deliberate a decision, don't have the time or the expertise to devote to the decision.

A few products almost never rise to a high-involvement status: Almost no one spends much time on mundane and repeat purchases such as soda or laundry detergent. Consumers don't search for external information on or reviews of these products, and they don't read labels to compare ingredients; they rely on *habit* and, especially, *brands* to guide their decisions. On the other hand, some product categories are almost never approached casually; choices of college, choices of cars, and home buying almost always involve high-involvement and deliberate consideration, including extended search and careful evaluation. This should not be taken to mean that involvement is determined by product category. Although product categories do have typical levels of involvement (e.g., very expensive products usually are associated with extensive decision making); there is substantial variance across customers with regard to their involvement depending upon their personal attributes and the personal situation.

TABLE NOTE 4-1 Sources in Consumer Information Search			
Sources of Information			
Internal		**External**	
Memory	Interpersonal	Public	Marketer-Controlled

Customer information search may tap a range of sources (Table 4-1); each type of source has different advantages, disadvantages, and consequent strategic implications. Customer information search can be limited and it can be constrained to "internal" sources, that is, to memory. Because of the overwhelming amount of information in the modern environment and because of growing consumer skepticism, it is increasingly difficult to gain consumers' attention or to earn a place in consumers' memory. Other sources of information include interpersonal sources—friends, neighbors, and colleagues. Marketers recognize the importance of inter-consumer or "word-of-mouth" communications. Firms such as Proctor & Gamble are enlisting armies of unpaid but well-organized, well-tracked, and well-attended consumers to "spread the word" about their products. Information search may also include public sources, such as Internet consumer review sites and consumer organizations, and "marketer controlled" sources—advertisements, Websites, salespeople, and published materials and manuals. Within this categorization, marketer-controlled sources face increasing clutter, diminishing attention, and growing skepticism.

ALTERNATIVE EVALUATION. As with information search, involvement levels and situational factors determine whether consumers will undertake extensive and demanding evaluations of purchase alternatives or routine processing that borders on no evaluation at all. Marketing researchers have proposed elaborate "information processing" models in which consumers gather information, weigh attributes, and determine finely grained rankings of alternatives. At the same time, research has shown that grocery shoppers spend, on average, less than six seconds making most purchase decisions; although shoppers may bring carefully thought-out lists to the store,

more than 70 percent of the purchase decisions are reported to be made after the shopper has entered the store.[11] What is more, many purchases, even big purchases such as automobiles, are often driven by emotions as much as or more than by "rational" processes.

One fundamental tenet of consumer behavior theory is that consumers form "attitudes" toward products and those attitudes drive behaviors, especially purchase behavior. Attitudes are relatively enduring summaries of whether something is good or bad, pleasant or unpleasant, and so forth. Consumers hold these evaluations in their heads across time (but not forever—attitudes "decay" if consumers aren't reminded of the product or brand). Elaborate models of attitude formation have been proposed and validated. For example, a well-known model of attitude formation hypothesizes that people hold *beliefs* about whether or not a product has certain attributes (things like power, comfort, reliability, and high price in case of a car) and also make *evaluations* of those attributes and about whether the attribute (power, comfort, reliability, price) is a good or bad thing for the product to have (power is likely a good thing; high price is usually bad). A consumer's attitude is supposed to be a direct mathematical function of those beliefs and evaluations.

This model of attitude formation is *highly rational and demanding*—it assumes that consumers will think and, in fact, think pretty hard about the purchase. This is not always true. In many instances consumers respond with a fairly automatic "feeling" about the product and act on that—with very little rigorous thinking or effort. That is, *emotional responses to products, brands, and consumption experiences also have powerful effects on consumer judgments and behaviors*, including purchase, repeat-purchase (loyalty), complaints, and recommendations. The two systems, that is, the rational thinking or "cognitions" and the more visceral and automatic feelings or "emotions," have been considered as distinct, although they interact and influence each other, and both are essential in understanding the way that consumers respond to marketing actions. They are sometimes thought of as "the head" and "the heart" or "gut feelings." In the literature on integrated marketing communications and advertising, a well-known framework is the FCB Matrix, so named because it was developed at that forerunner advertising agency by Richard Vaughn.[12] This framework organizes products by their typical level of involvement (high and low involvement) and whether the typical motivation for buying and consuming the product is emotional ("feeling products") or rational ("thinking products"). Frameworks, such as the FCB Matrix, guide the development of products and the development of communications programs to position the product and persuade consumers to think and feel about the products in desired ways.

Two additional ideas, brands and customer value, are important to understanding how consumers evaluate alternatives:

- **Brands.** Customers face an overwhelming array of information and make innumerable decisions, big and small, every day. They can't possibly think about all that information or reevaluate each decision. Therefore, consumers establish habits and "heuristics." Heuristics are shortcuts or "rules of thumb" used in decision making.[13] Brands are the most common "rule of thumb" in the marketplace. Brands tie current and future decisions to past experiences and satisfaction, simplify decision making, and offer reassurance. Although brands have been criticized as unnecessary and exploitive,[14] they are useful to customers and provide real value to customers. From a buyer behavior standpoint, brands simplify purchase decisions in an extraordinarily hectic, cluttered, and demanding environment. Brands offer reassurance and communicate more complex information in simplified ways.
- **Customer Value.** We define "value" as the difference between, or ratio of, the *benefits* that the customer gets from a product (and its consumption) compared with all the *costs* of

acquiring and consuming the product (including monetary costs, time, and effort). This is the balance of the "get" and the "give" from the customer's perspective.[15] The appraisal of value may be subjective. For example, something that is worth paying for to one consumer will be disregarded as unimportant by another. However, along with attitudes, those appraisals of value are essential in understanding consumers' decision making. Perfectly rational consumers will often pay more to get something more or accept less in order to save money. Many rational consumers will opt for cheaper alternatives that offer the same performance (including brand image as a "get" component) or similarly priced alternatives that offer better performance. Very few consumers will knowingly pay more for the same performance or accept less performance than they could have gotten for the same price. Those tradeoffs and choices combine to define a "value map" or space and to create a balance in the marketplace, a "fair value frontier" along which consumers willingly make choices and tradeoffs (Figure 4-3). Offerings that are below

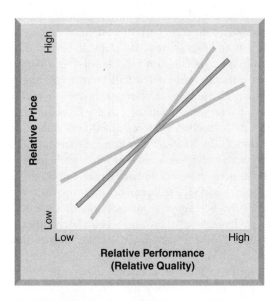

FIGURE NOTE 4-3 The Value Map: Tradeoffs along the Fair Value Frontier[16]

the frontier *gain* market share because they're more attractive to consumers. Offerings above the frontier lose market share—they are unattractive and unsustainable. The *slope* of the frontier reflects *price elasticity*—how much consumers are willing to pay (give) for incremental gains in performance (get); some frontiers will be relatively flat—a small change in price will justify a relatively large shift in performance.

PURCHASE DECISION.   Once the consumer has evaluated the alternatives, he or she must still decide *when to buy* and *where to buy.* That is, the "purchase decision" is about time and place, distinct from evaluations of alternative products (the "product decision"). Interestingly, although marketers spend enormous time and resources communicating with customers across settings, the time a consumer spends on any individual purchase at a grocery store is preciously short—three to six seconds—but more than 75 percent of specific product choices are made in the store (these statistics are for grocery stores and fast-moving consumer goods).[17] This indicates that the "point-of-purchase" is an important decision point, but also that those decisions are made quickly and with little effort.

More and more, consumers choose different channels for different parts of a purchase decision or process, and they move across channels several times within a single decision process. By this we mean that different "channels of distribution" ranging from brick-and-mortar stores, in-home repair services, to toll-free telephone help lines and the Internet can all deliver certain functional values (product information and training, financing, physical receipt or delivery, installation, user help, etc.). Consumers can use different channels to do different parts of the purchase and to access different sorts of value; they may, for example, choose one or more channels to "*shop*" and a completely different channel to *buy*, creating a disincentive for *any* channel to provide high service or, especially, free advice without somehow also generating revenue or capturing the customer's loyalty.[18] For example, when a customer can visit a full-service specialty store (e.g., a camera or stereo specialty shop), use the time and

expertise of the well-trained and expert service staff, and then go home and purchase the product at deep discount online, it puts the full-service specialty store's business model at risk, and that reality has ominous but still uncertain implications for the future retail landscape.

POST-PURCHASE PROCESSES.   Marketers that are interested in creating profitable long-term relationships with their customers need to understand post-purchase processes as well, for example, how they consume or use the product, how they form feelings of satisfaction or dissatisfaction, or whether they engage in word-of-mouth communications and why or why not they become loyal. Marketers are increasingly concerned not only with how to persuade consumers to purchase their products but also with understanding how customers *consume* and take value from those products. For example, clothing and clothing-care marketers remain concerned with understanding fashion marketing and merchandising, but they are also concerned with the entire "customer-value chain" from purchase and multiple wearing occasions and through garment care toward ultimate disposal (see Figure 4-5). Customer value is defined as what the consumer gets adjusted for what the consumer gives. The value-chain framework provides important, more granular insights into how the consumer gets benefits from a product and where and in what form the consumer feels the costs, including the financial, effort, and time costs of getting those benefits. This framework is an important overlay to the exploration for and framing of "customer insights." Whirlpool CEO David Whitwam described the appliance maker's reasoning for broad scrutiny of its consumers' value chains:

> We're now studying consumer behavior from the time people take off their dirty clothes at night until they've been cleaned and ironed and hung in the closet. What are we looking for? The worst part of the process is not the washing and drying. The hard part is when you take your clothes out of the dryer and you have to do something

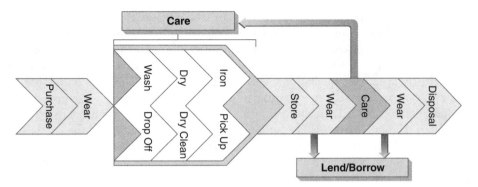

FIGURE NOTE 4-4 Hypothetical Consumer Value Chain

with them—iron, fold, hang them up. Whoever comes up with a product to make this part of the process easier, simpler, or quicker is going to create an incredible market.[19]

An important strategic consideration, especially in regards to innovations and truly "new to the world" products, is the fact that *changing consumer behaviors is extremely difficult*. Innovations are often classified along a continuum from *continuous* innovations that demand little change in the way customers consume and solve their needs through *dynamically continuous* innovations, all the way to *discontinuous* innovations, innovations that are truly new to the world and that require substantial changes in consumption patterns.[20] It has been shown that, even when innovations have substantial advantages over existing alternatives, consumers value existing ways of behaving and existing product alternatives over innovations that necessitate changes in behavior and that require abandoning existing, comfortable, and familiar ways of meeting needs. The tendency to stick with proven solutions has been attributed to *economic* costs of change (transaction costs, learning costs, and obsolescence costs or the sunk costs of equipment tied to existing solutions) and *psychological* costs related to a pervasive perceptual bias toward avoiding losses as opposed to seeking gains. These have been called the "endowment effect" and "status quo bias"—customers are more reluctant to give up what they have than they are eager to gain new advantages.[21]

CUSTOMER SATISFACTION. The marketing concept asserts that a marketing strategy and in fact the overarching strategy of the entire firm should be built around serving—or "satisfying" the customer needs. Satisfying the customer is an essential goal that should pervade strategic marketing. Extensive theory and observation across decades of research have confirmed that firms that satisfy their customers better prosper while those that leave customers dissatisfied fall short; those findings hold across consumer goods, services, and business-to-business markets. Customer satisfaction is the customer's evaluation (good to bad, pleasant to unpleasant) of a specific purchase or consumption experience. That is, satisfaction is how the customer feels about a specific product choice and usage. I may have an attitude toward a certain fast-food restaurant—I like its chicken sandwich and its friendly, fast service—but when I visit that restaurant on a specific occasion I form a related but differentiable evaluation *of that specific visit* (the sandwich tasted great and was fresh and hot; the service was excellent; and the server, remembering my last visit, gave me extra mayonnaise).

Customers evaluate purchases and consumption experiences and arrive at "satisfaction judgments" by comparing *what they actually received* or experienced with their subjective standard about *what they thought they'd get* or felt that they ought to have got. A customer comes to every purchase with some idea about what they think they'll get. If we go to a fine-dining steak restaurant to order a cheeseburger, we expect a certain sort of product and service; those expectations include what we think we should *pay* for the cheeseburger. If we go to a quick-service restaurant and order a cheeseburger, we have vastly different expectations. We might come away from a quick-service encounter having got a pretty unremarkable cheeseburger for less than a dollar, and, nevertheless, be *quite satisfied*—it was, after all, less than a dollar. On the other hand, we might spend ten times that amount on a cheeseburger at the full-service restaurant and receive a product many times the quality, with much more flavor and table-side service, and nevertheless come away far less satisfied *because our expectations were so much higher.* This framework has been tested and retested: *Customers form judgments of satisfaction by comparing what they get to what they thought they'd get.*

This understanding of customer satisfaction creates an interesting tension for marketing strategists, whose first concern is often to attract customers via appealing offerings, which would lead to extolling the virtues and, thereby, building high expectations. On the other hand, creating high expectations creates challenges—*the product has to deliver against those expectations* or risk dissatisfied customers. There may be situations when the strategist chooses to "under promise and over deliver."[22] There are many ways that a marketer can influence expectations and enhance resulting satisfaction. It has been shown, for example, that people waiting in line who are given an expected waiting time and then their wait is shorter than that "expectation" are more satisfied with the experience than other people who wait the same amount of time who were not told a longer wait time.[23] In any case, regardless of how the expectations are managed, the marketing strategist's challenge is almost always to somehow *exceed expectations.*

There may be many situations in which the marketer can't set modest expectations and then exceed them, but there are few situations in which the marketer would ever want to "over promise." That is a recipe for a short-term relationship with those customers, because customer satisfaction drives a range of important subsequent customer behaviors. Research has shown that satisfaction is an important intervening variable that drives subsequent price sensitivity, positive word of mouth, and *loyalty.* Loyalty itself, the tendency of customers to stay with a company or a brand, has been closely related to firm profitability, especially when considered together with customer-lifetime value. Another strategic consideration is the emphasis on understanding customer satisfaction and the role it plays in delivering quality products and exceptional service.

Factors Influencing the Purchase Decision Process

Customers make purchasing decisions within specific cultural/social, personal/individual, situational and commercial (marketer influenced) contexts such as (Figure 4-5)

- *Personal/Individual Factors.* Individuals come to purchase decisions with different personalities, such as their degree of introversion or extraversion, and motivational factors. All of those factors influence the way they consider options, make purchases, and use products.

FIGURE NOTE 4-5 Consumer Decision Making in Context

- *Cultural and Social Factors.* Factors such as national culture, regional culture, social class, and reference groups influence purchase decisions, product preferences, and consumption. People from different nations and regions hold different values, different norms of behavior and manners, and different aesthetic preferences and tastes.
- *Situational Factors.* Many factors are tied more to particular situations than to ongoing conditions or attributes of the consumer. Time pressure, resource or information availability, and immediate environmental factors (such as music, odor, colors) all affect purchases and consumption.
- *Marketing Actions.* Although all of these aforementioned factors have powerful influences on consumer decision-making and consumption patterns, the marketing strategist will recognize that the factors that influence decision making that are under his or her most direct control are the marketing mix; the product, the promotion and marketing communications, the people, the place or distribution, and the price. These are the "levers" and "dials" under the marketer's control that influence the consumer's purchase decisions.

ORGANIZATIONAL BUYING

In comparison to consumer markets, business markets are characterized by having fewer buyers and fewer transactions (but far *larger* transactions in dollar-value and quantity of goods per transaction). Business-to-business segments are easier to address (catalogue and target with customized communications). Other differences between consumer and business-to-business markets emphasize the differences in the way purchase decisions are made. Consumers, who as a rule make purchases as individuals, may use limited problem solving and rely on emotional responses in many situations; businesses are generally more thorough and more analytic, and often make purchases with teams or "buy

centers" and/or with professional purchasing agents using formal procedures and approved specifications. Business-to-business frameworks on buyer behavior include distinctions across types of purchases and across stages in the decision process as well as distinctions concerning roles in the purchase across members of the organization. As is the case with consumer behavior described above, many of these frameworks lend themselves to graphic presentations that clarify the relationship between stages in processes.

Stages in the Buying Process and the Sales Funnel

Like consumer decision making described above, organizational purchase decisions can be broken out into process models starting at need recognition and proceeding through formal need definition—something that is not necessary for consumer decision makers—and continuing through the specification of the solution to be sourced, the identification of viable suppliers or vendors for the purchase, the proposal specification and review, and the ultimate selection of a vendor and then review and feedback on performance (Figure 4-6). At the same time, and again parallel to the similar hierarchy of effects in consumer behavior, another process model can be created by organizing customers taken as segments along a continuum based on their relationship with the firm and its offerings. In business-to-business markets that process is usually called the "sales funnel."[24]

The Personal Selling Process

Organizational buyers are generally targeted with "push" communications strategies, that is, strategies designed to create demand at the next level in the channel of distribution relying heavily on personal selling and inter-firm partnering. Because of that reliance on sales, a third process model also offers perspective on business-to-business buyer behavior: the "Personal Selling Process." That framework organizes the various steps that the sales force can take, from prospecting, to assessing fit, gaining the initial order ("approach" and "closing") on to "fulfilling

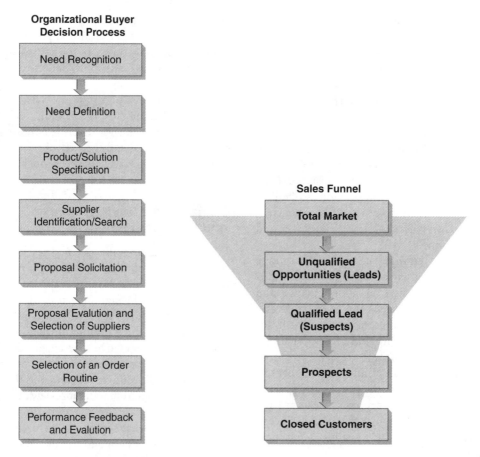

FIGURE NOTE 4-6   Organizational Purchase Decision Process and the Sales Funnel[25]

the initial order" to "delivering value" or "partnering" (Figure 4-7).[26]

To review and clarify these distinctions and very similar frameworks, the buying organization moves through a series of decision stages or steps that are summarized in the Organizational Purchase Decision Process (Figure 4-7). Those buying organizations themselves can be characterized by their relationship with the selling organization, from leads to suspects to prospects to customers within the Sales Funnel (Figure 4-7). It is important to note that, in the Sales Funnel, it is the various *accounts* (potential buying organizations) that are categorized within the levels of the funnel. At the same time, the various *steps that the selling organization can take* to move buyers from leads to customers are organized within

the "Personal Selling Process"; these are the things that the salesperson, sales team, or company can do to gain new business and to turn those accounts into loyal customers (Figure 4-7).

Types of Purchases

Organizations are, generally, more involved in every purchase decision than are individual consumers. In contrast to consumers, in organizational buying it is usually somebody's *job* to make the purchase, and companies have accounting regulations and reporting obligations that require specific and explicit purchasing policies and procedures. Nevertheless, organizational buyers certainly devote varying degrees of attention and resources to different sorts of

Sales Personal Selling Process

Prospecting

Assessing Fit

Gaining the Initial Order

Fulfilling the Initial Order

Delivering Value

FIGURE NOTE 4-7 The Personal Selling Process[27]

purchases. One of the best known representations of the different sorts of organizational purchases is the distinction between straight rebuys, modified rebuys, and new tasks. For new tasks, that is, for purchases that have not been made before, and especially for high cost/high risk purchases, organizations are likely to engage in all of the many steps in the purchase process with a great deal of attention. In straight rebuys, cases in which the firm buys the same item in the same quantities from the same vendor, only the essential steps are required. For modified rebuys, cases in which some element of the purchase changes (product form, quantity, or vendor), many of those steps may be reduced or even eliminated. As shown in Figure 4-8, the types of purchases and the steps in the purchase process can be joined to create the "Buygrid" framework, which shows that, generally, need recognition is necessary to prompt *any* purchase, even if it is as predictable as noticing that the copier paper supply is low or as routine as "every Monday we order a new supply of paper." Similarly, the selection of a product specification and order routine are required, even if they are the routine and automatic reorder. The other steps in the organizational purchase process are included as the newness and importance of the purchase increase.

Buy Centers

Another perspective on organizational buying is to understand that, unlike consumer markets, buying

		New Task	Modified Rebuy	Straight Rebuy
Buy Phases	Need Recognition			
	Need Definition			
	Product/Solution Specification			
	Supplier Identification/Search			
	Proposal Solicitation			
	Proposal Evaluation and Selection of Suppliers			
	Selection of an Order Routine			
	Performance Feedback and Evaluation			

FIGURE NOTE 4-8 The Buygrid Framework

decisions in organizations are most often made by *teams of people.* Some buying teams are formal and some are informal and emergent. Different people play different roles on those teams, and the roles themselves can be formalized or left informal and may be made explicit or left implicit. These teams have been labeled "buy centers," and several categories of roles have been identified in the literature, including initiators, users, deciders, buyers, influencers, and gatekeepers (Figure 4-9). Sometimes the same person will perform more than one of these roles, more than one person can play any given role (e.g., there can be multiple influencers), and sometimes certain roles will not be played in a given purchase:

Initiator.   The person in the organization who recognizes the need or conceives of the purchase.

Influencer.   The person whose expertise or opinion affects the purchase.

Decider.   The ultimate decision maker; has the authority to make the purchase decision.

Buyer.   The person who executes the transaction.

Gatekeeper.   Controls the flow of information within the team and access to the team from outside.

User.   The person within the firm who will actually use the product once it is purchased.

THE "PURCHASING AGENT MINDSET."   An interesting distinction is between users and "purchasing agents." A purchasing agent is employed to "buy" and to process purchase decisions and orders. The agent is, therefore, keenly aware of buying procedures and criteria. He or she may be highly trained in negotiations and the logistics of fulfillment. In general, purchasing agents tend to be process focused over outcome focused, not easily convinced to abrogate "procedure" to achieve more desirable ends, and a purchasing agent tends to be price conscious; often the agent is evaluated in part or even predominantly on savings achieved in the procurement process. After price, delivery and inventory replenishment tend to dominate purchasing agents' judgments. That mindset is noticeably different than that of users and initiators, whose focus may well be on performance and quality, and who may view price and procurement logistics as "necessary details."

In the buy center framework, a purchasing agent can play any role or several roles—or may not be involved in a decision at all. Generally, a purchasing agent, if involved, would play the role of the buyer. He or she might also be the gatekeeper and an influencer via the performance of tasks, including need definition, product/solution specification, and vendor identification steps. Although those steps may seem procedural, they can have enormous influences on the ultimate decision. Strategically, it is valuable to investigate the role that purchasing agents or "the purchasing agent mentality" will play in the target organizations' decisions. It is reasonable to segment organizational markets by purchasing process, buy center configurations and dynamics, and the role of purchasing agents in order to adapt and refine the selling process, and the composition of the offering and sales communications.

FIGURE NOTE 4-9   The Buy Center Framework[28]

Organizational Buyer Behavior and Personal Selling

Personal selling is the fifth P (for "people") in the marketing mix. A couple of the important trends in personal selling connect with organizational buying behavior: Personal selling has gone from a transaction- and commission-focused activity toward being a salaried, solutions-focused function. That solutions focus puts the salesperson in the role of a consultant as much as vendor and holds that sales accounts are the firms "partners"; success is seen as long-term relationships with customers for whom the firm can deliver real value in the form of solutions and expertise.

Summary

Understanding consumer and organizational-buyer behavior is a foundation for developing effective strategies and valued offerings. This note has presented a concise summary and outline of the extant knowledge that has emerged from decades of academic research focused on consumer and business buyers, their decision processes, and their behaviors. There are parallels between the two sets of buyers and the models that attempt to clarify their decision making. For example, an important factor is the degree of effort that the buyer puts into the purchase decision. In consumer markets that is often summarized as "consumer involvement," and it influences the amount of time and effort the consumer will spend on information search, alternative evaluation, shopping, and purchase. In business-to-business markets, purchases are differentiated as straight rebuys, modified rebuys, and new tasks, and the type of purchase drives the amount of time and energy the organization will devote to the purchase. In other regards the two types of buyers are quite different, and models have been developed to explain both. This note has taken a strategic and applied perspective on these ideas and has been limited by space and by the purpose of this book. There are many good and comprehensive textbooks and managerial trade books available that elaborate on and extend these important ideas.

Additional Resources

Rogers, Everett. *The Diffusion of Innovations.* 4th ed., New York: Free Press, 1995.

Moore, Geoffrey A. *Crossing the Chasm.* Revised ed. New York: Harper Perennial.

Schiffman, Leon, and Leslie Kanuk. *Consumer Behavior,* 10th Ed, Upper Saddle River, NJ; Pearson/Prentice Hall, 2010.

Solomon, Michael R. *Truth About What Customers Want.* Upper Saddle River, NJ: FT Press, 2009.

Tanner, Jeff, Earl D. Honeycutt, and Robert C. Erffmeyer. *Sales Management: Shaping Future Sales Leaders.* Upper Saddle River, NJ, Pearson/Prentice Hall, 2009.

Endnotes

1. See, for example, Leon G. Schiffman and Leslie Lazar Kanuk, *Consumer Behavior,* 10th ed. (Upper Saddle River, NJ: Prentice Hall, 2010); and Michael R. Solomon, *Consumer Behavior: Buying, Having, and Being,* 9th ed. (Upper Saddle River, NJ: Prentice Hall, 2011).

2. John A. Howard and Jagdish N. Sheth, *The Theory of Buyer Behavior* (New York: Wiley, 1969).

3. This basic framework is ubiquitous to contemporary consumer behavior textbooks; see, for example, Schiffman and Kanuk, *Consumer Behavior;* and Solomon, *Consumer Behavior.*

4. See Thomas E. Barry and Daniel J. Howard, "A Review and Critique of the Hierarchy of Effects in Advertising," *International Journal of Advertising* 9 (1990): 121–135; and Robert J. Lavidge and Gary A. Steiner, "A Model for Predictive Measurements of Advertising Effectiveness," *Journal of Marketing* 25 (1961): 59–62. Demetrios Vakratsas and Tim Ambler, "How Advertising Works: What Do We Really Know?" *Journal of Marketing* 63 (January 1999): 26–43.

5. The AIDA hierarchy is attributed to E. St. Elmo Lewis 1898, see Strong, Edward K., Jr., "Theories of Selling," *Journal of Applied Psychology,* 9 (February 1925): 75–86 (page 76); and Vakratsas and Ambler, "How Advertising Works."

6. See Thomas E. Barry and Daniel J. Howard, "A Review and Critique of the Hierarchy of Effects in

Advertising," *International Journal of Advertising* 9 (1990): 121–135; and, for a more recent compilations of perspectives, Vijay Mahajan, Eitan Muller, and Yoram Wind, eds., *New-Product Diffusion Models* (New York: Springer Science+Business Media, 2000).

7. See Everett Rogers, *The Diffusion of Innovations,* 4th ed. (New York: Free Press, 1995) and Thomas S. Robertson, "The Process of Innovation and the Diffusion of Innovation," *Journal of Marketing* 31, no. 1 (January 1967): 14–19.

8. See Abraham H. Maslow, "A Theory of Human Motivation," *Psychological Review* 50, no. 4 (1943): 370–396; and Abraham H. Maslow, *Motivation and Personality* (New York: Harper & Row, 1954).

9. See Maslow, "A Theory of Human Motivation"; and Maslow *Motivation and Personality.*

10. Russell. I Haley, "Benefit Segmentation: A Decision-oriented Research Tool," *Journal of Marketing* 32, no. 3 (July 1968): 30–3; 1 and Russell. I Haley, "Benefit Segments: Backwards and Forwards," *Journal of Advertising Research* 24, no. 1 (February–March, 1984); 19–25.

11. *The Economist,* 2005; Liljenwall, 2004

12. See Richard Vaughn, "How Advertising Works: A Planning Model ... Putting It All Together," *Journal of Advertising Research* 20, no. 5 (1980): 27–33 and Richard Vaughn, "How Advertising Works: A planning model revisited," *Journal of Advertising Research* 26, no. 1 (1986): 57–66.

13. Gerd Gigerenzer, Peter M. Todd, and the ABC Research Group, *Simple Heuristics That Make Us Smart* (Oxford, UK: Oxford University Press, 1999).

14. See Naomi Klein, *No Logo: Taking Aim at the Brand Bullies* (New York: Picador, 1999); cf., Johan Norberg, *In Defense of Global Capitalism* (Washington, DC: Cato Institute, 2003).

15. See for example, Bradley T. Gale, *Managing Customer Value,* (New York: Free Press 1994); Robert B. Woodruff , "Customer value: The Next Source for Competitive Advantage," *Journal of the Academy of Marketing Science* 25, no. 2 (Spring 1997): 139–153; Valarie A. Zeithaml, "Consumer Perceptions of Price, Quality, and Value: A Means-end Model and Synthesis of Evidence," *Journal of Marketing* 52 (July 1988): 2–22.

16. Bradley T. Gale, *Managing Customer Value* (New York: Free Press, 1994).

17. See Lars Thomassen, Keith Lincoln, and Anthony Aconis, *Retailization: Brand Survival in the Age of Retailer Power* (Philadelphia: Kogan Page, 2006).

18. Jeffrey Grau, Multi-channel Shopping: The Rise of the Retail Chains, *E-Marketer Report* (March 2006), www.emarketer.com/Reports/All/Multichannel_mar06 .aspx. Last accessed June 18, 2010.

19. Regina Fazio Maruca, "The Right Way to Go Global: An Interview with Whirlpool CEO David Whitwam," *Harvard Business Review* 72, no. 2 (March 1994): 134–145; quoted from page 143.

20. See Everett Rogers, *The Diffusion of Innovations,* 4th ed. (New York: Free Press, 1995); and Thomas S. Robertson, "The Process of Innovation and the Diffusion of Innovation," *Journal of Marketing* 31, no. 1 (January 1967): 14–19.

21. See John T. Gourville, "Eager Sellers & Stony Buyers: Understanding the Psychology of New-product Adoption," *Harvard Business Review* 84, no. 6 (June 2006): 98–106.

22. Tom Peters, *Thriving on Chaos: Handbook for a Management Revolution* (New York: Alfred A. Knopf, 1987): 96–98.

23. Regarding expectations and satisfaction with time in lines, see Piyush Kumar, Manohar U. Kalwani, and Maqbool Dada, "The Impact of Waiting Time Guarantees on Customer's Waiting Experiences," *Marketing Science* 16, no. 4 (1997): 295–314.

24. D. J. Dalrymple, W. L. Cron, and T. E. DeCarlo, *Sales Management* (Hoboken, NJ: John Wiley & Sons 2004).

25. See Patrick J. Robinson, Charles W. Faris, and Yoram Wind, *Industrial Buying and Creative Marketing* (Boston, MA: Allyn & Bacon, 1967); and Dalrymple, Cron, and DeCarlo, *Sales Management.*

26. Rosann L. Spiro, William D. Perreault Jr., and Fred D. Reynolds, "The Personal Selling Process: A Critical Review and Model," *Industrial Marketing Management* 5, no. 6 (December 1976): 351–363; and James C. Anderson, James A. Narus, and Das Narayandas (2009), *Business Market Management: Understanding, Creating, and Delivering Value,* 3rd ed. (Upper Saddle River, NJ: Pearson Prentice Hall), especially Chapter 8.

27. Ibid.; and Anderson; Narus; Narayandas, especially Table 8-1, page 330.

28. See Donald W. Jackson, Janet E. Keith, and Richard K. Burdick, "Purchasing Agents' Perceptions of Industrial Buying Center Influence: A Situational Approach," *Journal of Marketing* 48 (Fall 1984): 75–83. Wesley J. Johnston and Thomas V. Bonoma, "The Buyer Center: Structure and Interaction Patterns," *Journal of Marketing* 45 (Summer 1981): 143–156.

5

Competitor Analysis— Competitive Intelligence

In "The Art of War," one of the oldest and most successful books on military strategy, Chinese general Sun Tzu wrote: "If you know your enemy and know yourself, you need not fear the result of a hundred battles. If you know yourself but not the enemy, for every victory gained you will also suffer a defeat. If you know neither the enemy nor yourself, you will succumb in every battle."[1] Knowing the objectives, strategies, tactics, strengths, and weaknesses of the competitor is vital. For example, if you are Microsoft, producer of the market-dominating Web browser (Internet Explorer), you want to pay very close attention to what Google is doing with the development of its Chrome browser; Chrome represents an overt attack on Windows. If you are Google, you should be concerned with Microsoft's retaliatory response, Bing, produced in collaboration with Yahoo and intended to compete directly with Google's market-dominating search engine. Understanding the competition is vital to anticipating market actions and to constructing appropriate strategies and plans to succeed against those actions. A comprehensive competitor analysis includes the following four areas:

1. Long-term objectives and motivations of the competitor;
2. Strengths and weaknesses;
3. Strategies; and
4. Marketing tactics.

LONG-TERM OBJECTIVES AND MOTIVATIONS OF THE COMPETITOR

How competitors act and react in a market largely depends on their strategic objectives and on their motivations to engage in a business. Therefore, the first step of a competitor analysis should be the investigation of the long-term objectives. The objectives not only determine the strategy and likely tactical moves, but from them you can also derive what the motivations of your competitor are in a specific business or market. For example, if a market or segment is seen as the core business of a competitor, it will defend it with all possible means. If the strategic goal of a company is double-digit growth every year; and, if the company's strategic objective is to be among the top three players in terms of market share, then a business unit of that company that is in a low-growth market with a small market share will not receive much attention and resources, and can be more easily attacked. To identify the long-term objectives and motivations of a competitor, the following sources can be examined:

- Vision and mission statements;
- Annual reports;
- Press releases;
- Analyst reports; and
- Presentations and speeches of executives.

STRENGTHS AND WEAKNESSES

The second step of a competitor analysis consists of the assessment of strengths and weaknesses. This analysis helps you to (1) predict competitor's actions and initiatives—as they probably want to eliminate their weak points and to emphasize on their advantages and (2) to identify points of difference to position your products and services. The analysis consists of four steps:

- First, success factors in a market have to be determined;
- Second, the success factors are weighted according to their importance. Usually the

constant-sum scale is used: 100 points are divided among the success factors according to their importance; the higher the importance, the more points are assigned;
- Third, the competitor is rated on each success factor (e.g., using a 5-point scale, where 5 is excellent and 1 is very poor). Also rate your company on each success factor; and
- Fourth, multiply the rating by the importance weight. The importance weight indicates the relative advantage or disadvantage.

Figure 5-1 is an example. In the first column, the success factors in a particular industry are listed. The second column contains their importance. The performance of our company (We) and the competitor (Competitor A) is rated on a 5-point scale. Two weighted scores are computed: one for the competitor, and one for our company. The summed weighted scores indicate the overall performance of the two companies.

The best way to perform this analysis is by combining several sources of information, such as:

- Customer surveys (e.g., Assess brand image, service, product quality);

Critical Success Factors	Weight	Performance					Weighted Score	
		1	2	3	4	5	We	Comp. A
Brand Image	5						10	15
Product Innovation	10						20	30
Service	20						60	100
Extensive Distribution	15						30	60
Economies of Scale	30						60	90
Logistics	20						60	100
						Sum	240	395

We
Competitor A

FIGURE NOTE 5-1   Strengths and Weakness Analysis

- Sales force meetings (e.g., Sales people have close contact with the customers and are confronted every day with competitors' offerings, their strengths and weaknesses during sales negotiations);
- Analyst reports; and
- Discussions with shared suppliers, distributors, etc.

It is advisable to do this analysis as teamwork with experts from several functional areas that have competitor knowledge.

STRATEGIES

The next step, the analysis of the competitor's strategies, may be the most difficult. Ideally, you can use the data you have generated for your own portfolio analysis, customer value analysis, and so on, to create the strategy profile of your competitor. The strategy profile illustrates the strategic priorities and compares them with your own company. So, you can identify the areas of strategic overlap (i.e., where you follow the same strategy) and areas of difference. As you can also assume that your competitor uses the most essential tools for strategy formulation, you can try to decipher its strategic intent by looking through the lens of the competitor when you analyze the data. When, for example, the strategist creates a strength and weakness analysis, the question is: What would I do, if I were competitor A? A comprehensive strategy assessment leads to a strategy profile containing the following analyses:

- *Portfolio analysis:* Portfolio analyses organize a given firms' products or "strategic business units" (SBUs) according to the attractiveness of the market they serve and their strength in that market; the resulting categorization prioritizes the products/SBUs and directs investment (or withdrawal of support) across the various products. It is useful to understand how the competition prioritizes its products/SBUs for investment and other efforts. Therefore, it is useful to create a portfolio analysis of your competitor. It will give you insights into its

most likely strategic moves (growth, divestment, etc.) And, based on the positioning of the business units or products, you will be able to tell how balanced your competitor's portfolio is, in terms of cash flow and risk. Will your competitor have enough "cash cows" to generate financial resources for a growth strategy? Will your competitor have to invest in product development, as it has not enough "stars" in its portfolio? And so forth.
- *Customer Value Analysis:* If you create a customer value analysis, try to look at the positioning of the products from your competitor's point of view! How satisfied will it be with its positioning? Will it have to increase quality, or to lower prices?
- *Growth Strategy:* Try also to find out what the focus of your competitor's growth strategy is: market penetration, product development, market development, or diversification.
- *Marketing Approach:* Is your competitor's marketing approach undifferentiated or differentiated marketing? What are the target segments of your competitor?
- *Offensive Strategy:* What is the most likely "attacking" strategy of your competitor?
- *Defensive Strategy:* What is the most likely response to your strategic and tactical moves?

After having analyzed these strategy dimensions, you can create the strategy profile of your competitor, and compare it to your company (see Figure 5-2). Sources of competitor data for this analysis can be:

- Vision and mission statements,
- Annual reports,
- Press releases,
- Newspaper articles,
- Analyst reports,
- Trade shows,
- Fairs,
- Sales force meetings,
- Ex-employees,
- Shared suppliers,
- Shared customers, and
- Shared distributors.

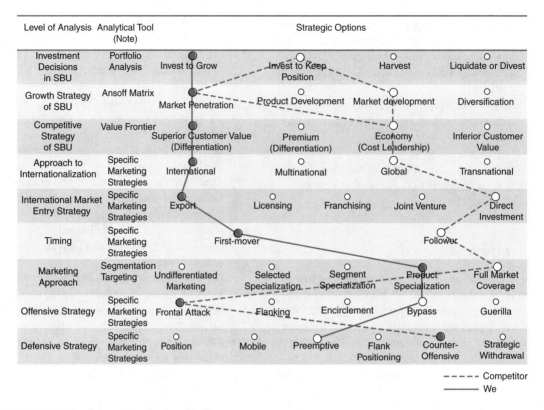

FIGURE NOTE 5-2   Competitor Strategy Profile

MARKETING TACTICS

The final part of the competitor analysis consists of the assessment of the individual marketing decisions. They relate to positioning, product and brand decisions, pricing, distribution and sales management, and communication. Where the previous analyses should help you to *predict* what the competitor's moves most likely are, in this step you assess what the competitors *actually do*. Sources can be:

- Price lists;
- Advertising campaigns;
- Promotions;
- Sales force meetings;
- Trade shows;
- Fairs;
- Shared customers; and
- Shared distributors.

Summary

A competitor analysis can be compared to a jigsaw puzzle. Each individual piece of data may be meaningless, and some pieces may be out of place, but accumulating all of the available data and organizing those data as nicely as possible in a noisy, chaotic context will nevertheless reveal important information about the competition and the future of the marketplace. The challenge is to collect as many of the pieces as possible, to assemble them correctly, and to create an overall picture of the competitor. The objective should be to clarify the competitions' long-term objectives and motivations, strengths and weaknesses, strategies, and tactics. The broad structure and basic tools outlined in this note will enhance those efforts.

Additional Resources

Armstrong, Scott, and Kesten C. Green. "Competitor-Oriented Objectives: The Myth of Market Share." *International Journal of Business* 12, no.1 (2007):117–136.

Champy, Jim. *Outsmart!: How to Do What Your Competitors Can't.* Upper Saddle River, NJ: FT Press, 2008.

Lehmann, Donald R., and Russell S. Winer. *Analysis for Marketing Planning.* New York: McGraw-Hill, 2008; especially Chapter 2—Defining the Competitive Set and Chapter 4 - Competitor Analysis.

Ohmae, Kenichi. *The Next Global Stage: Challenges and Opportunities in Our Borderless World.* Upper Saddle River, NJ: FT Press, 2010.

Endnote

1. Sun Tzu, *The Art of War,* Special Edition, trans. Lionel Giles (El Paso, TX: EL Paso Norte Press, 2005) 13.

6

Company Assessment— Missions and Visions

"McDonald's vision is to be the world's best quick-service restaurant experience. Being the best means providing outstanding quality, service, cleanliness, and value, so that we make every customer in every restaurant smile."[1]

"At IBM, we strive to lead in the invention, development, and manufacture of the industry's most advanced information technologies, including computer systems, software, storage systems, and microelectronics. We translate these advanced technologies into value for our customers through our professional solutions, services and consulting businesses worldwide."[2]

"Google's mission is to organize the world's information and make it universally accessible and useful."[3]

"Wal-Mart's mission is to help people save money so they can live better."[4]

H&M describes its mission as "Fashion and quality at the best price."[5]

Most successful organizations are driven by a commonly shared and inspiring vision such as the examples above. Without such guidance, it is easy to lose direction and purpose. It is rare to find a successful company today that does not have such vision. Decentralized companies that delegate decisions to business units, from business units to departments, and from departments down the line, will suffer if common long-term direction and goals are lacking. How can companies decentralize and increase responsiveness to new challenges, and at the same time have coordinated efforts, making sure that people in the far reaches of an organization know where it is heading? The development of a shared vision with a definition of the company's purpose, values, and long-term, visionary goals is an important response to this problem[6].

A strategy—in its broadest sense—is concerned with planning how a company will achieve its goals. There are three levels of strategies: corporate-level strategies, business unit strategies, and functional strategies (e.g., marketing, R&D, human resource, production). Having a clear vision and carefully crafted, sound strategies is one of the key success factors in a highly competitive environment.

VISION AND MISSION

The French writer Antoine de Saint-Exupéry once wrote: "If you want to build a ship, don't drum up the men to gather wood, divide the work, and give orders. Instead, teach them to yearn for the vast and endless sea."[7] This famous quote perfectly describes what a company's vision should do: It should organize and channel people's energy toward a direction to go. It communicates sense, and helps to actualize values, appealing to someone's heart and mind.[8]

A vision and mission statement should contain:[9]

- The core purpose of the company,
- The core values of the company,
- The visionary goal, and
- A vivid description of the envisioned future.

Core purpose

The core purpose of the company gives answers to questions like: What is the company for? What is the raison d'être of the company? Why should managers and employees put all their energy into the company and do more than the minimum required?[10]

The core purpose quickly and clearly conveys why the company exists; it is particularly motivating and inspiring if it is aimed at a higher ideal. It should be broad, fundamental, and enduring.

Examples:

- "We shall simplify the everyday activities of parents and children, making the most important years of life even more enjoyable" (Baby Bjorn, a Swedish baby products company).
- "We build families for children in need. We help them shape their own futures. We share in the development of their communities" (SOS Children's villages, an international nongovernmental social-development organization).
- "To experience the emotion of competition, winning, and crushing competitors" (Nike).

Core Values

Core values are those beliefs and moral principles that shape the company's cultures and guide employee's behavior. They define what a company stands for, how business should be conducted, and what is to be held inviolate. As Anita Roddick, founder of The Body Shop, puts it: "If business comes with no moral sympathy or honourable code of behaviours, then God help us all." As a small set of three to five timeless principles that have intrinsic value, core values need no external justification.[11]

Examples (look at the Web pages of these companies for a closer description):

SOS Children's villages

(www.sos-childrensvillages.org/Publications/Documents/_26J1-afJ_10A93C.pdf)

- Courage: We take action
- Commitment: We keep our promises
- Trust: We believe in each other
- Accountability: We are reliable partners

IKEA (http://franchisor.ikea.com/)

- Togetherness
- Cost-consciousness
- Respect
- Simplicity

The Body Shop (www.thebodyshop.com/_en/_ww/index.aspx)

- Activate self-esteem
- Against animal testing
- Protect our planet
- Support community trade
- Defend human rights

The core purpose and the values form the core ideology of the company that "provides the glue that holds an organization together through time."[12] Together, they preserve the authentic core of the company. However, a company can only sustain in the long run if it evolves. Therefore, the second element of a vision and mission statement is concerned with progress and development. It describes the envisioned future with a visionary goal, and a vivid description of what it will be like when the goal has been achieved.

Visionary Goal

The visionary goal is a clear and compelling, tangible and inspiring goal with a—at least virtual—finish line. It is challenging and ambitious enough that reason says "this is impossible" and intuition says "we can do it nevertheless."[13] It should be set high enough that people are motivated to put the maximum effort to achieve it and do more than a required minimum, and it should be set low enough that people see a realistic chance that it can be reached. The visionary goal should be so inspiring that people say "It's worth the effort; I want to be a part of it!"

Examples:

- "Every child belongs to a family and grows with love, respect and security." (SOS Children's villages)
- "Yomaha wo tsubusu! (We will crush, squash, and slaughter Yamaha)." (Honda)
- "To have any book ever printed, in any language, all available in under 60 seconds." (Amazon Kindle)
- "To organize the world's information and make it universally accessible and useful." (Google)

Vivid Descriptions

In order to make the company's vision and mission accessible to all employees, it should be translated to vivid pictures and words that describe the envisioned future in a way that captures the heart and soul of people. It must be authentic, passionate, and convincing.[14]

For example, from Coca Cola:

Our Mission   Our Roadmap starts with our mission, which is enduring. It declares our purpose as a company and serves as the standard against which we weigh our actions and decisions.

- To refresh the world . . .
- To inspire moments of optimism and happiness . . .
- To create value and make a difference.

Our Vision   Our vision serves as the framework for our Roadmap and guides every aspect of our business by describing what we need to accomplish in order to continue achieving sustainable, quality growth.

- *People:* Be a great place to work where people are inspired to be the best they can be.
- *Portfolio:* Bring to the world a portfolio of quality beverage brands that anticipate and satisfy people's desires and needs.
- *Partners:* Nurture a winning network of customers and suppliers, together we create mutual, enduring value.
- *Planet:* Be a responsible citizen that makes a difference by helping build and support sustainable communities.

- *Profit:* Maximize long-term return to shareowners while being mindful of our overall responsibilities.
- *Productivity:* Be a highly effective, lean and fast-moving organization.[15]

Together, the visionary goal and the vivid prescription form that part of the vision and mission statement that stimulates and ensures progress.

Criteria to Assess the Vision and Mission

The following criteria can be used to assess the company's vision and mission:

- Is the core purpose clear and compelling?
- Does the core purpose capture the heart and the soul of the organization?
- Is it motivating and aiming at a higher ideal?
- Is it broad, fundamental, and enduring?
- Are the values authentic and honorable?
- Are they timeless and able to guide behavior?
- Do executives and employees live up to the values?
- Do executives and employees accept and defend the values?
- Is the visionary goal long-term, inspiring, and challenging?
- Does the visionary goal inspire people?
- Do the vivid descriptions passionately convey the envisioned future?

CORPORATE STRATEGY

In a multi-business company, strategic management encompasses four major tasks at the corporate level:[16]

1. Providing a clear overall vision for the single business units, exercising guidance and control over the individual businesses;
2. Allocating resources to the single business units, thus managing the portfolio in a way that cash flow and risks are balanced, and sustainable long-term growth is achieved;
3. Managing linkages among the business units and exploiting synergies; and
4. Developing central competences and providing services and resources to the business units.

Hence, the following criteria are helpful to evaluate the corporate strategy:

1. Does the corporate headquarters have a clear overall vision or "strategic intent" for its business units?
2. Is the portfolio of business units balanced in terms of cash flow and risk?
3. Does the portfolio assure sustainable long-term development and growth?
4. Are synergies among the business units exploited?
5. Does the headquarters develop core competences, and does it provide valuable services and resources to the business units?

BUSINESS LEVEL AND MARKETING STRATEGY

The business level and marketing strategy describe how a business unit competes within a market, how it creates competitive advantages, and how it achieves its goals. A comprehensive business level and marketing strategy defines:

1. The customers the business will serve (Who?);
2. The geographic markets the business will serve (Where?);
3. The needs the firm will meet (What?);
4. The means the firm will employ (How?);
5. The business model that supports profitability (Why?);
6. The speed and sequences of actions (When?).

Each strategy is based on a thorough internal and external analysis, and should withstand the following test:[17]

1. Is the strategy aligned to the vision, mission, and corporate strategy?
2. Are the 5Ws and 1H clearly addressed?
3. Does the strategy exploit opportunities in the market?
4. Is the strategy aligned with the key success factors in the market?
5. Is the strategy built on core competences and strengths?
6. Are the differentiators sustainable?
7. Are the 5Ws and 1H internally consistent?
8. Does the company have enough resources to pursue and implement the strategy?

Summary

Companies need to establish a framework to guide the organization. Guidance consists of the company's vision for its future and a mission statement that defines what it is doing. This chapter has provided many examples of both.

Then, the sections on corporate strategy and individual business unit and marketing strategy spell out how the vision and mission will be achieved, and how the core values of the organization shape company actions.

Additional Resources

Campbell, Andrew, and Sally Yeung. "Creating a sense of mission." *Long Range Planning* 24, no. 4 (1991):10–20.

Collins, James C., and Jerry I. Porras. "Building Your Company's Vision." *Harvard Business Review* (September–October, 1996): 65–77.

———. "Organizational Vision and Visionary Organizations." *California Management Review* (Fall 1991): 30–52.

Endnotes

1. www.aboutmcdonalds.com/etc/medialib/aboutMc-Donalds/investors.Par.42274.File.dat/2001_Annual_Report.pdf. Last accessed on June 23, 2010.

2. www.company-statements-slogans.info/list-of-companies-i/ibm-international-business-machines.htm. Last accessed on June 23, 2010.

3. www.google.com/corporate/facts.html. Last accessed on June 23, 2010.

4. www.businessweek.com/the_thread/brandnewday/archives/2007/09/walmart_is_out.html. Last accessed on June 23, 2010.

5. www.e-pages.dk/hm/12/. Last accessed on June 23, 2010.

6. James C. Collin and Jerry I. Porras, "Organizational Vision and Visionary Organizations," *California Management Review* (Fall 1991): 30–52.

7. Antoine de Saint-Exup'ery, *The Wisdom of the Sands* (New York: Harcourt Brace & World, 1950), 2.

8. Hans H. Hinterhuber, *Strategische Unternehmens-führung, Band 1: Strategisches Denken,* 7 Auflage ed. (Berlin, New York: De Gruyter, 2004).

9. James C. Collins and Jerry I. Porras, "Building Your Company's Vision," *Harvard Business Review* (September–October, 1996): 65–77.

10. Andrew Campbell and Sally Yeung, "Creating a Sense of Mission," *Long Range Planning* 24, no. 4 (1991): 10–20.

11. Collins and Porras, "Building your Company's Vision."

12. Collins and Porras, "Building Your Company's Vision."

13. Collin and Porras, "Organizational Vision and Visionary Organizations."

14. Collins and Porras, "Building Your Company's Vision."

15. www.thecoca-colacompany.com/ourcompany/mission_vision_values.html. Last accessed on June 17, 2010

16. Robert M. Grant, *Contemporary Strategic Analysis,* 6th ed. (Malden, Oxford, Carlton: Blackwell Publishing, 2008).
Gerry Johnson, Kevan Scholes, and Richard Whittington, *Exploring Corporate Strategy: Text & Cases* (Harlow, England: Prentice Hall, 2008).

17. Adapted from D. C. Hambrick and James W. Fredrickson, "Are You Sure You Have A Strategy?" *Academy of Management Executive* 15, no. 4 (2001), 48–59.

7

Company Assessment— The Value Chain

"Competitive advantage cannot be understood by looking at a firm as a whole. Advantage stems from the many discrete activities a firm performs—designing, producing, marketing, delivering, and supporting products. Each of these activities can contribute to a firm's relative cost position and create a basis for differentiation."

MICHAEL PORTER[1]

A company can create competitive advantage when it is able to perform the individual activities of its "value chain" more effectively (differentiation advantage) or more efficiently (cost advantage) than its competitors. Developed by Porter,[2] the value chain organizes all of the activities a company performs in bringing a product or service to the market (see Figure 7-1). Value chain analysis has become exceedingly popular in the literature. A cursory search produces recent detailed value chain analyses of a wide variety of firms, including Marks and Spencer, British Airways, Apple Computer, 7-Eleven, Tesco, Emerson Electric, Wal-Mart, IBM, and others. The value chain distinguishes strategically relevant activities that *can* lead to cost or differentiation advantages in the market, and thus influence the product's margin. Value chain analysis allows the strategic planner to not only identify what activities can lead to advantage, but also facilitates identification of what activities for a particular firm *do* lead to advantage—and which do not. Primary activities are concerned with the creation or delivery of a product or service. Those activities typically include:

- *Inbound logistics:* Activities related to receiving, storing, and distributing internally the inputs needed to produce a product or service, including warehousing, stock control, and internal transportation systems.
- *Operations:* Activities related to the transformation of inputs into products, including production, assembly, packaging, equipment maintenance, quality assurance, etc.

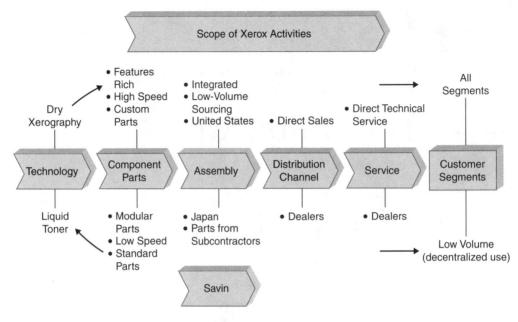

FIGURE NOTE 7-1   The Value Chain[3]

- *Outbound logistics:* Activities concerned with the distribution of the product, such as collection, storage, and delivery to the customer.
- *Marketing and sales:* Activities like market segmentation, targeting, positioning, sales management, advertising, pricing, and product and brand management.
- *Service:* Activities to enhance the value of a product, such as after-sales service, repair and maintenance, customer training, customer care, etc.

Support activities are needed to perform the primary activities and contribute to their effectiveness and efficiency. They are:

- *Firm infrastructure:* All activities and formal systems of planning, finance, quality control, accounting, information management, and so on.
- *Human resource management:* Activities related to the recruitment, training, development, and compensating people.
- *Technology development:* All activities related to know-how, research and development, product design, process improvement, and IT development.

- *Procurement:* Activities for acquiring resources as inputs for the primary activities, such as the selection of suppliers, negotiation of quality, prices, delivery terms, etc.

The individual activities of the value chain are strategically relevant because each of them can constitute a cost advantage or differentiation advantage, and in each of these activities a company can either win or lose money, depending how effectively and efficiently it performs them compared to the competitors.

Hence, a value chain analyses should answer the following questions:

1. *What are the activities of a company's value chain?* Figure 7-1 illustrates a generic value chain, which can be adapted to the industry and the company by adding, subtracting or renaming activities.
2. *Which of them are strategically important in the industry?* In this step, the strategic importance of the activities is assessed. This is important, as the nature of the industry determines which activities are critical to success.
3. *How well do we perform on the activities?* By comparing the individual activities with the

strongest competitor in the industry, the strengths and weaknesses of the company can be identified.

4. ***Which activities generate profits and which cause losses?*** When costs associated with each activity are analyzed, and when the value is generated in each activity can be measured, a company can determine where exactly it generates profits and where losses are incurred. This analysis requires detailed data that many information systems do not provide.

5. ***Which activities constitute competitive advantages or core competences?*** When a company shows stronger performance on an activity (more effectiveness or efficiency than a rival) that has high strategic importance, it has

a significant competitive advantage. If this activity or process cannot be imitated or substituted, it is a core competence.

6. ***Which activities should be outsourced?*** The value chain analysis can also be used to identify those activities that should be outsourced, for example, if a company has little competence in this activity and an outsourcing partner could do it more efficiently or effectively.

Figure 7-2 illustrates the value chain analysis of a pharmaceutical company. In this example, the strategic importance of the primary activities, the budget share of these activities, and the relative performance (compared to the strongest competitor) are shown. It illustrates whether the amount of money a company

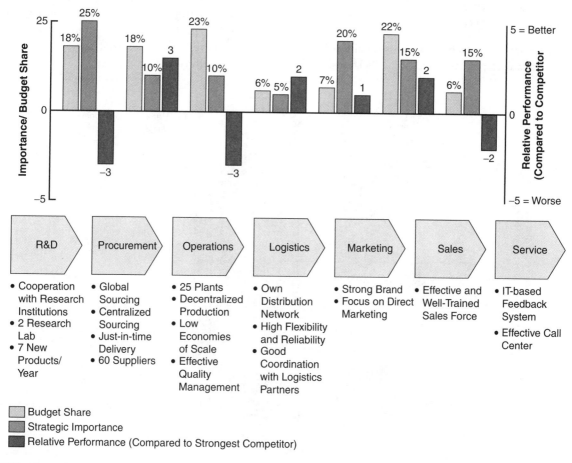

FIGURE NOTE 7-2   Analysis of the Value Chain of a Pharmaceutical Company[4]

invests in each activity and its performance are in line with the strategic value of this activity.

The following major conclusions can be drawn:

- R&D has the highest strategic importance (25%), but receives only 18 percent of the budget. As performance of R&D is below competition, more resources should be devoted to this activity to improve it.
- Operations constitute a major problem: It has very little strategic relevance (10%), consumes 23 percent of the budget, and performance is below competition. This activity obviously is a candidate for outsourcing.
- Also marketing seems to be unbalanced: It is of central importance (20%) but receives only 7 percent of the budget. As marketing, however, performs better compared to competition, no actions are necessary.

Another useful illustration of a value-chain analysis is the strategic priority analysis (SPA).[5] Using a two-dimensional matrix, where importance of the individual value chain activities is depicted along the x-axis and performance along the y-axis, four specific recommendations can be derived (Figure 7-3):

- **Quadrant I:** Activities evaluated high both in performance and importance represent opportunities for gaining or maintaining competitive advantages. These are the company's key strengths and it should "keep up the good work." Only marketing (and sales) in our example is located in this quadrant. This activity should be rewarded in future strategic planning.
- **Quadrant II:** Low performance on highly important activities demands immediate attention. We have great risk here. To enhance competitiveness, a company should improve these activities. If they are ignored, a serious threat is posed to the business. In our example, research and development, as well as service, need strong efforts to be improved.

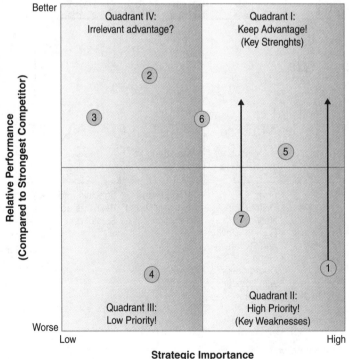

FIGURE NOTE 7-3   Strategic Priority Analysis (SPA)

- *Quadrant III:* These activities are both low in performance and importance. Usually, it is not necessary to focus additional effort here. These activities of the value chain are of "low priority." In the case of the pharmaceutical company, operations is positioned here. We are not very good at it, and it is not very important strategically.
- *Quadrant IV:* Activities located in this quadrant are rated high in performance, but low in importance. This implies that resources committed to these attributes would be better employed elsewhere. High performance on unimportant activities indicates a "possible overkill". Procurement and logistics are located in this quadrant. If resources were redeployed to quadrant I and II, the company would probably be better off.

The value chain analysis is an important tool for a number of other analyses, including, for example, identifying competitive advantages.

Summary

The ability of a company to understand the critical success factors in an industry, its own capabilities and competences, and through which activities it creates competitive advantages is essential in strategic management and marketing. The value chain is a systematic and useful tool to think through the ways in which a company delivers value to its customers, differentiates its products, and creates profits or losses. Applied in a systematic way (by answering the seven questions in this note), it leads to a profound strategic assessment of the company and to a sound basis for strategic decisions.

Additional Resources

Madsen, Benny, and Rob Brownstein. *The New Industrial Revolution: The power of dynamic value chains.* Ramsey, NJ: Arbor Books, 2008.

Hansen, Morten T., and Julian Birkinshaw. "The Innovation Value Chain," *Harvard Business Review* 85, no. 6 (June 2007): 121–130.

Heskett, James L., Thomas O. Jones, Gary W. Loveman, W. Earl Sasser Jr., and Leonard A. Schlesinger "Putting the Service-Profit Chain to Work," *Harvard Business Review* 72, no. 2 (March–April, 1994): 164–174.

Normann, Richard, and Rafael Ramirez. "From Value Chain to Value Constellation: Designing Interactive Strategy," *Harvard Business Review* 71, no. 4 (1993): 65–77.

Porter, Michael E., *Competitive Advantage: Creating and Sustaining Superior Performance* 2nd Ed. (New York: Free Press, 1985).

Endnotes

1. Michael E. Porter, Competitive Advantage: Creating and Sustaining Superior Performance, 2nd ed., (New York: Free Press, 1985).
2. Ibid.
3. Adapted from Porter, "Competitive Advantage."
4. Adapted from Müller-Stewens, Günter, and Christoph Lechner, *Strategisches Management—Wie Strategische Initiativen Zum Wandel Führen*, 3, aufl ed. (Stuttgart: Schäffer-Poeschel, 2005).
5. J. A. Martilla, and J. C. James, "Importance-Performance Analysis," *Journal of Marketing* 41, no. 1 (1977): 77–79.

8

Industry Analysis

Profitability varies significantly from industry to industry. The average return on invested capital (ROIC), that is, earnings before interest and taxes, in industries in the United States ranged from negative to more than 50 percent between 1992 and 2006.[1] The average profitability was 14.9 percent; airlines on average earned 5.9 percent, hotels 10.4 percent, grocery stores 16 percent, medical instruments 21 percent, pharmaceuticals 31.7 percent and soft drinks 37.6 percent. Obviously, from a profitability standpoint, there are some industries that are more attractive than others. To understand industry competition and profitability, Michael E. Porter developed an analysis framework (see Table 8-1) consisting of five forces that shape industry competition:[2]

- The bargaining power of buyers;
- The bargaining power of suppliers;
- The threat of new entrants;
- The threat of substitute products or services; and
- The rivalry of existing competitors.

These five forces drive the intensity of internal competition and overall industry profitability (as depicted in Figure 8-1).

They provide a framework for anticipating and influencing competition over time and are essential parameters to formulate a viable strategy. Hence, a thorough analysis and understanding of these five forces is of vital importance in strategy formulation. An industry analysis is carried out in five steps:[3]

1. Definition of the industry
2. Identification of participants (buyers, suppliers, competitors, substitutes, potential entrants)
3. Assessment of the drivers of competitive forces and of overall industry structure
4. Analysis of future changes in the industry
5. Identification of aspects of industry structure that can be influenced by competitors, new entrants, or by ourselves.

STEP 1

Is Red Bull's market the energy-drink market or the soft drink market? In the first case, Red Bull is the clear market leader of a fast-growing market. The major competitors are Monster and many other smaller brands. The target market is mostly male teenagers and twentysomethings, and people interested in extreme sports. In the second case, Red Bull is only a minor competitor of a fairly mature market, including products like carbonates, fruit juices and drinks, and also bottled water, competing against giants like

TABLE NOTE 8-1 Porter's Five Forces Analysis

Participant	Potential Entrants	Customers	Suppliers	Competitors	Substitutes
Key question	How likely is it that new competitors enter the industry?	How much of the value created do customers capture? How price-sensitive are they?	How much of the value created do suppliers capture?	How aggressively or "friendly" do competitors act and react?	How do potential substitutes threaten sales in an industry
Force	Market entry barrier	Bargaining power of customers	Bargaining power of suppliers	Rivalry among competitors	Threat of substitution
Drivers	• Economies of scale • Network effects • Customer loyalty and switching costs • Capital requirements • Incumbency advantages independent of size (e.g., proprietary technology, raw material sources) • Unique access to distribution channels • Restrictive government policy	• High concentration of buyers • Undifferentiated products • Low switching costs of buyers • Easy backward integration • Product represents significant fraction of cost structure or procurement budget • Buyers earn low profits or have to cut purchasing costs • Quality of products do not affect quality of customer's offers	• High concentration of suppliers • Suppliers do not depend on the customers for its revenues • High switching costs of customers • Highly differentiated products of suppliers • No substitute products • Easy forward integration	• Numerous competitors of equal size • Low industry growth • High exit barriers • Undifferentiated products, • Low switching costs • High fixed costs and low marginal costs • Perishable product	• Substitute offers an attractive price-performance trade-off • Low switching costs of buyers
Future development	Do market entry barriers change? Are new entrants attracted?	• Do suppliers change their strategy and structure? • Does their bargaining power change?	• Do customers change their strategy and structure? • Does their bargaining power change?	• Does competition change over time?	• Are new technologies arising that create new substitutes? • Do switching costs to substitute change?

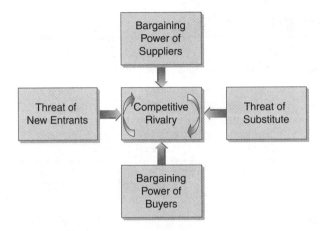

FIGURE NOTE 8-1 Five Forces Influencing Rivalry and Profitability[4]

Coca Cola and Pepsi who push their offerings to all soda drinkers.

Some arenas have well-defined boundaries with clearly identifiable competitors. Others have fuzzy boundaries and rivals are difficult to identify or anticipate. Therefore, the definition of the market arena is a crucial task and often not easy. The definition can be based on these four dimensions:[5] (1) the array of product or service categories (single product versus broad category); (2) the customers (single versus multiple segments); (3) geographic scope (regional, country-wide, global); and (4) activities in the value chain (many versus few).

STEP 2

In this step, the participants in the industry have to be identified by answering the following questions:

1. Who are the buyers?
2. Who are the suppliers?
3. Who are the competitors?
4. Which products or services are substitutes for the product in this industry?
5. Who are the potential entrants into this industry?

STEP 3

Now the analysis of the underlying drivers of each competitive force and the industry structure begins. This activity is usually the most interesting part of the analysis, as it reveals the forces that shape competition and industry attractiveness and provides a framework to anticipate and influence competition over time. Usually the analysis of the five forces is taken from the perspective of an incumbent (as in the following sections). But it can, of course, also be used to understand the challenges faced by a new entrant.

THREAT OF ENTRY. Whether or not existing competitors are threatened by new entrants largely depends on market entry barriers.

• Important market-entry barriers are economies of scale. Economies of scale exist when the unit costs of a product fall as a function of the firm's production volume. They can be achieved in most business functions (i.e., R&D, purchasing, production, marketing & sales). They accrue when fixed costs can be spread over a large sales volume, when purchasing discounts can be exploited, or when specialization advantages are present. In the pharmaceutical industry, for example, the development of a new drug costs on average $ 500 million. Therefore, a market leader has a huge cost advantage over a new entrant, as it can spread the fixed costs over a larger number of units and thereby reduce unit costs.

• Network effects constitute demand-side benefits of scale and arise when a buyers' benefit increases with the number of customers of a company. Credit card companies are more attractive the more contractual partners they have, and eBay has a competitive advantage because of its huge customer base.

- When customers are highly loyal to a vendor, or when they face high vendor switching costs, it is often difficult for outsiders to enter this market and attract buyers. Amazon.com, for instance, has very high brand recognition and a loyal customer base, which pose barriers for new entrants. In the enterprise resource planning software industry, customers have to invest much time to implement the software, to train the employees, and even to adapt internal processes. Hence, customers are reluctant to change suppliers after such investments.

- Another market entry barrier is capital requirements. Most Internet companies face minimal capital requirements when they enter the market, whereas entry into the auto industry requires billions of investments in R&D, production facilities, and so forth.

- Patented technologies, managerial know-how, access to raw materials, and learning-curve cost advantages are entry barriers independent of size that market leaders often can have.

- A strong market entry barrier can be limited access to distribution channels. In the beverage industry, for instance, restaurant chains usually have long-term contracts with their beer and soft drink suppliers. As a result, it is difficult for a new entrant in this industry to get access to this distribution channel.

- Finally, the government can impose market entry barriers. In Austria for instance, there is strong regulation of the pharmacy market. One person is allowed to own only one pharmacy. There must be a catchment area of a least 5,500 people for each pharmacy. And, there must be a special distance of at least 100 meters between each pharmacy. Obviously, this policy strongly restricts market entry of new competitors.

BARGAINING POWER OF CUSTOMERS. Customers can capture more value when they are able to force prices down and demand better quality or service. Customers have a high bargaining power:

- When customers are highly concentrated. High concentration can be found among grocery retailers in many European countries. In Austria, for example, the three biggest grocery retailers have a market share of more than 75 percent, and in Germany more than 60 percent. The German retailer Aldi (under its brand name Hofer in Austria) takes advantage of its size. Their relatively small outlets carry a limited assortment of only about 700 products (compared to more than 25,000 in a traditional supermarket), of which you find only one brand of sugar, four types of jelly, five types of soap, five types of pasta, and so forth. This strategy enables Aldi to sell more of each product, and therefore to negotiate lower prices. On average, the yearly purchase volume of each product is 30 million Euros, compared to 1.5 million Euros at Walmart.

- When the products of the rivals in the industry are standardized and undifferentiated. 90 percent of Aldi's products are store brands. As a result, its suppliers are interchangeable, and Aldi exerts greater power over them as a result of that interchangeability; if one supplier tries to resist Aldi's pressure, any other will do just as well.

- When there are low switching costs of buyers. This is the case for many undifferentiated components and parts in the automobile industry. The auto manufacturers keep a handful of suppliers, playing them off against each other, as they can easily switch from one supplier to another for these products. The furniture dealer IKEA uses the same strategy. It has more than 1,500 suppliers in 40 countries and some of them sell up to 100 percent of their output to IKEA. As there are relatively low switching costs for IKEA to change suppliers, the Swedish furniture dealer has an enormous bargaining power.

- When backward integration is easy. In that case a customer can continuously threaten to take over this element of the value chain and produce the product himself. In the soft drink industry, producers have long increased their bargaining power over the packaging manufacturers by threatening to produce packaging materials themselves.

Customers are hard negotiators when they are price sensitive. When they are price sensitive, they seek to create pressure to reduce procurement costs. This especially happens when:

- The product represents a significant fraction of the cost structure or the procurement budget.
- Buyers earn low profits or have to cut costs.
- In business to business markets, when the industry's products are inputs to customers own products and the quality of those inputs does not affect the quality of customers' own outputs (the firm's own products to its customer's).

BARGAINING POWER OF SUPPLIERS.   When suppliers have high bargaining power, they can charge higher prices, limit quality or services, and shift costs to their customers. This situation is the flipside of the customer's bargaining power. Therefore, most arguments that have just been made, apply for the bargaining power of suppliers, but now viewed from the perspective of the customer. Suppliers are especially powerful when:

- The supplier group is more concentrated than the industry to which it sells to or even reaches a near-monopoly position.
- The suppliers do not depend on single customers.
- There are high switching costs for customers.
- The products are highly differentiated or specialized to the specific needs of the customer or customer groups.
- There is no affordable substitute for the supplier's products or services.
- Suppliers can threaten to integrate forward, e.g., when customers make too much money compared to the supplier.

THREAT OF SUBSTITUTION.   Ease of substitution strongly reduces an industry's attractiveness and profitability. The threat of substitution is high when an alternative offers an attractive price-performance trade-off and when there are low switching costs to the buyer. ".Pdf" is a threatening substitute for print forms, and it strongly reduces demand in the printing industry. Voice-over IP is a strong substitute for mobile and fixed-line telephony.

RIVALRY AMONG EXISTING COMPETITORS. Rivalry can take numerous forms. It can lead to price wars, increased differentiation efforts, higher speed of innovation—all leading to lower industry profitability. Rivalry among existing competitors is particularly high when there are numerous competitors about the same size attempting to gain dominance over one another. Another factor increasing rivalry is industry growth. When a business is mature, companies can only grow by taking market share from competitors. High exit barriers, the flip side of entry barriers, may prevent companies from leaving the business—despite low profitability. Finally, high price competition can make an industry unattractive. Price competition especially occurs when markets are highly transparent (i.e., customers and competitors can easily see price cuts), when customers are price sensitive, the products are not differentiated, and when customers have low switching costs. If these characteristics are coupled with high fixed costs in an industry and perishable products, price wars are likely to occur. A good example is the airline industry: Fixed costs make up 60–70 percent of the traditional network airline's costs. The product is highly undifferentiated. There are low switching costs for customers, and the product is "perishable." In addition, customers are price sensitive, and, due to Internet booking systems, markets are highly transparent. These factors led to massive price competition in recent years and a major industry shakeout.

STEP 4

Once the industry structure and the major forces driving competition are understood, a careful look at possible future changes in the industry is in order. Five questions are appropriate:

- Do market entry barriers change? Are new entrants attracted?
- Do suppliers change their strategy and structure? Does their bargaining power change?
- Does the customer base change? Do they gain more power?

- Are there any new technologies arising that create new substitutes?
- Does competition change over time?

A helpful model for this analysis is the product lifecycle, which illustrates changing competitive conditions and strategies along the single phases of a lifecycle.

STEP 5

The industry analysis is a useful tool to:[6]

- Identify attractive industries, in which a company can invest

- Understand the forces that shape competition within an industry
- Better understand and predict changes that affect industry structure, profitability and the strategies of competitors
- Assess strengths and weaknesses of competitors in relation to these forces

It can also help managers to understand what they can do to influence the competitive forces, for example, how can market entry barriers be built? How can bargaining power be increased? How can we react to possible substitutes?

Summary

Industry analysis identifies the forces that shape industry attractiveness, especially the intensity of internal rivalry and resulting industry profitability, and the behavior of industry participants. By identifying the specific determinants of rivalry and profitability—customers' and suppliers' bargaining power, market entry barriers, substitution products, and rivalry among competitors—industry dynamics and competitors' strategies can be better understood and predicted.

The five forces analysis has become one of the most important tools in the strategic analysis of businesses and strategy. Some businesses will have the luxury of selecting industries to enter or invest in—others will not. Regardless of whether it is being used to select industries to compete in or simply to understand existing markets and competition, industry analysis within the five forces template is invaluable to strategy development and implementation.

Additional Resources

Day, George. "Assessing Competitive Arenas: Who Are Your Competitors?" In *Wharton on Dynamic Competitive Strategy*, edited by G. Day, D. J. Reibstein, and R. E. Gunther, 23–47. Hoboken, New Jersey: John Wiley & Sons, 1997.

Porter, Michael E. *Competitive Strategy: Techniques for Analyzing Industries and Competitors.* New York: The Free Press, 1980.
———. The Five Competitive Forces That Shape Strategy. *Harvard Business Review.* (January 2008): 78–93.

Endnotes

1. Michael E. Porter, "The five competitive forces that shape strategy," *Harvard Business Review* (January 2008): 78–93.
2. Michael E. Porter, *Competitive Strategy - Techniques for Analyzing Industries and Competitors* (New York: The Free Press, 1980).
3. Porter, "The five competitive forces."
4. Adapted from Porter, "The Five Competitive Forces"; figure is at page 80.

5. George Day, "Assessing Competitive Arenas: Who are your competitors?" in Wharton on dynamic competitive strategy, ed. G. Day, D. J. Reibstein, and R. E. Gunther (Hoboken, New Jersey: John Wiley & Sons, 1997), 23–47.
6. Gerry Johnson, Kevin Scholes, and Richard Whittington, *Exploring Corporate Strategy: Text & cases* (Harlow, England: Prentice Hall, 2008).

The Product Life Cycle

Every market is new at some point; *it has to start somewhere*. After that, inevitably, it evolves; and some important aspects of that evolution are similar across all or at least most markets. Every product moves through an introduction phase, a growth phase, a maturity phase, and ends with a decline phase. Each of these phases is characterized by changes in demand, competition, marketing tasks, and decisions. These changes during the "product life cycle" can be generalized across markets, and understanding *and anticipating* those changes is important for planning and for effectively adapting marketing strategies. This note summarizes: (1) the market factors that change as markets evolve; and (2) the effects of those changes on marketing strategies and on the marketing mix.

One essential proviso is that, in order to understand the product life cycle for any market, it is essential to first *define the market or the product under consideration*. Understanding life cycle effects at the various coexisting levels of the industry, the market, the product category, and the version allows for valid and valuable inferences. That is, there are life-cycle effects underlying the evolution of an industry, a specific market, a product form, and individual products. Each of these life cycles can provide insight for marketing strategy and tactics. But it is also important to keep the level of analysis in mind in identifying and drawing conclusions from changes in the market. An industry life cycle, such as that of the telecommunication industry, is much longer than a product life cycle, such as that of a specific generation of cell phones. And demand for a specific generation of cell phones depends on more specific factors (e.g., technology, price, competition), than demand for telecommunication in general that depends more on general need for telecommunication. It is also worth noting that not all products, and certainly not all industries, enter a "decline" stage in the life cycle. While industries such as beer and clothing have matured, and markets for beer are somewhat shrinking, these are really extended, and perhaps eternal, "maturities" rather than true declines. On the other hand, product forms such as "ice" beer and bell-bottom trousers have very specific life cycles ("fad" life cycles) that grow, mature, and decline toward obsolete fairly quickly.

CHANGES IN MARKETS ACROSS THE PRODUCT LIFE CYCLE

The single phases of a product life cycle differ in a number of important characteristics such as competition and assortment, customer behavior, segment configuration, distribution, etc. In the following sections we describe these characteristics.

Competition and Product Assortment

Initially there are very few offerings in any market. A market must begin with a single offering—at some point, someone offers *the very first version* of any new product, even if other entrants follow quickly. As a market grows, more firms offer more alternatives. Because consumers tend to be price insensitive in introductory and growth stages—they're still focused on the new benefits—margins tend to be high and those high margins attract competition and investment, including investment in production capacity to meet the growing demand for high-margin sales. During the growth phase, entry of each new competitor means the expansion of available assortment, and, importantly, each competitor offers a wider and wider variety of products, creating a rapid profusion in the variety of products available—and intensifying the rivalry for customers and for distribution (discussed below).

Eventually growth decreases and markets enter "maturity." One problem as a market enters maturity is that, production forecasters often miss the "inflection point" and regularly build capacity as if markets will continue to grow, if not forever, at least beyond the point that growth actually slows. This inevitably causes "pain" in the form of *excess capacity*. If competitors' excess capacity cannot be converted to other uses, for example, by producing other products with the same production facilities or by selling those facilities to other industries, those competitors will try to stimulate demand to maintain production, and

they tend to do so by lowering prices. Thus, competitors who would not otherwise resort to price competition end up "wrecking the market" in order to utilize their capacity—capacity that should not have been built in the first place.

These changes in the competitive landscape lead to some predictable changes in profitability (shown in Figure 9-1). Early in the product life cycle, firms must invest in order to develop products and to open markets. These investments represent negative profitability for the industry in the early stages. During the growth stage, firms take advantage of the investments and the product's newness to command fair margins and to reap profits. Profitability usually carries on into the early maturity stage. Later, in the late maturity stage and the decline stages, when industry-wide capacity is at its peak and as customers come to expect core benefits (discussed below), margins narrow, and price competition emerges to reduce profits. Nevertheless, average industry profits over any extended period should rarely be negative; that is, an industry will not lose money for long. Although increased price-based competition is typical, almost inescapable, and margins will necessarily narrow, competitors and rivals will exit an industry characterized by losses over any extended period.

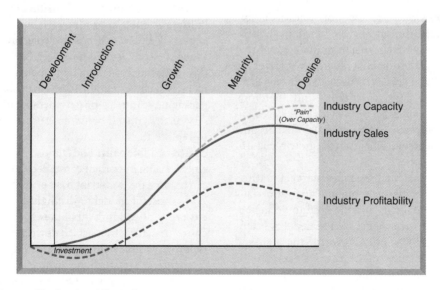

FIGURE NOTE 9-1   The Product Life Cycle

Customer Behavior and Segment Configuration

Across product categories, whether they are new technologies or not, several important changes in consumer behaviors emerge as the markets evolve; the most basic of these are simply logical and inevitable. In markets for truly-new products, that is, the markets for disruptive or "discontinuous" innovations, initial sales growth may be slow. Many consumers wait to see new products in use by others—that is, the majority usually prefers to "imitate" others rather than innovate. The rate of "penetration" or "diffusion" will accelerate as more consumers use a product and thereby create more opportunities for imitators to observe the product in use. That growth may literally be exponential in some phases for some markets, if a consumer shows the product to three others, and those three each buy it and tell three others who all tell three more, and so on; *but*, because markets and consumer resources are never unlimited, those periods of high growth do not last forever and, in some cases, may be very short-lived.

One important certainty about consumers and the product life cycle is that, as the life cycle progresses, consumers become more familiar with the product. Consumers are initially inexperienced with a product, but, as the market evolves, customers gain experience and expertise; inevitably, consumers' needs become more specific as they become more knowledgeable and sophisticated. Consumers who were initially satisfied by one basic offering begin to understand that they'd rather have a somewhat different version of the product or technology—something that more specifically meets *their* particular needs—and, therefore, *segments emerge from what were, in the early stages, undifferentiated markets*. Single segments often become two or more different segments in the growth phase of the product life cycle.

It is also true that, as some markets mature, multiple segments merge or join into one—especially as technology progresses and the need to decide between options in the product is alleviated. For example, in the late 1980s, BMW "owned" the high-end luxury/prestige segment of the American automobile market. "Yuppies" drove BMWs and accepted their high maintenance costs and lack of reliability as un-

avoidable. Then, in the early 1990s, Toyota introduced the Lexus brand of luxury sedans; Lexus's offerings were highly reliable and came with extraordinary service. The high-end luxury segment split into high-end performance (which BMW continued to dominate) and high-end reliability/comfort (won by Lexus). Lexus was positioned as a "cocoon" from the outside world.[1] In the early twenty-first century, however, BMW and others, such as Audi and Mercedes Benz, began to match Lexus's service and reliability, and segments that had been differentiable began to blur. An assortment of manufacturers took advantage of advances in production technologies to offer similarly reliable and comfortable cars with similar performance. It might be more accurate to say that the segments reconfigured, rather than merged. Luxury car buyers in America are still heterogeneous—and are still different from European luxury car buyers—but the basis of segmentation changed toward brand image and other differences.

Another factor that tends to drive a shift toward price-based competition across the product life cycle (along with over capacity, discussed above) is the fact that the attributes of a product that began as new-to-the-world and capable of differentiating one offering from another, eventually—sometimes very quickly—become "old hat." These benefits become expected as competition matches performance, making the benefits some "must have" attributes instead of "delighters"—that is, product attributes that are not expected and which positively surprise customers. When the core benefits have been "commoditized" in this way, other benefits, augmentations, and improvements—such as additional features or convenience and packaging features—or peripheral benefits—such as service, design, and brand image/social status—begin to replace the core benefits as drivers of consumer choice. Additionally, and almost inescapably, *price* emerges as an important consumer choice variable and can become the dominant basis of competition.

A useful model to distinguish between different types of product attributes is Kano's model of customer satisfaction, which describes three different types of product characteristics (see Figure 9-2). "Delighters" are attributes that cause satisfaction or even excitement if delivered, but that do not necessarily lead to dissatisfaction if not delivered. They are

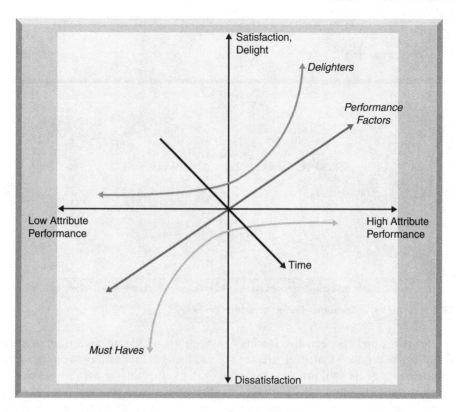

FIGURE NOTE 9-2 Kano's Model of Customer Satisfaction[2]

not explicitly expected and articulated. Overhead display in cars is an example. "Must haves" (basic factors) are minimum requirements that a product must fulfill. They do not lead to satisfaction if fulfilled, but lead to dissatisfaction if not present. An example is the brakes of a car. "Performance factors" are those attributes that lead both to dissatisfaction or satisfaction depending on how well they perform: The higher the product performance, the higher the satisfaction, the lower the performance, the lower the satisfaction. An example is fuel consumption of a car, battery life of a laptop, or resolution of a digital camera. This model is dynamic, that is, the three types of attributes change over time. What delights customers today (not expected product attributes, but those that surprise customers and create a "WOW-effect") become explicit expectations after some time and turn into "must haves".

These changes in the market and consumer behaviors are also related to a reality about research and development investments and returns. The rela-

tionship between inputs and outputs in research and development and new product development forms an "S-curve," which is a classic case of the "production function" relating inputs to outputs and of the law of "diminishing margin returns". Small investments may be inadequate to realize *any* results and getting started requires investment, but then there is a range of investments that will realize substantial advances. Eventually when the "low fruit" has been harvested and the most accessible innovations discovered, the successive generations of breakthroughs become more and more difficult to realize. Thus, at the same time when customers may be taking the old technology for granted, it becomes more expensive and takes longer to bring new technologies to market, further emphasizing the migration toward non-core features and peripherals.

Thus, as product life cycles evolve, so do the drivers of consumer preferences and choice (see Figure 9-3). Early in the life cycle consumers focus

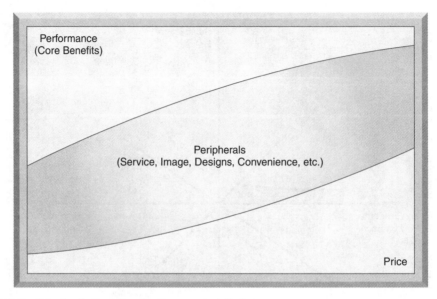

FIGURE NOTE 9-3 Criterion in Consumer Preferences and Choice

on product performance and core benefits. During growth and especially product maturity, greater consideration is given to "peripheral" product attributes such as service, comfort, convenience, nonfunctional design, and the like. Most importantly, price emerges as a more and more important decision criterion as the product life cycle moves forward; and price often becomes the *dominant* decision driver for many consumers in the later stages of the life cycle. This is especially true when core product attributes and benefits are so commoditized that they appear, largely, the same across alternatives (Figure 9-2). Attributes go from delighters/motivators (things that exceed customer expectations and move consumers to action) toward "must-haves" (things that consumers expect and take for granted), and the absence of a "must have" can dissatisfy customers, but the presence of which rarely satisfies or delights. This process of commoditization denotes a competitive environment where (1) product differentiation becomes very difficult, (2) customer loyalty and brand preferences erode, (3) competition is based primarily on price, and (4) where competitive advantages come from cost leadership[3]. As products move into the maturity phase of the life cycle, commoditization becomes a likely threat. There are basically three ways to delay the forces of commoditization: (1) Innovate: Introduce a new product with

new difficult to imitate features or upgrade existing product; (2) Bundle: Sell the commoditized product with a differentiated ancillary service that increases the value of the product (e.g., after-sales service) and motivates consumers to pay a price premium for more convenience; and (3) Segment: Try to segment the mature market and address customers that are less price-sensitive[4].

CHANNELS OF DISTRIBUTION. Gaining shelf space in traditional channels of distribution is a challenge for the most proven of brands. Getting distribution for new and unproven products that frequently require augmented customer service and "customer education" is especially challenging and creates a natural constraint on channel penetration in the introductory stages of the product life cycle. Often, new products are distributed through specialty channels, where sales staff have a particular interest and expertise in the product category; specialty sales clerks are often "product enthusiasts" themselves and serve as facilitators and even opinion leaders in their category. As a product gains acceptance, that acceptance and "track record" in the market combined with the substantial margins realized during the growth stage facilitate greater channel acceptance. Nevertheless, as markets grow, so does the competition and each competitors' assortment—leading to clutter and increased competition for shelf space amongst competitors, even as the overall product-category shelf space grows. In maturity, *fewer customers need the "hand holding"* that was necessary for early market offerings, and, as discussed above, more competitors tend to emphasize price; therefore, mass and lower-service retailers dominate the trade and discounters become a bigger factor. The emergence of Wal-mart as the dominant retailer in America, Aldi as the similar channel captain in Central Europe, and other large-scale discounters around the world, such as Tesco in the UK and Carrefour in Western Europe, have exacerbated and accelerated this "class-to-mass" effect across consumer-goods categories, leading to earlier and earlier emphasis on discounters. In later maturity and in decline, no-frills "discounters" and, more recently, direct retailers ("e-tailers") dominate many channels of distribution.

Summary of Changes in Market

Some basic logical and underlying realities drive a general market evolution or product life cycle (Figure 9-1), and there are predictable, although not uniform, patterns that provide important insight into what to expect as markets are created and as they grow, mature, and eventually decline (summarized in Table 9-1). The product life cycle forms an S-curve, demonstrating slow initial take-off, leading toward accelerated growth, but then, eventually, to slowing, maturity, and even decline as the market becomes saturated and alternatives are introduced. These changes in the market have important implications for viable marketing strategies and for the marketing mix—things that work in one stage may not work in another, and recognizing "inflection points" can generate great strategic advantage.

STRATEGIC IMPLICATIONS

Generic strategy frameworks generally stress two dimensions of strategy—competitive scope and competitive advantage. This book emphasizes these two as "who to serve/what need to meet" and "how to serve those customers/needs better than the competition and at a profit". Those two-dimensional frameworks are useful in organizing and summarizing changes in marketing strategies across the product life cycle; some strategies become more common and may generally be more effective (although it should be noted that the full range of strategies are often present in some form at most product-life cycle stages). Those generic strategy taxonomies do *not* isolate innovation as a separate dimension of strategy—the output of innovation is subsumed by "differentiation"—but it may be useful to view innovation as a

TABLE NOTE 9-1 Market Characteristics Across the Product Life Cycle

	Introduction	Growth	Maturity	Decline
Competition	None to limited	Growing; Larger players attracted	Intense	Concentrating and contracting
Industry capacity	Low; building	Increasing	Over capacity	Contracting capacity
Products	One to limited	Assortment/Variety increasing	Proliferation	Contraction/Consolidation
Customers/Benefits sought	Unsophisticated, uneducated, unaware	More sophisticated; Greater homogeneity More demanding	Price consciousness	Price Dominant
Segments	Gross	Emergence and Clarification		Agglomeration
Customer choice drivers (also see Figure II-8-2)	Core product benefits are delighters	Differentiate by new attributes (delighters); copycats emulate	Core benefits migrate toward "must haves."	Commoditization of core benefits; Differentiate by new, noncore attributes
Channels	Limited availability; Specialty	Broader distribution	Mass, discount and direct	More limited; Discount and Direct

TABLE NOTE 9-2 Marketing Strategies Across the Product Life Cycle

Dimension of Strategy	Stage in the Life Cycle			
	Introduction	**Growth**	**Maturity**	**Decline**
Scope (Who? What? Where?)	Targeting innovators and early-adopters but often via "shotgun" marketing mix.	Growing segments and greater heterogeneity; Opportunities for niche and mass strategies	Niche opportunities remain but become limited; **Mass dominates**.	Profitable survivor (consolidation)
Differential Advantage (What? Why?)	Core benefits (**Performance**) Speed-to-market	*Differentiation: core benefits*	*Differentiation: Peripheral benefits* **Price**	*Price*
Innovation	**Paramount;** "Basic" research and discontinuous breakthroughs	Differentiating/Features Innovation	Continuous innovation; Incremental benefits	Innovate to extend life cycle or breakthrough to new category

third dimension of strategy, when considering changes in viable and typical strategies across the life cycle. That is, strategies can be distinguished by the (1) scope of customers/needs they target, (2) basis of competition (differentiation versus cost/price), and also (3) *degree of innovation*, and these three characteristics of strategies are useful in considering what sorts of strategies are typically deployed and are most effective across the product life cycle.

Early in the product life cycle the scope of competition is notable, because the markets are small and narrow; however, the focus of most marketing programs must often be broad, because consumers are unfamiliar with the product and they cannot articulate the need. Marketing research, therefore, is challenging. It is difficult to focus communications and distribution even though the target segments—innovators and early adopters—are inherently narrow. As the market moves through introduction toward growth, it becomes broader and more differentiable—that is, there are more customers and they are organized into more distinct segments. As discussed above, when markets move toward maturity these segments become dynamic, and they are likely to split into more subsegments as consumers become more familiar with their needs and with the availability of product alternatives; however, but they may also merge as product features become less distinct and technology "overwhelms" the core needs. Finally, in terms of competitive advantage, early stages of the product life cycle emphasize innovation. The growth

stage is driven by firms attempting to differentiate their offerings in consumer perceptions. Later in the life cycle, innovation becomes less salient and becomes different. Instead of searching for and exploiting fundamental breakthroughs driven by basic research, firms focus on incremental innovation—new features and the adaptation and convergence of existing technologies—improvements that result from applied research and new product development. These strategic implications are summarized in Table 9-2.

TACTICAL IMPLICATIONS

The life cycle-related changes in the market, discussed above, and the different strategies firms pursue across the life cycle drive changes in the type of marketing mix and offerings that a firm can effectively offer. These implications are spelled out in Table II-8-3 and described in this section.

Introduction

Because the product life cycle's beginning is defined by a single new and innovative product, the number of products in the early stages is necessarily limited and focused on the new technology and its core benefits ("product performance"; see Figure 9-3). There are two basic pricing strategies that a firm may adopt in the introductory stage: (1) skimming and (2) penetration pricing. Skimming takes advantage of the newness of the technology and the relative advantage of the innovation to demand ("skim") higher prices and margins. Penetration involves low pricing intended to gain market penetration and the ensuing benefits of scale, brand awareness, and "installed base"—that is, lower penetration prices are designed to quickly gain as much market share as possible and should be supported with some assumed benefits of early market share. Early in the life cycle, promotions can rely on word of mouth more than at other stages—risk-averse customers are more likely to be persuaded by interpersonal communications (and observations of others adopting the product), and the early-adopters of something that is truly new are more likely to talk about it and pass along information. The channel strategy of any particular firm in a new market may be shaped by existing channel strengths and distribution coverage of similar products.

Growth

The growth stage emphasizes differentiation—as a strategy and across the elements of a marketing program. Product alternatives proliferate—new entrants bring new offerings and existing competitors offer a wider variety of products. Channels become more accessible to the category as it gains acceptance and wider market penetration, but competition within the category for space and attention within the channels becomes more intense. Prices supports fair margins but increased competition prevents exorbitant returns. Gaining market share in the growth stages is paramount in preparation for maturity and price competition. Market share leads to scale effects (economies of scale and learning) and grabbing market share in the early growth stage is less difficult than later in the life cycle.

Maturity

The maturity stage in the product life cycle is marked by increasing price competition evident in increasing consumer and trade promotions (i.e., price deals for customers and volume or price deals for channel partners, especially retailers in consumer goods channels and distributors in business channels). It is also characterized by an emphasis on peripheral benefits and new features on existing core products, brand-reinforcing communications programs (image-building and reminder) along with those price promotions, and accelerating product-form cycles. Customers no longer require education or "hand holding," they're familiar with the product, its underlying technology, and their own preferences across configurations. Therefore, mass and discount channels as well as low- to no-touch (direct) channels gain share, especially vis-à-vis high-support channels, such as specialty stores. Importantly, attention to loyalty-building tactics and customer satisfaction in this and earlier stages can drive significant competitive advantages in the maturity stage. That is, entering the maturity stage with a strong base of loyal customers or building that base in maturity can be a significant competitive advantage as markets move toward more intense rivalry with products that are inherently more difficult to differentiate.

Decline

Not all products enter a true decline stage—at least not inevitably. We have emphasized the notion that changes in underlying market realities (especially changes in the competitive landscape, and in the consumers' relationship with the product) inexorably drive changes in viable marketing strategies and effective marketing tactics, but it may be true that firm decisions and choices across marketing strategies actually accelerate the product life cycle in some instances. That is, the decline stage may, in some ways, be a "self-fulfilling prophecy"; once the competitor(s) in an industry decide that the industry is in a decline mode, their actions—especially withdrawing support for innovation and initiating price competition, may actually cause or at least exacerbate the decline. That is, forecasts of decline become a "self-fulfilling prophecy." Competitors "wreck the market" by moving too quickly and too willingly toward price competition, and viable entrants withdraw brand-building support in favor of harvesting profits from mature products (and shifting investment and attention toward "stars" and potential stars). In the maturity and decline stages of the product life cycle, viable strategies that are too often overlooked include consolidating brands into a "profitable survivor" portfolio (accumulating brands and encouraging exit by acquiring the competition and seeking benefits of scale across the expanded assortment), retrenching around core profitable and loyal

TABLE NOTE 9-3 Marketing Tactics Across the Product Life Cycle

	Introduction	Growth	Maturity	Decline
Products	Limited	Expand Assortment; Differentiated, especially by features	Full Assortment; Augmented with Service	Fewer; Technology may overwhelm and blur consumer needs
Price	Skimming or Penetration	Full (Collect margins and profits)	Increasingly Competitive	Price-based competition/Deal
Promotion	Informative; may be product category related more than specific product or brand. Interpersonal communications (and observations) very important. Public relations most viable.	Differentiation; Advertising and promotions geared to distinguishing products and brands.	Reminder/Competitive; Proliferation of price promotions	Reminder/Price
Distribution	Limited; Emphasis on specialty and on high service/high customer education	Expanding	Broadest; Shifting toward discount and lower service/less to no customer education.	Contracting; low to no service/support.

customers (which may move a "mass" or "multiple" segmentation scheme toward a focused or niche approach), and augmenting "commoditized" products with innovative new features and services rather than succumbing to the apparent inevitability of mutually-destructive price wars.

RECOGNIZING "INFLECTION POINTS"

All of these observations about differences in markets, strategies, and tactics across the product life cycle are of no value if the manager cannot recognize the stage of the life cycle a product offering is in and, especially, if the strategist cannot *anticipate and prepare for life cycle changes*. Generally, the introductory stage is obvious—the new technology emerges and receives media coverage. One of the attributes of the introductory and early-growth stages is the willingness of media to respond to public relations efforts with coverage; and sales begin slowly but accelerate as channel coverage expands. The move from growth toward maturity is less obvious and often more relevant to strategy and strategic success. Besides moderating sales growth—which is the definition of the passage from growth toward maturity, but which may often be disguised as a temporary adjustment or attributed

to external factors such as general economic cycles—there are several markers of maturity:[5]

- *Price Competition.* As discussed, two phenomena that may be harbingers of market maturity are the building of too much capacity at the industry level and the commoditization of core benefits in a category. Commoditization here refers to the fact and the perception by customers that all products deliver the same benefits. As discussed, these two phenomena lead toward price competition. Increased price competition or even just signs that price competition may be imminent should be forewarnings that maturity is imminent.
- *Buyer Sophistication.* Whether price competition seems imminent or not, increased buyer sophistication is an indicator of maturing markets. Sophisticated buyers tend to be better shoppers, buying what they need and unfazed by—and in fact unwilling to pay for—features or services that aren't relevant to them. Knowledgeable customers need little information and less service.
- *Substitutes Emerge.* Another mark of a maturing market is not only increasingly intense

rivalry amongst existing competitors but also increased availability of substitutes and increased buyer willingness to consider substitutes. This buyer acceptance of substitutes is a market condition related to increased sophistication and understanding of core needs. The availability of substitutes is an external condition that may *cause* maturity (it is not a result of maturity).

• ***Market Saturation/Fewer Growth Opportunities.*** Growth markets are driven by trial—large numbers of first time users being introduced to and then adopting the new product. In mature markets, most customers have tried the product and either adopted it or rejected it, and there are fewer opportunities to

grow via first-time trial, by developing new markets, or by targeting new segments.

• ***Customer Disinterest.*** Finally, a large segment of an active market being indifferent toward the technology or category is an indication of maturity. As discussed, it is relatively easy to gain media coverage for truly new products, and that is not only true for high-technology innovations. As markets move toward maturity, fewer mainstream media (in comparison to industry specific media) *are interested in* covering offerings and events in the sector. By the time markets reach maturity, buyer and media attention is elsewhere and the product is "yesterday's news." Signs that interest is waning may be warnings of impending maturity.

Summary

Product markets emerge, grow, mature, and decline over time. The product life cycle represents the typical moves of a product through these four phases and shows how sales volume, competition, and profits evolve. Thus, understanding the product life cycle is essential. The product life cycle stage fundamentally determines and constrains strategic and tactical alternatives. The single phases are characterized by differences in the competitive environment, priorities in strategic objectives, and cost and profit structures. Therefore, marketing programs must be adapted to the changing characteristics and challenges of each life cycle phase. Monitoring the environment for signals that a market may be approaching an inflection point, moving from one stage to another, particularly from growth to maturity, can offer crucial strategic advantage.

Additional Resources

Carpenter, Mason A., and Wm. Gerard Sanders. *Strategic Management. A Dynamic Perspective.* Upper Saddle River, NJ: Pearson Education, 2009.

Christensen, Clayton M., and Michael E. Raynor. *How to Avoid Commoditization.* Boston: Harvard Business School Press, 2003.

Hambrick, Donald C., Ian A. MacMillan, and Diana I. Day. "Strategic Attributers and Performance in the BCG Matrix: A PIMS-Based Analysis of Industrial Product Businesses" *Academy of Management Journal* 25, 3 (September 1982): 510–531.

Moore, Geoffrey A. *Crossing the Chasm* (Revised ed.). New York: Harper Perennial, 1999.

Moschis, George P. *Marketing Strategies for the Mature Market.* Westport, CT: Quorum, 1994.

Endnotes

1. Camilla Palmer, "Saatchi Creates Lexus 'Cocoon,' " *Campaign* 17 (May 3, 2002): 6.

2. Adapted from K. Matzler, H. H. Hinterhuber, F. Bailom, and E. Sauerwein, "How to Delight Your Customers," *Journal of Product and Band Management* 5, (1996): 6–18.

3. Henry Birdseye Weil, "Commoditization of Technology-based Products and Services: A Generic Model of Market Dynamics," (Working Paper # 144–96, The International Center for Research on the Management of Technology, Sloan School of Management, MIT, 1996).

4. John Quelch, *When Your Product Becomes a Commodity* (2007), http://hbswk.hbs.edu/pdf/item/5830.pdf. Last accessed on February 2, 2010.

5. Adapted from David Aaker, *Strategic Market Management*, 8th ed. (Hoboken, NJ: John Wiley & Sons, 2008), 65–66.

10

Experience Curve Effects on Cost Reduction

"Any customer can have a car painted any color that he wants so long as it is black," said Henry Ford about the Model T, the most influential car of the twentieth century. With his Model T, Henry Ford wanted to create a car that "will be low in price that no man making a good salary will be unable to own one—and enjoy with his family the blessing of hours of pleasure in God's great open spaces." By standardizing the product and taking advantage of cost savings through mass production, the price dropped from $850 when it was introduced in 1909, to $260 in the 1924.[1] Looking at the prices and the cumulative number of cars produced over time, one can note a remarkable relationship: Every time the cumulative output doubled, the prices of the car dropped by 15 percent (see Figure 10-1).

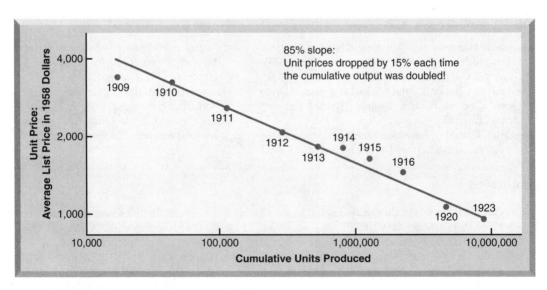

FIGURE NOTE 10-1   Price of Model T, 1909–1923[2]

EXPERIENCE CURVE EFFECTS AND UNIT COSTS

Henry Ford took advantage of an empirical general-ization, which the consulting firm BCG (Boston Consulting Group) later coined as the "experience curve." After observing the behaviour of unit costs in a number of industries like bottle caps, refrigerators, and integrated circuits, BCG generalized the regular-ity of reductions in unit costs with increased cumu-lative output in its "Law of Experience." Costs of value added (total cost per unit of production less the cost per unit of production of bought-in compo-nents and materials) decline by a fixed percent in real terms each time accumulated experience is doubled.[3]

Consider the example of the Photovoltaic Technology. In the 1950s, photovoltaic (PV) technol-ogy, commonly known as "solar cells," was developed to provide long-term power for satellites. The PV mod-ules house an array of solar cells that deliver direct cur-rent power. In the 1970s, companies started to offer PV technology for commercial applications (Harmon, 2000). Starting with a cumulative installed base of 15 MW_p (=Megawatt peak, where "peak watt" is de-fined as the power of full sunlight at sea level on a clear day) in 1983, the annual average growth rate was 15–16 percent. In 1995, the cumulative installed capac-ity reached 579 MW, which corresponded to just .02 percent of the global power generating capacity, and

TABLE NOTE 10-1 Cumulative Production and Costs for PV Technology

Cumulative PV Module shipments in MW_p	Module Costs (1994$/$W_p$)
0.25	51
0.5	41
1	32
2	26
4	20
8	16
16	13
32	10
64	8
128	7
256	5
512	4
1024	3,4

941 MW_p in 1998.[4] Table 10-1 shows the cumulative installed PV technology and the cost of a PV module, measured in dollars-per-peak-watt ($/$W_p$).[5] In 1976, at the outset of commercialization, module costs were $51/$W_p$; in 1998, it was $3.50/$W_p$. Applying the expe-rience curve to PV technology, it can be seen that the average "learning rate" (experience-curve effect) is 20.2 percent. Thus, every time the cumulative output is doubled, unit costs are reduced to 79.8 percent.

Figures 10-2 and 10-3 shows the experience-curve effect graphically. In the upper diagram the

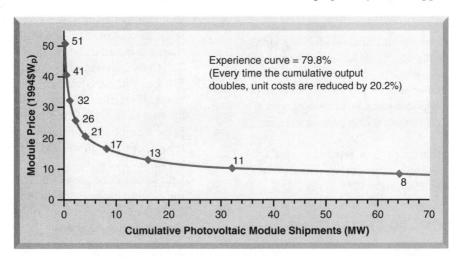

FIGURE NOTE 10-2 Experience Curve of Photovoltaic Technology

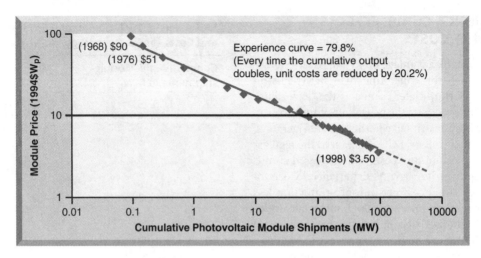

FIGURE NOTE 10-3 Experience Curve of Photovoltaic Technology

TABLE NOTE 10-2 Experience Curves for Selected Industries[6]

Industry	Experience Curve
Microprocessors	60%
LCDs	60%
Airlines	75%
Personal Computers	77%
DVD players/recorders	78%
Cars	81%
Color TVs	83%

vertical axis shows the unit costs (as of 1994) and the horizontal axis the accumulated volume of production. In the lower diagram, the relationship between the accumulated volume of production and the deflated unit costs is expressed in a log-log graph as a straight line, expressing a 79.8 percent experience curve.

The experience curve is dependent on the industry. Table 10-2 gives some examples of experience curves in different industries.

IMPLICATIONS FOR MARKETING

These experience curve effects occur as cost savings and are gained through activities such as learning, technical progress, product and process improvement,

specialization and redesign of labor, etc. It is important to note, however, that such cost reductions do not occur automatically; they require management and can be achieved only if all learning and improvement opportunities are exploited. The experience curve has a number of important implications:

- Growth is not an option in many markets. If a company grows slower than its competitors it has to expect a cost disadvantage.
- If market shares do not change over time, unit costs of competitors will remain the same.
- Profitability depends on experience curve effects, hence companies with higher market share can expect a higher return on investment
- The first-mover advantage can be important. Especially in industries with high experience-curve effects, first movers can try to gain market share quickly, create a cost advantage and prevent competitors from entering the industry by reducing prices along the experience curve.
- Unit costs can be predicted. This is important for a company's competitive strategy (especially the cost-leadership strategy) and valuable for pricing decisions.

Consider this example: There are three major and one smaller producer of Solar Cells. The experience curve is 79.8 percent. All of them had unit costs of $10

TABLE NOTE 10-3 Cost and Volume Comparisons of Selected Levels of Competition

Competitor	Cumulated production Volume (MW)	Sales volume in 2008	Market Share (%)	Unit Costs	Margin @ Unit Price $4.0
A	400	40	50	2.43	1.7
B	200	20	25	3.01	.99
C	100	10	12,5	3.77	.23
D	100	10	12,5	3.77	.23
	800	80			

when they entered the industry with a production volume of 5 MW (Table 10-3).

Figure 10-4 shows the experience curve and the relative cost position for each competitor. Given the current industry price, competitor A has the highest margin. Strategically, he could either take advantage of the higher return on investment and invest in further product or process improvement, or he could lower his prices, for example to $3.5. In that case he would still earn enough money and gain market share. Competitor C and D would not be able to produce and to sell at a profit and might decide to go out of business. Then, if competitor A continuously reduces his prices along the experience curve, he would prevent other competitors from entering the industry.

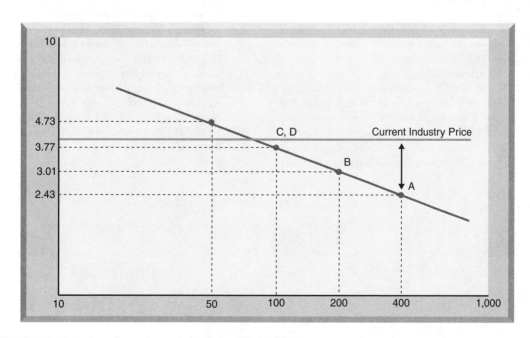

FIGURE NOTE 10-4   Experience Curve and Relative Cost Position

Summary

As companies get more experienced in the production of a product (or in any task), they *learn* and *become more efficient* at it. The associated cost savings have been labelled experience curve effects (or "learning curve effects"). Every time the cumulated output is doubled, unit costs drop at a regular rate. Computing and taking advantage of experience curve effects have important strategic marketing implications. It allows for the prediction of unit costs, it grounds the formulation of pricing strategies, it serves to help estimate competitor's cost advantages or disadvantages, and it can provide the firm with substantial and enduring cost advantages. Those cost advantages can be passed on as a price advantage (savings) from the customer's perspective, which should lead to higher unit sales, higher market share, and even greater experience (in a "virtuous circle") or reaped in higher margins and higher returns. The experience curve has become a major concept especially for companies that pursue a cost-leadership strategy.

Additional Resources:

Abernathy, William J., and Kenneth Wayne. "Limits of the Learning Curve." *Harvard Business Review* (September–October, 1974): 109–119.

Buzzell, Robert, and Bradley Gale. *The PIMS Principles: Linking Strategy to Performance.* New York: Free Press, 1987.

Carpenter, Mason A., and Wm. Gerard Sanders. *Strategic Management. A Dynamic Perspective.* Upper Saddle River, NJ: Pearson/Prentice Hall, 2009.

Swieringa, Joop, and Andre Wierdsma. *Becoming a Learning Organization: Beyond the Learning Curve.* Upper Saddle River, NJ: Addison-Wesley.

Endnotes

1. http://en.wikipedia.org/wiki/Model_T. Last accessed on July 28, 2008

2. Adapted from W. J. Abernathy and K. Wayne, "Limits of the learning curve," *Harvard Business Review* (September–October, 1974): 109–119.

3. B. Henderson,3/2006 "The Experience Curve Reviewed: History," in Carl W. Stern and Michael S. Deimler eds., *Perspectives on Strategy from The Boston Consulting Group* (New York: John Wiley & Sons, 2006), 12–14 and B. Henderson (1974/2006), "The Experience Curve Reviewed: Why Does It Work," in Carl W. Stern and Michael S. Deimler, eds., *Perspectives on Strategy from The Boston Consulting Group* (New York: John Wiley & Sons, 2006), 15–17.

4. C. Harmon, "Experience curves of photovoltaic technology" (Institute of Applied Systems Analysis, Laxenburg, Austria, 2000), unpublished manuscript.

5. Based on data used by Harmon, and estimations for missing data based on Harmon's computed overall experience curve effect of 20.2%.

6. Gottfredson M. Gottfredson, S. Schaubert, and H. Saenz, "The New Leader's Guide to Diagnosing The Business," *Harvard Business Review* (February 2008): 63–73.

Economies and Diseconomies of Scale

Former CEO of General Electric Jack Welch had an iron rule: "First, second, or out!" Each strategic business unit (SBU) was to achieve the first or the second market position—in terms of market share—or be divested or closed. Behind this dictum lay a simple observation: Return on investment is closely related to market share. In other words, size matters. Market leaders are usually more efficient than firms with lower share because they benefit from economies of scale. Economies of scale exist when each 1 percent increase in production volume results in an increase of less than 1 percent in the total cost of production. Each new unit, therefore, is less expensive to produce than the previous one. Economies drive industry concentration or consolidation, causing many markets like the car industry, airlines, the pharmaceutical industry, the telecommunications industry, aircraft production, and many others to be dominated by a few industry giants. These giants are often referred to as the "eight-hundred-pound guerrillas." Advertising costs in the United States soft drink industry is a good example of the effects of economies of scale (see Figure 11-1).[1]

A sixty-second television commercial can cost more than $5 million to produce. Coke and Pepsi spread those costs over a much larger sales volume. And they then negotiate volume discounts with the advertising agencies that produce the ads and the media (television networks) that run the ads. Therefore, advertising expenditures per case are below five cents, compared to about twenty cents for Schweppes, the producers of ginger ale and other mixers. Economies of scale can be achieved in a number of ways:[3]

1. *Cost Spreading.* This is particularly important in industries with high fixed costs. Examples of high fixed costs include research and development (R&D) costs in the pharmaceutical industry, high advertisement costs in the fast-moving consumer goods industry, and high manufacturing overhead (plant and equipment) in the auto industry.

   For example, development of the largest passenger airliner in the world, the Airbus A380, cost about €12 billion (roughly $18 billion US dollars). It was estimated that Airbus must sell 250 airplanes to break even; €48 million in R&D costs per unit. If Airbus sells 500 A380s, the development costs *per unit* would be cut in half. To benefit from economies of scale companies with high

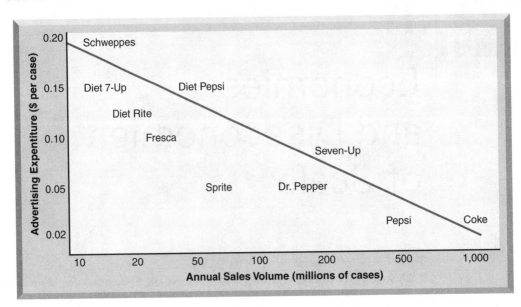

FIGURE NOTE 11-1   Economies of Scale in Advertising: The U.S. Soft Drink Industry[2]

fixed costs usually try to maximize volume output by serving very broad, even global market segments.

2. *Purchasing Power.* Another source of scale economies are the volume discounts that companies receive due to the size of their purchases and their bargaining power with vendors. Supermarket chains, fast food chains, car manufacturers and many other big companies are able to gain price and service concessions from suppliers due to the sheer volume of their purchases in both units and in dollars. Wal-Mart, the largest retailer ($400 billion in sales) in the world, is well known for using its purchasing power to achieve lower costs than many of its competitors.

3. *Specialization of Labor.* Economies of scale also occur because large companies with high volumes of production can divide labor into discrete activities which then are performed more efficiently. When complex processes are broken down into a few repeatable tasks performed by specialized workers with specialized equipment, time loss from switching from one activity to the next is avoided, and automation is possible.

4. *Specialization of Technology.* Large companies have more capital and can more easily afford expensive machines and technology that bring costs down.

Diseconomies of scale occur when various kinds of forces cause larger firms to produce goods and services at increased per-unit costs. In other words, each 1 percent increase in production volume results in an increase of greater than 1 percent in the total cost of production. If companies or plants exceed the optimal volume of production, costs can *increase* due to diseconomies of scale (see Figure 11-2) for the following major reasons:[4]

1. *Physical Limits to Efficient Size.* When the production volume exceeds capacity, additional investments have to be made; thus, additional fixed costs increase unit costs. Too much high-capacity utilization can prevent workers from having the time to maintain the machines and this can result in more machine breakdowns.

2. *Managerial Diseconomies.* Size can increase complexity and bureaucracy, and this can reduce the manager's ability to effectively manage an organization.

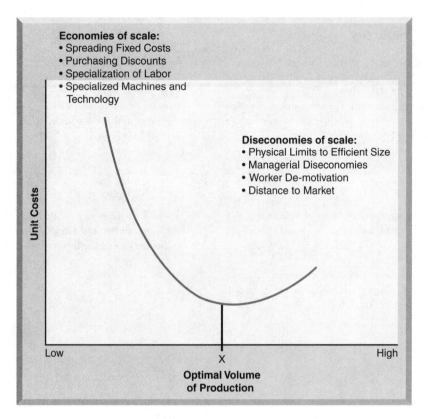

FIGURE NOTE 11-2 Economies and Diseconomies of Scale

3. *Worker De-Motivation.* In larger companies workers become segregated and communicate less with each other, the individual's contribution is diminished and increased specialization can lead to demotivation.

4. *Distance to Market.* Finally, diseconomies of scale can occur because of the physical distance of larger, centralized companies from the market which leads to higher transportation costs, less direct customer contact, etc.

Summary

Size can lead to cost advantages. Known as economies of scale, this important concept lies behind cost leadership strategies and mass marketing. The larger the market share and the production and sales volume, the lower the unit costs as, for example, fixed costs can be spread over a larger amount of units. However, if an optimal volume of production is exceeded, diseconomies of scale can occur. This can happen when physical limits to an efficient size are exceeded, when large organizations become complex and bureaucratic, etc. Marketing strategists need to know how costs behave depending on production volume, when they formulate their strategies (e.g., cost leadership versus differentiation, mass marketing versus targeting small segments) and when they determine prices of products and contribution margins.

Additional Resources

Barney, Jay B., and William S. Hesterly. *Strategic Management and Competitive Advantage.* Upper Saddle River, New Jersey: Pearson Education, 2006.

Carpenter, Mason A., and Wm. Gerard Sanders. *Strategic Management. A dynamic perspective.* Upper Saddle River, NJ, Pearson Education, 2009.

Haskett, James L., W. Earl Sasser Jr., and Joe Wheeler. *Ownership Quotient: Putting the service profit chain to work for unbeatable competitive advantage.* Boston: Harvard Business School Press, 2006.

Tom Peters "Rethinking Scale." *California Management Review.* 35, 1 (Fall, 1992): 7–29.

Endnotes

1. Robert M. Grant, *Contemporary Strategic Analysis*, 6th ed. (Malden, Oxford, Carlton: Blackwell Publishing, 2008).

2. Source: Ibid.

3. Adrian Haberberg and Alison Rieple, *Strategic Management. Theory and Application* (Oxford: Oxford University Press, 2008).

4. Jay B. Barney and William S. Hesterly, *Strategic Management and Competitive Advantage* (Upper Saddle River, New Jersey: Pearson Education, 2006).

12

Economies of Scope/Synergies and Virtuous Circles

Compared to economies of scale, which are driven by producing *more of a single product*, economies of *scope* are realized when producing *more than one product* makes the production of all units in the assortment cheaper. Whereas size and volume lead to economies of scale, diversity brings economies of scope. If producing product Y makes producing product X more efficient (cheaper per unit), that is an economy of scope.

Economies of scope are a form of "synergy" (from the Greek meaning "working together"). Synergies are realized when two (or more) inputs or activities (factors) come together or act together to result in output that is greater than the sum of the two factors taken separately [i.e., $(1+1) > 2$]. A good example of an economy of scope and synergy is the use of by-products from the production of one product in the production of another product (i.e., "by-product synergies"). Chaparral Steel, for example, realized improved efficiencies and reduced pollution by using slag "waste" from steel production in the production of Portland cement, another of its product lines. The productive use of the slag lowered the waste, and thereby the costs of steel production and the slag itself was a more efficient input than the lime it replaced, which in turn required less processing and lower energy inputs, thereby lowering the cost of cement production.[1] Economies of scope and synergies can be an important source of sustainable competitive advantages—and one that may be particularly difficult for competitors to replicate or substitute for. Chaparral's competitors who produced only steel or only Portland cement, for example, could not easily match the new efficiencies of by-product usage.

Economies of scope exist whenever there are cost savings from using a resource in multiple activities carried out in combination rather than carrying out those activities independently. There are basically six forms of synergies:[2]

1. ***Shared Tangible Resources.*** Unit costs can be reduced when tangible resources such as production plants, transportation systems, or information facilities are utilized across a range of products. The German car manufacturer Volkswagen, for example, reduced costs of the SUV Touareg by 30 percent by sharing resources, including production facilities with Porsche's SUV, the Cayenne.

2. ***Shared Intangible Resources.*** Hewlett Packard discovered that its inkjet technology could replace hypodermic needles or pills for the delivery of vaccines or

other medications. It used that intellectual property and innovation to develop patches for drug delivery. The medications in the patch are heated and then injected through the needles, delivering combinations of different drugs delivered at different times with dosages measured in a more controlled fashion.

3. *Pooled Negotiating Power.* By combining their purchases, different strategic business units can benefit from bulk discounts and from cost savings in transportation and logistics.

4. *Coordinated Strategies.* Multi-business-unit companies can coordinate market entry strategies, product development, pricing strategies, etc., to avoid duplication of efforts and to benefit from cross-selling etc.

5. *Vertical Integration.* Vertically integrated companies can benefit from a faster flow of products through the supply chain, reduced inventory costs, and improved market access.

6. *Combined Business Creation.* Diversified companies can combine the know-how and technologies of each business unit to create new products or businesses.

Economies of scope is a common reason for mergers and acquisitions, and for diversification strategies. When companies move into new products and/or markets which are related to the core businesses in one or more of the following ways, they can benefit from synergies.[3]

- *Customer assets:* Brand recognition, customer loyalty and trust can reduce costs dramatically when new products are introduced.
- *Channel assets:* Access to distribution channels and distributor loyalty facilitates the establishment of a dealer network and can help to overcome shelf-space restrictions for new products.
- *Input assets:* Knowledge of and access to supplier markets and cheap raw materials or components can also reduce costs and time to market.
- *Process assets:* Product or market-specific experience and know-how in, for example, production and marketing processes can facilitate the development and marketing of new products.
- *Market knowledge assets:* Knowledge of competitors, customers, etc. provides valuable insights into the marketing process.

Summary

While economies of scale arise when producing greater quantities of a single product, economies of scope come from selling a greater variety of products that share synergies. There are many ways to benefit from synergies, and for a marketing strategist it is important to know what types of synergies exist and to what extent they reduce costs. In practice, however, it is difficult to estimate the effect of economies of scope and to realize them. In most cases, companies tend to overestimate the potential of economies of scope.

Additional Resources

Carpenter, Mason A., and Wm. Gerard Sanders. *Strategic Management. A dynamic perspective.* Upper Saddle River, NJ: Pearson Education, 2009.

Markides, Constanctinos C., and Peter J. Williamson. "Corporate Diversification and Organizational Structure:

A Resource-based View." *Academy of Management Journal* 39, no. 2 (1996): 340–367.

Kaplan, Robert S., and David P. Norton. *Alignment: Using the Balanced Scorecard to Create Corporate Synergies.* Boston: Harvard Business School Press, 2006.

Endnotes

1. See Gordon Forward and Andrew Mangan, "By-product Synergy," *The Bridge* 29, no. 1 (Spring 1999): 12–15.
2. Michael Goold and Andrew Campbell, "Desperately Seeking Synergy," *Harvard Business Review* (September–October, 1998): 131–43.

3. C. C. Markides and P. J. Williamson, "Corporate Diversification and Organizational Structure: A Resource-based View," *Academy of Management Journal* 39, no. 2 (1996): 340–67.

13

Market-Share Effects

Most organizations want to have high market share, all else being equal, and some hold high market share as their primary objective. This may be the case because marketing managers are inherently competitive; in fact, marketing strategy is often analogized to competition in warfare and sports, with the "winner" being whichever firm has the greatest market share. Another reason for this focus may be the fact that "increasing market share" looks a lot like "increasing sales" on a day-to-day basis. In other words, as marketers strive to improve sales, they are also working to improve market share. Thus, the processes of increasing sales and increasing market share are inextricable, especially in low- or no-growth markets.

MARKET SHARE AS A STRATEGIC OBJECTIVE

Besides its appeal as a competition-oriented yardstick for one's own performance, market share for many companies is a strategic objective. Empirical studies have demonstrated that it is related to cost advantages and profitability, and many managers incorporate market-share effects into their strategic considerations. As empirical findings regarding market share are somewhat ambiguous and the use of market share comes with some problems, a more thorough, critical look at its effects and managerial implications is necessary.

Market Share and Cost Advantages

An improvement in market share signifies more than simply a "win" or a jump in sales figures. Because market share is a relative measure—in other words, it shows a firm's success *relative to the competition*—an increase in this measure should also lead to certain competitive advantages. For one, the firm with higher market share has, by definition, greater *scale*, and scale leads to advantages in learning and unit costs. In particular, scale effects (experience or learning curve effects and economies of scale) connect the number of units produced to lower per-unit costs, which offer a significant competitive advantage. The experience curve posits that the more often a task or operation is repeated, the lower will be the cost of completing it. Specifically, the relationship that has been observed is that each time cumulative volume is doubled, value added costs decline by a predictable percentage.

Economies of scale, on the other hand, arise, when unit costs decrease as output increases. In practice, the experience curve and economies of scale are related and often occur together. One way to think about the difference is that experience is based on number of units produced regardless of time and scale is based on number of units produced per period of time.

Market Share and Profits

The firm with lower costs can charge a lower price for its product (further increasing its unit sales, and thus its market share, in a virtuous cycle), or it can take higher margins at the market price. Experience curve effects also offer the benefits of *higher reliability and quality*. In other words, as a firm makes more units, its number of defects decreases and its "conformance" or uniformity across units increases. (Conformity is a dimension of quality, especially from an operations standpoint.). These basic share-profitability connections are illustrated in Figure 13-1.

Thus, increased market share seems to be a desirable outcome that is associated with specific competitive advantages. For this reason, many firms include market-share targets in their objectives and strategic planning. Extensive research has shown that market share and profitability do *correlate*—meaning that firms with higher market share *are*, in fact, more profitable. However, the relationship between share and profits is complex, and it is not clear whether market share actually *causes* higher profitability. It could be that the reverse relationship is true: Profitability may lead to higher market share, and other factors (such as higher quality products) may lead to the differences in *both* profits and share.

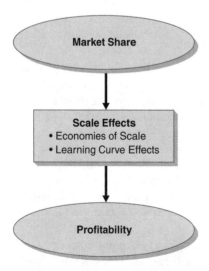

FIGURE NOTE 13-1   Market Share and Profitability
Higher market share leads to increased scale effects and lower costs—which leads to higher profitability.

Therefore, the correlation of share with profits may not be as straightforward as it first appears. For that reason, this note will briefly describe some important findings related to market-share effects and link those findings to their marketing strategy implications.

EMPIRICAL FINDINGS: THE PROFIT IMPACT OF MARKETING STRATEGY (PIMS) DATA

Research on business strategy in general and on the market share—profitability relationship in particular has been facilitated by compilation of the so-called Profit Impact of Marketing Strategy (PIMS) database. Collection of the PIMS data was initiated by Sidney Schoeffler in the 1960s at the request of General Electric, which had begun analyzing similar information about its own business units in the 1960s. In the early 1970s, the Management Science Institute at Harvard Business School, with Schoeffler's continued involvement, extended PIMS data collection across many more companies and industries. Then, in the mid-1970s, the Strategic Planning Institute, a not-for-profit organization, was created to facilitate the movement of the project from an academic to operating system. Today, the PIMS data include standardized information about 3,800 business units, including their income statement and balance sheet, quality and price data, new product development outcomes, data on market share and changes in share, and descriptions of markets, channels, and tactics for each business unit and its major competitors. Although the Strategic Planning Institute recently closed its North American offices, it continues to operate in Europe and to maintain the existing data base. The PIMS data have provided researchers with invaluable insight into the relationships between firm activities, strategies, and results, including the effects of market share on profitability.[1]

The PIMS data have led to several observations that are now axiomatic in strategy literature, including the fact that market attractiveness (growth and investment intensity) and competitive position (especially market share) are strongly correlated with profitability and returns. In fact, the market share—profitability relationship is so robust and so often replicated in the PIMS database that "PIMS" was sometimes mistakenly taken to stand for "Profit Impact of Market Share."[2] Various researchers adopting different assumptions, covariates, and statistical methods have offered different estimates of the market share—profitability relationship, but the absolute magnitude seems to be about three market-share points to one point in ROI (i.e., an increase of three percentage points in market share is related to a one-percentage-point increase in profitability; see Figure 13-2). Furthermore, a review of more than 48 studies and 276 reported share–profit elasticities that have been estimated using the PIMS and other data and found that, even with the influence of many diverse covariates taken into account, the relationship between share and ROI is still about five share points to one ROI point.[3] Nevertheless, there are several issues that must be highlighted when considering market share, especially when considering market share as the basis of a firm's marketing strategy. These include difficulty in defining what market is being shared; ambiguity in the causal direction of the relationship and the likelihood that intangible factors (such as product quality) drive both share and profits; and the fact that market share should be approached with caution as an external, competitor-oriented objective.

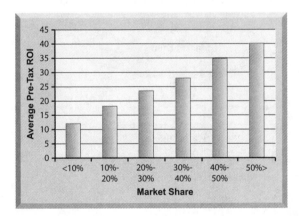

FIGURE NOTE 13-2   Market Share and ROI[4]
This figure suggests that as market share rises, pre-tax ROI does as well by a fairly predictable percentage. For example, a share of 10 percent or less obtains an ROI of a bit more than 10 percent, while a share of greater than 50 percent obtains an ROI of around 40 percent.

STRATEGIC IMPLICATIONS OF MARKET SHARE

A number of issues emerge, when companies use market share for their strategic considerations. They must be aware that market share depends on market definition, and that market definition can be a tricky task. Also, the causal direction between market share and profitability might be inverse, and market-share orientation might lead to an excessive competitor orientation. Finally, market share has several strategic implications that should be considered when strategies are formulated.

Defining the Market That Is Shared

Relating strategy and results to market share raises an important question: *For what market is the market share being computed?* Markets can be defined and labeled in many ways, and decisions about market definition can have powerful effects on strategic thinking and vision, objectives setting, and competitive actions. Market definition is obviously essential in the consideration of share as a means toward profits or as an evaluation metric. In fact, before computing market share, the denominator must be specified, and that specification will influence all subsequent considerations.

For example, Pepsi's Gatorade holds a dominant 75 to 80 percent share of the sports drink market in the United States (Coca-Cola's PowerAde is a distant second), and Aquafina, another Pepsi brand, is the U.S. market-share leader in bottled water, just ahead of Coca-Cola's Dasani (although this is not true in Europe). So, which "market" should Pepsi be concerned with, and under what circumstances? The Gatorade and Aquafina brand managers may argue for the "sports drink" or "bottled water" denominators, but the substantive benefits of market share—economies of scale in production and distribution, channel leverage, experience curve effects, and purchasing power—may not be achieved at the submarket or national level. Rather, they may accrue to the dominant overall U.S. beverage-category leader (Coca-Cola Corporation), or instead to the *global* beverage-category leader (also Coca-Cola). Thus, understanding the underlying drivers of share effects and the reasoning for holding share as an objective is crucial to defining the market for computing share effects. Moreover, an appropriate and clear definition of the market is essential to effective use of market share in strategy formation, implementation, and assessment.

Causation and Covariates

As previously mentioned, the causal direction of the relationship between market share and profitability is less clear than simple observations might suggest. That is, even though these two things unquestionably correlate, it is unclear whether market share *causes* profitability or vice versa. Alternatively, it is possible that this correlation could be "spurious" and explained by the fact that *both* market share and profitability are driven by other characteristics, such as product quality, management skill, organizational culture, access to scarce resources, or even luck.[5] Figure 13-1 illustrates these alternative explanations. In the figure, market share contributes to profitability via increased scale, but, at the same time, relationships exist between other variables (especially product quality) and both share and profits. As depicted in the figure, profitability and the resources it provides can also "feed back" to increased market share.

The complex relationships between market share, profitability, and other characteristics of a firm have been examined via extensive research using sophisticated statistical techniques. The conclusion, it seems, is that *all of these connections are real, at least in some degree and in some situations*. Indeed, more skillfully managed firms *do* enjoy both higher market shares and higher profitability, and better product quality *does* lead to both higher margins (which contribute directly to higher profitability) and higher market share. Thus, it is unsurprising that product quality, managerial skill, cost control, low-cost production, and advertising effectiveness *all* lead to *both* higher market share and higher ROI. The core connection between market share and profitability, mediated by the benefits of scale, is also real. Nevertheless, it remains unclear whether market share causes profitability or simply correlates with it, and even if one leads to the other, it may not be true that effective strategy can be developed based on the premise that increased share leads to increased profits.

Competitor-Oriented Objectives

Another problem with building strategy on market-share objectives is that market share is a *competitor-oriented objective*: It is inherently based on how the firm performs *in comparison with the competition*, rather than on how it delivers value to its customers, how it performs essential value-adding activities, or how profitable it is. That is, according to this view, market share is not itself about profitability; rather, it involves external phenomena and comparisons to

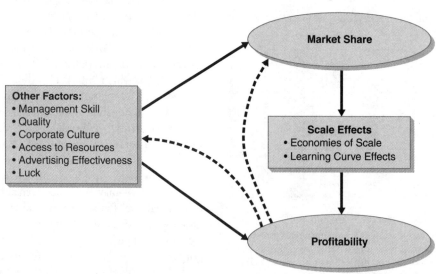

FIGURE NOTE 13-3 Possible Market Share—Profitability Relationships

others. Even more problematic is the fact that external, competitor-oriented orientations have been shown to result in *worse* performance across a variety of settings.

Wharton Business School Professor J. Scott Armstrong has reviewed and extended findings on the negative effects of competitor-orientated strategies. According to his results, and looking across many diverse tasks, people who adopt or who are manipulated into a competitor-oriented mindset realize inferior results compared to those who adopt internally focused objectives. Similarly, as per analysis of data from more than four decades of corporate performance by twenty Fortune 500 firms, those firms with competitor-oriented (market share) objectives fared worse than those with internal, profit-oriented objectives.[6] Importantly, these results relate to how strategy and objectives are established, not to the basic relationship between market share and profitability. That is, the question is not whether firms would, all else being equal, prefer higher market share; after all, most firms would always choose higher market share over lower market share. Rather, the question is whether firms are wise to establish strategic objectives around market share or to undermine other objectives, such as positioning and margins, to achieve market share? Armstrong's research indicates that internally focused objectives are far more effective than competitor-oriented objectives.

Market Share and Strategy

"First, second, or out."
Jack Welch, Former CEO
of General Electric (GE)[7]

Jack Welch's famous dictum for General Electric's (GE's) portfolio management practices grounded GE's strategy on the conviction that *market share leads to profits*, and behemoths like Wal-Mart, Microsoft, and Toyota seem to confirm that supposition. If market share doesn't make profits inevitable, it is certainly a powerful weapon to have in a brand's arsenal. For example, even if Coke and Pepsi fight for number one and number two in market share without gaining substantial advantage over each other in profitability, they are still the envy of Royal Crown

(RC) Cola, which can't wrest shelf space or media time from the two giants.[8] Similarly, Wal-Mart relies on its market dominance to apply purchasing leverage to lower costs, and its scale justifies investments, (both by it and by its vendors) in efficiencies such as RFID tag (radio-frequency identification tag) inventory tracking; Wal-Mart's purchasing leverage and investments in efficiencies then lead to even greater market share, more purchasing leverage, and yet more resources to invest in efficiencies—forming a classic virtuous cycle. In fact, market leaders, by definition, enjoy greater benefits of scale, including economies of scale and experience curve advantages, and they may also influence category-wide price points and promotion policies. Market leaders can also invest in category expansion—advertising and promotion that grows overall category sales—and retain the benefits of this expansion, whereas "also-rans" that invest in category expansion end up contributing to *other firms'* sales more than to their own.

Nevertheless, other examples emphasize that high market share is not the *only* way to achieve returns; indeed, they suggest that market share itself may not be enough, and some recent research has concluded that setting competitor-oriented objectives in general and market-share-based objectives in particular may actually be deleterious to firm performance. It is certainly true that many firms realize high returns without high market share and, conversely, that many high-market-share firms fail to garner high returns—or even *any* positive returns whatsoever. For example, at the same time that Toyota has succeeded as a market-share leader, GM has failed. Until very recently, General Motors was the leading producer of automobiles in terms of units sold. Still, despite this market share, GM was leaving customers dissatisfied and losing money. In the video game market, Sony (with its PlayStation 3) and Microsoft (with its Xbox 360) struggle to realize profits even though they dominate the market in terms of share; meanwhile, Nintendo, with the Wii system, is one of the most profitable companies in Japan.[9] Similarly, during the "Dot.Com" bubble of the late 1990s, many firms raced to capture market share but failed to focus on the immediate need to make money: "Speed was crucial in being first to market, and the key to success was to capture 'eyeballs' or visitors to your Web site. [It was believed that] eyeballs would lead to market share, which would eventually result in profits somewhere down the line."[10] Unfortunately, this belief failed to hold true for many Internet-based start-ups.

Given these scenarios, what conclusions can be drawn from the existing research on market-share effects? Market share certainly provides some specific benefits, including economies of scale, experience curve effects, and leverage to influence marketwide norms (such as price points and discounting patterns). These benefits may lead to marketplace and financial success. However, there is also evidence that share is not the only route to profitability and that the very act of defining strategy and objectives by market-share metrics may *hurt* performance. Many apparently contradictory cases—Toyota versus General Motors, Nintendo versus Sony and Microsoft, and the short-lived Dot.Com bubble—underscore the need to carefully consider use of market share as a strategy objective and to carefully examine assumptions about how share might drive or impede success.

So, with all else being equal, market share is an indicator of and correlates with profitability and affords a firm certain advantages in operations and in the market. However, market share is also an *outcome* of important strategic, managerial, and tactical accomplishments—that is, doing other more immediate tasks well *leads to* increased market share. Thus, market share itself may *not* be an effective means to success so much as it is a marker of success. In addition, market share can be a distracting and even misleading consideration in some instances. In particular, market share that is achieved ("bought") with low prices, meager or non-existent margins, and/or consequent degradation in product quality may be a Pyrrhic victory.

Some particular issues to consider when integrating market-share considerations into a strategy include the following:

- *Scale effects:* The chief precondition to using market share as an objective in strategy definition should be some well-tested expectation of substantial benefits from scale. Can the firm expect to learn in important competitive areas as it gains share and experience?
- *Dissuasion of competitors:* Often, market share can serve as a barrier to entry for competing firms. Thus, companies may seek to gain market share as a way to discourage new entrants and increased rivalry.
- *Standardization:* If an industry is expected to establish standards, then the firm with the highest market share for that industry will usually earn the power to influence or even lead the process of standard setting—and the abillity to dictate industry-wide standards is a powerful strategic advantage.
- *Ancillary sales:* Market share can establish an "installed base" of equipment and establish relationships with customers who will purchase ancillary products, supplies, or services from the firm. This is sometimes called "razor-blade economics," because razor companies often give away razors (the handles) with the expectation of future, highly profitable blade sales.
- *Customer "stickiness":* Customers gained via market-share oriented strategies must be retained as costs come down, margins go up, or competition in the market changes; otherwise, share-based strategies may be ill-advised.

Summary

Market share and profits move together (correlate), but the wisdom of using market share as a dominant strategic objective or of organizing marketing activities around gaining share is uncertain. Share that corresponds to other, well-thought-through strategies, especially to a strategy aimed at increasing production to realize the benefits of scale, may well be worth pursuing. Nevertheless, it may be wise to recall Edward Abbey's admonition: "Growth for growth's sake is the ideology of the cancer cell."[11] Setting market share as an objective or taking actions motivated primarily to gain share should be carefully considered and should be based on solid understanding, or at least on definite and well-tested assumptions about future profits.

Additional Resources

Armstrong, Scott, and Kesten C. Green. "Competitor-Oriented Objectives: The Myth of Market Share." *International Journal of Business* 12, no. 1 (2007): 117–136.

Buzzell, Robert D. "The PIMS Program of Strategy Research: A Retrospective Appraisal." *Journal of Business Research* 57, no. 5 (May 2004):478–483.

Buzzell, Robert, and Bradley Gale. *The PIMS Principles: Linking Strategy to Performance*. New York: Free Press, 1987.

Jacobson, Robert, and David A. Aaker. "Is Market Share All that It's Cracked Up to Be?" *Journal of Marketing* 49 (Fall 1985): 11–22.

Simon, Hermann, Frank F. Bilstein, and Frank Luby. *Manage for Profit, Not for Market Share: A Guide to Greater Profits in Highly Contested Markets*. Boston: Harvard Business School Press, 2006.

Endnotes

1. For more on the PIMS database, its history, and its content, see the Strategic Planning Institute's site at http://pimsonline.com/index.htm; also see Robert Buzzell and Bradley Gale, *The PIMS Principles: Linking Strategy to Performance* (New York: Free Press, 1987); and Robert D. Buzzell, "The PIMS program of strategy research: A retrospective appraisal," *Journal of Business Research* 57, no. 5 (May 2004): 478–483.

2. Ibid., p. 479.

3. See Buzzell and Gale, *The PIMS Principles*; and David M. Szymanski, Sundar G. Bharadwaj and P. Rajan Varadarajan, "An Analysis of the Market Share–Profitability Relationship," *Journal of Marketing* 57, 3 (July 1993): 1–18. Compare these results with those of Robert Jacobson and his colleagues, who, in questioning the causal nature of the market share–ROI correlation, arrived at substantially lower estimates of the relationship using several different assumptions and testing for effects on change in ROI.

4. From Buzzell and Gale, *The PIMS Principles*, page 9, Exhibit 1-2: Market Share and ROI (noting that this graph is "based on 4-year average of pretax, pre-interest ROI for 2,611 business units in the PIMS database).

5. See, for example, Robert Jacobson and David A. Aaker, "Is Market Share All that It's Cracked Up to Be?" *Journal of Marketing* 49 (Fall 1985): 11–22; David A. Aaker and Robert Jacobson, "The Financial Information Content of Perceived Quality," *Journal of Marketing Research* 31, no. 2 (May 1994, Special Issue on Brand Management): 191-201; Robert Jacobson and David A. Aaker, "The Strategic Role of Product Quality," *Journal of Marketing* 51, no. 4 (October 1987): 31–44; and Robert Jacobson, "Distinguishing among Competing Theories of the Market Share Effect," *Journal of Marketing* 52, no. 4 (October 1988): 68–80.

6. See J. Scott Armstrong and Kesten C. Green, "Competitor-Oriented Objectives: The Myth of Market Share," *International Journal of Business* 12, no. 1 (2007): 117–136; and J. Scott Armstrong and Fred Collopy, "Competitor Orientation: Effects of Objectives and Information on Managerial Decisions and Profitability," *Journal of Marketing Research* 33 (1996): 188–199.

7. Jeffrey A. Krames, *The Jack Welch Lexicon of Leadership: Over 250 terms, concepts, strategies & initiatives of the legendary leader* (New York: McGraw Hill, 2002), quoted on page 90.

8. "RC Cola Wins Suit Against Coca-Cola," *New York Times*, June 24, 2000, page 14.

9. J. Surowiecki, "In Praise of Third Place," *The New Yorker* (December 4, 2006)

10. Jeffry A Timmons and Stephen Spinelli, *New Venture Creation: Entrepreneurship for the 21st Century* (New York: McGraw-Hill/Irwin, 2004); 188.

11. Edward Abbey, *Voice Crying in the Wilderness (Vox Clamantis in Deserto): Notes from a Secret Journal* (New York: St. Martin's Press, 1990) 98.

14

Scenario Analysis

Scenario analysis is, essentially, an elaborate "if . . . then . . ." planning tool. It might be better described as an "*if . . . and if . . . and if . . . and if . . .* [all at the same time], *then . . .*" tool in which multiple forces ("drivers" of future conditions) are simultaneously combined to create rich "possible futures" or scenarios[1]. If forecasting asks "What will the world be like in the future?" scenario analysis asks "What *could* the world be like . . . and *what will we do* if that future comes about?" Scenario analysis also asks "What should we do *now* [or between now and then] to prepare, *just in case* the future looks that way?"

For example, if a regional home construction company wants to forecast interest rates, because interest rates have a strong impact on the building industry, the builder would base that prediction on trends in the economy and on inputs from economists and bankers. However, forecasting interest rates is challenging and expensive, and interest rates are not the only driver of any company's circumstances and strategic results. Other drivers for a builder might include the regulatory environment (such as local housing policies) and the competitive environment. Instead of forecasting specific variables, a marketing strategist might conduct a scenario analysis for the builder in which several levels of interest rates are incorporated (e.g., high, moderate, and low interest rates), along with two levels of competition (a large, national builder enters the market or no change in the competition), and a couple of possible regulatory shifts (such as continued pro-growth policies versus tightened regulations/slow-growth policies are enacted).

In scenario analysis, several concurrent factors or "drivers" such as interest rates, building regulations, and competitive intensity, are combined to create descriptions of complex possible "futures"—which may not come true, *but could*. In the real world, many factors change at the same time and many factors influence strategic results; scenario analysis captures that multifaceted nature of reality. Instead of focusing on a single factor, such as interest rates or even the economy, or describing multiple factors separately, scenario analysis brings the factors together to jointly describe a complex strategic context. For example, one scenario for the regional building company, discussed above, might encompass high interest rates, local governments constraining growth and limiting building permits, and a large builder entering the regional market. A more optimistic future might be low interest rates, moderate building permitted, and no new competition. These scenarios' multifaceted nature would enrich analysis in a realistic way and challenge assumptions, and broaden strategic thinking.

In this example three drivers, with three, two, and two levels or possible future conditions respectively, could generate 12 different scenarios. Not only would analyzing

12 scenarios be unwieldy, but also it is unnecessary. It is best to develop three or four complex scenarios for further consideration. Each plausible and internally consistent (but not real) scenario is then analyzed against the firm's strategies and *possible* strategies, and the most important drivers of the future and prudent actions to prepare for the future can be identified. By using scenario analysis, it becomes less important that any forecast—for interest rates or any other driver—be precisely right. Because several possible outcomes for each driver are included in the analysis, the process highlights the range of possibilities and the possible impacts of each driver as well as helps to identify feasible strategic responses to those eventualities.

THE SCENARIO ANALYSIS PROCESS

As powerful as it is, scenario analysis can nevertheless be reduced to a few basic steps:[2]

1. *Define the scope* of the analysis;
2. Identify the *drivers* of future strategic contexts;
3. *Select specific levels, changes, or events* within each driver to frame the future;
4. *Combine those drivers* and levels/changes/events to *develop comprehensive scenarios*;
5. *Select three or four scenarios* for analysis;
6. *Analyze and plan* for each selected scenario; and
7. *Integrate* results to identify near- and long-term directions, actions, and investments and to appraise strategic alternatives.

Define the Scope

Most scenario analyses in marketing strategy are focused on specific product offerings and their target markets. In order to encourage deep analysis, creative thinking, and relevance, the *sector* (markets/industries), the *environmental/internal factors* to be considered (at a broad level, such as economic, social, competitive, etc.), and the *specific timeframe* should all be spelled out at the outset. Scenario analysis can accommodate a variety of timeframes but is most useful for *longer-term strategizing*, and long-term horizons. Specific forecasts about various factors in the environment (interest rates, consumer preferences, attitudes etc.) may be quite accurate in the near-term but scenario analysis is more realistic and accurate in the long-term because it accommodates the inherent uncertainty of long-term forecasts.

Identify Drivers

What factors or forces *could* drive the firm's future or the industry—and which of those drivers are most important? Searching for the three to five most important drivers involves consideration of the various elements of the situation (the PEST domains of political/regulatory/legal, economic, social/cultural, and technical/physical as well as the competitive environment) and consideration of internal factors and initiatives with uncertain outcomes, such as new product development/R&D projects and human resource and training initiatives. That is, all drivers need not be external, but most uncertainties and uncontrollable drivers are external. In the example developed briefly above, there were three drivers (interest rates, building regulation, and competition); generally it is useful to include *at least* three and as many as five drivers.

Select Specific Levels, Changes, or Events within Each Driver

Many drivers have a continuous range of possible outcome levels—not all equally likely, but certainly a wide range of values the driver could have in the future. For example, inflation is, in reality, a continuum of percentage changes that can range from 0 (or even negative in those rare instances of "deflation") to 5, 10, or 15 percent—and the reality will certainly be measureable down to the tenth or hundredth of a percent (e.g., 6.9% or 3.48%). Creating specific scenarios for analysis and planning requires selecting *a few specific levels of each driver* to represent the whole range (e.g., low inflation will be 2%, moderate inflation will be 6%, and high inflation will be 12%). The chance that the analysts will have selected the exact level that eventually occurs is very low—but the chance that scenario analysis can select a set of specific values that, taken together, represent the range of possibilities is very high. The specific levels selected for analysis are not necessarily the "most likely"; they should be the levels that insure that the planning process considers the *whole range* of possibilities; they should also include levels or conditions that, even if unlikely, would have extreme impacts.

Combine Drivers into Scenarios

The next step is to select levels from each driver and combine those into *internally consistent* scenarios (Figure 14-1). Levels of some drivers may be incompatible with some levels of other drivers and are thereby *internally inconsistent*; national competition may not enter a market during a recession or downturn in the housing market. Therefore, high interest rates would be internally inconsistent with intensification of the competitive environment—that scenario wouldn't make sense.

Select Scenarios for Further Analysis

A very few drivers can quickly create an unmanageable number of scenarios (two drivers with two levels each and two drivers with three levels each yield

36 scenarios). Therefore, three or four scenarios should be chosen that *frame the range of possible outcomes.* That is, all of the possible scenarios define the universe of possibilities—but the analysis should consider a sample from that universe. In that way it is possible to dig deep into the selected scenarios rather than to skim a wider range. The ultimate reality will be different than *any* of those three or four fictitious scenarios—but three or four is enough to facilitate consideration of the range of possible futures and the implications of those possibilities for current and potential strategies. At this stage it is useful to *name* each selected scenario to help organize and enliven discussions, and each scenario should be expanded into a fully-developed narrative to enrich discussions.

Analyze each Scenario

"If these drivers worked out in this pattern to create this scenario, then a _____ strategy for this firm would be best, a _____ strategy will meet challenges in _____. The firm would want to have _____ between now and then." For each scenario,

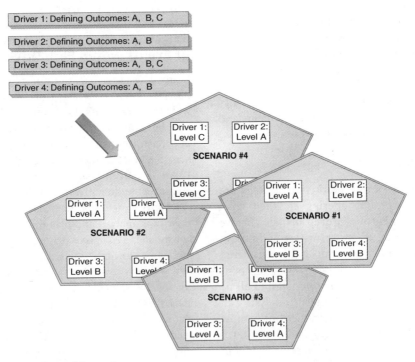

FIGURE NOTE 14-1   Drivers of Scenarios

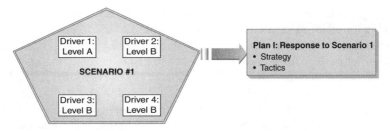

FIGURE NOTE 14-2 Analyze Each Scenario

how would the firm answer those related questions? Essentially, the analysts (or cross-functional team of strategists) assume the scenario will come true and plan for it. These analyses should consider the resulting industry structure (within a five-forces framework or otherwise), competitive actions and reactions, key uncertainties and risks, and the resulting impacts on the firm and its offerings. Existing strategies and alternative strategies should be tested within the "reality" of each scenario: *How will this strategy work in the future envisioned in the scenario? What would have to be done to make the strategy work better? What*

alternative strategy would work well? This process is graphed in basic terms in Figure 14-2.

Integrate Results

Analyzing across scenarios and plans allows the firm to identify near- and long-term directions, actions, investments, and to appraise strategic alternatives. As shown in Figure 14-3, this is a matter of integrating the results of all of the scenarios/plans and gleaning insights from commonalities and differences across them. Some insights come from what is very likely or

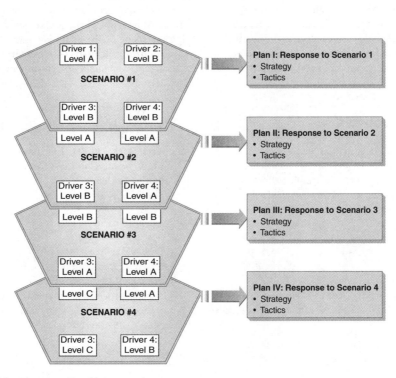

FIGURE NOTE 14-3 Integrate Results

what is common to many results, but others may come from the anomalies, the things that are true only if a certain set of outcomes occurs, and from considering very unlikely but potentially impactful possible futures. That is, the questions facing the analysts are not only about what strategy the firm would want to have pursued if the future ended up looking like any given scenario, likely or improbable; scenario analysis also offers the chance to look at low-cost/low-risk investments to position the firm to take advantage of improbable but potentially lucrative opportunities. Furthermore, it can also enable a company to take early, cost-effective steps to address potential threats and to preclude or cope with catastrophic scenarios.

The planning against the whole set of scenarios will identify likely events that should be dealt with as well as unlikely but potentially impactful events that should be prepared for regardless of their improbability. That is, things that are likely to occur require planning even if the impacts are not extraordinary; and unlikely events that would, if they occurred, "change the firm's world," so to speak, also require planning because of their potential impact.

Summary

Scenario analysis is a powerful framework for formalizing situation assessment, surfacing assumptions and important uncertainties, dealing with uncertainty and clarifying possible future events, and determining the firm's possible and preferred responses to those events. Scenario analysis clarifies the forces or drivers that shape *or could shape* the future operating context, promotes creative, long-range thinking, and produces robust, action-oriented "contingency plans." Business strategy applications of scenario analysis were pioneered by Royal Dutch Shell in the global oil industry to plan for catastrophes, wars, price shocks, supply disruptions, and the like. Regardless of the industry or the times, scenario analysis has the capacity to develop effective responses to concurrently evolving forces and for unlikely but potentially debilitating disruptions. Scenario analysis is done best by diverse teams of managers and experts "brainstorming." The more diverse the team in terms of functional area (marketing, operations, research and development, etc.), geographic location, and perspective, the broader the scope of the thinking will be—and broadening the scope of the analysis (in terms of time horizon and regarding elements of the environment considered) is critical to the quality of the outcomes.

Additional Resources

Lindgren, Mats, and Hans Bandhold. *Scenario Planning: The Link Between Future and Strategy*. Revised and updated ed. New York: Palgrave Macmillan, 2009.

Mercer, David. "Scenarios Made Easy." *Long Range Planning* 28, no. 4 (1995): 81–86.

Schwartz, Peter. *The Art of the Long View: Planning for the Future in an Uncertain World*. New York: Bantom Doubleday Dell.

Endnote

1. Paul J. H. Shoemaker, "Scenario Planning: A Tool for Strategic Thinking," *Sloan Management Review* (Winter 1995): 25–40.

2. This process is adapted from David Mercer, "Scenarios Made Easy," *Long Range Planning* 28, no. 4 (1995): 81–86.

MARKETING STRATEGIES

15

The Marketing Concept

"There is only one valid definition of business purpose: to create a customer. . . .

It is the customer who determines what a business is. It is the customer alone whose willingness to pay for a good or for a service converts economic resources into wealth. . . .

Because its purpose is to create a customer, the business enterprise has two—and only these two—basic functions: marketing and innovation. Marketing and innovation produce results; all the rest are 'costs.'"

PETER DRUCKER[1]

Managing a business is, without doubt, a complex undertaking involving diverse tasks across distinct functional areas ranging from financing the firm and making investments to managing operations and logistics, from tax and accounting matters to marketing and strategic issues. At any given moment every manager is faced with different, sometimes competing concerns across these functional areas. Individual executives, management teams, and whole corporate cultures tend to have distinctive priorities and approaches to problem solving; that is, they have distinct "orientations" and philosophies that drive what gets attention and what, on the other hand, gets neglected. These managerial orientations shape resulting strategies. Some firms focus on technical issues, logistics, and operations. Others emphasize financial management, and investments and returns dominate decision making. Some firms are driven by marketing and concern for customers. An important set of questions for management is: *What is the "best" executive orientation?* What factors should *lead* decision making and which should follow?

The marketing strategist's natural emphasis will be on the market and the customers—but there is also compelling evidence that a market focus and concern for the customer *should pervade the entire organization* and should guide the whole the strategy of an organization. The "marketing concept" holds that firms will be most successful at achieving goals, including profits, when they *orient around the consumers' needs* and align the entire organization, including production, finance, accounting, and marketing around satisfying those needs.[2] This is a "market orientation"—a *firm-wide customer and competitor* focus and coordination of activities[3]—and it has been shown to lead to superior firm-level performance, including profitability, ROI, and stock returns.[4]

A HISTORIC, EVOLUTIONARY ACCOUNT

Over time, dominant business philosophies, the prevailing priorities and problem solving modes of business leaders, have evolved. In the early twentieth century, demand for goods exceeded supply, and managers focused on efficient manufacturing and control; that is, their emphasis was on *production;* that period has been called the "production era." Henry Ford, founder of the Ford Motor Company and inventor of the modern "assembly line," is sometimes held up as the archetypical production-focused executive. When it was introduced in 1908, for example, the Model T was available in a variety of colors but painting the cars became a production bottleneck, requiring up to 18 days as each of five coats was hand painted and then allowed to dry.[5] Henry Ford's managerial orientation was clear when, in 1923, he wrote that:

> "Salesmen always want to cater to whims instead of acquiring sufficient knowledge of their product to be able to explain to the customer with the whim that what they have will satisfy his every requirement. . . . [I]n 1909 I announced one morning, without any previous warning, that in the future we were going to build only one model. . . . I remarked:
>
> 'Any customer can have a car painted any colour that he wants so long as it is black.'"[6]

In the mid-twentieth century, supply began to meet and exceed demand. Managers recognized that promotion and selling activities facilitated sales in competitive markets. Manufacturers had to inform and persuade customers to buy what they were making, especially instead of buying a competitor's offerings. Large dry-goods companies, including Pillsbury, Kellogg's, and Proctor & Gamble innovated their advertising and promotion strategies during what is now called the "sales era." A "sales orientation" begins with production and holds production paramount; that is, "*marketing makeable products.*"[7]

In the 1950s and 1960s, businesses and management experts recognized that production and selling, along with operations, finance, other core functions and strategic direction *all become more effective and more efficient if they began with a deep understanding of and emphasis on customer needs and wants.*[8] In 1960, Professor Ted Levitt of the Harvard Business School presented the logic of the marketing concept, especially in guiding firms and industries toward innovation and growth, and argued that "the organization must learn to think of itself not as producing goods or services but as *buying customers*, as doing the things that will make people *want* to do business with it."[9] This has been summarized as "*making marketable products.*"[10]

This historic account of the evolution of prevalent business philosophies may be allegorical; during the "production era" there were, of course, businesses that created products designed to meet customer needs and, on the other hand, there are firms that continue to prioritize production and efficiency over customer needs—without great disadvantage.[11] Henry Ford may, in fact, have been considering customer needs along with production efficiencies when he decided to paint all Fords black; the variety of colors used on earlier Model Ts had faded and cracked in use, and the "Japan black enamel" paints withstood the climate and wear best.[12] Nevertheless, it is certainly true that, whether or not businesses in general followed this evolution, many companies have progressed through very similar stages from internal, production-focused decision making toward a market orientation.[13]

Critics of the marketing concept have argued that it requires managers to focus on short-term and superficial customer needs and fads,[14] but that criticism confuses a market orientation with a short-term orientation. In fact, a market orientation should lead to the logical corollary that more substantive and compelling needs equate with more substantive and compelling market opportunities. As a result, solutions may well require longer term, more basic research. Customer needs are met by many types of innovation and exploration, including basic research. The marketing concept isn't to blame if firms overlook basic research in favor of less substantive but more immediate opportunities in applied new-product development. The preference for immediate opportunities is better attributed to forces ranging from Wall Street demands to human-resource evaluation cycles. These all contribute to a pervasive and detrimental short-term managerial time horizon.

It is useful to highlight some things that a market orientation *is not*. It is not an altruistic or feel-good mantra; it is a practical and pragmatic principle that has been shown to lead toward short- and long-term market success and profitability.[15] The market orientation doesn't imply that the firm should or could serve a need without realizing a profit—specifically, for most private organizations profitability must be a condition of serving a need. Additionally, a market orientation does not mean that the customer is "always right"; customers are *not* always right. In fact, firms may choose not to serve a customer, a segment of customers, or a type of customer for any number of reasons. Some customers are inherently unprofitable and firms are well advised to avoid those "devils." Other customers may simply be incompatible with the firm's offerings. Southwest Airlines is famous for its world class, no-frills but informal and fun service. Nevertheless, one customer was chronically dissatisfied, writing so many letters complaining about everything from boarding procedures to the color of the planes that she was given the nickname "Pen Pal." Eventually her dissatisfaction stumped the customer service staff, who kicked the letter up to CEO Herb Kelleher. Kelleher looked at the letter and the history of complaining and promptly responded: "Dear Mrs. Crabapple, We will miss you. Love Herb."[16] The marketing concept does not cede control to the customer, it doesn't require that service personnel put up with abusive behaviors,

and doesn't require the firm to meet every customer whim. It is more accurately understood as organizing and focusing strategy around meeting customer needs at a profit. All other activities are oriented around serving those customer needs at a profit, and no activity has value in and of itself if it is not contributing to meeting those needs at a profit.

The marketing concept also does not require that customers can articulate their wants, or that they even *know* what they will want or what will satisfy their need. Table 15-1 defines customer needs, wants, and demand. The marketing concept asserts that firms should begin strategic planning and managerial decision making with a keen focus on the customer needs that it aspires to serve. *Needs* are basic human requirements, starting with the most basic physiological needs required for survival but also including higher-level needs such as social needs. *Wants* are those needs translated into desire for specific solutions. *Demand* is that desire backed by the resources and willingness to buy. Most people are aware of basic needs—although psychological models of needs, such as Maslow's hierarchy,[17] hold that higher-level needs are subjugated to lower-level, more urgent needs; meeting basic needs may preclude attention to or even awareness of higher-order needs.[18] A starving person will not think about or even necessarily be conscious of their need for self-actualization, for example. A want is a need focused on a specific solution (product or brand); needs may manifest themselves in any number of wants. That is, any number of specific solutions might solve a need and, in the future, a need may be satisfied by products ("solutions" or wants) that customers can not yet describe or even imagine. Marketing research is not a prerequisite for action within a market-oriented firm (although marketing research is certainly invaluable in analyzing and planning investments in new products).

A focus on customer needs is invaluable in market definition and planning for growth. The firm that defines its market by the technology it produces will miss important opportunities as new technologies emerge to meet the same customers' needs. In the early twentieth century, for example, railroads defined themselves as being in the "railroad industry;" they operated heavy rolling-stock on iron rails moving people and goods from one place to another. Had they

TABLE NOTE 15-1 Needs, Motives, Wants, and Demand

Construct	Definition	Example
Need	Basic human requirements; "states of felt deprivation."[19]	Physiological (food, water), safety, belonging, ego-status or esteem (respect), self-actualization.
Felt need	Recognized gap between current situation and desired situation (e.g., hunger, loneliness); see "motive."	A lonely consumer feels a need to go out and meet people.
Motive	A need that is sufficiently pressing to direct the person to seek satisfaction of the need.[20]	
Latent need	Unrecognized or unconscious gap between current and desired state.	A lonely consumer too busy meeting critical needs, such as food, to think about social life.
Want	Needs *directed toward specific object/product* that can satisfy the need; "The form human needs take as shaped by culture and individual personality."[21]	A lonely consumer (person who needs belonging) wants to connect with others.
Apparent or State Want	A need-want linkage that the consumer is aware of and feels	A lonely consumer goes to a café for its sense of community
Unrecognized Want	A need-object relationship that has not been recognized because consumers don't understand or are unaware of the object/product	A lonely consumer (person who needs belonging) is unaware of online social networks that might meet that need.
Demand	Wants for specific object/product backed by an ability and willingness to pay; "Human wants that are backed by buying power."[22]	A consumer is thirsty, wants a cola, and has the money to purchase a cola

defined their industry as the "transportation industry," they might not have missed, as they did, the exodus of passengers from trains to cars and airplanes, or the shift of freight toward trucks.[23] Of course, the firm retains the prerogative and duty to define the needs it will meet—no firm can meet all customer needs—and it is also possible to define the scope *too broadly*. Nevertheless, a focus on customer needs offers an important perspective on market definition and in thinking about "what business the firm is in."

Summary

The marketing concept asserts that "achieving organizational goals depends on knowing the needs and wants of target markets and delivering the desired satisfactions better than competitors do."[24] It does not repudiate the necessity or importance of other functions, but it does argue that all functions should be aligned with a core purpose centered on the customer needs the organization will serve at a profit. Ultimately, the logic and force of the marketing concept and its emphasis on satisfying the customer was well-articulated by Sam Walton, founder of Wal-Mart, when he said:

> "There is only one boss. The customer. And he can fire everybody in the company from the chairman on down, simply by spending his money somewhere else."[25]

Additional Resources

Drucker, Peter. *Management.* New York: Harper & Row, 1973.

Levitt, Theodore. "Marketing Myopia." *Harvard Business Review* 38 (July–August, 1960): 24–47.

McGee, Lynn W., and Rosann L. Spiro. "The Marketing Concept in Perspective." *Business Horizons* 31, no. 3 (May–June, 1988): 40–45.

Slater, Stanley F., and John C. Narver. "Market Orientation, Customer Value, and Superior Performance." *Business Horizons* 37, no. 2 (1994): 22–28.

Endnotes

1. Peter Drucker, *Management* (New York: Harper & Row, 1973), 61.

2. See, for example, E. Jerome McCarthy and William D. Perreault Jr., *Basic Marketing*, 8th ed. (Homewood, IL: Irwin, 1984) 35.

3. Stanley F. Slater and John C. Narver, "Market Orientation, Customer Value, and Superior Performance," *Business Horizons* 37, no. 2 (1994): 22–28.

4. For reviews of the literature linking market orientation to firm performance, see for example Ahmet H. Kirca, Satish Jayachandran, and William O. Bearden, "Market Orientation: A Meta-Analytic Review and Assessment of Its Antecedents and Impact on Performance," *Journal of Marketing* 69 (April 2005): 24–41.

5. Thomas H. Klier and James M. Rubenstein, *Who Really Made Your Car: Restructuring and Geographic Change in the Auto Industry* (Kalamazoo, MI: W.E. Upjohn Institute, 2008).

6. Henry Ford (with Samuel Crowther), *My Life and Work* (Garden City, NY: Garden City Pub. Co., 1922), 71–72.

7. Robert H. Hayes and William J. Abemathy, "Managing Our Way to Economic Decline," *Harvard Business Review* 58 (July–August, 1980), 67–77.

8. Peter Drucker, *The Practice of Management* (New York: Harper and Row Publication, Inc., 1954), 37.

9. Theodore H. Levitt, "Marketing Myopia," *Harvard Business Review* 38, no. 4 (July–August, 1960): 45–56.

10. Robert H. Hayes and William J. Abemathy, "Managing Our Way to Economic Decline," *Harvard Business Review* 58 (July–August, 1980): 67–77.

11. Ronald A. Fullerton, "How Modern Is Modern Marketing? Marketing's Evolution and the Myth of the 'Production Era,'" *The Journal of Marketing* 52, no. 1 (January 1988): 108–125.

12. Klier and Rubenstein, *Who Really Made Your Car.*

13. Robert J. Keith, "The Marketing Revolution," *Journal of Marketing* 24 (January 1960): 35–38.

14. R. C. Bennett and R. G. Cooper, "Beyond the Marketing Concept," *Business Horizons* 22 (June 1979): 76–83.

15. For reviews of the literature linking market orientation to firm performance, see G. Tomas M. Hult, David J. Ketchen Jr., and Stanley F. Slater. "Market Orientation and Performance: an Integration of Disparate Approaches," *Strategic Management Journal* 26 (2005): 1173–118, and Ahmet H. Kirca, Satish Jayachandran, and William O. Bearden, "Market Orientation: A Meta-Analytic Review and Assessment of Its Antecedents and Impact on Performance," *Journal of Marketing* 69 (April 2005): 24–41.

16. Kevin Freiberg and Jackie Freiberg, *Nuts! Southwest Airlines' Crazy Recipe for Business and Personal Success* (Austin TX: Bard Press, 1996), 270.

17. Abraham Maslow, *Motivation and Personality,* 3rd ed. (New York: Addison-Wesley, 1987).

18. Ibid., page 57.

19. Philip Kotler and Gary Anderson, *Principles of Marketing*, 13th ed. (Upper Saddle River, NJ: Pearson Prentice Hall, 2009), 6.

20. Ibid., page 6.

21. Ibid., page 6.

22. Ibid., page 6.

23. Theodore H. Levitt, "Marketing Myopia," *Harvard Business Review* 38, no. 4 (July–August, 1960), 45–56.

24. Kotler and Anderson, *Principles of Marketing,* page 10.

25. Philip Verghis, *The Ultimate Customer Support Executive: Unleash the Power of Your Customer* (Summit, NJ: Silicon Press, 2006), 17.

16

What is a Marketing Strategy?

What is strategy? There are many definitions and conceptualizations of strategy and strategy means different things to different people. A simple and direct definition is: "Strategy is the coordinated means by which an organization pursues its goals and objectives."[1] It encompasses an integrated set of choices and decisions intended to support and advance the company's vision and objectives. A marketing strategy describes how to compete in a particular market or market segment. Hence, strategic marketing decisions address a range of issues and critical tasks, including

- The long-term direction of a company,
- The scope of the company,
- The identification and/or creation of competitive advantages,
- The maintenance and protection of those competitive advantages, and
- The identification and prioritization of opportunities and threats in the external environment, including
- The identification and prioritization of customer needs as well as expectations and the needs and interests of other stakeholders.[2]

A sound and compelling marketing strategy should consider all of these issues. It should fulfill three basic requirements:

1. It should be *comprehensive* and address the 5 Ws and 1 H (see Table 16-1);
2. It should be *integrative* in a way that the 5 Ws and the 1 H must fit together and reinforce each other; and
3. It should be *consistent* with the long-term vision, the core competences, and environmental opportunities.

A comprehensive marketing strategy must specify who, where, what, why, why, and how ("5 Ws and 1 H"):

1. *Who* the company will serve—the customer segments and products: A strategy requires a clear definition of the target market, the intended position within each market and the products and services that are tailored to it.
2. *Where* the firm will do business—the geographic markets and regions: Related to the first question is the definition of the geographic market— worldwide, country focus, regional focus, etc. This decision also involves setting priorities in market entry.
3. *What* needs the firm will meet—needs that a firm can meet better than the competitors and lead to a sustainable differentiation: This is a key question of

TABLE NOTE 16-1 The 5 Ws and 1 H of the Marketing Strategy[3]

"5 Ws and 1 H"		Typical Questions	Typical Analytical Tools
Who?	Who are the customer segments the company wants to serve, and what are the products and services?	• Which market segments? • Which product categories? • Which products and services? • Which technologies?	• Market segmentation • Targeting • Positioning • Portfolio analysis
Where?	What are the geographic markets a company wants to serve?	• Which Countries? • Which Regions? • Which distribution channels?	• Product-Market growth analysis • Place/distribution strategies

What?	What customers needs should the company meet?	• What are the differentiators?
		  ○ Quality
		  ○ Brand Image
		  ○ Design
		  ○ Functionality
		  ○ Price
		  ○ Service
		  ○ Customization
			• Positioning
			• Porter's generic strategies
			• The value frontier
			• Sustainable competitive advantages
			• Core competences

How?	How will we get there? Which core competences and activities of the value chain?	• Which core competences? • Which activities of the value chain? • Internal Development? • Strategic Alliances? • Joint Ventures? • Licensing? Franchising?	• Core competences • SWOT analysis • Value chain analysis
When?	What is the speed and sequence of the single moves?	• Speed of expansion • Sequence of initiatives	• Product-Market growth strategies • SWOT-Analysis

Why?	Why do we obtain our returns?	• What is the economic logic and what is the compelling business model?
		  ○ *Economies of scale*
		  ○ *Experience curve*
		  ○ *Economies of scope*
		  ○ *Price premiums*
			• Value chain analysis
			• Experience curve
			• Economies of scale
			• Economies of scope
			• The value frontier

strategy as it defines how a company creates a difference that it can preserve, and how it creates value to the customer.

4. *How* will the company serve the customers and needs—the means (core competences and activities of the value chain): A comprehensive strategy must also say *how* the company intends to achieve competitive advantages and deliver against the target customers' needs (through internal development of those competitive advantages, through outsourcing, or through collaboration with partners).

5. *When* the firm will act—the speed and sequence of the firm's actions: Without specification of the single steps and a time schedule, a strategy is not implementable, resources cannot be committed, costs for the single time periods of the strategic plan cannot be estimated, and the progress of implementation cannot be effectively monitored.

6. *Why* the firm will do these things—the compelling business model and economic logic: A sound strategy must explicitly explain why a company should earn returns with a specific strategy. Each strategy must be based on a sound economic logic, for example, lower costs through economies of scale or scope, higher price premium through super customer value, etc.

When formulating a strategy this summary framework offers a useful, comprehensive, and practical guideline. For each of the six elements (5 Ws and 1 H) you find typical questions that should be answered. The last column contains the analytical tools that can be used for the single decisions.

A good example of a comprehensive strategy is that of IKEA. The Swedish furniture retailer with about 130,000 employees, operating in 24 countries with a yearly turnover of over €21 billion (about $30 billion) has a clear and compelling strategy that has been consistent and enduring; its basic elements have been almost unchanged for more than 30 years. Guided by the vision to "create a better everyday life

for the many people . . . by offering a wide range of well-designed, functional home furnishing products at prices so low that as many people as possible will be able to afford them," each distinct element of the strategy is directed towards that vision. The single elements, illustrated in Figure 16-1 (the "hexagon" of strategy), fit together and reinforce each other.

Helmuth von Moltke, the famous Prussian field marshal (1800–1891) once defined strategy as "the evolution of the original guiding idea according to continually changing circumstances." Similarly, there is an old military axiom "the best battle plans never survive the first shot." These quotes emphasize a cardinal truth about strategies: They are not static, they're dynamic; strategies must evolve according to changing conditions!

Before any strategy is implemented it should be carefully tested for consistency and viability. The ultimate test is answering the following questions:

1. Is the strategy aligned to the vision, mission and corporate strategy?
2. Are the 5Ws and 1H clearly addressed?

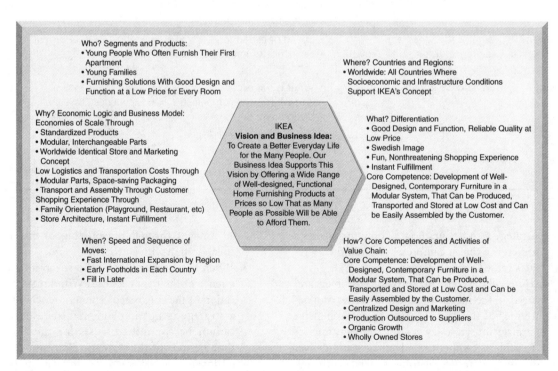

FIGURE NOTE 16-1   The "Hexagon" of Strategy (IKEA)[4]

3. Does the strategy exploit opportunities in the market?

4. Is the strategy aligned with the key success factors in the market?

5. Is the strategy built on core competences and strengths?

6. Are the differentiators sustainable?

7. Are the 5Ws and 1H internally consistent?

8. Does the company have enough resources to pursue and implement the strategy?

In summary, those six essential elements of a comprehensive marketing strategy can really be summarized under two broader headings:

- What customers/customer needs does the strategy target? and
- How does the firm serve those targets better than the competition at a profit?

When reviewing business proposals, venture capitalists sometimes reduce those two questions to "*Where's the pain?*" and "*Where's the magic?*" What needs will the venture target and how will it serve those segments/needs better than existing solutions? The two key elements are:

- ***Target Segments.*** Questions about *who* the firm serves, *when* the firm meets those needs (i.e., on what occasions), *where* it does these things (i.e., geographic markets) and, especially, *what* needs the firm meets are all essentially about what segments the business serves. *Where's the pain?* and

- ***Competitive Advantages.*** Questions about *how* the firm serves those target segments and their needs better than the competition, and *why* the firm does that (the business model or profit logic), are all really about what competitive advantages (resources or capabilities) the firm has or will build. *Where's the magic?*

A sound strategy must, eventually, reduce to *meeting some specific needs of some specific customers better than the competition within profitable relationships.*

Summary

A strategy is an integrated set of choices and actions pointed towards the vision and the long-term objectives of the company. It should be comprehensive, integrative, and consistent. By addressing the 5 Ws and the 1 H, the strategy becomes specific and actionable. By fitting those elements together and by matching them with the firm's long-term vision, with the firm's core competences, and with environmental opportunities, a strategy becomes viable and achieves it objective: to create long-term sustainable competitive advantages.

Additional Resources

Carpenter, Mason A., and Wm. Gerard Sanders. *Strategic Management. A dynamic perspective.* Upper Saddle River, NJ: Pearson Education, 2009.

Hambrick, D. C., and J. W. Fredrickson. Are You Sure You Have a Strategy? *Academy of Management Executive* 15 (2001): 48–59.

Porter, Michael. What is Strategy? *Harvard Business Review* 74, no. 6 (November–December, 1996): 61–78.

Porter, Michael. *Competitive Advantage: Creating and Sustaining Superior Performance.* New York: Free Press, 1985.

Endnotes

1. M. A. Carpenter and Sanders, W. G. *Strategic Management. A Dynamic Perspective* (Upper Saddle River, NJ, Pearson Education, 2009).

2. G. Johnson, K. Scholes, and R. Whittington, *Exploring Corporate Strategy: Text & Cases* (Harlow, England, Prentice Hall, 2008).

3. Adapted from D. C.Hambrick, and J. W. Fredrickson, Are You Sure You Have a Strategy? *Academy of Management Executive* 15 (2001): 48–59.

4. Adapted from Ibid.

17

Generic Strategies—Advantage and Scope

Over the years, many experts have tried to summarize *all possible strategies* within some reduced set of *characteristics* (dimensions) and/or *types* (categories). These efforts have generally converged on two fundamental characteristics of strategies that, together, delineate a limited number of categories of strategies; this précis of "generic" strategies has, as a rule, included about three or four broad types.[1] Although these characteristics and types have been labeled differently by different authors, their basic content appears robust across perspectives; the underlying logic makes it clear that, while strategies can also be described in other ways (in fact, strategies can be described in innumerable ways and countless specific strategies are feasible), these high-level characteristics and types are a useful starting place in understanding what strategies are possible, how they differ, and how they relate to each other.

The first characteristic or dimension along which all strategies can be described is the "basis of competition" or competitive advantage. Strategies can either emphasize *product differentiation* (which can take many forms, elaborated on below) or they can pursue *cost leadership* (which looks like "price leadership" from the customers' perspective). This distinction is logical; you can either compete on cost or you can compete on something else. The other principal way strategies can be differentiated is with regard to their *competitive scope*—the breadth of the market and range of customer segments that the strategy intends to serve. This note describes these two dimensions and also the types of basic strategies that they delineate: differentiation, cost leadership, and niche strategies. These are "generic strategies" because, at this high level of description, they distinguish a few very basic strategies that encompass all possible strategies. It is worth reiterating that, within these broad categories, there are almost infinite specific forms a particular strategy can take.

COMPETITIVE ADVANTAGE

Harvard Professor Michael Porter has argued that that "[a] company can outperform its rivals only if it can establish a difference that it can preserve."[2] Wal-Mart, Toys-Я-Us, and Black & Decker have advantages because of their size and the corresponding benefits of scale that give them the lowest cost structure amongst their competitors. Proctor & Gamble has unrivaled marketing and branding skills. Apple has similarly unparalleled design capabilities. Amazon.com has a sophisticated value chain that yields cash-flow, efficiency, and high-speed customization. *These companies are successful because*

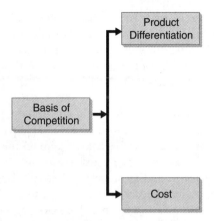

FIGURE NOTE 17-1 Basis of Competition: Cost Leadership and Differentiation

TABLE NOTE 17-1 Sources of Cost Advantages	
Economies of Scale	• Spreading fixed costs over large volume • Purchasing discounts/leverage • Specialization of labor • Specialized machines and technology
Economies of Scope	• Shared resources between products • Pooled negotiation power • Coordinated strategies between business units • Vertical integration • Combined business creation
Experience Curve Effects	• Improved skills and routines • Improved quality
Production Techniques	• Process innovation • Automation
Product Design	• Standardization of designs and components • Design to manufacture
Input Costs	• Location advantages • Access to low-cost inputs

they were able to create a sustainable difference. Creating a difference means either bringing an identical or similar product or service to market more cost effectively than the competitors (and therefore being able to charge the customer less or reap higher margins) or bundling unique benefits in an offering for which customers are willing to pay a price premium. These two strategies, cost leadership and the differentiation, are fundamentally different approaches to forging competitive advantage (Figure 17-1).

Cost Leadership

A cost leader typically offers a standardized, no-frills product; *adding 'frills' adds costs.* Wal-Mart is the classic cost leader, continuously innovating to reduce costs in its procurement, distribution, and logistics systems. The strategic objective of the cost leader is to deliver the products at lowest costs, to sell those products at the lowest price, and to communicate that proposition to price-sensitive markets. Such a positioning generally requires producing an undifferentiated offering (a commodity) and having a zealous focus on reducing costs. Potential sources of cost advantages are summarized in Table 17-1; many of those sources of cost advantage are tied to achieving scale advantage—that is, to being the biggest or among the biggest competitors in the market. Usually there is room for only one cost leader per industry; if there is more than one, a price war is likely. Because cost leadership, by definition, entails gaining competitive advantages through having

the lowest costs, because low costs are related to high scale, and because high scale is dependent on high market share, *market share becomes crucial to becoming and staying the cost leader.*

Cost leaders' products are highly standardized, with no-frills, and are usually produced for mass markets. Operational efficiency and process improvement are critical—the cost leader must excel in these areas. The cost-leader organization must run as a well-oiled machine to avoid inefficiencies, and its structure therefore is usually formal, standardized, and mechanistic. The dominant values are cost-consciousness, efficiency, and risk aversion. Cost leaders usually adopt a top–down approach and are authoritative to enforce smooth flowing, standardized processes, and consistency.

Differentiation

An advantage can be created when a company is able to deliver a superior product or service to the customer, for which the customer is willing to pay a premium because it better fulfills his needs. Superior value can stem from higher quality, better service, more features, more convenience, better brand image, and other distinctive qualities. Table 17-2 summarizes some selected sources of differentiation, including product and service quality, image factors (such as brand personality), and distribution qualities, all of which can, potentially, serve as points of differentiation. This assortment of potential points of differentiation emphasizes the range of ways that an offering can deliver superior satisfaction and greater value to customers.

A differentiation strategy requires almost the opposite skills and organizational characteristics than a cost-leadership strategy. Differentiation requires

---

TABLE NOTE 17-2 Common Bases of Differentiation

Quality in Goods[3]
- Performance
- Features
- Reliability
- Conformance
- Durability
- Serviceability
- Aesthetics
  - Form
  - Style
- Design
- Other Perceptions

Brand Personality[4]
- Sincerity
- Excitement
- Competence
- Sophistication
- Ruggedness

Quality in Services[5]
- Reliability
- Responsiveness
- Assurance
- Empathy
- Tangibles

Channel Functions
- Transactional functions
- Logistical functions
- Facilitating functions

---

continuous innovation and exceptional brand management; otherwise there is the chronic risk that a competitor will imitate or surpass the firm's offerings. A differentiated offering is typically highly sophisticated, depending on that technological superiority for strategic advantage, and it usually offers exceptional quality and/or a unique brand image—otherwise no customer would be willing to pay a the premium for it. To achieve and maintain these advantages, a differentiator must be *customer oriented* and *innovative* and must have special skills in brand management. To react to changing customer needs, to be innovative and flexible, these companies must have very flexible and organic organizational structures. To ensure fast information flow and customer orientation throughout the company, these companies often work with cross-functional teams, especially in product development. Dominant values of the organizational culture are risk taking, speed, flexibility, and experimentation—these are the ingredients of innovativeness. Leaders of differentiated organizations are often visionaries who involve employees in decision making and who encourage employees to innovate and generate creative ideas.

Cost Leadership versus Differentiation

The choice of a generic strategy has long-term consequences; in fact, it is usually irreversible, at least in the near- and mid-term. Importantly, the choice must be carefully thought through and should fit the company's strengths (or with strengths the company will develop). Table 17-3 describes and compares the two alternatives. Table 17-4 lists core functions of the firm—from manufacturing through sales—that must be carried out and distinguishes approaches to those tasks within cost leader and differentiation strategies. The table highlights the fact that the two strategies require quite different strengths and emphasize different, and in some instances conflicting approaches.

Hybrid Strategies

Some experts have argued that, in certain instances, companies can pursue a hybrid strategy that *simultaneously* seeks to achieve differentiation and

TABLE NOTE 17-3 Comparing Cost Leadership and Differentiation[6]

	Cost Leadership (or "Exploitative Business")	Differentiation (or "Exploratory Business")
Strategic Intent	Low cost, market share	Differentiation, innovation, price premium
Offering	Standardized, no-frills	Sophisticated, high quality, branded product
Critical Tasks	Operations, efficiency, process improvement	Customer orientation, product innovation, brand management
Organizing Structure	Formal, standardized, mechanistic	Flexible, organic, cross-functional product development teams
Organizational Culture	Efficiency, low risk, cost-consciousness	Risk taking, speed, flexibility, experimentation
Leadership Role	Authoritative, top down	Visionary, involved

TABLE NOTE 17-4 Generic Strategies and Their Requirements[7]

Function	Cost Leadership	Differentation
Manufacturing	Lean, automated, low cost, reliable quality	Flexible automation
Marketing	Emphasize value, reliability, and above all price	Emphasize unique product features and brand
R&D	Incremental product improvement, process innovation	New product development
Finance	Focus on low cost and stable financial structure	Enough funds for R&D
Accounting	Tight cost control, adopt conservative accounting principles	Accounting system that allows cost calculation for customized, complex products
Sales	Focus on value, reliability, low price, ubiquitous availability	Focus on uniqueness, brand, strong customer support

lower prices.[8] IKEA is an example of such a strategy; it has the lowest prices in the industry and is able to differentiate itself through design, image, and shopping experience. However, given the characteristics of these two strategies and their requirements (discussed above and summarized in Tables 17-3 and 17-4), it becomes clear that hybrid strategies are more the exception than the rule and that they are particularly difficult to execute. If it is not impossible, it is certainly extremely difficult to do both of these things better than the competition: Differentiation costs money, and costs necessitate higher prices. That unavoidable logic—and the contrasting, sometimes conflicting, attributes of successful cost leaders vis-à-vis differentiators—argues for treating

competitive advantage as a distinction rather than as a continuum and argues against straddling a cost-leadership and differentiation strategy. Michael Porter argued that firms that try to combine the two will end up "stuck in the middle":

"The firm stuck in the middle is almost guaranteed low profitability. It either loses the high-volume customers who demand low prices or must bid away its profits to get this business from the low-cost firms. Yet it also loses high-margin business—the cream—to the firms who are focused on high-margin targets or have achieved differentiation overall."[9]

One exception to the rule of choosing one or the other may be in an offering that is distinct for its low cost (and therefore low price to the customer) as well as differentiated by its high reliability and/or conformity. This is true because both costs per unit and reliability improve with scale. Costs go down and reliability goes up though experience curve effects and economies of scale. The more units of a standardized offering a firm produces, the lower the costs and, at the same time, the more reliable the units produced become. For example, Toyota produces more than 10 million small engines and vehicles every year. That industry-leading scale along with "the Toyota Way" of continuous improvement in manufacturing has led to Toyota and its brands (Toyota, Lexus, and Scion) leading the world not only in value pricing (not necessarily lowest price, but consistently great value for cost) as well as reliability and conformance.[10]

COMPETITIVE SCOPE

The second dimension or characteristic of strategies that has emerged across various frameworks and been well-established by many strategy experts is *competitive scope*, that is, the size and breadth of the market(s) the strategy means to serve—or target(s). Competitive scope may vary in terms of the number of customers the firm targets, the number of segments the firm targets, the heterogeneity of those different customers and segments, and the variety of needs that the firm endeavors to serve. Therefore, the dimensions and decisions that structure competitive scope are the same as those that define *market segmentation.*

Unlike the basis of competition, which we've argued above is best understood as a distinction between two mutually-exclusive alternatives, competitive scope can be thought of as a *continuum* covering a range of viable alternatives. That is, some firms serve mass markets with standardized offerings, some firms even target the whole world as a single market (these are called "global strategies"), while others serve very small markets or "niches" with highly customized, value-added offerings, and still others carve out any number of intermediate competitive scopes (Figure 17-2).

FIGURE NOTE 17-2 Scope of Competition

For example, Toyota is a global brand, taking advantage of scale effects to produce low-cost, high-value automobiles and light trucks. Toyota makes about 10 million vehicles a year. Porsche is a highly focused automobile manufacturer which produces about 100,000 vehicles a year.[11] Those two brands represent the extremes, a global mass marketer and a focused niche brand. (In point of fact, Porsche is also global in its operations and in the geographic dispersion of its distinctive market segment). But between Toyota and Porsche lies an assortment of other manufacturers and brands, each defining their competitive scope differently. BMW, for instance, produces about 1.5 million vehicles a year;[12] BMW's scale is more than 10 times that of Porsche but still only about a sixth of Toyota's. Thus, the competitive scope of a marketing strategy can vary along a continuum and there is less chance of getting caught in the "unprofitable middle" with regard to scope than there is with regard to the basis of competition (i.e., differentiation versus cost leadership). Companies that pursue a focus strategy try to serve a well-defined and narrow market segment more effectively or efficiently than an industry-wide competitor. A niche strategy is viable when segment-specific needs exist that an industry-wide supplier is not able to meet or not interested in meeting.

Is a Cost Focus Viable? Because of the close association between cost advantage and scale, a combination of cost leadership and a niche scope is difficult, but probably not impossible. In some markets—including automobiles—the cost leader actually offers an augmented product. The leading "economy car" manufacturers, such as Honda, Toyota, and General Motor's Chevrolet, offer products emphasizing price with practical functionality, but those products are also highly reliable and do offer elements of style and comfort beyond the "bare minimum." This leaves the extreme no-frills and absolute-low-cost market space under served. In India, the automobile manufacturer Tata has introduced the Nano, "the world's cheapest car." The Nano has a 35-horsepower, two-cylinder gas engine and is priced starting at 100,000 rupees (the equivalent of about $2,200 or €1,500).[13] This vehicle is targeted to a niche of customers in developing economies who use motorcycles as basic transportation but who would prefer to "upgrade" to a (very low-cost and bare-bones) car. Nevertheless, the far more usual sort of niche strategy offers differentiation tailored to a small but profitable segment's needs. It is essential that segment-specific needs exist, and that the focused company has the necessary skills and competences to satisfy them. Otherwise, industry-wide competitors can outperform the focused, niche offering due to cost advantages.

Summary

By combining two generally exclusive strategies, product differentiation or cost leadership, with the strategy's scope—the range of alternatives from a broad, mass target market to a narrow, niche target market—three competitive strategies emerge (see Figure 17-3): cost leadership, differentiation, or niche/customer-intimacy. Generally a niche or focused strategy is reserved for a combination of narrow focus and differentiation due to the strong connection between cost leadership and scale, but some niche-cost (or cost focus) strategies have been successful. Figure 17-3 clarifies these strategic alternatives.

These are meant to be *gross generalizations*; the "over simplification" is intentional, and it is clear that there are countless ways in which specific strategies can be different within these rudimentary but comprehensive buckets. Nevertheless, these distinctions are useful, as they create a valuable structure to initiate a high-level understanding of the breadth of strategies that may be created in a marketplace and the considerations that go with certain particular strategic orientations.

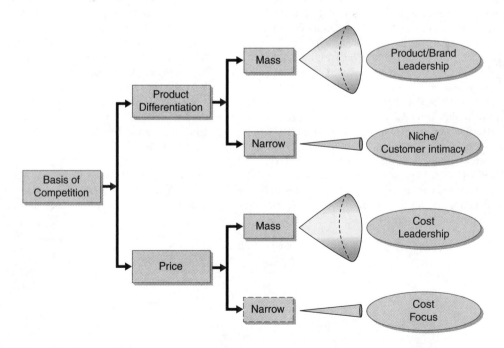

FIGURE NOTE 17-3   Generic Strategies

Additional Resources

Marr, Bernard. *Strategic Management Leveraging and Measuring Your Intangible Value Drivers.* Burlington, MA: Butterworth-Heinemann, 2006.

Porter, Michael E. "What Is Strategy?" *Harvard Business Review* (November–December, 1996): 61–78.

Porter, Michael E. *Competitive Strategy: Techniques for Analyzing Industries and Competitors.* New York: The Free Press, 1980.

Treacy, Michael and Fred Wiersema. *The Discipline of Market Leaders: Choose Your Customers, Narrow Your Focus, Dominate Your Market.* New York: Perseus Books, HarperCollins Publishers, 1995.

Endnotes

1. See, for example, Michael Treacy and Fred Wiersema, *The Discipline of Market Leaders: Choose Your Customers, Narrow Your Focus, Dominate Your Market* (New York: Perseus Books, HarperCollins Publishers, 1995); Michael E. Porter, "What Is Strategy?" *Harvard Business Review* (November–December 1996): 61–78. And Michael E. Porter, *Competitive Strategy: Techniques for Analyzing Industries and Competitors* (New York: The Free Press, 1980).

2. Porter, "What Is strategy?"

3. Adapted from David A. Garvin, "What Does 'Product Quality' Really Mean?" *MIT Sloan Management Review* 26, no. 1 (Fall 1984); David A. Garvin, "Competing on the Eight Dimensions of Quality," *Harvard Business Review* 65, no. 6 (November–December, 1987); and Philip Kotler and Kevin Lage Keller, *A Framework for Marketing Management*, 4th ed. (Upper Saddle River, NJ: Pearson/Prentice Hall, 2009).

4. From Jennifer Lynn Aaker, "Dimensions of Brand Personality," *Journal of Marketing Research* 8 (1997): 347–356.

5. A. Parasuraman, V. A. Zeithaml, and L. L. Berry, "SERVQUAL: A Multiple-item Scale for Measuring Consumer Perceptions of Service Quality, " *Journal of Retailing* 64, no. 1, (Spring 1988), 12-40; A. Parasuraman, V. A. Zeithaml, and L. L. Berry, "A Conceptual Model of Service Quality and Its Implications for Future Research," *Journal of Marketing* 49 (Fall 1985): 41–50.

6. C. A. O'Reilly III and Michael L. Tushman, "The Ambidextrous Organization," *Harvard Business Review* (April 2004): 74–81.

7. Adapted from Jay B. Barney and William S. Hesterly, *Strategic Management and Competitive Advantage*, (Upper Saddle River, New Jersey: Pearson Education, 2006).

8. Gerry Johnson, Kevan Scholes, and Richard Whittington, *Exploring Corporate Strategy. Text & cases.* (Harlow, England: Prentice Hall, 2008).

9. Porter, "Competitive Strategy."

10. See, for example, Jeffery K. Liker, *The Toyota Way: 14 Management Principles from the World's Greatest Manufacturer* (New York: McGraw-Hill, 2004).

11. Source: International Organization of Motor Vehicle Manufacturers, World Motor Vehicle Production (2008 Report), http://oica.net/wp-content/uploads/world-ranking-2008.pdf. Last accessed June 25th, 2010

12. Source: Ibid.

13. See, for example, Heather Timmons, "A Tiny Car Is the Stuff of 4-Wheel Dreams for Millions of Drivers in India," *The New York Times*, March 23, 2009, B4.

18

Generic Strategies—The Value Map

"Value" can be defined in many ways, but in marketing strategy it refers to customer perceptions that weigh or combine what the customer *gets* (the benefits or "performance" the customer receives) adjusted for what the customer *gives* (the costs, especially price, given in exchange for those benefits). That is, it is a ratio of the benefits divided by the price:

$$Value = \frac{\text{"Get"}}{\text{"Give"}}$$

The important thing is not how the firm or the marketing manager thinks about this equation, but how the customers think about it, and how they think about it *relative to other offerings in the marketplace.* Different customers and different segments of customers will value various benefits differently; for example, families usually think safety is very important in making a car purchase while other segments, such as young professionals, may value acceleration or comfort more highly. At the same time, although what the customer "gives" may be mostly about price, there are other costs, such as time and effort (convenience or inconvenience, required assembly, expected maintenance, and the like), and those are also part of the perceived price or "give" to the customer. Thus, what "value" means in a strategic context can be elaborated to:

$$Value = \frac{\sum[(Relative\ Benefits)^*(Importance\ Weight)]}{\sum(Relative\ Price + Other\ Costs)}$$

Customers understand that they can *get more* if they're willing to *give more*, and various alternatives in any market almost always offer varying degrees of benefits (performance or quality) at different price points. Customers' perceptions of value can be plotted into a two-dimensional space, give (relative price) versus get (relative performance/benefits), and there will be a segment-specific line or "frontier" along which customers can see fair tradeoffs between give and get. Figure 18-1 is a "value map" defined by those two dimensions—relative price and relative performance or quality—and shows a hypothetical "fair-value frontier."

For example, in the flat screen TV market, any customer knows they can buy a Funai, a Sony, a JVC, a Loewe and so on, as graphed in Figure 18-2. While some customers may choose a Funai, they understand that they could pay more and get more with another alternative. Similarly, Sony buyers know they could pay less and get less with either a Panasonic, or a Funai—or pay more and get a Metz. And so on. Thus, there is a frontier or equilibrium boundary along which customers choose *fair value*; a

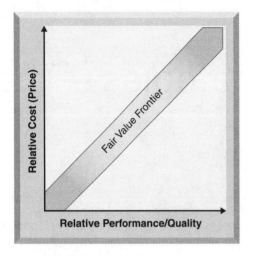

FIGURE NOTE 18-1 The Value Map and Value Frontier or Fair Value Zone[1]

position above or to the left of that frontier (toward the "northwest") reflects an inferior value—the customer could get more performance for the same price or pay less for the given performance. Only the constrained or poorly informed customers would willingly purchase a brand in this area, and that condition may not last for long. Anything toward the southeast is a superior value—it offers more than the

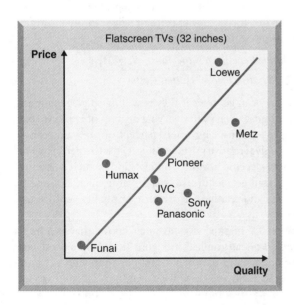

FIGURE NOTE 18-2 Value Map for Flat Screen TVs[2]

market had been offering for the same price or charges less for the same performance; this is where innovations often enter the market, by finding a way to deliver something more or a way to charge less.

The value frontier is the maximum performance or quality currently feasible at a given cost to the customer. Southwest Airlines created a new value proposition for airline customers; IKEA created a new value proposition with lower-priced knock-down furniture; Dell Computer did the same for PCs; and Wal-Mart did likewise for the world of re-tailing. In its own manner, each of these companies found a way to deliver superior performance at a lower price than its competitors. In particular, Southwest Airlines extended the value frontier at the low end of the airline industry and dramatically ex-panded demand for its flights. In contrast, Dell took advantage of the commoditization of the PC busi-ness to establish a new value frontier by selling prod-ucts directly to the customers, thus stripping out middleman costs that delivered few benefits to cus-tomers. Finally, Wal-Mart led mass retailers in the development of logistics, systems, and supply chain capabilities that allowed it to sell national brands for less than its competitors, thereby pushing the value frontier and eventually becoming the largest retailer in the world. But what exactly is a value frontier, and how is this concept useful to marketers?

The concept of the value frontier is a powerful tool for analysis and strategy formulation. It can be used to assess the value products or services create for the customer. This analysis is vital to marketing strategists, because value delivered to customers di-rectly influences market share and profitability. A customer value map is also useful in that it can assist marketers in developing clear and solid marketing strategies.

THE VALUE MAP AND CUSTOMER VALUE ANALYSIS

The pioneers of customer value analysis—Bradley T. Gale and Robert D. Buzzell[3]—carried out extensive research to measure the impact that customer value has on market share and profitability using the PIMS (Profit Impact of Market Strategies)[4] database. PIMS contains data on more than 3,000 business units from about 200 companies. To analyze the role of customer value in company success, Gale and Buzzell created a two-dimensional matrix and positioned each strategic business unit on this matrix based on the dimensions of "relative price" (price compared to competitors) and "relative quality" (quality compared to competitors). Gale and Buzzell then determined the average profitability (return on investment, or ROI, before interest and taxes) of the strategic business units in the four quadrants of the matrix (Figure 18-3).

The fair value line in Figure 18-1 indicates the points at which quality is balanced against price. Any product positioned to the left of the fair value line delivers low customer value. This product is either too expensive for its level of quality, or its quality is too low for its given price. Product positioned on this side of the line lose market share, which means that low profitability will follow. In contrast, any product on the right side of the fair value line creates high

customer value. These products will gain market share and earn a high return. As shown in the Figure 18-3, four basic strategies can be derived from this customer value map: the superior customer value strategy, the premium strategy, the economy strategy, and the inferior customer value strategy.

The Superior Customer Value Strategy

The superior customer value strategy is a combination of Michael Porter's cost leadership strategy and his differentiation strategy. With this strategy, the goal is to offer a product that not only performs better (i.e., offers higher quality, better brand image, better service, etc.) than those offered by competitors, but one that is also priced below the competitors' offerings. This is a particularly difficult position to achieve, because it requires both a cost advantage and a differentiation advantage. However, if a company succeeds in enacting this strategy, it is rewarded

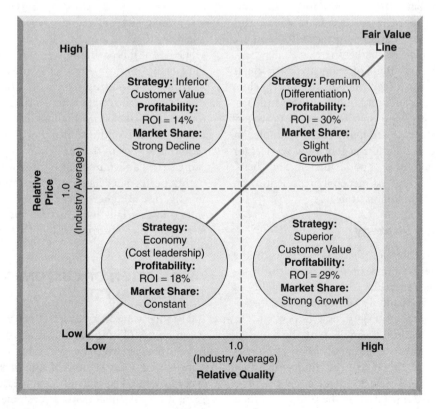

FIGURE NOTE 18-3   Strategies and Results within the Value Map[5]

with a strong increase in market share and, in turn, high profitability—on average, a 29 percent ROI (i.e., return on investment before interest and taxes).

Inditex, the parent company of highly successful apparel retailer Zara, has become the world's largest specialty fashion chain by creating superior customer value. Inditex can reportedly take a new fashion idea from concept to finished garment and distribute it to over 1,000 stores in about two weeks—this is truly fast fashion, as well as a significant differentiation advantage. Moreover, Inditex does this at very competitive prices due to its vertically integrated manufacturing and distribution system.

The Premium Strategy

The premium strategy comes close to the differentiation strategy—with one important difference. Specifically, it requires that a company is able to differentiate itself or its products in terms of quality, innovation, service, brand image, etc., *and* that customers are willing to pay a price premium for superior product performance. Products that are sold via this strategy on average earn a 30 percent ROI and are able to slightly increase market share.

One can easily think of many luxury products that employ this strategy, including Rolex watches, Bentley automobiles, and Louis Vuitton handbags. However, this strategy isn't just limited to luxury goods. Indeed, there are many other examples of both consumer and industrial goods and services for which companies offer "good," "better," and "best" products—with "the best" generally representing an exhibition of the premium strategy.

The Economy Strategy

Companies that position their products using the economy strategy compete on price, primarily by focusing on cost leadership. Although the quality of these products is balanced against their price, the average ROI using this strategy is only 18 percent. The reason for this low ROI is simple: With the economy strategy, price plays a dominant role, so price wars are a permanent threat to profitability. In other words, if companies want to increase market share, they usually do so by lowering the price—but their competitors often follow suit shortly thereafter.

Indeed, studies show that in the long run market shares remain unchanged, because competitors respond with price reductions to recover lost market share.

Dell Computer successfully exploited a cost leadership strategy for many years to become the market share leader in PCs. Later, the merger of HP and Compaq allowed HP to regain market share. In contrast, Wal-Mart has successfully adopted a cost leadership strategy over the years to deliver its economy strategy to consumers and become—and remain—the largest retailer in the world.

The Inferior Customer Value Strategy

Products positioned in the inferior customer value quadrant of the value frontier will not be able to contribute to a company's success unless the company has a monopoly, customers cannot switch to another product, or there is little market transparency and customers are not aware of better alternatives. This position usually is the worst in terms of market share and profitability; in fact, a strong loss of market share and a low ROI (on average, 14 %) are the typical consequences of this positioning. It might be argued that the North American automobile manufacturers got in trouble by offering inferior customer value for decades, with the result being a strong customer bias toward imports that led to those firms' difficulties in the first decade of this Millennium; Japanese brands had found ways to deliver greater reliability at the same price, and European brands were delivering higher performance and more desirable image and prestige for a higher price; the value frontier had shifted to the right and American brands were slow to adapt, thereby getting stuck in the "Northwest."

APPLICATION OF CUSTOMER VALUE ANALYSIS

A customer value analysis serves two purposes. First, it can be useful in the formulation of market data-based strategies, which are preferable to vague definitions or blurry descriptions of strategies. Second, this type of analysis helps identify clear measures to implement strategies. In other words, customer value analysis is a simple and straightforward tool to translate strategy into action. However, in order for an analysis to be successful, the marketer must have clear answers to the following questions, ideally based on market research data:

1. What is our target market?
2. Who are our competitors in the target market?
3. What are the customers' buying criteria?
4. How important is each of these criteria?
5. How do customers evaluate our product and the competitors' products on the basis of these buying criteria?
6. What are our prices and those of the competitors?
7. What is the customers' price sensitivity?

Strategy formulation based on the value frontier concept can be systematically accomplished using a number of single analytical tools over eight distinct steps of analysis. These steps are as follows

- Step 1: Definition of the target market
- Step 2: Identification of competitors
- Step 3: Identification of customers' buying criteria and their relative importance
- Step 4: Assessment of product performance and price
- Step 5: Calculation of relative quality and relative price
- Step 6: Estimation of customers' price sensitivity
- Step 7: Creation of the customer value map and formulation of strategies
- Step 8: Definition of an action plan using importance-performance analysis

Figure 18-4 also contains a worksheet that can be used for this purpose. Now, let's take a closer look at what each of the eight aforementioned steps entails, referring to Figure 18-4 as we proceed.

STEP 1: DEFINING THE TARGET MARKET. A good customer value analysis begins with the definition of market segments. This is a critical step and must be done carefully, because buying criteria and price sensitivity can differ significantly between segments. For instance, for sports car buyers (e.g., Porsche purchasers), characteristics such as engine power, acceleration, and brand image are typically important, whereas for family car buyers, traits like fuel consumption, space, and price are likely more important.

For the purposes of this example, we'll focus mid-level laptop computers, because they appeal to a broad, "all-round" segment.

STEP 2: IDENTIFYING COMPETITORS. The second step of the strategy formulation process involves identifying competitors within the market segment. For this task, the concept of strategic groups can be particularly helpful. A strategic group is a group of companies within an industry that pursue similar competitive strategies and have similar characteristics (e.g., size) and competences. These companies, therefore, offer similar products to similar customers and are in strong competition with one another. For our segment, we identified six major competitors: Samsung, Toshiba, Dell, IBM, HP, and Fujitsu Siemens (see Figure 18-4).

STEP 3: IDENTIFYING AND ASSESSING BUYING CRITERIA. Next comes a particularly crucial step in customer analysis: identification of the customers' buying criteria and their relative weights. This step usually requires market research in order to formulate a clear understanding what customers want, how they decide, and what is more (or less) important to them. Ideally, qualitative market research initially identifies the buying criteria (attributes). Then, by way of a subsequent quantitative, representative study, both the relative importance of these criteria and competitors' performance on these criteria are measured. There are several ways to assess the relative importance of these attributes, including:

- Conjoint analysis (a research technique that identifies customer preferences when attributes are considered simultaneously and interdependently);
- Rating scales (e.g., "How important is the battery of a laptop to you?"; 1 = not at all important, 5 = very important);
- Rank orders ("Please rank from 1 to 6 the following characteristics of laptop computers [1 is most important and 6 is least important]"); and
- Constant sum scales ("Please divide 100 points among the following characteristics so the division reflects the relative importance of each characteristic to you in the selection of a laptop.")

Customer Value Map
Product: Laptops
Segment: Middle-class, all round usage

Buying Criteria (non price)	Weight	Dell Inspiron 8600 Performance (1-5)	Dell Weighted Score	HP Pavillon zt3020 Performance (1-5)	HP Weighted Score	Toshiba Satellite p10-554 Performance (1-5)	Toshiba Weighted Score	Samsung P30 Performance (1-5)	Samsung Weighted Score	IBM R40 TR4BDGGE Performance (1-5)	IBM Weighted Score	Fujitsu Siemens AMILO P4 Performance (1-5)	Fujitsu Weighted Score
Performance	25	3	75	3	75	4	100	3	75	3	75	4	100
Handling	20	4	80	4	80	4	80	4	80	4	80	3	60
Screen	15	4	60	4	60	4	60	4	60	4	60	3	45
Versatility in use	10	4	40	4	40	3	30	3	30	2	20	3	30
Workmanship	5	4	20	4	20	4	20	4	20	4	20	4	20
Battery	10	4	40	4	40	3	30	4	40	4	40	2	20
Brand Image	15	2	30	4	60	1	15	1	15	5	75	4	60
	100												
Weighted Score			345,00		375,00		335,00		320,00		370,00		335,00
Relative Quality			1,00		1,08		0,97		0,92		1,07		0,97
Price			1500,00		1800,00		1600,00		1600,00		1500,00		1800,00
Relative Price			0,92		1,10		0,98		0,98		0,92		1,10

Weights	
Quality	40
Price	60
Sum	100

	Relative price	Relative Quality
Dell	0,92	1,00
HP	1,10	1,08
Toshiba	0,98	0,97
Samsung	0,98	0,92
IBM	0,92	1,07
Fujitsu Siemens	1,10	0,97

FIGURE NOTE 18-4 Worksheet for Customer Value Analysis

STEP 4: ASSESSING PRODUCT PERFORMANCE AND PRICE.   Product performance is best assessed using a rating scale (e.g., from 1 to 5, where 5 is best). In our example above (Figure 18-4), data on buying criteria and their relative weight, as well as on the performance of the single competing products, were taken from secondary market research on a European market.[6]

The second part of Step 4 is price assessment. Prices usually are easily available. In the case of complex price structures (e.g., bank services, supermarkets) instead of using actual prices, one can also estimate price levels (e.g., our price = 100, competitor's price level = ?).

STEP 5: CALCULATING RELATIVE QUALITY AND PRICE.   Next, in order to calculate the quality score of each competing product, the performance rating of each attribute must be multiplied by the relative weight of that attribute, and the resulting values must be added together. By themselves, the absolute individual quality scores and prices are not meaningful—they have to be compared to those of the competitors.

Therefore, a quality ratio and a price ratio are calculated. These ratios represent a product's quality score and price compared to the average of all products' quality scores and prices. In our example (Figure 18-5), HP's relative quality of 1.08 means that the quality is 8 percent higher than the average quality of the products, and its relative price of 1.10 means that the HP laptop costs 10 percent more than average.

STEP 6: ESTIMATING PRICE SENSITIVITY.   Customers' price sensitivity can simply be measured using a constant sum scale and a question similar to the following: "Please indicate how much weight you put on quality and how much weight you put on price in the selection of a laptop. Please divide 100 points between quality and price." In our example, let's assume that the customers are rather price sensitive. Thus, they place 40 percent of the weight of their buying decision on quality and 60 percent on price. Here—and in all cases—the slope of the fair value line will be equal to the percentage of the decision based on quality divided by the percentage of the decision based on price.

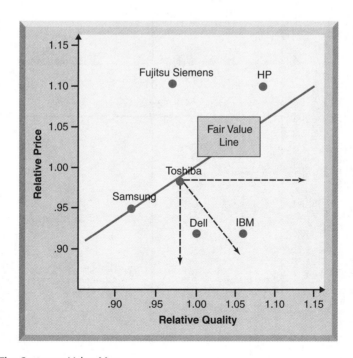

FIGURE NOTE 18-5   The Customer Value Map

STEP 7: CREATING THE CUSTOMER VALUE MAP AND FORMULATING STRATEGIES. At this point, the relative quality and relative price of each product can be used to create the customer value map (Figure 18-5). On this map, a "1" on each dimension indicates the average quality and average price of all products. As previously mentioned, the fair value line indicates the points at which quality is balanced against price. Products positioned to the left of the fair value line offer lower customer value, whereas those to the right of the line offer higher value. A flat fair-value line represents price-sensitive customers. If, for example, the price is increased by 10 percent, quality has to be increased by more than 10 percent, to, say, 20 percent, in order for the customer to continue to buy that product. When customers have low price sensitivity, the fair-value line is steep. Here, a low increase of quality will allow a disproportionately high increase of price.

Now the customer value map can be created and strategies can be derived. In our example, Fujitsu Siemens has a clear disadvantage, because its quality is too low and its price too high. In contrast, IBM has the most favorable position (i.e., it offers the highest customer value), followed by Dell. In this case, if, for example, Toshiba wanted to increase its market share, it would have three options: (1) lower prices, (2) increase quality, or (3) carry out a combination of price reduction and quality improvement.

STEP 8: DEFINING AN ACTION PLAN. The final step of customer value analysis involves defining an action plan. One especially useful tool for doing this is the importance-performance-analysis method.[7] For example, if Toshiba's strategy is to increase quality and position itself as the quality leader in the industry, it must determine how to enact this strategy. To do so, Toshiba should compare its product's performance

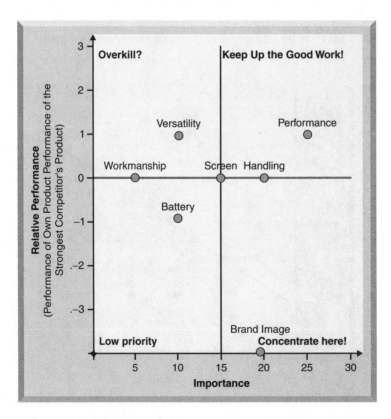

FIGURE NOTE 18-6 Importance-Performance-Analysis

attribute by attribute with that of its strongest competitor (IBM). Then, a matrix with attribute importance on the *x*-axis and attribute performance (compared to IBM) on the *y*-axis can be created. For the y-axis in our example (Figure 18-5), we use relative performance (Toshiba's performance score minus IBM's performance score). Four quadrants with the following implications are, therefore, identified:

- *Quadrant 1 (high importance –high performance):* These product characteristics or attributes (such as performance in Figure 18-4) are the competitive advantages. A company should keep up the good work here.
- *Quadrant 2 (high importance –low performance):* These product characteristics or attributes are the "burning fires". A company should take immediate action here.

- *Quadrant 3 (low importance –high performance):* A higher performance on unimportant attributes can represent a possible overkill. If costs need to be reduced, these are the best candidates to cut expenses.
- *Quadrant 4 (low importance –low performance):* Actions have low priority here, as these disadvantages are not very relevant.

In our example, Toshiba's priority should be to increase its brand image, which will have the strongest effect, followed by improving its products "handling" and screen.

After this final step, the customer value analysis is complete. Based on market-research data, a strategy has been formulated, and an action plan has been derived.

Summary

Value mapping is a useful tool that allows marketing strategists to define the relative positions of industry competitors on performance or quality, as well as on cost. The value frontier is the maximum performance or quality currently feasible at a given cost to the customer. Successful strategists attempt to find or create unique positions on the value frontier. The process by which this is achieved includes the definition of the target market; the identification of competitors; the identification of customers' buying criteria and their relative importance; an assessment of product performance and price; the calculation of relative quality and relative price; the estimation of customers' price sensitivity; the creation of the customer value map and formulation of strategies; and the definition of an action plan using importance-performance-analysis

Additional Resources

Gale, Bradley T. *Managing Customer Value.* New York: Free Press, 1994.

Buzzell, Robert D., and Bradley T. Gale *The PIMS Principles. Linking Strategy to Performance.* New York: The Free Press, 1987.

Endnotes

1. Bradley T. Gale, *Managing Customer Value* (New York: Free Press, 1994).
2. Based on N. N. "TV-Geräte im Test," *Konsument* 6 (2009). Also see Bradley T. Gale, *Managing Customer Value* (New York: Free Press, 1994).
3. R. D. Buzzell, and B. T. Gale, *The PIMS Principles. Linking Strategy to Performance* (New York et al.: The Free Press, 1987). B. T. Gale, *Managing Customer Value* (New York, Free Press, 1994).

4. Buzzell and Gale, *The PIMS Principles.*
5. Adapted from Buzzell and Gale, *The PIMS Principles*; and Gale, *Managing Customer Value.*
6. Sources: "Notebooks: Viel Leistung um wenig Geld," *Stern Markenprofile* 11 (2004); *Konsument* 4 (2004).
7. J. A. Martilla, and J. C. James, "Importance-Performance Analysis," *Journal of Marketing* 41, no. 1 (1977): 77–79.

19

Generic Strategies— Product-Market Growth Strategies

Most managers are wired to pursue growth. Even if it were not part of the innate competitiveness of free-enterprise managers and markets, growth is an important strategic objective. In fact, it is *imperative* for most firms for three reasons:

1. The only way to increase stock price, and thus shareholder value, is to grow faster in earnings and cash flows than shareholders expect. Current share prices already reflect expected growth; the only way to increase share prices is to *exceed* those growth expectations;

2. Growth equates to market share and scale; therefore, lower growth than the competition equates to exacerbating cost disadvantages as competitors gain experience and economies of scale; and

3. Even firms that might choose to forego growth must, nevertheless, continuously pursue new customers and new markets for its products simply to maintain sales volume. No company retains 100 percent of its customer base; therefore, new customers and new products are necessary to offset customer defections and attrition.

Of course, not *all* companies are *always* growing their sales and some may choose, at least for the short term, to forego growth. Later in this note we will briefly discuss non-growth strategies—"maintenance" and "retrenchment" strategies—but, for the reasons listed, those are anomalies. Most firms aspire to growth in sales, revenues, and profits for growth's sake and/or in response to the pressures articulated above.

The question, then, is *how* a company or a strategic business unit can achieve that vital growth? Professor H. Igor Ansoff proposed a simple, logical, and useful matrix to organize possible answers to this question. Logically, at any given time a firm is marketing its existing products to its existing markets. That's just the way it is, by definition. To grow, then, the firm must sell more of the same product to those same customers, sell its existing products to new customers, sell new products to existing customers, or sell new products to new customers. By combining those two dimensions, products (existing versus new products) and markets (existing versus new markets), the Ansoff Matrix defines four distinct growth strategies: market penetration, product development, market development, and diversification, as shown in Figure 19-1. These four growth strategies are described in more detail in the following sections.

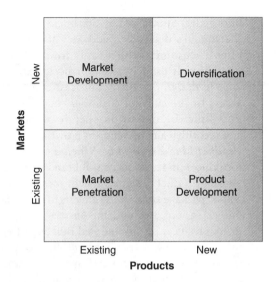

FIGURE NOTE 19-1 The Ansoff Product/Market Growth Matrix[1]

MARKET PENETRATION

The easiest and most promising way to grow is to increase sales of existing products in existing markets. As long as there is still some growth potential in existing markets, a company should prioritize this strategy. The company presumably has market knowledge, a developed and proven product, the necessary resources, and access to distribution channels. Customers know the brand, are familiar with the product and are, therefore, usually easier to stimulate to buy than new customers in a new market. Empirical studies indicate that "penetration" strategies have the highest success rate (50%) and require the lowest amount of resources of the four growth strategies[2]. There are several options to grow via market penetration:[3]

- *Increase Frequency of Use.* In this case, a company tries to persuade its customers to use its products more often. Diner's Club, for example, offers its credit card holders a rewards program. For each dollar charged, the customer earns a reward point, which then can be redeemed for a wide range of options, from frequent-flyer miles to brand-name merchandise to financial rewards. Hence, customers are motivated to use the credit card more often, instead of cash or instead of a competitor's card the customer might own.

- *Increase Quantity Used.* Another option to increase sales of an existing product to existing customers is to increase the quantity used. Amazon.com, for example, offers free shipping for most of its products if the total purchase is sufficient (€ 15 in Germany; $25 in the United States), and reminds customers of how much more they'd have to spend to get the free shipping. This policy increases sales, because many customers who would have bought a single item for € 15 or $25 or less decide to add another item to their "cart" to save on the shipping costs.

- *Convert Nonbuyers.* In any market there are customers that, for one reason or another, are nonusers of a product. If a company finds out the reasons for this, it can take measures to convert these customers. In many European countries the credit-card penetration rate is lower than in the United States. An Internet retailer that took payments only with credit cards would lose customers who didn't have cards, so Amazon.com has facilitated and promoted other payment methods, such as bank transfer after receipt of the product, to customers in central Europe.

- *New Applications.* Sales can also be increased when customers are shown new applications for existing products. Barilla, the Italian producer of pasta, offers a wide variety of recipes on the back of each package of pasta to stimulate its customers to consume more pasta. Danone increased sales of its brand "Fruchtzwerge" in Germany, a popular curd cheese product with fruit targeted to children, by showing in the TV ads a new application in summer. When "Fruchtzwerge" was put into the freezer, children could make their own tasty ice cream of it. Another example is the old Italian aperitif Aperol introduced in 1911. It used to be a regular aperitif sold mostly in northeastern Italy with a modest market share until a new product application was invented and promoted: Aperol Spritz, white wine with Aperol and soda water, became a refreshing orange flavor and low-alcohol cocktail and sales took off with yearly growth rates up to 70 percent in some countries.

- *Convert Lost Customers.* The average company has a customer turnover of 20 to 40 percent per year. A study by Marketing Metrics shows that on average there is a success probability of 60 to 70 percent to successfully sell again to existing customers, a 20 to 40 percent probability of successfully selling to lost customers, and only a 5 to 20 percent probability to win new customers. A mobile phone operator started to contact lost customers to find out the reason why they left the provider and tailored special offers to win them back; the success rate was between 15 and 20 percent.

- **Convert Competitor's Customers.** This, usually, is the most difficult way to grow as a company needs either a clear price advantage or a clear differentiation advantage. However, it can prove to be a successful strategy. A vendor of Enterprise Resource Planning (ERP) software realized that many small and medium-sized companies were dissatisfied with their ERP software and started to address them. As this company was very close to the market it could easily find out which of the companies were dissatisfied and why. Using this information it could target them and could turn these prospects, relatively easily, into customers.

PRODUCT DEVELOPMENT

To introduce modified, improved, or new products on existing markets is the second successful strategy with an average success rate of 33 percent. However, it takes on average eight times more resources than the market penetration strategy.

- **Product Improvements.** Adding new product features (e.g., digital camera to a cell phone) or improving product performance (e.g., fuel consumption of a car through the hybrid technology) is a typical strategy in a highly competitive market that came into its maturity phase of the product lifecycle. This way additional sales can be generated through a better differentiation of the product.
- **Product Innovations.** Synergies can be exploited when a company introduces a new product targeted to the existing customer base. In this case it leverages its brand equity and takes advantage of its market access and market

knowledge. Stimulated by Starbucks success, McDonald's decided to add McCafé and to offer its customers coffees and drinks. By simultaneously using its brand name, its experience in designing efficient processes, and its access to the existing customers base, it reduced the risk of new product development and identified a new avenue of growth.

- **Product Line-Extensions.** When a company introduces under its successful brand name in a given product category new flavors, forms, colors, package sizes, etc., it intends to grow via line-extensions. Red Bull, the Austrian energy-drink producer introduced Red Bull Sugarfree to address a new market segment. In addition to the Porsche Cayenne, Cayenne S, and Cayenne Turbo, the German car manufacturer introduced the new model Cayenne GTS to address the segment of SUV-Buyers who want to have a very sporty SUV, with fast acceleration and higher top-track speed similar to the Turbo, but at a lower price.
- **Cross Selling.** Cross selling in most cases offers very attractive opportunities for growth. Cross selling involves selling new products or services to its existing customers. Banks, for an instance, use cross-selling very systematically to increase sales by offering their customers services they have not used before. Amazon.com uses cross-selling when it tries to sell CDs or any other product to customers who have been buying only books so far. Cross-selling can be a very successful growth strategy when the customers are satisfied with the existing products and the relationship and trust their vendor.

MARKET DEVELOPMENT

The third growth strategy is market development; that is, expanding sales of existing products to new geographic markets (e.g., when Amazon.com entered China) or to new segments (e.g., when Amazon.com targeted business-to-business customers). This strategy requires building brand awareness and brand image, accessing new distribution channels, confronting new competitors, and often formulating new marketing strategies. Data show that, in comparison to market penetration, market development requires four times as much investment and the probability of success is only, on average, approximately 20 percent.

DIVERSIFICATION

Taking a new product to a new market is the strategy with the highest risk. It has the lowest probability of success (on average 5%) and needs the highest amount of resources (12 to 14 times as much as the market penetration strategy). There are different ways of diversification.

- *Related Diversification.* In a related diversification a company enters a new market with a new product attaining synergies by sharing assets or competencies across businesses. Synergies can be exploited by entering new markets with new products using a brand name (e.g., Richard Branson's Virgin Atlantic Airline, Virgin Records, Virgin Mobile UK, Virgin Express; not all the ventures proved to be successful), marketing skills, manufacturing skills, R&D skills, or taking advantage of economies of scale.
- *Unrelated Diversification.* In an unrelated diversification a company enters a new market with a new product not related to the existing product markets. In this case now synergies can be exploited and the venture is very risky as the company has no market knowledge and no product expertise.
- *Forward and Backward Integration.* Vertical integration is another potential growth strategy. Forward integration occurs when a company decides to move downstream the product flow (e.g., when it acquires retailers); backward integration means that a company moves upwards (e.g., when it acquires a supplier).

THE "Z" STRATEGY

Small firms and companies in mature industries often consider diversification as their only possible growth strategy. Especially when they missed to plan their growth strategically, they can find themselves in a situation where they need a new product and a new market at the same time. This, as Figure 19-2 shows, is a high risk strategy. The risk of diversification can be reduced when a company plans its growth across time. Before entering a new market with a new product,

	Existing Products		New Products	
Existing Markets	**Market Penetration:** • Increase Frequency of Use • Increase Quantity Used • Convert Non-Buyers • New Applications • Convert Lost Customers • Convert Competitor's Customers		**Product Development:** • Product Improvements • Product Innovations • Product-Line Extensions • Cross Selling	
	Probability of Success: 50%	Effort: 100%	Probability of Success: 33%	Effort: 800%
New Markets	**Market Development:** • Expand Geographically • Target New Segments		**Diversification:** • Related Diversification • Unrelated Diversification • Forward Integration • Backward Integration	
	Probability of Success: 20%	Effort: 400%	Probability of Success: 5%	Effort: 1200%-1400%

FIGURE NOTE 19-2   Strategic Planning within the Ansoff Matrix[4]

a company can develop a new product for the existing market, which it already knows, and in which it has brand image and access to distribution channels. In the next step, it can take the product that has been successfully introduced in the existing market to a new market. Alternatively, it could introduce an existing product to a new market to gain market knowledge, create brand awareness and brand image, get access to distribution channels, and then develop a new product for this market. Thus, it does not go directly from penetration to diversification, but reduces the risk of diversification by making a detour via one or both of the other growth strategies. This, however, has to be planned carefully and with a long-term perspective.

ADJACENCIES AND GROWING FROM "THE CORE"

Growth into either a new market or with a new product is less risky than diversification but that doesn't answer the question of what new market or new product to target for growth. *How should new markets or new products be selected?* A basic framework for answering that question is the notion of "adjacencies." Prominent strategy consultant and author Chris Zook has elaborated on and clarified this idea, arguing that firms should identify their "core," their

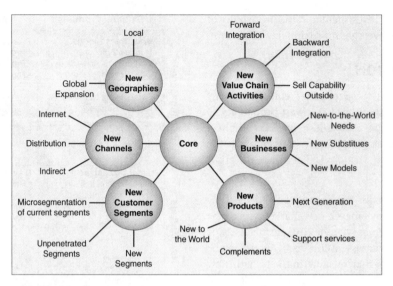

FIGURE NOTE 19-3 Building from the Core and Identifying Adjacencies[8]

essential, enduring, and defensible strengths, and grow by carefully defining that core and considering the distance or "steps" that any growth opportunity lies from it.[5] Of course, the first requirement in considering opportunities with regard to their relationship to the firm's core is to define that core rigorously and accurately. The company's core can be seen as its competitive advantages and market strengths: its most profitable customers, its key sources of differentiation, its core competencies, its most important products and the sources of profits ("profit pools"), its relationships with channels and other collaborators, its organizational culture, and any other assets such as patents, brands, or access to scarce resources that contribute to those core strengths.[6] Focus, that is understanding, protecting, and nurturing a strategic core is essential to success; Zook and his colleagues at Bain and Company studied data on more than 1,800 companies in seven countries with greater than $500 million in revenues and found that of the companies that could be described as "sustained value creators," those that had earned their cost of capital and realized growth of 5.5 percent or higher over the most recent decade, *78 percent had a single strong core and strong market leadership* (relative market share of greater than 1.2).

Once the firm has clarified its core strengths it should look for opportunities that build upon those strengths (that is, opportunities that are *adjacent to its core*). According to Zook, adjacencies can be found along any of six paths: new geographies, new value chain activities, new channels, new customer segments, new products, or new businesses (Figure 19-3). This six-strategy scheme corresponds closely with Ansoff's original two-dimensional summary: new geographies, new channels, and new customer segments are mostly about "new markets" (although new customer segments also includes what Ansoff labeled as market penetration in the form of increased sales to existing customers via "microsegmentation" of current segments), new products is simply product development, and new businesses and new value-chain activities are diversification. Zook studied 181 randomly selected adjacency moves by major corporations and found that for growth initiatives that were one step from the core, the success rate was 37 percent, for two-step moves it was 28 percent, and for three-steps it was less than 10 percent.[7]

NONGROWTH STRATEGIES

Most companies aspire to growth both for the inherent benefits of increased revenues and profits and in response to pressures, including investor demands, the need to achieve scale and its benefits, and the need to at least replace defecting customers, as discussed at the start of this note. Nevertheless, there are firms and situations for which growth is an unrealistic objective. Economic and competitive conditions may dictate, at least for certain periods, adopting a "damage control" strategy. Marketing strategy has long drawn on ideas about strategy from military and warfare strategists,[9] and a core idea in marketing as warfare is that there are times to act defensively. Defensive marketing strategies that are appropriate in times of low or no growth (or even decline) emphasize the need to identify the "high ground," the place where the firm has the most strength and the most likelihood of weathering the battle (with the intention, presumably, to "live to fight again another day" or resume growth in the future). Which customers are most attractive (loyal, profitable) and which strengths are most durable? Contracting

deliberately, rather than reactively, and concentrating on the most defensible market position, the most attractive customers, and the most resilient core strengths is necessary in times of defense and retrenchment (operationally, retrenchment also generally entails cost and asset reductions). One particular tactic is, generally, to avoid the temptation of retaining market size by discounting and degrading product quality. Discounting inferior products to maintain top-line sales can be a 'no win' situation, which fails to provide profits in the short term, dissatisfies customers and degrades the brand, and incites price wars and leads to pan-industry decline in the long run.

Summary

Growth is a pervasive objective in strategic marketing. There are only a certain number of ways to grow—market penetration, product development, market development, and diversification. Each of these is described in some detail in this note, along with a selected set of specific tactics for pursuing each general growth strategy. These growth strategies are not all equally attractive or sound—the further from the firm's "core" strengths the growth initiative reaches, the less likely it is to succeed. Identifying the core and building upon it is effective both in identifying opportunities for growth and in identifying defensible positions in times of retreat or retrenchment.

Additional Resources

Aaker, David A. *Strategic Market Management*, 7th ed. Hoboken. NJ: John Wiley & Sons, 2005.

Ansoff, H. Igor. "Strategies for diversification." *Harvard Business Review* (September–October, 1957), 113–24.

Becker, Jochen. *Marketing-Konzeption*. München: Vahlen Verlag, 2009.

Zook, Chris with James Allen. *Profit from the Core: Growth Strategy in an Era of Turbulence*. Boston, MA: Harvard Business School Publishing, 2001.

Zook, Chris. *Beyond the Core: Expand Your Market without Abandoning Your Roots*. Boston, MA: Harvard Business School Publishing, 2004.

Endnotes

1. Figure is from H. Igor Ansoff, "Strategies for Diversification," *Harvard Business Review* 35, no. 5 (September–October, 1957): 113–124; Figure is at p. 114.

2. Jochen Becker, *Marketing-Konzeption* (München: Vahlen Verlag, 2009).

3. Ibid.

4. Adapted from: H. Igor Ansoff, "Strategies for Diversification," *Harvard Business Review* (September–October, 1957): 113–24. Statistics on the probability of success and the effort relative to market penetration (set as 100%) are from Becker, *Marketing-Konzeption*.

5. Chris Zook and James Allen, *Profit from the Core: Growth Strategy in an Era of Turbulence* (Boston, MA: Harvard Business School Publishing, 2001); and Chris Zook, *Beyond the Core: Expand Your Market without Abandoning Your Roots* (Boston, MA: Harvard Business School Publishing, 2004).

6. See Chris Zook, "Finding Your Next CORE Business: What if You've Taken Your Core As Far As It Can Go?" *Harvard Business Review* 85, no. 4 (April 2007): 66–75 (with regard to defining the core, see especially page 68–69); and Chris Zook with James Allen, *Profit from the Core*, see especially page 13–17.

7. Chris Zook, *Beyond the Core*, page 88 (his Figure 3-1).

8. Chris Zook with James Allen, *Profit from the Core*, page 74.

9. See, for example, Philip Kotler and Ravi Singh, "Marketing Warfare in the 1980s," *Journal of Business Strategy* 1, no. 3 (Winter 1981): 30–41; and Al Ries and Jack Trout, *Marketing Warfare*, 20th anniversary ed. (New York: McGraw Hill, 2006).

20

Specific Marketing Strategies

Porter's framework of the "generic strategies" (cost leadership, differentiation, focus)[1] describes the most basic forms of a competitive strategy. A second framework, the "value frontier"[2] provides a structure to organize the ways that companies can compete based on relative price and relative quality. And, a third framework, "Ansoff's matrix"[3] shows how companies can systematically identify growth opportunities. These frameworks apply to generic strategies. Within these broad generic strategies, innumerable more specific options are available—and every firm will cobble together its own unique strategy as a combination of the characteristics presented in these general frameworks. These specific marketing strategies describe how companies can compete regarding timing, internationalizing, attacking, and defending.

TIMING

With regard to new products, services, technologies, or business models, a company can be either the first to market, capturing the first-mover advantage, or the follower, trying to learn from the first entrant and to imitate or even improve. The choice between a first-mover and a follower strategy is very difficult, as both strategies have particular advantages and disadvantages (see Table 20-1).[4]

The first mover often assumes a monopolistic position, and—at least theoretically—can charge price premiums. The first mover could also decide to enter with relatively low prices to gain market share. In that case, the first mover will benefit from experience-curve effects and scale economies. Another advantage of being a first mover is the access to critical resources, skilled labor, distribution channels, locations, and the like. Often, first movers can build a dominant brand and can create market entry barriers by establishing customer switching costs (e.g., contractual agreements or loyalty programs) or by setting new standards.

The first mover, of course, bears the full costs and the risks of the innovation, and has to educate the market, teach customers the new technology, deal with possible regulatory issues, and so forth. A follower, therefore, can "free ride" and learn from the first mover's mistakes. It has been estimated that the costs of imitation typically are only 65 percent of the cost of innovation[5]. However, if the first mover can establish market entry barriers, and take the most attractive market positions and segments, a follower will find it very difficult to build market share.

TABLE NOTE 20-1 First-Mover versus Follower Strategy

First-Mover Being first to market with a new product, service, business model, or technology	*Advantages* • Being monopolistic • Charging price premiums • Experience curve effects • Scale economies • Preemption of scarce resources • Reputation • Creating customer switching costs • Setting new standards disadvantages • Development costs • Market education costs • Risk of failure
Follower Entering a market as a follower with either an improved or lower priced version	*Advantages* • Free-riding • Learning disadvantages • Market entry barriers • Most attractive market position already taken • Most attractive customer segments already taken

INTERNATIONALIZATION

When a company internationalizes, it has four options (see Table 20-2):[6]

1. Build an international strategy;
2. Build a multinational strategy;
3. Build a global strategy; or
4. Build a combination of the above or a transnational strategy.

An internationalizing firm can take products developed for its home market and sell them abroad without adaptation to the foreign market. This approach is what many call an international strategy. This usually works only if foreign markets are not too different than the domestic market with regards to things like needs, tastes, consumer behavior, and competitors. A completely standardized approach has the advantage of higher scale economies, worldwide consistent brand image, and quality. The organizational structure associated with this strategy is very simple, as all important functions are centralized. With this approach it is also easier to transfer

products or technologies quickly and efficiently, and to effectively control what foreign subsidiaries do and how they implement the strategy. The Body Shop grew from a single store in the United Kingdom in 1978 to include more than 2,400 stores in 61 countries. The founder, Anita Roddick, established the company with a core value of non-animal tested cosmetic products. The marketing of that claim and other social and environmental causes proved to have international appeal. The company's name is now The Body Shop International plc.

A second approach is the multinational strategy. This approach, in which tailored strategies and marketing mixes are developed for different countries or regional markets, is appropriate if those markets are significantly different from the domestic market and/or from each other. Multinational strategies (which could really be labeled "multimix" strategies) are appropriate when local conditions (context factors such as regulations, culture, or climate), competitors, or market structures (e.g., distribution systems and industry structures) require an adapted strategy and a customized marketing mix. This

TABLE NOTE 20-2 Approaches to Internationalization	
International Products are developed for the domestic market and sold abroad with no alteration	*Advantages* • Scale economies • Consistency in brands and offerings • Ability to transfer products quickly and efficiently • Simple organization • Effective control *Disadvantages* • Differences in customer needs, markets, and competition ignored • Full potential of foreign market not exploited
Multinational Each foreign market develops customized strategies and offerings to fully adapt to the local requirements	*Advantages* • Full adaptation to and exploitation of local market *Disadvantages* • High product development and marketing costs • Little economies of scale • No consistent brand image, quality, etc. • Duplication of efforts • Little control over subsidiaries
Global Products are developed for the global market and companies sell "the same thing, the same way, everywhere"[7]	*Advantages* • Same as for international strategy, plus product developed for a global segment with the same needs everywhere • Centralized control and decision making *Disadvantages* • Assumes that national tastes and preferences are similar, and markets are homogenized
Transnational As much standardization as possible, as much adaptation as necessary	*Advantages* • Combines advantages of global and multinational strategy *Disadvantages* • Leads to complex organizational structures and a high need of coordination

adaptation of strategies and marketing programs to meet local conditions is intended to maximize sales in each market, but will also increase costs, including not only the specific costs of adaptation (changes to product specifications, foregone scale effects when production runs are shortened, and the costs of adapting packaging, advertising messages, and support materials to local markets) but also the costs of redundancies in R&D, new product development, and marketing mix development as each country "reinvents the wheel." Another risk of multinational strategies is confusion in brand building that may occur when a single brand is positioned differently or given different meanings across markets. Market boundaries are porous and customers often purchase product and are exposed to brand messages across markets; therefore, positioning a brand differently in different markets may lead to customer confusion and consequently to dilatation of the brand's equity. Nestlé is a good example of a multinational strategy. Only about 2 percent of Nestlé's sales are in its home market of Switzerland, while it employs nearly 300,000 people and has more than 500 factories in nearly 100 countries. Nestlé's extremely successful multinational strategy includes developing adapted products and marketing mixes to local conditions around the world–often via the purchase of local companies and brands. When products are developed for the global market (as opposed to for a local market and later sold internationally) and companies sell "the same thing, the same way, everywhere,"[8] a company adopts a global strategy. It is based on the observation that a global segment of customers with the same needs exists worldwide. This segment is addressed and a worldwide standardized product and marketing concept is developed. The advantage is full exploitation of scale economies, consistent brand image and quality, and centralized control. Most companies that adopt this approach, however, realize that differences in culture, consumer behavior, needs, preferences etc. still exist, and that a completely standardized approach has a high likelihood of failure. However, a company like Boeing has had a global strategy for years. The venerable 747 jetliner was, from its conceptualization and design, thought of as a global product. While many components of the plane are made around the world, the plane's assembly and control are centralized in the United States. Subsequently, that is also true of the 777 and soon to be produced 787 "Dreamliner."

The transnational strategy has emerged in recent years because many international companies discovered that neither complete standardization nor full adaptation is successful as a strategy. The transnational strategists adhere to the principle "as much standardization as possible, as much adaptation as necessary." They try to combine the benefits of a multinational and global strategy. They develop a core product or marketing concept with standardized core components or modules, which than can be adapted to local needs. This way they can exploit scale economies and customization advantages at the same time. This combination or transnational strategy, of course, requires much coordination between all the subsidiaries and the headquarters, and can lead to complex and sometimes bureaucratic organizational structures.

McDonald's International employs a transnational strategy that allows them to simultaneously standardize their operations while adapting to local tastes and customs. For, example, a McDonald's customer can get a lobster roll in Maine, but not a Big Mac in Mumbai—instead it is a mutton substitute (lobster is readily available and a local favorite in the State of Maine, especially with the considerable tourist trade while the cow is considered sacred in Hinduism, the primary Indian religion). Thus, while much of McDonald's menu is the standardized regardless of location, certain items are added or subtracted according to local tastes.

MARKET ENTRY STRATEGIES

When entering international markets, company executives must decide how many resources to commit, and how much control they want to have over their foreign activities. Resource commitment and control are both associated with risks and profits. Basically, five entry modes with specific advantages and disadvantages exist [9] (see Table 20-3):

1. Exporting;
2. Licensing;
3. Franchising;
4. Joint Ventures; or
5. Direct Investment.

Many companies start their first international activities with exports before they commit more resources to foreign markets. Indirect exporting through independent intermediaries and direct exporting through a home-based export department, foreign subsidiary, sales representatives or agents, entails limited risks. Limited resources are needed, and, therefore, this approach is very flexible. At any time, the company can intensify or limit its engagement without any major investments or losses. Exporting, however, is not suitable for every product, especially when high levels of service are needed. The exporter usually has no direct contact to the final customer and therefore will find it difficult to learn about needs and wants to adapt the product accordingly. Furthermore, the company fully bears the exchange rate risk.

Licensing is another entry strategy with limited risk and resource commitment. The licensor grants the right to use intellectual property (e.g., patents) or to manufacture and sell a company's product in a specified market against a royalty. Disney, for example, licenses its trademark and logos to manufacture apparel, toys, etc., for worldwide sales. The licensor benefits from the licensee's market

---

TABLE NOTE 20-3 Market Entry Strategies

Exporting
Indirect—through independent intermediaries
Direct—through home-based export
department, foreign subsidiary, sales
representatives, or agents

Advantages
- Low risk
- Few resources needed
- Little organizational complexity

Disadvantages
- Not suitable for complex products that need high levels
  of service
- No customer contact when indirect export
- Low exploitation of foreign market
- Exchange rate risks

Licensing
Issuing a license to a foreign company
to use a process, trademark, patent, or product

Advantages
- Low risk and few resources needed
- Allows quick entry in many markets simultaneously
- Licensee's knowledge of local market

Disadvantages
- Little control over activities of licensor
- Might create and educate a future competitor
- Low profits

Franchising
Offering a complete brand concept and
operating system to a franchisee against
a fee

Advantages
- Same as licensing, however higher control over franchisee
- Economies of scale through standardization
- Franchisee's knowledge of local market

Disadvantages
- Only for products and concepts that can be standardized
- Control of franchisee necessary

Joint Ventures
Joint venture with a local investor with shared
ownership and control

Advantages
- Pooling of competences (e.g., market access, technology)
- Lower risk and capital needed as for fully owned
  subsidiaries
- In many countries local partner required

Disadvantages
- High conflict potential regarding strategy, reinvestment,
  etc.

Direct investment
Direct ownership of a foreign production or
assembly plant

Advantages
- Full control
- Good relationships and better image with local authorities
  due to job creation

Disadvantages
- Highest risks
- High resource commitment

---

knowledge and market access. As few resources are needed, this approach allows for a quick entry into many foreign markets at the same time. The major drawback of this strategy is the limited control over the licensor, relatively low profits (typically a 2%–5 % royalty), and the risk that the licensor might become a potential competitor after termination of the licensing contract.

The difference between licensing and franchising lies in the offering of a complete brand concept and operating system to the franchisee. Franchising is very common in the fast food business. The franchisor provides training, marketing programs, and the whole business system against a lump-sum payment and a royalty fee. The advantages are similar to licensing. This market entry strategy usually works only for standardizable business systems and products. McDonald's, Dominos Pizza, and 7-Eleven Stores all employ franchise models. In most franchise relationships, the franchisor and the franchisee have a contractual relationship where the franchisor provides the franchisee with certain benefits described above but also has the right to enforce certain standards on the franchisee. It is a bit like a parent–child relationship. On the other hand, a joint venture, the next concept, is more of a marriage of equals.

A joint venture with a local investor with shared ownership and control is a desired option if the host country does not allow full ownership of a subsidiary by a foreign company. It is also desirable if competences, resources, or market access are missing, and a local partner is needed. In many cases that local partner provides market access and the international partner contributes technology and know-how. While this strategy allows the pooling of competencies and resources and promotes risk sharing, many joint ventures fail because of differences in culture, strategic priorities, and conflicts regarding reinvestment or repatriation of profits. Joint ventures are often common in the oil and gas industry as well as the automotive industry. The next level in market entry is full ownership.

Full ownership of a foreign production or assembly plant implies the highest level of resource commitment, risk, control, and profit potential, but also the lowest level of flexibility. Foreign direct investment also improves relationships with local authorities and image due to the jobs created and the investments made. Japanese automakers Nissan, Toyota, and Honda have all established U.S. assembly and marketing organizations. Likewise, IBM has company owned manufacturing facilities in more than 10 international countries.

OFFENSIVE AND DEFENSIVE STRATEGIES

Military science has proved to be very fruitful source for business strategists as many of its insights can be transferred to a business context. Business strategists and marketers have developed some concepts that describe how companies can "attack" their competitors or how they can defend themselves against the "aggressor."[10] Table 20-4 describes the characteristics for these strategies. Offensive or "attacking" strategies include:

1. The frontal attack, where a challenger tries to find a way to achieve an exploitable advantage over its target competitor. The "attacking" company can do so by massing its forces (which may include lower prices, new features, higher quality, or superior technology) against the strengths of the competitor. For example, Wal-Mart employed the capabilities (systems, logistics, and supply chain) it had developed serving rural USA customers to attack a much larger Kmart in the metropolitan areas of the country with "everyday low prices" and eventually won the war of the major discounters.

2. The flanking attack is executed by attacking segments and/or by addressing needs the competitor neglects. Often, the needs of later adopting segments are different from early adopters that were targeted by the first mover. The flank attacker focuses not on the established competitor's strengths but on his or her areas of weakness. Flank attacks work well when the incumbent is unwilling or unable to respond. Gillette, the long time market leader in the razor and blade business was surprised when Bic introduced the disposable razor, a clear flank attack that appealed to an emerging market segment and which the incumbent, Gillette, was reluctant to respond to initially.

TABLE NOTE 20-4 Offensive Strategies

Frontal attack Massing one's forces against the strengths of the competitor	• Must have a clear advantage (price, quality, financial strength, etc.), i.e., 3:1 advantage • Competitor should not be able to retaliate
Flanking Attacking segments or addressing needs that are neglected by the competitor	• Concentration of forces on competitor's weaknesses • Find segments that are not served well and develop them into strong segments
Encirclement Attacking at several fronts simultaneously	• Must have enough resources for a frontal attack in several segments where competitor has weaknesses • The encirclement must be comprehensive enough to overwhelm the competition
Bypass Gain strength in unserved markets to attack later	• Unserved or neglected markets must be found • They must allow to gain strength (develop and refine product, create brand awareness, gain financial strength, etc.) • These strengths must be transferrable to competitor's core market for an attack
Guerrilla Minor attacks on multiple fronts to demoralize competitor	• Find several weakly defended markets • Have enough resources to attack these "blind" spots • Be able to demoralize competitor to eventually prepare for a massive attack

---

3. The aggressor can attack on several fronts simultaneously, which is known as encirclement. Here, the plan is to surround the enemy with a variety of offerings directed at undeveloped segments of the market. Samsung has employed this strategy to become the worldwide leader in flat-panel television sets. The company offers a full range of both LCD (liquid crystal display) and plasma models, along with conventional sets. It passed Sony in 2006 to become the industry leader. The company focused on design, supplier relationships, and retail partners.[11]

4. The Bypass Strategy amounts to skipping over an adversary to attack elsewhere either through diversification into unrelated products or new geographies, or by leapfrogging into new technologies. The video game industry has been replete with technological leapfrogging, first by Nintendo leaping over Atari with next generation technology, then by Sega Genesis leapfrogging over Nintendo, then by Sony's Playstation leapfrogging Sega, and most recently the Nintendo Wii leapfrogging the Playstation.[12] In

each case, the new market leader used new technology to overtake the former market leader.

5. Finally, guerrilla warfare means that the aggressor launches many minor attacks at multiple fronts to demoralize the competitor and to eventually prepare for a massive attack. Southwest Airlines may be the ultimate guerrilla warrior. Beginning in Texas with the Dallas/Houston/San Antonio markets, the low-cost carrier has slowly but surely attacked city-pair markets and entrenched airline leaders (beginning with American and Branniff) to become the most valuable U.S. airline.

The attacked company has a number of options available to defend itself. Table 20-5 lists the characteristics of these strategies. They include:

1. Building a "fort" around the product (position). Anheuser Busch (AB) dominated the U.S. beer market for decades and built a fort around its domestic position. In the end, it failed to see the international threat that emerged and eventually led to its acquisition by In Bev, the Belgian

TABLE NOTE 20-5 Defensive Strategies

Position Building a "fort" around the current product	• All resources are used to defend the current product • A "fortification" is built • It is very risky to put all eggs into one basket (or behind the walls of one fort)
Mobile Diversify into new products and or markets to launch retaliatory strikes	• Defend current product • Exploit current strengths to diversify into new domains (products and or markets) • Defend or attack out of these new domains
Preemptive Defending by attacking	• Weaken competitor before he attacks
Flank positioning Develop defenders for uncertain eventualities	• Identify points of weaknesses • Develop defenders for potential attack
Counteroffensive Directly attacking aggressor	• Use all resources and strengths to attack competitor frontally or at selected points of weaknesses
Strategic withdrawal Withdraw from unimportant segments to concentrate resources for a counterattack	• Define unimportant segments and withdraw • Cumulate and concentrate resources on core products or segments • Counterattack out of core

powerhouse. It (AB) more or less had all its eggs in one basket—the United States—when the business was becoming a global game.

2. Diversification into new products and markets to launch retaliatory strikes (mobile). The mobile defense amounts to creating a moving target that is hard for a competitor to attack. After saturating the US toy market, Toys-Я-Us took its product (the toy supermarket) to new markets—first Canada, then Europe, then Asia. Later it developed a new product, Kids-Я-Us, and later Babies-Я-Us.

3. Weakening the competitor before it attacks (preemptive). In effect, the aim of this strategy is to attack an aggressive competitor by blocking its anticipated move before the competitor can mount its attack. A widely known example of such a preemption can be found in the software industry's practice of announcing new products well in advance of their actual (if ever) production thereby causing many customers of competitors existing products to wait for the anticipated new product. This practice has been referred to as offering "vaporware."

4. Preventively developing defenders for potential attack (flank positioning). Here the idea is to protect yourself by developing additional entries to cover weaknesses in the original offering. For example, Toyota's development of the high-quality and high-priced Lexus brand has often been referred to as the company's attempt to defend itself in the prestige segment—its exposed flank.

5. Counter attacking is often the response of a market leader when attacked. Examples would include significant price cuts, major promotional activities, product line improvements and extensions, and the like. Sometimes the result becomes a price war. In the Christmas season of 2009, Wal-Mart lowered its prices on the most popular books, and, later, DVDs, prompting Amazon.com and Target to counter attack with even lower prices. Wal-Mart then counter attacked them and the price war was on.[13]

6. Strategic withdrawal amounts to giving up an untenable position and freeing up the resources that had been deployed there to be used else-

where. For example, after more than a decade of trying unsuccessfully to build a strong position in Germany, Wal-Mart, the world's largest retailer, gave up and withdrew from the market. The company realized that the German retail business was very established, very entrenched, and already had many players such as Aldi, Lidl, and

Metro, that could match or beat Wal-Mart at their own game of lowest prices. Wal-Mart decided to redeploy those resources committed to Germany in other countries where its prospects appeared to be better. Likewise, IBM withdrew from the low-margin personal-computer business in order to redeploy its resources in more profitable areas.

Summary

These specific marketing strategies (timing, international, entry modes, offensive and defensive—the last two being military strategies, too) help to make consistent decisions and define patterns of actions that allow pursuit of long-term goals and the implementation of a general strategy.

Each of these individual strategies has advantages and disadvantages, and some of them have very clear requirements that must be fulfilled. Decisions to pursue any of them must be made in light of the general marketing objectives and strategy.

Additional Resources

Ansoff, H. Igor. Strategies for diversification. *Harvard Business Review* (1957): 113–124.

Cavusgil, S. T., G. A. Knight, and J. R. Riesenberger. *International Business. Strategy, Management and the New Realities.* Upper Saddle River, NJ: Prentice Hall, 2008.

Gale, B. T. *Managing Customer Value*, New York, 1994.

Johnson, G., K. Scholes, and R. Whittington, *Exploring corporate strategy. Text & cases*, Harlow, England: Prentice Hall, 2008.

Kotler, P. & Singh, R. (1980) Marketing Warfare in the 1980s. *The Journal of Business Strategy*, 1, 30–41.

Levitt, T. The Globalization of Markets. *Harvard Business Review* (1983): 92–102.

Porter, Michael. E. *Competitive Advantage: Creating and Sustaining Superior Performance*, (New York, Free Press, 1985).

Endnotes

1. Michael. E. Porter, *Competitive Advantage: Creating and Sustaining Superior Performance* (New York: Free Press, 1985.

2. B. T. Gale, *Managing Customer Value* (New York, 1994).

3. H. Igor Ansoff, "Strategies for Diversification," *Harvard Business Review* (1957): 113–124.

4. G. Johnson, K. Scholes, and R. Whittington, *Exploring Corporate Strategy. Text & Cases* (Harlow, England: Prentice Hall, 2008).

5. Ibid.

6. C. A. Bartlett, S. Ghoshal, and J. Birkinshaw, *Transnational Management* (Boston: McGraw Hill Irwin, 2004).

7. Ibid.

8. T. Levitt, "The Globalization of Markets," *Harvard Business Review* (1983): 92–102.

9. S. T. Cavusgil, G. A.Knight, and J. R. Riesenberger, *International Business. Strategy, Management and the New Realities* (Upper Saddle River, NJ: Prentice Hall, 2008).

10. P. Kotler, and R. Singh, "Marketing Warfare in the 1980s," *The Journal of Business Strategy* 1 (1980): 30–41.

11. "Samsung Edges Out TV Rivals," *The Wall Street Journal*, February 17, 2010, page B4.

12. "Changing the Game," *The Economist Technology Quarterly* (December 6, 2003): 16.

13. www.msnbc.msn.com/id/33721415/ns/business-retail/. Last accessed June 25, 2010.

STRATEGY FORMULATION

21

Market Segmentation

When addressing the market and developing a value proposition and marketing mix, a company has basically two options: mass marketing or segmented marketing. Mass marketing is a strategy that treats all customers as if they are the same—or at least treats all customers very similarly—with a standardized mix. This is a "one-size-fits-all" approach, with the same product, the same price, the same communications and sales effort, and the same distribution offered to all markets. Mass marketing is based on the desire to achieve scale effects (i.e., economies of scale, learning curve effects, and synergies) and preserve organizational simplicity and control. Within domestic markets, such as the United States or the European Union, many companies pursue mass strategies. Coca-Cola, for example, is often held up as the exemplary "mass marketer": Everybody drinks Coke, everybody's Coke is the same, everybody sees the same brand messages for Coke, and everybody finds Coke in the same places.

Nevertheless, for most companies, the world is not so simple. In fact, in the majority of markets, there are opportunities to gain advantage by adapting offerings to customer differences. Customers vary in their needs, tastes, preferences, and buying behavior. As a consequence, markets can be divided into homogeneous segments of customers with similar needs and behavior, with each segment clearly differing from the others. Adopting this approach allows a company to focus on the most promising market segments, tailor its offers to their needs and preferences, and to more effectively design and coordinate individual marketing activities to a specific target group.

In fact, even Coca-Cola's "mass marketing" strategy is more complex than it seems on first appraisal. At one time, the company's standardized offering was simple: Coke came only in six-ounce bottles and fountain syrup, and there were no alternative formulations. Over time, however, Coke's product lines proliferated, and currently, customers can choose from not only "regular" Coke but also Diet Coke, Coke Zero, Caffeine-free Coke, Cherry Coke, and Vanilla Coke in a variety of sizes and packages. When you consider Coke's international markets, adaptations in the company's so-called "standardized" marketing mix become even more striking. For example, there is a small group of enthusiastic consumers in the United States who covet Mexican Coca-Cola. The Mexican version of Coke is made with sugar instead of corn syrup and, therefore, tastes

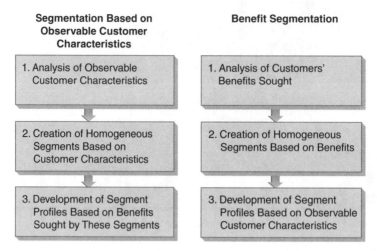

Segmentation Based on Observable Customer Characteristics

1. Analysis of Observable Customer Characteristics

2. Creation of Homogeneous Segments Based on Customer Characteristics

3. Development of Segment Profiles Based on Benefits Sought by These Segments

Benefit Segmentation

1. Analysis of Customers' Benefits Sought

2. Creation of Homogeneous Segments Based on Benefits

3. Development of Segment Profiles Based on Observable Customer Characteristics

FIGURE NOTE 21-1 Basic Segmentation Approaches[2]

different. According to a fan quoted in the *New York Times*, it is "a lot more natural tasting . . . [a] little less harsh" than the Coke sold in the United States.[1]

Thus, for a variety of reasons, including differing national commercial conditions, regulations, cultures, and available ingredients, even iconic Coca-Cola has adapted its flagship product to local contexts. This example emphasizes the fact that, in almost every market and for almost any marketer, there are substantial opportunities to be uncovered by segmenting markets and developing tailored marketing mixes for distinct segments.

APPROACHES TO MARKET SEGMENTATION

Today, strategists rely upon one of two basic approaches when they want to segment a market: either segmentation based on observable customer characteristics or segmentation based on underlying needs and "benefits sought." (See Figure 21-1 below). No matter which method is used, however, the process of segmentation entails six essential steps:

1. Identify effective segmentation variables
2. Group customers into homogenous segments
3. Create a detailed profile of the individual segments
4. Select the target segments
5. Create a sustainable positioning for the target segments

6. Develop a tailored marketing mix to reach the target segments

This note addresses only the first three steps. Targeting, positioning and the marketing mix are described in separate notes.

The overall objective of market segmentation is to tailor products and services (and the overall marketing program) to the needs of the individual segments. To do that profitably, all identified segments should possess the following characteristics:[3]

- *The segment should be internally homogeneous.* In other words, all customers within a particular segment must have similar needs and behaviors.
- *The segment should be externally heterogeneous.* This means that the members of one segment must differ in some way from the members of all other segments.
- *The segment should be accessible.* Accessibility is critical, because without it, a company cannot effectively address, reach, and serve the members of a segment.
- *The segment should be measurable.* This means that marketers must be able to identify and measure the segment's size, needs, and other characteristics.
- *The segment should be substantial.* Here, the segment must be big enough to be served at a profit.

- *The segment should be actionable.* Finally, if a segment is actionable, then marketers can tailor programs that serve it both effectively and efficiently.

SEGMENTATION BASED ON OBSERVABLE VARIABLES

Markets can be segmented based on any number of observable variables. Tables 21-1 and 21-2 give overviews and some examples of variables typically used to segment consumer and business markets, respectively. As demonstrated in the first table, these variables can be broadly classified as geographic, demographic, psychographic, and behavioral.

- *Geographic variables* (e.g., region, city size, population density) are the most basic descriptors of segments. Due to the increasing mobility of consumers and globalization of markets (which leads to stronger availability of global brands and diminishing cultural differences in many international markets or regions), this category has lost a great deal of its importance in market segmentation. In many cases, geographic variables are, therefore, combined with other variables to arrive at more meaningful market segmentation.
- *Demographic variables* (e.g., age, gender, family life cycle, income) are more powerful in predicting behavior than geographic variables

TABLE NOTE 21-1 Consumer Segmentation Variables

Segmentation Factor	Examples of Variables Used	Example of Application
Geographic	• Geographic region • City size or density (e.g., urban, suburban, rural)	In Austria, a major European tourist destination, vacationers are often segmented according to their country of origin (e.g., Italians, Germans, Scandinavians, Russians), because their needs, vacations styles, behavior, and so forth strongly correlate with their nationality.
Demographic	• Age • Gender • Family life cycle • Income • Occupation • Education • Social Status	Many banks use income and occupation to segment their customers for private banking services. Many producers of baby products segment the market according to age for products such as baby food, toys, safety seats, etc.
Psychographic	• Personality traits • Lifestyle • Attitudes about such factors such as self, family, and society	Some tourist destinations segment markets according to the lifestyle of guests (e.g., culture-interested, sports-interested, family-oriented, relaxation-oriented, outdoor-oriented)
Behavioral	• User status (nonuser, ex-user, potential user, first-time user, regular user) • Intensity of use (heavy versus light users) • Urgency, reason, cycle of demand • Attitude (enthusiastic through hostile) • Innovativeness (innovators, early adopters, early majority, late majority, laggards)	Some mobile phone operators segment the market using behavioral variables and create plans for heavy and light users, frequency and intensity of services used (e.g., phone, SMS), domestic or international calls, etc.

TABLE NOTE 21-2 Organizational Segmentation Variables

Segmentation Factor	Examples of Variables Used	Example of Application
Macro variables	• Demographics (size, industry, location) • Operating variables (technology, user/non-user status, capabilities) • Purchasing approaches (single versus multiple sourcing, centralized versus decentralized purchasing, purchasing criteria) • Situational factors (Urgency, order sizes, product application)	The Enterprise Resource Planning (ERP) Software market is segmented primarily based on company size as it influences: • Number of users • IT skills • Propensity to use ERP • Buying criteria • Customization Another frequently used segmentation variable for ERP software is industry, because industry type influences product requirements.
Micro variables	• Personal characteristics (motives, risk-taking tendencies, loyalty)	Some banks segment the market of corporate clients based on their risk-taking attitude and tailor financial products to either risk-taking or risk-avoiding customers.

and are included in most market segmentations. However, like geographic variables, they have declined in importance during the last few decades, because in most cases, they merely *describe* segments and do not actually *cause* differences in needs and behavior. Especially in developed countries, individuals have needs and adopt behavior independent of their demographic characteristics, and this has led to an increasing standardization of consumption modes across social classes, age groups, and so forth.

• *Psychographic variables* (e.g., personality traits, lifestyle) are often used when geographic and demographic variables fail to predict needs and behavior. Psychographic variables are tied more directly to attitudes, motivations, and behavior than the aforementioned categories of variables. However, their use is more difficult because it requires sophisticated market research techniques.

• *Behavioral variables* (e.g., user status, intensity of use) divide customers into homogeneous segments based on their consumer behavior, or their attitudes toward the use of, and response to, a product. These variables are directly related to purchase and consumption behavior

and are therefore well-suited to use in marketing strategy.

Table 21-3 gives an example of market segmentation in Alpine skiing tourism based on customer lifestyles. For each segment, there is a detailed profile of the customer complete with socio-demographic descriptors, preferred vacation style, preferred activities, and so on. These types of segment profiles are important to marketers when identifying target markets and tailoring marketing programs to those targets.

Conceptually, there is no difference between segmentation in business-to-business markets (b2b) and in consumer markets; in both cases, the logic is the same. However, the criteria that are used can differ greatly. One especially useful approach to segmenting b2b markets is the nested approach developed by Bonoma and Shapiro.[5] This approach is based on the premise that marketers should start with macro variables (e.g., demographics, operating variables, purchasing approaches, and situational factors) to find differences, and—if no differences are found—they should move on to consideration of personal characteristics. Let's consider this approach using Table 21-4 as an

TABLE NOTE 21-3 Lifestyle Market Segmentation in Alpine Skiing Tourism[4]

	Segment 1 "Pleasure Seeker"	Segment 2 "Work Oriented"	Segment 3 "Couch Potato"	Segment 4 "Family Oriented"	Segment 5 "Committed Helper"	Segment 6 "The Inconspicuous"	Segment 7 "Culture Interested"
Segment Size	12,2%	13,9%	13,5%	14,9%	13,7%	13,3%	18,4%
Lifestyle	Enjoying life, fun, variety seeking	Fulfillment in occupation, self centred	No pleasure seeker, frugal	Family is the center of interest	Socially and politically active and helping other	Living a simple and frugal life	Furthering knowledge, intellectual, culture interested
Socio-demographics	15 to 24 years, single, high school and trainees	24 to 44 years, high education, self employed or executives	35 to 44 years major part, but also 44 and up, married with children	35 to 44 years, married with children, high education	55 to 65 years, all types of employment	24 to 35 years, low education, skilled worker and employees	15 to 24 and 55 to 64 years, students and pensioners
Winter vacation style	fun and entertainment	emphasis on sports and relaxation	relaxation, gain new strength	relaxation	cultural experience, staying at home	no clear preferred vacation style	no clear preferred vacation style
Vacation activities	going out, attending local events, skiing, snowboarding	skiing, snowboarding, saunas, eating out	skiing, going for walks	saunas, thermal spas, skiing, going for walks	cross country skiing, ski touring	not very active in general	going for walks, relaxing
Vacation intensity (vacation/ short vacation)	1 vacation/ 2-3 short vacations	2-3 vacations/ 4 or more short vacations	1 vacation/ 1 short vacation	4 or more vacations/ 2-3 short vacations	2 -3 vacations/ no short vacation	no vacation/ either no short vacation or 2-3 short vacations	2-3 vacations/ 1 short vacation
Top five satisfaction drivers (correlation with overall satisfaction)	Ski resort (.501**) Shopping (.454**) Cityscape (.407**) Entertainment (.373**) Landscape (.284**)	Ski resort (.644**) Cityscape (.437**) Bad weather program (.388**) Comfort of accommodation (.358**) Peacefulness of destination (.343**)	Ski resort (0,601**) Cityscape (0,489**) Bad weather program (0,434**) Landscape (0,406**) Gastronomic quality (0,393**)	Ski resort (0,515**) Gastronomic quality (0,301**) Shopping (0,283**) Landscape (0,259**) Cityscape (0,223**)	Ski resort (0,518**) Comfort of accommodation (0,457**) Gastronomic quality (0,427**) Cityscape (0,398**) Bad weather program (0,396**)	Ski resort (0,668**) Cityscape (0,423**) Entertainment (0,404**) Bad weather program (0,312**) Landscape (0,294**)	Ski resort (0,511**) Cityscape (0,425**) Gastronomic quality (0,382**) Shopping (0,322**) Comfort of accommodation (0,313**)

TABLE NOTE 21-4 Segmentation of the European ERP-software market[6]

	Small Business Market	Mid-Market	Mid-Enterprise	Large Enterprise
Size	1-49 employees, < $25m revenue	50–499 employees, $25–250m revenue	500–5,000 employees, $250–500m revenue	>5,000 employees, >$500m revenue
Number of companies (Europe)	8.7m businesses	1.3m businesses	30,000 businesses	1,000 businesses
IT staff	One or a few, mostly single persons with multiple responsibilities	Small group of people, usually not involved in strategic decisions, no long-term IT strategy	Full line of IT staff	CIO with board participation, full line of IT staff
IT skills	Modest, learning on the job	Generalists, usually lack of specialization	Specialists	Highly skilled IT-staff
Buying criteria	Ease of use, price	Software depth, functionality, total cost of ownership	Software depth, functionality, total cost of ownership	Security, Software breadth and depth, functionality, total cost of ownership
Customization preference	Generic and less customized ERP system	High degree of integration	High degree of integration and customization	High degree of integration and customization, ERP important for competitive advantage
Competitors	Intuit, Sage	Exact, Sage, Scala	Intentia	SAP, Oracle

example. Working from the top to the bottom of the table, the marketer should begin by looking for demographic variables to segment the market. If this does not work, he or she should next look at operating variables, and then continue with purchasing approaches if there are no discernible differences in technology, user status, etc. As soon as the marketer finds one appropriate variable, he or she can then use that variable as the basis for market segmentation.

As another example, Table 21-4 describes the market segments for ERP-software. Here, firm size explains most differences between the segments and is the most appropriate variable. In a subsequent step, however, one might look at a second variable—such as industry—to refine the market segments even further.

SEGMENTATION BASED ON BENEFITS SOUGHT

As illustrated in the previous section, geographic and demographic variables are widely used for market segmentation, because they are easy to identify. Psychographic and behavioral variables are more relevant to needs and behavior, but they are more challenging to measure, and segments based on these variables are also more difficult to address. Thus, an alternative approach is that of *benefit* or *benefits-sought segmentation*. Benefits-sought segmentation begins with the *needs* and *wants* that are responsible for and explain differences in consumers' responses to the marketing mix. Because this approach uses causal instead of descriptive variables, benefit segmentation identifies more homogeneous

TABLE NOTE 21-5 An Example of Benefit Segmentation[7]

	The Worriers	The Health Conscious	The Sociables	The Sensory Segment	The Indifferent
Primary benefit sought	Decay prevention, sensitive teeth	Decay prevention	Cosmetic, brightness of teeth	Sensory, flavor	Economy, all-in-one
Demographics	Higher education, higher income	Families	Young people	Children, young people	Men
Price sensitivity	Low	Medium	Low–medium	Medium	High
Brand loyalty	High	High–medium	High–medium	Medium	Low
Behavior	Heavy users	Heavy users	Smokers, coffee and tea drinkers	Prefer spearmint toothpaste	Heavy user
Preferred outlet	Pharmacy, dentist	Drug store, supermarket	Drug store, supermarket	Supermarket	Supermarket, discounter
Typical brand	Rembrandt, Parodontax Med Sensodyne Med	Aronal and Elmex, Parodontax, Sensodyne	Macleans, Perlweiss	Colgate, Crest	Brands on sale
Lifestyle characteristic	Living a conscious life	Conservative	Active	Hedonistic	Value-oriented

segments. For instance, Table 21-5 presents a well-known example of benefits-sought segmentation of toothpaste consumers. The first three steps of the benefits-sought segmentation process are as follows:

1. Identification of the benefits sought (in the case of toothpaste, decay prevention, brightness of teeth, etc.) and assessment of the importance of primary benefit(s) to the individual segments.

2. Building of segments based on the primary benefits.

3. Creation of a detailed customer profile of each segment based on observable variables (e.g., demographics, behavioral variables).

   Steps 4 to 6, targeting, positioning, and the marketing mix are found in other notes.

Summary

Markets are almost never truly homogeneous; customers have differing needs and different wants and will, therefore, respond differently to the various elements of the marketing mix. A basic assumption of marketing is that customers will gravitate toward offerings that are best suited to their own needs and wants. However, customizing the marketing mix toward distinct needs and wants has inherent costs—including the cost of adapting the mix and the opportunity cost of foregone economies of scale, to name just a few. Still, the benefits of customization often outweigh the costs, and this is where segmentation becomes important. Segmentation is the essential first step in strategy formation—it entails differentiating relatively homogenous groups of customers (segments) within otherwise relatively heterogeneous markets based on their needs and wants, on the benefits they seek from a product, and on observable characteristics such as geographic location, demographic attributes, and lifestyles. The most widely used segmentation schemes are segmentation based on observable customer characteristics or segmentation based on underlying needs and "benefits sought." Regardless of how it is done, segmentation describes individual segments and allows companies to target them with adapted marketing mixes.

Additional Resources

Bonoma, Thomas V., and Benson P. Shapiro. *Segmenting the Industrial Market.* Lexington: D. C. Heath and Company, 1983.

Kotler, Philip and Kevin L. Keller. *Marketing Management,* 13th ed. Upper Saddle River, N J: Pearson Education, 2009.

McDonald, Malcolm, and Ian Dunbar. *Market Segmentation: How to Do It, How to Profit from It.* Burlington, MA: Butterworth-Heinemann, 2004.

Endnotes

1. Rob Walker, "Consumed-The Cult of Mexican Coca-Cola, *The New York Times*, 11 October, 2009, Sunday Magazine, MM22.

2. Adapted from Pierre-Louis Dubois, Alain Jolibert, and Hans Mühlbacher, *Marketing Management. A Value-Creation Process* (Houndmills, Basinstoke, Hampshire and New York: Palgrace MacMillan, 2007).

3. Philip Kotler and Kevin L. Keller, *Marketing Management*, 13th ed. (Upper Saddle River, NJ: Pearson Education, 2009).

4. Adapted from Kurt Matzler, Harald Pechlaner, and Gerald Hattenberger, *Lifestyle-typologies and Market Segmentation: The Case of Alpine Skiing Tourism* (Bolzano: EURAC, 2004).

5. T. V. Bonoma and B. P. Shapiro, *Segmenting the Industrial Market* (Lexington: D. C. Heath and Co., 1983).

6. Adapted from SG Cowen Research, European Observatory for SME, 2002, no. 2, IDC, Small Business Survey, 2002, www.erpsoftware360.com. Last accessed on June 29, 2010.

7. Based on Russel J. Haley, "Benefit Segmentation: A Decision-orietned Research Tool," *Journal of Marketing* (July 1968): 30–35. Jean-Jacques Lambin, *Market-driven Management* (Houndmills, Basingstoke, Hampshire: Palgrave Macmillan, 2007).

22

Loyalty-Based Marketing, Customer Acquisition, and Customer Retention

At any given time, a company has a certain "pool" of customers, otherwise known as its customer base. Not surprisingly, one basic objective of marketing is to grow this pool by acquiring (i.e., attracting for the first time) and retaining the "right" customers. Although a firm may have other objectives, and it may wish to attract anywhere from a very specific to a very broad group of customers, this basic idea of obtaining and managing a pool of loyal customers will underlie a great deal of the firm's marketing activities.

To understand loyalty-based marketing strategies, it is useful to think of a pool of customers as an actual pool or bucket of water—as long as that bucket that has an inflow (faucet) and an outflow (drain). Like water in a bucket, customers can "flow in" or come to a firm, but they can leave or "leak out" as well. Thus, there are two ways to increase the amount of water in the bucket: increase the inflow (turn up the faucet) or decrease the outflow (slow the drain and fix the leaks). For the firm, this equates to increasing the customer base by expending effort to attract new customers or by working to reduce customer loss.

Studies show that it can cost as much as 10 times more to attract a new customer than to keep an existing customer, and they additionally indicate that a 5 percent increase in customer retention can lead to a 25 percent to 90 percent increase in profitability.[1] Despite these findings, research has also revealed that firms spend the vast majority of their effort and marketing resources on customer acquisition; far less money and attention is dedicated to keeping existing customers. This emphasis is also true in the marketing management literature, where the majority of advice focuses on ways to attract new customers. This imbalance may have shifted somewhat since the mid-1990s, when loyalty-based marketing strategies first began to gain notice—in fact, industry continues to pay increased attention to retention and service quality yet today—but there is still a tendency for marketers to think about customer acquisition first while underappreciating the potential of existing customers.

THE LOGIC OF LOYALTY

Frederick Reichheld, author and consultant at Bain & Company, has been a leading voice in support of increased emphasis on customer retention strategies since the mid-1990s. Reichheld's book *The Loyalty Effect*[2] articulated the logic of focusing on customer retention, which goes beyond the hydraulic or "water-in-the-bucket" analogy offered earlier. According to Reichheld, companies miss an opportunity to spend marketing dollars effectively when they overemphasize customer acquisition at the expense of customer retention, because reducing customer defections may be more cost effective than increasing customer attraction (recruitment) and, just as importantly, because loyal customers may actually be *better customers* than "new customers" or customers who must constantly be "re-won." In fact, Reichheld reported several studies proving that loyal customers are worth more than new customers, and his research linked this higher value to a number of factors. In particular, loyal customers not only provide the base profit that all customers

presumably deliver, but they also buy more, cost less to serve, provide referrals, and pay a price premium. Furthermore, loyal customers spread their initial "acquisition cost" across more occasions (see Figure 22-1).

More recent research has tested the propositions that loyal customers drive increased profitability, cost less to serve, pay more for the same products, and "market the company" via referrals. Studies by Professors Werner J. Reinartz and V. Kumar found that average customer longevity and profits are correlated—that is, more profitable firms have more loyal customers (longer tenure) and less profitable firms have fewer loyal or more transient customers.[3] In addition, little evidence has supported the ideas that loyal customers are cheaper to serve or that loyal customers pay higher prices for given assortments of products. Finally, still other research has revealed that even though some loyal customers do give frequent (and valuable) recommendations, other loyal customers do not.

The ambiguous relationship between loyalty and referrals is clarified by the difference between

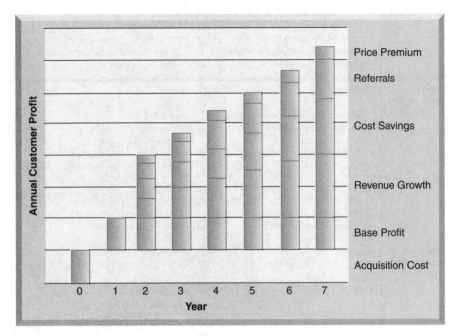

FIGURE NOTE 22-1   Why Loyal Customers Are More Profitable[4]

"attitudinal loyalty" and "behavioral loyalty." People who stay with a company or brand may be behaviorally loyal (and therefore return to the company over and over) because of attitudinal loyalty or for some other, less flattering reason, such as high switching costs, volume discounts, or another source of inertia. In comparison, people who are attitudinally loyal really like—or perhaps even *love*—the product or brand, and customers who love a product typically recommend that product to others. Moreover, these so-called "brand evangelists" or "brand ambassadors" are less price sensitive, more resilient to service failures, and more likely to increase their purchases across time than people who feel they are "trapped" with a product. This distinction between attitudinal and behavioral loyalty is important, because building attitudinal loyalty is invaluable. The same may or may not be true for behavioral loyalty.

Yet another important finding from recent studies is that loyalty—or the length of customers' relationships with a product—is not enough to drive profitability on its own. Rather, identifying and attracting customers who are both loyal *and* profitable—that is, customers who buy more products

with good margins and who buy fewer "loss leaders" (products with low or no margin)—is the key to long-term marketing success. In other words, loyalty is part of the picture, but it's not the whole picture. This logic is directly related to customer lifetime value, or the idea that marketers should estimate how much different segments of customers and different customers are worth across their lifetime with the firm in order to calculate "customer profitability," because thinking about the margin from specific transactions would yield an incomplete picture. Figure 22-2 presents Reinartz and Kumar's resulting matrix. As shown in the figure, each type of customer (organized by loyalty and profitability) requires different strategic actions.

BALANCING ACQUISITION AND RETENTION SPENDING

As previously mentioned, many firms tend to focus their time and money on acquiring customers rather than retaining them; in fact, one study found that 95 percent of marketing expenditures are focused on traditional customer acquisition

	Butterflies
	• Good Fit Between Company's
	  Offerings and Customers' Needs
	• High Profit Potential
	
	Action:
	• Aim to Achieve Transactional
	  Satisfaction, not Attitudinal Loyalty
	• Milk the Accounts Only as long as
	  They are Active
	• Key Challenge is to Cease Investing
	  Soon Enough
		True Friends
		• Good Fit Between Company's
		  Offerings and Customers' Needs
		• High Profit Potential
		
		Action:
		• Communicate Consistently but
		  not too Often
		• Build Both Attitudinal and
		  Behavioral Loyalty
		• Delight These Customers to
		  Nurture, Defend, and Retain Them

High Profitability		

**Low
Profitability**
	Strangers
	• Little Fit Between Company's
	  Offering and Customers' Needs
	• Lowest Profit Potential
	
	Action:
	• Make no Investment in These
	  Relationships
	• Make Profit on Every Transaction
		Barnacles
		• Limited Fit Between Company's
		  Offerings and Customers' Needs
		• Low Profit Potential
		
		Action:
		• Measure Both the Size and Share
		  of Wallet
		• If Share of Wallet is Low, Focus on
		  Up-and Cross-Selling
		• If Size of Wallet is Small, Impose
		  Strict Cost Controls

	Short-Term Customers	**Long-Term Customers**

FIGURE NOTE 22-2 Customers Differentiated by Loyalty and Profitability[5]

activities, whereas only 5 percent are focused on customer retention.[6] This suggests that firms are putting too much emphasis on attracting new customers, especially in light of the aforementioned logic of customer loyalty. The solution, however, is *not* to refocus all marketing dollars on loyalty/retention; rather, each firm must find a balance between its acquisition and retention efforts.

To understand why this balance is important, consider the following: Although a firm can continue to spend resources on customer retention and increase loyalty as it spends those dollars (Figure 22-3), its rate of return on that spending will inevitably diminish as customer loyalty approaches some upper limit. Thus, the key drivers of decisions about expenditures on acquisition and retention budgets should be customer loyalty and the proclivity of various segments to become loyal; customer lifetime value (CLV); and the overall marketing budget (i.e., the total budget to be spent on acquisition and retention).

Figure 22-3 shows that, for a hypothetical firm, increasing retention spending from €150 to €200 increases customer retention from about 67 percent to 70 percent. The key question, then, is how profitable are those 3 percent of customers who were retained by spending the marginal €50? The answer to this question requires more than just a cost-benefit analysis of the marginal retained customers—it also requires consideration of whether the return on those 3 percent of customers is worth more than the profitability of the new customers that could have been acquired with the €50 if those funds had been shifted to customer acquisition. In the example graphed in Figure 22-3b, the balance of customer lifetime value against the cost of retention appears to turn (become negative for margin-retained customers) at about €75 in retention spending; after that, the marginal benefits (contribution margins) are less than the marginal costs (retention spending). Of course, the converse question can and should be applied to resources spent on customer acquisition:

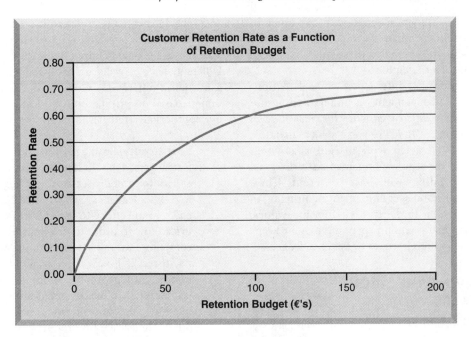

FIGURE NOTE 22-3A Returns on Investments in Customer Retention[7]

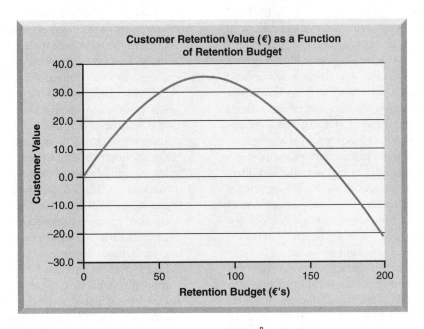

FIGURE NOTE 22-3B Profits on Investments in Customer Retention[8]

Are the new customers acquired with this expenditure more valuable than the old customers who would have been retained if these funds had been spent on customer retention?

This system of interdependent calculations and decisions is dependent on understanding not just CLV, but also *different customer lifetime values for different customers and customer segments.* That is, the segments attracted with margin acquisition spending and the segments retained with marginal retention spending will have different CLVs. Marginal acquisition spending might be bringing in new customers with fairly high lifetime values, whereas marginal retention spending may be keeping customers whom it would be better to let go.

IDENTIFYING THE "RIGHT CUSTOMERS"

"The customers who glide into your arms for a minimal price discount are the same customers who dance away with someone else at the slightest enticement"

Frederick Reichheld[9]

Believe it or not, there are some customers that a firm *doesn't want to attract,* retain, or do business with at all—and these aren't just the usual handful of "pains-in-the-neck." One such set of "wrong customers" consists of price shoppers. Unless a firm has consciously decided that its strategy is cost/price-based (such as Wal-Mart with its impressive logistics and buying-power cost advantages), those customers who are attracted by a price deal are unlikely to serve the firm's objectives. After all, the customers who are brought in by a price promotion are, by definition, most likely to be the same customers lured away by competitors' deals. Moreover, price is the easiest marketing tactic for competing firms to imitate. When one competitor competes on price—whether shrewdly or ill-advisedly—the rest of the industry can quickly follow suit; this is called "wrecking the market." In this situation, one competitor leads the industry into price competition, other competitors respond in kind, and the customers ultimately become accustomed to discounts and "trained" to shop for price.

But how can a firm determine which types of customers are "wrong" and work to eliminate them? The matrix presented above (Figure 22-2: Customers Differentiated by Loyalty and Profitability) is one tool. This matrix differentiates among four types of customers based on profitability and loyalty and spells out appropriate strategies for each sort of customer:

- Low-loyalty/Low-profitability customers ("strangers") should lead the firm to avoid, or at least to carefully reassess "loss–leader" offerings. Loss-leaders are items priced at or below costs in an effort to build "traffic"; that is, priced low in order to draw customers to the companies overall assortment, its Web site, or its stores. If loss leaders aren't leading customers into profitable shopping baskets of products (i.e., if the customers are just "cherry-picking" the loss leaders and not buying any other, higher-margin products), then the firm should eliminate the loss leaders.
- High-loyalty/low-profitability customers ("barnacles") present marketers with a trickier situation. Here, the first question is whether the low profitability is the result of "small wallets" (customers with little to spend) or low "share of wallet" (customers who spend on more profitable items elsewhere). In the first instance, small wallets, the appropriate strategy recognizes that customers are purchasing the precise assortment of products they need and that's likely *all* they'll ever purchase. Two viable strategies with those barnacles are: lower costs and sell the given, limited assortment profitability; or, avoid these customers altogether. On the other hand, if the issue is share of wallet, then the firm is looking at customers who are loyal, which is a big part of the battle and should make them attractive if not ideal, but who are spreading their purchases across vendors. The best strategy in that case is to target a greater share of wallet via "cross-selling" and to insure that the increased share of wallet is in more profitable items ("up-selling").
- Low-loyalty/high-profitability customers ("butterflies") buy full-margin items but, for some reason, are not loyal. A lack of loyalty can be

due to inherent attributes of the customers—for some reason their need for the firm's products is irregular—or their lack of loyalty can be due to the manner in which the firm meets their needs. That is, some customers may only experience the need for a company's products on an infrequent basis. In those cases there is little the firm can do (except enjoy the infrequent but profitable sales). On the other hand, some customers may have continuing needs for the products, but, upon meeting those needs from the given firm, they may either take their needs elsewhere or forego meeting the needs altogether for longer periods. That is, if butterflies are dissatisfied when dealing with the firm, they may go to the competition or exit the market. In those latter cases the butterflies represent an opportunity to improve the offering—either by improving the core product or by improving the surrounding service and customer experience—in order to develop those customers into "true friends."

- Of course, *the best customers of all are high-loyalty, high-profitability "true friends."* These customers should compel the greatest investment in communications, customer relationship management (CRM, discussed later in the note), and service. A great example of a strategy that focuses on this customer segment is the shift of resources in grocery stores from "express" lines (where customers with small purchases get the fastest service) toward better service (more registers, more clerks, and more baggers) for customers in the "regular" check-out aisles. One grocery store chain identified three large segments of shoppers: light spenders who spend about $20 a week; those who spend about $75 a week; and, a segment who spent about $150 every week. It actually *cost* the grocer $3 every time the low spenders visited the store; the stores made about $6 for every "$75 shopper" visit, and made, on average, $30 for every visit by a "big spender," yet the best and fastest checkout service was reserved for the light spenders. Although reducing "express lane" service might alienate Big Spender customers making a Light-Spender

shopping trip, and might slow service for the Big Spenders in the regular check-out lines, the implication of this segmentation scheme is that investments in service enhancement should be targeted at the "best customers," customers with full shopping carts.[10]

In recent years, American consumer-electronics retailer Best Buy also implemented a segmentation scheme based on this profitability/loyalty framework. The *Wall Street Journal* described Best Buy's thinking about its loyal-but-unprofitable barnacles (which they called "devils") as follows:

> The devils are the worst customers. They buy products, apply for rebates, return the purchases, then buy them back at returned-merchandise discounts. They load up on "loss leaders" . . . then flip the goods at a profit on eBay. . . .[11]

On the other hand, Best Buy also developed specific strategies for its high-loyalty, high-profitability customer segments. As described in the *Wall Street Journal*:

> Store clerks receive hours of training in identifying desirable customers according to their shopping preferences and behavior. High-income men, referred to internally as Barrys, tend to be enthusiasts of action movies and cameras. Suburban moms, called Jills, are busy but usually willing to talk about helping their families. Male technology enthusiasts, nicknamed Buzzes, are interested in buying and showing off the latest gadgets.[12]

Segmenting based on loyalty and profitability can, as Best Buy demonstrated, lead to an improved "inventory of customers." *Loyal and profitable customers are the "best customers,"* but tailoring marketing mixes to specific profiles of loyalty and profitability can also turn less desirable segments into lucrative customer bases, can help identify "lost causes"—segments that will never be the basis of profitable sales, and also help identify "follies"—unprofitable offerings that appeal to the wrong customers and that never generate ancillary, profitable sales.

TOOLS OF CUSTOMER LOYALTY: IMPROVING CUSTOMER SATISFACTION

"Do what you do so well that they will want to see it again and bring their friends."

Walt Disney[13]

Customer acquisition activities include almost all advertising, most personal selling (although salespeople can be redirected toward servicing accounts as well as closing deals), and traditional marketing communications, such as public relations and signage. In contrast, customer retention tends to involve initiatives that focus on improved service and follow-up, service recovery, product quality, and especially customer relationship management (CRM). One key to choosing from this range of potential loyalty tactics is to think about the influence various actions will have on customer satisfaction or "delight." The fundamental way to gain customers' affection or attitudinal loyalty is to deliver unique value—something they can't get elsewhere—and to exceed their expectations.

Indeed, customer satisfaction is a central idea in marketing. According to this view, the purpose of a firm is to serve the customer, and serving the customer well will engender customer satisfaction and, as a result, customer loyalty and recommendations (word of mouth). Customers form their satisfaction based on evaluation of how well a product, whether it is a good or a service, meets their expectations. If the product fails to meet expectations, customers will be dissatisfied—and, depending on their degree of displeasure, dissatisfied customers can become "brand terrorists," actively denigrating the brand or firm. If the product just meets expectations, customers will be minimally satisfied—but minimally satisfied customers are footloose customers, still shopping for a better experience. Finally, if the product exceeds expectations, customers will be satisfied and perhaps delighted—and delighted customers stay with the firm and sometimes even become "brand evangelists."

One interesting issue to consider is the interrelationship between the details of customer acquisition and the loyalty of the resulting customer pool.

Smart companies target customers who are likely to become loyal from the outset; that is, they seek out customers likely to end up staying with the firm. Past experience with similar customers is probably the best predictor of future experiences with various sorts of customers. Demographics can also predict future loyalty; older customers, rural customers, customers who are not well-educated, and women are all more likely to be loyal to a brand. Even the media through which customer-acquisition messages are communicated can predict loyalty. Customers acquired through price deals are least likely to be loyal, as discussed earlier, but it turns out that there are other cross-medium differences that predict loyalty as well. For example, a major insurance company analyzed its customers based on what media they'd responded to when acquired by the company. It turned out that direct mail customers (i.e., customers acquired via direct mail offering) were least loyal in the long term; customers who first saw an ad on television were more likely to become loyal; and customers acquired through word-of-mouth referrals from other customers were the most likely to be loyal in the long run.[14]

TOOLS OF CUSTOMER LOYALTY: CUSTOMER RELATIONSHIP MANAGEMENT

Another tool—or, really, *category* of tools focused on enhancing customer loyalty and profitability is Customer Relationship Management (CRM), which begins with collecting data on customer behaviors across "touch points"; touch points are the many and diverse places, ways, and times that customers interact with the firm from contact with a salesperson to visiting the website, visiting a salesroom, or calling a helpline. CRM also encompasses integrating and analyzing those data to derive actionable information or "customer insights." Those CRM analyses can include basic statistical analyses—correlations and cross-tabs, for example—to identify relationships or to describe segments, but CRM can also involve advanced and complex "data mining" analyses usually done by sophisticated experts; the marketing strategist need not become an expert in data mining to understand its results and to appreciate the value of the insights it generates in guiding marketing actions.

The actions that can be guided by CRM range from choosing target segments to customize offerings for specific chosen segments and even for specific customers. In the past, and still today in too many organizations, a customer might talk with an executive, talk with a salesperson, call in to a support desk, take delivery from a route driver, and have a repair or installation person on site all with the same vendor and never have those various contacts integrated into a single understanding of that customer or that customers' needs. The repair person might observe that the customer uses certain products more than others but needs specific add-on options to use them better and with fewer breakdowns. The executive might know that the customer is planning geographic expansion. The salesperson might know that the purchasing agent makes decisions in isolation and with little feedback from users. If all of those insights remain detached the company may be missing an opportunity to customize a solution that will help the customer grow, reduce frustrating breakdowns and downtime in their operations, and improve their purchasing processes to optimize their buying power and operational efficiency. That is, those disconnected understandings and insights represent lost opportunities.

Customer data are valuable in adapting and driving the marketing mix—what prices, products, communications, and distribution points should be targeted at which customers and when—and such data are invaluable in analyzing customers and segments with regard to profitability and loyalty and also in understanding how to target the right segments with the right offerings. CRM uses advanced information-management and communication technologies to track customer information across touch points, to systematically tailor new offers to individual customer, and to provide accurate and timely information on customer behavior, reactions to marketing campaigns, profitability, and so on to marketing strategists. These enhanced relationships should increase profitability and increase loyalty among the customers the firm wants. The accumulated data on customers' needs and profiles become a competitive asset or resource—something the competition doesn't have and is hard for the competition to recreate quickly. Thus, capturing data across customer touch points and mining those data for valuable (profitable to the firm) and valued (appreciated by the customer) insights tend to capture the customer (i.e., leads to durable and enduring customer relationships).

Despite CRM's promise and undeniable logic of capturing and analyzing data on all the various ways customers interact with the firm across the breadth and duration of their experience with the firm, early efforts to build CRM databases (data warehouses) and to cull those data for useful insights were expensive and frustrating. This may be partly due to the fact that early CRM initiatives were focused on the technology—on the hardware and software required to capture information about contacts and to build the large databases describing those contacts—and also because those data and the insights they produce were not distributed to all parts of the organization. That is, early CRM systems focused on the technology and not on getting the information into the right hands at the right time. More recent CRM investments have been more productive, and CRM is now a fundamental part of action-oriented marketing research and loyalty-based marketing strategies. It is a valuable tool in developing customer loyalty and in adjusting the marketing mix to attract the "right customers."

Summary

The idea that it is often more effective and more efficient to invest in retaining current customers rather than to invest those same resources in trying to attract ("acquire") new customers is not revolutionary, but, until fairly recently, it had been underappreciated in marketing practice and in the managerial marketing-strategy literature. Studies have shown that loyal customers are more valuable than short-term, transitory customers, and analyses have shown that firms with more loyal customers tend to be more profitable. It has also been shown that most firms over-invest in customer acquisition activities and under-invest in customer retention. It is also true that investments in customer retention, like investments in customer acquisition, tend to produce diminishing marginal returns and at some point investments in retaining the marginal customer will exceed the value of (profits from) that customer. Customer retention tools include enhanced ancillary services—improvements to the services that surround the core product often differentiate the offering and engender the greatest loyalty—and also include Customer Relationship Management or CRM

systems. CRM involves the collection and integration of data across customer "touch points" and the development of deep understandings of the customers at an individual and segment level from those data. CRM allows for improved targeting of the "right customers" (picking who to serve) and the customization of offerings (tailoring or personalizing the marketing mix) to maximize customer satisfaction, customer loyalty, and firm profitability.

Additional Resources

Reichheld, Frederick F. *The Loyalty Effect: The Hidden Force Behind Growth, Profits, and Lasting Value*. Boston, MA: Harvard Business School Press, 1996.

Reichheld, Frederick F. *Loyalty Rules! How Today's Leaders Build Lasting Relationships*. Boston, MA: Harvard Business School Press, 2001.

Greenberg Paul. *CRM at the Speed of Light: Essential Customer Strategies for the 21st Century*, 3rd ed. New York: McGraw-Hill/Osborne, 2004.

Endnotes

1. See Frederick F. Reichheld, *The Loyalty Effect* (Boston, MA: Harvard Business School Press, 1996); also see Frederick F. Reichheld, *Loyalty Rules!* (Boston, MA: Harvard Business School Press, 2001); and Frederick F. Reichheld, "Loyalty-based Management," *Harvard Business Review* 71, no. 2 (March–April): 64–73.

2. Ibid.

3. See Werner Reinartz, and V. Kumar, "The Mismanagement of Customer Loyalty." *Harvard Business Review* 80, no. 7 (2002): 86–94; and Werner J. Reinartz, and V. Kumar, "On the Profitability of Long-Life Customers in a Noncontractual Setting: An Empirical Investigation and Implications for Marketing," *Journal of Marketing* 64, no. 4 (October 2000): 17–35. Also see Larry Selden and Geoffrey Colvin, *Angel Customers and Demon Customers: Discover Which is Which and Turbo-Charge Your Stock* (New York: Portfolio, Penguin), 2003.

4. Reichheld, *The Loyalty Effect*, page 39.

5. Werner Reinartz, and V. Kumar, "The Mismanagement of Customer Loyalty," *Harvard Business Review* 80, no. 7 (2002): 93.

6. Martin Christopher, Adrian Payne, David Ballantyne, *Relationship Marketing* (Woburn, MA: Butterworth-Heinemann, 2001), 58

7. Adapted from Robert C. Blattberg and John Deighton, "Manage Marketing by the Customer Equity Test,"

Harvard Business Review 74 (July–August, 1996): 136–44. This graphic summary of Blattenberg and Deighton's ideas was created by Southern Methodist University Professor Jacquelyn Thomas (*personal communication*, March 8, 2010).

8. Adapted from Blattberg and Deighton, "Manage Marketing by the Customer Equity Test."

9. Reichheld, *The Loyalty Effect*, page 82.

10. James A. Tompkins, "Customer Satisfaction and the Supply Chain," in *The Supply Chain Handbook*, ed. James A. Tompkins and Dale Harmelink (Raleigh, NC, Tompkins Press, 2004). 11–18.

11. Quotes are from Gary McWilliams, "At Best Buy, Not All Customers Are Welcome—U.S. Retailer Tries to Outsmart Dogged Bargain-Hunters, Court Spenders Like 'Barrys' and 'Jills,'" *Wall Street Journal* (November 11, 2004).

12. Ibid.

13. As quoted in Rosalie Lober, *Run Your Business Like a Fortune 100: 7 Principles for boosting profits* (Hoboken, NJ: John Wiley & Sons, 2009), 223.

14. Peter C. Verhoef, Bas Donkers, "The effect of acquisition channels on customer loyalty and cross-buying," *Journal of Interactive Marketing* 19, no. 2 (2005): 31–43. L. O'Brien, and C. Jones, 'Do Rewards Really Create Loyalty?' *Harvard Business Review* 73, no. 3 (1995): 75–82.

23

Customer Lifetime Value

Marketing has been described as "the science and art of finding, retaining, and growing profitable customers."[1] Rather than focusing on discrete transactions, contemporary marketing thinking emphasizes the establishment, development and maintenance of long-term relationships as these usually are more profitable than short-term transactions. Instead of focusing on short term profits, marketers are interested in the long-term value—the lifetime value—of a customer relationship. The customer lifetime value is the net present value of future cash flows attributed to the customer relationship.

It is common wisdom that acquiring a new customer costs five to seven times as much as keeping an existing customer. Satisfied and loyal customers buy more often, buy higher quantities, recommend the product to their friends and relatives, are less price sensitive, less responsive to competitor's offers, and buy also other products from the company they are satisfied with.[2] Frederick Reichheld and W. Earl Sasser found that a 5 percent increase in the customer retention rate can boost profits by as much as 25 to 85 percent (in terms of net present value) depending upon the industry[3]. Hence, many marketing gurus call for "zero defections" in a customer relationship, or 100 percent loyalty. However, this is neither possible nor wise.

As not every customer relationship is profitable and as not every customer can be retained, it is crucial to determine their profitability and loyalty.

Hence, companies must focus on two important measures:

1. *Customer loyalty:* which of our customers are loyal, which are likely to switch to our competitors?
2. *Customer profitability:* considering all customer revenues and all customers' costs, which of our customers are profitable?

MEASURING CUSTOMER LOYALTY

There are several ways to measure customer's loyalty. The simplest way is to look at customer's repurchase behavior and to assess the retention rate, which represents the number of customers who repurchase the product or service. The retention rate, however, measures only "behavioral" loyalty and not "attitudinal" loyalty. Customers might repurchase a product not because they are truly loyal, or delighted by its quality, but because of situational constraints (e.g., there is no alternative), or out of convenience. True loyalty exists when customers also hold a favourable attitude towards the product. Hence, more effective measures of loyalty include measures of satisfaction or delight, or attitudes towards the product or company. Frederick Reichheld found that one of the best indicators for a company's growth is the number of customers who actively recommend the product or service to their friends. By asking the simple question: "How likely is it that you would recommend our company to a friend or colleague?" on a 0 to 10 scale, customers can be categorized into one of three groups: Promoters (9–10 rating), Passives (7–8 rating), and Detractors (0–6 rating). To calculate the Net Promoter Score—which is a strong indicator of a customer's attachment to a product or company—the percentage of Detractors is subtracted from the percentage of Promoters.

CUSTOMER PROFITABILITY ANALYSIS

It is crucial to determine the customer's profitability by analyzing customer revenues and customer costs. The key question is: What are the revenues of each customer and what are the costs of serving this customer? To answer this question, as many revenue and cost items as possible must be traced to individual customer. This can be done by using the following approach:[4]

> Revenues at list selling price
>
> −discounts
>
> =Revenues at actual prices
>
> −costs of goods sold
>
> =Gross margin
>
> −customer output-unit-level costs
>
> −customer batch-level costs
>
> −customer-sustaining costs
>
> =customer-level operating profit

In the first step, the discounts from the list selling price have to be deducted to determine the revenue at actual prices per customer. Then, costs of goods sold (direct costs attributable to the production of the goods sold; they include the materials cost along with the direct labor costs used to produce the good. Costs of goods sold exclude indirect expenses such as distribution costs and sales force costs) are deducted to compute the gross margin. In the next step, customer costs are subtracted from the gross margin to calculate the customer-level operating profit. Customer costs can be divided into three categories[5]:

- Customer output-unit-level costs (costs to sell each product to a customer, e.g., product handling costs),

- Customer batch-level costs (costs associated to a group of products sold to a customer (e.g., process orders, delivery), and
- Customer-sustaining costs (costs to support individual customers, e.g., customer visits).

Table 23-1 gives an example. It compares four different customers. Whereas customers A, B, and C are profitable, customer D produces losses to the company. This customer places more orders with lower values, receives more visits and higher delivery costs. From the analysis it becomes clear what could be done to make this customer profitable. The company could require the customer to make fewer purchases with higher volumes. This would reduce costs of order taking and delivery costs. Second, it could try to reduce customer visits and finally it could also try to reduce discounts.

CUSTOMER LIFETIME VALUE

The customer lifetime value is the net present value of the future cash flows that can be attributed to a customer relationship. To compute the customer lifetime value, we need to know (1) the customer level operating profit per year, (2) the length of the customer relationship, and (3) the appropriate discount rate. The following formula is used:

$$\sum_{t=0}^{t=n} = \frac{r_t - c_t}{(1 + i)^t} = r_{t_0} - c_{t_0} + \frac{r_{t_1} - c_{t_1}}{(1 + i)} + \frac{r_{t_2} - c_{t_2}}{(1 + i)^2} + \cdots + \frac{r_{t_n} - c_{t_n}}{(1 + i)^n}$$

where:

r_t = Expected revenues in year t
c_t = Expected costs in year t
i = Discountrate
t = Year
n = Length of relationship

Table 23-2 shows the customer lifetime value for each customer of our previous analysis, calculated for a time span of five years. In t_0 the company had to spend US\$ 5,000 to acquire each customer (e.g., customer visits, free samples, negotiation, opening the account), the discount rate is 10 percent, and it is assumed that the customer-level operating

TABLE NOTE 23-1 Customer Profitability Analysis

	Customer			
	A	B	C	D
Units sold	1250	1380	985	728
List selling price	55	55	55	55
Revenues at list prices	68750	75900	54175	40040
Discount	10%	12%	8%	8%
Revenues at actual prices	61875	66792	49841	36836,8
Costs of good sold ($42)	52500	57960	41370	30576
Gross Margin	9375	8832	8471	6260,8
Customer-level operating costs				
Order taking (number of orders)	20	24	15	30
$125 per order	2500	3000	1875	3750
Customer visits (number of)	6	5	4	8
$95 per customer visit	570	475	380	760
Delivery (delivery miles)	27	12	5	30
$2 per delivery mile	1080	576	150	1800
Expedited deliveries	2	0	1	2
$300 per delivery	600	0	300	600
Customer level operating profit	4625	4781	5766	−649,2

profit per customer remains the same. Of course, one can try to estimate how the customer revenues and customer costs develop over the time span. Sales can increase or decrease, cross-selling can be achieved, customer visits can be reduced or need to be increased, etc.

Scoring Models

Customer lifetime value analysis, as presented in the previous paragraphs, includes only monetary revenues and, therefore, may underestimate customer profitability. A more comprehensive approach is based on the following four components[6]:

1. *The core business potential.* This refers to the cash flow from products and services that form the core of the customer relationship.
2. *Cross-selling potential.* This refers to the cash flow from cross-selling, upgrading, a higher share of wallet.
3. *Networking potential.* This refers to the cash flow from new customer relationships through the customer's word-of-mouth, referrals, etc.

TABLE NOTE 23-2 Customer Lifetime Value Calculations

	t0	t1	t2	t3	t4	t5	CLV
Customer A	−375,00	4204,55	3822,31	3474,83	3158,94	2871,76	**17157,39**
Customer B	−219,00	4346,36	3951,24	3592,04	3265,49	2968,62	**17904,75**
Customer C	766,00	5241,82	4765,29	4332,08	3938,26	3580,23	**22623,68**
Customer D	−5649,20	−590,18	−536,53	−487,75	−443,41	−403,10	**−8110,18**

Customer acquisition costs of $5000 in *t0*

		Customer							
Criteria	Weight	A	B	C	D	E	F	G	Remarks
Core business potential	50%	6	4	6	8	2	10	7	10 = Annual sales volume = USD 100.000 5 = Annual sales volume = USD 50.000
Cross-selling potential	25%	10	6	6	5	6	4	3	10 = annual cross selling potential = USD 100.000
Networking potential	15%	8	5	5	...	...			10 = customer opens doors to additional prospects
Learning potential	10%	1	3	2	...				10 = Customer delivers valuable information for new product development, process improvement, or market
Overall score	100%	57.2	38.75	...	...				
10 = excellent, 0 = not at all attractive									

FIGURE NOTE 23-1 Assessing Customers' Attractiveness with Scoring Models

4. *Learning potential.* This refers to the cash flow from process and product improvements stimulated through the customer, market knowledge provided by the customer, etc.

Especially the networking potential and the learning potential are difficult to evaluate. Therefore, scoring models offer a good alternative (Figure 23-1). Each of the four components is weighted, and customers' attractiveness is assessed on a scale from 0 to 10. By multiplying the individual score of each customer with the weight and adding these numbers together, a weighted score is computed that indicates the overall attractiveness of each customer.

The Customer Portfolio

When the customer lifetime value or a score for the attractiveness of each customer is calculated, a company can devise marketing strategies for the customers or customer groups[7]. The portfolio approach is very helpful to allocate resources (e.g., time of salespeople) to the individual customers or groups of customers to increase the effectiveness of marketing initiatives. On the y-axis the customers' attractiveness (e.g., size, growth rates) is depicted, and the x-axis represents the share of wallet. Four types of customers can be identified: A-, B-, C- and D-customers.

Salespeople usually focus their time and efforts on A- and C-Customers. These are the "easiest" customers, as the company already has a high share of wallet. Doing business with these customers usually is easy going. Most salespeople avoid B-customers, as this is really hard work. They need a lot of time to be developed, competitors have a stronger position, and they are not easy to acquire. If a company, however, wants to grow, it has to focus on these customers. Figure 23-2 shows a customer portfolio of a specific

FIGURE NOTE 23-2 Customer portfolio

sales region. The numbers indicate the number of customers in each cell. The following strategies emerge: A-customers must be kept, B-customers must be developed, C-customers receive less attention and relationships with D-customers should be discontinued if such relationships are not profitable. In fact, some companies "fire" customers. ING, a Dutch direct bank, "fires" about 3,600 unprofitable customers of its 2 million customers every year. This saves the bank at least $1 million annually.

Summary

The establishment of profitable, long-term relationships with customers is at the core of modern marketing thinking. Hence, customer loyalty is a key objective. However, not every customer relationship is profitable. Therefore, besides monitoring customer loyalty, the analysis of customer profitability is a key issue. It can be measured through a customer lifetime value analysis—if all future cash flows that can be attributed to a customer are available—or using scoring models that also measure nonmonetary revenues such as word-of-mouth, or knowledge that is created through a customer relationship.

To prioritize marketing activities, a customer portfolio can be a helpful tool. Combining customer attractiveness (e.g., size, growth) with share-of-wallet in a two-by-two matrix, practical implications for customer relationship management can be derived.

Additional Resources

Bhimani, Alnoor, Charles T. Horngren, Srikant M. Datar, and George Foster. *Management and Cost Accounting.* Edinburgh Gate: Pearson Education Limited, 2008.

Ofek, Elie (2002), "Customer Profitability and Lifetime Value," *Harvard Business School Note 9-503-019.*

Reichheld, F. F. and W. E. Sasser. "Zero Defections: Quality Comes to Services." *Harvard Business Review* 68, no. 4 (1990): 105–111.

Stahl, Heinz K., Kurt Matzler, and Hans H. Hinterhuber. "Linking Customer Lifetime Value with Shareholder Value." *Industrial Marketing Management* 32, no. 4 (2003): 267–279.

Endnotes

1. Philip Kotler and Gary Armstrong, *Principles of Marketing* (Upper Saddle River, NJ: Prentice Hall, 2005).
2. F. F. Reichheld and W. E. Sasser, "Zero Defections: Quality Comes to Services," *Harvard Business Review,* 68, no. 4 (1990): 105–111.
3. Ibid.
4. Adapted from Bhimani, Alnoor, Charles T. Horngren, Srikant M. Datar, and George Foster (2008), *Management and cost accounting.* Edinburgh Gate: Pearson Education Limited.
5. Bhimani, Horngren, Datar, and Foster, *Management and cost accounting.*
6. Heinz K. Stahl, Kurt Matzler, and Hans H. Hinterhuber, "Linking Customer Lifetime Value with Shareholder Value," *Industrial Marketing Management* 32 no. 4, (2003): 267–79.
7. Elie Ofek, "Customer profitability and lifetime value," *Harvard Business School Note 9-503-019* (2002).

24

Competitive Advantages

Why are some companies more successful than others? What is the secret of earning above-average returns? In the strategic management literature there are two broad schools of thought that attempt to address these fundamental questions: the market-based view (MBV) and the resource-based view (RBV). The market-based view assumes that success depends on characteristics of the market or industry the firm competes in (industry attractiveness, industry structure, and the like), whereas the resource-based view regards a company's success as largely *self-determined*, dependent on its unique resources and capabilities.

THE MARKET-BASED VIEW

"Five forces analysis" is a good example of a market-based view of strategy development. In this framework, the interplay of five "forces" (bargaining power of suppliers, bargaining power of customers, threat of substitute products, rivalry among competing firms, and threat of new entrants) determines an industry's "attractiveness," or its competitive intensity and profitability. For example, in an industry with low barriers to entry (high threat of new entrants) such as the restaurant sector, competition is intense and profit margins are generally low, making it a somewhat unattractive industry for new investment. Thus, from the market-based perspective, the firm's success depends on its abilities to position itself in an attractive industry, to adapt to industry structures, and to develop strategies accordingly. Therefore, in the market-based view, strategy development should progress through four steps:

1. The company's environment should be analyzed (macro environment, industry, competitors);
2. The company should select attractive industries that promise above-average returns;
3. Strategies that are aligned with the industry structure should be developed; and
4. The company should develop or acquire the necessary resources and capabilities to implement those strategies.

THE RESOURCE-BASED VIEW

The resource-based view takes a very different view of strategy development and of the determinants of firm success. It argues that each company is a collection of unique resources and capabilities, and that those strategic resources of the company are the sources of above-average returns. In this framework, "unique" entails not only being different (unlike any other) but also being "valued" (being something that customers want and will pay for) and being *better than the competition*. Thus, a company has a "sustainable competitive advantage" (SCA) if it has resources or capabilities that are:

1. Valuable in the market (i.e., that they create value to the customers);
2. Rare (no other competitor has these resources);
3. Not imitable or substitutable (competitors have difficulty obtaining or developing similar/substitute resources or capabilities); and
4. Transferable to other markets or products.

When a firm possesses such sustainable competitive advantages it is, in a sense, a monopolist; it owns resources or capabilities (competitive advantages) that create value to the customers, and they cannot be imitated or substituted for by competitors. Of course, "sustainable" is a relative and an allusive quality; few advantages are truly sustainable in a long-term sense, and most are frustratingly short-lived. Within the resource-based paradigm, strategy development follows a completely different logic and process:

1. Strengths and weaknesses of the company are analyzed;
2. Based on strengths and weaknesses, competitive advantages are identified;
3. Industries, markets, and, especially, market segments are targeted in which these competitive advantages can be exploited;
4. Strategies for these industries and markets are developed and implemented based on the competitive advantages.

Thus, the resource-based view of the firm is less about "where you compete" and more about "how you compete." While it is still crucial to understand the company's environment and its industry (the core of the market-based view), the resource-based view has proven to be more effective in predicting firm-level success. Further, in most strategic marketing situations, choosing the industry is not an option—the imperative is on winning in the given industry; and the resource-based view of the firm starts with this perspective.

Identifying Competitive Advantages

In the long run, a company will be successful if it is able to deliver higher customer value than its competitors. This performance can either result from bringing a product onto the market more cost-efficiently, and, therefore, more cheaply, or from differentiating the product through a unique bundle of benefits for which the customer is willing to pay a price premium. A company has a sustainable competitive advantage if superior customer value is delivered more effectively and/or efficiently through a unique bundle of capabilities and resources that competitors do not have. And, which they cannot copy or which cannot be substituted with other capabilities and resources. Hence, a very practical way to understand and to identify competitive advantages is a three-step approach by answering the following questions:

Step 1. What do we do better than the competition? What are our competitive advantages?

Step 2. Which resources or capabilities are the sources of these advantages?

Step 3. Which of these resources or capabilities are valuable, unique, and not imitable or transferable to other industries or markets?

STEP 1. In the first step is to identify a prioritized list of customers' buying criteria (product features, product quality, service, convenience, brand image, price, etc.). Qualitative and open-ended methods are well-suited to generating the set of criteria and more quantitative methods, including ranking tasks and conjoint analysis, are proficient at gauging the weights customers place on the various attributes. Figure 24-1 presents a set of hypothetical attributes

Buying criteria	Weight
Fashionable design	30
Product quality	20
Brand image	15
Price	25
Assortment	10

FIGURE NOTE 24-1 Hypothetical Buying Criteria and Importance Weights for Costume Jewelry

or criteria for costume jewelry and the accompanying weights, which sum to 100 percent. In any application of this analysis, it is likely that the strategic marketer will want to see these attributes and especially their weights by segment. That is, different customers assess different attributes and place different importance on those attributes and understanding those differences at the segment or individual customer level is essential.

The next step is to compare the firm to its strongest competitor using these attributes and weights. That comparison should be done *from the customers' perspective*; that is, it doesn't matter whether the manager believes the firm is good at something, what matters is what the customers think or perceive, and, therefore, gauging customer perceptions instead of accepting an "expert opinion" or managerial viewpoint is essential. Figure 24-2 shows a hypothetical strength-and-weaknesses profile for a costume jewelry producer. Its competitive advantages against the strongest competitors are the fashionable design, the brand image, and the product quality; its weaknesses are the high price and (off-target or limited) assortment.

The next step is the analysis of the sources of these advantages by analyzing a company's value chain.[1].The value chain is a set of activities in which a company engages to develop, produce and market products. McKinsey and Company[2] developed a generic value chain consisting of six distinct activities that need to be carried out to bring a product into the market: technology development, product design, manufacturing, marketing, distribution, and service. Another widely used generic value chain was developed by Michael E. Porter. It consists of primary activities (that are directly related to the production and distribution of products) and secondary activities (that are needed to accomplish the primary activities). A company can decide how each of the single activities is carried out and which of these activities can be outsourced to other companies. Depending on how well a company performs on the single activities compared to the competitors, it can develop specific strengths and weaknesses, and can create and capture more value by being more effective or efficient than the competitors. The strategic importance of the single activities depends on the industry. In the pharmaceutical industry, research and development are key success factors. In retailing, procurement and inbound logistics are of strategic importance; and for a consulting firm, human resource management is essential. Hence, a company should rate the strategic importance of each activity and then examine each activity relative to competitors' abilities to identify strengths and weaknesses (see Figure 24-3).

The company in this example has three clear competitive advantages: technology development, operations, and marketing and sales. In the next step, we analyze the resources and competences that are the source of these advantages.

STEP 2.   What leads to the individual competitive advantages—from both a customer and value-chain perspective? To answer this question, we try to identify those resources and skills that account for the

Buying Criteria	Weight	Performance Compared to Strongest Competitor (−2 = Much Worse, 0 = About the Same, +2 = Much Better)					Weighted Score
		−2	−1	0	+1	+2	
Fashionable Design	30					●	60
Product Quality	20			●			20
Brand Image	15				●		30
Price	25	●					−25
Assortment	10	●					−10

FIGURE NOTE 24-2 Competitive Advantages from a Customer's Perspective

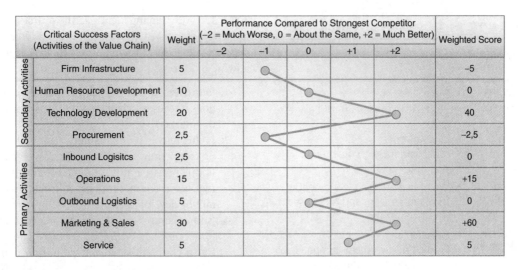

Critical Success Factors (Activities of the Value Chain)	Weight	Performance Compared to Strongest Competitor (−2 = Much Worse, 0 = About the Same, +2 = Much Better)					Weighted Score
		−2	−1	0	+1	+2	
Secondary Activities — Firm Infrastructure	5	●					−5
Human Resource Development	10			●			0
Technology Development	20					●	40
Procurement	2,5		●				−2,5
Primary Activities — Inbound Logisitcs	2,5			●			0
Operations	15					●	+15
Outbound Logistics	5			●			0
Marketing & Sales	30					●	+60
Service	5				●		5

FIGURE NOTE 24-3 Value Chain Analysis

company's strengths and competitive advantages. Step-by-step, the drivers for each competitive advantage are examined by asking questions like: Why do we have advantages in operations? Why are we able to continuously deliver higher product quality and more fashionable design than our competitors? The list of tangible and intangible resources in Table 24-1 and the list with examples of capabilities in Table 24-2 help to identify the sources of competitive advantages.

Tangible resources can be grouped into financial and physical resources. Financial resources can constitute a competitive advantage if companies have access to inexpensive capital or can more easily generate funds for their investments and strategies. Physical resources (e.g., locations, plants, raw materials) can either constitute a cost advantage or access to high quality inputs. For many companies, intangible resources (e.g., technologies, reputation, human resources) are more important than tangible resources. They are invisible and often more difficult to obtain or develop.

Tangible and intangible resources are not productive on their own; they only can constitute competitive advantages if companies are able to deploy them. As some companies are better able to exploit resources or are more effective in combining them, such distinctive capabilities can provide the basis of

TABLE NOTE 24-1 Examples of Resources[3]

Resources	Examples
Tangible resources	Financial resources • A company's ability to generate funds • Cash, securities Physical resources • Location • Sophistication of plant and equipment • Land, buildings • Access to raw materials
Intangible resources	Technological resources • Technologies • Patents • Research establishments • Technical and scientific employees Reputation • Brands • Customer relationships • Reputation among stakeholders Human resources • Training and experience of employees • Flexibility of employees • Commitment and loyalty of employees • Trust and cooperation

TABLE NOTE 24-2 Examples of Capabilities[4]

Functional area	Skill
Corporate function	• Financial control • Strategic management of business units • Innovativeness • Multidivisional coordination • Acquisition management
Management information	• Well-functioning management information system and MIS-based decision making
Research & development	• Research capabilities • Product development competences • Process development competences
Logistics	• Logistics competence • Process control • Interface management
Production	• Exploiting economies of scale • Continuous improvement • Flexibility
Product design	• Design skills
Marketing	• Brand management • Ability to react to market requirements • Customer relationship management
Distribution	• Efficiency in acquisition and order processing • Speed of distribution • Quality of customer service

superior performance. Such distinctive capabilities can be found in each functional area (see Table 24-2). Table 24-3 shows how sources of competitive advantages can be identified. It lists the resources and capabilities that lie behind the competitive advantages in our example.

Competitive advantages have the following characteristics: they are valuable, rare, not imitable and not substitutable, and are transferable to other markets or applications. Therefore, each source of competitive advantage is now investigated in light of these requirements.

STEP 3. After having identified the sources of competitive advantages, that is, resources and capabilities, we take each of them and try to answer the following questions:

1. Is this resource or capability valuable, that is, does it lead to a clear competitive advantage in the market?
2. Is this resource or capability rare, that is, does no competitor own these resource or capability?
3. Is this resource not imitable or substitutable, that is, do competitors have difficulties to obtain or develop them?
4. Is this resource transferable to other markets or products, that is, can it be leveraged and constitute a competitive advantage in new markets?

Figure 24-4 shows a simple tool that helps to identify competitive advantages based on these four questions. If resources or capabilities are valuable but not rare, they do not constitute a competitive advantage (e.g., highly skilled and experienced marketing people in our example). If they are valuable and rare, but easy to imitate or substitute, they constitute only a short-term advantage (e.g., sophisticated plants and quality management system). If they are valuable, rare and difficult to imitate or substitute, these resources or capabilities are the source of a long-term competitive advantage; if they are also transferable to other markets or products they can be leveraged and can be successfully used for a diversification strategy (e.g., grinding technology). The trend forecasting competence and the unique grinding technology are both competitive advantages, and as they can be transferred to different markets or products (e.g., crystal figurines, jewelry and accessories, home décor), where these competences are exactly needed, they can be leveraged to build the source of sustainable competitive advantage.

Thus, although many management teams hold somewhat inflated views of their firm's competitive advantages, usually those views are based on, at best, casual assessment. Identifying sustainable competitive advantage is not as easy as asking "What are we good at?" First, "good at" must be a *relative* assessment; specifically, it is *relative to the competition*. In addition, it is not enough to be good at something—to be an advantage, this "something" must be *valuable* to some set of customers and must also be something

TABLE NOTE 24-3 Competitive Advantages and Underlying Resources

Competitive Advantages from the Customer's Point of View	Resources and Capabilities Behind These Advantages
Fashionable design	• Trend competence: Ability to forecast trends in the fashion industry through a worldwide network with the leading trend researchers, designers, and artists
Product quality	• Technical sophistication of the plant and quality management system • Unique grinding technology that leads to superior quality of crystals
Brand image	• Marketing competence: Highly skilled and experienced marketing people • Decades of producing superior quality and excellent brand management skills • Customer Relationship Management System
Competitive advantages in the value chain	**Resources and capabilities behind these advantages**
Technology development	• First-mover in the development of the grinding technology with continuous investment and improvement of the technology • Highly skilled engineers
Operations	• Technical sophistication of the plant and quality management system
Marketing & Sales	• Highly skilled and experienced marketing people
Service	• Well-organized distribution and customer's service department

Resource or Capability	Is This Resource or Capability Valuable?		Is This Resource or Capability Rare?		Is This Resource or Capability Difficult to Imitate or Substitute?		Is This Resource or Capability Transferable?		Evaluation
	YES	NO	YES	NO	YES	NO	YES	NO	
Highly Skilled and Experienced Marketing Team	X			X		X	X		No Competitive Advantage
Trend Forecasting Competence	X		X		X		X		Core Competence!
Sophisticated Plants and Quality Management System	X		X			X	X		Short-Term Advantage
Unique Grinding Technology	X		X		X		X		Core Competence!
Brand Image: Superior Quality, Brand Management Skills...	X		X			X	X		Short-Term Advantage
Customer Relationship Management System	X			X		X	X		No Competitive Advantage
Highly Skilled Engineers	X		X			X	X		Short-Term Advantage
Excellent Distribution System and Customer Service's dpmt	X		X			X	X		Short-Term Advantage

FIGURE NOTE 24-4 Identifying Competitive Advantages

that the competition can't match, either by imitation or substitution. Finally, because of the imperative for growth in contemporary strategic management, the very best competitive advantages will also have "legs"; that is, they'll be exploitable in other, new markets, too.

The process of identifying sustainable competitive advantages, summarized graphically in Figure 24-5, begins with the identification of strengths and weaknesses. These strengths and weaknesses must be linked with the underlying resources and capabilities that generate the advantages. Finally, the strengths must be filtered against the further criteria of being valuable, not easily imitated or substituted for, and transferable. After that the firm can either find markets that will reward its current advantages or identify new advantages it should create in order to achieve success in its given markets (or, as is most often the case, do *both*). Thus, the resource-based view of strategy, and inside-out perspective, analyzes what the firm does best and what

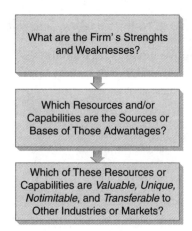

FIGURE NOTE 24-5   Identifying Sustainable Competitive Advantages

it needs to do best to target receptive industries, markets, and segments.

Summary

There are two broad approaches to assessing and developing strategies: the market-based view and the resource-based view. These two paradigms imply very different strategy-formation processes with fundamentally different starting points, as highlighted in Figure 24-6. The market-based view is an "outside-in" perspective; it begins with the

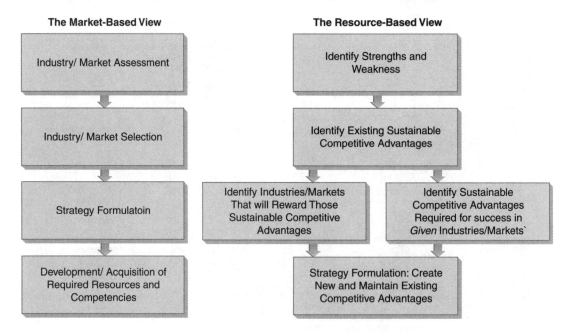

FIGURE NOTE 24-6   Distinct Strategy-Formation Processes Underlying the Market-Based and Resource-Based Views

assessment and selection of *where to compete*; the resource-based view is an inside-out process which begins with assessment of *how to compete*, that is with the firm's strengths, weaknesses, and competitive advantages. While it is important to understand the industries and markets in which the firm competes—and at certain junctures in the firm's growth it may be possible to actually select industries and markets in which to compete, making industry/market analysis even more central to strategy formulation, by far the more common circumstances that a strategic market faces involve succeeding in predetermined competitive contexts. That is, the marketing strategist does

influence where the firm competes, but those junctures do not occur frequently; succeeding within a given competitive fray is an ongoing challenge to most strategists.

Identifying sustainable competitive advantages requires understanding the firm's strengths and weaknesses and tying those strengths to the underlying resources and competencies that generate or support them. Strengths are only sustainable competitive advantages if they are valued by customers and hard or impossible to imitate or substitute for by the competition. The best competitive advantages are extended or transferred to new industries or new markets, especially in today's growth-preoccupied markets.

Additional Resources

Bailom, F., K. Matzler, and D. Tschemernjak. *Enduring success. What Top-Companies Do Differently.* New York: Palgrave Macmillan, 2007.

Barney, J. B. and W. S. Hesterly. *Strategic Management and Competitive Advantage.* Upper Saddle River, New Jersey: Pearson Education, 2006.

Porter, M. E. *Competitive Strategy: Techniques for Analyzing Industries and Competitors.* New York: The Free Press, 1980.

Porter, M. E. *Competitive Advantage: Creating and Sustaining Superior Performance*, 2nd ed. New York: Free Press, 1985.

Endnotes

1. M. E. Porter, *Competitive Advantage: Creating and Sustaining Superior Performance*, 2nd ed. (New York: Free Press, 1985).

2. See J. B. Barney and W. S. Hesterly, *Strategic Management and Competitive Advantage* (Upper Saddle River, New Jersey: Pearson Education, 2006).

3. Adapted from R. M. Grant, *Contemporary Strategic Analysis*, 5th ed. (Malden, Oxford, Carlton: Blackwell Publishing, 2005).

4. Adapted from Ibid.

25

SWOT Analysis

SWOT analysis—the systematic assessment of the firm's **S**trengths, **W**eaknesses, **O**pportunities, and **T**hreats and the recognition of their strategic implications—is a basic, often used tool of strategic thinking.[1] It may also be one of the most often misapplied.[2] The basic process of conducting a SWOT analysis begins with the identification of the firm's strengths and weaknesses, essentially an *internal analysis*, and of opportunities and threats in the environment, or an *external analysis*.[3] Too often, this is where the SWOT ends—with a description of the firm's strengths and weaknesses and an organized list of trends in the environment—and too often the firm's strengths are not really "strengths," but, rather, just a list of "things the firm does well." SWOT Analysis is only powerful when the analysis of strengths is rigorous. A strength isn't merely something the firm does well; it is something the firm does better than the relevant competition does it or, even better, *better than the competition does it or could adapt to do it*. Most importantly, the outcome of a SWOT Analysis is not merely descriptive—the outcome should be *prescriptive*, too. That is, once the description of Strengths, Weaknesses, Opportunities, and Threats is complete, SWOT analysis should lead to actions and strategies that are derived from the analysis.

Identifying strengths and weaknesses is principally an internal analysis but involves external comparisons, as well: *Nothing is a strength or a weakness except vis-à-vis the competition.* Opportunities and threats arise from the external environment. Therefore, a full environmental analysis needs to be done before the SWOT analysis can be carried out. Figure 25-1 organizes SWOT analysis graphically, emphasizing the role of internal and external analyses.

IDENTIFYING OPPORTUNITIES AND THREATS

"A pessimist sees the difficulty in every opportunity; an optimist sees the opportunity in every difficulty."

Winston Churchill[4]

Customer Assessment

Opportunities and threats are external phenomena. They may arise from many sources, including technology, the physical environment, the political/legal/regulatory environment, and the economy as well as from competitor actions. Still, although they may arise from many factors, those external events or trends tend to affect a marketing strategy *via their effects on customers.* That is, other external forces usually represent opportunities or threats because of the changes they produce in the way customers meet or can possibly meet a need. For example, the emergence of computer technology in and of itself didn't

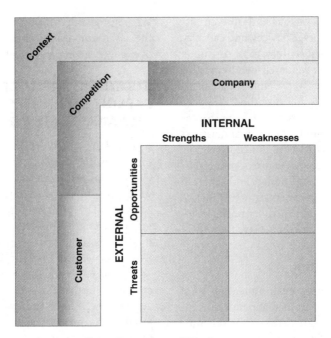

FIGURE NOTE 25-1 SWOT Analysis Identifying Strengths and Weaknesses

affect the typewriter industry. The emergence of computer technology influenced the typewriter industry *via changes in the ways that consumers met the need to create documents and manage information.* Technological change became an opportunity for IBM, a manufacturer of typewriters that developed computer technologies and competitive advantages in computers, and the same technological changes were a threat to other manufactures of typewriters who didn't have and didn't develop computer technologies. Therefore, considering *and continuously reconsidering* customer assessment and segmentation is essential to identifying opportunities and threats.

Segment Changes

Market segments are never static. Segments grow, shrink, and change their buying habits, preferences, and buying criterion. Importantly, segments can also *split* into subsegments or can *merge* or combine into a single, larger segments. For example, in many grocery-store markets, the dominant players were traditionally midmarket, traditional grocers with moderately large assortments. When a high-service player, such as

Harris Tweeter, entered a market, its presence, in a sense, *created* a high-service-seeking segment that had not existed before. Consumers couldn't have been high-service shoppers and might not even have known they valued high-service before a high-service alternative became available. The need for a high-service alternative was what would be labeled "latent," it may have been there but it wasn't actively driving shopping behaviors. Low-service/low-price competitors such as Food Lion and then Wal-Mart did the same thing with price-conscious shoppers. By offering a price-based alternative they "created" a segment based on latent, that is, previously unmet needs. Thus, what had been a relatively homogenous segment of grocery shoppers split into subsegments based on service and price; undifferentiated stores that didn't move with the market could easily be left in the unprofitable middle.

In other instances, previously different segments end up merging into larger segments based on products offering compound benefits. In the early-to mid-1990s, for example, the computer industry differentiated products based on processor speed. Some consumers desired the latest and greatest in terms of CPU speed, others were satisfied with slower speed but required various and different accessories—audio cards, storage devices, and capacity, etc. By the early twenty-first century, most consumer needs for processing power were well-met by existing processing speed. Far fewer were demanding cutting edge speed or even cared to improve the CPU speed and the cost of various accessories such as storage had come down to the point that most manufactures provided enough memory to satisfy most users. The basis of competition shifted from processing performance to convenience and design and segment structure shifted. Many consumer segments blurred into a single mass market and specialty business applications were based on new competitive factors.

Environmental Scanning

As noted, most changes in the environment manifest themselves in changes in consumer demand and consumer behavior, but many are tied to some other aspect of the environment. The competition is relevant to both strengths/weaknesses assessment (nothing is a strength or a weakness except as it compares with the competition). The competition is also important in identifying opportunities and threats; the competition can pose a threat and can, sometimes, create an opportunity (e.g., by withdrawing from a segment or market or by blundering with a product offering).

Wherever an opportunity or threat arises, monitoring the environment is essential to feed understandings of changes, trends, and events to SWOT analyses.

STRATEGIC IMPLICATIONS: EXPLOIT STRENGTHS; AVOID OR AMELIORATE WEAKNESSES

As noted above, SWOT analyses are not merely descriptions; they should *direct actions and resources.* One fundamental reality is that all four cells in the resulting two-by-two matrix are equally manageable or attractive. The marketing strategist is generally looking for strength-opportunity matches to exploit— that is a basic task of strategy formulation. Thus, SWOT analyses can be a very useful tool at the targeting stage. Weakness-Threat fits—a threat in the environment that exposes a weakness of the firm— generally need to be addressed or at least avoided (if avoiding the threat is a viable alternative). Figure 25-2 presents the strategic implications of SWOT analyses.

CONDUCTING A SWOT ANALYSIS

The basic steps in conducting a SWOT analysis are to:

1. Assess the firm's competitive advantages using the competitive advantage framework and/or comparing the value chains of the firm and its

	Strengths	Weaknesses
Opportunities	**Exploit:** Use Strengths to Take Advantage of Opportunities. *This is the Cell to Build Strategies on – Target Opportunities That are a Good Fit with the Firm's Strengths.*	**Develop:** Invest to Improve Weaknesses into Strength to Target the Opportunity and/or Overcome Weaknesses by Taking Advantage of Opportunities.
Threats	**Contend:** Use Strengths to Avoid Threats (Reduce Exposure to Threats), Turn Threats into Neutral Factors, or Even Turn Threats into Opportunities. (Defensive Marketing)	**Address/Avoid:** Address Weaknesses and/or Avoid Threats. If a Threat puts at Risk the Core Business, Then the Weakness Requires Investment; if the Threat does not Jeopardize the Core Business, Then the Weakness-Threat Situation can be Avoided.

FIGURE NOTE 25-2 Strategic Implications of SWOT Analysis

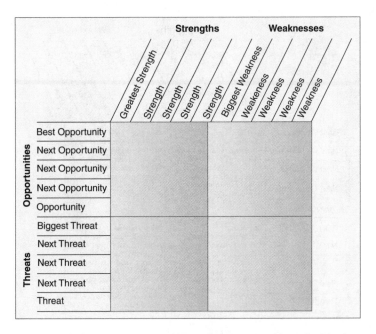

FIGURE NOTE 25-3   Strengths, Weaknesses, Opportunities and Threats Feed into the Matrix

competitors. Remember that the question isn't "is the firm good at this or that" nor "would the firm like to be the best at this or that." The question is "is the firm the best at this and how hard will it be for competitors to achieve parity?"

2. Study the environment for opportunities and threats with an emphasis on how changes will effect consumption in the relevant market and with regard to the relevant consumer needs;

3. Identify strategic alternatives and imperatives from the "fit" or match between the strengths and weaknesses—the internal analysis, and the opportunities and threats—the situation assessment; and

4. Prioritize, plan, and act.

Figure 25-3 shows a two-by-two matrix that matches strengths and weaknesses with opportunities and threats. Figure 25-4 shows the completed matrix with strengths and weaknesses and opportunities and threats *driving strategy and action*s. Note that, contrary to the way it is sometimes presented, the "descriptive" stages of a SWOT do *not* fill in the cells of this matrix—they go on the axes. Similarly, opportunities and threats are listed at the appropriate places along the OT axis. This correctly uses the SWOT framework to match and integrate external factors with internal attributes to drive strategic decisions. The cells are then used to list and then choose from strategic alternatives. Figure shows the generic format of this assessment.

Summary

SWOT analysis is a basic tool of strategic thinking but it is often misunderstood or misapplied. SWOT analysis is not merely descriptive of the situation; *it is prescriptive,* directing strategy formation. SWOT analysis is *a matching process,* meant to find opportunities that match or fit with the firm's strengths. Further, strengths aren't things the firm thinks it does well—to be effective foundations for strategy development, *strengths must be things the firm does better than the competition*—better than what the competition does today, than that for which the competition can develop competency in the future, and than the available substitutes. Thus, strengths are *sustainable competitive advantages*; things the firm does that customers value, that are rare, and that are hard to substitute for.

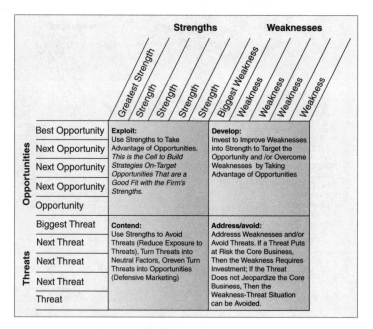

FIGURE NOTE 25-4   Strengths and Weaknesses, Opportunities and Threats Drive Strategies

Opportunities and threats are changes in the environment that generally manifest themselves as *changes in the way customers will or might meet their needs.* Changes in the context (political, economic, social/cultural, or technological/natural environments) or in the competition and competitive fray become opportunities or threats because they impact the way customers can meet their needs. Thus, SWOT is about exploiting opportunity–strength possibilities, identifying weaknesses that require development, or avoid a threat, and/or identifying threats to be avoided. All of those "matches" have important action-oriented strategic implications: *exploit, develop, contend,* or *avoid.*

Additional Resources

Andrews, Kenneth R. *The Concept of Corporate Strategy.* Homewood, IL: Irwin, 1971.

Fehringer, D. "Six Steps to Better SWOTs." *Competitive Intelligence Magazine* (January–February, 2007): 54.

Hill, Terry and Roy Westbrook "SWOT Analysis: It's time for a product recall," *Long Range Planning* 30, no. 1 (1997): 46–52.

Weihrich, Heinz. "The TOWS Matrix - A tool for situational analysis." *Long Range Planning* 15, 2 (April 1982): 54–66.

Endnotes

1. D. Fehringer, "Six steps to better SWOTs," *Competitive Intelligence Magazine* (January–February, 2007): 54.

2. Terry Hill and Roy Westbrook, "SWOT Analysis: It's Time for a Product Recall," *Long Range Planning* 30, no. 1 (1997): 46–52.

3. Kenneth R. Andrews, *The Concept of Corporate Strategy* (Homewood, IL: Irwin, 1971).

4. Richard M. Langworth, *Churchill by Himself: The Definitive Collection of Quotations* (New York: PublicAffair/Perseus Books Group, 2008), quoted at page 578.

26

Targeting

After a company has segmented its markets and has developed detailed segment pro-files, two important decisions have to be made:

1. Should the company adopt a differentiated or undifferentiated marketing approach?
2. If it adopts a differentiated marketing approach, which segments should be targeted?

The selection of the appropriate marketing approach and the decision about the target segment(s) require a thorough analysis of the market and the segmentation of cus-tomers into homogeneous segments (e.g., using demographic, psychographic, or be-havioral information). To make targeting decisions, a detailed evaluation of segment attractiveness and competitive advantages in those segments is required.

UNDIFFERENTIATED VERSUS DIFFERENTIATED MARKETING APPROACHES

The two basic strategies a company can adopt are undifferentiated and differentiated marketing[1] (see Figure 26-1). Undifferentiated marketing ignores segment differences and applies a "one-size-fits-all" approach: one product and one marketing program for all customers regardless of segment differences. This leads to benefits from scale, espe-cially economies of scale in research and development, production, advertising, distri-bution, and other overhead expenditures. Undifferentiated marketing also simplifies

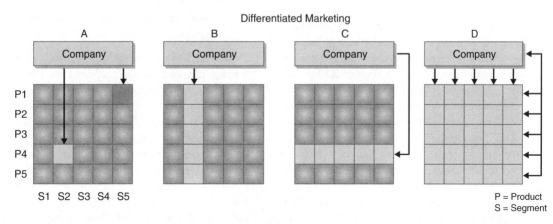

FIGURE NOTE 26-1 Differentiated Marketing Approaches[3]

organizational structures. An historical example of undifferentiated marketing is Ford's Model T. Henry Ford once wrote that "Any customer can have a car painted any color that he wants so long as it is black."[2] Coca-Cola once used this strategy, offering one single product and a single size—the famous green bottle—to the mass market. Increasing competition against differentiated products and the emergence of more idiosyncratic needs (such as family-size bottles, sugar-free drinks, caffeine-free drinks) has lead Coca-Cola to adopt a differentiated marketing approach.

Differentiated marketing means that a company develops adapted or customized marketing mixes for different target market segments (see Figure 26-1). As it tailors products and programs to the segments, it can better meet the segment-specific needs and requirements, and can, therefore, create superior value and demand price premiums. The downside of differentiated programs includes the higher complexity of the organization and of the product portfolio, the diluted benefits of scale, and, as a consequence, the higher per-unit costs. Differentiated marketing can consist of:

- **Selected Specialization.** The company selects and focuses on one or a few single segments (Case A in Figure 26-1). The Austrian company Emporia Telecom uses this strategy. It developed a cell phone for old people, with no digital camera, Internet access, or instant messaging capabilities. However, it does include a button to call relatives or friends in an emergency, is compatible with hearing aids, and can run on regular AAA batteries. It has big easy-to-use buttons, easy intuitive dialing, and big fonts. Thus, the product perfectly fits the needs of elderly people, a segment that has been ignored so far.
- **Segment Specialization.** A producer decides to serve several different needs of one segment and develops many products and marketing programs for this segment (Case B). Dr. Schär, an Italian company in the food industry, uses this approach. The company focuses on people with celiac disease that need a gluten-free diet (gluten is a protein present in certain cereals) and offers a comprehensive product portfolio,

including gluten-free flours, an extensive range of pasta and bread and a variety of bread substitute products, biscuits, snacks, pizza and ready-to-eat cookies as well as mixes to prepare delicious recipes at home. The specialization on this segment of people with celiac condition in the food market has been Schär's strategy for more than 25 years and has lead to its market leadership in Europe.
- **Product Specialization.** Focus on one product that is tailored to all market segments (Case C). Trek, one of the world-leading producers of bicycles is an example for this approach. It offers bikes for virtually all market segments: road bikes, mountain bikes, triathlon bikes, urban bikes, electric bikes, and cruisers; bikes for men, women, and kids; and bikes in several price ranges.
- **Full Market Coverage.** A company decides to address all market segments and develops all products the segment wants (Case D). This is Volkswagen's approach. With its brands (e.g., Volkswagen, Audi, Seat, Lamborghini, Porsche) it serves practically all market segments with a full range of products.

TARGET MARKET SELECTION

To identify the segments that should be targeted, two questions are of central importance:

1. How attractive are the individual segments to the company?
2. Does the company have competitive advantages in these segments?

These are the same questions, essentially, that shape the core idea of portfolio analysis: How attractive is a target and how strong are we vis-à-vis the requirements of that target? Hence, the same methodologies can be used for portfolio analysis and targeting.

In the first step, criteria for segment attractiveness are defined (e.g., segment size, segment growth rate, segment profitability, rivalry within the segment), they are weighted and evaluated (see Table 26-1). A weighted score can be computed that indicates the strength of each criterion in driving segment attractiveness.

TABLE NOTE 26-1 Evaluation of Segment Attractiveness

Segment Attractiveness Analysis

Criteria	Weight	Segment 1	Segment 2	Segment 3	Segment 4	Segment 5	Segment 6
Size	3	3	2	4	1	3	3
Growth	2	2	2	4	1	5	5
Profitability	5	1	2	3	2	4	2
Competition	3	4	1	5	1	5	3
Weighted Score		30	23	50	18	54	38

TABLE NOTE 26-2 Competitive Advantage Analysis per Segment

Competitive Advantage Analysis

Success Factors (Buying Criteria)	Performance*	Importance of success factor per segment**					
		Segment 1	Segment 2	Segment 3	Segment 4	Segment 5	Segment 6
Product Quality	2	4	1	3	1	4	2
Brand	−1	3	3	5	2	1	1
Price	−2	2	5	1	4	2	5
Technology	3	2	1	3	3	5	2
Service	0	2	1	2	2	2	3
Weighted Score		7	−8	8	1	18	−1

*Company Performance compared to strongest competitor (−3=much worse; 0= 3=much better)
**Importance of successs factor for segment (0=not at all; 5=very important)

The next step is to analyze whether a company has competitive advantages in the individual segments (see Table 26-2). To do this, first the success factors are defined (the *customers' buying criteria*). Then, for each segment, an importance weight is estimated. This is an important step, as the importance weights will vary greatly between the segments. Finally, the company compares itself against *the strongest competitor* on these success factors to find out whether it performs better or worse on each buying criterion. This can be done per segment (if there are different competitors in each segment) or against one competitor (if there is a single competitor competing for all the segments). Multiplying the weights with the scores and adding these numbers together, an overall score emerges that indicates the degree of competitive superiority or inferiority in each single segment.

Finally, the weighted scores of segment attractiveness and competitive advantages are used to position each segment in a portfolio (see Figure 26-2).

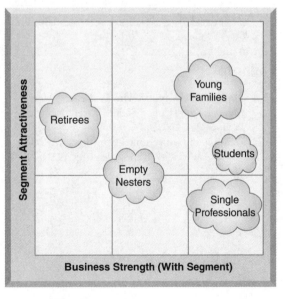

FIGURE NOTE 26-2 Hypothetical Segment Portfolio within GE/McKinsey Grid

The segments in the upper right quadrants are the most interesting candidates for target markets, as they are highly attractive and the company performs better on the success factors than the competitors.

For the target market selection the following additional criteria can be used:

1. *Synergies.* Are there any synergies (economies of scope) between the segments?
2. *Core competences.* Do the segments fit the company's core competences and core businesses?
3. *Strategic objectives.* Do the segments fit the strategic objectives of the company?

The final step in the STP-process (segmenting, targeting, positioning) is the development of a unique "position" in the minds of the customers. The goal of positioning is to establish a difference the company can preserve; the outcome is a customer-focused unique value proposition. Targeting is a critical task in this process; it matches the capabilities of a company with the needs of an attractive market and, therefore, requires careful attention.

Summary

Targeting is the second step in the STP-process. It builds on a division of the overall market into smaller, more homogeneous market segments and on a thorough description of these segments. A comprehensive profile of the segments is needed to determine their attractiveness and the competitive position in these segments. Segment attractiveness and the firm's competitive position can then be used to determine the target segments. In the next step a sustainable value proposition must be established that then guides the design and implementation of the marketing mix.

Additional Resources

Abell, Derek F. *Defining the Business: The Starting Point for Strategic Planning.* Upper Saddle River, New Jersey: Prentice Hall, 1980.

Kotler, Philip and Kevin L. Keller. *Marketing Management.* Upper Saddle River, New Jersey: Prentice Hall, 2009.

Endnotes

1. Philip Kotler and Kevin L. Keller, *Marketing Management* (Upper Saddle River, New Jersey: Prentice Hall, 2009).
2. Henry Ford (with Samuel Crowther), *My Life and Work* (Garden City, NY: Garden City, 1922), 71–72.
3. Adapted from Derek F. Abell, *Defining the Business: The Starting Point for Strategic Planning* (Upper Saddle River, New Jersey: Prentice Hall, 1980).

27

Positioning

"Positioning is not what you do to a product. Positioning is what you do to the mind of the prospect."

AL RIES AND JACK TROUT, *POSITIONING: THE BATTLE FOR YOUR MIND*[1]

Positioning is the final step in the strategy formation process (the "STP process" of Segmenting → Targeting → Positioning). Positioning spans and organizes all of the tactical elements of the marketing mix, such as price, product, promotion, etc. The purpose of positioning is to claim a unique and valued position *in the minds of the customers.* It answers the question: *How do we want to be perceived by our target market?* Generally, product positioning assumes that consumer's complex perceptions of products can be thought of as an actual, physical "space" – a two-dimensional or multidimensional space in which product locations and proximities depict the way consumers think about product characteristics and perceive products relative to each other. This is why product positioning is often captured in "perceptual maps" and terms such as "white space" (unserved or underserved markets) and even "position" itself analogize perceptions of products to actual spatial representations (see Figure 27-1: Perceptual Map of Women's Clothing Retailers in Washington, DC). Sometimes the characteristics that define a space (that is, the axes of the maps) are "real," tangible attributes of the products (such as "engine displacement," "screen resolution," or price), but consumers normally translate actual attributes into their essential benefits (such as "performance," "picture clarity," or "economy"); that is, consumers usually think in terms of the needs the attributes meet, not the actual attributes.

Positioning requires a thorough understanding of:

- The *needs* of the target market;
- *Competitor's positions* in the target market; and
- The firm's own *competitive advantages* and points of differentiation.

RELATED TOPICS AND TOOLS

Positioning involves the convergence of several analyses and strategic ideas discussed here. In particular, because it is tied to understanding *needs*, *competitors*, and the firm's *competitive advantages*, positioning relies on thorough customer analysis and marketing research, competitor analysis, and understandings of the firm's own strengths and

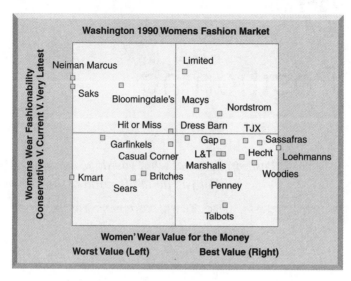

FIGURE NOTE 27-1 Perceptual Map of Women's Clothing Retailers in Washington, DC[2]

competitive advantages. As noted, successful positioning *claims a unique and valued place in consumers' perceptions;* the firm retains that position by "branding"—by marking or holding that position with a brand (a name, a logo or trademark, or other signals and a "meaning" that consumers retain across occasions).

SPECIFIC TOOLS FOR POSITIONING

There are four tools specifically related to, and especially important in, positioning products and brands in the market:

- Semantic scales;
- Customer value maps;
- Perceptual maps; and
- Positioning statements.

Semantic Scales

A very useful tool for brand positioning is semantic scaling. In a semantic-scale survey, customers are asked to rate alternatives with regard to a number of specific attributes. Those questions are usually formulated as bipolar items—that is, as questions with alternative words (such as hot versus cold, or powerful versus weak at each end or "pole"), and customers are asked to rate each alternative (each product) on a given scale (from, for example 1-to-5, or 1-to-7). For example, "How would you rate this furniture dealer

on a scale of 1 to 5, where is "1" means "exclusive" and "5" means "mundane?"

The attributes selected are intended to capture brand perceptions, and they do; but these attributes/items must be selected in advance by the researcher and may not capture the manner in which consumers combine attributes into perceptions. In particular, consumers often act on their perceptions of products benefits—benefits are what meet needs—but semantic scales are best in order to address perceptions of attributes. Data collected via semantic items can be used to create perceptual maps, to plot attributes into perceptual maps created via Multidimensional Scaling (MDS), or to compare alternatives along the selected attributes. Figure 27-2 shows the positioning of a producer of premium furniture and its competitor. The dotted line represents the ideal and intended position.

Customer Value Map

A basic positioning decision every company makes or should make is how to locate the product in the customer mind regarding the two cardinal buying criteria of overall quality and price. A company has the option of positioning their product as the price leader, the quality leader, or as some combination of those two high-level attributes. Figure 27-3 shows the price/quality position of flat screen television

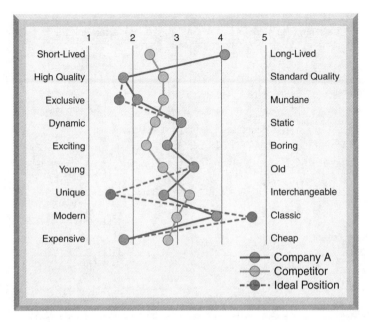

FIGURE NOTE 27-2   Semantic Scale Comparison of Premium Furniture Manufacturers

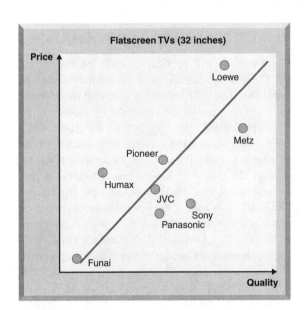

FIGURE NOTE 27-3   Price/Quality Positioning (i.e., Value Map) for Flat Screen TVs[3]

producers within a value map. Loewe's position is unfavorable; it has the highest price but not the highest quality. Metz and Sony are much better positioned; compared to their competitors and compared to their quality, their prices are relatively low.

Perceptual Maps and Multidimensional Scaling

Perceptual maps are graphical visualizations of customer's perceptions of products or brands. The Value Frontier is, in fact, a specific case of a perceptual map (with the axes stipulated as overall quality and price). A more complex way to position brands is multidimensional scaling (MDS). It allows the analyst to assess the similarity between brands in a multidimensional space and, instead of being specified by theory, it allows consumers to choose the dimensions upon which they evaluate the alternatives (and it identifies those dimensions for the strategic manager). The principle of MDS is very simple: The positions of the brands represent their similarity; brands that are closer together are more similar and brands farther away are less similar.

Figure 27-4 is an example using major European Alpine ski resorts.[4] Based on customers' evaluations of the resorts on a number of specific attributes (e.g., entertainment and nightlife, price, quality of the slopes), a perceptual map was created for two segments (skiers aged 50 years and above on the left, and skiers aged 25 years or less on the right). The horizontal axis separates the two ski resorts and places St. Moritz (Switzerland) on the left and Toggenburg (Switzerland) on the right, indicating that these two ski resorts are perceived as the

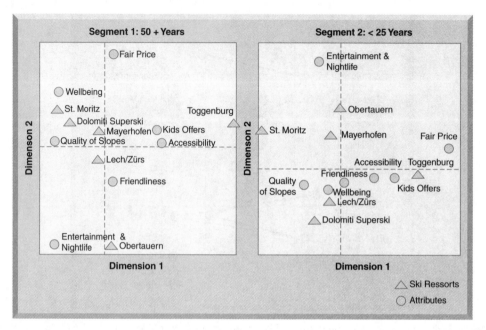

FIGURE NOTE 27-4 Perceptual Maps of Ski Resorts in Two Market Segments[5]

most dissimilar. St. Moritz and Dolomiti Superski (Italy) are positioned very closely to each other. Mayerhofen (Austria) and Lech/Zürs (Austria) are also perceived to be very similar.

The distance of a ski resorts from the attributes, which have also been plotted into the maps, indicates the strength of the perceptions on that attribute. St. Moritz's shows very strong associations with well-being and quality of slopes, and weak associations with entertainment and nightlife. Toggenburg is perceived as a child-friendly ski resort and also as easily accessible. The segment of the young skiers (<25 years) shows quite a different perceptual map. Again, St. Moritz and Toggenburg are the most dissimilar ski resorts, but their relationships with the attributes differ from the corresponding perceptions in the 50+ segment. St. Moritz has strong associations with well-being and quality of slopes, but is also seen as very expensive. Among <25 skiers, Lech/Zürs has a very strong position regarding well-being, quality of slopes and friendliness. These differences show how important it is to analyze brand perceptions of specific market segments. Not only do they differ regarding their needs (their "ideal" products are discussed below), they may also differ regarding their basic perceptions of the assortment and the important dimensions.

TARGET SEGMENTS AND POSITIONING

Consumers' "ideal" products can also be understood via the perceptual mapping techniques described here. The statistical analyses underlying the identification of consumers' ideal products (or "ideal points" in the perceptual maps) are beyond the scope of this book (and beyond the concern of most marketing strategists). It can, nevertheless, be invaluable to plot ideal products into these same product spaces or perceptual maps. The "ideal point" isn't the consumers' "favorite" from among the offered assortment (products already in the market); in fact, there doesn't have to be any offered product that meets the consumers' ideal preferences. The ideal point is the product that, *if it were offered*, would be the favorite of the consumers of a particular segment; in fact, the *perfect* product. Figure 27-5 shows where in the perceptual space of Washington area retailers the ideal retailer of the five segments would fall (the *size* of the circle depicting each segment reflects that segment's size).

POSITIONING STATEMENTS

These analytical tools—perceptual maps, semantic scales, and multidimensional scaling—reveal the current positions of products offered in a market as

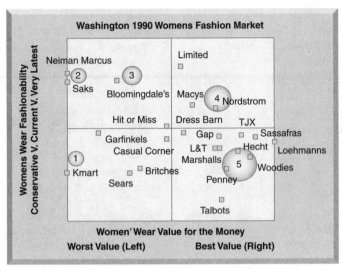

FIGURE NOTE 27-5   Perceptual Map with Segments Plotted Within Space[6]

perceived by customers. Once a strategy has been chosen to target a position—that is, once the target position has been established, the marketing plan or strategy should generate a written statement of that intended position. These codifications of intended product positions are called "positioning statements." They should capture in one or two sentences the intended position and should also convey the brand's differentiation from its competitors. Selva, an Italian producer of high-quality furniture, describes its positioning as:

> "For nearly forty years now, the name Selva has been a trademark for the pinnacle of creativity, unique variety, and fantastic quality. To reach that point, it has been the very special interplay of tradition and innovation that provides the very particular Selva touch. Tradition means that we are absolutely committed to the classic virtues. And throughout the world, that has made us an appreciated and reliable partner."

Red Bull, the Austrian inventor of energy drinks, positions its core product as a functional beverage with a unique combination of ingredients. It has been specially developed for times of increased mental and physical exertion. The positioning statement states:

> "Red Bull Energy Drink vitalizes body and mind. This is achieved through the following product characteristics: It

increases performance, increases concentration and reaction speed, improves vigilance, improves the emotional status and stimulates metabolism."

A positioning statement expresses the singular characteristic of a product or a brand aiming at establishing unique, sustainable, and positive associations in the minds of the customers. A positioning statement should be:[7]

- Relevant, that is, it must emphasize attributes that are important to the customer;
- Distinctive, that is, it must emphasize attributes that are superior to competitors;
- Believable, that is, the brand must provide a compelling reason for being superior;
- Feasible, that is, the positioning must be backed-up by superior product attributes or capabilities;
- Communicable, that is, the superiority must be easy to explain; and
- Sustainable, that is, the position must be easy to sustain and difficult to imitate.

Most positioning statements specify the target segment, the brand being positioned, the product category within which it is being positioned, the point of difference or "unique selling proposition," and the reason to believe. For example, many experts and firms use some version of a generic statement such as:

> For (*definition of target consumers/segments*), (*Brand X*) is (*definition of frame*

of reference and subjective category) which gives the most... (promise or consumer benefit/point of difference) because only (Brand X) is (reason to believe).[8]

Key elements in these statements are the promise and the reason to believe—these specify and substantiate the intended position (of Brand X in this market, specified as the "frame of reference," for these consumers/segments). Positioning statements may also specify the "brand meaning" or "brand personality" of the intended positioning. At Johnson & Johnson, for example, positioning statements include a well-known personality, not as the intended spokesperson (most often these celebrities have no formal relationship with the brand and, in fact, some are historical figures), but rather to richly capture and communicate the "brand personality."

Summary

There is an old adage that "Segmentation is the tough job, and positioning is easy." Positioning really represents the sum total of all of the marketer's actions on each of the elements of the marketing mix, the 5 Ps. If the marketer has a well-defined target segment with well-defined needs and wants, then getting the Ps right (right product at right price in right place, with right amount of information for the customer to make an intelligent decision, at the right time) should be relatively easy. On the other hand, if the marketer doesn't understand the segmentation and the market structure, then getting the Ps right—the positioning—is just a guessing game. While there are many tools available for use in positioning products, services, and brands, marketing strategists should remember this basic rule. We position to a segment, not the other way around. In other words, the process involves segmenting, then targeting, and finally positioning.

Additional Resources

Kapferer, J-N. *The New Strategic Brand Management*, 4th Ed. Philadelphia, PA: Kogan Page, 2008.

Kotler, P., and Keller, K. L. *Marketing Management.* Upper Saddler River, NJ: Pearson Education, 2009.

Ries, A., and J. Trout. *Positioning: The Battle for Your Mind.* New York: McGraw-Hill, 1981.

Tybout, A. M., and B. Sternthal. "Brand Positioning," in *Kellogg on Branding*, edited by A. M. Tybout and T. Calkins, 11- 26. New Jersey: John Wiley & Sons, 2005.

Endnotes

1. Al Ries, and Jack Trout, *Positioning: The Battle for Your Mind* (New York: McGraw-Hill, 1981), 24.

2. Lawrence J. Ring and Douglas J. Tigert, "Store Wars Around the Beltway: Women's Fashions in Washington D. C., 1990 (A)" case number W&M-M-109, pp. 35–36, Copyright 1990 by the Sponsors of the Graduate School of Business Administration of the College of William and Mary, and the Sponsors of Babson College.

3. Based on N.N. (2009) TV-Geräte im Test. *Konsument.* Also see Bradley T. Gale, *Managing Customer Value.* (New York: Free Press, 1994).

4. See R. Faullant, K. Matzler, and J. Füller, "A Positioning Map of Skiing Areas Using Customer Satisfaction Scores," *Journal of Hospitality & Leisure Marketing*, 16, (2008): 230–245.

5. Adapted from: Ibid.

6. Lawrence J. Ring and Douglas J. Tigert, "Store Wars Around the Beltway: Women's Fashions in Washington D. C., 1990 (A)" case number W&M-M-109, pp. 35–36, Copyright 1990 by the Sponsors of the Graduate School of Business Administration of the College of William and Mary, and the Sponsors of Babson College.

7. P. Kotler, & K. L. Keller, *Marketing management* (Upper Saddler River, NJ: Pearson Education, 2009).

8. J-N. Kapferer, *The New Strategic Brand Management*, 4th Ed. (Philadelphia, PA: Kogan Page, 2008), 178; and A. M. Tybout and B. Sternthal, "Brand Positioning," in *Kellogg on Branding*, ed. A. M. Tybout and T. Calkins (New Jersey: John Wiley & Sons, 2005), 11–26, see pages 12–13.

IMPLEMENTATION

28

Customer-Oriented Market Research

Effective strategic marketing requires persistent and thorough attention to the customer and to customer needs—*that's "the marketing concept."* A customer focus pervades our strategic marketing framework, by design, taking different forms at different points in the process. Some distinctions across market research activities and related terminology are summarized in Table 28-1. Market research includes studying events and trends in the general environment (situation assessment), including events and trends with regard to competitors and in the "general context," summarized by the mnemonic PEST (Political/regulatory/legal, Economic, Social/cultural, and Technical/natural/physical). Marketing research also encompasses customer assessment, the wide-ranging search for social trends and customer insights. Those applications of marketing research to situation assessment and, in particular, to customer assessment are inductive, exploratory, and less structured.

Marketing research also encompasses research focused on specific problems or on guiding specific marketing-mix activities. This note links focused *customer-oriented market research* to marketing strategy; this is the issue-specific research that (1) segments and targets customers, (2) shapes specific marketing programs and tactics (positioning and the marketing mix), and (3) evaluates those activities against standards and objectives for use in assessment and adjustment. This note takes a strategic marketer's perspective, emphasizing how to manage the research function. It is not about how to *do* market research; it is about how to *manage* market research and how to integrate market research into strategic planning (See Figure 28-1).

Table 28-1 highlights the pervasive role of market research in strategy formation, implementation, and assessment. Market research is a required input to segmenting customers based on consequential differences in needs and responses to the marketing mix. Market research is similarly essential to developing marketing mixes; it tests and directs everything from new product development and pricing to advertising, sales, and distribution. Finally, assessment and adjustment requires rigorous measurement and a "dashboard" of marketing metrics including outcomes such as customer satisfaction, customer

TABLE NOTE 28-1 Customer Consideration in the Strategic Marketing Process

Customer-Oriented Marketing Research			
	Situation Assessment	*Customer Assessment*	The broad, exploratory, and inductive study of customers in general to identify (1) *trends* in needs and demand, and (2) *customer insights*.
	Strategy Formation and Implementation	*Segmentation, Targeting, and Positioning*	Ongoing as well as focused research identifying differences across customers/consumers with regard to needs and descriptive characteristics and linking those differences to existing or achievable competitive advantages.
		Positioning and the Marketing Mix	Focused research to pretest and refine tactics including price, promotions and advertising, new products or product modifications, and merchandising programs and to gauge the effects of those tactics on achieving the desired positioning.
		Customer Relationship Management (CRM)	Ongoing data collections tied to specific accounts, customers, or consumers that serves to tailor offerings (personalize or customize offerings) and direct investments and efforts toward the "right" customers and segments.
	Assessment & Adjustment	*Customer- and Market-Oriented Metrics*	Focused and ongoing research collecting information on customer responses to the marketing mix including measures of satisfaction, loyalty, profitability, and revenues.

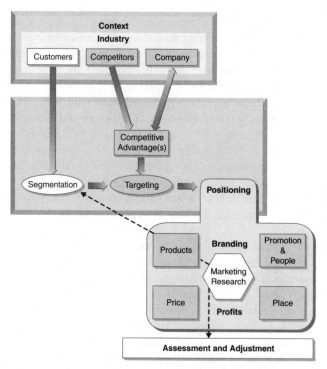

FIGURE NOTE 28-1 Market Research Supports Various Stages in Strategic Planning

profitability, and customer loyalty measures that gauge how the firm is doing with its customers).Still, *every* problem doesn't require formal market research. Before discussing market research from a strategic perspective, it is worthwhile to clarify some considerations about when market research is required and when it may not be necessary or wise.

WHEN TO DO MARKET RESEARCH—
AND WHEN NOT TO

Obviously, every marketing decision *doesn't* require formal market research; in fact, in many situations, traditional market research may be inaccurate and misleading. Decisions about when to undertake market research and when *not* to invest in market research should be based on considerations of:

- Whether or not the information can realistically be researched; for example, whether or not customers can be realistically expected to know or estimate their responses to a proposed marketing action; and
- Whether or not the *benefits* outweigh the *costs* of doing the research.

When a product is truly "new to the world" customers may not understand it well enough to predict their responses. Sony executive, Kozo Ohsone, observed that "When you introduce products that have never been invented before, what good is market research?"[1] When Sony introduced the Walkman personal music player into the market, market research had determined that customers would not buy a tape player that did not record; Sony management trusted its instincts and went ahead and launched the now legendary device— without recording capabilities—despite those research findings. Similarly, market research on the phone answering machine found that customers thought it would be rude to have a machine answer their phone. Today, of course, most phones have voicemail.[2] The understanding that, in some cases, customers can't accurately respond to new product ideas and that the knowledge and the "instincts" of experts, including marketing managers and channel partners, may be more accurate in predicting market responses is especially relevant to the marketing of radical innovations.

Additionally, before investing in market research, the marketer should weigh the costs against the benefits of the effort. The costs of market research include financial costs—market research can be very expensive—as well as the *time* required to conduct the research (including managerial time and delays in taking the contemplated actions). The benefits of market research are its support for decision making and the reduction of risk. Risk assessments should be multifaceted, taking into account both the probability of an outcome (its likelihood) and the consequences of the risk. Market research may be wasted on refining elements of a marketing program that can be easily adjusted after "launch," on reducing the risk of highly unlikely outcomes, or on reducing risks that will in any case have inconsequential impacts on the program or the firm. Those deliberations are especially relevant when speed-to-market is critical. A study by Arthur D. Little & Company found that 92 percent of all new cereals launched in the market failed despite the best market research efforts, leading cereal marketers to reduce their expenditures on market research in favor of cutting the costs of launching a new cereal and increasing the agility and flexibility of their manufacturing operations.[3] Introducing new products into actual markets and "seeing what sticks" may, in many cases, be more efficient and more effective than investing in expensive and time-consuming market research and test markets.

One interesting observation in this regard is that modern business education and culture seems to teach managers not to trust their instincts or expertise. That is probably a good thing in many situations; good market research should suffer less bias than managerial judgment. Nevertheless, in some cases managerial expertise or "gut feel" is accurate, more accurate than customers themselves can be in some situations. Further, for some decisions, managerial expertise can be "close enough"; more research may tweak and refine a decision but those tweaks and refinements may not produce much in terms of substantive improvements or increased sales. For example, Sony co-founder Masaru Ibuka wanted to extend Sony's competence in magnetic recording, which had been focused on audio recording, into video recording. Traveling in the United States to research the concept, he observed people buying paperback books at the airport and easily carrying those books in their pockets, briefcases and pocketbooks. Without further market research to validate or fine-tune the concept, he decided that the Betamax video-tape cassette should be the size of those paperback books. Returning to Japan, he challenged the research and development team to come up with Betamax; he took a book he'd purchased at the airport in New York out of his pocket, "This is the size I need for the cassette."[4] Although Betamax eventually lost out to the VHS format, that outcome was unrelated to the size of the cassette. Ibuka understood the appropriate role of managerial judgment and expertise in directing certain details of the marketing programs—further research might have changed the size and shape of the Betamax cassette, but the size and proportion of Mr. Ibuka's book was an *adequate.*

THE MARKET RESEARCH PROCESS

When market research *is* appropriate and needed, it should be clearly based on a specific understanding of the issue, opportunity, or problem that is to be researched and with a detailed understanding of the managerial decision to be guided by the research. Figure 28-2 presents two versions of the same basic, strategic market research process. The four-step process on the left, adapted from Philip Kotler and Gary Armstrong's classic *Principles of Marketing* textbook,[5] is a traditional view of the Market Research flow: The first step is to define the problem and the objectives of the research. Subsequent steps plan and execute a data-driven project that addresses those problems and objectives, leading toward a summary report.

The process graphed on the right in Figure 28-2 is adapted from an article, "Backward Market Research," by Alan Andreasen[6] in which he argued that "Only by first thinking through the decisions to be made with the research results will the project be started with a high likelihood of actionability."[7] Andreasen argued that the manager should not only spell out the issue or problem to be addressed by the research, but should also carefully tie the research *to specific managerial actions* (the "implementation" or "actionability") that are possible depending on the outcomes of the research, and even go so far as to *draft the eventual report*—including the tables for presenting quantitative results—before developing

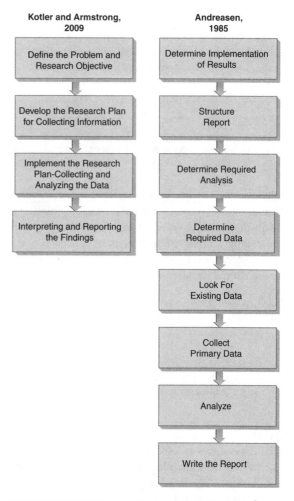

FIGURE NOTE 28-2   The Market Research Process[8]

and executing the research plan. Andreasen's framework emphasizes the need to hone in on what, exactly, could be done differently depending on the results of this research and the need to think ahead about how the research will address the issue and how the recommendations will be communicated.

Most of the remainder of these marketing-research process steps are "technical"—sampling plans, data collections, and statistical analyses that are the purview of research staff and vendors—but an appreciation of the need to link investments in research to specific issues and feasible strategic actions, discussed above, and a broad understanding of the ways different research approaches link with different issues and produce different sorts of information are invaluable to guide decision making to effective and efficient strategic management.

Questions and Issues that Market Research Can Address

In science there are two types of "errors": Type I errors are when the research finds positive results for something that is, in fact, not true (these are also called "false positives"); and Type II errors are those that reject hypotheses that are really true ("false negatives"). A third sort of error, not as often discussed in the research literature, is a "Type III error": *finding the right answers for the wrong questions.*[9] Market researchers should be particularly attentive to Type III errors when structuring the parameters of a research project. There are at least three broad categories of questions that market research can address:

- Market Questions:
  - Demand forecasting: What is the size of the market? What are the sizes and growth rates of the different segments? How will markets/segments respond to the offerings?
  - Describe competition and context (see Table 28-1: the row "Situation Assessment");
  - Needs identification and segmentation: What do customers need and care about, and how much do they care? How do customers differ in regards to those needs and "importance weightings?"

- Mix/Program Questions:
  - The effect of various marketing mix elements: What is the best product, message, channel, or price? What is the best combination of these interdependent tactics?
- Assessment and Adjustment Questions:
  - Market Share: How are we doing vis-à-vis the competition? How are we meeting our objectives?
  - Performance: Success in meeting customer needs: How do our customers feel about us (customer satisfaction)? How loyal are they? How profitable are they?

Types of Research

Market Research can have three basic formats:

- *Exploratory.* We have separated out customer assessment, which is certainly exploratory research, as a distinct set of processes. Exploratory research is also part of market research. Exploratory research uses less structured and wide-ranging methods to identify issues for further research without imposing *a priori* structure or hypotheses on the data collection or the respondent. In market research, focus groups, depth interviews, and other methods may all be useful, *especially at the front end of a project*, to explore customer experiences and the underlying factors driving observed phenomena, and to generate specific issues for further research.
- *Descriptive.* Descriptive research characterizes the *who, what, when,* and *where* of the market (but not the *why*—why implies causation, which is discussed below). Descriptions are most often of markets, segments, or specific customers and their *size, attitudes* and *preferences,* and *behaviors* or other characteristics important to strategy and marketing-mix management.
- *Causal.* Causal research is the *why* of a marketplace phenomena. It relates two or more variables and isolates the *causal* factors. Causal research identifies the event (or "cause") and its consequence ("effect"). Experiments are the most common form of causal research. Experiments are research designs in which one group of customers or one market is exposed to one level of a variable (a promotion, a price level, or an advertisement) while another group is not, (making it the "control group") or in which different groups are given different levels of a variable (different prices, for instance, or different advertisements).

Types of Data

There are several ways to differentiate sources of and types of data. Some data are *internal* to the firm—and most firms can find out a lot just by analyzing data they already have "in house"—and other data are *external* to the firm. Generally, because internal data are more readily at hand (although not necessarily "easy" or free to access), it is a good idea to start by asking "what do we already know" and to thoroughly analyze internal data *first*, before investing in gathering external data. It is also generally true that firms underappreciate the informational value of internal data, such as shipments, inventories, and returns. The Japanese tend to rely on hard data along with channel partners (conversations with and visits to distributors and retailers) more, in making decisions—than do American managers.[10]

A second distinction across data is between *secondary* data, preexisting data already collected for some other purpose either by the firm or elsewhere, and *primary* data, data collected specifically for the project and issue at hand. As with the internal–external distinction, there is a general rule that looking at secondary data first is a good idea. Secondary data may not be free or immediately available, there may be costs to obtaining secondary data and it may take some time, but secondary data are generally cheaper, easier, and faster to access than primary data. For example, a firm might want to know how much has been paid in taxes on the sale of alcohol in a certain jurisdiction in order to estimate the size of the market for adult beverages; obtaining those secondary data may require sending a paid staff researcher to Alcoholic Beverages Commission (ABC) and could involve fees for the reports, but those costs and time required would be less than doing a survey to estimate the size of the market. On the other hand, primary data would be customized to the specific research issue being addressed; if the product being considered is high-end tequila, for example, a primary data collection such as a consumer survey could ask how much premium tequila the customer has consumed or intends to consume, providing more specifically relevant information (e.g., than simple tax receipts would). In addition, some secondary data can be a little outdated (e.g., tax receipts for the current year may not be available), and others can be quite outdated (e.g., the U.S. Census is collected every ten years), but primary data will be up-to-date. Table 28-2 summarizes these basic distinctions between secondary and primary data.

TABLE NOTE 28-2 Primary versus Secondary

	Cost	Time Required to Obtain	Timeliness	Customization
Secondary:	Low	Quick	Can be Outdated	Low to None
Primary:	High*	Delayed	Current	High

*Costs of primary Market Research are high in both *monetary* terms and in terms of *managerial time and effort* and with regard to *delays in taking action.*

Another distinction across data is between *qualitative* and *quantitative* data. Every marketer can appreciate that a customer's reaction to almost any consumption experience, from dining at a fine restaurant to purchasing raw materials for a plant, is going to be hard to summarize with a single, simple number. Customer satisfaction, for example, is certainly a much "richer" experience than a single number (e.g., on a scale of 1–10) can possibly describe. Nevertheless, in order to test hypotheses and evaluate concepts in large, random samples and in order to compare responses across customers, marketers frequently must use simple, forced-choice scales to gauge and analyze phenomena such as customer satisfaction.

Qualitative data are those data that are developed from observation or via textual, verbal, and open-ended responses methods; qualitative data tend to be subjective and imprecise and are not easily compared or generalized across customers, but qualitative data can provide invaluable depth and vividness. Quantitative data are responses that are provided or can be summarized *numerically*, and quantitative methods are conducive to statistical analysis, enabling generalization of results across larger groups ("populations"). The ability to compare data across customers, for example the ability to compare customers across time (e.g., last year versus this year) or across segments, and the ability to "generalize" to all customers in a target population (a segment or a market) support the use of quantitative data in many market research applications.

Generalizability is an important idea. Because qualitative techniques require a lot of the respondent's time, thought, and energy, it is often impossible to develop qualitative data from adequate sized, truly-random samples. Only when each member of a population (the overall group the researcher is interested in) has had an equal chance of being selected for a data collection can its results be generalized to the population. If the researcher selects and pays eight retirees that she or he personally knows to attend a focus group, she or he only knows *what those eight retirees think* about the product or advertisement— they weren't selected randomly and they are a very small sample, so we can't generalize to all retirees. If we randomly sample from all of the retirees in a market and survey a large enough number of them regarding their responses to a new product idea, our results will be quantitative and, although not rich (e.g., a rating of a new product might be an 8.73, versus a 7.49 for an alternative, or a 23% "definitely will try"), those results will be *generalizable* to all retirees in the market—we would know that there is a significant probability that all retirees will prefer one product to the other or will try the product.

Thus, as summarized in Table 28-3, there is an inherent tradeoff between the richness of qualitative data and data collection methods and the generalizability and comparability of quantitative data. As a general course of action, market research projects should begin with qualitative research in order to

understand the issues and problems better and from the customers' perspective and to confirm that the issues the manager thinks are important are important from the customers' perspectives, too. If the researcher believes that the problem is with a certain aspect of the product (e.g., the size of the package), and doesn't go out to interview customers to let *them* describe what *they* see as the problem (e.g., package resealability), a resulting survey may be ineffective at describing the problem or selecting solutions. The general flow should be from qualitative research in small, nonrandom samples toward quantitative methods in larger and random samples.

Various specific types of data combine these characteristics—internal/external, secondary/primary, and qualitative/quantitative—in different ways. Some data, like syndicated data (i.e., scanner data or panel data), are external/secondary/quantitative data tied to observations of consumers' behaviors recorded electronically (in the case of scanner data) or via surveys (in the case of panels). Other data, such as sales-force feedback, are internal/secondary/qualitative. Other sorts of data can combine these characteristics in innumerable ways but all can be characterized using these three qualities and those characterizations are useful in understanding the data's content, their usefulness in strategic planning, and their limitations.

Data Analyses

As noted, it is generally *not* the marketing strategist's job to design or execute the data collection in a research project nor is it the strategist's job to analyze those data, but it is important to understand some specific analyses that are especially useful in strategic marketing planning. Three market research analyses are important for the strategic marketing to understand:

- Syndicated data and associated analyses, such as All Commodity Volume (ACV), Brand Development Indices (BDI), and Category Development Indices (CDI);
- Perceptual Maps, including those developed from direct items (such as, "On a scale of 1–7, how heavy is beer X?") or from indirect "paired comparison" ("How similar or dissimilar are beers X and Y?") using multidimensional scaling (MDS);

TABLE NOTE 28-3   Qualitative versus Quantitative

	Richness	Generalizability	Comparability
Qualitative	High	Low to None	Low
Quantitative	Low	High	High

- Conjoint analysis, which pulls apart customer preferences along specific attributes when customers consider those attributes in conjoint with (or "simultaneously and interdependently with") other attributes; and,
- Experiments, which allow the researcher to identify with certainty which actions or other variables cause what outcomes (e.g., to determine with certainty that a change in price leads to higher sales).

This section briefly describes each of these three specific sorts of research and analysis; Appendix C explains them in greater (but still high-level and strategic) detail.

SYNDICATED SOURCES Syndicated data are collected by third parties (not the customers, not the trade (retailers), and not the company itself), usually one of a very few large market research companies (Information Resources Incorporated [IRI] and ACNielsen dominate the market). Syndicated data have grown dramatically with technological advances over the past few decades and today researchers have access to hundreds of terabytes of data. These data include *scanner data*, the data recorded each time a UPC code (Uniformed Product Code or bar-scan) is passed over a checkout scanner at a grocery store, from retailers across the country (but missing Walmart's data—they compile their own scanner data for their own suppliers' use). Those scanner data are augmented with information about "causes" or events such as coupons, price promotions, and the like to allow for analysis of sales patterns across time and in correlation with price and promotion tactics. Other data offered by these third-party research syndicators include *panel data*, which results from a panel of consumers tracking their actual purchases, including the retailers they purchase from, across time. *Single-source data* combine panel data (tacked purchases and purchase venues) with surveys of things like demographics and lifestyles, and also augments those data with consumer media usage (television watched, newspapers read, etc.). These syndicated data are powerful tools in understanding the links between segments, media, marketing actions (especially price and price promo-

tions but also advertising), and purchase behaviors as well as for describing retail coverage.

PERCEPTUAL MAPS. One of the most useful ways to present and to think about competitive position in the marketplace is to translate positions in consumer perceptions to position in a two-dimensional map (a plane), with products and customer preferences graphed into that space. The usefulness of maps in understanding actual positions held in customers' minds is well-established (Even though it is unlikely that many customers carry such "maps" in their minds, they do perceive the various products in relationship to each other and to some salient characteristics—and the maps capture that reality). It is, therefore, reasonable to conceptualize targeting (directing marketing programs at segments) and competitive differences (relationships amongst products and brands) within these two-dimensional representations. Figure 28-3 is a two-dimensional map of perceptions of woman's magazines in the United States. It shows that a certain set of magazines, including Vogue and Cosmopolitan, are perceived as upscale fashion magazines while another cluster, including Ladies' Home Journal and Redbook, are viewed as downscale service magazines. "Joint space" maps allow the researcher to also place characteristics (such as "sophisticated," "stylish," etc.) and customers' "ideal points" into these maps—usefully showing how perceptions of product alternatives and attributes correspond with product attributes and customer preferences. Two commonly applied approaches to creating perceptual maps are (1) structured or semantic items mapped into Cartesian Coordinates and (2) multidimensional scaling which derives "similarities" from less structured customer responses that tap into the dimensions along which customers perceive the product category when they are not given dimensions but must develop there own.

CONJOINT ANALYSIS Another invaluable class of analyses addresses how customers evaluate and choose across products when those products are made up of multiple attributes, when those attributes must be considered together, and when preferences with regard to those attributes involve trade-offs across attributes. For example, everyone would like a car that handles really well. Everyone would also prefer a car that can carry a lot of luggage. But customers know that if they want handling, they must give up some cargo capacity (and vice versa). It is physically impossible to get a great handling car that also has the maximum cargo capacity. In other cases those trade-offs are based on price; even if a car that could do everything—handle well and move lots of things—were possible, most customers know it would cost a lot and they aren't willing to pay for it. In this way, different customers and different segments of customers have different preference. The perfect car for one segment will embody a certain set of trade-offs. Young families frequently trade off handling and performance for cargo space and fuel economy. On the other hand, young single professionals probably will prefer handling and performance. Conjoint analysis, which takes its name from the fact that multiple attributes are considered "in conjoint" or simultaneously and interdependently, is capable of identifying the trade-offs or "value func-tions" of different customers and different segments, gauging the importance different segments place on different attributes, and identifying each segment's perfect product or "ideal point." Those pieces of in-formation can be invaluable in new product develop-ment, integrated marketing communications, and other positioning activities.

EXPERIMENTS.   Experiments are a powerful tool to fine-tuning marketing programs and linking specific actions (causes) with specific outcomes (effects). Managers have been encouraged to turn to experi-ments more as technology has allowed for the easier targeting of different groups with different actions. For example, the Internet allows for quick changes in the way products are described and priced. By vary-ing the presentation and price across consumers the researcher can link specific changes in the marketing mix to specific outcomes (usually those outcomes are desired customer responses such as sales or satisfac-tion). If customers are "assigned" to different "cells"

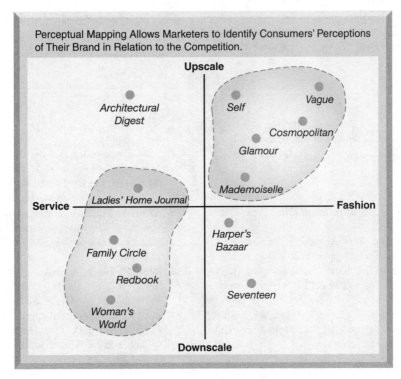

FIGURE NOTE 28-3   Perceptual Map of Woman's Fashion Magazines[11]

or treatments randomly then differences in their responses (higher sales, greater satisfaction) can be attributed to the treatment variable (different price, different advertisement) with confidence.

Summary

The marketing strategist at any medium-to-large firm *should not* be designing research, collecting data, or analyzing results, but she or he *should* be expert in what sorts of research are possible, what sorts of information those research alternatives can provide, and how *market research should drive strategy development, implementation, and assessment.* Managers at small firms may actually conduct research themselves, and there are many sources available to guide the details of those activities. In any case, market research should start with a clear understanding of the problem or issue to be addressed and the managerial actions that may be guided by the research. The marketing strategy itself should be based on and tested against data.

This note has presented a high-level perspective on when to do research, why to do research, how to manage the research effectively and efficiently, and on *what the compelling link is, between research and strategy in a market-driven firm.* The only way to develop, implement, monitor, and adjust the appropriate marketing mix toward achieving a desired marketing strategy is by means of rigorous marketing research.

Additional Resources

Larreche, Jean-Claude. *The Momentum Effect: How to Ignite Exceptional Growth.* Upper Saddle River, NJ: Wharton School Publishing, 2008.

Malhotra, Naresh K. *Marketing Research: An applied orientation,* 6th ed. Upper Saddle River, NJ: Pearson/Prentice Hall, 2010.

Vitale, Dona. *Consumer Insights 2.0: How smart companies apply customer knowledge to the bottom line.* Ithaca, NY, USA: Paramount Market Publishing, 2006.

Endnotes

1. Willard I. Zangwill, "When Customer Research Is a Lousy Idea," *Wall Street Journal* (March 8, 1993): A12.
2. Ibid.
3. Ibid.
4. See Akio Morita, *Made in Japan* (New York: E.P. Dutton, 1986), 112.
5. Philip Kotler and Gary Armstong, *Principles of Marketing,* 11th ed. (Upper Saddle River, NJ: Pearson/Prentice Hall, 2009), 106; compare that with Alvin C. Burns and Ronald F. Bush's 11-step elaboration on the same underlying flow of tasks and analyses, in Alvin C. Burns and Ronald F. Bush, *Market Research,* 6th ed., (Upper Saddle River, NJ: Pearson/Prentice Hall, 2009).
6. Alan R. Andreasen, "Backward Market Research," *Harvard Business Review* 63, no. 3 (May–June, 1985): 176–182.
7. Ibid., page 180.
8. The six-step process on the left is from Kotler and Armstrong, *Principles of Marketing,* page 106. The eight-step process on the right is adapted from Andreasen, "Backward Market Research."
9. Allyn W. Kimball, "Errors of the Third Kind in Statistical Consulting," *Journal of the American Statistical Association* 52, no. 278 (June 1957): 133–142.
10. Johny K. Johansson and Ikujiro Nonaka, "Market Research the Japanese Way," *Harvard Business Review* 65, no. 3 (May–June): 16–19.
11. Michael R. Solomon, Greg W. Marshall, and Elnora W. Stuart, *Marketing: Real People Real Choices,* 6th ed. (Upper Saddle River, NJ: Prentice Hall, 2009), 219.

29

Brands and Branding

"If this business were split up, I would give you the land and bricks and mortar, and I would take the brands and trade marks, and I would fare better than you."

JOHN STUART, CEO OF QUAKER (CA. 1900)[1]

According to the American Marketing Association, a brand is: "A name, term, design, symbol, or any other feature that identifies one seller's good or service as distinct from those of other sellers. The legal term for brand is trademark."[2] This useful but narrow definition focuses on the specific indicators of brands (name, term, symbol, etc.) and the functions of brands in the marketplace. Brands are also complex social phenomena. As concepts in customers' minds (and hearts), brands have rich symbolism and meanings that go beyond their identifying function. That social symbolism and meaning is, to varying degrees, beyond the marketing strategist's or the brand manager's control. Nevertheless, the essential strategic roles of a brand are to identify the product and its producer to consumers, to differentiate the offering in a valued way, and to command margin—and these are roles that the marketing manager must shape and control.

BRAND MARKS AND THE FUNCTIONS OF BRANDS

In the movie *50 First Dates* (2004), Henry, played by Adam Sandler, falls in love with Lucy, played by Drew Barrymore. The theme of the movie is that Lucy suffers an unusual memory disorder as a result of a car accident. She awakes every day with no memory of the day before—in Lucy's mind each morning is the morning before the accident. Consequently, Henry must reintroduce himself and win Lucy's heart anew every day. Marketing would be like *50 First Dates* if marketers couldn't build brands to identify their products to customers across occasions and to capture the benefits—the "brand equity"—earned by delivering satisfying customer experiences. From the customers' perspective, shopping and buying would involve reevaluating every option on every occasion—the absence of brands would make it difficult to ever routinely repurchase alternatives that served well in the past (or to avoid alternatives that disappointed). Branding is not always generated by the brander. In the old Soviet Union, there was an interesting historic instance of consumer generated "branding." There, when products were supposedly identical and "unbranded" and could have been produced anywhere, consumers figured out how to decipher barcodes in order to identify goods from factories that produced higher-quality items.[3]

Brands are manifest in an offering's characteristics that mark or identify it in consumer perceptions, that distinguish it from other offerings, and that retain a valued place in customers' minds across occasions. A brand's identifying characteristics usually include the brand name (or "trade name"), logos and marks ("trademarks"), and distinguishing features such as packaging, colors, and even sounds.[4] That commercial identity is not dissimilar to an individual's personal identity; we know a person by their name but we may also recognize them by their attire, their posture or gait, their voice, even associated smells and sounds.

Coca-Cola, for example, is a trade name—as is Coke—but Coca-Cola is also identified by the distinctive red, "Spencerian cursive" logo, by its packaging (especially the "contour bottle"), and by slogans such as "It's the Real Thing" and "Open Happiness." Intellectual property law not only protects trademarks and trade names, it protects "trade dress," the distinctive configuration of *nonfunctional* elements such as package shapes, designs, colors, materials, and sounds. Owens Corning has, for example, protected their pink fiberglass insulation coloring,[5] and NBC trademarked its station-break "chimes."[6]

Thus, a straightforward way to understand what a brand is and what can be protected as a trademark, trade name, service mark, or trade dress is to understand that *a brand is the producer's and the product's commercial identity.*[7] Table 29-1 summarizes some essential benefits of brands to both marketers and customers. For customers, brands offer efficiency and assurance in overwhelmingly complex lives; brands may also offer abstract benefits, including comfort, risk reduction, and self-expression. To the marketing strategist, brands embody and retain the benefits, including loyalty and margins, from "a job well done," and can serve to facilitate distribution and accelerate new product launches (brand extensions). This information-value or commercial-identity role of brands is a good foundation for understanding brands, but it is narrow and legalistic; brands also serve to deliver value to consumers *in and of themselves* and hold rich and influential meanings of their own.

BRAND MEANING AND BRAND EQUITY

"What's a brand? A singular idea or concept that you own inside the mind of the prospect."[9]

Al and Laura Ries, authors and marketing experts

The functional or information-value view of brands, explicated above, is useful—an essential part of branding is this notion of commercial identity—but it leaves out some important roles that brands play in the modern marketplace and in contemporary culture. Brands hold *meaning* that can encompass a variety of aspects from functional and hedonic benefits to social significance and symbolism, and those meanings reside in the minds of consumers.

Professor David Aaker, a leading authority on branding, defines brand equity as the "set of brand assets and liabilities linked to a brand, its name and symbol that add to or subtract from the value provided by a product or service to a firm and/or to that firm's customers."[10] Thus, brand equity is a summary of brand meaning/associations along with brand

---

TABLE NOTE 29-1 The Benefits of Brands[8]

Benefits to Customers	Benefits to Markets/Firms
• Efficiency: Reduce demands on information search/cognitive processing	• Responses to marketing mix
• Assurance: Confidence and comfort in purchase	• Loyalty
• Social signals/symbolic value	• Prices and margins
• Personal identity and self-image	• New-product launches and brand extensions
	• Effectiveness and efficiency of distribution/trade programs

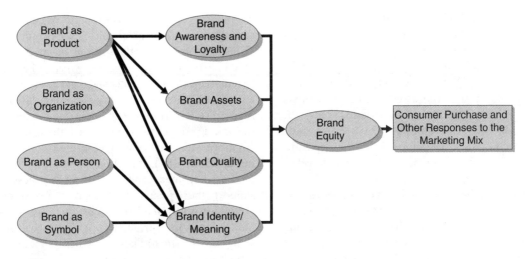

FIGURE NOTE 29-1   Brand Meaning and Brand Equity

awareness, brand loyalty, brand quality, and other "brand assets," ranging from protected trademarks and proprietary technology to the strength of long-term relationships with distribution partners (channel presence). Professor Aaker also distinguishes four aspects of a brand's identity or "brand meaning":

- The "brand as a product" (attributes and benefits such as hard-disc memory, taste, or reliability);
- The "brand as an organization" (ties to the identity and heritage of the parent organization);
- The "brand as a person" (includes the brand personality, for example, "rugged," and the brand-customer relationship, such as "friend"); and
- The "brand as a symbol" (brand meaning and the connection of that meaning to the customer's self-image; for example, youthful, prestigious, practical).

All these potential aspects of brand identity may not be relevant to every brand. The roles of brand identity and brand equity in driving desirable responses to the marketing mix, including especially purchase behavior, are diagramed in Figure 29-1.

These definitions and the graphic organization of these variables impose specific labels and roles on things that, in reality, have overlapping and blurred meanings. For example, "the brand as product" includes "product quality," which also contributes to brand loyalty and to brand equity. These joint connections are shown as shaded links in Figure 29-2 to illustrate the complexity of the interrelationships. Differentiating these abstract ideas too narrowly could reduce to a semantic muddle: is there really a difference between "identity," "meaning," and "equity"? The answer is that, although some of these may be fine lines to draw, *the higher-level ideas are substantive and important for marketing strategists to understand*: consumers *do* hold in their minds different perceptions like awareness, beliefs about quality, feelings of attachment and loyalty, and diverse associations ranging from "prestigious" and "traditional" to "cool" or "stylish." Those perceptions and predispositions are not only real, they are *invaluable* to the firm—they drive differences in responses to the marketing mix, in purchase behaviors, and in margins.

WHO OWNS THE BRAND?

> *"Brand equity is the sum of all the hearts and minds of every single person that comes into contact with your company."*
> Christopher Betzter[11]

Brands as products delivering functional and hedonic (emotional) benefits are, in general, things that a marketer can influence, if not control. Brand "meanings," brands as "symbols," and brands as means of self-expression all begin to suggest richer cultural roles for brands. In fact, brands may *begin* with producers and marketers, and brand managers may *influence* the brand's meaning, but *brands belong to the consumers* who use them and who assign meaning to them. Major brands, including Timberland boots, the Cadillac Escalade, and Pabst Blue Ribbon beer have all taken on meanings and gained traction in segments the branding organization never imagined or targeted. Timberland's CEO Jeffrey Swartz once acknowledged, "Timberland is being adopted by a consumer that we didn't know existed relative to our target audience."[12] He meant that Timberland had become a fashion brand for many consumers as opposed to a functional footwear product which it was intended to be.

Some brands have become the focal point of "brand communities," communities that deliver complex personal, psychological, and social benefits to their members. Owning a Harley Davidson, for example, has utilitarian value (a Harley Davidson takes its owner from point A to point B), hedonic value (riding a Harley Davidson evokes feelings of joy and freedom), and self-expressive benefits (owning a Harley Davidson may tell others the rider is a "rugged individualist"). Further, Harley Davidson riders are a community of people who identify with the brand and with each other and who take value from their membership in that community. The brand has even become so intertwined with some consumers' self-concepts that they tattoo the brand logo on their bodies. These consumer-centered aspects of brand meanings are more difficult to manage; in a sense, brands can take on "lives of their own" with consumers. Nevertheless, from a marketing strategist's perspective, there *are* marketing tools that influence consumers' perceptions of brands, that connect brands to purchase and loyalty, and that build strong, enduring brands. The next section clarifies the tools the marketing organization and strategist can use to build, shape, and profit from strong brands.

BUILDING BRANDS

The marketing strategist has numerous tools to build a brand—but building or maintaining a brand must begin with *a clear understanding of what the brand is meant to be in consumer perceptions.* That is, before de-veloping any creative advertising copy or clever sponsorships for a brand, before hiring a spokesperson or choosing a promotion, the strategic position that the brand intends to claim in the marketplace must be determined, based on customer and competitive analyses, and should be recorded in a 'positioning statement'. A complete positioning statement usually specifies: the brand/product to be positioned, the market (the "frame of reference"), the target segment(s) and target needs (the "target"), at least one "point of difference" or "brand promise," and the "reason to believe" that supports those points of difference.[13] A positioning statement isn't intended for customers to see—although it may be distributed to vendors such as advertising agencies and to channel partners—it is intended as an internal record of what the brand is meant to be. It serves to keep the various tactics "on strategy," and it fosters institutional memory of what the brand is and, often just as importantly, what it is *not*. For example, many experts and firms use some version of a generic statement such as:

> For (*definition of target consumers/ segments*), (*Brand X*) is (*definition of frame of reference and subjective category*) which gives the most . . . (*promise or consumer benefit/point of difference*) because only (*Brand X*) is *reason to believe*).[14]

Once the desired position has been determined and spelled out in a positioning statement, the marketing strategist has a variety of tools to use in "claiming" and reinforcing the brand's position. The product itself has an enormous impact on the brand in customer perceptions. Additionally, brand managers generally emphasize the promotion mix or "integrated marketing communications" to build and hone brand image. Figure 29-2 organizes the many controllable factors that can influence brand identity/meaning, brand equity, and brand strength:

- **The Product Itself.** There is no evidence as convincing to the customer as their experience with the brand itself. In order to be credible, the core product must live up to the brand promise. Hayes Roth, chief marketing officer at Landor Associates summarized this truth: "In the end, all of the fine promises and business and marketing acumen come down to one simple question:

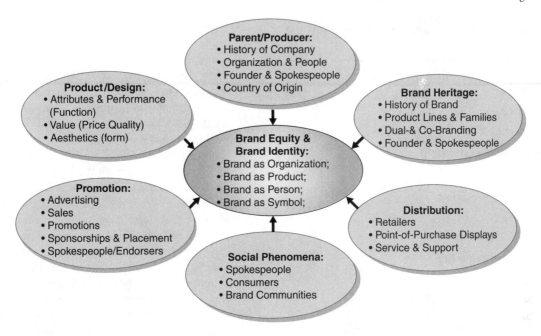

FIGURE NOTE 29-2   Building Brand Identity and Brand Equity

Does my actual experience with the brand meet or exceed my expectations?"[15] Consequently, the primary and essential element in brand building is the product itself, and the surest way to dilute brand equity is for the product to fail to live up to the brand promise. "Design" encompasses both form and function—how the product works (functional benefits), how it is experienced (i.e., aesthetically and emotionally via its look, feel, touch), and how the two work together. The control wheel on Apple's iPod is a great example of the fusion of form and function to create a unique consumer experience.

- *Promotion/Integrated Marketing Communications.* One of the overarching, organizing principles of integrated marketing communications is that those communications should *contribute to building the brand* and to claiming a unique and valued place in consumers' perceptions. The key to that investment is a unified voice; a consistent, compelling, and focused message repeated and reinforced at every point of contact. Within the promotion mix, price promotions have been contrasted with "brand building" investments, such as advertising, be-

cause it has been argued that price promotions may damage brand image and brand equity. Brand building, positioning, and integrated marketing-communications strategies are inseparable. For example, McDonald's presents a consistent and focused message across all of its integrated marketing communications that it delivers consistency at a great value.

- *Parent/Producer Organization.* Apple makes well-designed, user-friendly products with trendy cachet. Anheuser-Busch is the classic American brewer. BMW makes high-performance cars. Many companies have well-established reputations tied to their histories and core competencies. Those corporate reputations can be advantages, or, in certain cases, they can also be detriments for subordinate products and brands. Table 29-2 presents various aspects of corporate image that can influence product brand images. The country of origin will also contribute to product brand equity and is an element of parent organization reputation and legacy; country of origin can be a positive influence on the brand's meaning, as in the case of Italian shoes or German cameras, but it can

TABLE NOTE 29-2 Dimensions of Corporate Image[16]

Common Product Attributes, Benefits, or Attitudes

- Quality
- Innovativeness

People and Relationships

- Customer Orientation

Values and Programs

- Concern with the Environment
- Social Responsibility

Corporate Credibility

- Expertise
- Trustworthiness
- Likability

also be a detriment, as has become the case for American automakers.

- **Brand Heritage.** Many brands build on strong brand heritages—they have a history of sustained and consistent presence in the market. That heritage was perhaps best illustrated in the case of New Coke and Coca-Cola; although consumers supposedly preferred the taste of Pepsi to (old) Coke, the heritage of the brand and its assimilation into American culture had secured a place in the hearts of consumers. Coca-Cola was deeply ingrained in American culture. Coke had appeared in popular media from Andy Warhol lithographs to Bob Dylan songs, and when Coca-Cola tried to adjust the taste it found out quickly that customers wanted their familiar Coke. In fact, the Coke consumers rose up in disgust and bombarded Coke's head office in Atlanta with their complaints about the change in the product. Clearly, some brands have heritages that have integrated them into the common vernacular, and others have shorter histories that, nevertheless, carry over into every new endeavor. Apple's relatively brief but focused and consistent record of offering convenient, reliable, and trend-setting devices imparts new offerings with that heritage identity.

- **Distribution.** An underappreciated element in brand building and also a potential trap toward brand destruction is the selection, affiliation with, and control of channel partners. Especially in instances of products requiring knowledgeable sales support, products augmented by high-levels of service, and products pursuing prestige positions in the marketplace, channel partners can be a powerful means for building and reinforcing the brands promise. Stihl, the premium chain saw brand has always insisted that its channel partners provide significant after sale service and support. Conversely, partnering with the wrong channel partners can be harmful to the brand and the business. Snapper, the manufacturer of premium lawn equipment, made the extraordinary decision to *stop* selling through Wal-Mart in 2002 just as Wal-Mart was offering to expand its outdoor power-equipment category around Snapper lawnmowers. Snapper CEO Jim Wear said:

  > "We're not obsessed with volume. We're obsessed with having differentiated, high-end, quality products . . . If a brand is going to stand for being high end, with special features, catering to a particular kind of customer, that wasn't compatible with selling though Wal-Mart."[17]

- **Social Phenomena.** Other consumers of the brand, the brand in popular art, and affiliated spokespeople all influence brand meaning and brand associations. For example, despite the fact that Cadillac's traditional target markets are older and suburban and that the company's cars are perceived as "your grandfather's car,"[18] the brand's SUV Escalade has become popular with highly-successful athletes and celebrities, and that has fed broader popularity with young, urban consumers. The Escalade brand manager conceded: "It has been the vehicle of choice among some Hollywood folks and athletes, even though we've never particularly marketed it that way."[19]

The marketing strategist has numerous tools to utilize in building a brand. These elements cannot be treated as disconnected or be managed separately.

Disney CEO Michael Eisner summed it up: "A brand is a living entity—and it is enriched or undermined cumulatively over time, the product of a thousand small gestures."[20] Consumers' impressions of the brand are inclusive and cumulative; building a strong brand requires consistency and long-term commitment across the big campaigns and all the small details.

MEASURING BRANDS

Like most things in strategic marketing planning, brands can be and should be measured and monitored rigorously. Measuring brands can be approached in at least two basic ways:

- Consumer-level brand meaning, brand equity, and brand strength; and,
- Firm- or brand-level value.

Consumer-level brand meaning and brand equity focus on the beliefs, attitudes, and behavioral tendencies that exist in consumers' minds. Firm- or brand-level value deals with the financial impacts of the brand on the financial performance and the value of the firm.

Consumer-Level Brand Meaning, Brand Equity, and Brand Strength

Brand equity is complex—it includes basic brand awareness but also brand associations and the meanings that a brand holds in consumers' minds, and it includes consumers' loyalty to the brand and their perceptions of the brands quality or objective attributes. There are various measurement approaches that gauge these different and disparate aspects of brand equity. As each brand is unique and as not all aspects of brand equity are relevant to every brand, the measurement of brand equity should be tailored to the individual brand. Nevertheless, there are some well-accepted measures of various aspects of brand equity. Things like awareness, quality, and loyalty are basic concepts in marketing research—for example, brand awareness is often measured as "unaided recall" and "aided recall," that is, the proportion of consumers who mention the brand without being prompted and those who recognize it when prompted. Quality is a belief system related to product-category-specific attributes and performance: *How reliable is Brand X? How well does Brand Y remove dirt? Employees at Brand Z are polite.*[21]

TABLE NOTE 29-3 Brand Personality[22]

Factors	Facets	Traits*
Sincerity	Down-to-earth	Down-to-earth; Family-oriented; Small-town
	Honest	Honest, Sincere, Real
	Wholesome	Wholesome, Original
	Cheerful	Cheerful, Sentimental, Friendly
Excitement	Daring	Daring, Trendy, Exciting
	Spirited	Spirited, Cool, Young
	Imaginative	Imaginative, Unique
	Up-to-date	Up-to-date, Independent, Contemporary
Competence	Reliable	Reliable, Hard-working, Secure
	Intelligent	Intelligent, Technical, Corporate
	Successful	Successful, Leader, Confident
Sophistication	Upper class	Upper-class, Glamorous, Good looking
	Charming	Charming, Feminine, Smooth
Ruggedness	Outdoorsy	Outdoorsy, Masculine, Western
	Tough	Tough, Rugged

*The Brand Personality Scale consists of these 42 "traits" rated as to "How well does this describe [Brand]; traits can then be summed to facets and factors.

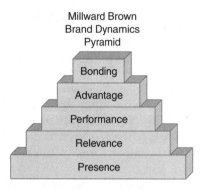

Millward Brown
Brand Dynamics
Pyramid

FIGURE NOTE 29-3 Millward Brown's BrandDynamics® Model

Well-established measures are available for brand meaning, especially for "brand personality." Jennifer Aaker's Brand Personality Scale (Table 29-3) illuminates the measurement of brand meaning and highlights the breadth of human-like qualities a brand can hold. The five factors—sincerity, excitement, competence, sophistication, and ruggedness—are the highest-level structure. Facets and traits expand those factors into greater detail. While any brand can be described on these traits, not all these traits are relevant to every brand.

Brand strength is a reduction of brand equity to the basic drivers of customer behavior. It is usually modeled using a hierarchy of effects similar to those used in advertising to set objectives and track customers from unaware through awareness and knowledge to interest, preferences, and eventually trial and loyalty. One of the best-known commercial gauges of brand strength is Millward Brown's BrandDynamics® model (Figure 29-3), which encompasses "presence" (awareness), "relevance" (interest), "performance"

(understanding the brand's attributes and benefits), "advantage" (preference), and "bonding" (loyalty), and awards one "score" per level of the relationship.

Advantages of hierarchical models of brand strength, such as Millward Brown's BrandDynamics,® include their capacities to compare competitive brands and to assess the results of specific marketing programs and investments. For example, if a firm determined that it needed to increase awareness and, therefore, undertook a mass advertising campaign—a promotion-mix emphasis well-suited to increasing awareness (but less adept at converting interest to purchase) and loyalty—the "before" and "after" assessment of brand strength would capture their success (Figure 29-4). In this fictitious example, bonding and advantage are largely unaffected by the campaign, relevance and especially presence are dramatically improved.

Brand Valuation[23]

Brand strength is important for building brands, and measures of brand strength are indispensable in comparing competitive brands and in evaluating specific marketing investments, but there is another perspective on measuring brands that approaches the issue from a very different angle: *What is a brand worth taken as a whole? What does a brand contribute to the firm's financial value?* This is referred to as "brand valuation." Of course, what a brand is worth to the firm is, in reality and as a marketing strategist would recognize, the sum total of all the consumer perceptions—all that brand strength manifest in thousands, even millions, of consumer behaviors. That is, although it is a different measurement approach, the brand is valuable to the firm because it can be expected to generate sales and command margin in the future, and those sales and

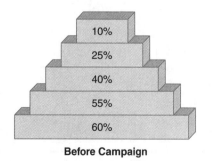

Before Campaign

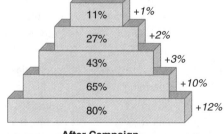

After Campaign

FIGURE NOTE 29-4 Hypothetical Effect of a Communications Investment on BrandDynamics®

margins are the product of cumulative individual-level feelings about the brand.

The strongest global brands are worth billions of dollars each to their parent corporations; Business Week and the global brand consultancy Interbrand, for example, value the Coca-Cola/Coke brand at more than $66 billion.[24] Brand valuation can be approached in many ways, and several consulting and advertising agencies generate slightly different but very similar annual rankings.[25] They all attempt to gauge the *aggregate, discounted financial value of the brand to the corporation*.[26] That is, these methods view the brand as a source of revenue spread out across time—and they estimate what future flows of revenue are worth in current terms ("Appendix A: The Basic Financial Math for Marketing Strategy" includes a much detailed discussion of discounting future revenue to its "net present value").

The Business Week/Interbrand rankings calculate how much of the firm's market capitalization and sales stream are due to the specific brands (many companies own multiple brands, so brand revenues are parceled out from total revenues), and then attempts to identify how much of those earnings are attributable to the brand. To accomplish this, variable costs and capital investments in the brand are differentiated from revenues due to the intangible assets, including the brand. Finally, earnings due to parent activity and the like are also removed from the calculation. Then, Interbrand calculates the present value of those revenues, discounting out the time value of money and risks to the brand.[27] Distinguishing future revenues attributable to the brand from those resulting from proprietary technology and other tangible and intangible assets is inherently subjective, but in any case these brand valuation efforts tend to triangulate on which brands are the most valuable, and these efforts emphasize another approach to understanding how important brands are to firm success and wealth creation.

Summary

Brands have benefits for both branding organizations and customers. They serve as commercial identities that retain the value of marketing investments across time; brands that deliver satisfactory experiences are rewarded and those that disappoint are avoided. Brand value can be a substantial asset to companies and brand meaning can deliver real benefits to consumers beyond core product attributes or performance. There are a variety of tools available to the marketing strategist to shape and maintain the value of the brand—the most prominent are encompassed in the marketing mix of product, promotion, price, and place—and there are social and cultural roles of brands that are somewhat beyond the control of the parent organization. In general, brands are derived from decisions about positioning—brands are the "place holders" that embody the position the strategy targets in the market—and brands are shaped by and should direct all of the tactical elements of the marketing mix.

Additional Resources

Aaker, David. *Building Strong Brands.* New York: Free Press, 1996.

David Aaker. *Managing Brand Equity.* New York: Free Press, 1991.

Kapferer, Jean-Noel. *The New Strategic Brand Management,* 4th ed., Philadelphia, PA: Kogan Page, 2008.

Keller, Kevin Lane. Strategic Brand Management, 3rd ed. Upper Saddle River, NJ: Pearson/Prentice Hall, 2008.

Tybout Alice M., and Brian Sternthal. "Brand Positioning." In *Kellogg on Branding,* edited by Alice M. Tybout and Tim Calkins, 11–26. Hoboken, New Jersey: John Wiley & Sons, 2005.

Endnotes

1. www.brandchannel.com/papers_review.asp?sp_id= 357. Last accessed on July 11, 2010
2. From the American Marketing Association's online dictionary found at www.marketingpower.com/_ layouts/Dictionary. zaspx?dLetter=B. Last accessed June 19, 2009.
3. The Economist, "Warfare in the aisles," 375, no. 8420 (April 2, 2005; Special Section): 6–8.

4. In the United States, the Lanham Act defines protectable marks as "any word, name, symbol, or device, or any combination thereof" (15 USC §§ 1114-27). The World Trade Organization's *Agreement on Trade-Related Aspects of Intellectual Property Rights*, defines a trademark as encompassing "any sign . . . capable of distinguishing the goods or services of one undertaking from those of other undertakings."

5. See, for example, Samuels, Jeffrey M. and Samuels, Linda B. "Color Trademarks: Protection Under U.S. Law," *Journal of Public Policy and Marketing* 15, no. 2 (Fall 1996): 305–07.

6. U.S. Trademark Registration No. 0523616

7. See, for example, Ralph S. Brown Jr., "Advertising and the Public Interest: Legal Protection of Trade Symbols," 57 Yale Law Journal 1165, 1167 (1948), reprinted in 108 Yale Law Journal 1619, 1621 (1999).

8. Adapted from David Aaker, , *Building Strong Brands* (New York: Free Press, 1996); David Aaker, *Managing Brand Equity* (New York: Free Press, 1991), p. 9.

9. Al Ries and Laura Ries, *The 22 Immutable Laws of Branding* (London: Harper Business, 1999) 172.

10. Aaker, *Building Strong Brands*; Aaker, *Managing Brand Equity*.

11. Dick Martin, *Rebuilding Brand America* (New York: AMACOM Books, 2007), 95

12. Michel Marriott, "Out of the Woods," *New York Times*, November 7, 1993, Section 9, page 1.

13. See Alice M. Tybout and Brian Sternthal, "Brand Positioning,' in *Kellogg on Branding*, ed. Alice M. Tybout and Tim Calkins (Hoboken, New Jersey: John Wiley & Sons, 2005), 11–26.

14. J-N. Kapferer, *The New Strategic Brand Management*, 4th ed. (Philadelphia, PA: Kogan Page, 2008), 178; and Tybout, and Sternthal, "Brand Positioning," see p. 12–13.

15. Peter Walshe, "Ten-year trends: Rise of Machines and Mobile Technology," The Financial Times (April 2008)

16. Kevin Lane Keller, *Strategic Brand Management*, 2nd ed. (,Upper Saddle River, NJ: Prentice-Hall, 2003), 545.

17. Charles Fishman, *The Wal-Mart Effect* (New York: Penguin Press, 2006) 119–120

18. David Menzies, "It Don't Mean a Thing If It Ain't Got That Bling," *National Post*, October 24, 2003 (Toronto).

19. Robert Strauss, "MARKETING; Appealing to Youth, Selling to the Not-So-Young," *New York Times*, October 22, 2003, Section G, page 37.

20. Interbrand, *The Brand Glossary* (Hampshire UK: Palgrave Macmillan, 2007).

21. The final example item is from a specific measure, the "ServQual," which measures *service* quality along five dimensions: reliability, assurance, tangibles, empathy, and responsiveness. See A. Parasuraman, Leonard L. Berry, and Valarie A. Zeithaml, "A Conceptual Model of Service Quality and Its Implications for Future Research," *Journal of Marketing* 49, no. 4 (1985): 41–50; A. Parasuraman, Leonard L. Berry, and Valarie A. Zeithaml, "SERVQUAL: A Multiple-Item Scale For Measuring Consumer Perceptions of Service Quality," *Journal of Retailing* 64, no. 1 (1988): 12–40; for a review, see Francis Buttle, "SERVQUAL: Review, Critique, Research Agenda," *European Journal of Marketing* 30, no. 1 (1996): 8–31.

22. Jennifer L. Aaker, "Dimensions of Brand Personality," *Journal of Marketing Research* 34, no. 3 (August 1997): 347–356, especially Figure 1, page 352 and Appendix A, page 354.

23. See Kusum L. Ailawadi, Scott A. Neslin, Donald R. Lehmann, "Revenue Premium as An Outcome Measure of Brand Equity," *Journal of Marketing* 67 (2003): 1–17; V. Srinivasan, Chan Su Park, and Dae Ryun Chang, "An Approach to the Measurement, Analysis, and Prediction of Brand Equity and Its Sources," *Management Science*. 51, no. 9 (September 2005), 1433–1448.

24. Burt Helm, Best Global Brands BusinessWeek, (September 18, 2008) www.businessweek.com/magazine/content/08_39/b4101052097769.htm. Last accessed on July 11, 2010

25. Compare the data in Table V-11-4 with rankings by Young & Rubicam's Landor

26. Technical valuations, such as those used for balance sheet reporting, litigation, and tax planning categorize "brand value" as falling into the accounting category of "unrecorded, intangible assets." These issues are largely beyond the scope of this book, and there is little agreement on the correct or generally-accepted way to do this. For more information see Mary E. Barth, Michael B. Clement, George Fosthr, and Ron Kasznik. "Brand Values and Capital Market Valuation." *Review of Accounting Studies* 3, no. 1/2 (1998): 41–68.

27. www.businessweek.com/magazine/content/08_39/b4101056103890.htm?chan=magazine+channel_special+report. Last accessed on July 11, 2010.

30

Products—New Product Development

New products—usually understood as products that are for less than five years on the markets—make up an increasingly large share of sales across companies and industries. In many leading firms, new products contribute more than 50 percent of overall sales volume.[1] New product development, however, is a risky process. Studies show that for every seven new product ideas, on average of not more than four enter the development stage, one-and-a-half are launched and *only one succeeds*. Others speak of a failure rate up to 45 percent or 55 percent.[2]

However, only 10 percent of all new products are truly innovative.[3] Most new products that are called an innovation are, in point of fact, merely line extensions, continuous improvements, or revisions of existing products. A study by the PDMA (Product Development Management Association) has shown that of all new products, 4 percent are repositionings, 9 percent are cost reductions for the firm through new production processes but not new product developments in the sense of new product features, new design or the like, 20 percent are new product lines (i.e., new to the firm but not new to the market), 23 percent are product improvements, and 34 percent are additions or subsets of existing product lines.[4] Just 10 percent are "new to the world."

As product lifecycles become shorter and rivals are increasingly faster to copy new products, time to market becomes crucial. This implies that companies do have less time for extensive market research, or concept testing. Striving for higher customer value often means higher development and production costs. And if a company wants to keep development costs down, it has less time and resources to design new products in a way that they can be produced at low costs. The majority of large companies have introduced systematic processes for new product development; about 60 percent use a systematic blueprint or roadmap for moving a new product project through the various stages of new product development.[5] Through systematic new product development processes, companies want to achieve that

- There is a steady stream of new and promising ideas into the pipeline of the product development process
- These ideas are screened for customer benefit, feasibility, and market potential systematically and early enough (before resource are committed to poor ideas)
- The product concept is market oriented and has a unique selling proposition
- The selling price, production costs, and market demand are such that the product can be sold at a profit
- The concept is extensively tested before market introduction to make sure that it is accepted by the customers and that the marketing plan works.

THE NEW PRODUCT DEVELOPMENT PROCESS

A systematic product development process consists of several phases: idea generation, idea selection, concept development and testing, business analysis, prototype and market testing, and product launch. Each has some important tasks to fulfill and is characterized by important challenges (see Table 30-1).

TABLE NOTE 30-1 Phases in the New Product Development Process

Phase	Task	Challenge
1. Idea generation	This phase aims at collecting as many promising ideas for a new product or service as possible. The starting point is unsolved customer needs.	• Generate as many good ideas as possible • Unleash creativity • Use all internal and external sources for new product ideas (customers, suppliers, distributors, technology, R&D, marketing)
2. Idea selection	In the idea selection phase, ideas are eliminated that do not deserve additional resources and attention and the most promising ideas are selected for the next phases of the development process	Identify ideas • That create customer value (address a real unsolved need) • For which a substantial market exists (size and growth of the market) • That can be profitably produced and marketed (competitive situation) • That fit the vision and strategy of the firm
3. Concept development and testing	Develop the marketing and engineering details	Specify • The target market and product positioning • Product attributes • Unique selling proposition • Prove feasibility • Estimate production and marketing costs • Test product idea with customers, distributors, experts, etc.
4. Business analysis	Create a business plan, estimate resources needed, and profitability	Determine • Selling price • Costs • Sales volume • Breakeven and profitability
5. Prototype and market testing	Develop a physical prototype and test it in a typical usage situation	Get feedback • On market acceptance • For necessary adjustments • On marketing concept in a test market To refine • Product and • Marketing campaign
6. Product launch	Launch product and marketing campaign	Executive marketing campaign, react flexibly to competitor moves, changing market conditions and needs

Idea Generation

The so called "fuzzy front end" of innovation (all activities from the search of new opportunities until the development of a product concept) usually is not very capital intensive, but it can consume up to 50 percent of the development time. In this phase, ideas are developed and it is decided whether or not further resources are invested in the further development of this idea.[6] Therefore, it can be very crucial for the success of the entire process. Ideas for new products can come from many sources inside or outside the company, from engineers, suppliers, scientists, distributors, or customers. Companies use creativity-generating techniques with internal and external groups and focus groups, conduct in-depth interviews with customers, analyze customers' problems and complaints, use surveys, observe online communities and brand communities or integrate lead users (highly innovative customers that have their own ideas for new products), and observe competitors to get ideas for new products.

A logical starting point for the idea generation phase are unsolved customer needs. In this context, the Kano-model of customer satisfaction can help to identify promising ideas (Figure 30-1). It distinguishes three types of product attributes:

- Basic factors (must haves) are minimum requirements. The fulfillment of basic requirements is a necessity, but an insufficient condition for customer satisfaction. Basic factors are entirely expected. The customer regards them as prerequisites; they are taken for granted. If basic factors are already fulfilled, an increase of their performance usually does not increase the customer benefit. If however, basic factors are not yet fulfilled, this offers great opportunities for a product innovation. When the French ski producer Salomon entered the ski industry in the 1990s, it discovered that a basic need of the skiers was not fulfilled. Most skiers had difficulties to ski well on hard and icy slopes. The edge grip of the ski was a basic factor. Salomon invented a new technology, the monocoque ski with dramatically improved edge grip, and had a tremendous success. Within a short time,

Salomon became a leading producer of skis and all other ski manufacturers had to switch to the new technology. Salomon was able to discover and satisfy a not yet fulfilled basic requirement.

- Excitement factors (delighters) are the factors that increase customer satisfaction if delivered but do not cause dissatisfaction if they are not delivered. Excitement factors are not expected, they surprise the customer and generate "delight." Delighters typically are latent, not articulated customer needs and add value to the core product. In the car industry, delighters play an important role to differentiate the product. GPS, head up displays, infotainment systems, etc., are features that fall into this category.

- Performance factors (the more the better) lead to satisfaction if performance is high and to dissatisfaction if performance is low. In this case, the performance–overall-satisfaction relationship is linear and symmetric. These attributes usually are explicitly expected. Gas mileage of a car, battery life of a laptop, and the weight of a mountain bike are examples of performance factors.

For product development, the following implications emerge from Kano's model: Basic factors establish a market entry "threshold." If they are delivered at a satisfactory level, an increase in performance does not lead to an increase in customer satisfaction. Typically, performance factors are directly connected to customers' explicit needs and desires. They are typically clearly stated and articulated by the customer. Therefore, a company should be competitive with regard to performance factors. Excitement factors are unexpected and surprise the customer. As they generate "delight", a company should try to stand out from the rest with regard to these attributes.[7] It is important to emphasize the dynamic nature of these product requirements. What delights customers today, become explicit expectations after some time, and eventually turn into basic factors. Wireless LAN and free Internet in hotels is a good example. When the first hotels introduced it, it delighted customers. It soon became an

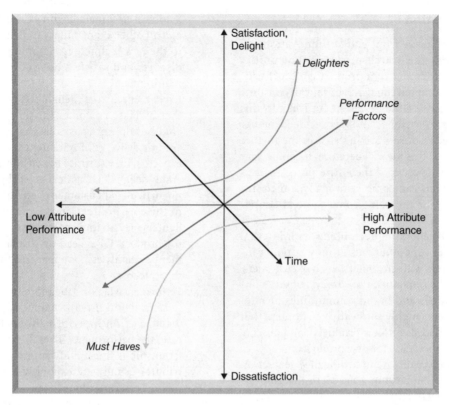

FIGURE NOTE 30-1 The Kano Model[8]

explicit expectation and many hotel guests consider it as a basic feature today.

Idea Selection

The challenge in the second phase of the new product development process is to select those ideas that are promising enough to be pursued and to eliminate those that do not deserve additional resource commitment. This is a critical task, because, if not done carefully, good ideas might be killed or poor ideas might enter the next phase—concept development—and waste resources. Therefore, a systematic approach to a preliminary assessment of an idea's potential is advisable. Many companies use an idea rating matrix as shown in Table 30-2. Success criteria are defined, weighted, and each idea is evaluated. A weighted score is computed and a minimum threshold is defined (e.g., a weighted score above 6) that must be met to enter the next phase of product development.

Concept Development and Testing

For the remaining ideas, product concepts are developed and preliminarily tested. The target market has to be clearly defined; product attributes must be specified to achieve a unique selling proposition, technical and economic feasibility must be proved, and the prototype should be tested with customers. In this phase, trade-offs among needs and features have to be made. Usually not all needs can be addressed economically, and sometimes needs contradict each other (e.g. weight and battery life of a laptop). An important principle in this phase is: Every product feature causes costs, but not every product feature generates value to the customer. Hence, a careful examination of the cost–utility relationship of the single features is important. Conjoint-analysis is a widely used tool in this phase. It helps to measure the utility a customer attaches to varying levels of product attributes.

TABLE NOTE 30-2 Idea Rating Scheme

Success Criteria	Weight	Idea 1	Idea 2	Score (0–10) Idea 3	Idea 4	...
Superior customer benefit	0, 4	4	7	2	8	...
Potential market size	0, 3	5	4	5	5	...
Competitive situation	0, 1	8	3	4	6	...
Fit vision and strategy	0, 2	2	6	3	7	...
Weighted Score		4, 3	5, 5	3, 3	6, 7	...

More and more companies use the Internet and virtual reality to test concepts. When Audi developed a new infotainment system, it decided to integrate customers into the development process.[9] It devised a virtual lab as a web-based platform in order to generate ideas, configure a product, and test its acceptance. It attached importance to addressing customer groups with different levels of innovative ability. Lead users were to provide inspiration for future infotainment systems, early adopters were to configure aspects of functionality using a virtual prototype, such as navigation, telematics and voice control, and heavy users in the low-end segment were to provide input as to the weaknesses of the existing system. These different customer groups were found on various portals (e.g., www.autobild.de, www.tt-owners-club.de, www.automotor-und-sport. de). The results were impressive: The lead users provided visions about the infotainment of the future, the early adopters provided input about configuration of it, and the heavy users provided clues as to its acceptance in the mass market.

Business Analysis

For product ideas that "survive" the concept and testing phase, a detailed business analysis must be carried out. The exact price must be determined, the sales volume as well as costs and profits have to be estimated. A particular challenge in this phase is the estimation of demand. Not all customers react to innovation with the same speed; some need years until they take an interest in it. Innovators are adventurous and prepared to take risks, they are the first to buy an innovation. Early adopters accept new ideas early, but are more careful and also frequently are opinion leaders. And the mass market often reacts with an enormous time lag to innovations. Therefore, quantitative and representative market research studies cannot really help in the innovation process. On the contrary, if one tries to interview a representative cross section of customers about their desires or tries to test the potential of an innovation on them, the results can be misleading.[10] Products such as the Sony Walkman, the SMS (Short Message Service), or the Blackberry would never have come to market as the market-research studies showed that these products had no potential.

Prototype and Market Testing

For those products that prove to be promising after a thorough business analysis, a physical prototype is developed and tested in the typical usage situation. Before the product is introduced, customer feedback is sought to make final adjustments of the product and marketing plan. This can be done by bringing customers into laboratories where they test a prototype. Philips, for example, has such a laboratory in Klagenfurt, Austria. They have a panel of women who are invited every time they have developed a new prototype of epilators. In the laboratory the women test the prototype and give feedback about the functionality, handling, etc. Other companies give the prototype to customers to test it at home. Often, test markets are used. These are representative cities or regions where the product is introduced accompanied with all marketing activities that are planned for this product. This way trials, repeat purchases, purchase frequency, etc., can be tested.

Product Launch

The product launch phase usually is the most costly phase. Advertising, promotion, and other communications of a major new consumer packaged good can cost up to $100 million in the first year; marketing expenditures of new food products represent up to roughly 60 percent of the first year's sales volume.[11] Of particular importance in the product launch decision is timing. As a first entrant, a company can benefit from the first-mover advantages (e.g., acquiring the most attractive customer segments, locking up key distributors and suppliers, gain market share, and benefit from scale economies). As a follower, one can learn from competitor's mistakes and free ride. Another critical question is internal cannibalization. When a new generation of products is introduced, they can replace the old products. If the new product *only* substitutes for the old product and does not increase sales or generate marginal profits, then the company is no better off; this is called "cannibalization." New product launches often involve some degree of cannibalization with the critical question being whether or not that cannibalization is strategically justified by marginal (i.e., new) sales and profits. GM's 2009 Chevrolet Traverse crossover, for instance, not only competes with other larger crossovers such as the Mazda CX-9, Ford Flex, and Toyota Highlander. Under the skin, the seven-passenger crossover wagon Traverse is nearly identical to GM's Saturn Outlook and other GM vehicles and is expected to cannibalize sales and marketing budgets from these cars that are made on the same platform.

Earlier, Table 30-1 summarized the phases of a new product development process, with the challenges that have to be addressed in each single one. The individual steps in this process may be reiterated as needed. If, for example, the physical prototype turns out to be technically unfeasible or is not accepted by the customers, a new concept needs to be developed. Also, some steps might be eliminated to reduce time. Some companies try to reduce time to market by overlapping several activities of the process and completing them at the same time (concurrent engineering).

RESEARCH VERSUS DEVELOPMENT

The two words, "research" and "development" are almost always used together in the everyday business lexicon to refer to a single undifferentiated set of activities—in fact, they're regularly shortened to "R&D" with little thought about why there are two parts to the description—but "research" and "development" can be distinguished, and the difference can have significant strategic implications. Research refers to more basic explorations while "development" refers to more applied and incremental and tactical new product development and "design."[12] Research and development range from basic "research" that involves explorations of fundamental ideas and that advances in theory to applied "development" that takes known technologies and applies them to specific problems or product applications, as shown in Figure 30-2. Basic research is often conducted at universities or in very specialized laboratories. Applied research is usually done by corporate departments or teams and even by managers and entrepreneurs in commercial settings.

This distinction between theoretical research and applied and incremental development has strategic implications. Different mixtures or "R&D orientations" are appropriate for different strategies and are more effective or less effective depending on the product's stage in the product life cycle. Most new industries emerge from breakthroughs gleaned from basic research. If a firm wants to be a "pioneer" or "first mover" it must invest in basic research to ensure that, if it isn't the one to develop the basic technology, it isn't far behind. "Fast followers" and "late movers" let others do the basic research; they focus on adapting and improving those breakthroughs, and on taking advantage of earlier entrants' mistakes and learning. More mature markets generally compete

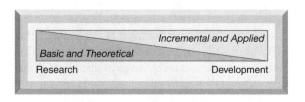

FIGURE NOTE 30-2   Research versus Development as a Continuum

by incremental improvements and product augmentations anchored in development or design. Nevertheless, firms in mature industries may invest in basic research to "shift the product life cycle curve," to extend the product lifecycle, or to "change the game" by forging new markets or "blue oceans." The most important aspect of integrating this continuum from basic theoretical research to applied incremental development is to have an understanding of exactly what the investments are meant to contribute to the strategy and to then shape the activities to conform to that purpose. Firms that need product modifications but that invest in abstract experiments or, conversely, that need the "next big idea" but that study mundane and well-known technologies are likely to fail.

DESIGN

In the past, "design" meant different things to different people (it often meant different things to different people *in the same firm*): industrial designers typically focused on the "form" in the form-versus-function distinction,[13] whereas engineering designers focused on function and the practical issues such as "design for manufacturability."[14] The newer, integrated view looks at *both* and, importantly, does so from a customers' point of view while also taking into account the firm's strategy and other considerations. That is, the term "design" has been broadened to recognize the essential process of integrating *both* nonfunctional or aesthetic elements of the product (i.e., the form) with the functional elements to create enhanced customer experiences and customer value. Professors Michael Luchs and Scott Swan have offered a new, more holistic and relevant definition of design (based on an extensive review of how the process has been defined in the literature):

> "Product design refers to both a process, integral to the definition and realization of a firm's strategy, and the outcome of the process; where the process includes analysis of the internal and external context, strategy development, and the definition and realization of the finished product; and the "product" refers to the product's form, i.e., its physical manifestation

and/or servicescape, the product's function, i.e., its capabilities, and the integrative properties of the combination of both form and function."[15]

Thus, design or "product design" as a process is a broad, holistic, and integrative set of activities linking the new product development process to the customers and to the firm's strategy from the onset. The outcome, or product, of design may be a tangible good and/or service or the combination of goods and services, and the design elements include its form, its function, and the vital interactive effect of both. These elements include, among other things, usability, ergonomics and haptics, form and aesthetics, packaging, materials, and other elements of sustainability as well as core technology and functionality. Because customers engage with the whole product, not its parts, the holistic perspective on design is invaluable to enhancing the customer's experience and to creating customer value. This understanding of the product design process, therefore, is broader than mere new product development as it has traditionally been understood; it extends backwards into strategy formation and forward into marketing research and methods for understanding how customers use and take value from the product and even how customers dispose of the product.

Apple's iPod is a great example of the more integrative and more comprehensive design orientation leading to great strategic success. Apple took existing technology and, rather than maximize functionality and then fitting it into a form (the traditional, form-follows-function approach), Apple took into account the entire product from a consumers' point of view. The result was a simplified set of features, an intuitive interface, a form that conveyed the simplicity and elegance of the underlying technology, a highly functional accompanying Web site, and a "cool" aesthetic that improved the business model for Apple and increased value to consumers. While none of the underlying elements were groundbreaking on their own, providing all of them in an integrated experience set Apple apart, and has opened doors to subsequent products that exhibit a similar design philosophy (the iPhone and iPad). The iPod wasn't an isolated tactical or product decision, but a superbly conceived design strategy consistent with and adding to the Apple brand.

DIMINISHING MARGINAL RETURNS IN R&D

Research and development efforts, like a lot of investments, conform to the law of diminishing marginal returns, which holds that "As successive equal increases in a variable factor of production, such as labor, are added to other fixed factors of production, such as capital, there will be a point beyond which the extra, or marginal, product that can be attributed to each additional unit of the variable factor or production will decline."[16] That is, there is a range of inputs to R&D that achieve a certain level of outputs, and then the output from each marginal input begins to diminish. In practice, there is often a converse relationship, too—some minimal investment is required to get any benefits. To even *begin* doing research in areas like genetic therapy or nuclear power generation, investments below that threshold will likely be ineffective or wasted entirely. These realities produce an s-shaped relationship between inputs and outputs (shown in Figure 30-3 with the inputs along the horizontal and outputs on the vertical axis). As shown, as inputs initially increase, the outputs produced are low; but once some threshold is reached, outputs rise dramatically across a range of inputs. Then a second inflection point is reached and marginal returns diminish in accordance with the law of diminishing

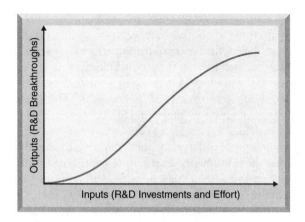

FIGURE NOTE 30-3   Diminishing Returns on R&D Investments

marginal returns. In the strategic management of research and development, this means that if the firm can't afford the minimum threshold amount to do R&D well, it should not do it at all. It also means that some "breakthroughs" will be achieved more easily than others and that a strategy that is grounded on breakthrough research and development may have its limits. At some point, the next breakthrough will be much more expensive to achieve than the earlier breakthroughs—if it is achievable at all. This problem of diminishing returns on R&D investments is exacerbated by the reality that early breakthroughs are more likely to meet pent-up customer demand but later, incremental advances don't enjoy that eager customer reception because the basic need has already been met.

Summary

Thus, the new product development process has traditionally been organized into several phases: idea generation, idea selection, concept development and testing, business analysis, prototype and market testing, and product launch. Each of these phases or steps has an important role in delivering successful new products to market that are consistent with the firm's strategy and with customers' needs. "Research and development" intended to create new products is often reduced to a simple, undifferentiated idea within the organization, but a continuum can be drawn between basic theoretical research and applied development, and different orientations along that continuum are appropriate and effective for different strategies; choices of

R&D emphasis have important implications for marketing strategy and the success of the firm. New product development and research and development have traditionally been set aside as a distinct functional area within the firm but a more integrative and broader view of product development has emerged under the rubric of "product design" that promises to integrate new product development into every step of strategy formation, from situation assessment to market research and operations. This note has reviewed the traditional new product design process and briefly outlined some of the challenging ideas involved in a design-oriented strategic focus.

Additional Resources

Bailom, Franz, Kurt Matzler, and Dieter Tschemernjak. *Enduring success. What top-companies do differently.* New York: Palgrave Macmillan, 2007.

Füller, Johann and Kurt Matzler. "Virtual Product Experience and Customer Participation—A chance for customer-centred, really new products." *Technovation,* 27 (2007): 378–87.

Kano, Noriaki. "Attractive Quality and Must Be Quality." *Hinshitsu* [Quality], 14, no. 2 (1984): 147–56 (in Japanese).

Luchs, Michael and Scott Swan (forthcoming). Working paper version available at Mason School Web site: mason.wm.edu/faculty/documents/**product_design_**

swan.pdf. Product Design since Bloch: Analysis of 14 Years of Research and the Emergence of Product Design as a Field of Marketing Inquiry," *Journal of Product Innovation Management* (1995).

Matzler, Kurt and Hans H. Hinterhuber. "How to Make Product Development Projects More Successful by Integrating Kano's Model of Customer Satisfaction into Quality Function Deployment." *Technovation* 18, no. 1 (1998): 25–38.

Trott, Paul. *Innovation Management and New Product Development,* 4th ed. Harlow, England: Prentice Hall, 2008.

Endnotes

1. Paul Trott, *Innovation Management and New Product Development,* 4th ed. (Harlow, England: Prentice Hall, 2008).

2. For a review see Robert G. Cooper, *Winning at New Products,* 3rd ed. (Cambridge, MA: Perseus publishing, 2001).

3. Paul Trott, *Innovation Management and New Product Development,* 4th ed. (Harlow, England: Prentice Hall, 2008).

4. Abbie Griffin, "PDMA Research on New Product Development Practices: Updating Trends and Benchmarking Best Practice," *Journal of Product Innovation Management* 14, no. 6 (1997): 429–58.

5. Robert G. Cooper, Scott J. Edgett, and Elko J. Kleinschmidt "Optimizing the Stage-Gate process: What best-practice companies do-I," *Research Technology Management* (September–October 2002): 21–27.

6. Trott, *Innovation management.*

7. Kurt Matzler et al., "How to Delight Your Customers," *Journal of Product and Band Management* 5, no. 2 (1996): 6–18.

8. Adapted from Noriaki Kano, "Attractive Quality and Must Be Quality," *Hinshitsu* [Quality] 14, no. 2 (1984): 147–156 (in Japanese); and Kurt Matzler and Hans H. Hinterhuber, "How to Make Product Development Projects More Successful by Integrating Kano's Model of Customer Satisfaction into Quality Function Deployment," *Technovation,* 18, no. 1 (1998): 25–38.

9. Johann Füller and Kurt Matzler, "Virtual Product Experience and Customer Participation—A Chance for Customer-Centred, Really New Products," *Technovation* 27, nos. 6/7 (2007): 378–387.

10. Franz Bailom, Kurt Matzler, and Dieter Tschemernjak, *Enduring Success: What Top-Companies Do Differently* (New York: Palgrave Macmillan, 2007).

11. Philip Kotler and Kevin L. Keller, *Marketing management,* 13th ed. (Upper Saddler River, New Jersey: Pearson Education, 2009).

12. Marc A. Annacchino, *New Product Development: From Initial Idea to Product Management* (Amsterdam: Elsevier, 2003) 18–20.

13. See, for example, Peter H. Bloch, "Seeking the Ideal Form: Product Design and Consumer Response," *Journal of Marketing* 59, no. 3 (1995): 16–29.

14. James G. Bralla, *Design for Manufacturability Handbook,* 2nd ed. (New York: McGraw-Hill Professional, 1998).

15. Michael Luchs and Scott Swan (forthcoming) Working paper version available at Mason School Web site:: mason.wm.edu/faculty/documents/**product_design**_swan.pdf. Product Design since Bloch: Analysis of 14 Years of Research and the Emergence of Product Design as a Field of Marketing Inquiry," *Journal of Product Innovation Management* (1995).

16. Roger LeRoy Miller, *Economics Today,* 15th ed. (Boston, MA: Addison-Wesley, 2010), 588.

31

Products—Innovations

What is an innovation? When marketing strategists talk about "innovations" they're usually referring to "discontinuous innovations"—products that are truly "new to the world" and that change the way a customer need is met. In marketing strategy, the degree of innovation is not generally thought of in terms of the underlying technology. Although products such as hybrid-powered cars are generally viewed as very innovative and the underlying technology may be groundbreaking, the marketing of a product like hybrid cars may not be "innovation marketing" per se. People buy and consume hybrids in much the same way that they bought and consumed their previous, gas-only cars. Even if they stop at gas stations less often, they bought the car from the same sort of dealer, they have the car serviced in a similar way as they would have maintained any earlier car, and they drive it and it takes them places in almost exactly the same manner that their earlier cars did.

DEGREES OF NEW PRODUCT INNOVATION

For marketing strategy, an "innovation" is defined by *the degree of change in consumer behavior or "consumption patterns" required to adopt it, consume it, and meet a need with it* (Figure 31-1). Consumption patterns include the actual behaviors required to use the product as well as the knowledge required and the ancillary equipment and installations required. "Discontinuous innovations" or "disruptive technologies" require *substantial* changes in consumption patterns (they *disrupt* consumption patterns and they disrupt industries and markets). "Continuous innovations" offer incremental value without major or sometimes even noticeable changes in consumption patterns, and "dynamically discontinuous innovations" fall in between (they change consumption behaviors and change the way the need is met, but only to a limited degree). This may seem like a semantic exercise, assigning labels and definitions to ranges along a continuum, but it is strategically important to consider the degree of change in

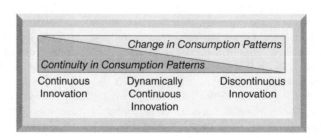

FIGURE NOTE 31-1 Degrees of New Product Innovation

consumption patterns that an innovation requires of the customers. This attribute of an innovation—required changes in consumption patterns and behaviors—determines important aspects of the marketing programs and strategies that will be effective or ineffective in supporting it. The "diffusion of innovations" framework, presented in this note, is most relevant to marketing *discontinuous* innovations. Strategies for incremental, continuous innovations are less likely to be effectively based on the diffusion-of-innovation dynamics.

CUSTOMER VALUE AND PRODUCT INNOVATION

A useful framework for understanding new product innovation in strategic marketing is the "customer value frontier." Value is defined as what the customers get adjusted for what the customers give—or *relative performance* adjusted for *relative price*. In most markets there are offerings that are low in price but also low in relative performance/quality, other offerings that offer "more for more," that is, that offer some more features of performance at a higher price, and then some offerings that offer very high performance for quite a bit higher price. These two aspects of the offerings in any market can be used to create a two-dimensional space or map, as shown in Figure 31-2, in which the axes are relative price (on the vertical) and relative performance/quality (on the horizontal). In that space there are trade-offs that customers understand and are willing to make—that is, there is an equilibrium frontier or zone in which customers and marketers understand that the trade-offs are "fair." Customers may not personally choose to pay less to get less or to pay more to get more, but the trade-off is nevertheless understood as fair and justifiable.

There are also regions in that "value map" within which the trade-offs are *not* sustainable. Products in

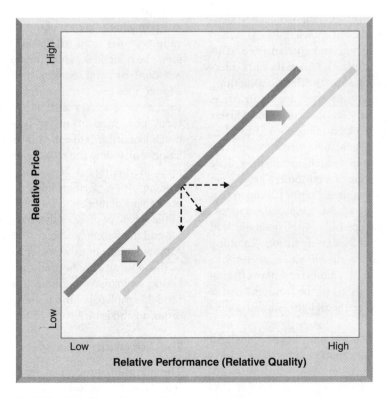

FIGURE NOTE 31-2 The Value Frontier and Innovation

the upper-left (the "northwest") quadrant are charging more than products in the lower-left (the southwest) quadrant but are offering only the same performance/quality. *This is not viable in the long term*; customers will find the offerings in the lower left and choose to save and/or find offerings in the upper right and choose to pay the same but get more.

On the other hand, products in the lower right (the southeast) are offering *more* performance than products in the southwest but at the same relative price; they can also be seen as offering the same quality as products in the northeast but at a *lower price*— either way, more-for-the-same or the-same-for-less, these products have found a way to dominate their competition. *These are innovations!* They will draw sales and gain market share until the competition catches up.

Of course, it isn't easy to offer more for less— but that is what entrepreneurship and innovation require. If the firm itself isn't innovating, it can be sure that the competition *is or will be soon.* When Wal-Mart introduces electronic inventory tracking systems enabled by RFID tags (radio-frequency identification tags) on pallets of merchandise, or when Apple adds features, style, and convenience to its iPod, iPhone, and iPad product lines, they are offering the same goods for a lower price or something more than the competition offers for a fair price. Wal-Mart's extraordinary logistics backbone delivers the same products that customers could buy elsewhere at lower prices. Apple's intuitive interfaces and distinctive designs offer "much more for a little more"; that is, something that customers perceive as unique and valuable at a price they're willing to pay. That attracts customers and, eventually and inevitably, it attracts competition—which should lead to further innovation. The competition "catching up" can be understood as *the fair value zone shifting to the right*—as the market adjusts to new offering that appear to the southeast of the frontier, what is considered "fair" shifts to the right to establish a new equilibrium.

One way of understanding innovations and how innovations enter the market and affect a market is to view them as changing or "destroying" the structure of a market and the way the market is defined. As discussed, they offer customers more performance for

the same price or they charge less for the same performance. Those superior offerings attract customers to their better value propositions, and in the long term shift competition toward that new equilibrium. Thus innovation can be thought of as continuous "creative destruction"; in the words of renowned economist Joseph Schumpeter, innovation is the

> process of industrial mutation—if I may use that biological term—that incessantly revolutionizes the economic structure *from within*, incessantly destroying the old one, incessantly creating a new one. This process of Creative Destruction is the essential fact about capitalism. It is what capitalism consists in and what every capitalist concern has got to live in.[1]

THE DIFFUSION OF INNOVATIONS

The "diffusion of innovations" refers to the speed at which a truly new product (or an idea, for that matter) spreads through or "diffuses" into a market. Much of what is known about the diffusion of innovations comes from studies of the agricultural sector—the basic ideas and much of the early research was done by rural sociologists studying patterns of adoption for new farming methods and technologies such as weed sprays and crop varieties. Because, it turns out, innovations diffuse through markets much like diseases like the flu spread through populations (including the reliance on interpersonal contact), marketing has also adopted knowledge from epidemiology. Epidemiology uses sophisticated mathematical models to forecast the rate and severity of the spread of diseases through populations of people and marketing has borrowed some of that math. Although many of those models go beyond the scope of this note and are beyond the needs of most marketing strategists, one basic framework, the "Bass Model," emphasizes the underlying mechanisms of diffusion and is invaluable in forecasting.

The Adoption Process

The adoption process of an innovation includes stages that a consumer moves through on their way from unaware of a new product to eventual (hoped

FIGURE NOTE 31-3   The Adoption Process

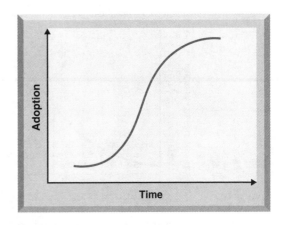

FIGURE NOTE 31-4   The Diffusion S-Curve

for) adoption and loyalty. The consumer must start out unaware of the product and therefore the first objective of the marketing program for innovations must be to gain awareness in target markets. Consumers then move from susceptible—that is, having the need and in the target market but unaware—through awareness, interest or understanding toward an evaluation (an attitude) eventually to trial and adoption (Figure 31-3). It is important for the marketing strategist to recognize where consumers are in that process—and to recognize that different consumers, different proportions of consumers, and different segments of consumers will be in different stages at any given time. Different tools and different messages are required for consumers in different stages of the adoption process.

Not all consumers are equally likely to adopt a new technology as others, certainly not at the same time. Some consumers are more likely to adopt; they will buy the new product when it is very new, while others will wait for different periods of time. Much of the study of the diffusion of innovations has been the study of *who will adopt when* and, importantly, what a marketing strategist can and should do differently when dealing with different types of adopters at different times in the diffusion of an innovation. In general, the diffusion of an innovation into the market across time forms and S-shaped

curve (Figure 31-4). At first only a few consumers will buy the product—it is untried and they can't see anyone else using it, but someone has to be the first to buy. As more people try a product and adopt it the speed of that adoption increases—the curve turns more sharply upward because, as more people adopt the product, others see it in use, distribution broadens (it is easier to get), and perceptions of risk diminish (it's been "tested" by others). Eventually that diffusion starts to "max out"; most of the people who have the need and the means have purchased the product, more of the product's sales become repurchases, and the rate of new adoption inevitably flattens. At some point, everyone in the market who was ever going to try the product has tried it and the only new customers are new to the market.

Types of Consumers

One of the most important understandings to come out of the study of farmers' adoption of new agricultural methods was the recognition that markets can be segmented into groups of consumers (farmers) who will adopt new technologies at different stages in the diffusion lifecycle. Some consumers are inherently more likely to adopt a new technology—and some are very unlikely to be "innovative." Some of those differences are general—they're true across product categories and across innovations—and some are product category specific. The most basic segmentation scheme regarding adoption of a new product presents five types of consumers: innovators, "early adopters,"

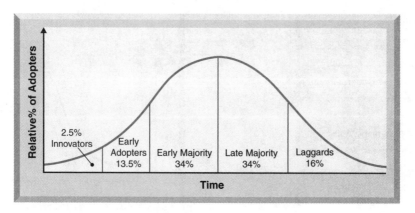

FIGURE NOTE 31-5 Segments Based on Propensity to Adopt Across Time

the "early majority," the late majority, and laggards (Figure 31-5; Table 31-1). In general, and unsurprisingly, innovators and early adopters tend to be younger, better educated, more affluent, and more open-minded, and innovators and early adopters for any particular product category tend to be more involved in the product and more attuned to product-category-specific media.

There are some important strategic differences between these segments. Innovators are too "out there"; they typically do *not* influence as many other consumers—certainly not as many as the early majority influence; because they are so involved in the product category and have such a specialized knowledge, their needs are simply different. They also don't tend to be as well-connected to

TABLE NOTE 31-1 Characteristics of Adoption Segments

Adoption Segment	Bass Model Label	General Characteristics	Strategic Implications
Innovators	Innovators	Younger, highly involved in the product category. Less socially connected than Early Adopters. Individualistic.	Great source of new-product ideas—less important to accelerating the diffusion of the product.
Early Adopters (Opinion Leaders or Gatekeepers)		Young, better educated, more affluent, *socially connected*. Extraverted. Moderate- to high-category involvement.	*Critical* to gaining market foothold and to influencing later adopters.
Early Majority	Imitators	Deliberate but open-minded. Moderately interested in the product category.	
Late Majority		Conservative and skeptical. Low product category involvement. Risk averse.	
Laggards		Older, less well-educated, lower incomes, risk-averse, low interest in product category.	

broader social networks. Innovators *can* provide important design feedback and may be the source of innovative ideas, that is especially true in the current reality of "Web 2.0," in which online consumers "co-create" and collaborate in new product development, but they're less influential on other adopter segments.

The early adopters are sometimes referred to as "opinion leaders" or "gatekeepers." Those labels emphasize the important role this segment plays in marketing and in the success or failure of truly new products. Like innovators, these consumers are younger, better educated, more affluent, more open minded and more highly involved in the product category. Unlike innovators, these consumers are also well-connected in social networks and tend to talk with *and influence* many other consumers.

The bell-shaped curve is simply the S-curve—not coincidentally exactly the shape of the "product life cycle"—but instead of graphing cumulative sales it graphs trial by period. Figure 31-6 shows the same phenomenon with the vertical axis capturing cumulative (percent of total) trial. We highlight that relationship to emphasize the relationship between diffusion and the product lifecycle. The product lifecycle graphs cumulative total sales—the diffusion process addresses cumulative trail. By adding "adopters" or repeat sales, the diffusion curve maps directly to the product lifecycle. By graphing trial as period specific rather than cumulative, the five

adopter categories can be connected to the product lifecycle in the same way.

Importance of Two-Step Communications

When thinking about marketing communications the tendency is to think first about marketer-controlled communications—messages created by the marketing organization to send to consumers and potential consumers via some media such as newspapers, television, or the sales force. Nevertheless, the most important and persuasive information that consumers receive about a product, especially a truly new innovation, is received *from other consumers.* In addition, some of the most important information consumers use in decision making is from *observing* other consumers using a product (rather than from overt, explicit communications or traditional word-of-mouth communications). That is, some information consumers transmit *overtly*—by telling others about the product; but another influential source of information is simply observing the product being used or seeing another consumer with the product. This process is called the "two-step communications." The first step is the marketing effort—traditional elements of communications such as sales, advertising, and public relations—and some customers do respond to marketer-controlled communications and try the product. Nevertheless, the communications

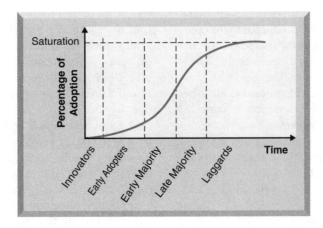

FIGURE NOTE 31-6 Cumulative Adoption and Adoption Segments

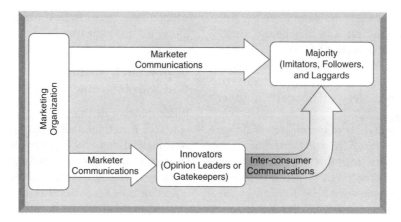

FIGURE NOTE 31-7   "Two-Step" Communications

process that actually drives most customer behavior is one that is mediated by a second step, the processing of the information via *other customers* (shown graphically in Figure 31-7).

Both explicit inter-consumer communications (consumers telling other consumers something or sending a message to other consumers) and observations of other consumers' behaviors are especially powerful mechanisms via which truly innovative new products gain acceptance and thereby diffuse into the market. For older technology and familiar brands it is difficult to motivate consumers to talk about the product and, although it is still possible to observe the product in use, these observations are less important. There are older product categories such as fashion and clothing, which defy that general rule—purchases are still strongly influenced by opinion leaders within a mediated, two-step process even though fashion is not a new or technologically sophisticated category. Nevertheless, for truly new products, inter-consumer communications are especially persuasive and, conversely, marketer-controlled communications (ads, sales messages, etc.) are not particularly persuasive. Communications mediated by third-party news organizations, that is, news reports that result from public relations efforts, are more persuasive than paid-for communications such as advertisements, but are still less influential than inter-consumer communications and observed behaviors. Importantly, not all inter-consumer

communication is positive—in fact, negative word of mouth is considered to be more influential than recommendations and dissatisfied consumers are far more likely to talk about their experience than satisfied customers.

Attributes of the Product/Innovation

Various characteristics of the product or the innovation influence the rate at which that innovation diffuses through the market. Some of these attributes can be addressed or changed by the marketing strategist to increase the rate at which consumers adopt the new product—and it should be remembered that, while we talk about the "rate of adoption," marketers should equate that diffusion with rate of "sales growth"—*each trial is a sale and every adopter is a loyal customer.* While some attributes of an innovation can't be changed—a new medicine, for example, may be inherently risky and there is nothing anyone can do about that riskiness—other attributes of an innovation may be "manageable," such as the financial risk (which can be mitigated by lowering the price or offering guarantees or warranties). So, although discussed as a separate topic here, it is important for the marketing strategist to understand that some of these "attributes of the product" that drive the rate of diffusion are under the influence of the marketing manager and are therefore part of the "marketing program" discussed after this.

- *Relative Advantage.* The first and most obvious attribute of an innovation itself that is related to its speed of diffusion is the "relative advantage" the new technology offers over existing, "old" technologies. This is not surprising but is important to consider: The enhancement in the way consumers meet a need and the significance of the met need to the consumers will, in large part, drive acceptance of the innovation, and these two attributes (advantage over existing technologies in meeting a need and the salience of the need to consumer) equate to "relative advantage."
- *Trialability.* If consumers can try a product without committing to adopting it or committing to a large purchase or effort to try it, they will be more willing to "sample" and evaluate the product. Innovations which require complete conversion or even large purchases will diffuse more slowly due to the increased price, the increased risk, and the increased effort required to try without perfect knowledge.
- *Complexity/Ease of Use.* The more complex an innovation is, the slower and less willing customers will be to try the innovation. The simple and easier to use the technology is, the more readily customers will try it. This may seem obvious, but, in too many instances, marketers have adopted the attitude that "customers should just know how to use the product," instead of recognizing that it is the marketers' job to ensure that the product is easy for customers to understand and to use.
- *Observability.* Innovations that can be seen in use will diffuse into a market more quickly than products that are not visible. The logic underlying the two-step process of communications and the effect it has on diffusion is that some consumers—in many markets for disruptive technologies most consumers will use other consumers as "testers" for the innovation. Either deliberately or unconsciously, customers will think "I don't want to be the first to try that innovation" but, once they've seen someone else trying the product, they will perceive the risk to be lower and may also believe that information and assistance will be available more readily from others.
- *Compatibility.* The less the degree of change—and the lower the price of change required to try a product, the more likely customers and consumers will be to try. Innovations which require major changes—either to behaviors or to other systems—will be less readily tried.
- *Risk.* There are many forms of risk perceived by customers—financial risk, physical (health and welfare) risk, social risk, etc.—and the greater the risk of any sort the less likely customers are to try the innovation.
- *Network Effects.* Some of the substantive, core benefits of an innovation may also go up with wider market adoption via "network effects"; for example, owning the first fax machine had few benefits to the innovative firm that bought it—until others bought faxes. The utility of owning a fax machine was greatest when, eventually, fax machines became pervasive.

ATTRIBUTES OF THE MARKETING PROGRAM AND LINKS TO MARKETING STRATEGIES

All of the elements of a marketing strategy and the tactics of a marketing offering can influence the pace of product diffusion and the resulting realized market size. Most of those relationships can be understood as influencing that diffusion via the reality of and/or consumers' perceptions of the characteristics of the innovation, described above. That is, changing the actual relative advantage, trialability, complexity/ease of use, observability, compatibility, risk, and network effects or changing consumers' perceptions of those things will speed diffusion. Marketers can change the size of product packages or offer smaller minimum order quantities to create easier trialability. Product names can be displayed more prominently to enhance observability. Lower prices for first-time buyers and money-back guarantees increase trialability and lower risk. Increased channel support and training for sales clerks improves understanding (i.e., reduced perceived complexity). Another way to think about the influence of mix decisions on the diffusion of innovation is to consider the two segments modeled in the Bass Model: marketing mix elements can influence innovation or can affect imitation (or might augment both). Some elements may be specifically developed, for example, to facilitate word of mouth and observability. Agricultural supply companies develop programs via which opinion-leader farmers host events to display innovations and also offer discounts to farmers who post signage in their fields making otherwise unobservable choices, such as those about fertilizers and seeds, visible to passersby. Some of these mix decisions are tactical while others may demand distinct strategies. For example, pricing to accelerate diffusion precludes "skimming" strategies in pricing and developing knowledgeable sales support from channel partners precludes intensive, mass distribution.

Summary

Innovation involves the creation of something new that customers will value more than they do their previous alternatives. Innovation is an essential element of free markets and competition. As Joseph Schumpeter recognized, innovation "incessantly revolutionizes the economic structure *from within*"[2]; that is, markets are constantly evolving as competitors and new entrants offer more for the same price or the same for lower prices.

Marketing strategists must understand: how different customers react to innovations, including the adoption process at the individual customer level, differentiable segments of customers based on their propensity to adopt, and the essential role of inter-customer communications in driving adoption. Strategists should also understand how different attributes of the innovation and different elements of the marketing mix such as price and integrated communications can influence the adoption and diffusion of innovations. That is, although the diffusion of innovations into a market is influenced by some factors largely outside the marketers' direct control, there are controllable tools available that influence those customer and market reactions, and the successful strategist will have a keen appreciation of those tools and their limits. This note has summarized these ideas and frameworks and connected them to the strategic marketing process.

Additional Resources:

Moore, Geoffery A. *Crossing the Chasm: Marketing and Selling High-Tech Products to Mainstream.* New York: Harper Business, 1991.

Mohr, Jakki J., Sanjit Sengupta, and Stanley Slater. *Marketing of High-Technology Products and Innovations.* Upper Saddle River, NJ: Pearson/Prentice Hall, 2010.

Rogers, Everett M. *Diffusion of innovations,* 5th ed. New York: The Free Press, 2003.

Endnotes

1. Joseph A. Schumpeter, *Capitalism, Socialism and Democracy* (New York: Harper, 1975; originally published in 1942), 83.
2. Ibid.

32

Products—Product Portfolios

Most companies produce and sell more than one product or service, and many companies have more than one business unit. Those collections of products and businesses are referred to as "product portfolios." Marketing strategists must make important and inevitable decisions about how to allocate cash, expertise, time, and other scarce resources across individual products and business units. Different products and different strategic business units (SBUs) require and justify different levels of investment. In addition, those investment priorities change across time as markets, products, industries, and customers evolve. Marketing strategists need ways to decide which products justify more resources to grow, which products should merely hold their market position, and even which products should be withdrawn from the market.

When facing these decisions about investments and withdrawal of investments across the product portfolio, it is useful for managers to consider two fundamental questions: "How strong is the product/SBU in its market?" and "How attractive is the market?" (or "How likely are we to win at this game?" and "How nice would it be to win at this game?"). These two considerations—the product or SBU's *strength* in the market and the market's *attractiveness*—are, of course, complex questions, especially if a company has dozens of products or business units to manage. Fortunately, there are several straightforward models managers can use to address these questions. Two of the most widely used and well-tested models are The Boston Consulting Group (BCG) portfolio matrix and the GE (General Electric)/McKinsey Portfolio Planning Grid. Both hold these two questions as central to decisions about whether to grow a business, or maintain it, or withdraw:

1. How attractive is the market?
2. How strong is the product/SBU in the market?

These frameworks differ in their complexity or "granularity" of the analyses and the resulting strategic recommendation.

THE BCG MATRIX

One of the earliest portfolio models was the BCG matrix, developed by The Boston Consulting Group in the 1960s.[1] It remains the best known and most often applied. Several terms now part of everyday business jargon originated with the BCG matrix, including "cash cow," "harvest," and "dog." The BCG matrix is an uncomplicated description of strength and attractiveness. It uses just one variable, *market growth rate,* to summarize attractiveness.[2] Using growth rate as the single characteristic that makes a market attractive can be justified because, for one thing, growing markets offer opportunities of investments, which promise higher returns later on than low-growth markets. Additionally, during the growth phases of the product life cycle, market share can be gained by expanding capacities earlier than competitors, ensuring product availability, and managing sales effectively—all reasons to increase investments in higher-growth markets. Further, in high-growth markets, competitors may not react as intensely when they lose market share, because, even if their sales increase below market growth, the sales do increase. In a no-growth market, increases in sales can only be achieved by reducing the competitors' sales—and competitors are likely to feel the losses more acutely and to respond to actual losses in sales more intensely.

The BCG matrix uses *relative market share* as the single marker or the product or SBU's strength. This, too, is true in as far as it goes. Relative market share corresponds to relatively greater scale (production volume). That is, the higher a product or business unit's relative market share, the lower its relative unit costs and the higher its relative margins. All of these things are "relative" in that they're specific to the comparison with the competition. The original

BCG framework defines relative market share as the sales volume of an SBU divided by the sales volume of the *largest competitor*. Therefore, the largest firm in a market will have a relative share greater than one, and all the other entrants will have relative market shares of less than one. The BCG model combines the two questions—attractiveness and relative strength as indicated by market growth and relative market share—into a two-by-two matrix (shown as Figure 32-1. Products or SBUs in each quadrant necessitate different strategic orientations, have investment requirements, and present different cash-flow challenges and opportunities.

Applying the BCG Matrix

To better understand the strategic and investment implications of the BCG matrix, we may start by considering the information in Table 32-1, which describes the growth rates and market shares for ten SBUs and their respective markets within a single consumer electronics company. Figure 32-2 displays that product portfolio within the BCG Matrix. The size of each circle in the matrix represents that business unit's share of the company's overall sales volume. The following strategic implications emerge for each quadrant:

- *Question marks (low market share/high market growth; in the electronics firm example these are flat-screen TVs and game consoles):* Business units in this quadrant are usually in the early phase of the product lifecycle. As the market grows, investments in capacity expansion, marketing, distribution, and related activities are required. Cash flow is usually negative. It is vital to grow faster than the market; otherwise, the market leader cannot be caught. As their name indicates, "question mark" business units have an unsure and risky future. If they are able to build market share, they become the stars and, eventually, the cash cows of the future; if not, they become dogs and cash drains.
- *Stars (high market share/high market growth; here, car navigation):* These strategic business units are the market leaders in high-growth markets. As the market continues to grow strongly, they need high investments.

FIGURE NOTE 32-1 The BCG Matrix[3]

TABLE NOTE 32-1 Growth Rates and Market Shares for Selected Units of a Consumer Electronics Company[4]

Business Unit	2002	2006	2006/2002 (%)*	2007	2007/2006 (%)*	2011	2011/2007 (%)*
CRT TV	2781	745	−28,1	331	−55,6	26	−47,1
Flat-screen TV	330	4041	87,1	4601	13,3	5200	3,1
DVD Player/Recorder	725	646	−2,8	525	−18,7	840	12,5
Digital Still Cameras	870	1988	22,9	2062	3,7	1760	−3,9
Digital Multimedia Player	77	695	73,3	681	−2	620	−2,3
Personal Audio	483	877	16,1	835	−4,8	730	−3,3
Home HiFi	1233	775	−11	711	−8,3	670	−1,5
Game Consoles	210	487	23,4	705	44,8	570	−5,2
Recording Media Digital	229	1008	22,3	993	−1,5	1420	8,7
Car Navigation	180	748	42,8	1010	35	610	−5

Market volume (in Million. EUR)

*Compound annual growth rate (CAGR)

Business Unit	Sales 2006 (Million. Euro)	Profit 2006	Sales 2006 Strongest Competitor
CRT TV	12	−2,5	16
Flat Screen TV	330	48	913
DVD Player/Recorder	92	12	180
Digital Still Cameras	312	9,8	188
Digital Multimedia Player	118	35	90
Personal Audio	210	54	128
Home HiFi	72	−23	144
Game Consoles	150	−2,2	336
Recording Media Digital	99	7,5	188
Car Navigation	336	−33	212

Cash flow usually balanced or slightly positive. The strategy should emphasize maintaining market position into the next phase of the product life cycle; if this occurs—if the star can strengthen its market-share leadership, these products/SBUs become cash cows as market growth rate inevitably declines.

- *Cash cows (high market share/low market growth; here, digital still cameras, personal audio, and digital multimedia players):* These products/SBUs need little investment because the market is mature—but that does not mean

they require no investment at all. In fact, one of the first rules of portfolio management and differential investment should be "feed your cows first." These products should have a cost advantage based on their greater scale and, therefore, they should generate a large cash surplus that can be invested in question marks and stars (even after receiving the level of investment required to maintain the cash cow).

- *Dogs (low market share/low market growth; here, recording media digital, home HiFi, DVD player/recorders, and CRT TVs):* Holding a

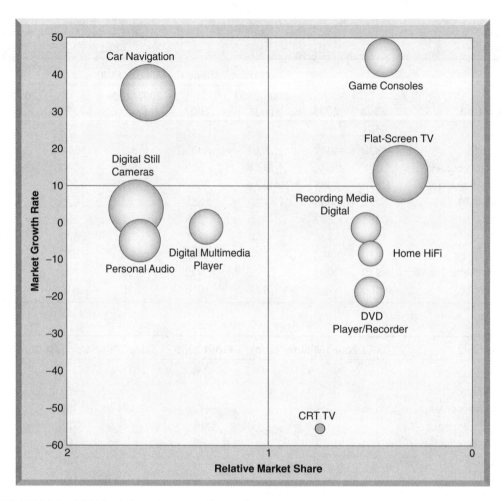

FIGURE NOTE 32-2   BCG Matrix for a Consumer Electronics Company

weak position in an unattractive market should be a sure warning against further investment ("good money after bad"). Dogs are candidates for withdrawal and divestment, especially if a product is at the end of its lifecycle (e.g., CRT TV). Still, divestment decisions are more complex than simply "sell or don't sell." For example, in the late 1990s Novartis and AstraZeneca each had agribusiness divisions they had identified as being unrelated to their core businesses and suitable for divestment. The two firms joined to divest their respective units into a single business that could establish strengths and synergies based on size and interproduct economies of scope. The resulting entity, Syngenta, quickly became a market leader in agribusiness and agrichemicals.[5]

A well-managed portfolio is characterized by balanced cash flow and balanced risk, and it has business units in each quadrant (including dogs, as long as they are profitable). Thus, for the company in this example, portfolio analysis suggests adopting the following strategies:

- Withdrawing from the CRT TV market
- Keeping the home HiFi and DVD player/recorder business units as long as they are profitable

- Investing in the recording media digital business unit, because the long-term perspective is attractive (as evidenced by growth during the period 2001–2007)
- Using cash generated by the personal audio and digital multimedia player business units to increase market share of the game console and flat-screen TV units and to maintain the leading position of the car navigation unit

Limitations of the BCG Matrix

The BCG matrix is widely known and often applied; as noted, it has added to the common business vernacular and it is a basic concept in strategic management. Nevertheless, it has certain limitations that managers should be aware of, including the following:[6]

1. The use of market growth rate and relative market share may be oversimplifications; they certainly are simplifications. In reality, whether a market is attractive can depend on many factors such as market size, competitive intensity, and average profitability as well as growth rate. Furthermore, competitive advantages (relative strength) may not only depend on relative market share but may also result from distinctive R&D capabilities, marketing capabilities and relationships, loyal customer bases, and other attributes. The BCG framework assumes that market growth rate and relative market share are enough, or that they, in fact, capture the effects of these other sources of attractiveness and strength—and either of these assumptions may not always be true.

2. The BCG matrix treats relative market share as a proxy for cash generation. It also treats market growth rate as a proxy for cash usage, because slow-growth markets are mature and presumably don't require much investment. Unfortunately, this is a problematic assumption, because mature markets are often competitive and, therefore, require cash. For instance, airlines and car manufacturers immediately come to mind. These businesses can be said to be quite mature, but they also require huge capital investments to replenish airlines and invest in the latest technology to manufacture cars, respectively. Another anomaly is Microsoft, which has a high growth rate but low cash usage.

3. Using relative market share only makes sense when economies of scale and experience curve effects play a major role. In industries in which size does not lead to cost advantages, relative market share is not a good indicator for competitive advantages.

4. Not only the variables but also the specific values or cut-off points along the axes of the matrix are somewhat arbitrary.

   a. *Relative Market Share.* Defining market shares and splitting the y-axis of the matrix into high and low growth can present problems. First, for many companies, reliable market share data is not available, and second, markets can be defined broadly or narrowly (e.g., beverages, soft drinks, or energy drinks in the case of Red Bull). Market share can be high or low depending on this definition of the market, and that adds an element of subjectivity to the BCG framework which has not always been adequately appreciated.

   b. *Market Growth Rate.* The original BCG framework suggested a 10 percent market growth rate as a threshold to differentiate between "high" and "low" growth markets, and that criterion is better understood as dependent upon the market and the times: a 5 percent growth rate may be high in the food industry but low in the consumer electronics industry, and a flat growth rate might be an achievement in a major recession but a setback in a high-growth economic cycle.

5. The BCG portfolio framework ignores synergies between business units or products. Hence, it does not consider the ways in which divesting one business unit can affect other business units if those units share fixed costs or produce products that complement each other.

6. Finally, the BCG Matrix is a *snapshot*; it captures the state-of-market growth and market share *at a specific time*, and does not consider changes or trends in the market or in the product/SBU's strength.

These cautions indicate that the BCG Matrix should not be used for making decisions but as a guide to discussions that will lead to decisions. In any case, the BCG Matrix remains one of the most durable, well-known, and functional frameworks in the strategy literature, and terms such as "cash cow" and "dog" have become part of the ubiquitous business vernacular.

GE/MCKINSEY PORTFOLIO PLANNING GRID

A second framework for managing and prioritizing multiple products or SBUs within the single firm's assortment is the GE/McKinsey Portfolio Planning Grid (also referred to as the GE Business Screen Matrix, the "Stoplight Grid" due to its adoption of green, yellow, and red to emphasize its strategic implications, and, henceforth in this note, abridged to the GE/McKinsey Grid); it was developed subsequent to the BCG Matrix and it follows from that now-classic scheme. GE/McKinsey Grid is a somewhat more complex and detailed matrix, addressing the "reductionist" nature of the BCG Matrix (which reduces business strength to just relative market share and market attractiveness to just market growth rate). It was developed by McKinsey and Company, the international strategic consulting firm, for GE in order to evaluate business units, to evaluate the balance and allocation of resources across the overall portfolio of business units, and to assist in setting appropriate performance targets across products and units. The GE/McKinsey Grid is based on some of the same assumptions as the BCG matrix—especially the assumption that investment levels across products or SBUs should be a function of business strength and market attractiveness—but it incorporates more variables into the two main axes (business strength and market attractiveness) and it offers a more granular distinctions across product/SBU positions within the resulting space. The GE/McKinsey Grid is shown in Figure 32-3.[7]

		Industry Attractiveness		
		High	Medium	Low
Business Strength	High	• Grow • Seek Dominance • Maximize Investment	• Identify Growth Segments • Invest Strongly • Maintain Position Elsewhere	• Maintain Overall Position • Seek Cash Flow • Invest at Maintenance Level
	Medium	• Evaluate Potential for Leadership Via Segmentation • Identify Weaknesses • Build Strengths	• Identify Growth Segments • Specialize • Invest Selectively	• Prune Lines • Minimize Investment • Position to Divest
	Low	• Specialize • Seek Niches • Consider Acquisitions	• Specialize • Seek Niches • Consider Exit	• Trust Leader's Statesmanship • Sic on Competitor's Cash Generators • Time Exit and Divest

FIGURE NOTE 32-3   The GE/McKinsey Portfolio Planning Grid[8]

Applying the GE/McKinsey Grid

To compile the GE/McKinsey Grid, six steps are necessary:

1. Define and weight *market attractiveness* markers;
2. Define and weight *business strength* markers;
3. Evaluation each product's or SBU's market attractiveness and business strength;
4. Compute weighted scores for market attractiveness and relative competitive position;
5. Position business units in the portfolio;
6. Derive strategic implications of positions within matrix.

There are a number of variables than can be used to mark or assess market attractiveness and relative business strength (we'll refer to these as "markers"). The BCG Matrix incorporates just one of those variables for each two axes, and those may be the most powerful variables in explaining strength and attractiveness, but they are certainly not the only variables that lead to strength or attractiveness, and, in fact, it is likely that the "best" variables to consider depends upon the industry, the firm, and the situation. Table 32-2 lists some common indicators of business strength and industry attractiveness. As noted, the variables chosen in any particular analysis and the relative weights put on those variables varies across different types of industries and should be selected carefully, customized to the particular firm and its circumstances. Each of the chosen markers of market strength and business attractiveness may not be equally important. Different variables should be assigned different *importance weights* or "weights" based on the degree to which they determine or influence the superordinate variable (market attractiveness or business strength).

After choosing the markers and assigning each marker an importance weight, each product or SBU should be evaluated on those factors (e.g., with a 0–100 score), and a weighted score can be computed by multiplying the evaluation score by its weight, as in Table 32-3. For some factors, the scores can be determined from hard numbers (e.g., market growth and market size). For other factors, managerial judgment might be called upon (e.g., R&D capabilities or environmental impact.) The weighted scores can then be used to position the business units in the matrix. Finally, strategies can be derived based on each unit's position, as in Figure 32-4.

Advantages and Limitations of the GE/McKinsey Grid

As illustrated by the example, the GE/McKinsey Grid is more comprehensive and more detailed than the BCG Matrix. It has the advantage of taking into account more market and company information and it leads to more specific strategic recommendations. Furthermore, the GE model can be applied at the level of business units, product lines, or single products, and it can even been adapted to a number of other applications, such as the following:

- Customer portfolios (by considering customer attractiveness and relative competitive position)
- Segment portfolios (by considering segment attractiveness and relative competitive position)
- Country portfolios (by considering market attractiveness and relative competitive position)

TABLE NOTE 32-2 Common Markers of Market Attractiveness and Business Strength

Market Attractiveness	Relative Competitive Position
• Market growth	• Market share
• Market size	• Product quality
• Profit margins	• R&D capabilities
• Competitive intensity	• Marketing capabilities
• Market entry barriers	• Brand awareness and image
• Cyclicality of life cycle	• Production capabilities
• Environmental impact	• Cost efficiency

TABLE NOTE 32-3 Assessment of Market Attractiveness and Relative Competitive Position

Business Unit: Flat-Screen TVs
Assessment of Market Attractiveness

Criteria	Weight (%)	Evaluation/Remarks	Score (0–100)	Weighted Score
Market growth	30	Highly growing market in growth phase of the life cycle: CAGR 2002–2006 = 87%; 2006–2007 = 13%; Projected CAGR 2007–2011 = 3.1%; growth is going to slow down in the coming years (CAGR = Compound Annual Growth Rate)	90	27
Market size	25	Market size in 2006 = 4,000; only 15% of households own flat-screen TVs; still very high potential	100	25
Competitive intensity	10	Strong, suppliers of CRT TVs have already switched to flat-screen	30	3
Profit margins	20	Price wars not yet to be expected, high growth rate in Euro sales volume due to higher prices for high-end products: unit increase 2002–2006 = 5%, increase of Euro sales volume = 54%	80	16
Market entry barriers	15	Medium to high, biggest market entry barriers are access to distribution channels, economies of scale, and brand name	60	9
	100			80

Business Unit: Flat-Screen TVs
Assessment of Relative Competitive Position

Criteria	Weight (%)	Evaluation/Remarks	Score (0–100)	Weighted Score
Relative market share	30	Low relative market share (.36); strong cost disadvantages due to lower economies of scale and experience curve effects	10	3
R&D strengths	15	Low, behind competition in introducing new technologies or upgrading technologies, R&D budget only 1/3 of strongest competitor	10	1,5
Marketing capabilities	20	Brand awareness and brand image according to market research clearly below competition, lower marketing budget than strongest competitors	15	3
Distribution and sales	25	Limited access to distribution channels, listed in only 3 of 7 major distributors of consumer electronics	10	2,5
Production capabilities	10	Medium, high investments in capacity enlargement, production technologies	50	5
	100			15

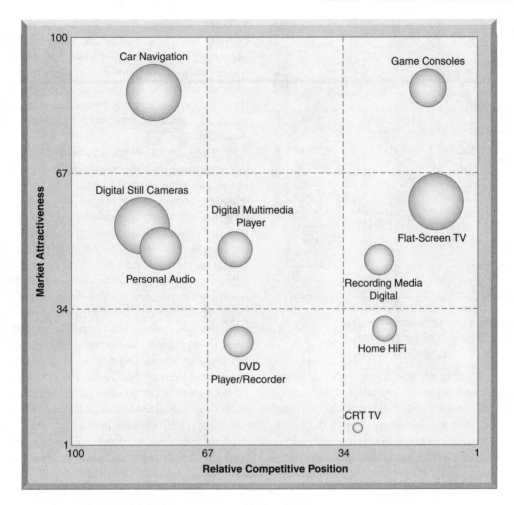

FIGURE NOTE 32-4 GE/McKinsey Grid for a Consumer Electronics Company

In such applications, customers, segments, or countries are rated on attractiveness and business strength:

- How much would we like to succeed with this customer (with this segment or in this country)? and
- How likely are we to succeed with this customer (with this segment or in this country)?

Companies will, generally, want to balance these two considerations when targeting customers, segments, or countries and when deciding which business strengths (competitive advantages) to invest in.

For example, in Figure 32-5, segments are arrayed by their attractiveness and the strength of the

business in that segment. Segment attractiveness might be a function of size, price insensitivity, lack of appropriate offerings in the marketplace (they're "under-served"), or a number of other qualities. Business strength might be a function of such things as current market penetration (share), fit between competitive advantages and the segment's needs, proximity or access to the segment, and the like. This firm would then assess the array to choose target markets and to prioritize the development of new or future strengths. This firm should likely target the "Retirees," if it hasn't already. The firm should avoid allocating resources toward attracting the "Single Professionals"; they are a bad fit with the firm's

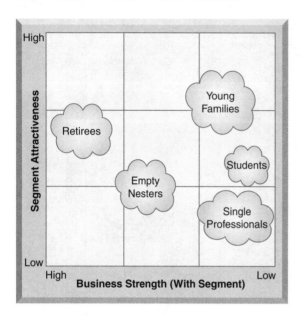

FIGURE NOTE 32-5 GE/McKinsey Grid for Hypothetical Segments of Customers

more money to spend, are less price sensitive, tend to be more loyal, or somehow are attractive in an important way). Very similar analyses could assort specific customers or entire countries with regard to their attractiveness and the firm's strengths to serve them, aiding in everything from account selection in sales force management to planning for international expansion.

The GE/McKinsey Grid also has some important limitations. In particular, because the assessment factors have to be selected, weighted, and evaluated by managers, there is greater subjectivity in this model at each step in the process than in the BCG Matrix (note that the subjectivity of distinguishing the distinct products or strategic business units and defining the market for each product/SBU is an issue in both analytic frameworks). This subjectivity is especially problematic when planners are inexperienced and when they evaluate *their own* business units. Unsurprisingly, when these analyses are done by product or SBU managers, their evaluations commonly avoid placing business units in a weak competitive position and/or in unattractive markets. Finally, like the BCG Matrix, the GE/McKinsey Grid is most often a snapshot of strength and attractiveness at a particular time, unless trends are specifically incorporated into the summary variables (i.e., unless trends in business strength variables or market attractiveness variables are specifically incorporated into the analysis).

strengths and are, in any case, an unattractive target market. The firm might be well-advised to develop strengths that would fit well with the "Young Families" or "Students" because, although the firm's strengths and offerings are not currently well-suited to those segments, those segments are the most attractive in the market (maybe they are growing, have

Summary

Portfolio logic arrays competitive position against market attractiveness in matrix form. The growth/share matrix (a crossing of the concepts of product/market evolution and cost and share leverage) offers generic strategies for four (BCG) to nine (GE) polar product/market positions. Where the BCG model is based on two dimensions, market growth rate and relative market share, the GE model is based on multiple dimensions summed to two: market attractiveness and competitive position. However, market growth rate is but one measure of market attractiveness—there are many others. Likewise, relative market share is just one measure of competitive position and there are many others. The nine GE positions more or less map to the four position of the BCG model, just with

more granularities. In the simplest case then, for BCG we have the following summary:

- Low share/high growth—the question mark or problem child, which either needs significant investment to improve position (build share) during market growth, or probably should be divested. Often, this quadrant can be viewed as cash flow negative.
- High share/high growth—the star, whose share should at least be maintained and should continue to receive enough investment dollars to maintain or increase its distance from competitors. This quadrant is likely a cash flow neutral one as we are reinvesting whatever we make.

- High share/low growth—the cash cow, which should get just enough investment to maintain share and because of low growth, market maturity, and low cost (further down the cost curve) should throw off significant cash to fund either other stars or problem children.

- Low share/low growth—the dog, which should eventually die, it is just a question of how fast, because it has neither leverage from cost or share nor the advantages of a growth market.

Additional Resources

Day, George S. "Diagnosing the Product Portfolio." *The Journal of Marketing*. 41, no. 2 (April 1977): 29–38.

Hax Arnoldo C., and Nicolas S. Majluf. "The Use of the Industry Attractiveness-Business Strength Matrix in Strategic Planning." *Interfaces* 13, no. 2 (1983): 54–71

Hedley, Barry. "Strategy and the 'Business Portfolio.'" *Long Range Planning* 10 (February 1977): 9–15.

Zook, Chris, with James Allen. *Profit from the Core: Growth Strategy in an Era of Turbulence* (Boston, MA: Harvard Business School Publishing).

Endnotes

1. Barry Hedley, "Strategy and the "Business Portfolio," *Long Range Planning* 10 (February 1977); 9–15.
2. Ibid.
3. The BCG Portfolio Matrix from the Product Portfolio Matrix, © 1970, The Boston Consulting Group.
4. Data source: BITKOM (2007), Die Zukunft der digitalen Consumer Electronics. Berlin: BITKOM.
5. Patricia Anslinger, Justin Jenk, and Ravi Chanmugan, "The Art of Strategic Divestment," *Journal of Applied Corporate Finance* 15, no. 3 (2003): 97–101.
6. Adrian Haberberg and Alison Rieple, *Strategic Management: Theory and Application* (Oxford: Oxford University Press, 2008).
7. See Arnoldo C. Hax and Nicolas S. Majluf, "The Use of the Industry Attractiveness-Business Strength Matrix in Strategic Planning," *Interfaces* 13, no. 2 (1983): 54–71; Darrell Rigby, *Management Tools 2003: An Executive's Guide* (Two Copley Place, Boston: Bain & Company, 2003); S. Robinson, R. Hitch, and D. Wade, "The Directional Policy Matrix—Tool for strategic planning," *Long Range Planning* 11, no. 3 (1978): 8–15; Michael G. Allen, "Diagramming GE's planning for What's Watt," *Strategy & Planning* 5, no. 5 (1977): 3–9.
8. Adapted from Allen, "Diagramming GE's planning."

33

Pricing Strategies

Of all the marketing mix elements, price is the one (and only) that generates revenues. Price is usually the easiest element of the mix to set and adjust—and is the easiest competitive action to *imitate*. A company's pricing policy can make or break the bottom line.[1] Pricing changes have a stronger impact on profits than revenue increases or reductions in the costs of goods sold. On average, a 5 percent increase in selling price increases earnings before interest and taxes (EBIT) by 22 percent, whereas increasing sales (revenue) by 5 percent increases EBIT by 12 percent, and a 5 percent reduction in costs of goods sold increases EBIT by just 10 percent.[2] Price is also important as a compliment to other mix elements in shaping customers' perceptions of the offering, its quality, and its value and, therefore, setting pricing objectives must be done within the context of the intended positioning and the overall strategy. The following four steps are central to effectively developing pricing strategies and tactics:

1. Define Price Objectives;
2. Analyze Key Elements of Pricing Situation;
3. Define the Pricing Strategy; and
4. Set the Price and the Pricing Tactics.

PRICE OBJECTIVES

Pricing objectives are derived from the marketing strategy and the positioning decisions the firm has made. Pricing decisions can have short-term or long-term objectives. Two common short-term objectives are survival or maximum current profit:[3]

- *Survival.* In the short run, sales contribute to survival as long as all variable costs are covered. That is, if price is at least as much as the marginal cost of creating each additional unit, then the sale of any additional unit contributes *something* toward overhead. Therefore, the *minimum* price (the "floor price") is the amount of direct variable costs. In the long run, however, prices must be set in such a way that, in aggregate across the assortment, all the *fixed costs* are also covered and the company earns a profit.
- *Maximum current profit.* When a company knows the precise cost and demand functions for its products and markets, it is possible to set price to maximize profits. In reality, however, these parameters are very difficult to gauge precisely. Furthermore, a company that maximizes current profits might sacrifice long-term profits by, for example, ignoring competitor actions.

Three long-term objectives include building market share, market skimming, market penetration, and product positioning:

- **Building and protecting market share.** Low prices can serve to build and to protect market share. By increasing market share, companies expect to lower unit costs due to economies of scale and experience curve effects. A market leader can discourage competitors to enter the industry by cutting prices further as costs fell with increasing experience.
- **Market skimming.** Customers' price sensitivity depends on the product lifecycle and varies across market segments. Many companies "skim" the market by setting high prices for an innovation at the beginning of the lifecycle and targeting price insensitive segments. Later they plan to lower prices step by step to target other customer segments' differing willingness to pay. A skimming strategy foregoes volume for margin.
- **Market Penetration.** The converse of a market skimming strategy (above), which forgoes sales volume to skim high prices from price-insensitive customers, a market penetration strategy entails setting a relatively low price and accepting that lower unit margin in order to gain market share rapidly (i.e., in order to penetrate the market). This strategy is based on the recognition that volume leads to the benefits of scale, including economies of scale and learning curve or experience effects, and that those benefits of scale include lower unit costs. Further, the first brand to penetrate a market enjoys primacy effects including brand equity and customer stickiness (customers who have purchased a product and tend to stay with the brand, sometimes due to inertia and sometimes due to "installed base" of ancillary or support equipment).
- **Product positioning.** The price is an important positioning variable. A premium price can serve to position the product as the quality leader in the category. In many categories, especially those in which intrinsic quality is difficult

to judge, price is an important quality cue; customers may not only infer quality during shopping but may also actually perceive more expensive alternatives as actually being of higher quality or greater prestige while consuming the product. A low price, on the other hand, can increase brand awareness and the product visibility.

ELEMENTS OF PRICING DECISIONS

After the objectives have been formulated, at least four key elements of a pricing should be analyzed:[4] the firm's *costs* and cost structure, its *customers*, its *competition*, and the *legal and ethical implications* of the decision and strategy.

Costs

In the first step, fixed and variable costs are determined. Next, given a certain selling price, the contribution margin (selling price less variable costs) and the break-even-volume (fixed costs divided by contribution margin) can be calculated. A company can also set a profit goal; in this case the target profit is added to the fixed costs to calculate the breakeven volume. In a second step, cost-volume-profit (CVP) analysis can be used to answer questions like: "If prices are raised by 10 percent, how much sales volume can the company afford to lose, if overall profits are at least to be maintained?", or "If prices are reduced by 10 percent, to what extent does sales volume need to increase if overall profits are to be maintained?" CVP analysis builds on some basic, immutable accounting relationships between price, sales and production in units, and costs. For example, total sales revenue is equal to price (per unit revenue) times the number of units sold. Total variable cost (the total of those costs that vary directly with units produced) is equal to variable costs per unit times the number of units sold. Overhead is equal to both marketing overhead (advertising costs, sales force expenses, etc.) and general administrative overhead. Figure 33-1 organizes these relationships graphically. These basic relationships allow for accurate assessment objectives, such as breaking even and

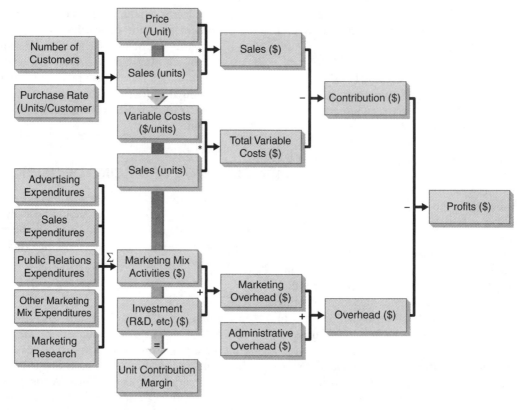

FIGURE NOTE 33-1 Cost-Volume-Profit Relationships

target profits, and of the effects of proposed changes in price on changes in units sold (demand) and on profitability.

The following example illustrates these analyses:

Sample Cost-Volume-Profit Analysis

A mechanical engineering company has developed a new device to test the crashworthiness of car components using simulation software. The marketing strategy is to sell this device to auto manufacturers. The CVP parameters are shown in Table 33-1.

One of the first questions management would want to ask would be *how many units of the software they would need to sell to "breakeven"*; that is, to have revenues exactly equal to total

TABLE NOTE 33-1 Cost-Volume-Profit Parameters for a Sample Analysis

Fixed costs (e.g., R&D, production facilities, marketing):	$4,100,000	
Target profit	$2,000,000	
Variable costs (e.g., variable manufacturing & marketing costs)	$77,000	
Selling price	$120,000	
Contribution margin	$43,000	(35.8%)

costs (variable costs per unit times units produced plus fixed costs or overhead):

$$(\bar{P}^*Q) = (VC/u^*Q) + FC$$

We can solve this equation for Q (the breakeven quantity in units) by subtracting (VC/u * Q) from both sides and then dividing by (P − VC/u), leading to the breakeven formula:

$$Q_{be} = \frac{FC}{\left(\bar{P} - \dfrac{VC}{u}\right)}$$

If management wanted to change that analysis slightly to include target profit—that is, to ask how many units sold would cover all costs plus contribute the target profit, the breakeven formula could be adjusted to include target profit with the fixed costs (p denotes "profit" or, in this case, target profit):

$$Q\pi = \frac{FC + Target\ Profit}{\left(\bar{P} - \dfrac{VC}{u}\right)}$$

Plugging in the data from the example presented in Table 33-1, the mechanical engineering company would use compute:

$$Q_{be} = \frac{\$4,100,000}{\$120,000 - \$77,000} = 96$$

To calculate the level of sales/production required to breakeven and make the desired target profit ($2,000,000) the formula is adjusted:

$$Q\pi = \frac{\$4,100,000 + \$2,000,000}{\$120,000 - \$77,000} = 142$$

These illustrative calculations assume that variable costs per unit and overhead stay the same across levels of production. Variable cost usually is static across only some specific range of production; those costs will go down with increasing production or scale due to economies of scale and learning or experience curve effects. Likewise, the costs of many

elements of overhead will, in reality, look like steps across levels of production; a certain investment in overhead is able to support certain levels of sales and production; when sales and production levels go over that level or capacity then the overhead must be expanded in increments or "steps."

Cost-Volume-Profit Analysis is also invaluable in evaluating the effects of price changes. Any change in price is likely to have a direct effect on demand: A price increase will increase revenue and margin per unit and, as a rule, lower demand; and a price decrease will lower revenues per unit but increase demand. The trade-offs in price changes and consequent changes in demand can also be evaluated directly using the basic CVP logic.[5]

Customers

Many companies use markup pricing to determine the selling price; whatever the costs of the product are, they mark that amount up a set percentage to arrive at the list price. Others use "market pricing," or mark-to-market, charging a traditional or "everybody's doing it" price. These are simple and low-risk methods, but they don't consider the customers' *perceived value* or *willingness to pay* from the customers' perspective, and therefore may miss opportunities. More sophisticated considerations are not based on the product's cost but begin, instead, with the customers' willingness to pay and the customers' perceived value and value function to determine prices.

Table 33-3 presents real data from the automobile industry, showing that a car feature's costs do not correspond to customers' willingness to pay. For example, customers are willing to pay €340 for the metallic color option, which costs just €20 to add to the vehicle, while they are only willing to pay €260 for a sunroof, but adding a sunroof costs the manufacturer €350. If the manufacturer charged a set percentage mark-up on the color and the sunroof they'd be leaving a lot of money on the table when selling the metallic color and likely dissuading customers from purchasing the sunroof option altogether. Margin is the difference between costs and price; in Table 33-2 margins are shown as percentages of selling price. For example, customers are willing to pay €340 for the

TABLE NOTE 33-2 Product's Cost versus Willingness to Pay for Car Components[6]

Product Feature	Customer's Willingness to Pay	Product Costs	Margin
Metallic color	340	20	94%
Light-alloy wheels	220	140	36%
Air condition	750	550	27%
Sun roof	260	350	−35%
Navigation System	310	450	−45%

metallic color option; if the pricing manager used willingness to pay instead of some predetermined markup, the price for the color would be € 340. The metallic color costs just € 20 to add to the vehicle. Thus, the margin is € 320, a 94 percent margin (320 margin/340 price = 94% percentage margin).

This same logic can be used in new product development to set target costs for alternatives; when developing a new product, target costs are often an important starting point. For example, if the marketer has determined that customers are willing to pay € 310 for a navigation system but the current alternatives cost € 450 to add to a vehicle, as shown in Table 33-3, the new product development project might focus on developing a barebones navigation system that satisfies customer needs but that also costs less than € 310 to produce.

Competitors

The third element of a pricing decision is competition. Important questions include: *What are the competitors' prices? What are competitors' costs and, therefore, their floor prices? What are their pricing strategies, tactics, and intentions?* Although price-setting *collusion* is illegal, price *signaling* is an important reality in interpreting competitive strategies and intentions and in setting prices. The various rivals in a market signal their pricing policies and intentions to customers and to competitors via statements and actions. Advertising "we match all competitors' prices," for example, may signal to customers that a retailer is the low-price alternative but that policy signals competitors that dropping price will not lead to sustainable advantage; the expectation is that everyone will therefore maintain pricing norms.

Unfortunately, an insidious pattern in many competitive markets is the tendency to follow the competition into *price wars*. During the Christmas retail-season of 2009, for example, Walmart.com, the retailing behemoth's online store, marked down the ten best selling books in its assortment to $10. Amazon.com responded to the "opening salvo" and matched Wal-Mart's prices on the same 10 titles. Wal-Mart then dropped its price to $8.99, which Amazon again matched. (Target got into the fight with an $8.99 price point.) Wal-Mart dropped its price to $8.98 (a penny below Target's price). Amazon and Target did not counter the $8.98 price. Of course, none of these competitors made any money on sales at the low-price point. Nevertheless, Wal-Mart succeeded in signaling to customers and competitors that it was a serious player in the online-book sector. Amazon succeeded in signaling that it would respond to any competitive price threat. Target stayed in the game. Who lost this price war? In the long run, small book retailers lost to the large online players, and consumers may have lost, too. The online price competitors signaled to each other and the world that they would not be beaten on price—and all entrants are now, it seems likely, preparing to compete on something else.[7]

Legal and Ethical Considerations

Finally, legal and ethical issues also need to be considered in setting prices. Legal constraints proscribe overt price collusion between competitors, predatory pricing, deceptive pricing, price fixing in channels of distribution, and price discrimination across customers or channels. These myriad laws and regulations are complex and dynamic. For example, in the United States *any* price fixing between vertical channel members, most commonly a manufacturer setting a minimum price for its distributors or retailers, was illegal *per se* for almost a century. Recently, however, the United States Supreme Court changed its interpretation of those laws, allowing manufacturers to, in some cases, implement pricing policies on its resellers.[8] In Europe, on the other hand, many countries still prohibit "sales" (temporary price reductions on items or on entire assortments) and presale price announcements, a regulation that dampens price competition among retailers.[9]

Ethical standards should shape *all* managerial and strategic decision making, as they should personal decision making, and that includes pricing decisions. One of the most notorious cases of unethical and ill-advised strategic decision making relates to the earlier example of customers'-willingness-to-pay and the cost-of-automobile options. In the early 1970s, Ford Motor Company recognized that there might be safety issues with the subcompact Pinto's gas tank rupturing in relatively low-speed collisions.[10] Ford executives made the cost-benefit calculation that the cost of adding safety features, which was at most $11 per car and likely a lot less, outweighed the benefits of saving the victims' lives and wellbeing, which were callously appraised at a little more than $200,000 per life and $67,000 per burn victim. Ford argued that car buyers were not interested in paying more for safety features; CEO Lee Iacocca was quoted as saying "Safety doesn't sell."[11]

In hindsight it is clearly appropriate to criticize Ford and Iacocca—the company and its executives failed to apply the same standards to their professional decision making that they would, presumably, have applied instinctively to their personal behaviors—but in the context of the commercial, legal, and regulatory environments of the time, their decisions seemed prudent. Nevertheless, as with all marketing-strategy decisions and as with all professional behavior, ethical standards should have prevailed over cost-benefit analyses, worries about retooling costs, prevailing regulatory standards, or perceptions of customers' willingness to pay. Ford's analyses and rationale were documented in a memorandum that laid out the cost-benefit analysis, and when it was revealed in a prominent expose by Mark Downie in *Mother Jones*,[12] it triggered an embarrassing and expensive public furor, a costly recall, and extended legal difficulties. The Pinto brand was destroyed; it was soon withdrawn from the market by Ford. The Ford brand itself was damaged. Even without those fiscal and brand losses, Ford, the Pinto, and the decisions made with regard to gas-tank safety remain emblematic of shortsighted overemphasis on analysis and underappreciation of the role of managerial and personal ethics in price and strategy setting.

DEFINE THE PRICING STRATEGY

The company's pricing strategy has to be in line with the core strategy of the business unit. A differentiation strategy, for example, implicates a premium price strategy; a cost leadership strategy usually means low prices. Hence, the core strategy defines the pricing objectives, and the pricing objectives together with customer, cost, competitor, and legal and ethical aspects set the framework for the pricing strategy. There are several important concepts that can shape the pricing strategy:

1. The value map;
2. Skimming versus penetration strategies;
3. Razorblade pricing;
4. Price promotions versus brand building; and
5. Premium/prestige pricing.

The Value Map

In most markets, and for most product categories, customers shop for more than the lowest price; fully aware customers *will deliberately pay more to get more*, but informed customers will *not* pay more to get the same, or pay the same (or more) to get less. For example, in the automobile sector, customers who buy a BMW know that they could pay less and get a Toyota or pay more and get a Porsche—or pay even more and get a Ferrari. Those are rational trade-offs, and BMW's customers have chosen their preference. There are stated or implicit trade-offs that customers make when choosing to pay more and get more or to pay less and get less and the value functions that underlie those trade-offs in any market serve to shape a "value frontier" or natural boundary along which customers will make trade-offs. Products that lie to the southeast of that frontier are naturally more attractive—they exceed the value function by offering more quality/performance for the same price or the same quality/performance for a lower price. Offerings that lie to the northwest of the frontier are inherently inferior, dominated by some alternative that offers the same quality/performance for lower price or more quality/performance for the same price. This reality, shown in Figure 33-2, can be used to set pricing strategy and is useful for describing differences across strategies:

- Product A is positioned as the premium brand in the market—it offers the highest quality (differentiation) at the highest price;
- Product C is the price leader—it offers the least quality/performance but offers it at the lowest price;
- Product B's strategy offers superior customer "economy," sometimes called "value" pricing— this offering is to the southeast of the frontier and should be attractive to a large segment of the market because it pushes the value frontier toward the right (offering more quality/ performance for the same price or the same quality/performance for a lower price).
- Product D's position is unfavorable; it offers low-customer value and there are alternatives along the value frontier that dominate it on both quality/performance and price.

The value map is a very practical tool to define the pricing strategy, as it contains all essential information: competitor's quality, competitor's prices, customer's price sensitivity (slope of the fair-value line) and customer value.

SKIMMING VERSUS PENETRATION PRICING. When a new product is introduced, that is, early in the product lifecycle, a company can opt for one of two basic pricing strategies. The choice has implications for operations and the achievement of scale and should be driven by careful consideration. With a skimming strategy, the company sets a high price to "skim" profits from customers with low price sensitivity and high, unmet need for the new product and its advantages. After that market segment has been served, the price is usually lowered so that segments with lower willingness to pay can afford the product. There are a number of requirements for success with a skimming strategy, including a substantial market of customers with low price sensitivity and high unmet needs, a truly innovative product with substantial

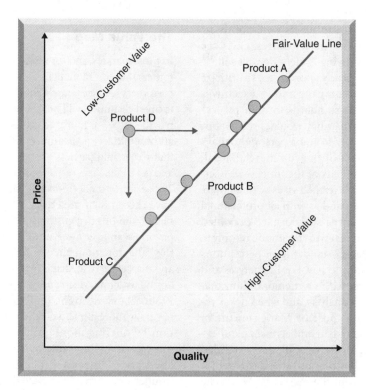

FIGURE NOTE 33-2 The Value Map

advantages and a relatively low risk of imitation, and relatively high market-level barriers to entry (see Table 33-3). Essentially, skimming is possible when the producer has power: a product with real advantages that customers want and will pay for and that others can't copy.

A penetration pricing strategy, on the other hand, aims at quickly gaining substantial market share with a relatively low price. It is used when economies of scale and experience curve effects are available, when a substantial number of customers are price sensitive, when imitation or substitution risk is high, when competitors face low barriers to entry, and when the company is financially strong (because, with a penetration price, contribution margins are lower and, therefore, breakeven volume is high). A penetration strategy basically sets a price that doesn't attract competition and sets production objectives that achieve the cost benefits of volume quickly (which then further dissuades competitors), and requires subsidizing the introductory stage—when costs are still high—in order to gain market presence and the long-term advantages of scale.

"RAZORBLADE" PRICING. Another strategic pricing idea that can be powerful in certain industries and for certain products is "razorblade" or

"razor-and-blade" pricing, sometimes called "freebie marketing." Economist call this a "cross subsidy;" the discount or "freebie" is subsidized by the margins on required supplies. Traditionally, dating back to King Gillette, the inventor of the safety razor, manufacturers have discounted or given away the razors (the handles) with the expectation that those handles would lead to future, plentiful, and profitable sales of the full-margin blades (razor handles are usually cheap, relatively simple to manufacture, and durable, while blades are more expensive, precision manufactured from higher-value materials and need to be replaced frequently).[13] Today, cell phones, water-purification systems, and single-serve "pod" coffee brewing machines are all discounted below costs (and are sometimes free) in strategies designed to lock in a stream of revenues from monthly-calling plans for those cell phones, filters for the water purification systems, and coffee pods for the brewing machines.

Some contemporary strategies are variations of that basic razorblade pricing model. For example, Skype gives away its Voice-over-Internet-Protocol (or VoIP) telephone software and service, anticipating that sufficient customers will upgrade to its premium, for-fee versions to create overall profitability, but there is no requirement that any customer upgrade to

TABLE NOTE 33-3 Skimming versus Penetration Strategy

	Skimming	Penetration
Costs	• Economies of scale and experience curve effects unimportant	• High economies of scale • High experience-curve effects
Customer	• Low price sensitivity • Price is indicator for quality • Early adopter of innovations	• Very price sensitive • Innovation aversive • Trial purchase should be stimulated
Competition	• High prices of competitors • Low risk of imitation • Low risk of substitution • Short product lifecycle (risk of obsolescence before break even) • High market-entry barriers	• Low prices of competitors • High risk of imitation • High risk of substitution • Long product lifecycle • Low market-entry barriers
Company	• Highly innovative product • Differentiation strategy • High-quality and premium brands • Small capacities	• Large capacities • Strong distribution network • Financially strong (low contribution margins, high investments in capacity)

use and take full value from its basic product. RyanAir, the European discount airline, charges below-cost fares—many flights are essentially "free" except for required taxes—but then it charges for almost every additional service, from baggage check-in to snacks, and bombards passengers with offers and advertisements throughout their travel experience; nevertheless, the traveler who doesn't require checked baggage service, who isn't hungry, and who ignores the sales pitches and promotions can take advantage of the travel service itself at the low fare.

Price Promotions versus Brand Building

An important tension that must be considered relates to the short-term benefits of price-based promotions—things like price-off specials at the point of purchase, coupons, and volume deals (buy-one-get-one-free deals or "BOGOs," extra-volume packs, and the like)—and weighing those benefits against their costs and their long-term effects and against alternative investments in promotions that may have more muted but more enduring positive effects. Price-based promotions do have an immediate and often dramatic effect on customer behaviors—*stuff moves off the shelf on discount*—but those are short-term effects. Unfortunately, those short-term effects are made all the more attractive because of the incentive and evaluation systems within which many product managers work, which are often tied to quarterly or annual sales rather than to longer-term brand building. Nevertheless, price-based promotions deteriorate more quickly than investments in brand-building tools like advertising, public relations, experiential promotions, and even sampling. Price-based promotions have certain obvious short-term costs: lost revenue and margins, and the sales lift of price-based promotions are more short-lived than other investments. Price-based promotions can even have negative effects on sales in the long term. Reasons for those long-term and potentially harmful effects of price-based promotions on sales and the brand include

- *The Price–Quality Relationship.* Customers often use price as a signal of quality, so discounting the product lowers their perceptions of the product's price and, therefore, its quality;
- *Resentment.* Customers come to expect the reduced price and may resent the "price increase" to what the manufacturer believes is the "regular" price; and
- *Accelerating/Waiting.* Customers learn to buy ahead when a product is on discount and to wait when it is not. That is, they shift purchases across time in order to take advantage of price-based promotions.

As shown in Figure 33-3, although brand-building investments such as advertising do decay over time, those effects are long term and gradual and do not decay at the same rate or to the same degree.

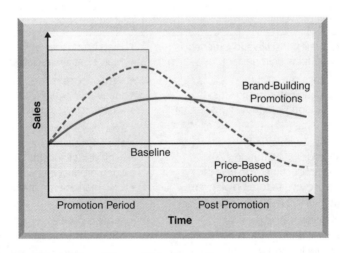

FIGURE NOTE 33-3   Short- and Long-Term Effects of Price Promotions

Another pricing strategy, appropriate for certain brands in certain product categories and for certain customers, prestige pricing, the use of price as an indicator of quality, performance, and status. Quality and performance refer to the actual, physical quality of the product. Status refers to the use of products to seek or communicate social standing or "success." Inferences about both quality/performance and status are drawn from a variety of product-related cues ranging from spokespeople, advertising content, and other consumers of the product to its places of distribution, packaging, *and price.*

Consumers are frequently unable to judge the "actual" quality of various products due to a lack of expertise or the inability to inspect or try a product in advance of purchase. Wine is a good example; most consumers do not understand France's traditional *Appellation d'origine contrôlée* (AOC) wine certification and quality system, nor can they be familiar with the innumerable varieties, vintages, and brands produced across the many wine-making regions of the world. By necessity, many consumers rely on a small set of familiar brands, on point-of-purchase merchandising and in-store information, *and on price.* In this case, rather than reviewing price with simple "minimization" criteria, wine shoppers use price as an indicator of quality. This is true across a variety of other product categories as well.

An illustrative case of prestige pricing combined with packaging and selective distribution to create a exclusive status image is grappa. Grappa is a brandy made from grape pomace—the dregs of wine making, including grape skins, seeds, and stems—drunk by Italian peasants since the twelfth century. In the late 1980s, producers softened grappa a little, to make it more palatable to upscale tastes, packaged it in elegant designer bottles (including some in hand-blown Murano glass), and put outlandish prices on it (often more than $150 per bottle in the United States). One grappa, Fratelli Marolo, was packaged in "heavy Baccarat crystal decanter decorated with 18-karat gold" and sold in the early 1990s for as much as $2,800 a bottle.[14] Grappa quickly became a fashionable and trendy drink in the New York and Hollywood high society. As one restaurateur observed, grappa was transformed from a "hard liquor for strong, poor, earthbound people to

an elegant, fruity and pricey spirit of considerable appeal to the affluent, urbane international consumer."[15] Prestige pricing is about understanding when and how consumers use price as a cue for quality, scarcity, and prestige, and then using price along with the other elements of the marketing mix to achieve that premium positioning.

SETTING AND ADJUSTING THE PRICE

The final price must be consistent with the core strategy and with the pricing objectives. Competitive reactions, changes in consumer and buyer behavior, variations in demand and in costs, and other changes, however, require that a company adapts prices to changing circumstances. There are a number of tactics that can be used to respond to such challenges,[16] such as:

- *Price discounts and allowances* (e.g., quantity discounts, seasonal discounts);
- *Promotional pricing* (e.g., cash rebates, low-interest financing, longer payment terms; discussed above);
- *Price differentiation* (e.g., customer segment, channel, location, or time differentiation);
- *Price bundling and complementary pricing* (e.g., low price for inkjet printers, high price for ink cartridges); and
- *Yield management* (e.g., setting prices depending on the booking situation of an airline, i.e., low prices for travelers who buy the ticket well in advance, and high prices for those who book later)

The short- versus long-term implications of discounts and price-based promotions were discussed above; in general, discounting is very persuasive with regard to motivating purchase behavior but can be damaging to the long-term health of the brand and the firm. When price adjustments are applied, it is of utmost importance that its effects on demand and on profits are estimated. Depending on the contribution margin, it may well be that a 10 percent discount requires a 50 percent increase of sales volume if overall profits are to be maintained (see CVP analysis, above).

Summary

Pricing is too often an afterthought to strategic planning. Managers routinely rely on their cost structure or market norms to set prices, but pricing can be a powerful element of a coherent strategy. Prices can accelerate cash flow or hasten the benefits of scale. Price can attract customers and price can engage customers in long-term and profitable relationships. Price can signal quality, and price-based promotions can signal mediocrity and teach customers to shop by price rather than for benefits. As this note has reviewed, effective pricing strategies consider costs, customers, competitors, and positioning objectives to maximize profits within long-term relationships.

Additional Resources

Dolan, Robert J. and Hermann Simon. *Power Pricing*. New York: Simon & Schuster, 1996.

Guidry, F., J. Horrigan, and C. Craycraft. "CVP analysis—A New Look," *Journal of Managerial Issues*. 74–85, 10 , no. 1 (1998).

Thomas T. Nagle, John Hogan, and Joseph Zale. *The Strategy and Tactics of Pricing: A Guide to Growing More Profitably*, 5th ed. Upper Saddle River, NJ, Prentice Hall, 2010.

Hinterhuber, Andreas. "Towards Value-Based Pricing—An Integrative Framework for Decision Making." *Industrial Marketing Management* 33 (2004): 765–778.

Endnotes

1. Robert J. Dolan and Hermann Simon, *Power Pricing* (New York: Simon & Schuster, 1996).

2. Andreas Hinterhuber, "Towards Value-Based Pricing—An Integrative Framework for Decision Making," *Industrial Marketing Management* 33 (2004): 765–778.

3. Adapted from Philip Kotler and Kevin L. Keller, *Marketing Management*, 13th ed. (Upper Saddle River, NJ: Pearson Education, 2009).

4. Adapted from David W. Cravens and Nigel F. Piercy, *Strategic Marketing*, 8th ed. (Boston: McGraw Hill, 2006). And Hinterhuber, "Towards Value-based Pricing."

5. F. Guidry, J. Horrigan, and C. Craycraft, "CVP Analysis—A New Look," *Journal of Managerial Issues* 10, no. 1 (1998): 74–85.

6. Source: Simon, Kucher & Partners, a Germany-based consulting firm

7. See James Surowiecki, "Priced to Go," *The New Yorker* 85, no. 36 (November 9, 2009), and Brad Stone and Stephanie Rosenbloom, "Price War Brews Between Amazon and Wal-Mart," *The New York Times*, November 24, 2009, page A1.

8. *Leegin Creative Leather Products, Inc. v. PSKS, Inc.* [2007] 551 U.S. 877.

9. See, for example, "Shop-worn arguments," *The Economist* 386, no. 8561 (January 2008): 46.

10. See Mark Downie, "Pinto Madness," *Mother Jones* 2 (September–October, 1977): 18–32; and, Matthew T. Lee, "The Ford Pinto Case and the Development of Auto Safety Regulations, 1893-1978," *Business and Economic History* 27, no. 2 (Winter 1998): 390–401.

11. Ibid.

12. Ibid.

13. Gordon McKibben, *Cutting edge: Gillette's Journey to Global Leadership* (Boston: Harvard Business Press, 1998)

14. G. Buchalter and J. Levine, "Italian White Lightning," *Forbes* 147, no. 4 (1991): 94–95. Online database EBSCOhost, *Academic Search Premier.*, www.epnet.com/ehost/login.html. Last accessed on July 10, 2010.

15. Al Bassano, "Grappa: Italian 'White Lightning' Goes Upscale," *Beverage Network*, (March 2005) available at www.bevnetwork.com/pdf/mar05_grappa.pdf and www.bevnetwork.com/monthly_issue_article.asp?ID=106. Last accessed (both) on July 10, 2010.

16. See for example Philip Kotler and Gary Armstrong, *Principles of Marketing* (Upper Saddle River, NJ: Prentice Hall, 2005).

34

Promotion and People— Integrated Marketing Communications

"Doing business without advertising is like winking at a girl in the dark. You know what you are doing, but nobody else does."

STUART HENDERSON BRITT, 1956[1]

Today, Professor Britt's observation about advertising applies more accurately to the whole assortment of marketing communications tools, which includes everything from advertising, point-of-purchase displays, and price-off coupons to press releases, the "placement" of products in movies, and consultative sales initiatives. Doing business without an effective program to communicate the firm's value proposition to customers is like "winking in the dark." Integrated marketing communications—*how the firm tells its target customers about its offerings and value propositions and moves customers to purchase*—are essential to strategic success. The "integrated" characterization emphasizes the fact that customers have many "points of contact" with a firm across a variety of occasions and a variety of media. Each of those occasions is an opportunity to build equity with the customer. In an effective strategy, each of these points of contact will deliver consistent, even synergistic messages and experiences that build on each other to develop and reinforce a singular position for the brand. Entire courses and texts are available on these topics.[2] This note is a strategic overview highlighting the range of tools and basic strategic frameworks of integrated marketing communications.

THE COMMUNICATIONS MIX

Although consumers watch more television than ever (today Americans averaged more than four-and-a-half hours of television *per day*[3]), mass media has fragmented, and media habits have changed. Television channels have proliferated—the average American home receives almost 125 channels[4]—and "viewing," which was once a family event, now may mean anything from having the television on as "background" for other activities to recording shows to watch at different times and on different devices. Other technologies, including the Internet, personal music players, satellite radio, and video games have all taken consumers' time away from traditional broadcast media. In this fragmented media environment, marketers can no longer rely on advertising to reach mass audiences efficiently; instead, they utilize an increasingly diverse set of communications tools appropriately mixed to develop truly integrated marketing communication programs.

The communications mix has traditionally been defined as comprising advertising, personal selling, sales promotions, and public relations. In addition, new hybrid tools have emerged, including event and "experiential" promotions, "brand ambassador" programs, and the Internet. Labeling or categorizing these and other new tactics is not particularly important and novel sorts of communications appear everyday, but understanding differences in the way the tools affect customers is invaluable. Table 34-1 presents basic characteristics of the core elements of the communication mix and summarizes their strengths and weaknesses:

- *Advertising.* Advertising entails communicating messages via paid-for, impersonal media (television, radio, newspapers, etc.) in which the sponsor is identified or known. Because advertising includes everything from multi-million-dollar television commercials shown on the Super Bowl to weekly grocery inserts in local newspapers, it is a very broad category, and difficult to treat as one. In general, it is effective at building awareness and interest and for communicating vivid images and ineffective at communicating extensive information. Advertising suffers from significant waste, clutter, and consumer skepticism.

- *Direct.* Direct communications such as direct mail, telemarketing, and e-mail contacts are perhaps a form of advertising. However, they are distinct in that they take advantage of advances in computer and database power to *target customers* with communications that are "personalized" (but usually not truly personal) and to *track customer responses* to those communications. Marketers have the ability to collect, maintain, and analyze large databases of

customer contact information and to buy similar customer data from a variety of vendors. Using those data to target customers with messages as well as to customize offerings is a powerful tool, but it has also spawned overwhelming clutter and increasing resentment. Direct marketing messages, especially electronic points of contact, are unique in their ability to track responses and to connect directly with order taking and fulfillment.

- *Sales.* Sales or "personal selling" involves individualized and interactive (two-way) communications, including one-on-one meetings, presentations, and personal communications targeted to the individual customer or "account." Sales programs are capable of communicating and customizing large amounts of information (from the marketer to target customer *and from the customer to the marketer and firm*). Personal selling is effective at moving customers to trial and adoption—that is, personal selling is capable of "closing the deal" and follow-on support. Personal selling is poorly suited to creating broad awareness or interest because, although absolute costs of sales programs can be modest, especially compared with those for advertising, the cost per exposure (the cost of each sales call or contact) is generally high. The structure of sales relationships for many business-to-business products has deepened toward consultative "partnerships," with sales engineers working closely with customers to create customized solutions to their problems, sometimes even maintaining offices in the customers' facilities.

- *Sales Promotions.* Sales promotions are short-term incentives intended to move customers to "action" (to purchase). Sales promotions include offers to consumers and to retail partners or "the trade." The variety of creative sales promotions has expanded a great deal and the distinction between sales promotions and other promotion mix elements, including advertising, has blurred. Price-based consumer sales promotions (coupons, deals, and volume deals such as "bonus packs") are effective at increasing

TABLE NOTE 34-1 Characteristics of the Elements of the Communications Mix

CHARACTERISTICS	ADVERTISING		DIRECT		PROMOTION				PERSONAL SELLING	PUBLIC RELATIONS	INTER-PERSONAL	
					Point of Purchase	Consumer Price Promotions	Sampling	Trade Promotions			Word-of-Mouth	Viral
Mass v. Addressable	Mass	Mass	Mass	Mass	Mass	Mass	Addressable	Mass	Individual	Mass	Addressable	Mass
Paid/Unpaid Media	Paid	Paid	Paid	Paid	Paid	Paid	Paid	Paid	Paid	Unpaid	Paid	Paid
One-Way v Interactive	One-Way	One-Way	Trackable	Interactive	One-Way	One-Way	One-Way	Trackable	Interactive	One-Way	—	Two-Way
Awareness (Persuasive)	☆											
Interest (Persuasive)												
Decision/Trial (Persuasive)					☆	☆	☆	☆	☆			
Adoption (Persuasive)												
Information Content												
Vivid/Image		☆										☆
Credibility										☆	☆	
Control									☆			
Reach	☆			☆								
Waste			☆						☆			
Clutter												
Absolute Expense												
Cost per exposure												

☆ - Outstanding strength.

Strength | Weakness

301

sales in the short term but also have notewor-thy shortcomings in the longer term. These shortcomings include foregone revenue, degradation of brand image (due to price–quality inferences), and "training" cus-tomers to expect deals and to hasten or delay purchases (i.e., to buy earlier or later to take advantage of promotions). The trade-offs between brand building and price-based pro-motions will be discussed further below.

• **Public Relations.** Public relations encom-passes the management of the firm's complex relationships with its many "publics" or con-stituencies, including regulators, public inter-est groups, the media, and customers. Public relations includes "publicity," which specifi-cally entails efforts to gain *mediated coverage,* especially by journalists (i.e., "press coverage"), that appears as articles or segments in unpaid-for space (in newspapers or electronic media) rather than in paid-for (advertising) space. Publicity has great *credibility* because of its mediated quality but there is an intractable *loss of control* with that mediation; journalists can report negative stories as easily as they can pos-itive stories. Publicity is most effective for in-novations that compel interest; the press is less likely to cover more mature products.

• **Inter-Customer Communications.** The impor-tance of communications *between customers* has increased in the contemporary climate of media fragmentation, clutter, and filtering. "Buzz" marketing includes interpersonal communica-tions (literally word of mouth), electronic inter-customer communications, including the mass forwarding of content and messages ("viral" marketing) and inter-customer obser-vations, which are especially important in the diffusion of new-to-the-world, disruptive inno-vations. Inter-consumer communications are powerful—buyers trust and respond to recom-mendations and to complaints heard from other customers far more readily than they re-spond to paid-for communications from mar-keters—but inter-consumer communications are also the least controllable element of the communication mix.

Each of these categories of tools in the mar-keter's repertoire perform some tasks well and other tasks less well (see Table 34-1). For example, point-of-purchase promotions , which encompass in-store merchandising (e.g., displays, shelf-coupons, and sig-nage), are good at influencing cross-brand decisions and moving consumers to act, but they are not good at creating awareness or building category demand, and they can get lost in the clutter of the contempo-rary shopping environment. Imaginative and re-sourceful new tactics are being devised everyday that do not necessarily fit neatly into a single category in the traditional communication-mix framework but that are, nevertheless, persuasive and effective. Today, few communication programs rely on only one or even just a couple of the tools in the communication mix. The best are truly "integrated" campaigns in which multiple tools are used *and coordinated* so that customers' contacts with the firm are consistent and "on strategy" and so that the tools interact to create and reinforce a strong message and to claim a singular position in consumer perceptions.

For example, in 2007 Unilever's AXE® brand of men's hygiene products—which targets men from 11 to 24—created carnival-like "experiences" on university campuses across the United States, invit-ing students to, among other things, jump into (and become part of) an enormous ice cream sundae complete with sauces and whipped cream, to mud wrestle, and to take part in an enormous food fight. Afterwards, students washed off in glass-walled showers using AXE® shower gel and received AXE® samples and gifts (see Figure 34-1). The events were tied to a campaign that included the creation of the *World's Dirtiest Film* starring David Spade and featur-ing video segments submitted online by consumers, and product placement on relevant television shows, such as "Jimmy Kimmel Live" as well as print and television advertising designed to drive traffic to as-sociated Web sites. The events spawned buzz and newspaper coverage on campuses. College papers major national media, including the New York Times,[5] wrote articles about the on-campus events surrounding the AXE campaign. Were these events and online collaborations "advertising," "sales pro-motions," or "publicity"? *It didn't matter!* They were imaginative (and a bit risqué), they cut through the

FIGURE NOTE 34-1   AXE® Campus Event

clutter, they reinforced a consistent message claiming a unique place in the target consumers' perceptions ("*fun in the 'mating game'*"), and importantly, the program increased brand awareness, brand understanding, and sales.

THE COMMUNICATIONS MANAGEMENT PROCESS

In order to create, manage, and evaluate a successful integrated marketing campaign, the manager should proceed through a process of specifying the target segments, gauging those customers' current relationship with the product or brand, establishing strategic objectives, setting the campaign budget, implementing the program, and finally evaluating the effort. Even ongoing, continuous communications programs, such as routine sales activities, will benefit from periodically going through these steps.

1 Specifying the Target Market and Segments

Targeting is the "matching" of some segment of customers and their specific needs with the firm and its sustainable competitive advantages. The crucial question in targeting is: *What specific needs of which specific customers can the firm meet better than the competition at a profit?* Spelling out the target market and target segments/needs is the essential first step in any communication program. A number of basic characteristics of the target market, buyer behavior, and the product itself dictate fundamental differences in appropriate and effective communication mixes available to the marketer:

- *Type of Market.* Businesses buy differently than consumers, and, as a result, B2B markets are different than consumer markets. Businesses use purchasing agents and "buy centers," teams of users and experts, to make large, generally more expensive purchases often based on technical specifications and explicit procurement procedures. B2B communications are, therefore, dominated by personal selling.

- **Target Market Concentration and Addressability.** The more concentrated a market is and the more easily addressed the entities in the market are, the more likely it is that personal selling can be used to engage the market. "Addressability" refers to the ability of the marketer to identify and list or catalogue the members of a target market segment. For example, a pharmaceutical marketer can easily obtain a list of medical practices and doctors, complete with contact information and specialization such as pediatrics or geriatrics. On the other hand, it would be nearly impossible to create a similar database of all mothers of ill toddlers or all elderly citizens. The physicians market is highly addressable while the patient market is not easily addressed.

- **Order Size/Cost.** Within both business and consumer markets, the size of a typical order and especially the total cost and margin of orders drive differences in the way buyers behave and the sorts of communications that can be used to connect with consumers. Expensive goods and high total-cost orders often require personal sales, and their margins justify and support sales efforts. Lower-cost goods are less well-suited to personal selling but do respond to wide reach, low-cost-per-exposure communications such as advertising and sales promotions.

- **Type of Product.** Not only do the cost, typical order size, and typical margin influence the types of communications programs that can and should be used effectively, so do other characteristics of the product such as technological sophistication or complexity, required customer support and installation, and the need for customization. Complex products require more information and significant training (or "hand holding"), and information and training are best delivered via personal selling. Products that require customization or

tailoring are also a good fit with personal selling and less well-suited to mass communications. Marketers of low-cost, low-tech, low-risk, and low-involvement products, on the other hand, may well use mass forms of communications to remind consumers of the brand and can give the brand with emotional or social meaning.

- **The Stage in the Product Lifecycle.** Innovations in the early stages of the product lifecycle require more "hand-holding" and technical support. As the product lifecycle evolves, customers gain experience and expertise and need less sales and service support or hand-holding. At the same time, in the introductory stage, innovations may command greater attention from the media, making the use of publicity viable, and from customers who will more readily engage in inter-customer communications. Later in the lifecycle core benefits become widely available across product alternatives, peripheral benefits and attributes, including brand image become more important, and advertising can serve to build brand image and to remind customers of the need and of the brand.

- **Available Commercial Infrastructure and Cultural Differences.** In adapting communications to the international markets or in developing global campaigns, it is important to recognize that many economies lack the communications infrastructure enjoyed in the developed world. In the developing world, mass media are gaining penetration and more and more of the population has access to radio, television, and newspapers, but that reach is still far lower than it is in the developed world. Similarly, direct communications that rely on the Internet or postal services are less reliable and have lower reach in the developing world. Even across developed, industrialized economies, customers respond differently to different promotion mix elements and certainly to different "copy" or arguments in persuasive messages, and those cultural differences will also drive differences in effective communication programs.

TABLE NOTE 34-2 Customer Readiness/Response Hierarchy Models

Business to Business			Consumer	
Decision Process[6]	**Sales Funnel**[7]	**Hierarchy of Effects**[8]	**Consumer Decision Making Process**[9]	**Adoption Process**[10]
Problem Recognition	Leads	Awareness	Need/Problem Recognition	Awareness
General Need Description		Knowledge	Information Search	Interest
Product Specification	Suspects	Liking	Evaluation of Alternatives	Evaluation
Supplier Search		Preference		
Proposal Solicitation	Prospects	Conviction		Trial
Supplier Selection	Customers	Purchase	Decision	
Order Routine Specification				Adoption
Performance Review			Post-Purchase Behaviors	

2 Determining Customers' *Current* Relationships with the Product/Brand

Shaping integrated communications programs within the context of the overarching marketing strategy, setting appropriate objectives, and evaluating results all require gauging the consumers' current (pre-program) relationships with the product/brand and the purchase decision (consumer "readiness to buy" or readiness). Table 34-2 presents some "hierarchical" or process models of consumer decision making for both business-to-business and consumer markets. Although many such models have been proposed in the literature, they all break down the customer–product relationship into phases or steps, from unaware of the product or the need through awareness and evaluation toward purchase and, ultimately, adoption and "loyalty."

Some strategies and associated communications programs will involve reinforcing or changing a brand's position in consumers' perceptions; in those cases, objectives should be specified in terms of consumers' perceptions and changes in those perceptions, often captured within perceptual maps. Positioning is a combination of several factors, including the targeted customers and their needs, the firm's value proposition, and the intended brand definition—what the brand will promise to deliver better than the competition.

It is also important to gauge the customers' psychological relationship with the need, the product or brand, and the purchase. What are the customers' *motives* for making purchases? How do consumers go about making decisions in this product category? A variety of frameworks for categorizing customer motives and linking those motives to communications efforts have been proposed, most of which address, in one way or another, differences in consumer *involvement* with the product and the decision and distinguish elements of both *thinking* and *feeling* in the way consumers relate to the need and the product. One of the best known, the FCB Grid, will be presented in a little more detail below in this note.

3 Setting Objectives

Any integrated marketing campaign should specify objectives in measurable and specific terms. As a core objective, many communications programs will have customers moving from their *current* readiness or relationship with the decision, established above, toward some *desired* state of readiness, whether that is greater awareness, heightened interest, more inquiries, greater preference, or simply increased sales. As noted, objectives may also include the desired *position* in customer perceptions that the product or brand will claim or "own." Objectives for an integrated communications program should be *specific* and *measurable* and almost always require that baseline or "before" levels be well established.

4 Setting the Budget

There are a few basic approaches to setting communications budgets. Many of these are "reactive"—spending all that the firm can afford, spending a stipulated percentage of sales, or matching the competition (competitive parity). Another approach, objective-based or *task-based* budgeting, is more *proactive*, although the resulting budgets are usually modified by the reality of scarce resources and competing priorities within the firm. Task-based budgeting begins with a set of tasks or objectives that the strategy seeks to accomplish, such as increasing consumer awareness, generating sales leads, or simply boosting sales, and then "backs-up" to the communications activities necessary to accomplish those tasks. Those activities might include things like advertising messages, "mail drops" (direct mailings), or cold calls by the sales force. Once objectives have been translated into specific tasks, it is relatively straightforward to calculate the total budget. Task-based budgeting is preferable to reactive methods such as percent of sales from a strategic point of view because it begins with strategy-related objectives and works its way, via costing out specific activities, to the required resources.

A second set of budgeting considerations is *across tools* or elements of the promotion mix (for example, between sales and advertising or between price promotions and brand-building activities) and between customer acquisition and customer retention. Both of these allocations can be informed by comparing expected returns against costs. Specifically, if the strategist understands the lifetime value of its customers and knows or can estimate the number of customers acquired by each tool under consideration, it is relatively straightforward to compute the expected Return on Investment (ROI) for each tool (advertisements, promotions, etc.) and to make informed choices about investments in those activities. Similarly, if those "yields" and returns are known for elements of an integrated communications program, they can be easily compared with increased profits from enhanced customer retention.

5 Implementing the Program

From a strategic perspective, the critical tasks in integrated communications management focus on specifying the target markets/segments, determining where the target customers are in relationship to the decision and the purchase, and establishing the strategic objectives and budgets. Implementing a communications program is tactical—and complex. There are whole industries devoted to providing communications services, including advertising and public relations firms, direct marketing agencies, media brokers, and agents and distributors who will handle sales as well as distribution functions. It is, nevertheless, important for the strategist to understand the whole communications process and to oversee the tactical implementation of the campaign with emphasis on staying "on strategy."

6 Evaluating the Communications Effort

Measuring the effectiveness and return on a communication program is essential for adjusting and improving communications and to justifying investments. One of the most difficult arguments to make within a firm is for long-term, brand-building investments. Although brand-building activities may not be linked directly to immediate sales or profits, that doesn't mean that brand building doesn't drive sales and financial results, especially long-term results, and it doesn't mean that the long-term and short-term effectiveness of communications programs can't be measured or linked to financial contributions (i.e., "returns" or "return on investment").

Evaluating the effectiveness of a communications effort is predicated on specifically describing the target markets and segments and the pre-campaign relationship of those customers with the product or brand (steps one and two above) and setting detailed, measureable objectives for the campaign (step three above). Establishing customers' pre- and post-campaign relationship with the product generally requires marketing research and, specifically, survey research.

Marketing ROI, or "return on marketing" is a powerful tool for marketing strategists. Return on

Investment is a ratio—the profit earned divided by the investment made to achieve that profit:

$$\text{Marketing ROI} = \frac{\text{Profits}}{\text{Investment (Costs)}}$$

Profits are *not* simply sales or gross revenues—profits are *net contribution* or units sold multiplied by average margins (margin being price minus unit costs). From a strategic perspective, these computations should take into account the *lifetime value of the customer—how much does each acquired customer provide for the firm across the lifetime of his or her relationship with the brand?* This computation—the lifetime value of a customer—can be done for different levels of "readiness" (such as awareness, liking, or commitment; See Table 34-2, above). How much is a percentage gain in awareness worth in increased sales and in increased margins? Knowing what a percentage change in a level of readiness is worth in sales across time (the lifetime value of those customers) allows communications campaigns to be expressed in Return on Investment (ROI) or Return on Marketing Investment (ROMI). If the firm invests $10 million in a campaign that increases awareness by 1 percent, which might for example equal 10,000 customers becoming aware of the brand, and each customer who is aware of the brand has a lifetime value of $150, than the campaign would have a ROI or ROMI of 1.5 (15 million divided by 10 million). This ROI can be compared to alternative uses of the resources (the $10 million), including other communications campaigns or alternative investments.

SOME SPECIFIC STRATEGIC COMMUNICATIONS ISSUES

The following sections detail four specific strategic communications issues, including (1) push versus pull, (2) promotions versus brand building, (3) customer motives and decision making, and (4) business-to-business (B2B) motives and buyer behavior.

Push versus Pull

A basic distinction in marketing communications is between "push" and "pull" strategies. When the focus of a communications program is on building demand at the consumer level it is a "pull" strategy; the consumer demand *pulls* the product through the channel of distribution. That is, distributors, wholesalers, and retailers are motivated to stock and sell the product because of the downstream demand. Sometimes that demand will manifest itself in actual requests from consumers to retailers to stock a product; retailers would then ask their wholesalers for the product, wholesalers would ask their distributors or brokers, and so forth. While the idea that consumers literally request the product may help illustrate the idea underlying a "pull" strategy, actual consumer requests aren't necessary or even typical. Usually a pull campaign builds demand at the level of the ultimate consumer using mass communications tools like advertising while also selling to distributors, wholesalers, and retailers to persuade them to stock and sell the product, often using evidence from research and other markets to show that consumers will buy the product once it's on the shelves. It is the *relative emphasis* on generating demand at the consumer level that distinguishes a "pull" strategy.

A "push" strategy, on the other hand, emphasizes building demand in the channel of distribution, especially at the next level "down" the channel. The manufacturer emphasizes sales efforts directed toward distributors; distributors then sell to wholesalers who sell to customers or retailers (who sell to consumers). Those selling efforts persuade the channel members to stock and sell the product and then the channel members' sales force works to sell the product to the next channel entities. Push strategies emphasize direct selling and trade promotions, and are typically found in B2B markets.

Although "push versus pull" makes for a neat dichotomy, most marketing communications campaigns include elements of *both*, and the real distinction is a matter of degree. For example, Coca-Cola, an iconic global consumer brand famous for massive advertising and consumer-marketing programs, also has an elaborate and highly regarded sales organization working closely with channel members, from bottlers to distributors, retailers, and restaurateurs, to build distribution and facilitate consumption. Similarly, although selling military planes is a long, intensive "push" process of lobbying and bidding to governments, Northrop Grumman, Boeing, and other large defense contractors in the United States also uses mass media, including advertising in major national newspapers, to reinforce the brand and to build goodwill amongst opinion leaders, lawmakers, and the general public.

Promotions versus Brand Building

Another basic distinction can be drawn between "brand-building" efforts, including advertising, on the one hand, and price-based promotions. Price promotions such as deals (price-off programs), coupons, and bonus packs tend to have an immediate and marked impact on sales—there is no question but that consumers do buy products "on deal" (i.e., when those products are offered with special price deals). Nevertheless, price promotions can have important negative effects in the long term. The first and most obvious negative effect is the inherent loss of revenue—price promotions, by lowering the price, lower the revenue realized for the product. Other possible negative effects are more subtle and less immediate. Lowering the price for a specific period of time may shift sales forward in time; that is, some customers who buy on deal would have bought later (when the product would be offered at full price). As price promotions become more common and predictable, consumers may also shift purchases out in time to wait for the next deal rather than buy at full price. This purchase shifting may compound the loss of revenue, distort demand, and disrupt production planning. Additionally, price is an important signal of quality—especially in some product categories where consumers lack the ability or expertise to judge substantive quality. By lowering the effective price, price promotions can diminish consumers' perceptions of the product's quality in the long term.

Another set of long-term and undesirable effects of price promotions relates to "trade promotions," deals offered to channel partners, especially retailers, such as price reductions ("case allowances" and extra product deals), as well as cooperative advertising participation, contests, and slotting or shelving fees (direct payments for stocking consideration). Trade promotions can quickly become expected, a necessary part of doing business with the retailers, and are hard to control. It is hard to insure that consumers get some or any of the benefit of trade promotions. Often retailers drop incentives directly to their own

bottom line, and some channel members "divert" promotions to other retailers and to other markets. In fact, an entire industry called "diverting" has emerged in which one retailer will take advantage of a trade promotion offered to it, such as discounts for volume orders, and then resell inventory via intermediates ("diverters") who then resell to other retailers and to other geographic markets for whom the promotion was never intended. The fact that trade promotions become expected rather than exceptional and motivating, and that many customers misdirect trade promotions, doesn't make it easy for manufacturers to decline to participate—trade promotions have become part of the "ante," a necessary prerequisites of doing business with some retailers. Some large retailers, including Wal-Mart, have recognized that trade promotions distort their business model and may distract energies from core value propositions. Wal-Mart accepts no trade promotions (and doesn't allow its buyers to accept gifts or other consideration from its vendors). The company which is the largest retailer in the world has been able to "own" the position of "everyday low prices" in the marketplace while other retailers deal and do time-specific promotions.

Customer Motives and Decision Making

Customers are motivated by different things and to different degrees depending on the product category and occasion as well as on the customers themselves. Some consumers react more to emotional messages while others respond to rational appeals (the "facts and figures"). Similarly, customers do not bring the same level of *interest* or *attention* to all purchases or to all product categories. Some products, such as laundry detergent, are inherently uninteresting—marketers call that level of interest, involvement, or enthusiasm for a purchase or a product "involvement"—while others are inherently engaging, such as cars and movies. Even though some products may be more engaging, customers also vary in their degree of involvement within product categories; some people are movie junkies or car enthusiasts while others far less engaged, even uninvolved with these products.

Many frameworks have been proposed to gauge consumers' purchase and consumption motives in order to develop appropriate communications messages. One of the best known is the FCB Grid, which

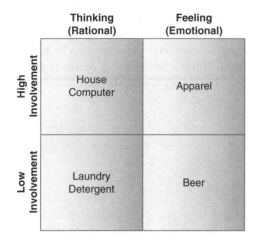

FIGURE NOTE 34-2 The FCB Grid

makes basic distinctions between thinking and feeling products on one axes and high versus low involvement products on the other (Figure 34-2). Richard Vaughn introduced this now-well-known framework while he was the director of research at Foote Cone & Belding advertising agency.[11] In this framework, products like cameras and life insurance are high-involvement/ thinking products; customers generally learn (think) about these products, form a preference (feel), and then buy or "act." Perfume and apparel are examples of high-involvement/feeling products; the purchase process for these "affective" product categories usually follows a "feel-learn-act" flow in which customers' emotions are the primary and most influential factor. Low-involvement/thinking products, or "habitual" purchases, including mundane household consumables such as detergent and groceries, follow a "do, learn, feel" process in which trial may precede evaluation and feelings (and feelings are low-intensity preferences). Finally, low-involvement/feeling products are items such as liquor and candy, and the consumer decision process is most often do-feel-think; rational evaluations come after the act and the feelings (which often involve satisfaction or self-indulgent pleasure).

The FCB Grid is just one prominent framework for classifying and understanding customer motivations and tying those motives to differences in suitable and effective communications programs. Many other frameworks have been proposed,[12] but the basic implication of these tools is that customers are motivated by different things for different products.

It is also true that different customers on different occasions are going to be motivated by different things; for example, there are certainly some occasions where some customers will purchase candy in a very rational (thinking) and highly involved manner. These motives are generally consumer motives— they apply less well to B2B products, most of which are fairly rational or "thinking" products and are purchased initially in a highly analytic fashion even if they later become "straight rebuys" (or habitual purchases); B2B motives are discussed below.

Understanding customer needs, customer motives, and the purchase decision process of the product's customers informs the development of the integrated marketing communications program. Vaughn linked the FCB Grid to advertising copy (messages and creative content): Messages focus on the decision process (e.g., thinking-feeling-doing) and persuasive content expected to influence the relevant processes. Understanding the motives and decision-making process can also influence decisions about the overall promotions mix; for example, sales are effective in influencing rational, thinking purchases but are usually less persuasive with regard to feeling decisions or low-involvement purchases.

B2B Motives and Buyer Behavior

Most industrial or B2B purchases are approached in a relatively high-involvement (at least for the initial purchase) and highly rational/thinking manner, but there are important distinctions in the B2B sector just as there are in consumer products and purchase decisions. Understanding how B2B customers make decisions, how they fashion specifications and proceed through the buying process, and what motivates or drives B2B purchases is important. Buying processes and motives will be different by product category and by firm (or segment of firms). When purchasing the same products, for example, some firms will use a purchasing agent from the outset (and those purchases will, therefore, be driven by price and efficiencies such as delivery time and quantity) while other firms will begin with "buying centers" to determine requirements, set specifications, issue requests for proposals (or "RFPs"), and ultimately to make the purchase decision. Buying centers are teams working, either formally or informally, to make purchase decisions for an organization. There are many roles in buying centers, from "users" (the people who will ultimately make use of the purchased good or service and who influence the purchase through that application role), influencers (experts in some aspect of the purchase), gatekeepers (people who control the flow of information in the organization), and "buyers," the people who will ultimately commit the organization to the purchase. In order to communicate with organizational buyers effectively, it is necessary to understand the buying criteria, the buying process, and the various roles in that buying process.

Summary

Managing the communications mix and integrated marketing communications is an essential part of marketing strategy; the strategist must understand integrated marketing communications at the strategic level. This includes understanding the variety of communications tools, the integration of these tools, and basic processes for managing and evaluating communications programs that build on and reinforce a unique and valued position in consumer perceptions. Integrated marketing communications require deep and broad understandings of consumer motives, buying behaviors, and relationships with the need, the product, the brand, and the purchase decision.

Additional Resources

Clow, Kenneth E., and Donald E. Baack. *Integrated Advertising, Promotion and Marketing Communications*, 4th ed. Upper Saddle River, NJ: Prentice Hall, 2010.

Dye, Renée. "The Buzz on Buzz," *Harvard Business Review* 78, no. 6 (November-December, 2000): 139–146.

Lenderman, Max. *Experience the Message: How Experiential Marketing Is Changing the Brand World*. New York: Carroll & Graf, 2006.

Endnotes

1. T*he New York Herald Tribune*, October 30, 1956.
2. Kenneth E. Clow and Donald E Baack, "*Integrated Advertising, Promotion and Marketing Communications*," 4th ed. (Upper Saddle River, NJ: Prentice Hall, 2009).
3. www.screentime.org/index.php?option=com_content&task=view&id=7&Itemid=14. Last accessed on July 10, 2010.
4. See "Average U.S. Home Now Receives a Record 118.6 TV Channels" at: www.nielsenmedia.com/nc/portal/site/Public/menuitem.55dc65b4a7d5adff3f65936147a062a0/?vgnextoid=fa7e220af4e5a110VgnVCM100000ac0a260aRCRD. Last accessed on July 10, 2010.
5. See Shain Bergan, "UA Students Take AXE to Dirtied Selves on Mall," *The Arizona Daily Wildcat*, November 7, 2007; and Louise Story, "Advertising; The Campaign Is Clean, The Stunts, Fairly Dirty," *The New York Times*, September 28, 2007.
6. Patrick J. Robinson, Charles W. Faris, and Yoram Wind, *Industrial Buying Behavior and Creative Marketing* (Boston: Allyn & Bacon, 1967).
7. D. J. Dalrymple, W. L. Cron, and T. E. DeCarlo, *Sales Management* (Hoboken, NJ: John Wiley & Sons, 2004).
8. Robert J. Lavidge, and Gary A. Steiner, "A Model of Predictive Measurements of Advertising Effectiveness," *Journal of Marketing* (October 1961): 59–62.
9. F. Nicosia, *Consumer Decision Processes* (Englewood Cliffs: Prentice Hall, 1966).
10. Everett M. Rogers, *Diffusion of Innovation* (New York: Free Press, 1962); also see Note II-9: New Products and the Diffusion of Innovations.
11. See Richard Vaughn, "How Advertising Works: A Planning Model . . . Putting It all Together," *Journal of Advertising Research* 20, no. 5 (1980): 27–33 and Richard Vaughn, "How Advertising Works: A Planning Model Revisited," *Journal of Advertising Research* 26, no. 1 (1986): 57–66.
12. See, for example, John R. Rossiter, Larry Percy, and Robert J. Donovan, "A Better Advertising Planning Grid," *Journal of Advertising Research* 31 (October–November, 1991): 11–21.

35

Place—Distribution

Channels of distribution involve *how a product is delivered from the producer to the customer and all the functions that add value within that process.* Traditionally, the marketing management literature has emphasized the distribution of *goods* (physically tangible products) toward end consumers via wholesalers, distributors, agents, brokers, and retailers. Advances in technology and in logistics along with the increased importance of services (intangible products) in modern economies have reshaped and, in particular, *shortened* many channels. Multiple channels, in which the same product is made available through different and sometimes competing distribution paths, have proliferated as have hybrid channels in which different paths deliver different parts of the overall bundle of value-adding functions. Charles Schwab, for example, not only offers the convenience of trading online, by phone or in person, but—using offline and online tools—also provides advice and information through online portfolio consultation, along with investment courses that their Learning Center hosts. Airlines sell their tickets online, through their own sales offices, independent travel agencies, tour operators and brokers. An example for hybrid channels is Nestlé's revolutionary coffee brand Nespresso. The coffee machine, developed by Nestlé and licensed to leading producers of household appliances, is mainly sold through household appliance retailers and the Internet. The individually portioned aluminium coffee capsules, however, are exclusively sold through the Internet-based Nespresso Clubs, and through the Nespresso Boutiques, and a limited number of brick-and-mortar stores.

In many industries, the Internet has revolutionized distribution systems by not only lowering costs, allowing for more effective direct marketing, and addressing new customers segments, but also increasing market transparency and reducing customer's switching costs. In the Airline industry, for instance, the Internet has saved airlines roughly $10 to $15 per booking. The increased price transparency, however, forces some Airlines to sell a ticket on the Internet an estimated $50 to $100 lower than tickets purchased through other channels.[1]

Distribution issues are too often treated as mundane or as established "givens," and the literature commonly treats "place" as a one-way, producer-toward-the-consumer flow, usually adopting the producer's "downstream" perspective. These viewpoints overlook important aspects of and opportunities in distribution in contemporary marketing strategy. Precipitating or at least anticipating changes in distribution systems has created substantial competitive advantages for many firms. For example, being the first mover into valuable distribution space can fashion a barrier to entry for later movers. Coca-Cola's' early move into vending-machine distribution in Japan created a long-lived advantage—today Coke has more than a million vending machines in Japan, and enjoys a 50 percent market share.[2] When Netscape entered the software market with its Navigator® browser, it also innovated in the way software was distributed (and priced). Rather than battle established software vendors for space in bricks-and-mortar retailers, Netscape offered the Navigator® browser for "free but not free" via download over the Internet:[3] Navigator® was "officially" priced at $39, but many target segments—including educators, students, and not for profits—were given free copies and everyone was offered a 90-day free trial. Netscape's business model was based on revenue from sales of their business and Web-server software. Meanwhile, competitors whose business models were tied to traditional channels and to revenue from software sales were slow to respond. Between its launch in 1994 and early 1998, more than 94 million users had downloaded Navigator®[4].

Many firms' core business models and strategies center on their own roles in distribution and the manner in which they add value within larger channel systems. Dell Computers' "Dell Direct" model is a noteworthy example of a strategy based on the firm's role within a larger supply chain. As the personal-computer (PC) market evolved, Michael Dell recognized that consumers no longer required "hand holding"; as the PC product lifecycle evolved customers were willing and able to buy direct but they wanted customized machines. In addition to selling customized products directly to consumers, the Dell Direct model also involves partnering closely with vendors to accelerate inventory. Michael Dell described that model:

> The supplier effectively becomes our partner. They assign their engineers to our design team, and we start to treat them as if they were part of the company. For example, when we launch a new product, their engineers are stationed right in our plants. ... So it's not, "Well, every two weeks deliver 5,000 to this warehouse, and we'll put them on the shelf, and then we'll take them off the shelf." It's, "Tomorrow morning we need 8,562 and deliver them to door number seven by 7 A.M."[5]

The Dell Direct model is so efficient that Dell makes money on the "float"; customers' payments are received almost immediately (via credit card payments and transfers) while vendors are paid on terms.[6] To customers Dell looks like the customized/direct alternative in the PC market—and from the customers'

perspective that's what they are—but their overall strategy is as an efficient value-adding player within the channel from manufacturer to customer.

In summary, many strategists have found advantage by challenging assumptions about and anticipating changes in the manner via which products are distributed. Marketers continue to face challenges and to find opportunities in *getting the product to the customer*. A foundation to understanding how channels work and to identifying opportunities and threats in distribution is an understanding of the basic functions of value-adding activities that channels perform. This note reviews those basic value-adding functions and how technology and other dynamics are changing the way those functions are performed, and then outlines strategic considerations and alternatives in channels of distribution.

CHANNEL FUNCTIONS

To get a product from the manufacturer to the customer, regardless of the length of the channel, the number of entities in the channel, the type of product, or the type of customer, certain things have to happen—somewhere in the channel these things have to occur for an efficient and effective delivery of the product to occur. For example, the product must be physically moved to the customer; it must be transported to the location where the customer needs it when the customer needs it. The customer must pay for the product, either in advance, on delivery, or on terms. Also, the assortment of complimentary products and services required to use and derive value from the product must be made available. All of these and more are the essential "channel functions"; valuable benefits that a channel of distribution as a whole provides to the customer and the marketer. Some of these functions are not relevant to some products or for some customers, and a single channel member doesn't necessarily even often provide all of these functions—*but these things need to be done somewhere in most channels*.

Different channel members may provide different channel functions depending on the product category and even the brand within a product category. For example, Dell customizes and ships PCs directly to customers using delivery services such as UPS to physically move its computers from the manufacturer to the customer; Dell's logistics partners even assort various components of the order, such as workstations and screens, from vendors for Dell—and Dell uses direct communications, including the Internet and toll-free telephone services, to provide customer support. Hewlett Packard (HP) competes directly with Dell in the PC market, but unlike Dell, HP distributes its computers through retail stores, delivering computers in bulk to distribution centers from which they are shipped to individual stores, and using retail sales personnel and the retailers' customer-service staff for selling and support. Both of these strategies are viable and have been successful, but they approach distribution and service in very different ways that create very different value propositions for the PC customer.

Understanding the strategic issues involved in channels of distribution begins with an understanding of the functions channels provide or can provide. There have been many comprehensive lists and frameworks of channel functions proposed in the marketing literature; they all emphasize the breadth and diversity of value-added activities that take place between the manufacturer or marketer and the customer. Table 35-1 is an inclusive list of channel functions organized into three overarching categories: transactional functions, logistical functions, and facilitating functions. Some of these "functions" overlap—for example, financing is often a part of selling and involves risk taking—but this extensive inventory provides a thorough conceptual perspective on the sorts of value-adding activities the channels provide.

TABLE NOTE 35-1 Functions Performed by Channels of Distribution and Channel Entities[7]

Transactional Functions

- *Buying*—Taking title (possession) and making payment to vendor/manufacturer
- *Selling*—Providing title to buyer, accounting and managing receivables
- *Risk Taking*—Assuming ownership risks of obsolescence, spoilage, shrinkage, etc. as well as other risks associated with other functions below (e.g., credit risks associated with financing)

Logistical Functions

- *Transporting*—Physically moving products toward the customer and place of need
- *Assorting*—Bringing together diverse products (creating assortments) to meet simultaneous or related needs
- *Storing*—Holding products until needed (time convenience)
- *Location*—Locating products where needed (place convenience)
- *Sorting* or "breaking bulk"—making product available in desired quantities or volume

Facilitating Functions

- *Financing*—Providing and managing credit and assuming credit risk
- *Grading*—Converting heterogeneous supply into homogeneous supply
- *Assuring*—Providing and backing warranties, guarantees, promised repairs and replacements, etc.
- *Maintenance and Repair*—Regular or scheduled maintenance and exceptional repair
- *Installing and Tailoring*—Installation, customization, fitting, etc.
- *Promoting*—Marketing communications, including advertising, personal selling, and promotions and provision of required customer information to persuade customers to buy and rebuy
- *Negotiating*—Creating dialogue and bargaining to identify interests and reach agreement
- *Matching*—Fitting diverse customers with diverse product alternative in conditions of scarcity
- *Training*—Technical training for customers and staff, help-desk support, etc.
- *Marketing Research*—Understanding the customers, competition, and market and communicating that information to manufacturers, suppliers, and other channel partners
- *Disposal*—The repurchase and disposal of customers' previous equipment or product

TRANSACTIONAL FUNCTIONS.   Taking possession and then selling goods involves managing numerous specific transactions and tying up capital and cash flow. Having layers of distributors is valuable for the manufacturer because it reduces the number of transactions (and therefore the bookkeeping and overhead) and it accelerates cash flow; the manufacturer usually receives payment before the ultimate customer buys the product. Taking possession of goods also involves inherent possession-related risks including spoilage, obsolesce/changes in tastes, and shrinkage (theft).

LOGISTICAL FUNCTIONS.   A fundamental function of channels is the physical distribution of the product. Logistical functions (i.e., "logistics") encompass the following: (1) getting the product to the *place* the customer experiences or meets the need (2) providing service at the *time* the customer experiences the need (3) providing the right size or quantity of the product that meets the customer's needs, and (4) providing *other products* and accessories required to meet the need or set of needs.

FACILITATING FUNCTIONS.   Although transactional and logistical functions may be the traditional core functions of distributors—the "nuts and bolts" of channels—facilitating functions such as financing, promoting, and servicing and supporting the installed base can be the most valuable and the hardest-to-bypass functions that channel members perform. Many distributors and retailers "own the relationship" with the customer via these value-added activities.

DISTRIBUTION DYNAMICS

Although sometimes disparaged as redundant or noncontributing profiteers—as in this vintage 1920 headline from the New York Times—channel entities ("middlemen") invariably provide valuable functions or they are circumvented or replaced by market dynamics. If manufacturers find that they can provide a function or bundle of functions on their own and no longer require a distributor or agent, they integrate forward. If a retailer finds that it can deal directly with manufactures and therefore does not need distributors, it deals directly with manufacturers. Farmers, for example, have organized into cooperatives to integrate forward into distribution—and

have enjoyed the increased margins while also assuming the increased headaches of assorting, selling and promoting, logistics, dealing with spoilage, and providing customer service.

Changes in the competitive environment and, especially, in technology have caused channel structures to change and some channel members have become obsolete or redundant. Modern computational and database power, the proliferation of consumer credit cards and electronic banking, the wide-availability of rapid-delivery services such as UPS and FedEx, along with the emergence of the Internet as a widely available two-way tool for marketing and communications have allowed many organizations to sell directly to their customers and to manage those numerous accounts themselves. At the same time, the emergence of huge retailers such as Aldi in Europe and Wal-Mart in the United States has consolidated channel "power" at the retail level and increased the importance of key account management—that is, the emphasis on a few large retail accounts that comprise the vast majority of sales. This has decreased the ability of small retailers to compete and made "jobbers," small distributors who called on individual retail accounts and assisted in the management of inventory and merchandising, obsolete. While these changes threaten small players, such shifts also create opportunities, especially for firms that consolidate across a level of the channel (horizontal integration, i.e., taking over or merging with another firm in the same industry) or integrated backwards and/or forwards (vertical integration, i.e., owning its upstream suppliers or its downstream buyers).

Channel structures continue to evolve due to technological and competitive forces. Channel structures are also influenced by factors like the emergence of large, efficient third-party logistics suppliers (3PLs), the maturation of many consumer products (e.g., consumer electronics and personal computers) toward lifecycle stages at which consumers are comfortable with lower and less hands-on service and with purchasing items without personal inspection. These changes have led some channel entities to lose share and profitability—their basic business models have been challenged—but others have grown and profited. Thus, the creative marketing strategist may find opportunities as well as hazards in the changing dynamics of marketing channels. Three related forces underlie channel dynamics and distribution outcomes for firms: channel power, channel control, and channel conflict.

- *Channel Power.* Channel power is "the ability of a particular channel member to control or influence the decision making and behavior of another channel member, or one channel member's potential for influence with another channel member."[8] There are several types of or sources of channel power: (1) reward, that is, offering positive outcomes such as payment, margins, or traffic, (2) coercive, that is, punishments such as withdrawal of products or of support, (3) expert, that is, the ability to provide scarce and valuable expertise, (4) legitimate, that is, ownership, legal/contractual, etc., and (5) referent, that is, offering benefits via affiliation such as prestige. In consumer goods, large manufacturers once had channel power over their retail partners (the "trade")—every grocer needed to have Coca-Cola in its assortment to meet their consumers' needs, so Coke had power over those retailers and could set the terms of trade. Consolidation in the grocery trade and the emergence of Wal-Mart, Target, and others as retailing behemoths has shifted that power toward those fewer retail "key accounts." Understanding where power resides in a channel *and why* is important to managing distribution and to identifying opportunities for channel-structure shifts.

- *Channel Control.* Channel control, "the actual impact that a channel member achieves on an associated channel member's beliefs, attitudes, and behavior"[9] varies as an outcome of channel power and as a function of prices and margins for the product, and the length of the channels. Many firms that require close control forge direct or exclusive channels but others distribute through arms-length channels but provide control through intensive, company-owned services. Frito-Lay, for example, sells through groceries, discounters, and convenience stores but controls product quality, merchandising, and inventories via its intensive network of 10,000 route salespeople who call directly on stores on a daily basis.

- *Channel Conflict.* Channel conflict, "disagreement among marketing channel members on goals and roles—who should do what and for what rewards,"[10] can occur between levels of the channel (e.g., between manufacturer and distributor), between members at the same level in a channel (amongst distributors), or between different channels. Conflict can arise from different objectives. For example, in fast-food franchise systems conflict arises because of conflicting goals: the franchisor (the brand) wants to maintain and grow market share and absolute sales levels—franchisor revenues are tied to franchisee's gross sales and royalty rates—but franchisees need to maintain margins rather than top-line revenues. Conflict can also arise from perceived competition. When Nike opened its Niketown retail outlets, motivated as much by its interest in building the brand through consumer experience, retailers carrying the brand perceived Niketown as competition.[11] Channel conflict can be expensive in terms of lost support and goodwill as well as in lost sales and reduced channel coverage.

STRATEGIC CHANNEL CONSIDERATIONS

There are a variety of issues to be considered in establishing and managing channels of distribution, including especially customer needs as well as the desired brand position, and costs and margin structures:

- **Customer Needs and Behaviors.** One essential driver of the channels required by a firm, a product, or a brand is the *target customer needs*, especially (a) needs for information, guidance, customization, and installation at the time of the purchase, (b) needs for the provision of or availability of service and support after the purchase, and (c) needs for convenience and extensive availability. Needs for selling and service support correspond with more limited, exclusive distribution. Needs for convenience and availability drive broader, "intensive" distribution.
- **Brand Positioning.** Just as people are known by the company they keep, brands are known by the company *they* keep, and choosing channel partners connects the brand with channel partners (distributors and retailers) and with the *other brands* in the channel partners' assortments. Premium hair care products, for example, often choose to distribute only through salons to affiliate with the salons' perceived expertise, exclusivity, and style. Those same brands might decline to distribute through discounters to avoid being perceived as ordinary or cheap.

  Choosing channel partners also links the brand, the firm, and the firm's business model to the channel partner and its business model. Firms selling through Walmart, for instance, often claim that Walmart forces a continued emphasis on cost reduction at the expense of quality.
- **Costs and Margin Structures.** Consideration of the costs of distribution—and deliberation of possible savings in distribution—should begin with consideration of *the functions that are performed in the channel*, where they are performed, how well they are performed, and how well they meet customer needs. The marketing organization "pays" for distribution in two ways: directly in the actual expenses associated with managing and maintaining distribution, and indirectly in the form of margins retained

by the entities in the channel (such as wholesalers, distributors, and retailers) as they resell and mark up the marketing organization's products. Direct channel-management costs include selling expenses, logistics expenses, and promotions to channel members' sales forces and service personnel. Prominent costs incurred by channel members in delivering value-adding functions include transportation and handling, order processing and account management, accounts receivable management, and inventory management and carrying costs.

These considerations influence choices across distribution alternatives, discussed next.

STRATEGIC CHANNEL ALTERNATIVES

Structuring channels within any given marketing strategy entails consideration of at least two parameters: distribution intensity and channel structure and ownership. These "decisions," which may be constrained for a number of reasons such as being late to market (preferred channels are "taken") or available resources, are shaped by the considerations outlined above: customer needs, desired brand positioning, and cost structures as well as channel power, control, and conflict.

- **Distribution Intensity.** Channel coverage can vary from exclusive distribution systems in which only selected stores carry a product, such as that for Rolex watches, to intensive distribution that can approach being iniquitous (seeming to be available "everywhere)," such as Coca-Cola's objective of having every consumer be "within arm's reach of desire" (i.e., within an arm's reach of a Coca-Cola product).[12] Generally, four factors drive greater exclusivity in distribution: the amount of effort buyers will expend in "shopping" for a product, the required service and support from channel members required by customers, the degree of "prestige" positioning sought, and the desire to maintain price points and margins.
- **Channel Structure/Ownership.** There are several sorts of relationships and bases for cooperation that a marketer can forge with channel partners, ranging from fully independent (arms-length) to full ownership. In traditional,

arms-length channels the various channel members act independently, motivated by self-interest (profits, margins, etc.), and do not coordinate activities other than as mutual interests and transactions dictate. These channels require investment in selling and account management, but do not require large capital investments and are generally cheaper to establish. At the other extreme are company-owned channels. Control is highest in company-owned channels; in fact, control is *absolute* within parameters of organizational control. Company owned systems such as Red Lobster restaurants and Starbuck's cafés enjoy greater control than franchised competitors, such as McDonald's and Dunkin' Donuts, and far greater control and market presence than firms selling through independent channels. On the other hand, capital investments are much greater and costs are generally higher, too, to operate company-owned channels and flexibility is constrained.

- *Multiple Channels.* An alternative to design a single distribution system that is becoming more common, given changes in competition and technology, is for firms to distribute through more than one channel at the same time (Figure 35-1). In a multiple-channel set up customers may choose their channel, but, at least in theory, they source all of the value-adding channel functions from that specific channel (which is the distinction between "multiple" and "hybrid" channels, discussed below). In practice, many consumers use higher-service channel members for shopping (to benefit from sales advisory service) and then resort to low-service discount channels for purchase, leading to predictable channel conflict and inescapable channel modifications. In fact, channel conflict is a significant problem with multiple channel distribution. Partners who add value see discount and direct channels as unfair competition. To deal with this conflict, some brands have created different products for different channels. Levi's, for example, has created lower-quality jeans for sale through discounters like Wal-Mart while continuing to offer higher-quality jeans through department and clothing stores. Of course,

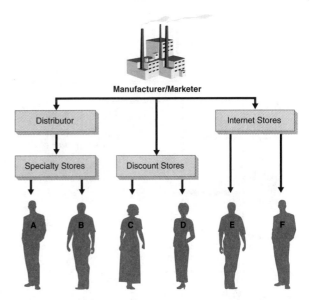

FIGURE NOTE 35-1 Multiple Channels of Distribution

that tactic introduces a real threat of brand dilution and consumer confusion.

- *Hybrid Channels.* "Hybrid" is sometimes used to refer to multiple-channel systems (described above), but there are also emerging channel structures in which different, complementary functions are delivered to the same customers through different, parallel channels (Figure 35-2); this is conceptually and strategically different from delivering all functions through alternative channels to different customers. We use "hybrid" to refer to the latter, that is to the structuring of distribution so that the same customers receive different channel functions—which add up to the complete bundle of customer requirements—via different channels.

For example, high-end consumer electronics firms such as Bose (consumer audio equipment), Lexmark (printers), and Linksys (computer peripherals) distribute through the Army and Air Force Exchange Service (AAFES, the on base "PX" stores), but those stores do not provide adequate selling or service support at the point of purchase. Customers require information and support to understand the product benefits, to make informed choices across alternatives, and to use the products once purchased.

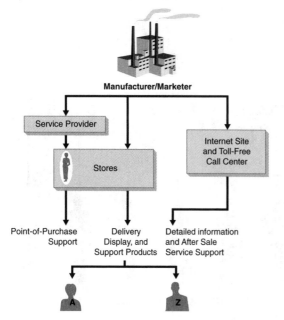

FIGURE NOTE 35-2   Hybrid Channels of Distribution

TABLE NOTE 35-2 Hypothetical Needs and Importance for Two Segments	
Repair Trade (Mom & Pop Plumbers)	
Availibility	1
Assortment (Breadth of inventory)	2
Location	3
Customer Service	4
Price	5
DIY (Do-it-Yourself Customers)	
Price	1
Customer Service	2
Assortment (Complementary products)	3
Location	4
Availability	5

These brands contract with Military Sales and Service (MSS) to provide point-of-sale support (simplified graphically in Figure 35-2). Therefore, the clerks working with the customers on the floor are not AAFES employees; they're MSS staff working on behalf of Bose, Lexmark, Linksys or other contracted brands.

STRATEGIC DISTRIBUTION DECISIONS[13]

Making strategic channel decisions—including designing new channels and making reorienting existing channels—begins with thorough analysis of customer needs with regard to the functions that channels provide. *What do customers need and want from the product's distribution system?* Thus, the first step in this process is to describe the firm's target segments with regard to their channel-function needs. Because needs are an essential descriptor in any segmentation classification, it is likely that differences in channel-function-related needs influenced the segmentation scheme adopted in the firm's strategy development but, in designing channels, those segments' specific channel-function-related needs should be analyzed or re-analyzed in detail and each segment's priorities, or rank-ordered needs should be spelled out.

A "big box" home improvements retailer might, for example, have identified two key plumbing-supply

segments: small plumbing repair contractors ("Mom and Pops") and Do It Yourselfers (DIYs). These segments' needs are different (Table 35-2). Small plumbing repair contractors need the *exact* part for a problem *quickly*—their time is money, to them and to their customers. Many of their customers are in emergency situations requiring immediate remedy; they can't wait for a part to come in. In addition, when a plumber is charging $45 an hour (or more) and passing parts costs through to the customer (who has a leaking toilet or water all over the kitchen floor), the price of a part or fixture is not a prominent consideration. On the other hand, DIYs are less likely to be repairing urgent plumbing problems, but they are, almost by definition, *price conscious*; they're doing this job themselves and often to save the money. The DIY segment also needs and expects customer service and informative sales assistance. DIY consumers are not "on the clock" and, although convenience matters, plumbing supplies are shopping goods to them; location and immediate availability are less important. These priorities are shown in Table 35-2 as rank orderings for both segments.

The next step in designing or modifying distribution systems is to benchmark both the firm's and its competitors' capabilities at delivering those salient customer needs. The big-box retailer might well determine that it delivers superior customer service—especially vis-à-vis plumbing supply houses that are not geared toward consumer retail merchandising, and the big box likely offers lower prices. Nevertheless, the big

Repair Trade (Mom & Pop Plumbers)		
Availibility	1	High←7 − [6] − 5 − 4 −(3)− 2 − 1→Low
Assortment (Breadth of inventory)	2	High←7 − [6] − 5 − 4 −(3)− 2 − 1→Low
Location	3	High←7 − 6 − [5] − 4 −(3)− 2 − 1→Low
Customer Service	4	High←7 − 6 −(5)− 4 − [3] − 2 − 1→Low
Price	5	High←7 −(6)− 5 − [4] − 3 − 2 − 1→Low
DIY (Do-it-Yourself Customers)		
Price	1	High←7 −(6)− 5 − [4] − 3 − 2 − 1→Low
Customer Service	2	High←7 − 6 −(5)− 4 − [3] − 2 − 1→Low
Assortment (Complementary products)	3	High←7 − [6] − 5 − 4 −(3)− 2 − 1→Low
Location	4	High←7 − 6 − [5] − 4 −(3)− 2 − 1→Low
Availability	5	High←7 − [6] − 5 − 4 −(3)− 2 − 1→Low

○ = "Big Box" Discount Home Improvement Retailer
☐ = Plumbing Supply Houses

FIGURE NOTE 35-3   Firm and Competitor Capabilities on Functions by Segment and Priorities

box's assortment and availability—the breadth of parts available and on-site—are inferior to those specialized plumbing-supply houses, and that its locations are only slightly more convenient than those of the plumbing-supply houses. Figure 35-3 shows a format for making these comparisons graphically. The big-box retailer's capabilities are shown in circles, plumbing-supply houses' capabilities in squares.

The next step is to generate alternatives. Looking at the Mom and Pop's requirements, for example, it is clear that inventory and convenience are the driving forces. Possible solutions would center on improving the availability of parts in a product category that can involve numerous low-priced SKUs ("stock keeping units," i.e., distinct items in the inventory). Investments in increased inventory, inventory management/warehousing technology, and logistics as well as innovations such as single parts that can be adapted to fit many repair needs might all be viable alternatives to consider. These alternatives may well include both multiple- and hybrid-channel configurations. This step should begin with the segment-by-segment analysis of customer needs vis-à-vis channel functions and generate as wide-ranging and inclusive a set of alternatives as possible.

Next, those various and numerous alternatives should be analyzed against their expected costs and benefits. What do the various options cost in financial terms, in terms of managerial resources and attention, and in terms of channel conflict and motivation? For example, investments in broader availability (stocking more parts in each store) are mostly about space and inventory carrying costs—things that can be readily quantified. Offering express/dedicated check-out and special contractor pricing may, on the other hand, have both monetary and consumer-goodwill costs; customers who are *not* offered discounts or special services may resent that lack of consideration. Channel conflict may be a greater threat in channels where members previously enjoyed exclusive rights to sell a product in certain markets; they will resent new programs that create multiple-channels targeting customers who they had invested in and that they believed were theirs. Of course, cost-benefit analyses also require careful quantification of the benefits of each alternative. Benefits may include greater customer satisfaction and loyalty, enhanced reputation and value, and increased sales but all those benefits should, in the final analysis, be quantified as increased margins and profits. Finally, decisions can be made based on those "costed-out" analyses. That is, this process should facilitate informed and systematic choices across feasible distribution alternatives and should lead to systems that optimally meet customers' real needs for the values created by channel functions.

Summary

Channels of distribution are rapidly changing due to competitive and customer considerations as well as changes in technology. Understanding those changes and the strategic opportunities they present begins with an understanding of the value-adding functions performed by channels—the entities that don't provide real value and irreplaceable value are likely to be bypassed and eliminated. Channel dynamics include issues of power, control, and conflict—understanding who has power and control and anticipating and managing conflict are important to effective distribution. Finally, managing channels and making choices across channel alternatives should begin with careful assessment of customer needs in relation to channel functions and analysis of alternative mechanisms for delivering those value-adding functions to various segments.

Additional Resources

Coughlan, Anne, Erin Anderson, Louis W. Stern, and Adel El-Ansary, *Marketing Channels*, 7th ed. Upper Saddle River, NJ: Pearson/Prentice Hall, 2006.

Kasturi Rangan, V. with Marie Bell. *Transforming Your Go-to-Market Strategy: The Three Disciplines of Channel Management.* Boston: Harvard Business School Publishing, 2006.

Rolnicki, Kenneth. *Managing Channels of Distribution: The Marketing Executive's Complete Guide.* New York: AMACOM, 1997.

Endnotes

1. Joseph B. Myers, Andrew D. Pickersgill, and Evan S. Van Metre, "Steering customers to the right channels," *McKinsey Quarterly* 4 (December 2004): 36–47.

2. The Coca-Cola Company, "Coca-Cola Celebrates 50 Years of Innovation in Japan," news release, June 26, 2007; David B. Yoffie, "Cola Wars Continue: Coke and Pepsi in the Twenty-First Century," Harvard Business School case no. 9-702-442 (Boston, MA, 2002)

3. David B. Yoffie and Michael A. Cusumano, "Building a Company on Internet Time: Lessons from Netscape," *California Management Review* 41, no. 3 (1999): 8–28; and David B. Yoffie and Michael A. Cusumano, "Judo Strategy: The Competitive Dynamics of Internet Time," *Harvard Business Review* 77, no. 1 (January–February, 1999): 70–81.

4. Ibid.

5. Joan Magretta, "The Power of Virtual Integration: An Interview with Dell Computer's Michael Dell," *Harvard Business Review* 76, no. 2 (March–April, 1998): 72–84, see page 75.

6. www.crn.com/it-channel/193200086;jsessionid=IBCNVLJSLFFNCQSNDLPSKHSCJUNN2JVN. Last accessed on July 10, 2010

7. The American Marketing Association specifies eight "universal channel flows: physical possession, ownership, promotion, negotiation, financing, risking, ordering, and payment," www.marketingpower.com/_layouts/Dictionary.aspx?dLetter=C#channel+flows. Last accessed on July 10, 2010); This table elaborates on those eight "flows", adapting from: from V. Kasturi Rangan, *Designing Channels of Distribution,* Note - 9-594-116 (Boston, MA,: Harvard Business School Press 1994); Gary Armstrong and Philip Kotler, *Marketing: An Introduction*, 9th ed. (Upper Saddle River NJ: Pearson/Prentice Hall, 2009), 295; and Roger A. Kerin, et al., *Marketing,* 8th ed. (New York: McGraw-Hill Higher Education, 2005).

8. www.marketingpower.com/_layouts/Dictionary.aspx?dLetter=C#channel+power. Last accessed on July 10, 2010.

9. www.marketingpower.com/_layouts/Dictionary.aspx?dLetter=C#channel+control. Last accessed on July 10, 2010

10. Armstrong and Kotler, *Marketing*, page 297.

11. T. Collinger, "Lines Separating Sales Channels Blur: Manufacturers, Direct Sellers, Retailers Invade Each Other's Turf," *Advertising Age* 34 (March 30, 1998).

12. Mark Pendergrast, *For God, Country and Coca-Cola* (New York: Basic Books, 2000), 9

13. This section is adapted from the work of Professor V. Kasturi Rangan. See V. Kasturi Rangan, *Reorienting Channels of Distribution,* Note 9-594-118 (Boston, MA: Harvard Business School Press, 1994); Kasturi Rangan, *Designing Channels of Distribution;* and Erin Anderson, George Day, and V. Kasturi Rangan, "Strategic Channel Design," *MIT Sloan Management Review* 38, no. 4 (Summer 1997): 59–69.

DOCUMENTATION, AND ASSESSMENT AND ADJUSTMENT

36

Budgets, Forecasts, and Objectives

Executing a marketing strategy and implementing a marketing mix requires resources—the strategy and mix are, of course, expected to *generate* revenues that more than offset the associated expenditures, but they will nevertheless also necessitate *investments*. Therefore, a strategy and marketing-mix plan must be translated into the specific expenses expected to be associated with the activities (*budgets*) and projected revenues expected to result from those activities (*sales forecasts*). Once those plans have been established they should be translated into desired outcomes and measures of those outcomes (*objectives and metrics*). Whereas "goals" are the general, long-term desired conditions (often part of or implicit in corporate mission and visions), "objectives" are the more specific and desired results tied to specific timeframes (These two words are synonyms in the common English-language dictionary, but they are typically used to denote this "general" versus "specific" distinction in the strategy literature).

MARKETING PLANNING AS AN ITERATIVE PROCESS

The relationships of strategy to marketing mix implementation, budgets, forecasts, and objectives underlie the strategic-marketing-management model that organizes this book, summarized in Figure 36-1, and are emphasized in Figure 36-2: The organization's missions, vision, and goals shape its strategies, which, in turn, shape general objective that drive the development of the marketing mix (i.e., specific tactics, including products, prices, promotions and people, and distribution or "place"). The marketing mix must be elaborated into a budget and projected into forecasts of results, which lead to specific objectives tied to definite metrics. At the same time, the objectives, which are themselves related to the mission, vision, and goals and to the strategy, shape the development of the marketing mix. Section V of this book gives details of the strategic considerations involved in establishing and managing the marketing mix. This note focuses on forecasting, budgeting, and establishing specific objectives and metrics for moving

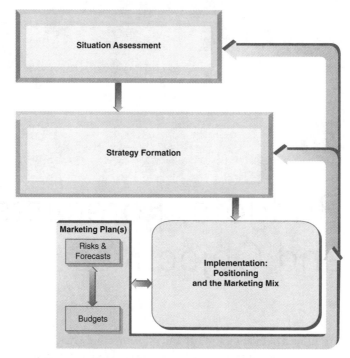

FIGURE NOTE 36-1   Summary of the Strategic Marketing Process

forward to effective implementation and to facilitate subsequent assessment and adjustment.

Planning the marketing mix, budgeting, forecasting, and objective setting are *inseparable* and *iterative processes.* That iterative nature of these processes is important to emphasize. Effective planning will link specific activities and investments—for example, the commitment of ten salespeople costing $1 million, or four quarterly coupon/price promotions at $1 million—to specific expected benefits or forecasted outcomes (e.g., a number of new retail accounts, or a specific level of increased sales and new customers). That is, various activities and their associated costs should be linked, as closely as possible, to their forecast effects. Such links between inputs and outputs may be based on assumption—some assumptions are inevitable in developing forecasts—but they may also be based on observations of past effects and on marketing research. Then, marketing mix and budget decisions can be adjusted to *optimize* their

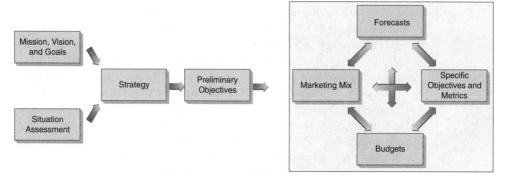

FIGURE NOTE 36-2   Planning the Marketing Mix, Forecasting, Budgets, and Objectives

forecasted effectiveness. Budget level and allocation questions—*Is an investment in new salespeople worthwhile? Are 10 new salespeople more effective than four quarterly coupon promotions? Should we commit or request the resources to do both?*—can be posed and tested based on understandings of their forecasted impacts, and the resolution of those iterative, maximization analyses should be incorporated into resulting plans.

Thus, marketing mix development, budgeting, and forecasting are inextricably linked and should be done iteratively within *pro forma* analyses to develop and optimize investments and to arrive at effective objectives and metrics. The first step is to outline a preliminary marketing mix derived from strategic planning. That outline specifies a certain set or "mix" of activities, facilitating the estimation of the costs for those activities (a budget) and allowing the effects of those activities to be estimated (a forecast). That mix is then adjusted or optimized within *pro forma* models, including forecasts, budget implications, and resource constraints. Once an optimal mix is determined, forecasts and budgets can be finalized and a set of objectives established (Figure 36-3).

Forecasting

A sales forecast usually contains two parts: the *market forecast*, which estimates future sales for the entire market or industry, and the *sales forecast*, which estimates the sales and the market share of the particular company and its products. There are two ways to obtain those forecasts: primary research and secondary research. In primary research the firm develops its own forecast based on customer surveys, expert opinions, estimates of sales force, and the like. In secondary research, forecasts are acquired from specialized vendors (market research firms and industry experts) that regularly estimate sales trends in the industry. There are many methods that companies use to forecast sales: They can be based on customer data (e.g., assessment of buying intention), expert opinions (e.g., sales force estimates), or historical data (e.g., time-series analysis). Table 36-1 gives an overview of these sales forecasting methods with their strengths and weaknesses.

Sales forecasts are an essential input to the formulation of marketing objectives and setting objectives, but objectives and budgets also impact forecasts. Without realistic assumptions about market size and trends, it is impossible to set realistic sales targets. The results of a sales forecast predict future sales *given a specific marketing mix* or effort; forecasts usually begin by estimating how sales will evolve without changing the marketing mix or committing additional resources, or with a specific proposition about marketing mix effort based on strategic considerations. Subsequently, if sales forecasts are short of the strategic objectives, the manager will consider additional and new marketing initiatives and, therefore, revise the budget which will in turn influence sales forecasts. Thus, forecasting, setting objectives, and budgeting are dynamic and iterative rather than sequential activities.

It is also invaluable to develop, as specifically as possible, estimates of the effects of specific mix elements and allocated resources on sales. For example, historic data, managerial judgment, and/or marketing research can be used to develop an estimate of the relationship between advertising expenditures and sales, sales-force effort and sales, price promotions and sales, and the like. In this way, specific marketing mixes and expenditures (budgets) can be forecast onto future sales, revenues, and profits at a more detailed level. Such forecasts of "return on marketing investments" by marketing mix element are not always possible and are not always precise, but these are the basis for modeling the effects of different marketing mix combinations and permutations and for thereby performing *pro forma* analyses to optimize the effectiveness of the marketing mix expenditures.

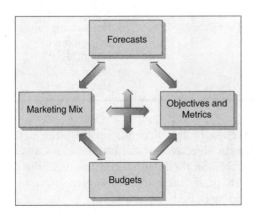

FIGURE NOTE 36-3 Marketing Mix, Forecasts, Budgets, and Objectives

TABLE NOTE 36-1 Sales Forecast Methods[1]

Method	Description	Strength	Weakness
1. Assessment of buyer's intentions	In a representative survey, customers are asked to indicate their intention to buy a specific product in the next period of time	• Works well for products, which purchases are planned in advance (e.g., industrial products, consumer durables) or for new products • Forecasts are directly derived from customers' buying intentions	• Requires representative, and reliable market research • Can be costly and time consuming
1. Sales force estimates	Sales people estimate the future sales they can make	• Sales people usually have important insights in their markets, competition etc. • Estimates available for individual sales territories • Easy to do	• Estimates might be biased, as sales people want to have the objectives set low enough
2. Expert opinions (such as "Delphi surveys" in which estimates are aggregated, sent back, refined in several iterative rounds)	Experts (e.g., dealers, distributors, trade associations, consultants) are asked to estimate future sales	• Utilizes "collective" wisdom of experts • Relatively easy and quick	• Can be costly • Difficult to find and motivate experts
3. Market tests	The company chooses representative markets (e.g., cities, regions) where the product is introduced with the full marketing plan (or variations to test the effect of single activities) and tests the market reaction	• Works well for new products • Effectiveness of marketing activities can be tested	• Expensive and time consuming • Competitors get to know your strategy
4. Time-series analysis	Statistical methods (e.g., exponential smoothing, econometric models) are used to predict future sales from historical data	• Less subjective	• Not suitable for innovations (no historical data) • Requires sophisticated statistical skills

Budgeting

As noted, establishing marketing budgets, forecasting results, and setting marketing objectives go hand in hand. These activities make up the heart of the marketing plan. The marketing plan specifies what the objectives are and how they should be achieved, and estimates the costs for each marketing task. The marketing budget depends on the strategies, the strategic objectives of the business unit and, unavoidably, on the financial constraints of the company. Basically, there are four ways to determine the marketing budget:

- ***Extrapolation:*** Building upon the previous year's budget as a base, those allocations are either increased or decreased by a certain amount or are left unchanged. This approach is problematic as it does not explicitly consider marketing objectives, changes in strategies, costs, or adjustments to the competition or to evolving opportunities.

- **Percentage of Sales/Profits:** The marketing budget is determined as a percentage of the projected sales or profits. This is an uncomplicated method but it reverses "cause" and "effect." Sales are a *result* of marketing activities, not vice versa.

- **Target Costing:** The company determines the target sales volume and determines the target profit. The remaining resources—after profits are taken from projected sales—are the *de facto* marketing budget. This approach applies the "all-you-can-afford method" and similar to the "percentage of sales approach" it does not consider the causal relationship between marketing budget and the target sales or profits.

- **Bottom-up Budgeting:** This approach derives the required marketing budget from the objectives of the business unit. It determines all marketing activities that are needed, calculates the costs for each and the total marketing budget is computed. The bottom-up approach requires a breakdown of all the specific expenses for the marketing department, including salesforce expenses, market research, advertising, public relations, promotions, and marketing overhead. Bottom-up budgeting is the most effective but is also the most complex. It highlights the need to integrate objective setting, to develop the marketing mix, and to establish the budget based on those drivers.

Costs for all marketing activities can be divided into direct marketing costs (e.g., promotions, discounts, folders), semi-fixed marketing costs (such as media advertising, public relations), and fixed marketing costs (including marketing department overhead, sales force management expenses, marketing research and the like). Once all tasks and activities are determined, the costs are estimated. Table 36-2 contains the marketing budget of a business unit broken down to marketing budgets for the single segments, and an estimation of segment profitability. Segment four

produces a loss, all other segments are profitable. Overall, the business unit targets are met. Marketing budgets usually are established for one year. However, market developments should be monitored in shorter time intervals (e.g., on a monthly or quarterly basis), so that the marketing managers can react if competitor's actions, changes in market demand, etc., require immediate action and a change in marketing plans.

Objectives

To be effective, objectives should be **S**pecific, **M**easureable, **A**chievable, **R**elevant, and **T**ime-specific, or "SMART." That is, the more specific, measureable, achievable, relevant, and time-specific an objective is, the better it guides action and investment, the more motivating it is, and the better it facilitates assessment and adjustment. Vague objectives lead to confused and ineffective effort, discourage initiative, and complicate diagnosis and remedial action.

The marketing function must contribute to the overarching objectives of the business unit; the business unit in turn contributes to the overall vision and mission of the company. This hierarchy of goals is important, as only marketing objectives that are consistent with the business unit strategy and the overall company mission and vision contribute to the long-term success of the firm. Well-managed companies translate visionary goals into long-term strategic objectives of the business units, and systematically derive objectives for the various business functions, including marketing, from those business unit objectives (see Figure 36-3). Hence, marketing objectives are derived from business unit objectives. In the example shown in Table 36-3, business unit objectives are specified in terms of profit, ROA, market share, and sales volume.

These business unit objectives now have to be translated into marketing objectives. There are three types of marketing objectives which should be specified at the overall level and at the segment level:[2]

- Profit objectives (e.g., profits, return on assets, return on sales, contribution margin, net marketing contribution);
- Sales objectives (e.g., sales volume, unit sales, market share); and

TABLE NOTE 36-2 Sample Marketing Budget

Buaness Unit 1: Net Marketing Contribution

	Segment 1	Segment 2	Segment 3	Segment 4	Total
Total market					
Volume (units)	480,000	1,300,000	250,000	860,000	2,890,000
Average unit price ($)	120	145	120	125	133
Dollar sales (millions)	57,600,000	188,500,000	30,000,000	107,500,000	383,600,000
Company Sales					
Average unit price ($)	125	138	118	126	130
Units sold	101,376	218,551	82,627	68,254	470,808
Market share (% units)	21.1	16.8	33.1	7.9	16.3
Sales revenue (millions)	12,672,000	30,160,000	9,750,000	8,600,000	61,182,000
Market share (% dollar sales)	22.0	16.0	32.5	8.0	15.9
Cost of Goods sold (millions)	8,236,800	19,604,000	6,337,500	5,590,000	39,768,300
Gross profit (millions)	4,435,200	10,556,000	3,412,500	3,010,000	21,413,700
Direct marketing costs					
Promotions	120,000	350,000	60,000	120,000	650,000
Discounts	60,000	160,000	35,000	50,000	305,000
Folders and mailing	40,000	110,000	20,000	50,000	220,000
Misc.	50,000	100,000	25,000	45,000	220,000
Semi-fixed Marketing Costs					
Media advertising	450,000	1,200,000	200,000	400,000	2,250,000
POS	100,000	250,000	60,000	95,000	505,000
Public relations	20,000	50,000	10,000	20,000	100,000
Fixed marketing costs					
Marketing department	120,000	240,000	60,000	120,000	540,000
Salesforce	240,000	480,000	120,000	240,000	1,080,000
Market research	50,000	125,000	25,000	45,000	245,000
Misc.	10,000	30,000	5,000	10,000	55,000
Total marketing expenses	1,260,000	3,095,000	620,000	1,195,000	6,170,000
in % of sales sale revenue	9.94	10.26	6.36	13.90	10.08
Net Marketing Contribution	**3,175,200**	**7,461,000**	**2,792,500**	**1,815,000**	**15243,700**
Other operating expenses	2,150,000	6,900,000	1,450,000	1,900,000	12,400,000
Net profit (before taxes)	**1,025,200**	**561,000**	**1,342,500**	**−85,000**	**2,843,700**
Assets	11,200,000	19,800,000	5,200,000	10,900,000	47,100,000
Return on assets (%)	**9.15**	**2.83**	**25.82**	**−0.78**	**6.04**
Return on sales (%)	8.09	1.86	13.77	−0.99	4.65

• Customer objectives (e.g., brand awareness, positioning, customer satisfaction, loyalty, cross-buying, share of wallet).

The marketing manager now must specify how the single market segments, or customers, contribute to the overall objective. This requires three basic steps:

1. Set profit objectives per segment;
2. Determine sales volume and market share needed to achieve that target profit; and

TABLE NOTE 36-3 Example of Business-Unit Objectives

Profit (before taxes):	$ 2,800,000
Return of Assets (ROA):	6%
Market share:	16%
Sales volume:	$ 61,000,000

3. Specifying levels of brand awareness, brand image, purchase rates, customer satisfaction, and customer loyalty needed to achieve the target market share.

For step number three, specifying levels of hierarchical customer "readiness," staircase analysis is a useful framework. Staircase analysis estimates the hierarchical components that influence future sales volume (illustrated in Figure 36-4):

- *Market Potential*—the maximum of all customers who could possibly purchase in the product category;
- *Actual Market*—the number of customers who actually buy the product category;

- *Brand Awareness*—the percentage of the customers of the actual market that are aware of the brand;
- *Brand Image*—the percentage of customers that know the brand and also find it attractive
- *Purchase Rate*—the number of customers that actually bought the product
- *Share of Wallet*—the company's share of the customer's annual purchase volume
- *Repurchase rate*—the number of customers who buy again
- *Cross-Buying Rate*—the number of customers that buy more than one product category from a specific supplier.

Another powerful and systematic method for developing specific objectives is "Cost-Volume-Profit" logic (or the Net Marketing Contribution (NMC) approach[3]). This framework decomposes marketing strategy's contribution to the overall profits of a business unit into its subordinate parts and thereby helps to identify various possible measures to improve profits:

$$Profit = Contribution (or NMC) - Overhead$$

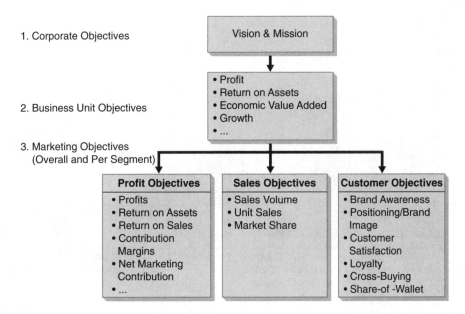

FIGURE NOTE 36-4 The Hierarchy of Objectives

Contribution = Sales − Total Variable Costs
= [(Unit Volume × Unit Price) −
(Unit Volume × Unit Variable Costs)]

Note that Unit Price minus Unit Variable Cost equals Unit Contribution Margin, another important concept in marketing and managerial accounting.

Profits, or "Net Marketing Contribution," can be broken down to identify the universe of feasible strategies for increasing profits (see Figure 36-6). Each cell in this tree represents an opportunity to increase overall profitability. For example:

- Overall profitability can be increased by increasing net marketing contribution or by decreasing overhead (expenses that do not vary with the marketing strategy, e.g., R&D, corporate overhead);
- Net marketing contribution can be increased by increasing sales revenue or by lowering total variable cost (or "costs of goods sold;" i.e., total cost or producing a product that varies directly with the volume sold, such as materials costs, direct labor, transportation, and other direct variable costs);

- Sales revenue can be increased by increasing sales in units or by increasing price;
- Sales in units can be increased by increasing the number of customers or by increasing those customers purchase rate.

Other logical contributors to profitability via this cost-volume-profit "tree" are not shown but can be readily deduced to extend the reasoning. For example:

- The number of customers can be increased by acquiring more new customers or by retaining more of the firm's existing customers;
- Purchase rate can be increased by increasing average purchase volume or by increasing purchase frequency; and,
- Sales in units can be increased by increasing overall market demand (i.e., increasing the size of the 'pie') or by increasing market share (the firm's piece of that pie);
- New customers can be acquired from competitors or by converting nonusers.

In this way the effects of various marketing tactics can be linked to overall profitability and subordi-

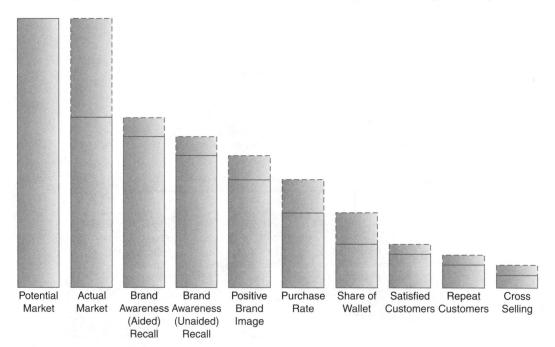

FIGURE NOTE 36-5   Staircase Analysis

nate objectives through these cost-volume-profit relationships. It is important that objectives are specific, measureable, achievable, relevant, and time-specific.

Finalizing the Marketing Mix

Once specific objectives are formulated, the marketing mix can be finalized. Note that the process of making forecasts, setting objectives, and creating a budget *began* with an understanding of a strategic objectives and the establishment of a preliminary marketing mix. Initial forecasts were then based on that draft marketing mix and on an understanding of the effects of each tactic on resulting sales revenues and profits. With the budget, forecasts, and objectives refined and adjusted, a final marketing mix emerges. That final marketing mix, by the way, then solidifies the final budget, final forecasts, and specific objectives.

If the overall target market share is 16 percent, the target ROA 6 percent, and the target sales volume is $ 61,000,000, the marketing manager has to specify the objectives for each market segment and how they should be achieved, for example:

- The amount of promotions to stimulate trial purchases;
- The amount of discounts;
- The amount of folders and mailings to create awareness; or
- Media advertising to create brand image.

The following example illustrates the logic:

1. Determine the objective: Segment 2 currently has a market share of 14 percent and it has to be increased to 16 percent (see Table 36-1 which contains the targets and the budget) to reach the overall target of the business unit.

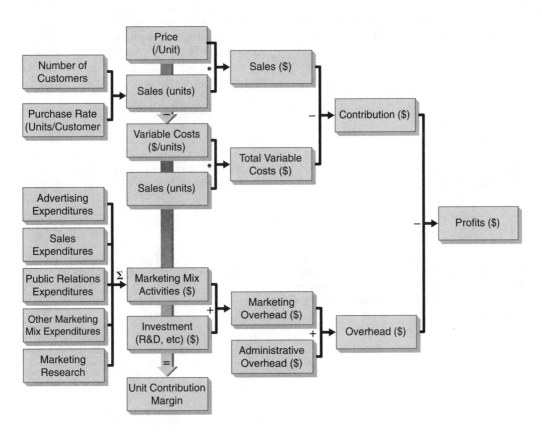

FIGURE NOTE 36-6   The Marketing Profit Tree

2. Determine the number of customers to be acquired: Currently, the sales volume to segment 2 is $26,390,000 (191,232 units). It has to be increased to 218,551 units (+27,318 units). The average customer buys 1.5 products per year. Therefore, 18,213 new customers have to be acquired.

3. Determine the necessary marketing activities: A mix of marketing activities is necessary to acquire new customers (media advertising, folders, and mailings to create brand awareness, promotions, and discounts to stimulate trial purchases, etc.). It is estimated that, on average, $35 have to be spent to acquire a new customer (advertising, folders, promotions, discounts, etc.)

4. Establish the budget: The marketing budget for new customer acquisition, therefore, is: 18,212 × $35 = $637,420.

Of course, a number of additional marketing activities are necessary to keep brand awareness high, to react to competitor's marketing moves, to keep loyal customers, and to achieve other objectives. For all these activities, costs are estimated and combined into a comprehensive marketing plan (see Table 30-2).

Summary

The strategic marketing process ties situation assessment—including scrutiny of the organization's mission, vision, and goals—to strategy formation, and that strategy drives the development of a marketing mix, including the traditional summary "Ps" (promotion or integrated marketing communications and people, product, place or distribution, and price). Diligent and effective strategic management requires that the implementation plan, the tactics, be linked with forecast results and detailed budgets, and then those plans, forecasts, and budgets be fleshed out in specific and measurable objectives. These various deliverables—a detailed implementation plan, an associated budget, a set of related forecasts, and specific and measureable objectives—be generated through iterative and interconnected analyses that optimize the expected impact of the investments. These then become the basis for assessment. Comparing realized results against objectives using the specific metrics, identifying gaps, and formulating remedial plans is the essence of assessment and adjustment but is impossible if appropriate and measurable objectives were not derived from the marketing mix plan in advance.

Additional Resources

Best, R. J. *Market-Based Management*. Upper Saddle River, NJ: Prentice Hall, 2005.

Lambin, J.-J. *Market-Driven Management*. Houndmills, Basingstoke, Hampshire: Palgrave Macmillan, 2007.

Endnotes

1. Adapted from D. W. Cravens, and N. F. Piercy, *Strategic Marketing* (Boston: McGraw Hill, 2006).

2. J.-J. Lambin, *Market-Driven Management*, (Houndmills, Basingstoke, Hampshire: Palgrave Macmillan, 2007).

3. Roger J. Best, *Market-based Management* (Upper Saddle River, NJ: Prentice Hall, 2005).

37

Staircase Analysis

To translate a strategy into *action,* clear marketing objectives must be established. *What specifically is each action intended to accomplish?* Objectives can be *financial,* which is related to profitability and returns; *operational,* including inventory turns, conformance, and the like; or *market-oriented,* such as sales volume (units or dollars), market share, brand image, customer satisfaction, and so on. A simple mnemonic for evaluating objectives is "SMART": objectives should be **S**pecific, **M**easureable, **A**chievable, **R**elevant, and **T**ime-specific (although they are synonyms in the common language, by convention in the strategy literature "objectives" are more specific and shorter-term than "goals," which are longer-term and tied directly to the organization's mission and especially vision). Objectives must be set high enough to motivate people to achieve them and low enough so that they are realistic and not frustrating to employees. They should be relevant (it is not useful to give people objectives that are not related to things they control) and time-specific. In many companies, strategies fail because managers are not able to develop and communicate useful (SMART) objectives.

An extremely useful tool for formulating objectives is *staircase analysis.* Staircase analysis addresses "specificity" by breaking down the flow, "staircase" (Figure 37-1) or "funnel" (Figure 37-2) through which the total potential market—the largest and most inclusive understanding of the market—is narrowed down to the firm's actual customers and those actual customers are sorted out by "share of wallet," "satisfaction," "loyalty," and "cross-buying." Staircase analysis accentuates the "steps" that lead to a purchase decision, and its structure highlights the *gaps* where potential sales are lost (and where investments and improved efforts can therefore *improve* sales and profitability). The logic of the staircase analysis is simple; it is organized by the following questions:

1. What is the market potential?
2. What is the actual market?
3. What is the brand awareness in the market?
4. How many of the customers who know my brand find it attractive?
5. How many of the customers who find my brand attractive have bought it in the last year?
6. What is my share of wallet of these customers?
7. How many of these customers were completely satisfied?
8. How many of these customers will buy again?
9. How many of these customers also buy other products of my portfolio?

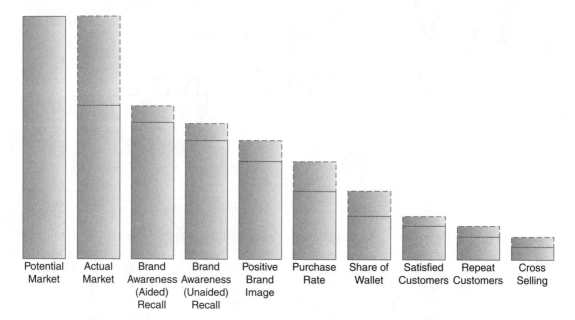

FIGURE 37-1 Generic Staircase Analysis

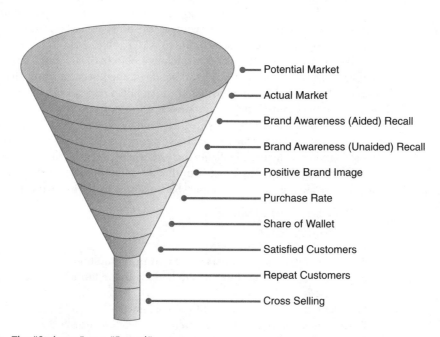

FIGURE 37-2 The "Staircase" as a "Funnel"

By answering these questions, it is easy to spot the steps where market share is lost along the single steps of the "staircase." We can define realistic objectives to close the gaps; and if we find the reasons why some of the gaps are so big, we can take the right measures to close them. Figure 37-3 shows the staircase-analysis for an online bookstore in a European market. Going through the following questions, the staircase has been built, marketing objectives have been set, and measures to close the gaps have been derived.

1. *What is the market potential?*
   The market potential consists of all potential buyers or users of a product who have the need, the resources necessary to use the product, and the ability to pay.[1] In the case of our example above, an online bookseller, it was found that the target market consists of 71 million potential customers. The average annual spending of each customer is €60. Hence, the potential of this market is €4,260 million.

2. *What is the actual market?*
   In the case of our online bookseller, not all potential customers can be accessed—but only those who have Internet access (67% of the population). Therefore, the actual market consists of 47.6 million buyers. The online bookstore loses 23.4 million buyers, which corresponds to €1,404 million of market potential, as it addresses only Internet users. The distinction between the actual market and the potential market is important, as in this case an increase of the Internet penetration in the target market could dramatically increase the size and prospects of the market.

3. *What is the brand awareness in the market?*
   There are two methods to measure brand awareness: unaided recall and aided recall. Unaided recall is a technique to test brand awareness of the target market without giving the customers the brand name (e.g., which online bookstores do you know?), whereas aided

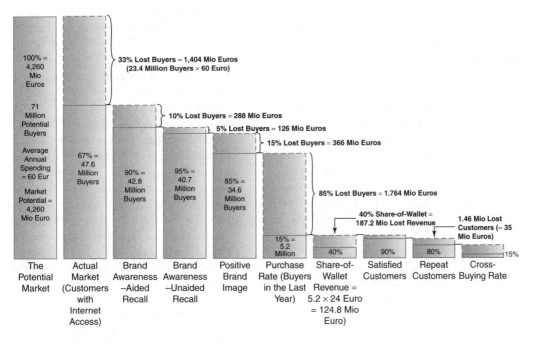

FIGURE 37-3   Example of a Staircase-Analysis: An Online Bookstore

recall tests brand awareness by showing the consumers a list of brands and asking them to tell which of them they know. Aided recall is always higher than unaided recall. A big difference between unaided and aided recall means that the brand is not strong, and it does not automatically come into mind when consumers think about a product category. In our example, unaided recall is 90 percent. This number means that the company loses 10 percent of potential customers (€288 million) at this stage. Of those consumers who know the brand, 95 percent do so without being given a list of online bookstore brands. Overall, this company loses €414 million of potential revenues as not all Internet users know the brand.

4. *How many of the customers who know my brand find it attractive?*
Brand awareness is not enough. To be successful, potential customers must find the brand attractive. Therefore, the next stage of the staircase analysis tests how many of the consumers who know a brand and also find it attractive. In our example, the market research has shown that the brand not only has high brand awareness, but also that the majority of customers find it attractive (85%). Hence, at the stage between brand awareness and brand attractiveness, only 15 percent of potential customers are lost (€366 million).

5. *How many of the customers who find my brand attractive have bought it in the last year?*
The next step of the staircase analysis assesses how many customers who find the brand attractive actually buy it. If there is a huge gap between these steps, a company has to find the reasons for this and needs to try to close the gap. In our example, only 15 percent of the potential customers who find the Internet bookstore attractive have bought books from it in the last year. Hence, it lost 1,764 million of potential revenue at this stage. Market research identified the following main reasons:

1. 55 percent of the nonbuyers do not own a credit card;
2. 19 percent did not find the book they wanted;
3. 12 percent do not want to pay with credit card on the Internet;
4. 14 percent of the nonbuyers do not trust an online vendor or are reluctant to buy a product they cannot see and touch before buying.

6. *What is my share of wallet of my customers?*
The share of wallet is the amount of business a company gets from a customer. In our example, the online bookstore's share of wallet is 40 percent. We can determine this because the average sales volume per customer is €24, and the average customer spends €60 a year for books: €24 /€60 s = 40 percent share of wallet. The share of wallet is an important indicator for possible growth, as it tells the company how much growth potential can be exploited without having to acquire new customers. At this stage, the online bookstore loses €187.2 million of revenue as it captures only 40 percent of its customers' annual spending for books.

7. *How many of our customers are completely satisfied?*
Customer satisfaction is one of the most important marketing objectives. It gives immediate and precise feedback on whether the company is able to fulfill the customer's needs. Customer satisfaction is a driver of repurchase, of positive word of mouth, and of cross-buying.

8. *How many of our customers will buy again?*
Another critical performance indicator is the retention rate. A company with a retention rate of 70 percent has lost more than 80 percent of its customers after five years; a company with a retention rate of 80 percent has lost two thirds. As every lost customer has to be replaced in order not to lose business and as on average it costs five to seven times as much to acquire a new customer than to keep an existing one, a high retention rate is a critical success factor. In our case, the online bookstore loses €1.46 million of business with its retention rate of 72 percent (80% of the 90% satisfied customers buy again) within the first year.

9. *How many of my customers buy also other products of my portfolio?*

Cross-buying means that a customer also buys other products of a vendor's portfolio. Cross-selling usually is a very effective means to increase sales as the company can use an existing customer relationship, its brand image, trust, and distribution channel to generate additional sales. There are different ways to compute a cross-selling or cross-buying rate (e.g., percentage of customers who buy more than one product of my portfolio and average number of products customers buy from my portfolio). In our case, the cross-buying rate means that 40 percent of the customers buy more than books (e.g., CDs).

Based on market research, the staircase has been built. In the next step, we can formulate marketing objectives. To do so, we need to set priorities to make our marketing efforts as effective as possible. The best way to achieve that is to look at the gaps between the stages of the staircase and to focus on the biggest ones. Next, we define realistic objectives for them:

1. Keep brand awareness at this level.
2. Keep the positive brand image.
3. Increase to purchase rate from 15 percent to 25 percent within two years.
4. Increase share of wallet from 40 percent to 50 percent within two years.
5. Increase the retention rate from 80 percent to 85 percent within two years.
6. Increase the cross-buying rate from 15 percent to 40 percent within two years.

If our market research has also revealed why the single gaps are so high (e.g., the reasons for the low purchase rate), the right measures can be taken to reach the objectives.

Summary

The Staircase Analysis approach provides a framework emphasizing objective criteria such as retention rate, share of wallet, purchase rate, and so forth so that managers can easily visualize the connections between these sequential outcomes and business performance. Objectives can then be set to improve business performance one step of the staircase at a time. Staircase Analysis is a great example of a "process model" using hierarchical logic to summarize the funneling of a *total market*—the "total potential market" and the "actual market"—down through levels of awareness (aided and unaided) and desire (positive brand image), toward eventual action (purchase, share of wallet) and adoption or loyalty (satisfaction, repeat purchase, and cross-buying). Similar hierarchies are used to model advertising and promotion effects in the flow of consumers from unaware to purchase and adoption[2] and, in B2B settings, to model the progression of business customers from "unqualified lead" to "suspect" to "prospect," and finally to "closed customer" (purchase).[3] A given business or product manager may adjust the steps to better suit the flow of customers through the purchase process or sales funnel for a particular business. The logic and rigor of staircase analysis is indispensable in thinking strategically and in granular detail about desired effects in the marketplace and in tying investments to measurable outcomes.

Additional Resources

Barry, Thomas E., and Daniel J. Howard, "A Review and Critique of the Hierarchy of Effects in Advertising." *International Journal of Advertising* 9 (1990): 121–135.

Lehmann, Donald R., and Russell S. Winer, *Analysis for Marketing Planning.* (New York: McGraw-Hill, 2008).

Tanner, Jeff, Earl D. Honeycutt, and Robert C. Erffmeyer, *Sales Management: Shaping Future Sales Leaders* (Upper Saddle River, NJ: Pearson/Prentice Hall, 2009).

Endnotes

1. D. R. Lehmann and R. S. Winer, *Analysis for Marketing Planning* (New York: McGraw-Hill, 2008).

2. See Thomas E. Barry and Daniel J. Howard, "A Review and Critique of the Hierarchy of Effects in Advertising," *International Journal of Advertising* 9 (1990): 121–135; and, for a more recent compilations of perspectives, Vijay Mahajan, Eitan Muller, and Yoram Wind, eds., *New-Product Diffusion Models* (New York: Springer Science+Business Media, 2000).

3. See Patrick J. Robinson, Charles W. Faris, and Yoram Wind, *Industrial Buying and Creative Marketing* (Boston, MA: Allyn & Bacon, 1967); and D. J. Dalrymple, W. L. Cron, and T. E. DeCarlo, *Sales Management* (Hoboken, NJ: John Wiley & Sons, 2004).

38

Assessment and Adjustment

A well-known management adage holds that "if you can't measure it, you can't manage it."[1] During the marketing planning process (reiterated in Figure 38-1), long-term strategies are translated into specific shorter-term marketing activities (positioning using the marketing mix) accompanied by budgets, forecasts, and objectives. This note focuses on that essential step: translating marketing mix activities into budgets, forecasts, and objectives. That process is inherently interactive; changes in one element—the objectives, planned mix, budgets or resulting forecasts, can impact each of the other elements.

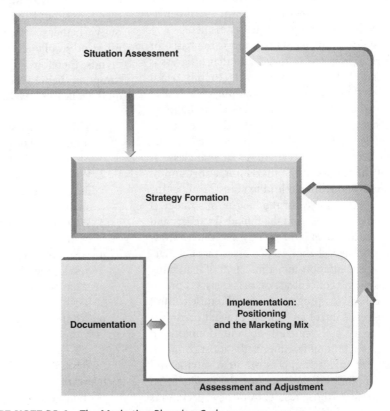

FIGURE NOTE 38-1   The Marketing Planning Cycle

To be effective, objectives should be "SMART": **S**pecific, **M**easureable, **A**chievable, **R**elevant, and **T**ime-specific. The specific, measurable, and time-specific characteristics of good (smart) objectives flow into the assessment and adjustment stage of the strategic planning framework. Without specific, measureable, and time-specific objectives it is hard to tell whether the firm has achieved what it set out to achieve and impossible to attribute gaps in the planning to specific problems or failures. Therefore, a useful complement to the axiom quoted above, about measurability, may be Yogi Berra's slightly tangled quote: "if you don't know where you're going in life, you're liable to end up somewhere else"[2] (by which he apparently meant that, if you don't know where you're going, you'll never know if you've gotten there[3]). Thus, the necessary first steps to effective assessment come well before the assessment, even before the implementation of the plan to be assessed, when the assumptions that guide it and the specific outcomes that it is intended to achieve are spelled out carefully and clearly along with the specific metrics that will inform their eventual assessment.

It guides implementation and is the basis for monitoring progress. To make sure that progress is made and that a company reacts to important changes in time, a continuous planning cycle is necessary, as shown in Figure 38-1. Based on the long-term strategy, which usually extends beyond one year, yearly marketing plans are developed, implemented, evaluated and revised. A systematic assessment of the results of the marketing effort and of market conditions should lead to adjustments of the marketing plan or even of the long-term strategy, if important deviations from the intended strategy and the plan are found, or if the premise on which a strategy is formulated, change. Hence, assessment of marketing implementation and adjustment of marketing activities should concentrate on two areas: (1) premise control and (2) progress control. Premise control and progress control are similar to what organizational theory calls single-loop and double-loop learning. Single-loop learning is the most common style of learning: it simply is problem solving and program calibration. We measure the results of an action, compare those results to prior expectations or forecasts, and modify our actions to close the gap

between expected and obtained outcomes. This is *progress control*. Double-loop learning is more than fixing a problem and changing behavior to obtain expected results; double-loop learning questions the fundamental values, assumptions and policies that are behind those actions. This is the principle of *premise control*. Every strategy is based on specific assumptions; premise control means testing and questioning those values, assumptions and policies, including the overarching strategy behind a particular marketing mix.[4] The next sections elaborate on premise control and process control, the two basic levels of assessment and adjustment.

PREMISE CONTROL

Each strategy is based on a set of assumptions about opportunities and threats, industry development, competitor strategies, consumer behavior, and so on. Consequently, a strategy can be pursued only as long as these premises do not change. Premise control therefore should check systematically and continuously whether or not the assumptions during a planning and implementation period are still valid.[5] A premise therefore starts with an explication of the assumptions behind each strategy. This should be done on the following levels:

1. What are the assumptions about future opportunities and threats stemming from the analysis of the macro environment?
2. What are the assumptions about the industry development stemming from the industry analysis?
3. What are our assumptions about the behavior of our competitors?
4. What are our assumptions about the market development?
5. What are our assumptions about customer behavior?
6. What are our assumptions about our own competences, strengths, weaknesses, etc.?

Table 38-1 clarifies the logic of the analysis. For each level of the analysis (macro-environment, industry, competition, etc.), the assumptions (strategy premises) are explicated. In the next step, it is analyzed

TABLE NOTE 38-1 Example of Premise Control

Level of Analysis	Strategy Premise	Change	Impact
1. Macro environment	1. Exchange rate USD/Euro 1.60 2. New production technology lowers cost of goods sold by 10%	1. USD/Euro 1.45 2. Introduction of new technology delayed for 2 years	1. Loss of competitiveness in Europe due to strong dollar; 12.4 million less profits in Europe 2. COGS higher than planned, contribution margin 18% lower than planned
2. Industry level	3. Diffusion of product substitute slow in 2009 (4 % market share) 4. Bargaining power of buyers does not change	3. Product substitute gains market share quickly (8%) 4. Buyers form buying associations unexpectedly	3. Rapidly declining sales (20%) due to substitution 4. Price reductions of up to 5% required
3. Competition	5. Main competitor keeps prices high 6. New generation of products introduced in 2011	5. Main competitors lowers prices by 10% 6. New generation of products introduced already in 2010	5. Price reduction necessary, loss of customers expected
4. Market	7. Market growth 12%	7. As expected	6. No changes
5. Customers	8. High loyalty due to high switching barriers and no available substitutes	8. Due to substitution product and price strategy of competitor, high customer churn	7. New customer acquisition must be doubled to compensate for customer migration
6. Company	9. We can generate enough cash flow from Business Unit X to finance the acquisition of company 10. We can keep our cost leadership due to economies of scale and the 70% learning curve, as we have the highest market share	9. No changes 10. Experience curve is only 80%; competitor X has increased market share via an acquisition	8. No changes 9. Competitor X has significant cost advantages now

whether any changes can be observed, and if so, how these changes impact the strategy, the marketing plan, and its implementation. The strategy of the company in Table 38-1 is based on a number of assumptions, including:

1. The U.S. dollar (USD)/Euro exchange rate will remain 1.60;
2. A new production technology lowers costs of goods sold by 10 percent;

3. The diffusion of a product substitute is slow (4% market share); and
4. Bargaining power of customers does not change.

The premise control, however, reveals that a number of these planning assumptions are not valid anymore. They have a substantial impact on the strategy (last column of Table 38-1) and lead to a revision of either the marketing plan or of the overall strategy.

PROGRESS CONTROL USING FINANCIAL RATIOS AND MARKETING METRICS

Progress control should measure how well a marketing plan is executed, whether the objectives are achieved, and whether the marketing strategy is still on target. The focus should be on financial ratios and on marketing metrics. Each marketing manager should be concerned about the overall financial ratios of a company for two reasons. First, marketing contributes to the financial performance of a company and second, financial performance (e.g., liquidity) can constrain or permit marketing strategies and activities.

Marketing performance metrics measure the factors that actually drive financial profits of a company. They include four areas of metrics (see Figure 38-2): (1) market metrics measure market conditions and a company's performance in the market; (2) competitive metrics measure how well a company performs compared to competitors; (3) customer metrics measure the company's performance on a customer level and (4) marketing profitability metrics assess marketing's financial success.[6] The marketing metrics discussed in this section are only a selection of all available metrics. We tried to focus on the most relevant ones.

Financial Ratios

Financial ratios are based on accounting information. Most of them are most meaningful when they are used on a comparative basis (compared with industry standards, prior periods, competitors, and previously established plans or budgets). Differences in accounting practices and principles however can lead to differences in ratios between companies. Financial ratios, therefore, must be used and interpreted with caution.

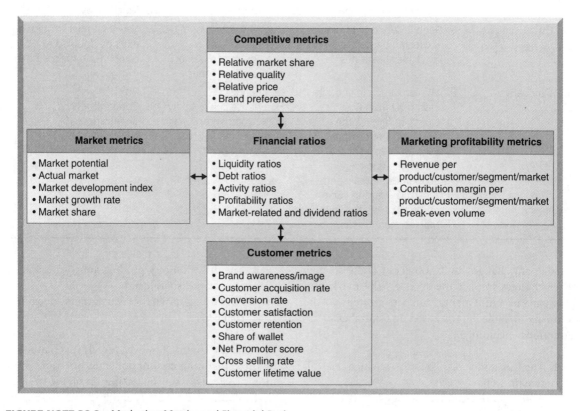

FIGURE NOTE 38-2 Marketing Metrics and Financial Ratios

There are five major groups of financial ratios.

- Liquidity ratios measure whether a company is able to meet its current financial obligations; they focus on the size of, and the relationship between current assets and current liabilities.
- Debt ratios indicate the company's ability to repay long-term debt.
- Activity ratios (or investment utilization ratios) assess the effectiveness of a company's use of its resources.

- Profitability ratios relate the income earned with the amount of resources used to generate this income.
- Market-related and dividend ratios measure to what extent a company generates value for its shareholders.

Table 38-2 gives an overview of the most important financial ratios, their calculation and description of their informative value.

TABLE NOTE 38-2 Important Financial Ratios[7]

Ratio	Formula	Informative Value
1. Liquidity ratios		
• Current ratio	$\dfrac{Current\ Assets}{Current\ liabilities}$	Indicates the firm's ability to meet its current financial liabilities with assets that can be converted to cash in a short term.
• Quick ratio (acid-test ratio)	$\dfrac{Current\ assets\ -\ inventory}{Current\ liabilities}$	Indicates the firm's ability to pay off short-term obligations using liquid assets (without relying on sales of inventory)
• Inventory to net working capital	$\dfrac{Inventory}{Current\ assets\ -\ current\ liabilities}$	Indicates the extent to which the firm's working capital is tied up in inventory
2. Debt ratios		
• Debt-to-assets-ratio	$\dfrac{Total\ debt}{Total\ assets}$	Indicates how much of the firm's total assets are financed by debt
• Debt-to-equity-ratio	$\dfrac{Total\ debt}{Total\ stockholder's\ equity}$	Compares how much the firm is financed by debt with how much it is financed by equity
• Long-term debt to equity ratio	$\dfrac{Longterm\ debt}{Total\ shareholder's\ equity}$	Indicates the balance between debt and equity in the firm's overall capital structures
• Times-interest-earned	$\dfrac{Profits\ before\ interest\ and\ taxes}{Total\ interest\ charges}$	Measures the firm's ability to meet all interest payments
• Fixed charge coverage	$\dfrac{Profits\ before\ taxes\ and\ interest\ +\ lease\ obligations}{Total\ interest\ charges\ +\ lease\ obligations}$	Measures the firm's ability to meet all of its fixed-charge obligations

(Continued)

TABLE NOTE 38-2 *(Continued)*

Ratio	Formula	Informative Value
3. Activity ratios		
• Inventory turnover	$$\frac{Cost\ of\ goods\ sold}{Inventory}$$	Indicates how quickly a company is able to convert inventories to cash; or whether a company has excessive inventory or perhaps inadequate inventory
• Fixed-assets turnover	$$\frac{Sales}{Fixed\ assets}$$	Measures the effectiveness of the firm in utilizing its plants and equipment
• Total assets turnover	$$\frac{Sales}{Total\ assets}$$	Measures the effectiveness of the firm in utilizing total assets
• Days' receivables	$$\frac{Net\ Sales}{365} = Average\ day's\ sales$$ $$Day's\ receivables = \frac{Accounts\ receivable}{Average\ day's\ sales}$$	Measures the amount of time that elapses between sales and receipt of payment
• Working capital turnover	$$\frac{Sales}{Average\ current\ assets - Average\ current\ liabilities}$$	Measures the speed with which funds are provided by current assets to satisfy current liabilities
4. Profitability ratios		
• Gross profit margin	$$\frac{Sales - Costs\ of\ goods\ sold}{Sales}$$	Indicates the total margin available to cover operating expenses and yield a profit
• Return on sales (ROS)	$$\frac{Profits\ after\ taxes}{Sales}$$	Indicates after-tax profits per dollar of sales; neither a high nor a low return on sales necessarily indicate good performance, it depends on the amount of investment.
• Return on total assets (ROA)	$$\frac{Profits\ after\ taxes}{Total\ assets}$$	Measures the net return on total investment of the firm
• Return on stockholder's equity (ROE)	$$\frac{Profits\ after\ taxes}{Total\ stockholder's\ equity}$$	Measures the net return on stockholder's investment in the firm.
• Return on invested capital (ROIC)	$$\frac{Net\ income}{Total\ liabilities\ and\ stockholder's\ equity - Current\ liabilities}$$	Relates all net income to all resources committed to the firm for long periods of time.

TABLE NOTE 38-2 *(Continued)*

Ratio	Formula	Informative Value
5. Market-related and dividend ratios		
• Earnings per share	$$\frac{Profits\ after\ taxes\ -\ preferred\ stock\ dividends}{Number\ of\ shares\ of\ common\ stock\ +\ equivalents}$$	Indicates the earnings returned on the initial investment.
• Price earnings ratio	$$\frac{Market\ price\ per\ share\ of\ stock}{Earnings\ per\ share}$$	Measure of the price paid for a share relative to the annual profit earned per share; indicates whether investors pay a relative high or low price for the stock.
• Dividend yield ratio	$$\frac{Dividends\ per\ share}{Market\ price\ per\ share}$$	Indicates the annual dividend payment as a percentage of the price per share.
• Dividend payout	$$\frac{Dividends}{Profits\ after\ taxes\ (available\ to\ common\ shareholders)}$$	Shows the proportion of net income paid out in dividends.

Marketing Metrics

Whereas financial ratios indicate a company's or a business unit's performance, marketing metrics measure those factors that *drive* a firm's performance. There are many marketing metrics available; like a lot of managerial data, it would be easy for the sheer volume of those metrics to become overwhelming. Therefore, two critical, related strategic marketing tasks are to *identify the information needed by managers* and, based on that, to *select the appropriate performance metrics* to monitor performance. Whether individual performance metrics are appropriate or not depends on the strategy. If, for example, a business unit follows a growth strategy, performance criteria such as relative market share and customer acquisitions are important; whereas for a harvest strategy in the maturity phase of the product life cycle, customer retention and cross-selling might be more appropriate. Table 38-3 contains four categories of marketing metrics, with their formula, and a brief description.

TABLE NOTE 38-3 Marketing Metrics

Metric	Formula	Informative Value
1. Market metrics		
• Market potential	*Number of potential customers X average sales volume per customer*	Indicates the maximum potential of a market if all potential consumers buy the product or service
• Actual market	*Number of buyers X average sales volume per customer*	Indicates the actual market demand (e.g., on a yearly basis)
• Market development index	$$\frac{Actual\ market}{Market\ potential}$$	Indicates the market saturation.

(Continued)

TABLE NOTE 38-3 *(Continued)*

Metric	Formula	Informative Value
• Market growth rate	$\dfrac{Actual\ market\ t1\ -\ Actual\ market\ t0}{Actual\ market\ t0} \times 100$	Indicates the market growth in percentages
• Market share (units)	$\dfrac{Unit\ sales\ of\ company\ X}{Overall\ unit\ sales\ in\ market\ X}$	Indicates a company's share of the overall market measured in units sold
• Market share (volume)	$\dfrac{Sales\ volume\ of\ company\ X}{Overall\ sales\ volume\ in\ market\ X}$	Indicates a company's share of the overall sales volume in a market
2. Competitive metrics		
• Relative market share (units)	$\dfrac{Unit\ sales\ of\ company\ X}{Unit\ sales\ of\ strongest\ competitor}$	Indicates a company's or product's competitive position in terms of unit sales
• Relative market share (volume)	$\dfrac{Sales\ volume\ of\ company\ X}{Sales\ volume\ of\ strongest\ competitor}$	Indicates a company's or product's competitive position in terms of sales volume
• Relative price	$\dfrac{Unit\ price\ of\ company\ X}{Unit\ price\ of\ strongest\ competitor}$	Measures a product's price competitiveness
• Relative quality	$\dfrac{Quality\ score\ of\ company\ X}{Quality\ score\ of\ strongest\ competitor}$	Measures perceived quality of a product (e.g., on a scale from 1 to 5) compared to competitors
• Brand preference	$\dfrac{Brand\ preference\ of\ company\ X}{Brand\ preference\ of\ strongest\ competitor}$	Indicates brand superiority by relating the number of customers who prefer the brand of company X to the number of customers who prefer the competitor's brand
3. Marketing profitability metrics		
• Revenue per product/ customer/ segment/market	$\dfrac{Revenue\ per\ product,\ customer,\ etc.}{Overall\ revenue}$	Indicates the importance of each product, customer, segment, etc., for the overall sales volume of the company
• Total contribution margin	$Sales\ revenue\ -\ total\ variable\ cost$	The total contribution margin indicates the fraction of sales that contributes to the offset of fixed costs. It can also be calculated per product, customer, segment, or market
• Contribution margin ratio	$\dfrac{Unit\ price\ -\ variable\ cost\ per\ unit}{Unit\ price}$	The contribution margin ratio indicates the product's contribution to offset fixed costs as a percentage of unit price
• Break-even market volume	$\dfrac{Fixed\ costs}{Price\ per\ unit\ -\ variable\ cost\ per\ unit}$	Indicates how many units must be sold in order to break even (cover total costs)

TABLE NOTE 38-3 *(Continued)*

Metric	Formula	Informative Value
4. Customer metrics		
• Brand awareness ratio	*Number of customers that know my brand* / *Total number of customers*	Indicates the company's communication effectiveness
• Brand preference ratio	*Number of customers that prefer my brand* / *Total number of customers*	Indicates the attractiveness of the offer to the customer.
• Customer acquisition rate	*Number of new acquired customers* / *Overall number of existing customers*	Measures a company's effectiveness in acquiring new customers
• Conversion rate	*Number of customers that bought my product* / *Total number of customers*	Indicates the company's effectiveness in converting customers (from lookers to buyers)
• Customer satisfaction rate	*Number of satisfied customers* / *Number of overall customers*	Indicates the ability to satisfy customer's needs
• Customer retention	*Customers that repurchase the product* / *Number of customers*	Measures the company's ability to keep customers
• Share of wallet	*Purchase volume of customer X* / *Overall purchase volume of customer X*	Indicates the untapped sales potential per customer.
• Net promoter score	*Customers who recommend my product* / *Overall number of customers*	Measures the psychological commitment of a customer to a brand/company.
• Cross selling rate	*Number of customers who buy more than one of the offered products* / *Overall number of customers* *or* *Average number of offered products bought by customer*	Indicates the company's ability to exploit customer relationships.
• Customer lifetime value	*Net present value of all profits a customer produces over time*	Indicates a customer's profitability and attractiveness.

Summary

Developing a sound marketing strategy and a sound marketing plan is only half of the marketing success. To make sure that strategy and plans are on target, continuous assessment is necessary. A marketing manager must always monitor whether the premises of the strategy are still valid, and should revise the strategy or plan accordingly when those conditions or assumptions change. Progress of implementation and success should be measured to make sure that everything is on track. Peter Drucker once said: "If you can't measure it, you can't manage it!" There are

many marketing metrics available, and you have to be very careful in the selection of the metrics for a number of reasons. First, using too many metrics might lead to "paralysis by analysis." Second, if you decide to use specific metrics to assess performance, you have to be aware that employees will focus on these metrics as they know that they are measured against them. If salespeople's performance is measured on their sales volume, they will maximize sales volume, if they are measured on contribution margins, they will maximize contribution margin, and if they are evaluated on their customer's satisfaction, their focus will change again. Third, you have to make sure that metrics don't contradict each other. Especially short- and long-term effects have to be considered. Maximizing market share in the short run (i.e., by reducing prices) might damage the long-term brand image. The challenge is to select and focus on a limited set of appropriate metrics. This selection of metrics depends on the strategy and their measurability.

Additional Resources

Best, Roger J. *Market-based Management.* Upper Saddle River, NJ: Pearson, Prentice Hall, 2009.

Hitt, M. A., R. D. Ireland, and R. E. Hoskisson.*Strategic Management. Competitiveness and Globalization,* Mason, OH:, Thompson South-Western, 2005.

Schreyögg, G. and H. Steinmann. "Strategic Control: A New Perspective." *Academy of Management Review* 12 (1987): 91–103.

Endnotes

1. David A. Garvin, "Building a Learning Organization," *Harvard Business Review* 71, no. 4 (July–August, 1993): 89.

2. Quoted by Lewis Timberlake (with Marietta Reed), *Born to Win: You Can Turn Your Dreams into Reality* (Carol Stream, Il: Tyndale House, 1986) 38.

3. Ibid.

4. See Chris Argyris and Donald A. Schön, *Organizational Learning: A Theory of Action Perspective* (Reading, MA.: Addison Wesley, 1978).

5. G. Schreyögg, and H. Steinmann, "Strategic Control: A New Perspective." *Academy of Management Review* 12, (1987): 91–103.

6. R. J. Best, *Market-based Management* (Upper Saddle River, NJ: Prentice Hall, 2009).

7. Adapted from R. N. Anthony, D. F. Hawkins, and K. A. Merchant, *Accounting* (Boston: McGraw-Hill, 2007); M. A. Hitt, R. D. Ireland, and R. E. Hoskisson, *Strategic Management: Competitiveness and Globalization* (Mason, Ohio, Thompson South-Western, 2005); and D. W. Cravens and N. F. Piercy *Strategic Marketing* (Boston: McGraw Hill, 2006).

APPENDIX A

Basic Financial Math for Marketing Strategy

PART ONE: COST-VOLUME-PROFIT LOGIC

There are some fundamental relationships among prices, volume, and costs that define the income statement and drive profitability. These relationships are logical—you can deduce them by thinking about the way a business works and the way its accounts are defined and relate to one another. In fact, understanding their interrelationships can illuminate important aspects of business plans and differentiate alternatives in strategic planning. These terms and their interrelationships are defined below:

- Total revenue (R; the total amount of money taken in) equals average price ($\bar{P}$; the average amount received for each individual unit sold) multiplied by quantity sold (Q; the number of units sold):

$$R = \bar{P} * Q$$

"Selling prices" are generally stated for each level of distribution. So there may be a manufacturer's selling price, a distributor's selling price, and a retail selling price. In that respect, the selling prices may be thought to codify "outbound logistics" to channel members and customers. For example, when Perdue Farms was considering whether to enter the chicken hot-dog business, their analysts estimated they could sell 200,000 pounds of this product each week at a manufacturer's selling price of $0.75 per pound. This level of sales would have resulted in total revenues of 200,000*$0.75, or $150,000 per week (which, when multiplied by 52, equates to $7.8 million per year in total revenue). In that same example, the distributor's selling price was expected to be $0.80 per pound and the retail selling price was expected to be $1.23 per pound.

- Total variable costs (TVC; the costs of goods sold) equals variable costs per unit (VC/u; the cost of each unit sold) multiplied by quantity sold (Q):

$$TVC = VC/u * Q$$

Variable costs represent the costs of material and labor coming into the firm—its "inbound logistics" in its value chain. Variable costs are cost that vary with volume. To return to the previous example, Perdue Farms' analysts estimated that the variable costs per unit for chicken hot dogs would be $0.582 per pound (including processing and packaging), and $0.582 multiplied by 200,000 pounds per week would yield a total variable cost of $116,400 per week (or $6,052,800 per year).

- Total costs (C; the overall total paid out to operate the business) equal total variable costs (TVC) plus total fixed costs (FC or "overhead"; costs that don't vary with production or change across levels of sales):

$$C = TVC + FC$$

Fixed costs do not vary with volume. As more units are manufactured and sold, fixed costs remain the same. Fixed costs represent the value chain "operations" of the firm. In Perdue's case, total fixed costs related to the chicken hot dogs amounted to $1.2 million for marketing, $60,000 in salaried expenses, and $22,500 in depreciation, for a total of $1.285 million in total fixed costs. Therefore, the total costs were equal to $6,052,800 ($TVC$) plus $1.285 million ($FC$), for a total of $7,337,800.

- Total revenues (R; money in) minus total costs (C; money out) equals profit (π; the money the firm can keep):

$$R - C = \pi$$

In the Perdue example, the profit is therefore equal to $7.8 million (in total revenue) minus $7,337,800 (in total costs), for a final value of $462,200.

These relationships are fairly straightforward, and they make sense if we think about what goes into each variable or "account" and how revenues and costs are incurred. Despite its apparent simplicity, this cost-volume-profit logic (presented graphically in Figure A-1) and its application to marketing strategy can be extremely informative. In fact, cost-volume-profit logic facilitates sensitivity analysis and underlies breakeven analysis—two basic ways of evaluating investments, including capital outlays and marketing expenditures and alternatives.

As Figure AA-1 illustrates, several of the basic components involved in cost-volume-profit logic (shown as nodes in the graphic) can be broken out even further. For example, as stated earlier, revenue equals average price times quantity sold ($R = \overline{P} * Q$), and quantity sold itself can be broken down to the number of customers (C) multiplied by the average purchase quantity (PQ):

$$Q = C * PQ$$

This greater detail underscores two basic ways to grow sales: Either attract more customers or sell more products per customer (increase use). For instance, in the aforementioned example, Perdue debated whether to market its chicken hot dogs to heavy users (who might consume as much as one pound per week) or to light users (who might only use one pound per month). Clearly, selling to a few "heavy users" is worth as much as or more than selling to many "light users".

It is useful here to think about the revenues per pound and per user as well as the total revenues that might be expected. In other words, there is valuable information in both aggregate and unit-level analyses. Figure AA-1 shows both. At the aggregate level, unit-level price is multiplied times quantity sold and unit-level variable costs are also multiplied times quantity sold to arrive at sales (total revenue) and total variable costs. This allows for dynamic modeling. For example, if price changes, quantity sold also changes, and, as a result, revenues and costs change in concert. Typically, as price is increased, quantity sold decreases. In Purdue's case, one alternative possibility that was considered was to market to light users at a much higher price, say $0.90 per pound

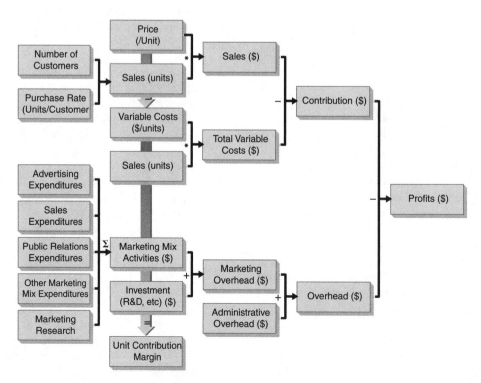

FIGURE AA-1   Cost-Volume-Profit Relationships

instead of $0.75. The company expected that at the higher price, demand would be much lower but that the higher price would compensate with increased revenue per pound sold.

It is also helpful to understand that unit-level revenue (price) minus variable costs per unit yields a value known as the "contribution margin"—or the contribution of each unit to covering overhead. Contribution margin per unit is a key measure; it almost always varies across the firm's assortment of products and product bundles, and understanding which products make more money and which make less, and what roles each product plays within the overall assortment and strategy, is invaluable. In the Perdue example, the contribution was equal to the manufacturer's selling price ($0.75 per pound) minus the variable costs ($0.582 per pound) for a value of $0.168 per pound.

Cost Structures

Costs or expenses can be thought of as falling into two categories: variable and fixed. Variable costs are costs directly associated with a unit of product sold. For example, if a store sells a dress, it incurs the cost of that dress. If it doesn't sell the dress, the dress stays in inventory and the costs are not incurred (leaving out the cash-flow implications of buying and storing the dress to have at the ready). However, the store had to have clerks available as well as the store facility itself, whether or not a customer came in to buy the dress, so salaries and rent are fixed costs—in other words, they do *not* change with every unit sold. Figure AA-2 illustrates these basic relationships.

Of course, some costs are neither perfectly variable nor completely fixed; costs can also be mixed, semi-variable, step-function, and so forth. These variants are not hard to incorporate into cost-volume-profit thinking. For example, if the store can sell 20 dresses per clerk and it must schedule another clerk when sales are expected to exceed 20 (and yet another clerk on very busy days when sales will exceed 40, and so forth), then fixed costs become a step function.

Sensitivity Analyses

The relationships spelled out in the previous sections allow us to create dynamic models—models in which changes in one variable or assumption change the whole system—and also to perform sensitivity analyses. Sensitivity analyses are "what-if" analyses in which changes in specific variables are modeled out to determine their impact on other variables and, ultimately, their effects on profits. In this regard, it is worth noting that quantity sold (Q, or "Sales" in Figure AA-1) *appears twice in the model*: both revenue ($R = \bar{P} * Q$) and total variable costs ($TVC = VC * Q$) are a function of Q. This makes sense, because both revenues and costs are direct functions of the number of units that are sold. Also, in the real world, the quantity sold is typically related to price; in most cases (but not all), if the price is lowered, then the quantity sold will increase. Similarly, there is a relationship between another variable—one not expressly included in these models—and quantity sold. That variable is quality. In general, the higher the quality of a product (at a given price), the

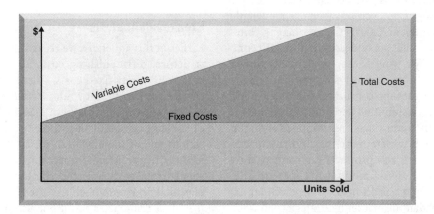

FIGURE AA-2 Simple Variable-, Fixed- and Total-Cost Structure

higher the quantity sold and, most likely, the higher the variable costs per unit.

Thus, these basic formulas allow us to perform "what-if" analyses. What if we lower the price (and keep quality constant) and assume sales increase by some certain percentage? What if we raise the quality 20 percent (and assume variable costs also go up exactly 20%), raise the price 10 percent, and assume sales increase 8 percent (after all, we're increasing quality by more than we're increasing price)? Of course, we often have good marketing research data regarding how much sales will increase or decrease given specific changes in price, quality, and marketing expenditures—but sometimes, we must live with informed assumptions. If these assumptions are sensible and ranges of possible outcomes are considered (via sensitivity analyses), then the possible outcomes are likely well covered. Still, it is important to understand the interrelationships in cost-volume-profit thinking and to "surface" (i.e., state clearly) and make an effort test all related underlying assumptions.

Elasticity

Elasticity refers to responsiveness of demand. In other words, elasticity is a measure of changes in demand/sales due to changes in any marketer input, including things like advertising, sales effort, and so forth. In economics, the term "price elasticity of demand" relates the demand for a commodity, such as gasoline, to changes in the price of that commodity. Gasoline demand, for example, is not terribly elastic because consumption is partly discretionary, partly a function of long-term decisions (such as the length of one's commute), and partly tied to ongoing commercial activities that are not easily adjusted. In contrast, demand for wine is more elastic, because a large portion of this demand is discretionary and, when the price goes up, consumers can quickly adjust their wine consumption and find substitutes.

A firm often must make assumptions about or perform research to determine the elasticity of demand for its particular products (as compared to broad categories of commodities). There are also other change-effect relationships very similar to price elasticity that the marketing strategist will want

to estimate or measure as well. For instance, how much do sales (demand) increase given a change in advertising? How much do sales drop given a cut in personal selling efforts? How much will demand fall if quality or service is pared back? In each of these cases, elasticity is defined by the general formula:

$$E = \frac{\Delta Q}{\Delta P} \quad \text{or} \quad E = \frac{\Delta Q}{\Delta I},$$

where E is elasticity, Δ ("delta") is change, Q is quantity demanded, P is price, and I is the more general variable "input"—in other words, the input that the firm changes, whether it be the price, advertising, sales, quality, or something else. Drawing on basic algebra, this same equation can be reformulated as:

$$\Delta Q = E \times \Delta I$$

by multiplying each side by ΔI. Thus, if a firm has a series of observations about quantities sold at different levels of the input, it can estimate E by running regressions; here, E is simply the beta (β) for I regressed on Q.

Even if the strategic marketer is unfamiliar with the underlying math of regression, the logic of these relationships remains straightforward: *How does Q change when some input I is changed?* For example, in the chicken hot dog example, the question might be "How does the quantity purchased change as the price per pound of chicken hot dogs is either raised or lowered?" Estimating these relationships and understanding the effects of changes in the various components of the cost-volume-profit relationship is fundamental to sensitivity analysis.

Breakeven Analysis

Earlier in this appendix, we recognized a simple cost structure, distinguishing costs as purely variable costs and purely fixed costs. (Again, variable costs change with each unit sold, whereas fixed costs do not change across any level of sales.) Although costs can behave differently than these two simple classifications, use of these two categories allows us to determine the point in sales at which total revenue is equal to total costs (variable costs times quantity sold plus total fixed costs)—that is, the point at which the firm does not make a profit but also does not take a loss. This is also known as the breakeven point, and it can be calculated as follows:

$$R = C\,(\pi = 0)$$

We know that revenue equals average price times quantity sold, that total cost equals total variable costs (TVC) plus total fixed costs (FC), and that total variable costs equals variable costs per unit times quantity sold:

$$R = \bar{P} * Q$$
$$C = TVC + FC$$
$$TVC = VC/u * Q$$

Using basic algebraic principles, we can combine these equations as follows:

$$C = VC/u * Q + FC$$

Therefore, at breakeven, revenue is equal to total variable costs (TVC) plus total fixed costs (FC):

$$(\bar{P} * Q) = (VC/u * Q) + FC$$

and profit (π) is zero. We can solve this equation for Q (the breakeven quantity in units) by subtracting ($VC/u * Q$) from both sides and then dividing by ($P - VC/u$):

$$Q_{be} = \frac{FC}{\left(\bar{P} - \dfrac{VC}{u}\right)}$$

Figure AA-3 shows breakeven graphically. Breakeven (in units) is an important sales level to determine. Strategic marketers want to understand breakeven because it represents the point at which capital investments (such as new plants or equipment) and program investments (such as advertising or research and development) are paid back without a profit, but without a loss either. Marketers will also want to know how changes in price affect payback. An increase in price will steepen the total revenue line because each incremental unit of sales brings in more. However, the price increase may also reduce the likelihood of achieving a given level of sales in units.

To return to the Perdue Farms example, our breakeven quantity, Q_{be}, will be equal to our FC ($1.285 million) divided by the value we get when we subtract our VC ($0.582 per pound) from the manufacturer's selling price ($0.75 per pound). To simplify, this quantity is equal to $1.285 million divided by $0.168, which gives us a value of £7.686 million per year (or £147,000 per week).

Margins and Mark-ups

Above we defined a margin—in particular, the "contribution margin"—as the difference between the price per unit and the total variable costs per unit ($CM = P - VC/u$; see Figure AA-1). In certain cases, the contribution margin is the difference between what a reseller, such as a retailer, pays for a product and the sales price (e.g., if a store sells a dress for $100 and its

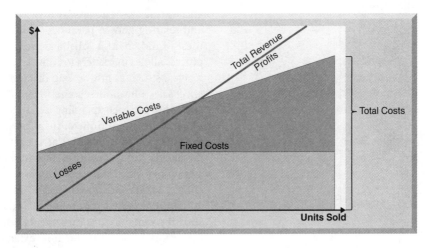

FIGURE AA-3 Breakeven Analysis

cost for the dress was $50, its contribution margin is $50). Still, it is worthwhile to clarify some particular uses of the term "margin" and to distinguish it from the term "mark-up," if only because these terms are often confused and do have specific and different meanings.

A margin, as stated, is the difference between sales price and total variable costs. If margin is expressed as a percentage, it is always the difference divided by the total selling price. Remember, margin is **not** the difference divided by the costs. That is, in Figure AA-4, margin is equal to B divided by A (i.e., $\frac{B}{A}$), not B divided by C ($\frac{B}{C}$). In comparison, mark-up is the amount over costs that a firm, usually an entity in the channel of distribution (such as a retailer), adds onto what they paid for a product to arrive at the selling price. Markup can be attributed to the value created by particular operations. Thus, the retailer's margin and its markup are the same amount of money in dollars *and* in percentage terms. Usually, markup is expressed as a percentage; it is the amount of profit divided by the selling price of the unit sold. This is often confusing, because it seems logical that markup would be on the cost as in the cost plus the markup. *It is not.* In retailing in particular, markup is always expressed as a percent of selling price—and thereby related as a percent of selling price. Because both markup on selling price and markup on cost are conventionally expressed as percentages, the result of

using the wrong reference point (denominator) would be dramatic and would cause confusion.

Because gross margin (the total contribution of sales toward fixed costs) is equal to average price ($\overline{P}$) multiplied by quantity sold (Q), gross margins and changes in gross margin can be readily graphed in a two-dimensional space defined by average price and quantity sold. Figure AA-5 shows such a graph comparing gross margins for sales of a product with costs of $100, comparing sales at a price of $200 (where quantity sold is estimated to be 1,000) with sales at a price of $150 (in which case the contribution margin has been cut from $100 to $50 and quantity sold is estimated to be 1,500). The graph highlights the reality that, at the reduced price (and reduced contribution margin), the firm realizes increased sales in units (from 1,000 to 1,500) and increased sales in dollars (from $200,000 to $225,000), but the gross contribution margin drops from $100,000 to $75,000.

Part One Summary

As illustrated in the preceding sections, cost-volume-profit logic—the relationships among revenues, costs, volume (sales), and profits—is fundamental to analyzing marketing programs, comparing alternatives, and formulating marketing strategies. This logic does not involve complicated math, but it usually involves making some well-founded assumptions, surfacing those assumptions (i.e., articulating the assumptions and testing them against reality as far as possible), and relating known parameters, links, and plans to these fundamental business relationships. This process allows marketers to consider a wide variety of scenarios such as how a drop or raise in price would affect sales. Or, another scenario might explore the relationship between spending a particular amount on a marketing communications program (marketing overhead), and sales level at a particular price to 'breakeven' on the investment and thereby to begin adding to profits?" "If we add a product with a different price and contribution margin and it cannibalizes a certain assumed percentage of existing sales but adds the remainder as incremental sales, is the firm better off launching the line extension or not?" Having a solid, even intuitive understanding of the

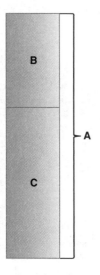

FIGURE AA-4   Margin and Markup

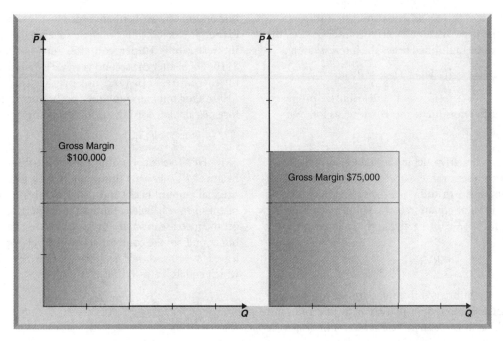

FIGURE AA-5 Graphic Representations of Gross Margins

logical relationships integrated in "cost-volume-profit" framework is therefore an invaluable tool to analyzing alternatives and thinking strategically.

PART TWO: THE TIME VALUE OF MONEY

Money changes value across time—in fact, it is almost always true that any amount today will be worth more in the future. For example, if a business takes out a loan today for some amount of money, say $100,000, it must repay *more than $100,000* in the future. If the company were only going to pay back an identical amount ($100,000), there would be no incentive for the lender to make the loan. In fact, given the reality of inflation—the fact that things generally become more expensive across time—the lender would actually lose money if it gave the borrower money today and only got that same amount back later. Because of these concerns, lenders must charge some additional interest rate (on top of inflation) that represents the *profit* on a loan. (After all, if a lender only charges the rate of inflation, it will still have no incentive to commit its money and take on the risks of the loan to get back

essentially exactly what it lent). Thus, a loan's interest rate over-and-above inflation can be thought of as the "price" the lender charges for the loan.

As previously mentioned, money changes value across time, and, as a rule, it takes more money in the future ("future value") to equal a given amount of money today ("present value"). It is not difficult to understand the basic logic of this "time value of money" and to translate these ideas into simple formulas. In fact, these formulas are programmed into most spreadsheet applications and are easy to apply. The following sections explain the logic of the underlying algorithms, because it is useful to understand this logic before applying the spreadsheet tools.

The Basic Logic and Formula

If a bank loans a company $100 today and the simple interest rate is 10 percent, then in one year, the repayment amount will be $110—that is, $100 today equals $110 in one year at 10 percent interest. In this situation, the present value (PV) is $100; the interest rate ($i$) is 10 percent; and the future value (C) is $110.

If we express this as an equation, the future value equals the present value itself plus interest (i.e., the present value multiplied times the interest rate):

$$C_1 = [(PV)_0 * 1] + [(PV)_0 * i]$$

Basic algebra (specifically the distributive property) allows us to reformulate this equation as follows:

$$C_1 = PV_0 * (1 + i)$$

It is similarly uncomplicated to work out a formula for present value—or the amount some future payment is worth today—by dividing each side of the future value equation by $(1 + i)$ (i.e., multiplying both sides by $\frac{1}{(1 + i)}$ to arrive at the following:

$$PV_0 = \frac{C_1}{(1 + i)}$$

These straightforward formulas are for future value *after just one year* and for present value of an amount that will occur in *one year*. The subscript indicates the point in time or "period." Here, zero (0) is the present (zero periods have passed so far), so PV_0 is actually redundant, and C_1 indicates future value after one period; in this example a period is equal to one year— but the formula and logic can be applied to analyses in which the unit of time (i.e., "period") is something other than a year, such as a month or a day.

Multiple Years

Of course, people are frequently interested in thinking about the value of money received in *more than one year*. What if we wanted to calculate the present value of money received in two years, for example? In this situation, we can use C_2 to denote the future value after two periods—here, two years because we're defining each period as equal to one year in our analysis. (Note that such analyses can also be done with months as the unit of time.) Similarly, C_3 would denote a lapse of three periods; and so on.

We can figure out how much some amount today would be worth in *two* periods by remembering that, if we invested an amount today in, say, a bank, we'd want to have the bank add the interest after one period—or "compound" our investment— and then compute the second-period interest using

our original investment amount *plus* the amount we earned in period one. So, if we invest $100 and the interest rate is 10 percent, after one year we have $110. Then, after the second year, we earn ten percent on the entire $110 (and not on the just original $100). Our total amount after both years can therefore be calculated using the following formula:

$$C_2 = [[PV]_0 \times (1 + i) \times 1] + [[PV]_0 \times (1 + i) \times i]$$

Here, we're computing the end-of-the-*first*-year balance $(PV_0(1 + i))$ times one (which gives us the original amount back) and also multiplying the end-of-the-*first*-year balance times the interest rate (i) to get the increase in value. Again, we can use basic algebra to pull out the common term $PV_0 * (1 + i)$, which leaves $(1 + i)$ and we'd get $[[PV]_0 * (1 + i)] \times (1 + i)$ which equals $[[PV]_10 * (1 + i)]^{*2}]$. So:

$$C_2 = PV_0 * (1 + i)^2$$

and therefore:

$$PV_0 = \frac{C_2}{(1 + i)^2}$$

We can now create a general formula by recognizing that the key to compounding interest is simply multiplying by $(1 + i)$. Compounding across two periods was achieved by multiplying times $(1 + i)^2$; thus, compounding across three periods would be achieved by multiplying $(1 + i) \times (1 + i) \times (1 + i)$ or $(1 + i)^2$, and compounding across n periods would be achieved by multiplying times $(1 + i)^n$. So, the general forms of the relationship between present value and future value are:

$$C_n = PV_0 * (1 + i)^n$$

and:

$$PV_0 = \frac{C_n}{(1 + i)^n}$$

These equations use the subscript n to indicate some indeterminate number of periods, n, so C_n is the generic "future value after some number of periods n."

Annuities

Often in business and certainly in marketing, the manager is not just analyzing the present value of a single future amount received (or paid) in time period n. Instead, the issue is valuing some stream of revenues that recur across n periods of time—that is, the concern is for valuing a series of payments or profitable sales on a recurring basis. For example, banks make loans and expect to be paid back with a series of regularly recurring loan payments. Similarly, a marketer who wins a customer's loyalty—his or her repeated patronage across time—has a recurring stream of margins that have some specific present value (see Note IV-3, Customer Lifetime Value). These recurring streams of revenue are called annuities, and the present value of an annuity is referred to as the "net present value" (*NPV*), which is simply *the sum of the present values of each payment*. Thus, if a marketer knows that a customer will buy one unit every year for three years and the margin or profit on each sale is $10 at a 5 percent interest rate, the net present value of that three-year annuity could be computed using the formulas above. In fact, the NPV is simply the sum of three present value computations:

$$NPV_0 = \frac{C_1}{(1+i)^1} + \frac{C_2}{(1+i)^2} + \frac{C_3}{(1+i)^3}$$

which, in our example, yields the following:

$$NPV_0 = \frac{10}{(1+.05)} + \frac{10}{(1+.05)^2} + \frac{10}{(1+.05)^2}$$

$$= \$27.23 \ (not \ 30!).$$

Thus, the general formula for net present value is simply:

$$NPV_0 = \sum_1^T \frac{C_n}{(1+i)^n}$$

where sigma (Σ) denotes *sum* (add these terms all together) and the whole formula denotes "the sum of the values of this formula from $n = 1$ to $n = T$," with T representing the number of periods. That is why we use C for what's been labeled "future value"—C denotes a future "cash flow." It is important to remember that, if the period for analysis is *months* instead of years, then the interest rate (i) should be the annual interest rate divided by 12. Similarly, if you're using quarters, the interest rate is the annual interest rate divided by 4, and so on.

If an annuity is going to involve some initial investment—as annuities usually do—than an extension of this logic and formula is to include the initial investment as C_0 (value today), which is usually negative (i.e., it is a cost, not a revenue):

$$NPV_0 = -C_0 + \sum_1^T \frac{C_n}{(1+i)^n}$$

or

$$NPV_0 = \sum_1^T \frac{C_n}{(1+i)^n} - C_0$$

because C_0 would normally be negative (i.e., an investment or cost, not an inflow of cash). For example, if the initial investment to achieve a three-period annuity of $10 per period at 5 percent interest is $15, the formula would be:

$$NPV_0 = C_0 + \frac{C_1}{(1+i)^1} + \frac{C_2}{(1+i)^2} + \frac{C_3}{(1+i)^3}$$

and the calculation would be:

$$NPV_0 = \frac{10}{(1+.05)} + \frac{10}{(1+.05)^2} + \frac{10}{(1+.05)^3} - \$15$$

which equals $12.23.

Part Two Summary

The relationships above and the corresponding formulas are really all it takes to understand the logic and the underlying the concepts of future value, present value, and net present value (the present value of an annuity). This logic and these formulas are the very basis for thinking about "the time value of money." As stated previously, money changes value across time, and the time value of money is an essential concept in business—especially for marketers, who must think strategically about pricing, future prices and future costs, delayed payments (financing), and recurring streams of revenues, such as rents and customer lifetime value (*CLV*). Of course, the time value of money is also important when thinking about borrowing for cash flow and for capital budgeting tasks. This value is easily computed in any spreadsheet application, but it is still useful to understand the time value of money conceptually before running those computations.

APPENDIX B

Strategic Marketing Plan Exercise

A major objective of this text is to provide you with the process, concepts, and tools needed to develop a strategic marketing plan. What follows in this note is a "paint-by-number" set of worksheets that will assist you in developing, as an exercise, a strategic marketing plan for a specific product or market.

All strategic marketing plans are fundamentally similar, varying in the degree of specificity required as a function of the planner's predilections and corporate policy. The following worksheets provide an overview of planning considerations and tentative decisions for a particular line of business.

There is no expectation that you will have all of the specific data and information necessary to make your planning precise. You may have to make estimates and judgments. However, this exercise will reveal the areas in which you need particular kinds of data or information. For example, you may be able to give only nominal estimates of your competitive advantages here (using a plus or minus to indicate whether you are in a better or worse position than specific competitors), but you could gather more precise ordinal data via marketing research in your actual planning process.

THE STRATEGIC MARKETING PLAN ASSESSMENT

All strategic marketing plans pose and answer three fundamental questions:

- Where are we now?
- Where do we want to go?
- How do we get there?

In fact, these three questions form the basic structure of this exercise. You could use the worksheets to help prepare a strategic marketing plan for any business unit, line of business, product, or market.

A. Situation Assessment: Where Are We Now?

The exercise begins by asking you to consider the question "Where are we now?" This exercise is called the "Situation Assessment." **Worksheet A-1** asks you to provide a business definition describing the business in which your company wants to be involved. You should refer to the particular line of business here, not the company as a total organization. Your business definition should be specific; it is not enough to simply say the company will "provide solutions." You must specify the kinds of solutions it will provide to different types of people or organizations and the ways in which these will differ from the competition.

Next, you will provide a market profile with **Worksheet A-2**. This profile must assess the overall market and define it in terms of the relevant or "served" market. For example, at the broadest level, Federal Express serves the "rush" market with its overnight delivery services. However, the relevant market that Federal Express wishes to serve is the time- and reliability-sensitive market for small packages (under seventy pounds) and documents. This more precise market definition defines the relevant market that Federal Express wishes to serve.

In the market profile, you must *estimate* market size, share, and growth, and give an indication of the life cycle stage for the product market. You should also designate your company's largest competitor and its share relative to that competitor.

Worksheet A-3 requires you to segment the overall market that you have identified. This is often the most time-consuming task in the exercise, but it is a critical one. The worksheet includes some basic instructions to refresh your memory about approaches to market segmentation, and gets you started by asking you to list some differences across the total market.

You will then assess differences in the benefits sought by each market segment with **Worksheet A-4**. If there are no differences, then your segmentation approach is flawed. On the other hand, all segments may benefit the most from a single attribute but vary in terms of the other attributes. The cell entries on the worksheet are rank orders of the benefits for each segment.

Worksheet A-5 continues the "Where are we now?" exercise by asking you to describe buyer behavior and determine what the decision-making process is in each segment. It may be similar across segments, but you should still examine the decision-making unit (DMU) and the decision-making process (DMP). In many products or markets, the Chooser (i.e., the person or persons responsible for the decision to buy from you versus another vendor) may be different from the users (i.e., the individuals who will actually use or consume your services). It is sufficient to indicate job titles to characterize the DMUs. You may wish to characterize the DMP in terms of time (long or short term), complexity, or qualitative factors (routine or modified rebuy, new task, political, performance, etc.)

Worksheet A-6 asks you to assess the individual market segments that you have identified and define them in terms of the relevant market. This is similar to the work you did in **Worksheet A-2**, and it may be helpful for you to refer to the information about the total served market in that worksheet and break it down by market segment.

Next, you will develop an overview of the environment in **Worksheet A-7** based on three analyses:

- Market trends (What are the crucial current and potential trends in the overall market?)
- Competitive trends (What are the crucial elements of competitors' strategies and where are they heading?)
- Segment/customer trends (What are the crucial trends that best describe segment and customer trends that affect your marketing planning in the product or market?)

Worksheet A-8 asks you to provide a relative assessment of how your company stacks up against its major competitors. First, you will list the competitors in the product or market. Then, for each competitor, you will indicate with pluses and minuses whether your company is better (+) or worse (−) on each benefit (from **Worksheet A-4**) and give brief examples where you can. Note that specific, ordinal data could be gathered to provide a more precise determination of your relative ranking on each benefit.

Worksheet A-9 continues the assessment of your company versus its competitors by asking for your overall judgment about the company's relative strength against each competitor in the market segments in which you compete. You will use pluses and minuses in your assessment again, and your judgments may heavily reflect those you made in **Worksheet A-8**. Once again, give brief examples to illustrate your points where you can. Note that market research could be used to more precisely describe the nature and extent of your relative position in this grid.

Worksheet A-10 continues the situation assessment by asking you to construct one or more perceptual maps and indicate your company's relative position on each map versus its competitors. Each map is, in effect, a cross-section of a customer's brain and should reflect how customers perceive the company relative to the competition. This will require you to choose dimensions; for example, individual customers may perceive various competitive options in terms of size (so the dimension might be "large to small") and in terms of focus (so the other dimension might be "general purpose to specialized purpose"). You may have multiple perceptual maps for each segment if you have many significant *dimensions* or characteristics.

Worksheet A-11 completes the Situation Assessment with a "SWOT" analysis (Strengths, Weaknesses, Opportunities, and Threats) by segment and for the overall market. To a large extent, this exercise will provide a quick summary of the analyses you have completed to this point.

Worksheet A-12 extends the situation assessment to portfolio analysis and establishes a transition from "Where are we now?" to "Where do we want to go?" This worksheet consists of five pages:

1. Market Attractiveness/Competitive Position Portfolio Model Development Process (This page lists the steps involved in the process.)
2. Market Attractiveness/Competitive Position Criteria Examples (This page lists ideas for increasing the attractiveness and strength of your company.)

3. Market Attractiveness/Competitive Position Model Input Criteria Evaluation Development (This page asks you to establish which of the criteria from page two you will use to improve the market attractiveness and competitive position of your company and to complete steps two and three from page one.)

4. Market Attractiveness/Competitive Position Graph (This page asks you to determine the relative position of strategies for improving market attractiveness and competitive position and to complete steps four and five from page one.)

5. Market Attractiveness/Competitive Position Graph Prescriptions (This page provides an example of strategies and their likely positions in each of the nine portfolio matrix boxes.)

Worksheet A-1

A. Situation Assessment: Where Are We Now?

1. Business Definition (Product, Line of Business, Industry Segment)

Worksheet A-2

A. Situation Assessment: Where Are We Now?

2. Total Market Profile

a. Size (Units and/or $)
b. Share: i. Now: ii. Sought in Three Years:

c. Growth
 	
   Trend
 	
   APGR, 3 years

d. Life Cycle Stage
e. Largest Competitor   Your Company's Relative Share

Worksheet A-3

A. Situation Assessment: Where Are We Now?

Segmenting the Market

Now that you have described the TOTAL relevant or "served" market, your task is to subdivide the market into the most appropriate and useful segments. This is a difficult task and demands careful analysis from all team members. You should start by listing the areas of differences across the total market. For example, the market may vary by size of firms, nature of business, decision-making units, decision criteria, and so on. Next, you should evaluate these market differences by the criteria for segmentation, including:

- Are the segments reachable, differentially responsive to some elements(s) of the marketing mix, and likely to be profitable given different costs that may be associated with starting each of them with different mixes?
- Are the segments reasonably exclusive, yet mutually exhaustive? Are excluded segments ones that your company is just as happy to walk away from?
- Which segmentation approach presents the greatest "product-company-market fit?" In other words, which approach makes the most sense in terms of how your company is set up now, how well established it is (compared to its competitors) in each segment, and what barriers to competitive entry are in each segmentation approach?
- Which segmentation approach fits with your company's LOB mission, goals, and resources? For example, you might define segments that your company has not traditionally served but may choose to serve given their growth potential, possibilities for add-on business later, fit with other corporate business, etc.

Try sequential segmentation: start with broad industry descriptors, proceed through company characteristics, and try uncovering some differences due to desired benefits of needs. The result may well be a multidimensional segmentation. Note that you will complete **Worksheets A-4** through **A-6** using your segmentation approach. You might look at these forms now to help you get started.

Segmenting the Market

3. List Some Differences Across the Total Market:

Worksheet A-4

A. Situation Assessment: Where Are We Now?

4. Customer Analysis: Benefits Sought

Customer Benefits Sought	Segment A	Segment B	Segment C	Segment D	Segment E

NOTE: Rank the order of benefits *for each segment*.

Worksheet A-5

A. Situation Assessment: Where Are We Now?

5. Analysis of Decision Makers in Each Segment

	Segment A	Segment B	Segment C	Segment D	Segment E
Decision Making Unit (DMU) (Buyers, Influencers)					
Decision Making Process (DMP)					

Worksheet A-6

A. Situation Assessment: Where Are We Now?

6. Segment Profiles

	Total	Segment A	Segment B	Segment C	Segment D	Segment E
Size (Units and/or $)						

Share
  Now
  Sought in Three Years						

Growth
  Trend
  APGR, 3 years						

Life Cycle Stage						

Largest Competitor
  Today/Future
  Your Relative Share						

Worksheet A-7

A. Situation Assessment: Where Are We Now?

7. Environment: Our Relative Position Vis-À-Vis Markets, Competitors, Segments, and Customers

- Market Trends

- Competitive Trends

- Segment/Customer Trends

Worksheet A-8

A. Situation Assessment: Where Are We Now?

8. Competitive Analysis

Major Competitors	Major Benefits				
	Benefit 1	Benefit 2	Benefit 3	Benefit 4	Benefit 5

Worksheet A-9

A. Situation Assessment: Where Are We Now?

9. Strength of Competitors by Segment

Major Competitor	Segment A	Segment B	Segment C	Segment D	Segment E

+ We are BETTER   − We are WORSE

Worksheet A-10

A. Situation Assessment: Where Are We Now?

10. Competitive Positioning (Axis relates to benefits by segment)

Map #1   Map #2   Map #3   Map #4   Map #5

Worksheet A-11

A. Situation Assessment: Where Are We Now?

11. SWOT Analysis: Strengths, Weaknesses, Opportunities, Threats

	Strengths	Weaknesses	Opportunities	Threats
Overall Market				
Segment A				
Segment B				
Segment C				
Segment D				
Segment E				

Worksheet A-12

A. Situation Assessment: Where Are We Now?

**MARKET ATTRACTIVENESS/COMPETITIVE POSITION PORTFOLIO
MODEL DEVELOPMENT PROCESS**

Situation Assessment

STEP 1: Establish the level and units of analysis (business units, segments, or product-markets).

STEP 2: Identify the factors underlying the market attractiveness and competitive position dimensions.

STEP 3: Assign weights to factors to reflect their relative importance.

STEP 4: Assess the *current* position of each business or product on each factor, and aggregate the factor judgments into an overall score reflecting the position on the two classification dimensions.

Strategy Development

STEP 5: Project the future position of each unit, based on forecasts of environmental trends and a continuation of the present strategy.

STEP 6: Explore possible changes in the position of each of the units, and the implications of these changes for strategies and resource requirements.

MARKET ATTRACTIVENESS/COMPETITIVE POSITION CRITERIA EXAMPLES

ATTRACTIVENESS OF YOUR BUSINESS	STRENGTH OF YOUR COMPETITIVE POSITION
A. **Market Factors** • Size (Dollars, Units) • Size of Product Market • Market Growth Rate • Stage in Life Cycle • Diversity of Market (Potential for Differentiation) • Price Elasticity • Bargaining Power of Customers • Cyclicality/Seasonality of Demand	A. **Market Position** • Relative Share of Market • Rate of Change of Share • Variability of Share Across Segments • Perceived Differentiation of Quality, Price and Service • Breadth of Product • Company Image

MARKET ATTRACTIVENESS/COMPETITIVE POSITION CRITERIA EXAMPLES

ATTRACTIVENESS OF YOUR BUSINESS	STRENGTH OF YOUR COMPETITIVE POSITION
B. Economic and Technological Factors • Investment Intensity • Nature of Investment (Facilities, Working Capital, Leases) • Ability to Pass Through Effects of Inflation • Industry Capacity • Level and Maturity of Technology Utilization • Barriers to Entry/Exit • Access to Raw Materials	**B. Economic and Technological Position** • Relative Cost Position • Capacity Utilization • Technological Position • Patented Technology, Product or Process
C. Competitive Factors • Types of Competitors • Structure of Competition • Substitution Threats • Perceived Differentiation Among Competitors	**C. Capabilities** • Management Strength and Depth • Marketing Strength • Distribution System • Labor Relations • Relationships with Regulators
D. Environmental Factors • Regulatory Climate • Degree of Social Acceptance • Human Factors Such as Unionization	

MARKET ATTRACTIVENESS/COMPETITIVE POSITION MODEL
INPUT CRITERIA EVALUATION DEVELOPMENT

MARKET ATTRACTIVENESS — X AXIS

CRITERIA	HIGH	MEDIUM	LOW
Opportunity Size			
Opportunity Growth			

POSITIONS CAPABILITIES — Y AXIS

CRITERIA	HIGH	MEDIUM	LOW
Skills to Support Segment			

(continued)

MARKET ATTRACTIVENESS/COMPETITIVE POSITION GRAPH

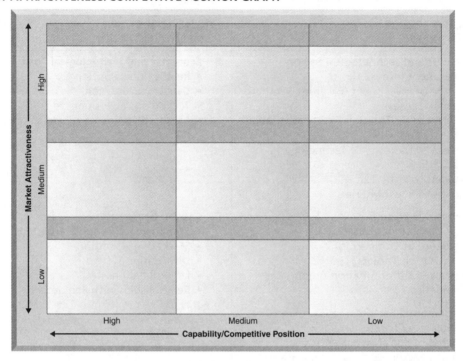

PRESCRIPTIONS

	High	Medium	Low
High	**Reinforce** • Invest to Grow at Maximum Digestible Rate • Concentrate Effort on Maintaining strength	**Invest to Build** • Challenge for Leadership • Build Selectively on Strengths • Reinforce Vulnerable Areas	**Exploit Industry Attractiveness** • Specialize Around Limited Strengths • Seek Ways to Overcome Weaknesses • Withdraw if Indication of Sustainable Growth are Lacking
Medium	**Build Selectively** • Invest Heavily in Most Attractive Segments • Build up Ability to Counter Competition • Emphasize Profitability by Raising Productivity	**Manage Earnings** • Protect Existing Program • Concentrate Investments in Segments Where Profitability is Good and Risk is Relatively Low	**Limit Expansion or Harvest** • Look for Ways to Expand Without High Risk; Otherwise Minimize Investment and Rationalize Operations
Low	**Protect & Refocus** • Manage for Current Earnings • Concentrate on Attractive Segments • Defend Strengths	**Preserve Cash Flow** • Protect Position in Most Profitable Segment • Upgrade Product Line • Minimize Investment	**Divest** • Sell at time That will Maximize Cash Value • Cut Fixed Costs and Avoid Investment

Market Attractiveness

Capability/Competitive Position

B. Proposed Strategy: Where Do We Want to Go?

Once you have fully assessed your company's market and position in the market, you are ready to propose a strategy (**Worksheet B-1**). The term "strategy" refers to your company's *overall plan of action*. It should be distinguished from "tactics," which are expedients for carrying out strategies, and "objectives," which are near-term, measurable, desired end-results. Objectives may be qualitative (e.g., increases in customer satisfaction), but they should always be measurable (e.g., a 20 % increase in satisfaction measures).

Typically, marketing strategies involve some plans regarding products and services and/or markets. Strategies designed to exploit current markets with current products or services are "market penetration" strategies; plans to develop new markets or focus on particular markets are "market development" or "market segmentation" strategies. Some other examples of strategies include "new product" or "product development" strategies, and "diversification" strategies, which involve simultaneous moves into new markets with new products or services.

Still other marketing strategies include "market dominance," "low cost/lost price," "product differenti-

ation," and "control of supply or distribution." There are many other strategies, too, and it is up to you to rationalize the strategy you choose based on the Situation Assessment to this point. The fourth and fifth pages of **Worksheet A-12** should be very helpful in determining your company's strategy.

Once you have clearly stated your company's strategy, the next step is to make it more explicit by specifying objectives (also on **Worksheet B-1**). As discussed earlier, these are near-term (usually one year), measurable, desired end-results, usually expressed in terms of market share, some financial measure, and/or additional, qualitative measures

Note that strategies precede objectives here. Some individuals might believe that objectives should be set first and strategies then specified to achieve those objectives. This approach is perfectly acceptable—strategies and objectives are derived hand in hand, in strategic market planning.

Finally, you will assess risks on **Worksheet B-2**. To do this, you must ask yourself what types of things might happen that would jeopardize the strategy and threaten your company's ability to achieve its objectives.

Worksheet B-1

B. Proposed Strategy and Objectives: Where Do We Want to Go?

1. **Strategic Statement (Overall and/or by Segment):** Remember, "Strategy" refers to the overall plan of action, e.g., penetration, segmentation, new products, diversification defense, flanker, etc. "Tactics," to be specified later, refers to near-term specific actions or maneuvers that you will employ to carry out your strategy.

2. **Objectives (Overall and/or by Segment):** Remember, "objectives" are near-term, measurable, desired end-results. They may be qualitative, but some objectives must be quantitative.

Worksheet B-2

B. Proposed Strategy and Objectives: Where Do We Want to Go?

3. Risk Analysis

Event or Assumption	Likelihood of Occurrence	Possible Impact	Contingency Plan

(continued)

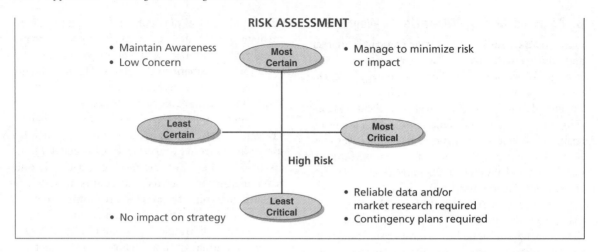

RISK ASSESSMENT

- Maintain Awareness
- Low Concern

Most Certain

- Manage to minimize risk or impact

Least Certain

Most Critical

High Risk

- No impact on strategy

Least Critical

- Reliable data and/or market research required
- Contingency plans required

C. Marketing Tactics: How Do We Get There?

After your company's strategy is set, you must turn your attention to specifying the market program your company will use to carry out its strategy and achieve its objectives in the context of the situation you have described and assessed. **Worksheet C-1** asks you to consider and describe what will be required in terms of the "marketing mix" and internal operations support.

Note that "internal operations support" refers to "What will be done when and by whom," and the other elements parallel what we have described as the marketing mix.

The financial consequences described in **Worksheet C-2** require you to give some preliminary thought to the costs of your company's marketing programs by segment. Again, precision is not expected here, but you should have some idea of costs, margins, and expenses that will enable you to give reasonable estimates that describe your expectations.

Worksheet C-1

C. Marketing Tactics: How Do We Get There?

1. Marketing Mix

	Segment A		Segment B		Segment C		Segment D		Segment E	
	Current Position	Plan	Current Position	Plan	Current Position	Plan	Current Position	Plan	Current Position	Plan
Product: What Is Your Company Selling?										
Service Maintenance/ Customer Support										
Distribution										
Communications										

	Segment A		Segment B		Segment C		Segment D		Segment E	
	Current Position	Plan	Current Position	Plan	Current Position	Plan	Current Position	Plan	Current Position	Plan
Pricing Strategy/ T & C										
Internal/Operations Support										
Channel Design										

Worksheet C-2

C. Marketing Tactics: How Do We Get There?

2. Financial Consequences (Enter numbers where you can, use the icons below, or invent your own.)

	Segment A	Segment B	Segment C	Segment D	Segment E
Share of Market					
Relative Share of Market					
Sales					
Margins (%)					
Marketing Expenses					
Contribution after Marketing Expenses					

Faster Than Market

Same as Market

Slower Than Market

Hockey Stick Change (Up or Down)

Staircase Change (Up or Down)

Most Important Objective for Each Segment

GETTING STARTED

Remember, this is a template designed to get you started with building a strategic marketing plan. By the time you have completed all of the worksheets in the template, you will have used many of the major concepts and tools from this text and applied them to a specific business. This template should also help you understand the kinds of information required for sound strategic marketing planning and get you started on your way toward completing a preliminary strategic market plan. You may be somewhat uncomfortable making estimates instead of using "real" data, but you will learn where in the process you need precise data, what kinds of data would be most helpful, and how these data are used in strategic marketing decision making.

APPENDIX C

The One-Page Memo

Tom Peters and Robert Waterman, in their now-classic book "In Search of Excellence," included a section on the value of a "bias for action," and highlighted the value of the one-page memo as a tool for effective, action-oriented communications and for clarifying thinking:

> "John Steinbeck once said that the first step toward writing a novel is to write a one-page statement of purpose. If you can't get the one page clear, it isn't likely you'll get far with the novel.... It's little wonder that key assumptions get lost in a 100-page investment proposal. The logic probably is loose. The writing most likely is padded. The thinking is almost by definition shoddy. And, worse, the ensuing debate about the proposal among senior executives and reviewers is apt to be similarly unfocused."[1]

One-page memos are *required* at Proctor & Gamble, one of the world's preeminent consumer marketing companies, and they are invaluable for any company and any marketing strategist. Distilling the essential ideas of an analysis or arguments for a proposal down to one-page is not easy. It actually takes a lot longer to create a one-page memo than it does to write longer reports, but the exercise enhances communication and persuasion. Additionally, the process almost always leads to *better underlying ideas*, forcing managers to clarify their thinking, surface and examine their assumptions, and test their own decision-making criteria and processes.

WHAT TO INCLUDE/USE OF APPENDICES

Creating a one-page memo does *not* require that all the relevant information be included on that one page. A lot of important data can be appended to the memo. Any data that are attached should be clearly cited and explained in the body of memo. The writer shouldn't just point the reader to an appendix (e.g., "Financial statements are attached") but, rather, should summarize and interpret the attachments (e.g., "The impact on financial performance, shown

in the Appendix, will be lower per-unit margins but higher net contribution and profitability"). The one-page memo should point the readers to the important information and must tell them what that information means. Of course, those appended materials should also be relevant, readable, and succinct.

COMMUNICATING AND SELLING YOUR IDEA

The process of writing a one-page memo is interwoven with the process of making decisions and thinking about persuading others to endorse the ideas the memo conveys. The "others" being persuaded are usually busy and are often higher in the organization than the writer. In fact, thinking about who exactly the memo is targeting and exactly what action is being proposed—*Who do you want to do what?*—is an important an important first step in framing the task of creating a one-page memo. Other initial considerations should include determining exactly what it is that is being recommended—*What is it the memo wants to have happen?*—and what the most compelling arguments for doing that are. This analysis—who the intended decision makers are, what it is the memo recommends they do or that they approve, and what the essential arguments are for doing that—leads to considerations of persuasive strategy: What do those readers care about? That is, what are the readers' needs and motivations? What does the reader need to know? What reactions might the reader have—and how can undesirable reactions be anticipated and cut-off?

CREATING THE ONE-PAGE MEMO

PREPARATION AND ORGANIZATION. The first steps in preparing a one-page memo, steps which precede any writing, are to decide:

- *Who* your reader is/readers are;
- What are the reader's *needs and motivations*—what drives this audience to act or not act;

- What is *the objective*; what does the memo recommend (specific actions, approvals, etc.);
- What the reader *needs to know*;
- What will *persuade/motivate the reader* to take desired action; and,
- *Possible reader reactions* –questions, concerns, and reservations;

Once this context has been fleshed out in some detail, then the writer can begin to gather specific elements of the memo. The first step is to organize, analyze, summarize, and prioritize the information. Organizing is part of the preparation for writing—the writer must be confident that he or she has all of the facts and that those facts supported by data are "on hand"—and it is an important step in persuasion process. It should include sorting facts as supportive or contrary and by importance and power to persuade the intended audience. This should produce an ordered summary of the key pieces of information—or "key points" for the memo.

WRITING THE MEMO. When the information and key points have been organized, analyzed, summarized, and prioritized, the memo writer should outline the memo *in detail.* Any good piece of communications has an underlying, organizing outline. This outline may be in the memo writer's head, but that invites negligence. Explicit outlines are most useful when they are written and available for reference in the next stages, the drafting, and review, and rewriting of the memo itself. Outlines are not "set in stone," but maintaining an explicit outline while writing is an important practice for producing clear, concise, and persuasive memos.

In summary, during the writing process you must:

- Organize, analyze, and summarize information—without putting it into a memo or worrying about how it will appear in the memo;
- Prioritize information—what is more important and what is less important;
- Create a detailed outline of the memo;
- Draft the memo;
- Review the memo—step back and review the memo for form and substance. In at least one review the writer should very deliberately adopt

the intended readers' perspective or "point of view." *How will they [or he or she] interpret the memo?* Will they be inclined to agree or predisposed to argue against the recommendations? How do the facts stated in the memo correspond to the reader's prior understandings?); and,
- Rewrite—and rewrite, *and rewrite.*

A generic outline of every one-page memo is not really possible, because each memo has a particular purpose and the outline will change depending on that purpose, but at least one outline that works in many strategic business settings includes:

   I. *The Idea:* What are you proposing?
  II. *Background:* What facts and events have led to this being important?
 III. *Details: How it will work?*
  IV. *Motivate the Audience:* Who will benefit and how will they benefit?
   V. *Next Steps.* Who has to do what and by when for this to happen?

A more detailed version of this generic outline is included as Table C-1 below.

Summary

In summary, marketing managers usually influence the broader organization and make things happen not by claiming resources or commanding action—in most organizations they do not have that sort of authority—but rather by *persuading* the organization to commit resources and people to support proposals and programs. Learning to communicate persuasively in concise memos can be a powerful tool in that process. It can also be invaluable in organizing and directing the marketing effort; staff and field sales people do not have time to read lengthy missives, but they must be managed, informed, and motivated—all of which entails effective communications from the marketing manager. This note presents some basic guidelines with regard to creating a one-page memo—a well-tested format made famous Proctor & Gamble, recommended notably in "In Search of Excellence." The keys to creating an effective memo are: (1) careful preparation, (2) consideration of the audience and the audience's motivation to read and respond to the memo, and (3) pithy composition.

TABLE C-1: Detailed Outline of a One-Page Memo

1. Opening/'The Whole Idea'

"I recommend . . ." "This memo recommends . . ."
- Succinct statement of exactly:
  - What you're recommending and when;
  - Why you're recommending it—What do you expect the recommended action will accomplish;
  - Expected impact;
  - Action/decision expected of the reader, assuming agreement (exactly what you want the reader to do); and
  - Key next step and timing if reader agrees.
- Concurrences of others; as required (1 sentence).

2. Background

Briefly explain what the issue is all about to get reader up to understanding speed and put recommendation in perspective.
Include, if appropriate:
- Project description;
- Past history/experience;
- Current situation;
- Define the issue (the problem, the opportunity, or the need and its causes or roots);
- Solution requirements: What is required in terms of resources or changes, and when will those requirements be needed; and,
- Any pertinent statements of strategy, principles or objectives.

3. Recommendation/How it works/How it will work

Briefly outline entire recommendation. Cover all important elements. Define the solution. Include:
- Objectives;
- Strategic focus;

- Implementation plan;
- Financial implications;
- Impact on other functions/brands/businesses; and
- Evaluation/measurement—criteria of success.

4. Basis for Recommendation/Key Benefits

Concise statement of most important rationale for the recommendation.
"The most important reasons for this recommendation are . . ." (typically 2 or 3 justifications, in priority order).

5. Discussion

Briefly identify, if appropriate, and address:
- Reasons for not doing the recommendation;
- Arguments against;
- Major disadvantages—the con's;
- Major risks/concerns and how plan to manage those risks;
- Important (and obvious) alternatives to recommendation—"Alternative options considered include . . ."
- Implications of rejection of recommendation—consequences of not doing;
- Key issues—key factors for success and problems expected;
- All basic assumptions; and
- Any feasibility issues.

6. Next Steps & Timing

Briefly identify what happens next, when it should happen, and who is responsible. The more specific these steps, schedules, and responsibilities are, the better.

Endnote

1. Thomas J. Peters and Robert H. Waterman Jr., *In Search of Excellence: Lessons from America's Best-Run Companies* (New York: Harper & Row, 1982), 151.

APPENDIX D

Case Analysis and Action-Oriented Decisions

This book presents a paradigm—a way of seeing the world and a framework for addressing strategic marketing problems—that dovetails with one of the core teaching methods in business education, the case method. Our strategic-thinking/problem-solving framework, presented in the first section of this book, is about recognizing issues and identifying the appropriate tools, theories, and frameworks to develop strategies, exploit opportunities, avoid threats, solve problems and take action. Those tools, theories, and frameworks are themselves presented in the thirty-eight short notes that make up the remainder of this book, *Strategic Marketing*.

This appendix focuses specifically on ways to approach and analyze challenges, opportunities, threats, and problems that are *presented in written cases.* Therefore, the appendix will be especially useful to students who are required to analyze written cases and come up with action-oriented recommendations to the challenges therein. It also will be useful to students who are participating in marketing-strategy simulations involving a sequence of analyses, decisions, and simulated actions. Like the case method itself, this note is really about *making action-oriented decisions* in general; therefore, it will also be valuable to practicing marketing strategists. After all, the whole point of studying a case in the "business-school world" is as practice for addressing similar challenges in the "real world." Thus, marketing strategy students and managers alike will find this note and this approach to decision making invaluable in addressing the opportunities, threats, and problems of marketing strategy.

ACTION-ORIENTED DECISION MAKING

Action-oriented decisions are decisions that specify something that should be done. In other words, these decisions identify one or more actions that should be taken. Action-oriented decisions can be compared, in particular, with descriptions, evaluations, and plans to decide:

Descriptions are simply statements of fact and organizations of the facts. Some professionals create value by analyzing, organizing, and stating facts, *but that is not strategic management decision making.*

Evaluations are assessments of whether something is good or bad, to be desired or to be avoided. Many people make their living as critics, inspectors, or judges by offering evaluations of what others have done, *but that is not management.*

Plans to decide are about delaying decision making; for instance, a person might say, "I think we should meet another time to look at this again" or "I think we should do more research." Sometimes, decisions must be delayed and research can be invaluable, but delays and further research are not strategic management decision making.

Thus, managers don't just issue descriptions and evaluations or make plans to decide. Rather, *managers direct and take action*—which means that strategic marketing managers direct strategic marketing actions. For managers, the more specific an action recommendation is the better it is; ambiguous decisions and indefinite strategies are unsound and ineffective. In the framework that organizes this book, broad strategies synthesize and align specific actions or tactics. Either without the other is insufficient: Actions that are not organized and aligned within a cohesive strategy are ineffectual, and strategy that isn't translated into specific, structured actions is no strategy at all. Thus, strategic marketing management is about making action-oriented decisions, which, in the framework of this textbook, include both clarification of an organizing strategy *and* specification of the tactical details (in as much as is possible). Like strategic marketing management in practice, case analysis in marketing strategy education requires action-oriented decisions and should avoid being satisfied with description, evaluation, or planning.

THE CASE METHOD

> *"If you hold a cat by the tail, you learn things you cannot learn any other way."*
>
> Mark Twain

Some knowledge can't be "told"; instead, it must be learned by experience. Thus, one of the core pedagogies in business education is the case method. The choice to teach management via cases is motivated by the recognition that management is about *problem solving*, and problem solving is better learned by doing than by listening. That is, problem solving is both a process and a skill and, and as such, it can only be mastered by practice and feedback. Theory will inform that practice, but it can't replace it. Another reason to teach with cases is that doing so not only incorporates an "answer"—a theory or framework that is appropriate to the situation—but it also necessitates *first coming up with the question*. This is appropriate, because before real-world managers can address challenges and opportunities and solve problems, they must first identify the question(s); that is, they must recognize opportunities, threats, and problems and choose the appropriate tools (theories and frameworks) to bring to bear on those issues.

Learning golf is a good metaphor for learning managerial decision making. Golf can be described in terms of physics and biomechanics: Striking the golf ball with a club at a certain angle and certain velocity leads to the ball traveling in a certain direction at a certain speed and rolling or stopping in a certain way. One can learn *about* golf by reading or attending a lecture, and that lecture would be interesting and informative, but no one ever learned *to* golf in the classroom or laboratory. Rather, one learns to golf by golfing, even if it is on the practice range. This example reflects a core tenet of the philosophy behind the case method: As a process and a skill, management is best learned by applying theory to practice, and the case method gives students experience in action-oriented decision making.

The Role of the Professor

Still, with both golf and management, it is not enough to merely practice—practice alone is inadequate. A golfer needs to practice *doing things right*—applying certain techniques and seeing the results of those applications. When a person practices doing things poorly, he or she only ingrains bad habits. As professional golfer Henry Longhurst observed, "They say 'practice makes perfect.' Of course, it doesn't. For the vast majority of golfers it merely consolidates imperfection."[1]

Based on that same logic, the case method must be informed by theory and guided by skillful discussion leadership in order to be effective. Analyzing cases without guidance would be frustrating and would only ingrain bad habits. Case-learning leadership is the responsibility of the professor. In the case method, the professor is usually reluctant to over-control a case discussion—too much direction weakens the effect of having students gain experience attacking the challenges and problems themselves—but he or she does know at least two important things going in that the student may not. First, the professor knows the problem-solving process and has experience guiding students through it. Second, the professor knows at least a subset of the theories, tools, and frameworks that might be productively applied to the case. Thus, the case method and marketing simulations are experiential, but they are safe and directed experiences, done without real investment or real risk (because there is rarely any real money at stake) and under the supervision of someone who has an idea of how the process could be done well.

Inefficiency in the Case Method

Most of the frameworks and lessons conveyed through a case discussion could be summarized in much shorter lectures—so why use the case method? In short, the case method is valuable because it both teaches those frameworks *and* provides experience applying those frameworks to messy, ambiguous situations that mirror the realities faced by managers. In doing so, the case method provides students with experience making and defending action-oriented decisions. Furthermore, there is rarely a definite "right answer" to a case. Instead, as with any real-world administrative situation, there are likely to be *many* possible good and defensible answers. In fact, there may be several ways to define the problem or problems in a case, and, needless to say, several possible answers or solutions once a problem is defined. This ambiguity can be frustrating to students, but it mirrors the real world of strategic management.

This absence of a single right answer leads to another quality of case teaching that most students will notice and some will find frustrating: It is often difficult to come out of a particular case discussion with a clear understanding of what "the lesson of the day" was. Taking notes and summarizing a case discussion can be frustrating. Nevertheless, these aspects—the absence of a right answer or even a single correct view of the problem; ambiguous and incomplete information; and the presence of distracting information—are all aspects of the real world. Insofar as management education is intended to prepare students to manage in the real world, with all of its ambiguity and misinformation, the case method, even with its accompanying frustrations, is an appropriate and effective pedagogy.

Cases

A case can be described as a verbal photograph of a particular decision-making situation, real or invented (but nevertheless realistic), at a particular moment in time. The case presents the reader with more or less the same information that was available to the decision maker at the time. Some cases can be "tools-oriented," meaning they present data meant to support specific analyses and lead toward "correct answers," but these sorts of cases are unusual and especially rare in marketing strategy. Instead, most cases are descriptions of credible, complex situations that a strategist has faced or might face. Some data in a case may not be particularly relevant—like real management, part of learning via cases is dealing with distractions, messy information, and potential misdirection—but most cases will not present *false* information. Some cases may stop there, with the description of good or bad management, but these sorts of "illustration" cases

are also rare in marketing strategy. Rather, the most common type of marketing strategy case will present a situation and a challenge (an opportunity, a threat, or a problem of some sort) and then challenge students to analyze the path that led to the current situation and to identify solutions in the form of forward-looking action recommendations. Thus, there are at least three types of cases—tools-oriented, illustrations, and problem cases. Most cases used in teaching marketing strategy present problems and call for rigorous analysis and action-oriented decision making.

LEARNING VIA THE CASE METHOD

Because of its discussion format and its other differences from lectures and traditional pedagogies, the case method relies on the preparation, analysis, and contributions of students to advance the learning process. If the professor or discussion facilitator does the work—summarizing the issues, working through the analysis, or offering a solution—then the case is reduced to little more than an elaborate example. Therefore, the advantages of the case method are diluted or lost if students do not thoroughly prepare in advance and then vigorously participate in case discussions.

Preparation

A detailed plan for analyzing cases in preparation for class discussions is presented later in this appendix. This plan involves two elements: things to accomplish (outcomes), and a process (steps) to move through the case analysis to accomplish those things. Things to be accomplished include becoming familiar with the situation, identifying the issues (opportunities, threats, problems, and challenges), evaluating alternative courses of action, and recommending a specific course of action. The specific course of action should include appropriate tactical detail, including acknowledgment of trade-offs and uncertainties and consideration of ensuing assessment and measurement. At the same time, it is possible to identify a series of steps for working through the case and producing the outcomes just discussed. The steps to producing these outcomes include:

1. An initial reading of the case;
2. A subsequent, much more thorough reading, including taking notes and identifying things to come back to for subsequent analysis;
3. The analyses themselves including digging deeply into and reformulating the facts and assumptions, performing computations, and creating summaries; and
4. Synthesis of the analyses which includes making and supporting recommendations fleshed out into specifics as much as possible and as far as is appropriate, and elaborating trade-offs, uncertainties, and measurement.

These outcomes and steps are organized in Table AC-1. Of course, these are only guidelines—some cases will not require each step or each outcome, and some steps may be done in a different order and can certainly be repeated—but in general, these

TABLE AC-1 Making Decisions and Analyzing Cases

Outcomes

Steps	Situation Assessment	Issue/Problem Identification — Major/Surface	Minor/Root	Objectives	Analysis — Facts	Assumptions and Missing Data	Alternatives	Analyses	Recommendation(s)	Details/Tactics	Trade-offs and Uncertainties	Evaluation and Measurement
First Read/Skim												
Document	X	X										
Scrutinizing Read/Scrutinize												
Document	X	X	X	X	X	X	X					
Analyze/Deep Dig												
Document			X	X	X	X	X	X				
Review/Synthesis												
Document									X	X	X	X

objectives and this process will be part of any thorough case analysis.

Things to Avoid

There are also a few things *not* to do when analyzing a case and preparing for discussion. For one, the student should not research additional information or more recent data on the case facts, and the student should not, in as much as is possible, assume the role of a critic reviewing prior management or past decisions described in the case. The case is meant to be complete on its own, so getting on the Internet or going to the library and augmenting case facts (or, especially, finding out what has happened to the protagonist, the company, or the industry since the case was written) is "out of bounds." *Stick to the case facts!* (Of course, the professor may abrogate this rule in certain, deliberate instances.) Generally, it is assumed that the case facts are adequate to support the discussion and the learning objectives, so digging up additional information can make the class discussion uneven, because other students will not have the new data, or may have their own "new information". The idea is for all students to be playing with the same deck of cards or to have the same information.

Beyond not researching information outside of the case unless instructed to, students should also avoid being unduly skeptical and thereby missing out on the experience. In the arts, theater, and literature there is an expression—the "willing suspension of disbelief"[2] that gets at the fact that, in order to enjoy a work of art such as a play or a piece of literature the members of the audience must be inclined to put aside their skepticism and to believe the story no matter how seemingly far-fetched or unrealistic. For example, if the audience looks for the guide wire, they will not enjoy Peter Pan's flight. Similarly, in case discussions, sticking with the case facts and suspending disbelief are important to learning and to enjoying the process. The student should not say, "Well, if this were the 'real world,' I'd get on the phone and find out this, that, and the other." Rather, students should assume they have all the information they can get, and they should see what they can learn from making action-oriented decisions based on these facts.

Finally, it is also important to recognize that, in almost all instances, the lesson of the case is not to point out what previous management did wrong (or right); instead, it is to figure out *"Where do we go from here?"* Previous management was rarely "dumb"—and saying "the old boss was dumb" is unbecoming and unproductive in both the business world and the classroom. In actuality, previous managers likely made decisions based on the best information they could gather and within their understanding of the situation and their knowledge of sound strategic business practices and theories. Instead of judging past decisions, students should build on the best information they can gather (specifically from the written case) and apply their understanding of the situation and their growing knowledge of business practice and theory to create a forward-looking plan for success.

Thus, when analyzing a case and preparing for case discussion, the student is expected to come to class well prepared, having thoroughly analyzed the case and gone beyond the facts to analysis, action-oriented recommendations, and considerations of implementation and control. The student should stick with the case facts and suspend disbelief. The student also should view him or herself as taking on the role of the protagonist in a forward-looking, proactive way, and he or she should avoid simply criticizing or critiquing past decisions.

Case Discussion and Class Participation

With regard to classroom discussion of a business case, there are a few simple rules that will lead to success. Of these rules, two are particularly important. The first critical rule is "Come prepared," as described earlier in this appendix. The second critical rule is "Offer your ideas to the class discussion." After all, the professor doesn't want to hear about your shyness, nor does he or she want you to approach after class with an insight that everyone would have benefited from in class—this will only highlight the lost opportunity. Remember, *every student brings a unique perspective and can present valuable understandings to every case discussion.* One way or another, timidly or boldly, all students must enter the discussion and offer their inputs, otherwise the class will suffer for the lost insights and the individual students will lose an opportunity to test their ideas (and almost certainly suffer lowered grades as a result).

Of course, there are good and bad ways to participate in class. For one, students should remember that professors can distinguish contributions that are meant to gain "air time" from thoughtful input that moves the discussion forward. As much as case professors don't like to have a student come in after class and talk about their introversion, they also hate to learn about someone's extraversion in the middle of the case discussion. *Don't talk just to talk!* Class participation isn't about quantity; *it's about quality.* Offer well-thought-through ideas concisely and at the appropriate time. Build on what's been said— don't take the discussion back to what you wanted to say at an earlier juncture. If you didn't get called on, then you missed that chance, so simply move forward with the discussion. Also, don't move to a *new* issue unless the current topic is at, or at least moving toward, resolution. If you believe it's time to move on, then it's a good idea to preface your comment with a motion to change to a new topic ("Can we shift to considering X?" or "I think we need to talk about Z before we can decide Y"). This helps everyone track the discussion and gives the discussion leader (and your classmates) a chance to delay the shift if they think it should be put off.

Professionalism and Respect

All of the aforementioned classroom skills (moving discussions ahead, refraining from moving discussions backward, and shifting topics appropriately) require listening and respect. Respect for your classmates and for the instructor is of utmost importance in a discussion-based learning environment. Remember, discussion is about ideas and analyses. You can criticize someone's idea, offer alternatives to their analysis, or even question their understanding of the facts, but no student should ever criticize another student as a person or participant. *There is no room for personal attacks or disparagement in the classroom!* Any such characterization of a person and certainly any effort to stifle contribution are out of bounds. This level of respect should extend to the instructor as well. Leading a case discussion is a tricky undertaking. Tracking contributions, managing the discussion, keeping the learning objectives in sight,

and tracking evaluations of student contributions while ceding control of the discussion to the class require a lot of skill and a thorough understanding of the topic, the case, and the participants. Be sure to respect everyone in the room and work *with* the instructor to move the process ahead while keeping the discussion professional and pleasant.

CASE ANALYSIS

As described above and summarized in Table AC-1, the process of understanding and analyzing a case can be broken out as iterative readings, reviews, and analyses leading toward an action-oriented decision and plan. These steps may be slightly different or progress in a somewhat different order for different cases, but this is a reliable, general approach.

Recall that the first step in the systematic approach to case analysis is reading through a case at least once just to get the "lay of the land," or the so-called "view from 30,000 feet." Doing so gives the reader an overview of the firm, the protagonist, the industry, and the broad issues at play in the case. Then the student should read the case again, digging into the details, confirming or refuting first impressions, taking notes, and identifying analyses that may be feasible and relevant (but not yet stopping to perform those analyses). It is a good idea, in going through these initial iterative reviews of the case, to take notes and document the issues, facts, and assumptions of the case on paper.

Having skimmed the case and then studied it carefully, it's now time for the student to go back to specific data and facts in the case to perform the analyses and organize information and assumptions. Once the analyses have been performed, the student must make a decision, and that decision should be fleshed out into appropriate details, depending on the case, the amount of detail included, the purpose of the case analysis, and its place in the course. As with any plan, the uncertainties in the case should be elaborated and the contingency plans articulated. This series of related steps will produce a set of structured outcomes or "deliverables," as described in subsequent sections.

Situation Assessment

The first thing to be achieved in reviewing a case is an understanding of the situation. This book has presented a framework for organizing situation assessment: specifically, the situation includes the general context (divisible into the political/regulatory/legal environment, the economic environment, the social/cultural environment, and the technical/physical/natural environment); the competitive situation; the company itself (including its missions and goals, competitive advantages, and strengths and weaknesses); the industry the company competes in or could compete in; and the customers the company serves or might serve. Although a case is a "snapshot" of a situation, the situation is never actually static, so one important aspect of marketing strategy is to recognize the changes in the environment and the effects of those changes on strategy. Hence, a crucial set of related questions in developing and maintaining effective marketing strategy—and in analyzing a marketing strategy case—is as follows:

- What is the situation (context, industry, competition, customers, and the company itself)?
- What has changed or is changing in the situation? Where are those changes and trends headed?
- How have those changes impacted the firm's customers, its strategy, and its competition?

Problem Identification

As noted above, there are often *multiple* reasonable ways to interpret and define "the problem" in a case analysis or in the real world of applied strategic management. Identifying the problem and organizing multiple problems in a logical order by importance is often more than half the battle. Frequently, if the problem has been clearly and correctly specified, the analyses may become "workmanlike" and relatively straightforward.

In identifying the problem or problems, it is useful to distinguish high-level or surface problems from underlying root problems, as well as to differentiate causes from symptoms. Symptoms may at first appear to be "the problem." For example, a first read of many marketing strategy cases will reveal that sales are failing to meet expectations, and in some cases, they may even be declining. Falling sales are almost always a problem, but they're also likely to be the outcome of some other problem, such as an unsound strategy, poor product quality, or a bad fit between the

offering and the customers' needs and wants. Given these sorts of situations, it is important to flesh out an understanding not only of the immediate, surface problems, but also of these problems' underlying root causes.

A useful framework for identifying issues is to organize those issues into a "gap analysis." Gap analysis identifies the difference (or "gap") between *where we are* and *where we want to be*. A strategic gap or planning gap is the gap between actual and desired results along any strategic objective or marker of strategic success, such as sales, market share, profitability, or returns. Gap analysis can also be applied to a process or logical chain connecting managerial objectives to actual outcomes and customer responses.

A well-known example of a process-based gap analysis comes from services marketing. Professors Valarie A. Zeithaml, Leonard L. Berry, and A. Parasuraman have presented a logical framework linking management's perceptions of customer expectations, management's specifications of service quality, delivered service quality, customer perceptions of delivered service quality, and customer expectations, shown in Figure AC-2.[3] A "service-quality gap" can occur at any of the five major linkages shown in this model, and any gap can contribute to lowered customer satisfaction. This framework illustrates gap analysis applied to a system of relationships and linkages involved in delivering value and executing strategy.

It is also important to *prioritize* issues and problems in both case analyses and strategic management. One especially useful way to organize and prioritize issues is Pareto analysis, which can be presented as a Pareto chart and is built on the Pareto principle. Also referred to as the "80/20 rule," the Pareto principle states that, for most phenomena, roughly 80 percent of the effects or outcomes are attributable to roughly 20 percent of the causes or inputs. In marketing, the Pareto principle leads to the rule of thumb that 20 percent of your customers account for 80 percent of your sales (and also that 20 percent of your customers generate 80% of your complaints).Therefore, Pareto principle implies that 20 percent of the issues in a particular situation are related to 80 percent of the problems—which also means solving 20 percent of the problems will account for 80 percent of the solution. This principle

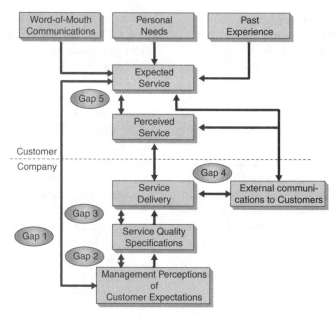

FIGURE AC-1   Zeithaml, Berry, and Parasuraman's Service Quality Gap Framework[4]

In this example, Gap1 is between managements perceptions of customer expectations and their actual expectations, Gap 3 is the difference between specified service quality and delivered service quality, and so forth.

does not always hold true in specific terms, but in nearly all situations, some small amount of the total causes and issues almost always accounts for a disproportionate amount of the effects or outcomes. Figure AC-2 shows a simple hypothetical Pareto analysis and highlights its utility; here, solving the first and second issue solves half the problems, while solving the first four issues (of 20 total issues) solves

80 percent of the problems. As shown in the figure, if the manager can focus on only one issue, focusing on root cause 1 in the hypothetical scenario will resolve almost 30 percent of the problem, whereas solving root cause 13 will only address one percent of the problem. Thus, Pareto analysis facilitates the prioritization of underlying problems and the maximization of return on problem-solving effort.

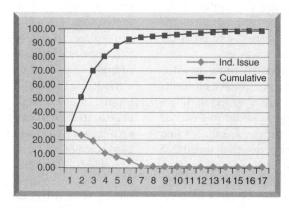

FIGURE AC-2   A Hypothetic Pareto Chart.

The first several issues (the horizontal axis) alleviate more a disproportionate percentage of the problems (the vertical axis)

Another useful tool that serves to organize and summarize these first two steps, situation assessment and problem identification, is SWOT analysis. In any SWOT analysis, the "strengths" and "weaknesses" are aspects of the situation that are *internal* to the company. Still, identifying strengths and weaknesses does require reference to the competition, because it is not enough just to be good at something—rather, the firm must be better than the competition or the competency is not really an exploitable strength. In contrast, "opportunities" and "threats" in SWOT are *external* aspects of the situation. Opportunities and threats may arise from the context (i.e., "PEST" analysis) or from the competition, but their effects on the firm are usually felt via customers and their behaviors. For example, even if an opportunity arises because a competitor withdraws from the market, that competitive change actually connects to the firm and its strategy as an opportunity (that is, as newly unmet demand).

Identification of Facts, Assumptions, and Opinions

As shown in Table AC-1 and described earlier, analyzing a case involves multiple, iterative readings moving from familiarization toward deep understanding and analysis, accompanied by increasingly detailed note taking or "documentation." The core of that process involves identifying and organizing the case facts, surfacing assumptions, and distinguishing fact from assumption. Assumptions and opinions are sometimes presented in the case, or they may be necessitated by the issues in the case. In either situation, documenting the assumptions facilitates going back to those assumptions to consider their impact on resulting decisions. Assumptions put forward in a case text are generally stated equivocally or as personal beliefs—for example, "Fran [the protagonist] believed that . . ." or "The market was thought to . . ." Another source of assumptions is the student's own analysis of the issues. There will be many situations in which the student has to make assumptions or "educated guesses" in order to proceed with an analysis of the case—and documenting these necessary assumptions ensures that the student can support his or her analyses in a presentation or discussion and return to these assumptions and challenge them after any initial analyses are complete.

Clarify the Objectives

What is the protagonist or the firm trying to accomplish? When considering a case, these sorts of objectives may seem obvious—but if they are obvious, then it should be easy enough to make them explicit. Frequently, however, trying to clarify a simple statement of the objectives leads one to the recognition that the objectives at play in a particular situation are more complex than first thought. Some objectives may conflict or be mutually exclusive. For example, raising margins and raising unit sales/market share are common objectives in marketing strategy, but they are not compatible objectives; one is generally counter to the other. It may also be true that the objectives can be organized in a means-end hierarchy. Increasing margins or increasing market share are, for example, usually seen as "means" to the "end" or ultimate objective of increasing profits and returns. Organizing objectives in a hierarchy helps prioritize the objectives and make it easier to decide between conflicting objectives. Thus, clarifying objectives is worthwhile, even if the objectives might seem obvious, and it often helps in the process of sorting through case facts and tying these facts to relevant elements of a decision.

Specify Alternatives

What are the *possible* courses of action? It is useful to deliberately delay settling on a decision or choosing an alternative course of action until after thoroughly and creatively cataloging the full range of alternatives. Once a manager or an analyst has chosen his or her preferred direction or alternative, he or she is likely to focus on facts and arguments that support the decision and to see confirming evidence more keenly than counter evidence. In fact, he or she may not recognize or integrate contrary evidence at all; that is human nature. Thus, in making any decision, it is valuable to first flesh out as wide a range of alternative actions as is possible before analyzing each for viability and merit.

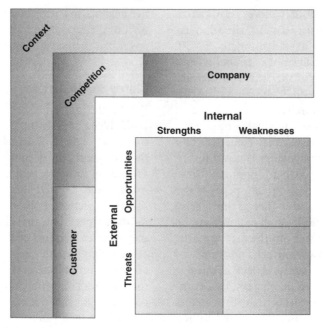

FIGURE AC-3   SWOT Analysis

Strengths and weaknesses arise in the context of comparing one's company with the competition, while threats and opportunities arise in the context the externalities of competition and customer and the external environment.

Evaluation and Analyses

This textbook consists of a planning model that ties directly to specific analytic tools and frameworks. These tools range from quantitative formulas for things like breakeven volume and net present value (NPV) of a stream of revenues, to taxonomies, organizing schemes, and definitions such as SWOT analysis, five-forces industry analysis, and the like. Although these may not be all of the tools and frameworks of strategic marketing, they are among the most important ones. Similarly, the word "analysis" has several meanings but, at its core, it involves separating a whole into its component parts and then examining those parts of the whole and their relationships. In strategic marketing, analysis may include separating the situation, facts, and assumptions using a conceptual framework or it may involve computing figures and ratios using formulas and relationships among variables. This textbook includes thirty-eight notes on various frameworks, theories, and tools that embody the core knowledge in strategic marketing. Applying these tools to the facts and data in a case is

essential to arriving at good decisions and forging effective strategic marketing plans.

Make the Decision

What is the best course of action? When the objectives in a situation are clear, the problem or problems have been stated, and the analyses have been performed, then the decision may be relatively clear. It is important to emphasize, yet again, that the decision should be action oriented. Action-oriented decisions are decisions that specify something that should be done and are not satisfied with mere descriptions, evaluations, or plans to decide. The more specific an action recommendation is, the better it is, and the framework that organizes this book specifies that broad strategies synthesize and align specific actions or tactics. Therefore, when analyzing a strategic marketing case, the "decision" should actually be a plan, complete with an organizing strategy and specification of tactical details. How does that strategy translate into specific tactics? Not all cases will involve all tactics—some may be focused on a particular area of strategic marketing management—but all cases should include opportunities to learn and to add value to the discussion by fleshing out general plans into as detailed and specific a single plan as possible within the learning context and the place of the case in the course.

Consider Contingencies

What might go wrong? What should be measured to monitor progress and warn of problems? How would changing earlier assumptions change a decision? It is at this stage in the process that the importance of documenting assumptions is revealed. At this step, by going over earlier assumptions and connecting them to the analyses (with an understanding of which analyses were most influential in driving the decision), it is possible to perform "sensitivity analysis" in which the relationship between the assumption and the outcome are tested. For example, suppose a case analysis included the computation of customer lifetime value (CLV) with an assumption that customers would stay with the brand for an average of five years. Suppose further that the computation was critical in deciding how much to invest in acquiring new customers in the current strategy. Then, a good way to test the resulting decision against changes in the assumption would be to create a spreadsheet with the duration of the customer's relationship with the brand as a variable parameter. By changing the assumption (e.g., testing CLV with three-year and seven-year time frames), the analyst can test the effects of the assumption, and of violations of that assumption, on the decision.

Summary

The case method is used in management education to give students experience applying neat, orderly theories and frameworks to messy, disorganized information and data. Learning through case analysis can be inefficient and frustrating, but it can also be tremendously rewarding. This note has presented a short description of the case method and the philosophy that underlies its use, and most importantly, it has advanced a concise "plan of attack" for addressing problems and opportunities in written cases that will also be useful for managers who are addressing "real-world" strategic marketing challenges.

Legendary American football coach Pop Warner once said, "You play the way you practice."[5] In football and other sports, it turns out that players who loaf in practice also underperform on game day (i.e., in actual competition). Similarly, if a student looks for the easy way through a case, fails to prepare, or "sits out" during a class discussion, that student is likely to continue ducking responsibility in his or her career as well. The case method is about practicing a managerial perspective; the student must become an active learner and should tackle the case in the same manner that he or she hopes to attack his or her imminent role as a manager, strategist, and leader in the business world. In the case method, the student's personal gain and the entire class's learning depend on each individual preparing rigorously and contributing unhesitatingly to the discussion.

Endnotes

1. Leon Z. Seltzer, *Golf: The Science and the Art* (Mustang, OK: Tate Publishing & Enterprises, 2007), 22.

2. Nineteenth-century English poet and literary critic Samuel Taylor Coleridge coined this term in describing "that willing suspension of disbelief for the moment, which constitutes poetic faith." See *Biographia Literaria* (Middlesex, England, UK: The Echo Library, 1817/2007), 118.

3. See, for example, A. Parasuraman, Valarie A. Zeithaml, and Leonard L. Berry, "A Conceptual Model of Service Quality and Its Implications for Future Research," *Journal of Marketing* 49, 4 (Fall 1985): 41–50 and Valarie A. Zeithaml, A. Parasuraman, Leonard L. Berry, *Delivering Quality Service: Balancing Customer Perceptions and Expectations* (New York: The Free Press, 1990).

4. Parasuraman, Zeithaml, and Berry, "A Conceptual Model of Service Quality," figure is from page 44.

5. Quoted by Michael Benson, *Winning Words: Classic Quotes from the World of Sports* (Lanham, MD: Taylor Trade /Rowman & Littlefield, 2008), 146.

INDEX